To Fred –

to increase your appreciation of unions.

John Foss

Labor Relations

Development, Structure, Process

Eleventh Edition

John A. Fossum

Center for Human Resources and Labor Studies

Carlson School of Management

University of Minnesota

The McGraw-Hill Companies

LABOR RELATIONS: DEVELOPMENT, STRUCTURE, PROCESS, ELEVENTH EDITION

Published by McGraw-Hill, a business unit of The McGraw-Hill Companies, Inc., 1221 Avenue of the Americas, New York, NY 10020.

This book is printed on acid-free paper.

1 2 3 4 5 6 7 8 9 0 QFR/QFR 1 0 9 8 7 6 5 4 3 2 1

ISBN 978-0-07-802915-8

MHID 0-07-802915-5

Vice President & Editor-in-Chief: *Brent Gordon*
Vice President & Director Specialized Publishing: *Janice Roerig-Blong*
Publisher: *Paul Ducham*
Sponsoring Editor: *Daryl Bruflodt*
Director of Marketing & Sales: *Jennifer J. Lewis*
Senior Project Manager: *Lisa A. Bruflodt*
Design Coordinator: *Brenda A. Rolwes*
Buyer: *Susan K. Culbertson*
Media Project Manager: *Balaji Sundararaman*
Cover Design: *Studio Montage, St. Louis, Missouri*
Cover Image: *© Getty Images*
Typeface: *10/12 Palatino*
Compositor: *Cenveo Publisher Services*
Printer: *Quad/Graphics*

Library of Congress Cataloging-in-Publication Data

Fossum, John A.
Labor relations : development, structure, process/John A. Fossum.—
11th ed.
p. cm.
ISBN-13: 978-0-07-802915-8 (alk. paper)
ISBN-10: 0-07-802915-5 (alk. paper)
1. Industrial relations—United States. 2. Collective bargaining—United States. 3. Labor unions—United States. I. Title.

HD8072.5.F67 2012
331.0973—dc23 2011026573

www.mhhe.com

Labor Relations

Development, Structure, Process

Eleventh Edition

John A. Fossum

Center for Human Resources and Labor Studies

Carlson School of Management

University of Minnesota

The McGraw-Hill Companies

LABOR RELATIONS: DEVELOPMENT, STRUCTURE, PROCESS, ELEVENTH EDITION

This book is printed on acid-free paper.

1 2 3 4 5 6 7 8 9 0 QFR/QFR 1 0 9 8 7 6 5 4 3 2 1

ISBN 978-0-07-802915-8

MHID 0-07-802915-5

Vice President & Editor-in-Chief: *Brent Gordon*
Vice President & Director Specialized Publishing: *Janice Roerig-Blong*
Publisher: *Paul Ducham*
Sponsoring Editor: *Daryl Bruflodt*
Director of Marketing & Sales: *Jennifer J. Lewis*
Senior Project Manager: *Lisa A. Bruflodt*
Design Coordinator: *Brenda A. Rolwes*
Buyer: *Susan K. Culbertson*
Media Project Manager: *Balaji Sundararaman*
Cover Design: *Studio Montage, St. Louis, Missouri*
Cover Image: *© Getty Images*
Typeface: *10/12 Palatino*
Compositor: *Cenveo Publisher Services*
Printer: *Quad/Graphics*

Library of Congress Cataloging-in-Publication Data

Fossum, John A.
Labor relations : development, structure, process/John A. Fossum.—11th ed.
p. cm.
ISBN-13: 978-0-07-802915-8 (alk. paper)
ISBN-10: 0-07-802915-5 (alk. paper)
1. Industrial relations—United States. 2. Collective bargaining—United States. 3. Labor unions—United States. I. Title.

HD8072.5.F67 2012
331.0973—dc23 2011026573

www.mhhe.com

About the Author

John Fossum is a Professor Emeritus of Human Resources and Industrial Relations in the Center for Human Resources and Labor Studies, Carlson School of Management, at the University of Minnesota. He began his academic career in 1972 at the University of Wyoming, and in 1974 he moved to the Business School at the University of Michigan. In 1983, he joined the faculty of the University of Minnesota, from which he retired in 2008. Professor Fossum received his BA (economics) from St. Olaf College from Northfield, Minnesota, his MA (industrial relations) from the University of Minnesota, and his PhD (labor and industrial relations) from Michigan State University. In addition to his teaching and research at Minnesota, he served as Director of the Industrial Relations Center (recently renamed the Center for Human Resources and Labor Studies)—a teaching, research, and outreach unit involved with all facets of employment issues—and chair of the Department of Human Resources and Industrial Relations for eight years; as Director of Graduate Studies in Human Resources and Industrial Relations—with programs enrolling more than 225 masters and 15 doctoral students—for four years; and as Associate Dean of Faculty and Research of the Carlson School for two years. He has held visiting faculty appointments at UCLA and Cornell University and is appointed as a Visiting Professor at Szkoła Glówna Handlowa (SGH-Warsaw School of Economics). During the fall semester 2001, he was a Fulbright lecturer at SGH. Additionally, he has taught students and faculty at other universities and programs in Austria, China, France, Poland, and Ukraine. In 1981 to 1982, he was chair of the Personnel/Human Resources division of the Academy of Management, a scholarly organization of academics engaged in research and teaching across a broad spectrum of organizational practices, and was later a member of the executive board of the Industrial Relations Research Association. His research and writing cover a broad set of employment issues.

To all my parents—Peter, Almeda, Herb, and Jane

To Alta for 47 years (and counting) of vigilance, support, and love

To Andy and Amy, Jean and Steve for their accomplishments

To Megan and Kristen for tenacity, charm, and humor

To Georgie Herman, a national treasure among dedicated librarians

And to Solidarność (the free Polish trade union movement) for its central role in overcoming totalitarian rule in Eastern Europe and validating the essential role of democratic trade unions in creating and maintaining a free society.

Preface

The eleventh edition of *Labor Relations: Development, Structure, Process* is being published 34 years after I began to work on the first edition. At that time, most labor relations texts were primarily descriptive, focusing on laws, their interpretation, and the process of negotiation and contract administration. They didn't pay much attention to the results of research studies, particularly from basic behavioral and economic research.

A confluence of fortuitous circumstances catalyzed this project. First, Jim Sitlington, who was then an editor for Business Publications, Inc. (BPI), lived in Ann Arbor, Michigan. I was an assistant professor in the Business School at the University of Michigan. BPI was then a recently created subsidiary of Richard D. Irwin, Inc., a dominant publisher of business and economic texts. One of BPI's major objectives was to develop a broad set of competitive texts for business courses. Jim regularly visited the business school at Michigan looking for potential authors. He suggested to me that BPI needed a labor relations text to fill a major gap in its list. As an untenured assistant professor, I demurred. In addition, my primary teaching assignment was the required organizational behavior (OB) course for first-term MBA students. But he had planted the seed of potential interest.

Second, one of the faculty members in our department, Dallas Jones, was eligible for a sabbatical leave the following year. He taught all of the labor relations courses that our department offered. For him to go on leave, someone from within the department would need to teach his courses. No one else had the preparation or interest, and I was eager to get some time away from the required Organizational Behavior (OB) course, so I volunteered. This meant that I would have to spend all of my time during the coming summer preparing to teach his courses. The work necessary to do that could serve as the basis for preparing a text.

Third, the business school at Michigan had an excellent special collection library—the Industrial Relations Reference Room—staffed with a dedicated group of librarians led by JoAnn Sokkar. The material that I needed not only to give the book the institutional and legal perspective that others had but also to incorporate more broadly based behavioral and economic theory and research was immediately at hand.

So I decided to do it. Cliff Francis, BPI's president, and I began with basically a "handshake" relationship, perhaps neither of us recognizing the actual risks we faced. With the great help of others mentioned below, and after two years of work, the manuscript went to the publisher in 1978 and was first published in 1979. The market reacted very positively to the risks that we had taken. The time was right for a new approach, and we were rewarded with increasing numbers of adoptions.

Much has changed since the first book appeared. The corporatist period in U.S. labor relations was ending at that very point. The employment and industrial structure of the U.S. economy began to change in an accelerating manner, and the prevalence of unionized employment in the private sector declined markedly. Increasing attention began to be paid to the financial performance of private sector firms, and negotiations with unions and resistance to new unionization became much more adversarial in many instances.

Economic globalization has grown rapidly. While producers, customers, and suppliers have increasingly crossed national boundaries in their transactions, labor organizations have not, which has decreased their power to bargain.

The book has changed over time to recognize and incorporate these changes. The eleventh edition includes a large number of updates and changes—particularly the increasing importance of health care costs, access, legislation, and regulation; the growing crises in financing public sector pensions in many jurisdictions; the rapidly expanding use of arbitration as a final forum for deciding statutorily based employment claims; and the shift in emphasis in regulation and enforcement of labor law issues from the Bush to Obama administrations.

The Online Learning Center that accompanies this text (www.mhhe.com/fossum11e) includes password-protected teaching supplements for instructors and chapter quizzes for students.

I hope that you will see this book as presenting a perspective that reflects and balances the viewpoints of both labor and management and includes economic, institutional, legal, and behavioral perspectives. In developing my approach to this book, I am indebted to many institutions and individuals—my graduate school professors at the University of Minnesota and Michigan State University; my academic colleagues at the University of Michigan, UCLA, the University of Minnesota, and the institutions at which I have visited; and human resource and labor relations managers and specialists and national and local union representatives and members who have provided me with insights and background information.

In an age of mergers and acquisitions, it's important to trace the family tree of a surviving project. The first three editions of this text were published by BPI, but by the fourth edition, BPI had been reabsorbed into Irwin, which in turn was sold to Dow Jones. By the time the fifth edition came out, Dow Jones had sold Irwin to the Times Mirror Corporation. Between the sixth and seventh editions, Times Mirror sold its business and economics text business to McGraw-Hill, which has published the eighth, ninth, tenth, and eleventh editions. Thus, over the 33 years this book has been in print, it has been published by three different houses under four different owners.

Many academics have provided reviews and feedback on earlier editions. I am particularly indebted to the reviewers of the first edition, Hoyt

Wheeler of the University of South Carolina (and my first faculty industrial relations colleague as we began our careers at the University of Wyoming) and I. B. Helburn of the University of Texas. The second edition was aided by suggestions and comments from Jim Chelius (Rutgers), Sahab Dayal (Central Michigan), and George Munchus (Alabama at Birmingham). The third edition benefited from reviews by George Bohlander (Arizona State), Richard Miller (Wisconsin), Edmond Seifried (Lafayette), and Bobby Vaught (Southwest Missouri State). The fourth edition was helped by comments and suggestions from Edward Reinier (Southern Colorado) and Jack Steen (Florida State). The fifth edition was reviewed by Frank Balanis (San Francisco State), A. L. "Bart" Bartlett (Penn State), Bill Cooke (Wayne State), Robert Seeley (Wilkes), Ed Suntrup (Illinois at Chicago), and R. H. Votaw (Amber), and provided particularly helpful comments on specific portions of the text. The sixth edition was assisted by comments from Alison Barber (Michigan State), Robert Bolda (Michigan–Dearborn), Michael Buckley (Oklahoma), Constance Campbell (Georgia Southern), Paula Phillips Carson (Southwestern Louisiana), Paul Clark (Penn State), Harry Cohany (Towson State), Millicent Collier (Chicago State), Pete Feuille (Illinois), Robert Forbes (Oakland), Gilbert Gall (Penn State), Denise Tanguay Hoyer (Eastern Michigan), Foard Jones (Central Florida), Gundars Kaupin (Boise State), William Livingston (Baker College Flint), Michael Long (Oakland), Kathleen Powers (Willamette), Gary Raffaele (Texas at San Antonio), Jerald Robinson (Virginia Tech), Stephen Rubenfeld (Minnesota–Duluth), Donna Summers (Dayton), Henry Testa (Herkimer County Community College), Herman Theeke (Central Michigan), Hoyt Wheeler (South Carolina), and Harold White (Arizona State). The seventh edition benefited from feedback from Donna Blancero (Arizona State), Paul Clark (Penn State), Jack Kondrasuk (Portland), Gary Raffaele (Texas–Arlington), Ed Suntrup (Illinois–Chicago), and Mark Widenor (Oregon). The tenth edition reviews of Brian Heshizer (Georgia Southwestern State University), David Piper (Indiana University of Pennsylvania), and Janet Solomon (The George Washington University) were very helpful. The eleventh edition was reviewed by Brian Heshizer (Georgia Southwestern State University), Meika McFarland (Albany Technical College), George Munchus (University of Alabama at Birmingham), Edward O'Dower (Ottawa University), and Joseph Piergiovanni (Delaware County Community College). John Weimeister has contributed strong editorial assistance over several editions and began his career in publishing as a sales representative for BPI while I was working on the first edition. Over the years, as Michigan State graduates, we have actively rooted against Michigan and have mostly commiserated about the outcomes. Lori Bradshaw organized and developed the revision.

Reference materials are particularly important in preparing a text, and reference librarians are very helpful in identifying and locating new information. While the Internet has facilitated a great deal of research, it in no way replaces a well-managed library. I have been assisted by many individuals in preparing this text. For the first two editions, Phyllis Hutchings, JoAnn Sokkar, and Mabel Webb of the Industrial Relations Reference Room at the University of Michigan provided this assistance. Editions three through eleven were aided by Brenda Carriere, Jennifer Clement, Georgie Herman, Mariann Nelson, Christine Schonhart, and Brenda Wolfe of the Industrial Relations Center (now Herman) Reference Room at the University of Minnesota.

Finally, I owe a permanent debt to the parents of my family, both my wife's and mine, for providing me with the examples and support to undertake an academic career; to my wife, Alta, who has made the personal sacrifices of moving several times, has subordinated her interests during times when I was writing, and has offered the wisest counsel; and to my children, Andy and Jean, of whom I am immensely proud.

John A. Fossum

Table of Contents

About the Author iii

Preface v

Chapter 1
Introduction 1

Contemporary Labor Relations 4
What Unions Do 5
Collective Behavior 7
  Group Cohesiveness 7
  Class Consciousness 7
  External Threat 8
Why Workers Unionize 9
  Catalyst for Organization 9
  Individuals and Union Organizing 10
Beliefs about Unions 13
  Willingness to Vote for Union Representation 14
  The Local Community 16
  Union Member Beliefs 16
Unions, Their Members, and Decision Making 16
Labor Unions in the "New Normal" 17
Why Has the Labor Movement Been in Decline? 18
  Transformation in Industrial Relations Systems 20
  What Should Unions Do? 22
Summary and Preview 23
  Plan of the Book 24
Key Terms 26
Selected Web Sites 26

Chapter 2
The Evolution of American Labor 27

Union Philosophies and Types in the United States 28
Early Unions and the Conspiracy Doctrine 29
  Philadelphia Cordwainers 29
  Commonwealth *v.* Hunt 29
  Pre–Civil War Unions 30
The Birth of National Unions 31
  The National Labor Union 31
  The Knights of Labor 32
  The American Federation of Labor 33
Labor Unrest 34
  The Industrial Workers of the World and the Western Federation of Miners 36
  The Boycott Cases 39
  Early Legislation 40
Trade Union Success and Apathy 40
  World War I 40
  The American Plan 41
  The End of an Era 42
Industrial Unions 42
  The Industrial Union Leadership 42
  Organizing the Industrial Workforce 43
Legislation 44
  Norris-LaGuardia Act (1932) 45
  National Industrial Recovery Act (1933) 45
  Wagner Act (National Labor Relations Act, 1935) 45
Employer Intransigence 46
  Constitutionality of the Wagner Act 47
Labor Power 48
  World War II 50
  Reconversion 51
Changing the Balance 51
  Taft-Hartley Act 52
  The New Production Paradigm 53
Retrenchment and Merger 53
  Merger 53
  Corruption 54
  Landrum-Griffin Act 55
Public Sector Union Growth 55
  Federal Executive Orders 55
  Civil Service Reform Act 56

Labor in Crisis and Transition 56
Rising Employer Militancy 56
Striker Replacements 57
New Union Leadership 58
Summary 59
Discussion Questions 60
Key Terms 61
Selected Web Sites 61

Chapter 3
Employment Law and Federal Agencies 62

Overview 62
Railway Labor Act (1926) 64
Norris-Laguardia Act (1932) 66
Wagner and Taft-Hartley Acts (as Amended) 68
Definitions 68
National Labor Relations Board 70
Unfair Labor Practices 70
Representation Elections 73
Unfair Labor Practice Charges and NLRB Procedures 73
Right-to-Work Laws 73
Religious Objections to Union Membership in Health Care Organizations 73
Federal Mediation and Conciliation Service 74
National Emergency Disputes 74
Suits, Political Action, and Financial Relationships 74
Summary and Overview 74
Landrum-Griffin Act (1959) 75
Bill of Rights for Union Members 75
Reports Required of Unions and Employers 75
Trusteeships 76
Other Federal Laws and Regulations 76
Byrnes Act (1936) 76
Copeland Anti-Kickback Act (1934) 76
Racketeer Influenced and Corrupt Organizations Act (1970) 76
Other Major Employment Laws 77
Effects of Implementation of Laws 82
Federal Departments and Agencies 82
Department of Labor 82
Federal Mediation and Conciliation Service 86
National Mediation Board 86
National Labor Relations Board 87
Pension Benefit Guaranty Corporation 90
Labor Law Reform: A Continuing Controversy 90
Trade Treaties 92
Summary 92
Discussion Questions 93
Key Terms 93
Selected Web Sites 93

Chapter 4
Union Structure and Government 94

The Local Union 94
Local Union Democracy 96
Functional Democracy 98
Independent Local Unions 101
National Unions 101
National Union Goals 103
National Union Jurisdictions 104
National Structure 105
National-Local Union Relationship 113
National Union Headquarters Operations 114
National Union Governance and Politics 116
National Unions and Public Policy 117
The AFL-CIO 117
The Change to Win Coalition 118
State and Local Central Bodies 119
Overview of the Union Hierarchy 120
National Union Mergers 120
Union Finances 121
Financial Malfeasance 122
Pension Administration 123
Summary 123
Discussion Questions 124
Key Terms 125
Selected Web Sites 125

Chapter 5
Unions: Member and Leader Attitudes, Behaviors, and Political Activities 126

The Individual and the Local Union 127
Joining, Socialization, and Leaving 127
Member Participation 130
Commitment to the Union 135
Local Union Effectiveness and Member Behavior 139
The Individual as a Union Officer 139
Stewards 139
Local Officers 141
National Unions and Their Environment 142
Employment Law and Administration 143
The Economy 143
Globalization and Organized Labor 144
Political Action 146
Lobbying 152
Use of Union Dues for Political Activity 154
Summary 154
Discussion Questions 155
Key Terms 155
Selected Web Sites 155

Chapter 6
Union Organizing Campaigns 156

Organizing and Union Effectiveness 157
How Organizing Begins 157
The Framework for Organizing 158
Representation Elections 160
Bargaining-Unit Determination 163
Legal Constraints 163
Jurisdiction of the Organizing Union 164
The Union's Desired Unit 164
The Employer's Desired Unit 165
NLRB Policy 166
Other Issues in Unit Determination 168
The Railway Labor Act and Airline Mergers 169
The Organizing Campaign 170
Employer Size and Elections 172
General Organizing Campaign Rules 173
Union Strategy and Tactics 175
Management Strategy and Tactics 182
The Role of the NLRB 184
Election Certifications 184
Setting Aside Elections 185
The Impact of Board Remedies 185
Election Outcomes 186
Other Types of Representation Changes 187
Contextual Characteristics Related to Election Results 187
First Contracts 189
Summary 191
Discussion Questions 191
Key Terms 192
Web Sites 192
Case: GMFC Custom Conveyer Division 193

Chapter 7
Union Avoidance: Rationale, Strategies, and Practices 195

Historical Overview 196
Capitalistic and Trade Union Philosophies 196
Employer Resistance before World War II 196
The Corporatist Period 197
Union-Free Employment 198
The Economic Rationale 198
Inflexible Rules 199
Profitability 199
Shareholder Value 199
Company Investment Decisions 200
Industrial Structure 200
Union-Free Approaches 201
Environmental Factors Associated with Union Avoidance 201
Wage Policies 202
Nonwage Policies 203
Employment Security 204
Employee "Voice" Systems 205
Other Innovative Techniques 208
Developing Practices in Nonunion Employee Relations 209

Preventive Programs 211
Management Campaign Tactics in Representation Elections 212
Decertifications 214
Job Structuring 215
Summary 215
Discussion Questions 216
Key Terms 216
Case: Locating the New Recreational Vehicle Plant 217

Chapter 8
The Environment for Bargaining 218

The Legal and Political Structure 219
Regulation of Employment 220
Waxing and Waning of Corporatist Approaches in U.S. Labor Relations 222
Public Policy and Industrial Organization 223
Competition and Concentration in Markets 224
Regulation and Deregulation 225
Global Competition 226
Labor Force Demographics and Employer Growth 228
Changes in Consumer Demand 229
Employer Interests 230
Labor as a Derived Demand 230
Labor-Capital Substitution 233
Labor Markets 235
Employee Interests 236
Union Interests 237
Bargaining Power 237
Ability to Continue Operations (or Take a Strike) 238
Union Bargaining Power 240
Bargaining Structures 240
Multiemployer Bargaining 241
Industrywide Bargaining 243
National/Local Bargaining 244
Wide-Area and Multicraft Bargaining 244
Pattern Bargaining 245
Conglomerates and Multinationals 246
Coordinated Bargaining 247
Craft Units within an Employer 249
Centralization and Decentralization in Bargaining 249
Changes in Industrial Bargaining Structures and Outcomes 250
Public Policy and Court Decisions 251
Influence of Bargaining Power and Structure 252
Summary 253
Discussion Questions 254
Key Terms 254
Case: Material Handling Equipment Association Bargaining Group 255

Chapter 9
Wage and Benefit Issues in Bargaining 256

Union and Employer Interests 257
Components of Wage Demands 257
Equity 257
Ability to Pay 258
Standard of Living 259
Pay Programs 259
Pay Level 261
Pay Structure 262
Pay Form 268
Pay System 278
Union Effects on Pay 286
Union Effects on Pay Levels 286
Union Effects on Pay Structures and Inequality 292
Union Effects on Pay Form 293
Union Effects on Pay Systems 294
Union Effects on Firm Performance 295
Productivity 295
Organizational Investment and Growth Decisions 296
Profitability and Returns to Shareholders 297
Wage Clauses Found in Contracts 299
Summary 299
Discussion Questions 300
Key Terms 300
Web Sites 300
Case: Health Care Bargaining and the PPACA 301

Chapter 10
Nonwage Issues in Bargaining 302

Nonwage Provisions of Current Contracts 303
Union and Management Goals For Nonwage Issues 304
Design of Work 304
Work Design History 305
Hours of Work 310
Federal Wage and Hour Laws 310
Collective Bargaining and Work Schedules 311
Entitlements to and Restrictions on Overtime 311
Shift Assignments and Differentials 311
Alternative Work Schedules 311
Paid Time Off 312
Length of Contracts 313
Union and Management Rights 313
Discipline and Discharge 314
Grievance and Arbitration 315
Strikes and Lockouts 316
Union Security 316
Working Conditions and Safety 318
Seniority and Job Security 319
Layoff Procedures 319
Promotions and Transfers 320
Time Away from Work 320
Effects of Unions on Nonwage Outcomes 320
Union Influences on Hiring 321
Promotions, Transfers, and Turnover 322
Retirement Programs 324
Job Satisfaction 324
Summary 326
Discussion Questions 327
Key Terms 327
Case: GMFC Attitude Survey 327

Chapter 11
Contract Negotiations 328

Management Preparation 330
Negotiation Objectives and the Bargaining Team 330
Reviewing the Expiring Contract 330
Preparing Data for Negotiations 331
Identification of Probable Union Demands 331
Costing the Contract 332
Bargaining Books 335
Strike Preparation 338
Strategy and Logistics 338
Union Preparation 339
National-Level Activities 339
Local-Level Preparations 340
Negotiation Requests 341
What Is Bargaining? 341
Behavioral Theories of Labor Negotiations 343
Distributive Bargaining 343
Integrative Bargaining 344
Attitudinal Structuring 344
Intraorganizational Bargaining 347
Bargainers and the Bargaining Environment 348
Attributes of the Parties 348
The Process of Negotiation 350
Perceptions of Bargainers 352
The Roles of the Actors in Negotiations 353
Contract Negotiations 354
Initial Presentations 354
Bargaining on Specific Issues 355
Tactics in Distributive Bargaining 355
Committing to a Position 356
Deadlines 356
Settlements and Ratifications 357
Nonagreement 358
The Bargaining Environment and Outcomes 358
Summary 360
Discussion Questions 361
Key Terms 361
Mock Negotiating Exercise 362
A. Contract Costing 362
B. Approach 368
C. Demands 368
D. Organization for Negotiations 370
E. Negotiations 371
F. Additional Information 371
Agreement between General Manufacturing & Fabrication Company, Central City, Indiana, and Local 384, United Steelworkers of America AFL-CIO 376

Chapter 12 Impasses and Their Resolution 399

Impasse Definition 399
Third-Party Involvement 400
Mediation 400
Mediator Behavior and Outcomes 401
Mediator Backgrounds and Training 404
Mediator Activity 404
Fact-Finding 406
Fact-Finding and the Issues 406
Interest Arbitration 407
Review of Third-Party Involvements 407
Strikes 409
Strike Votes and Going Out 409
Picketing 411
Slowdowns 413
Corporate Campaigns 414
Coordinated Campaigns 415
Employer Responses to Strikes 415
Rights of Economic Strikers 419
Evidence on the Incidence, Duration, and Effects of Strikes 420
Boycotts 426
Lockouts 427
Perishable Goods 427
Multiemployer Lockouts 429
Single-Employer Lockouts 429
Bankruptcies 430
Summary 432
Discussion Questions 433
Key Terms 433
Selected Web Sites 433
Case: GMFC Impasse 434

Chapter 13 Union-Management Cooperation 435

Labor and Management Roles and the Changing Environment 435
Organizing and the Evolving Bargaining Relationship 436
Preferences of Management and Labor 437
Levels of Cooperation and Control 437
Integrative Bargaining 438
Mutual-Gains Bargaining 439
FMCS Innovations 440
The Use and Effects of Interest-Based Bargaining 442
Creating and Sustaining Cooperation 444
Methods of Cooperation 446
Areawide Labor-Management Committees 446
Joint Labor-Management Committees 447
Workplace Interventions 448
Alternative Governance Forms 455
Union Political Processes and the Diffusion of Change 455
Management Strategy 457
Research on the Effects of Cooperation across Organizations 457
Research on the Long-Term Effects of Cooperation 460
High-Performance Work Organizations 462
Workplace Restructuring 462
The Legality of Cooperation Plans 463
Employee Stock Ownership Plans 464
The Diffusion and Institutionalization of Change 465
Maintaining Union-Management Cooperation in the Face of External Change 466
Summary 466
Discussion Questions 467
Key Terms 467
Selected Web Sites 467
Case: Continuing or Abandoning the Special-Order Fabrication Business 468

Chapter 14 Contract Administration 469

The Duty To Bargain 469
Conventional Contract Administration 470
Empowered Work Environments 470
Issues in Contract Administration 470
Discipline 471
Incentives 471
Work Assignments 472

Individual Personnel Assignments 472
Hours of Work 472
Supervisors Doing Production Work 473
Production Standards 473
Working Conditions 473
Subcontracting 473
Outsourcing 474
Past Practice 474
Rules 474
Discrimination 474
Prevalence of Issues 475
Grievance Procedures 475
Steps in the Grievance Procedure 475
Time Involved 479
Methods of Dispute Resolution 481
Project Labor Agreements 481
Grievance Mediation 481
Wildcat Strikes 482
Discipline for Wildcat Strikes 483
Employee and Union Rights in Grievance Processing 484
To What Is the Employee Entitled? 484
Fair Representation 485
Grievances and Bargaining 487
Union Responses to Management Action 487
Fractional Bargaining 488
Union Initiatives in Grievances 489
Individual Union Members and Grievances 490
Effects of Grievances on Employers and Employees 493
Summary 495
Discussion Questions 496
Key Terms 496
Case: New Production Equipment: Greater Efficiency with Less Effort or a Speedup? 496

Chapter 15
Grievance Arbitration 498

What Is Arbitration? 498
Development of Arbitration 499
Lincoln Mills 499
Steelworkers' Trilogy 499
Boys Markets *Relaxes Norris-LaGuardia* 501
14 Penn Plaza *and Deferral of Statutory Grievances to Arbitration* 501
Additional Supreme Court Decisions on Arbitration in Unionized Firms 502
NLRB Deferral to Arbitration 504
Arbitration Procedures 505
Prearbitration Matters 505
Selection of an Arbitrator 505
Sources and Qualifications of Arbitrators 507
Prehearing 510
Hearing Processes 511
Representatives of the Parties 512
Presentation of the Case 512
Posthearing 512
Evidentiary Rules 512
Arbitral Remedies 514
Preparation of the Award 514
Procedural Difficulties and Their Resolutions 515
Expedited Arbitration 517
Inadequate Representation 518
Arbitration of Discipline Cases 518
Role of Discipline 518
Evidence 519
Uses of Punishment 519
Substance Abuse Cases 521
Sexual Harassment Violations 521
Fighting 522
Work-Family Conflicts 522
E-Mail Abuse 522
Arbitration of Past-Practice Disputes 523
Arbitral Decisions and the Role of Arbitration 525
Summary 525
Discussion Questions 526
Key Terms 526
Selected Web Sites 526
Cases 526
Case 1 526
Case 2 527
Case 3 528
Case 4 529

Chapter 16
Public Sector Labor Relations 530

Public Sector Labor Law 530
Federal Labor Relations Law 531
State Labor Laws 532
Public Employee Unions 536
Bargaining Rights and Organizing 543
Public Sector Bargaining Processes 544
Bargaining Structures 544
Management Organization for Bargaining 544
Multilateral Bargaining 544
Bargaining Outcomes 546
Union-Management Cooperation 550
Impasse Procedures 552
Fact-Finding 552
Arbitration 553
Strikes 559
Summary 561
Discussion Questions 562
Key Terms 562
Case: Teacher Bargaining at Pleasant Ridge 562

Chapter 17
A Survey of Labor Relations in Market Economies 565

The Development of Labor Movements 566
The Structure of Labor Movements 568
Works Councils 569
Globalization 571
Organizing and Representation 575
Bargaining Issues 578
Bargaining Structures 580
Impasses 583
Union-Management Cooperation 584
Contract Administration 587
Public Sector Unionization 587
Comparative Effects of Unionization 587
Summary 592
Discussion Questions 592
Key Terms 592

Glossary 593

Author Index 605

Subject Index 611

Introduction

In unionized employers, **labor relations** is the ongoing interchange between the **union** and the **employer** that identifies their common and specific interests and creates mechanisms to clarify, manage, reduce, and resolve conflicts over their specific interests. Federal and state laws and regulations and common law establish the basic rules and define and shape the rights and responsibilities of employers and unions in how labor relations is conducted. These laws and regulations are ultimately the product of the democratic political process and jurisprudence as influenced by culture, economic performance, and beliefs about how individual rights can be protected and social justice enhanced.

The basis for the practice of labor relations within a unionized employer is a contract negotiated by the parties. Contracts spell out the rights and obligations of each during the period of time in which they are in effect. Contracts are renegotiated periodically to take into account changing goals and objectives of the parties and changes in the economy and society.

While the practice of labor relations is governed by a fairly stable set of laws and regulations, and its processes and activities are relatively common across employers, practices within employers are, to some extent, unique due to differences in the specific goals of each employer and the union that represents its employees. Within larger employers that operate several **establishments,** labor relations can vary depending on what each produces and whether different unions represent employees in different establishments.

In nations where free markets and the rule of law exist, there are legal means and practical incentives for businesses to incorporate. Incorporation creates a legal entity that can act as if it were a person. Individual investors in a corporation have limited liability—they cannot lose more than their original investments. Many individuals and organizations can collectively own a corporation, and each can sell its shares to new owners at any time while the corporation continues. Stock markets create the opportunity to make ownership highly liquid by providing an institutionalized mechanism for the purchase and sale of shares. Investors often further reduce their risks by diversifying their ownership across several corporations.

Large corporations generally have many owners or shareholders, most of whom do not materially participate in the corporation's day-to-day business. Operational decisions are made by managers hired by the shareholders' elected board of directors. Shareholders who are dissatisfied with corporate performance can either sell their shares or combine with others to oust the current board and its managers. Shareholders are primarily interested in the corporation's financial performance, particularly as reflected in the price of its stock. Higher profitability, cash flows, returns on invested capital, and growth rates typically lead to higher share prices. Minimizing the costs of inputs relative to the price of outputs is an important goal for managers in seeking to improve profitability. Labor costs are one of the inputs to be minimized. Shareholders may also decide, collectively, to sell their interests to another company that seeks to acquire its assets. They may do so over the objections of their current management, employees, and/or other stakeholders.

Enterprises employ workers to produce the goods and services that will be sold to ultimately yield a profit. Public and nonprofit organizations also have goals and objectives that are accomplished through employees' efforts. Employers would like complete freedom to alter the terms and conditions of employment in their workplaces, as necessary, to maximize returns on investments and/or achieve organizational goals.

While labor is somewhat mobile, with workers able to move between employers as opportunities occur, it is less mobile than financial capital. Workers have investments in houses, occupations, family ties and friendships in a local community, and other intangibles. They would like to reduce the risks associated with employment—particularly the risk that their employers will radically change the terms and conditions of employment.

Unionization offers employees a method for countering employers' powers to unilaterally change employment conditions. It is, to an extent, the corollary of incorporation. Members elect officers and may hire agents to bargain an employment contract with the owners' managers. Unionization introduces democracy into the employment relationship. Employees determine, first, whether a majority desires to be represented; second, who to elect as leaders or hire as agents; third, what workplace issues are most important to them; and fourth, whether to accept a proposed contract or to collectively withhold their labor.

Unions develop to counter employer power by exerting control over the employer's labor supply. Unions emphasize the need to create and maintain solidarity among members of the working class to effectively assert power in the workplace. In general, they favor greater equality in pay across employees and greater worker control of the work environment. Unions also stress the importance of continual improvements in living standards for their members, best attainable through increases in their pay.

Higher pay and other improvements in employment, other things equal, lead to lower returns to capital. Thus, the goals of capitalists and unionists are inevitably in conflict.

In democracies, laws and regulations ultimately reflect the will of the electorate. If employment conflicts exceed what voters will tolerate, or if the conflicts' results are manifestly different than desired and highly important relative to other issues, voters will elect leaders who promise change in the desired direction. Thus, the limits within which unions and employers develop their particular relationships are defined by public policy. How much conflict exists depends on how able the parties are to accommodate the goals of their opposite numbers while achieving their own. Within the limits imposed by public policy, unions and employers are free to devise and implement their own relationships, usually through a negotiated contract together with each party's management mechanisms to administer, interpret, and enforce the agreement. This text focuses on the bases of the underlying conflicts, the tactics the parties use to gain power to achieve their goals, and how the process works in an ongoing relationship.

An important point to consider in studying labor relations is that employers can exist without unions, but unions cannot exist without employers. Thus, where public policy permits, it's to be expected that most employers will try to avoid unionization, to look for opportunities legally to remove unions if they exist in their workplaces, and to minimize their impact if they do. Unions, on the other hand, rarely try to eliminate a unionized employer in which they represent workers. If a unionized employer is eliminated, the jobs the union represents are also simultaneously eliminated, weakening the union's long-run power.

It is also important to remember that a corporation's shareholders ultimately control decisions about its direction, investments, and existence—whether to continue operations, sell, or liquidate—depending on which best meets their interests. Managers are employed to determine how best to implement these decisions, but unless the managers are also shareholders, they have no independent ability to determine the distribution of profits. In addition to being expected to achieve certain operating results, managers might also be expected to either solicit or consider possible sales of all or part of the firm if that would provide greater benefits to shareholders.

While this introduction has focused on the private sector, there are many parallels that can be drawn for labor relations in the public sector. Where permitted, public sector unionism has grown rapidly so that the number of union members in the public sector is about equal to the total of private sector members.

Public sector labor relations are more complicated, as we will show in Chapter 16. Part of the complication is due to the fact that voters are not exactly like shareholders and that successful union political activity may lead to the "board of directors" (elected officials) who direct and review managerial actions boosting the unions' bargaining agenda.

Unions are simultaneously economic and political organizations. As economic actors, unions seek to control the supply of labor to employers in order to improve economic returns for their members. To accomplish this, they also seek to create and maintain power to influence the direction of laws and regulations, to provide a vehicle for advancing their leaders' and members' purposes, and to survive and grow. Conflicts may exist between union levels as national union goals may not completely agree with goals at the local level.

Employers have corporate goals and objectives with regard to unions and coping with unionization and **collective bargaining. Line managers** have production and sales goals that must be achieved. Achievement is facilitated or inhibited by how successfully labor relations (or **employee relations** in a nonunion environment) is practiced. In larger employers, **human resource** or **industrial relations managers** and staff assist the organization by negotiating and administering collective bargaining agreements and advising and assisting line managers in dealing with interpreting and implementing the contract while pursuing organizational goals.

CONTEMPORARY LABOR RELATIONS

Labor relations and employment in the United States have changed markedly since 1980. Unionized employment, in both the proportion and number of workers, has declined substantially due to a shift from manufacturing toward services, the increasing intellectual content of jobs, the globalization of manufacturing, geographic shifts in the concentration of employment toward less unionized regions of the country, fewer successes in organizing large units of employees, and an overall decline in union organizing activity.[1] Unionization in other developed economies has also declined. Global economic development and competition, freer trade, and an emphasis on corporate financial performance have strongly influenced employment patterns and reduced union bargaining power.

To survive, unions must generate economic benefits for their members. To achieve gains, unions need to be able to exert bargaining power through some degree of labor supply control, and employers must be profitable enough to pay for the gains. Today's global economy, combined with the elimination of anticompetitive regulations in several major industries, has reduced union bargaining power because unions don't control labor supply on an international basis and the costs of increased benefits cannot readily be passed on to consumers.[2]

[1] H. S. Farber and B. Western, "Ronald Reagan and the Politics of Declining Union Organization," *British Journal of Industrial Relations*, 40 (2002), pp. 385–401. See also R. J. Flanagan, "Has Management Strangled U.S. Unions?" *Journal of Labor Research*, 26 (2005), pp. 33–63.

[2] M. L. Wachter, "Judging Unions' Future Using a Historical Perspective: The Public Policy Choice between Competition and Unionization," *Journal of Labor Research*, 24 (2003), pp. 339–357.

Since the late 1970s union-management relations have become increasingly adversarial in the United States. Union bargaining power has declined. Employers resisted unionization more vigorously and, when labor market conditions permitted, reacted strongly to potential and actual strikes by threatening to use or hiring replacement workers. Additionally, some employers have adopted human resource management practices that increase the extent to which employees are involved in the management of their workplaces and pay attention to improving factors that could lead to declining employee satisfaction.

Union representation has declined from 35 percent in 1955 to a little more than 12 percent now. The declining size means unions exert less influence on employment practices through "spillovers" than they did in the past. A **spillover** occurs when a unionized employment practice is adopted by nonunion employers in order to avoid unionization by copying what unions have won for their members. Some U.S. unions are attempting to increase their influence on U.S.-based multinational corporations by assisting foreign unions in organizing the corporations' offshore employees—especially in low-wage developing economies.[3]

WHAT UNIONS DO

Unions evoke controversy. Many people have strong positive or negative opinions about their tactics and effects. Unionization creates monopoly power through contracts by fixing wages for a specific period of time (usually above the market clearing wage). It also provides employees a voice in how the employment relationship is implemented in their workplaces. Thus, unions benefit their members **(monopoly power),** at the expense of higher costs, and benefit the public by requiring that employers respond to employee grievances **(voice power).**[4] Union monopoly power costs less than 1 percent of gross domestic product (GDP). Administration costs in obtaining and exercising monopoly power are less than 0.2 percent of GDP. The higher wages and benefits that union members receive, relative to their nonunion counterparts, are probably more than eight times larger annually than the cost of their union dues.[5]

Large differences exist in the degree of unionization across industries and occupations. Some of the differences across industries relate to their

[3] M. Fong and K. Maher, "U.S. Labor Leader Aided China's Wal-Mart Coup," *The Wall Street Journal*, June 22, 2007, p. 1.

[4] R. B. Freeman and J. L. Medoff, *What Do Unions Do?* (New York: Basic Books, 1984).

[5] C. M. Stevens, "The Social Cost of Rent Seeking by Labor Unions in the United States," *Industrial Relations*, 34 (1995), pp. 190–202. The impacts estimated have been reduced from the 1995 findings to account for declining union wage premiums and proportion organized since the study was published.

TABLE 1.1 Changes in Employment and Union Membership, 1983–2009 (in thousands)

Source: Condensed from B. T. Hirsch and D. A. Macpherson, *Union Membership and Earnings Data Book 1994: Compilations from the Current Population Survey* (Washington, DC: Bureau of National Affairs, 1995); and U.S. Bureau of Labor Statistics data on union affiliation of employed wage and salary workers by occupation and industry, http://stats.bls.gov/news.release/union2.t03.htm, updated January 22, 2010.

	Employment		% Union Members	
Sector	**1983**	**2009**	**1983**	**2009**
U.S. total	88,290	124,490	20.1	12.3
Private sector	72,656	103,357	16.5	7.2
Public sector	15,634	21,133	36.7	37.4
Industry				
Agriculture	1,446	1,045	3.4	1.1
Mining	872	662	20.6	8.6
Construction	4,609	6,613	28.0	14.5
Durable goods manufacturing	7,930	8,438	25.9	10.8
Nondurable goods manufacturing	11,294	5,016	29.2	11.2
Transportation	3,627		49.9	
Transportation and warehousing		4,258		25.8
Communications and public utilities	1,435	1,994	45.2	21.3
Information		2,790		10.0
Wholesale trade	3,657	3,386	9.3	4.9
Retail trade	14,510	14,465	8.6	5.3
Finance, insurance, and real estate	5,709	8,236	3.4	1.8
Services	15,146		9.5	
Professional and business services		11,325		2.3
Education and health services		19,289		8.6
Leisure and hospitality		11,352		3.1
Other services		5,598		2.9
Federal government		3,594		28.0
State government		6.294		32.2
Local government		11,244		43.3

varied mix of occupations, ages, and employment practices. Unionization is more prevalent where jobs require employer-specific knowledge and where internal workplace rules more strongly influence employee outcomes.[6]

Over the past 26 years the proportion of employees represented by unions has decreased. As Table 1.1 shows, this decrease is largely related to industrial and occupational employment changes. During the 1983–2009 period, employment increased by over 36 million while union membership declined by about 7.8 percent. In the private sector, there are almost 4.7 million fewer members, and the proportion who are members declined by more than half, from 16.5 to 7.2 percent. Public sector unionization increased slightly from 36.7 to 37.4 percent. About 1,476,000 employees whose employment is in a unionized establishment choose not to be union members.

[6] G. Hundley, "Things Unions Do, Job Attributes, and Union Membership," *Industrial Relations*, 28 (1989), pp. 335–355.

COLLECTIVE BEHAVIOR

If employees are dissatisfied with their present employment, one might ask why they don't change employers. Some employees may believe that alternative employment that matches their skills will be hard to find where they live, particularly if the skills are specific to their employer. Others believe that they might be able to exert collective pressure to relieve the dissatisfaction. Thus, people can express dissent about their workplace in two ways—either by quitting (exit option) or by trying to reform it (voice option).[7] Forming a union creates a collective voice to influence change at work.

Group formation is a necessary precursor to unionization in the United States. Groups form because of mutual interests or similarities among their members and a desire to direct common effort toward maintaining or changing some condition that affects them. They also form in response to perceived danger or threat. Management "by fear" may lead to a collective response from group members. "Wagon-circling" is a pervasive phenomenon that occurs when a group perceives danger.

Group Cohesiveness

One of the characteristics that defines a cohesive group is a high degree of similarity in the values and behavior of its members. One of these values may be class consciousness. Age, seniority, and other background characteristics are also probably quite similar. Cohesive groups usually have a leader or group of leaders that strongly reflect the values of the group and are deferred to by other members of the group. Cohesiveness may also be a function of a perceived external threat. Unions emphasize the need for cohesiveness to members through calls for "solidarity" during periods of threat.

Class Consciousness

Class consciousness has often been suggested as a catalyst for the formation of unions. Employees and employers often come from different social classes, and if mobility between classes is perceived as unlikely and if income inequality is high, class consciousness and a perception of inequity are more likely to develop. Unionization is viewed as a means for equalizing power in dealing with employers. Americans are highly individualistic, however, and American unions have generally followed pragmatic, business-related agendas, downplaying class consciousness.[8] At the same time (and as will be noted later) specific differences that exist between managerial and employee privileges and outcomes are frequently used to raise class consciousness during organizing campaigns. To the extent that

[7] A. O. Hirschman, *Exit, Voice, and Loyalty* (Cambridge, MA: Harvard University Press, 1970).

[8] M. J. Piore, "The Future of Unions," in G. Strauss, D. G. Gallagher, and J. Fiorito, eds., *The State of the Unions* (Madison, WI: Industrial Relations Research Association, 1991), pp. 387–410.

FIGURE 1.1
Hypothetical Relationship between Threat and Cohesiveness

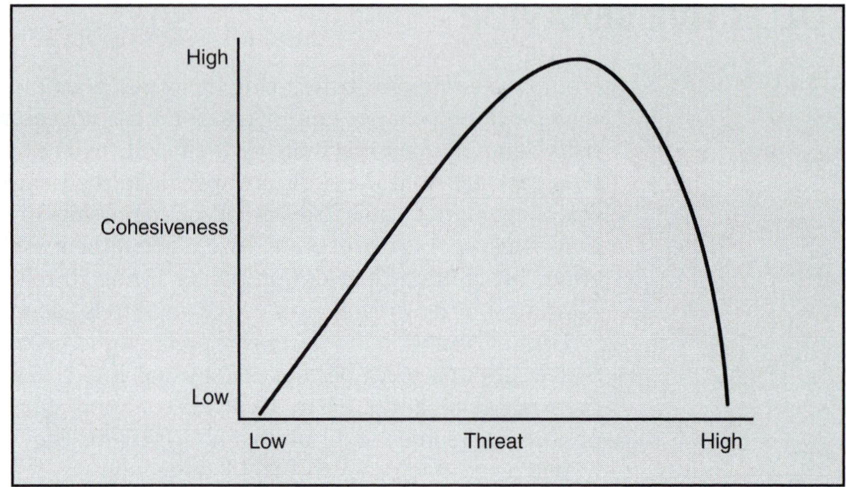

there are large or changing differences between managers and workers within the same organization in terms of the distribution of pay, safety, and employment security, class consciousness is increased and the demand for unionization increases. To the extent that these situations are ameliorated and/or other mechanisms such as human resource management practices that are more friendly to employees are implemented, demand for unionization will be low.[9]

External Threat

If external threat increases cohesiveness, will greater threat continue to increase cohesiveness, or is some limit reached? If a worker thinks that negative outcomes will occur for one who acts alone but not for a similarly acting group, then belonging to the group has positive consequences, and cohesiveness would be expected to be high. If an employer is unwilling to grant a wage increase to a single employee and dares the employee to quit, the same employer might not be willing to risk denying a collectively demanded raise if the alternative is a strike.

How far would group members be expected to go in individually sacrificing for the good of the group? When the costs of membership outweigh the benefits perceived from remaining a group member, cohesiveness will break down. As Figure 1.1 shows, the hypothetical relationship between threat and cohesiveness is an inverted *U*.

Unions can't ensure similar backgrounds among their members because management makes hiring decisions and unions are obligated to admit all

[9] B. E. Kaufman, "The Future of Private Sector Unionism: Did George Barnett Get It Right after All?" *Journal of Labor Research*, 22 (2001), pp. 433–457.

employees who want to join. To maintain cohesiveness, unions must continually convince employees they will receive greater employment benefits through continued unionization, often casting management as a threat to those benefits. To maintain cohesiveness through perceived threat, an adversarial relationship follows. Thus management actions against individuals or the group may benefit the union because management action can then be rebuffed, modified, or rescinded through group action.

WHY WORKERS UNIONIZE

Employees become union members through one of three processes. First, nonunion employees may organize a union to bargain collectively for them. Second, employees in a unit covered by a collective bargaining agreement may decide to join the union. Third, newly hired employees may be required by the collective bargaining agreement where they work to join the union (to the extent of paying dues) as a condition of continued employment.

Catalyst for Organization

The interest among employees in unionization is related to a number of demographic, economic, and attitudinal factors. In general, women, minorities, and senior workers are more interested in union representation. Job content, experience, younger age, social-democratic political beliefs, lower education, and lower personal income also relate to a willingness to form or join a union.[10] Lower satisfaction with career prospects and higher perceptions of job stress are also related to an interest in representation.[11] Workers in companies with innovative human resource management practices are less likely to desire unions.[12]

Employees are more likely to unionize as job dissatisfaction increases. The presence of *any* organizing activity is related to lower satisfaction as compared to units where it does not occur. Employees are more likely to vote for unions due to dissatisfaction with employment conditions rather than job task characteristics. Dissatisfaction with **job security,** economics, and supervisory practices were most predictive of a pro-union vote across a set of studied elections.[13] The presence and level of organizing

[10] J. Fiorito, D. G. Gallagher, and C. R. Greer, "Determinants of Unionism: A Review of the Literature," in K. Rowland and G. Ferris, eds., *Research in Personnel and Human Resource Management*, vol. 4 (Greenwich, CT: JAI Press, 1986), pp. 269–306; and S. M. Lipset and I. Katchanovski, "The Future of Private Sector Unions in the U.S.," *Journal of Labor Research*, 22 (2001), pp. 229–244.

[11] B. A. Friedman, S. E. Abraham, and R. K. Thomas, "Factors Related to Employees' Desire to Join and Leave Unions," *Industrial Relations*, 45 (2006), pp. 102–110.

[12] J. Fiorito, "Human Resource Management Practices and Worker Desires for Union Representation," *Journal of Labor Research*, 22 (2001), pp. 335–354.

[13] J. M. Brett, "Why Employees Want Unions," *Organizational Dynamics*, 8, no. 4 (1980), pp. 47–59.

activity in various units of a large multilocation company were predicted by poor supervision, co-worker friction, amount of work required, lack of advancement, bad feelings about the company, physical surroundings, and nature of the work.[14]

Dissatisfaction alone does not automatically mean a union **organizing campaign** will result or a **representation election** will be won by the union. Two conditions have to exist to predict organizing attempts and a union win. First, employees have to be dissatisfied and believe they are individually unable to influence a change in the conditions causing their dissatisfaction. Second, a majority of employees have to believe that collective bargaining would improve conditions more than changing jobs and that its benefits outweigh the costs.

Individuals and Union Organizing

Several factors influence the organizing process. Dissatisfaction is consistently associated with interests in unionizing and is also consistently associated with turnover.[15] Since both unionization and turnover are predicted by dissatisfaction, organizing involves other influences as well, with employees believing that their individual outcomes are best leveraged by collective action to improve the outcomes of all employees in the unit, rather than by quitting.

A unionization model suggests that gaps between expectations and achievements motivate employees to find ways to eliminate them. They may first try nonadversarial methods to accomplish change. If they are frustrated, or if part of a gap is due to a perceived threatening environment created by the employer, they may prepare to act against the employer. Decisions leading to readiness are made by assessing conditions that facilitate and inhibit action (see Chapter 6). Workers are expected not only to judge whether they expect outcomes would be better or worse if unionization occurs but also to be influenced by their political and/or ideological beliefs.[16] Figure 1.2 displays this relationship. The figure contains a "rational calculation" box. The next section examines how this calculation is made and displays the process in Figures 1.3 and 1.4.

In an organizing campaign, workers must decide whether unionization is in their interest. To make this decision, they assess whether the likely outcomes of unionization will be positive or negative and whether

[14] W. C. Hamner and F. J. Smith, "Work Attitudes as Predictors of Unionization Activity," *Journal of Applied Psychology*, 63 (1978), pp. 415–421.

[15] J. M. Carsten and P. E. Spector, "Unemployment, Job Satisfaction, and Employee Turnover: A Meta-Analytic Test of the Muchinsky Model," *Journal of Applied Psychology*, 72 (1987), pp. 374–381.

[16] H. N. Wheeler and J. A. McClendon, "The Individual Decision to Unionize," in G. Strauss, D. G. Gallagher, and J. Fiorito, eds., *The State of the Unions* (Madison, WI: Industrial Relations Research Association, 1991), pp. 47–84.

FIGURE 1.2 **An Integrative Model of Factors Related to the Decision to Support Unionization**

Source: H. N. Wheeler and J. A. McClendon, "The Individual Decision to Unionize," in G. Strauss, D. G. Gallagher, and J. Fiorito, eds., The State of the Unions, Madison, WI: Industrial Relations Research Association, 1991, p. 60. Copyright © 1991 The Industrial Relations Research Association (now known as the Labor and Employment Relations Association) Champaign, IL. Reprinted by permission from the publisher.

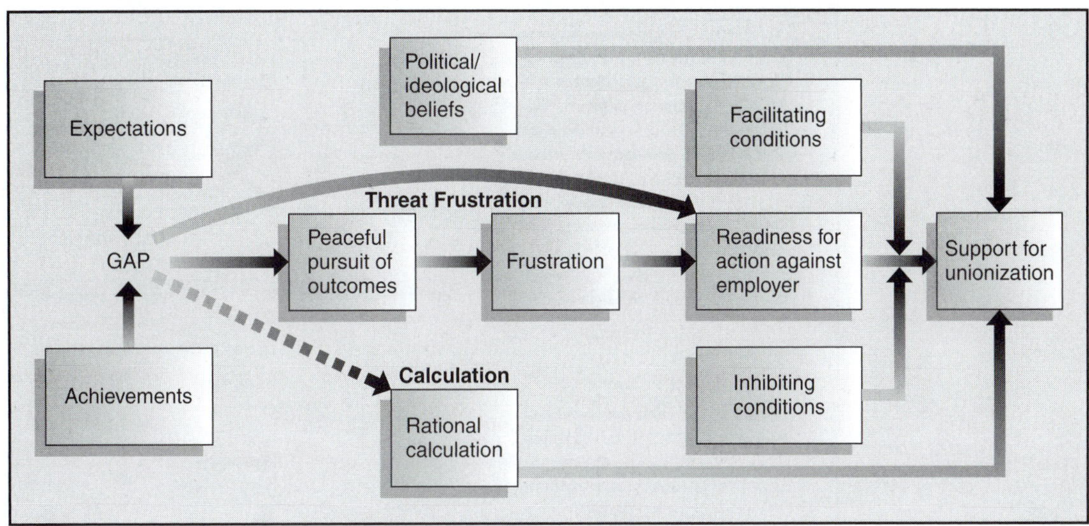

FIGURE 1.3
Rational Calculations

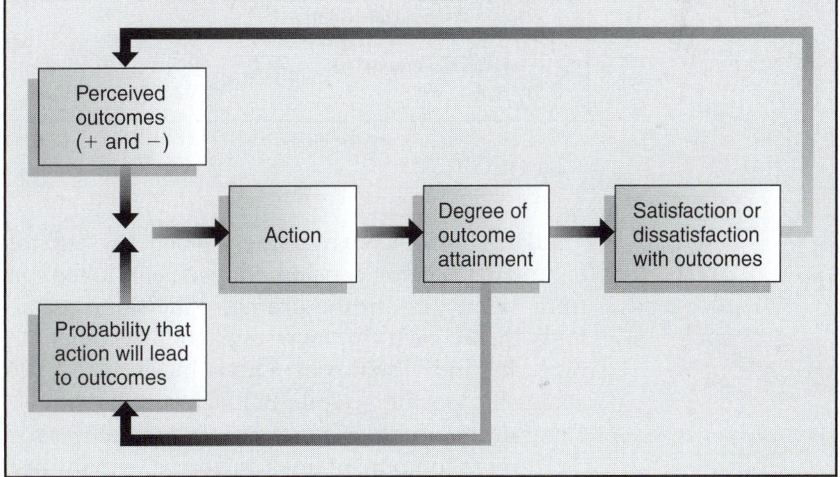

it's likely that working for or voting for a union will lead to positive or negative outcomes. Workers are likely to consider how satisfied they are presently with the issues the union is raising, how successful they have been in having their complaints dealt with by their managers, and what efforts and risks will be necessary if they work in support of unionization. Figure 1.3 outlines a model of an individual's decision process.

FIGURE 1.4
Beliefs about Organizing

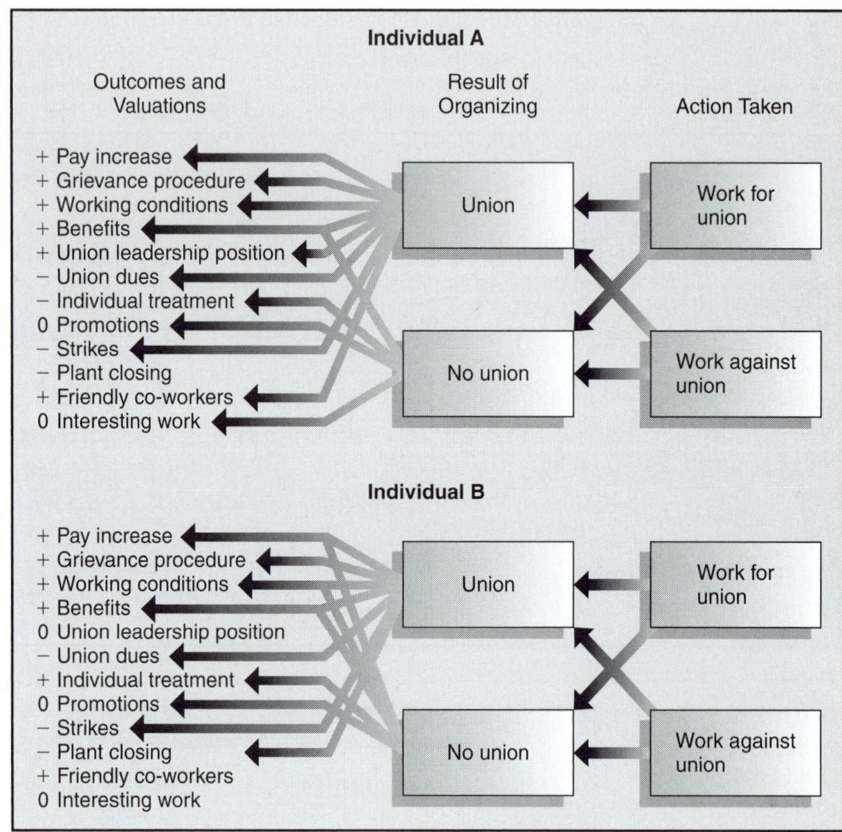

Figure 1.4 depicts a hypothetical belief system for two employees where organizing is being considered. Each employee evaluates likely outcomes from organizing. In the example, the same set of outcomes is specified for both, but each employee evaluates the outcomes differently, reflecting his or her individual preferences. Individual A positively values a union leadership position, while B attaches no positive or negative value to it. Other differences also exist, such as preferences for individual treatment.

The next component links outcomes with the result of an action—in this case, success or failure in organizing. For individual A, success in organizing is associated with six positive and two negative outcomes. Failure to organize leads to one positive, one negative, and two neutral items. If individual A believes taking action will increase the likelihood of unionization, he or she will likely be an activist because a greater net balance of positive outcomes results from a union. Individual B, on the other hand, expects four positives and three negatives from a union and four positives and one neutral from no union. B would be predicted to oppose the union.

Some consequences could follow directly from actions taken rather than their results. For example, if individual A thinks neither working for nor working against the union will affect the organizing campaign outcome, then no effort would be expected. Why? It's easier. But effort would be predicted from individual A if A thinks it's necessary for unionization and believes his or her effort will contribute to winning the election.

Some might argue that this model makes it difficult to predict what people in a group will do. This is the case if group members have diverse backgrounds or widely differing beliefs as to what actions will lead to results or what outcomes will follow from results. However, a number of things probably reduce this diversity.

Employees often see avenues other than union membership to attain valued outcomes from employment. For example, if promotions based on individual merit and interesting work are highly valued but seen as unattainable on jobs likely to be unionized, then many employees desiring them would probably leave. Positive past job outcomes are increasingly valued by employees. Thus, unionizing attempts may begin because management withholds rewards or changes the system so that rewards differ from what people in the jobs have learned to value.

Union organizing campaigns are aimed at increasing perceptions that unions can help attain positive and avoid negative employment outcomes and create more homogeneous attitudes and behaviors. Both labor and management attempt to direct employees toward a stronger belief that unionization will have positive and negative consequences, respectively.

Examining the perceptions and choices individuals make about unions should make it clear that, before unionization is possible, employees must hold a common belief that a union will benefit them. This means a large heterogeneous unit would probably be difficult to organize, whereas a smaller, more stable work group should be easier. Even considering differences among individuals, however, people likely take into account not only their own probable gains and losses but also the opinions of family and other workers important to them.[17] Thus, differences among members of a bargaining unit after unionization may be substantial and must be considered by the union in its representational activities.[18]

BELIEFS ABOUT UNIONS

Each of us has beliefs about the appropriate role of unions in society. These beliefs result from our upbringing and experiences, involvement with union members, work in unionized or nonunion employers, and gains or costs we perceive to be associated with organized labor.

[17] See D. Knoke, *Organizing for Collective Action* (New York: Walter de Gruyter, 1990).

[18] L. A. Newton and L. M. Shore, "A Model of Union Membership: Instrumentality, Commitment, and Opposition," *Academy of Management Review*, 17 (1992), pp. 275–298.

A 2009 Gallup Poll survey found that 48 percent of respondents approved of labor unions while 45 percent disapproved (the rest were neutral or expressed no opinion). Respondents expected that unions will be weaker nationally in the future (48 vs. 24 percent that expected stronger unions) and preferred that unions would have less influence in the future (42 vs. 25 percent desiring greater influence). Respondents agree that unions are instrumental in helping their members to achieve employment goals (66 vs. 28 percent who believe they mostly hurt their members) while a majority believes that unions hurt the economy in general and employees who are not represented.[19]

At the same time, job satisfaction is also in decline. A Conference Board survey in 2009 found that only 45 percent of respondents were satisfied with their jobs. They also were less satisfied with job security, their work-related extrinsic rewards, and their managers. This was the first time that the survey found less than half of respondents were satisfied with their jobs. Both those who approved and disapproved of unions believed employees need protection from employers, and close to half of those who disapproved still felt that, without unions, laws and benefits employees have gotten would be weakened or repealed and that laws enabling employees to organize should be strengthened.[20]

In general, opinion evidence finds that employees believe they need to have more influence in how workplaces are organized and operated. Dissatisfaction with their employment is closely linked to a lack of trust in employer promises and to poor management-employee relationships. Employees believe cooperation with management is important, but many feel management is unwilling to work closely with employees.[21] Table 1.2 illustrates the gap between perceived importance of wanting and having employee influence in the workplace.

Willingness to Vote for Union Representation

When people are asked whether they would vote for a union to represent them, about one-third respond yes. Pro-union sentiments are influenced by the perceived power of the labor movement and its instrumentality for worker gains and also by specific beliefs employees have about how unions affect their personal intrinsic and extrinsic outcomes and introduce more fairness in the workplace.[22] In addition, perceptions that unions are

[19] L. Saad, "Labor Unions See Sharp Slide in U.S. Public Support," Gallup Poll, September 3, 2009 (Princeton, NJ: Gallup).

[20] J. M. Gibbons, *I Can't Get No … Job Satisfaction, That Is* (New York: Conference Board, 2010).

[21] R. B. Freeman and J. Rogers, *What Workers Want* (Ithaca, NY: Cornell University Press, 1999), pp. 39–64.

[22] S. P. Deshpande and J. Fiorito, "Specific and General Beliefs in Union Voting Models," *Academy of Management Journal*, 32 (1989), pp. 883–897.

TABLE 1.2 Beliefs about Wanting and Having Influence in the Workplace

Source: R. B. Freeman and J. Rogers, What Workers Want (Ithaca, NY: Cornell University Press, 1999), pp. 48–49. Copyright © 1999 by Russell Sage Foundation. Used by permission of the publisher, Cornell University Press.

	Wanting Influence	**Having Influence**	**Average Gap**	**Individual Gap**
	Percentage of workers for whom it is very important to have a lot of influence	Percentage of workers with a lot of direct influence and involvement	Difference between "Wanting influence" and "Having influence" columns	Percentage of workers with less involvement than they want
Deciding what kinds of benefits are offered to employees	60%	6%	54%	83%
Deciding how much of a raise in pay the people in your work group should get	41	6	35	76
Deciding what training is needed for people in your work group or department	62	29	33	53
Deciding how to work with new equipment or software, if needed	52	28	24	46
Setting goals for your work group or department	55	32	23	43
Setting safety standards and practices	55	35	20	45
Deciding how to do your job and organize the work	76	57	16	31
Setting work schedules, including breaks, overtime, and time off	42	30	12	47
Average	55%	28%	27%	53%

working to better the lot of all working people positively influence an interest in voting for representation.[23] Some of the decline in union membership may relate to changing perceptions about unions. Between 1977 and 1984, beliefs about unions' abilities to improve employment conditions fell, while job satisfaction increased for nonunion employees and decreased for unionized employees.[24] Even those dissatisfied with their

[23] J. Fiorito, "Unionism and Altruism," *Labor Studies Journal*, 17, no. 3 (1992), pp. 19–34.

[24] H. S. Farber, "Trends in Worker Demand for Union Representation," *American Economic Review*, 79, no. 2 (1989), pp. 161–165.

jobs are less likely to be interested in unionization than they would have been in the past.[25]

The Local Community

Local community attitudes affect union power. Unions influence the community's political makeup. The depth of support for the union among its members and citizens who may not be union members influences the union's ability to gain important collective bargaining outcomes. Community influence is most likely when an unfavorable outcome of a labor relations dispute threatens the community.[26] Union action may also influence public policy decisions on potentially favorable tax abatements for employers.[27]

Union Member Beliefs

Union members place the highest priorities on the way their union handles grievances, their ability to get feedback from their union, additional fringe benefits, their ability to have a say in the union, better wages, and job security. Union member preferences for bargaining outcomes will be covered in detail in Chapters 9 and 10. Union members are generally satisfied with the performance of their unions, particularly on economic issues. Ninety percent of union members say they would vote to continue unionization in their workplaces.[28]

Among a sample of public sector union members who could choose to join or not join the union that represented them, satisfaction with the union's performance was related to beliefs in the goals of the union movement and endorsement of the union's preferred positions on promotions and job security. Less favorable attitudes were found among those who joined for social reasons or who felt pressured to join.[29]

UNIONS, THEIR MEMBERS, AND DECISION MAKING

To understand the activities of unions, it's necessary to recognize that officers are elected and contracts require ratification by the members. Bargaining units are not organized until a majority of employees desire

[25] H. S. Farber and A. B. Krueger, "Union Membership in the United States: The Decline Continues," in B. E. Kaufman and M. M. Kleiner, eds., *Employee Representation: Alternatives and Future Directions* (Madison, WI: Industrial Relations Research Association, 1993), pp. 105–134.

[26] J. A. Craft, "The Community as a Source of Union Power," *Journal of Labor Research*, 11 (1990), pp. 145–160.

[27] B. Nissen, "Successful Labor-Community Coalition Building," in C. Craypo and B. Nissen, eds., *Grand Designs: The Impact of Corporate Strategies on Workers, Unions, and Communities* (Ithaca, NY: ILR Press, 1993), pp. 209–223.

[28] Freeman and Rogers, *What Workers Want*, p. 69.

[29] M. E. Gordon and L. N. Long, "Demographic and Attitudinal Correlates of Union Joining," *Industrial Relations*, 21 (1981), pp. 306–311.

representation, officers are elected or defeated by majorities of **local union** members, and contracts are ratified by a majority of union members in the bargaining unit. Ultimately, the policies of large national unions are influenced strongly by the actions of majorities of local union members.

For union decisions that require voting, it's helpful to understand the **median voter** concept.[30] To obtain a majority in any decision in which the alternatives lie on a continuum, the chosen alternative must be favored by the person who occupies the middle political position on that issue since a majority requires 50 percent plus one. Thus, to predict the outcome of an election or ratification, an analyst must understand the preferences of the middle person on a continuum of attitudes toward an issue. The median voter concept will be discussed at several points in this book when we examine union decision making.

LABOR UNIONS IN THE "NEW NORMAL"

The 1980s was a decade of accelerating decline for organized labor as economic changes, coupled with employer and governmental initiatives, surprised unions and eroded membership. The 1990s left unions facing crucial structural and functional problems even as the economy generally prospered. The 2000s was a decade of economic malaise bracketed by the dot.com bubble crash and 9/11 attack at the beginning and the subprime mortgage-spawned financial crash at the end. The 2010s began with a weak economic recovery under way, high unemployment with only tepid job creation, record domestic fiscal deficits, debt crises in several Euro zone countries, growing fiscal difficulties in states and local governments, a rapidly increasing bulge of retirees in all developed Western economies, and increasingly partisan politics in Washington. Some have dubbed this scenario the "new normal," as if these conditions will dog the country for the foreseeable future.

How unions will fare in the new normal depends on a number of factors, particularly whether the American electorate and workforce sees the new normal as something they are willing to endure as their future way of life. What the electorate decides will have significant spillovers to the workplace. There is an apparently profound current disconnect between the average citizen and his or her legislative or congressional representative. If there is a secular movement toward replacing incumbents with progressive legislators, then laws and regulations to facilitate organizing will be enacted, but so, too, will social programs that reduce the need for workers to organize to obtain the outcomes they would get from the legislation. In other words, employment will be increasingly regulated by government

[30] M. D. White, "The Intra-Unit Wage Structure and Unions: A Median Voter Model," *Industrial and Labor Relations Review*, 35 (1982), pp. 565–577.

with less need for unions except to influence economic outcomes—which is increasingly difficult in a global economic environment. If there is a secular movement toward conservatism, then regulations will be relaxed and employers will increase their opposition to unions, and even public sector unions may be in retreat as legislators insert themselves into bargaining to reduce public sector pensions and benefits toward private sector level coverage, or even seek to limit or eliminate collective bargaining rights for public sector employees. How this plays out will depend on where voters place the greatest blame for the economic debacle that began in 2008—laissez-faire capitalism and regulatory neglect or interventionist deficit spending of federal politicians.

WHY HAS THE LABOR MOVEMENT BEEN IN DECLINE?

Some suggest the U.S. legislative climate, along with declining membership, has retarded organizing, representation, and bargaining outcomes relative to the past and compared to Canada.[31] One perspective traces the decline to aggressive employer actions to fight organizing campaigns, build new plants where they will not be initially unionized and where antipathy toward unions probably exists, and violate or ignore labor laws aimed at protecting collective bargaining.[32] An alternative position is that larger numbers of employees were unionized in the past than wanted to be represented, partly because of coercive organizing tactics in which union members refused to deal with nonunion employees. Legislation outlawing this behavior coincides with the beginning of the decline in unionization.[33] Still another position argues that the relative satisfaction of nonunion employees has increased to become substantially equivalent to that of unionized workers, particularly along economic dimensions, eliminating the motivation to organize.[34]

It's argued that the employment relationship in union and nonunion firms is substantially different. Nonunion employees may be treated more consistently in promotions and pay increases, have more involvement in managing production, be subject to fewer rules, and have a more leisurely

[31] G. N. Chaison and J. B. Rose, "New Directions and Divergent Paths: The North American Labor Movements in Troubled Times," *Labor Law Journal*, 41 (1990), pp. 591–595.

[32] R. B. Freeman, "Contraction and Expansion of Unionism in the Private and Public Sector," *Journal of Economic Perspectives*, 2, no. 2 (1988), pp. 63–88; P. C. Weiler, "Governing the Workplace: Employee Representation in the Eyes of the Law," in B. E. Kaufman and M. M. Kleiner, eds., *Employee Representation: Alternatives and Future Directions* (Madison, WI: Industrial Relations Research Association, 1993), pp. 81–104.

[33] M. W. Reder "The Rise and Fall of Unions: The Public Sector and the Private," *Journal of Economic Perspectives*, 2, no. 2 (1988), pp. 89–110.

[34] Farber and Krueger, "Union Membership Decline."

work pace.[35] Finally, it has been suggested that the workplace governance paradigm is changing away from unionism as a mechanism for gaining voice and that unions might not be the best platform for representing the plethora of interests among groups of employees. Beginning in the 1960s, laws and regulations have been increasingly implemented to establish the legal rights of a variety of groups among employees identified by race, gender, ethnicity, disability, and in some jurisdictions sexual orientation. Groups of employees coalesce around common interests or group membership to pressure their employers to address employment issues of particular interest to their groups.[36]

A historical perspective suggests that the relatively small proportion of the workforce belonging to unions is strongly related to the economic history of the United States. While U.S. unions have waxed and waned at various points during the past two centuries, several conditions may have prevented their empowerment. First, employers fiercely protected, and unions ceded to them, the capitalistic, market-driven system the United States has embraced. Thus, prices, and ultimately wages, are controlled by the market rather than by collective bargaining or administrative order. Second, with the exception of the skilled construction trades, employers have always controlled the content of jobs. Even skilled trades have been increasingly defined by employers through attempts to blur their boundaries. Third, employers have historically been involved with the U.S. educational system, especially the high schools, colleges, and universities that have the closest relationship to developing skills of future employees. Ironically, given organized labor's strong advocacy of free public education, this has occurred within both private and public school systems. Fourth, business has been strongly involved with government in advocating legislation, in providing executives for public policy positions, and in using the courts to litigate labor problems. Fifth, and probably most telling, the large middle class in the United States has had strong interests in efficiency and productivity. If the middle class perceives income distribution as fair, then support for collective bargaining will not be strong.[37]

The fifth point—the effect of the middle class—appears to be the most important (recognizing that it's also related to the others). The future ability of the labor movement to exercise monopoly power depends on a class consciousness developing or a perception by the middle class that income is unfairly distributed. If the middle class decreases in size relative to the

[35] J. Evansohn, "The Effects of Mechanisms of Management Control on Unionization," *Industrial Relations*, 28 (1989), pp. 91–103.

[36] M. J. Piore and S. Safford, "Changing Regimes of Workplace Governance, Shifting Axes of Social Mobilization, and the Challenge to Industrial Relations Theory," *Industrial Relations*, 45 (2006), pp. 299–325.

[37] For a provocative expansion of these issues, see D. Montgomery, *The Fall of the House of Labor* (New York: Cambridge University Press, 1987).

upper and lower classes, then the lower class could exert more power through unions because efficiency claims would not be as strong. If the income distribution is perceived as unfair, as median voters, the middle class may seek collective bargaining as a method for restoring an appropriate balance. Recent econometric studies find that income inequality has increased as union coverage declined. A comparison of the United States and Canada shows that inequality is substantially lower in Canada, which has a larger proportion of unionized employees.[38] However, two scholars, who earlier saw differences in institutions between the United States and Canada being related to differences in levels of unionization, now predict continuing decline for private sector unions in both countries unless there is a major upswing in organizing activity and success.[39] Organizing activity is financed by current union members. Increasing unionization in the industry or community where one is employed can positively influence wages and benefits, but organizing elsewhere may have little additional value unless it's highly pervasive. The resources necessary to successfully organize would require large contributions from current members.[40]

As will be noted at several points in later chapters, the difference in average wage rates between unionized and nonunion workers in similar occupations is greater in the United States than in virtually every other developed economy. The relative magnitude of this difference in the United States may help explain the greater resistance of U.S. employers to unionization since union wage differentials directly reduce profitability.[41]

Transformation in Industrial Relations Systems

From the end of World War II until the late 1960s, the American economy led the world in innovation and productivity. However, the 1970s and early 1980s found the United States lagging in productivity and gripped in a period of high inflation and low profitability. Part of this was due to substantial real increases in the price of oil following political turmoil in the Middle East that contributed to the establishment of the OPEC oil cartel. Automobile manufacturers in particular lost considerable market share because their products not only had lower gas mileage but also were of substantially lower quality than comparably priced imports. Japanese manufacturers established a growing reputation for high quality and productivity. American manufacturers sought to imitate the workforce

[38] J. DiNardo and T. Lemieux, "Diverging Male Wage Inequality in the United States and Canada, 1981–1988: Do Institutions Explain the Difference?" *Industrial and Labor Relations Review*, 50 (1997), pp. 629–651.

[39] J. B. Rose and G. N. Chaison, "Unionism in Canada and the United States in the 21st Century," *Relations Industrielles*, 56 (2001), pp. 34–62.

[40] H. S. Farber and B. Western, "Accounting for the Decline of Unions in the Private Sector, 1973–1998," *Journal of Labor Research*, 22 (2001), pp. 459–485.

[41] Flanagan, "Has Management Strangled U.S. Unions?"

flexibility, team-based work designs, and higher skill requirements found among Japanese manufacturers. These major discontinuities in the American economy shifted the initiative in employee relations from labor to management—a trend that has continued to the present.[42]

Presently, the greatest challenge facing private sector unions is the continually increasing globalization of production. As will be noted in more detail in Chapter 8, competition from foreign labor reduces union bargaining power and can lead to the loss of jobs. One study found that for any industry in which more than 10 percent of goods were produced in low-wage countries, these low wages influenced U.S. wage rates for production employees in those industries.[43] At the same time, shifting lower-skilled production work to offshore facilities increases the amount of skilled work available in the United States assuming that lower production prices, and hence lower product prices, increase demand and enable the firm to expand. While major employers have increasingly exercised global options, unions around the world have maintained jurisdictions largely within their own countries. In fact, within North America, unionization has become more country-specific during a period in which employment and plant location alternatives have increased.

In understanding the threats facing unions in maintaining or increasing membership, it is important to understand that in many cases economics are international while politics are local. When an employer decides to outsource or move production abroad, the decision frequently sets up internal competition among employees to retain jobs. Often, unionized workers from two different local unions of the same national will offer competitive concessions in order to have their plant be the one that remains open. This may increase job security for the winners, but it erodes union bargaining power on a companywide basis. Companies may also seek tax concessions from governments representing a particular country or geographical region in deciding where to locate.

Bargaining power is higher for unions that represent workers who must deliver services directly to the consumer. For example, at the time this book was revised, U.S. domestic air travel could not be provided by foreign carriers, and baggage handlers were always domestic workers. Unions representing these workers are less vulnerable to international comparisons, but they may be vulnerable to nonunion entries in their industries. We would expect these unions to have greater survival

[42] For a theoretical approach to understanding these changes, see C. L. Erickson and S. Kuruvilla, "Industrial Relations System Transformation," *Industrial and Labor Relations Review*, 52 (1998), pp. 3–21. For an intensive exploration of the changes, see T. A. Kochan, H. C. Katz, and R. B. McKersie, *The Transformation of American Industrial Relations* (New York: Free Press, 1986).

[43] R. B. Freeman, "Are Your Wages Set in Beijing?" *Journal of Economic Perspectives*, 9 (1995), pp. 15–32.

opportunities in the future. The same would hold true for local construction. Once a site has been selected, there is no geographic competition unless the employer imports workers from other locations.

What Should Unions Do?

The challenge to unions involves membership. Traditionally, membership depended on employment in a workplace governed by a collective bargaining agreement. If employment was lost, membership often terminated. Only in the building trades, the maritime unions, and some entertainment unions does membership survive after employment with a particular employer ends. The reason for this difference is that union **hiring halls** were the primary source of employees in these industries. If future employees have increasingly temporary ties to an employer, more unions may need to take on the same features as the building trades. They could offer continuity in benefits and training programs to improve occupational skills and to enable members to excel in comparison to nonmembers. If industrial unions don't offer these services and act only as a collective bargaining agent, they will find it increasingly difficult to attract members in a transient employment environment.

With the increased mobility of capital experienced during the last 30 years, one source of potential union power and solidarity could be the development of community-based movements.[44] These could reinforce the resolve of employees in employers with difficult labor relations problems, reduce the ability to hire replacement workers for strikers, and galvanize a united local policy on employment.

The labor movement has increased its attention to organizing, particularly among professionals and low-paid service workers, but has been notably unsuccessful, with the rate of new organizing falling at about the same rate as overall membership.[45] It sees formidable barriers in its path, particularly the vigor of employer anti-union campaigns and what it considers the lax enforcement of existing labor law and protection of concerted activity. At the same time, there has been little showing of grass roots demand for representation except in specific situations involving low-wage service workers, who are frequently recent legal or illegal immigrants.

Within the labor movement, there is a great deal of debate about the strategy organized labor in the United States should adopt for the future. There has been a lot of internal strife in the labor movement related to the belief by some union leaders that insufficient effort and an ineffective strategy have led to the failure to organize. The Change to Win coalition (covered in greater detail in Chapters 2 and 4) has implemented a variety of community organizing tactics to successfully organize custodial

[44] Nissen, "Successful Labor-Community Coalition Building," and Piore, "The Future of Unions."

[45] Flanagan, "Has Management Strangled U.S. Unions?"

workers in several major U.S. cities. However, it has experienced its own internal difficulties that will be covered in Chapter 4. As we note in Chapters 4 and 5, labor has always been politically active, almost always casting its lot with the Democratic Party. However, since the passage of the Wagner Act in 1936 (covered in Chapters 2 and 3), no major laws and regulations have been enacted that enhance union power vis-à-vis employer power. Thus, unions have not generally benefited much from a Democratic president and/or Congress, but they have been at risk from Republican presidents and/or Republican majorities in Congress. As we will also note in Chapters 3 and 6, the "winner-take-all" rules in union representation elections mean that union members who are not in represented units cannot invoke their union's power on their behalf, contrary to what occurs in several European Union countries.

Should unions in the future increasingly cooperate with management in the workplace, maintain the status quo, or become more militantly adversarial?[46] In society as a whole, should unions adopt a "value-added unionism" approach, aiming to increase mutual gains for both employers and employees as a vehicle for enhancing relevance for organizing and reducing employer opposition, or should they shift their approach from traditional "business unionism" toward "social movement unionism," in which industrial and social justice become the touchstones to catalyze organizing?[47] For the latter to occur, a national class consciousness would need to develop. If income inequality were to increase and occupational mobility were to stagnate, this outcome might be possible. For value-added unionism to take hold, unions would need to find a way to enhance productivity at rates greater than employer-designed human resource management systems could deliver.

Summary and Preview

The evidence indicates that dissatisfaction leads to interest in organizing. For the most part, the general public sees unions and their leaders as beneficial to the public interest but also likely to increase tensions in the workplace. A significant minority of unorganized employees say they would vote for union representation if an election were held in their work unit.

Cohesiveness appears to be a necessary property for successful organizing. Similarities among group members and external threats have a positive influence on cohesiveness. The adversarial role that unions take is likely to enhance the cohesiveness of their memberships.

[46] See S. Estreicher, "Strategy for Labor," *Journal of Labor Research*, 22 (2001) pp. 569–580, for a conversation among unionists representing each of these three views. For a complete and provocative view see H. N. Wheeler, *The Future of the American Labor Movement* (Cambridge, UK: Cambridge University Press, 2002); and A. Verma, S. Wood, and T. Kochan, eds., "Union Decline and Prospects for Revival," *British Journal of Industrial Relations*, 40, no. 3 (2002).

[47] B. Nissen, "The Recent Past and Near Future of Private Sector Unionism in the U.S.: An Appraisal," *Journal of Labor Research*, 24 (2003), pp. 323–338.

This book examines the historical development of the labor movement, the structure of unions and institutions involved in labor relations, and the processes of collective bargaining, including the identification of bargaining issues, negotiations, and contract administration.

Plan of the Book

The title, *Labor Relations: Development, Structure, Process*, indicates a focus on the employment relationship in unionized settings. The words following the colon establish the topical flow of the book and indicate the necessity of understanding foundations before applications.

Development

The present state of the labor movement and collective bargaining results from a variety of economic and social situations in which strategic choices were made by labor leaders and managers. In examining the development of the labor movement, the conditions related to the initial formation of unions must be understood. Public opinion influenced the response of public officials toward the subsequent formation of unions and their operation.

Other areas of interest concern the reactions of employers to unions. Where did unionization begin? In what industrial sectors have unions been most prevalent? How have the parties adapted to each other over the long run? What are the present stances of employers toward unions, and where are the greatest changes occurring?

Chapters 2 and 3 address development issues, tracing the historical evolution and present public policy environment in which American labor operates. Although union activity has occurred throughout the nation's history, effective labor organizations are about 125 years old. These chapters indicate that labor law and its enforcement have played an important role in the conduct of labor relations. The development chapters trace societal and economic changes and detail the statutes that have contributed to the development and particular shape of collective bargaining in the United States—in particular, legislation passed in the 1930s to protect employees in forming unions and engaging in collective bargaining contributed to union growth. The current interpretation of statutes may be hastening the decline.

Structure

The examination of union structure focuses on the office and institutions that make up the labor movement or have major impacts on it. In this regard, the last part of Chapter 3 details the federal institutions involved in regulating collective bargaining. Chapter 4 lays out the structure of the various organizational levels of the labor movement and identifies the location of its power centers. Chapter 4 also discusses the organizational structure of several national unions, the roles played by union officers, and the causes and consequences of the recent increase in union mergers. Chapter 5 examines the attitudes and activities of union members and the political activities of unions. The various structures within which negotiations between labor and management take place are detailed in Chapter 8.

Process

The greatest emphasis in this text is on process. The discussion of process concerns methods used to organize employees into unions, identifies issues of importance in bargaining, explains the organization and processes involved in negotiations, and details how labor and management deal with differences that occur during bargaining and after a contract has been signed. These areas are covered in Chapters 6 through 15.

Special Chapters

The last two chapters of the book involve special issues that cut across development, structure, and process. Chapter 16 covers differences in collective bargaining in the public sector. Chapter 17 examines some of the differences between unions and labor relations in the United States and other industrialized nations.

Preview

In this text, each chapter begins by introducing the subject and highlighting some major issues that should be explored to gain an understanding of the development, structure, or process of labor-management relations.

Most chapters end with discussion questions. These either relate to relatively broad issues raised in the chapter or ask that a position be formulated for labor or management on one of these issues. Many chapters also conclude with case material. A continuing running case will be based on a simulated organization, General Materials & Fabrication Corporation (GMFC), a heavy-equipment manufacturer. Other cases or incidents involving different types of employers are also included. The first case involving GMFC follows Chapter 6. Later, a mock negotiation exercise, contract administration cases, and cases discussing arbitration issues arising from the contract are presented. These cases should help you gain a greater appreciation of the process involved in the collective bargaining relationship.

Some chapters also have reference lists of Web sites. However, they are not extensive lists because Web addresses are often subject to change, especially those for topical materials.

Point of View

Most readers of this book are or have been employed, but most have probably not been union members, and most do not expect to be union members. But readers have likely formed attitudes toward labor unions and collective bargaining through information provided by the news media.

Media attention is usually focused on unusual events. In labor relations, this usually means a major negotiation, a strike, a lockout, or an unlawful-practice charge. The media shouldn't be faulted for this—excitement draws viewers and sells newspapers, but it does not reflect day-to-day labor relations in the United States. Overt disagreement occurring in strikes, lockouts, and unlawful practices, is relatively infrequent.

This text includes information to increase your ability to understand labor relations as it is practiced in the United States. This understanding must be based on the evolution and development of the labor movement to its present form, the subject matter and jurisdiction of labor law, and the practices of the two major parties in the process—management and labor.

The subject should be interesting. In teaching courses in organizational behavior, human resource management, and labor relations, I have found most students are more intrinsically interested in labor relations than in the other two, perhaps because we are likely to have strong attitudes about what we think are the proper roles each party should take in the process and notions about which side should be blamed for the problems surrounding labor relations. I do not expect your basic posture toward labor relations to change as a result of either this book or the course you are taking, but I expect you will gain a far greater understanding of why the parties act as they do.

Key Terms

Labor relations, *1*
Union, *1*
Employer, *1*
Establishment, *1*
Collective bargaining, *4*
Line manager, *4*
Employee relations, *4*
Human resource manager, *4*
Industrial relations manager, *4*
Spillover, *5*
Monopoly power, *5*
Voice power, *5*
Job security, *9*
Organizing campaign, *10*
Representation election, *10*
Local union, *17*
Median voter, *17*
Hiring hall, *22*

Selected Web Sites

www.bls.gov
www.unionstats.com

The Evolution of American Labor

Labor relations in the United States is as old as the nation. The American labor movement's goals and methods have been shaped by the events, leaders, philosophies, and tactics that led to its initial successes. Major milestones include the development of local **craft unions,** the formation of **national unions,** the creation of the **American Federation of Labor (AFL),** industrial violence and the overcoming of employer resistance, federal laws curtailing injunctions against union activities and enabling representation, the creation of the **Congress of Industrial Organizations (CIO),** the merger of the AFL and CIO, and its breakup through the defection of the national unions that formed the **Change to Win (CTW)** coalition in 2005.

Waves of immigration and major economic panics have strongly influenced the course of development and success rate of organized labor. Throughout most of its history, the American labor movement has been predominantly results-oriented rather than ideologically oriented. Surviving labor organizations have adapted to change and been responsive to member needs.

As you study this chapter, consider the following questions:

1. How have laws, public policy, and public opinion changed over time? Consider the influences of employers, unions, legislators, judges, and the news media.
2. What ultimate form did the American labor movement develop?
3. What types of events contributed to and detracted from union growth? Do these still operate in the same manner?
4. How have the personalities of the major actors within the labor movement contributed to union growth?
5. Why have American unions generally accepted the capitalist system?

UNION PHILOSOPHIES AND TYPES IN THE UNITED STATES

Since the union movement began, certain values have influenced its development. Their intensity has varied across time and between labor organizations, but they underlie the actions of all. The values can be summarized as follows: In society there is a productive class that ultimately creates the tangible products or delivers the services people demand. Labor is thus the ultimate creator of wealth and entitled to its returns. Society generally includes a monied aristocracy that owns the means of production and controls much of society's wealth. Unless major efforts are exerted to avoid it, education is unequal and undemocratically provided. Class distinctions exist, and the goals of workers and employers differ. Thus, trade unions are necessary to protect workers' rights.[1]

In most democracies, unions have favored **corporatism,** in which unions, employers, and the government are jointly involved in governing the employment relationship.[2] Unions have led the political struggle to establish laws and regulations requiring minimum standards for the terms and conditions of employment and to require consultation and bargaining with management where employees desire them. As Chapter 17 will note, corporatism still prevails in some parts of the European Union, but it has eroded in the United States since the 1960s.

Unions' strategies can be characterized within four categories. **Uplift unionism,** concerned with social issues, is aimed at the general betterment of educational and economic outcomes and labor-management systems for workers. **Revolutionary unionism** is primarily oriented toward changing the fabric of society, overthrowing the capitalist system, and replacing it with worker control of industry. **Business unionism** involves the representation of employees' immediate interests, primarily the regulation of wages, hours, and terms and conditions of employment. This philosophy was typified by Adolph Strasser, one of the AFL's founders, in 1883, when he testified in Congress, "We have no ultimate ends. We are going on from day to day. We are fighting only for immediate objects—objects that can be realized in a few years." **Predatory unionism** occurs when the union's prime goal is to enhance itself at the expense of the workers it represents.[3] No U.S. union exists in an absolutely pure form. Most take a business unionism approach: concerned with immediate goals, accepting the system as it is, and working for union goals within that system.

[1] M. F. Neufeld, "Persistence of Ideas in the American Labor Movement: The Heritage of the 1830s," *Industrial and Labor Relations Review*, 35 (1982), pp. 207–220.

[2] See N. Lichtenstein, *The Most Dangerous Man in Detroit: A History of Walter Reuther and the UAW* (Charlottesville: University of Virginia Press, 1995), for examples of this philosophy.

[3] R. F. Hoxie, *Trade Unionism in the United States* (New York: Appleton-Century-Crofts, 1921).

EARLY UNIONS AND THE CONSPIRACY DOCTRINE

The genesis of the American labor movement parallels the birth of the nation. In 1778, New York **journeyman** printers won a wage increase through collective action.[4] But for the next 100 years, the union movement did not grow at the same pace as the nation due to adverse legal decisions, the predominantly rural nature of 19th-century America, and substantial numbers of relatively unskilled immigrants competing for jobs at relatively low wages.

Philadelphia Cordwainers

The Federal Society of Journeyman Cordwainers (shoemakers) was organized in Philadelphia in 1794.[5] It formed as a result of changes in the way shoes were marketed. Until about 1790, journeymen almost exclusively manufactured "bespoke" (i.e., custom) work. Master shoemakers took orders and supplied material to the journeymen, who produced a pair of shoes or boots for an agreed-on wage. Days or weeks might elapse between the order and the finished shoes. Because this was inconvenient and expensive for customers, the masters developed three other market classes: "shop," "order," and "market" work. Shop work was for the master's stock, order work was for wholesalers, and market work was for the public market. Each was priced lower than its predecessor, and masters differentiated wage rates depending on the market being supplied. The journeymen cordwainers responded by attempting to fix wages for shoemaking at the rate for bespoke work.

The cordwainers' concerted refusal to work at rates that varied depending on the market for their output was seen by the employers as a criminal conspiracy. A court found that the cordwainers' collective actions in pursuit of their personal interests contravened the public's interests and was hence a criminal conspiracy. Each member of the union was fined $8 (see Exhibit 2.1).[6] Thus, the **conspiracy doctrine** was established, under which a union could be punished if either its means or its ends were deemed illegal by the courts. This legal interpretation of union activities persisted in some forms into the first third of the 20th century.

Commonwealth v. *Hunt*

The conspiracy doctrine was softened substantially in 1842 when the Massachusetts Supreme Court overturned the conviction of Boston Journeymen Bootmakers' Society members for refusing to work in shops

[4] U.S. Department of Labor, Bureau of Labor Statistics, *A Brief History of the American Labor Movement*, Bulletin 1000, rev. (Washington, DC: U.S. Government Printing Office, 1970), p. 99.

[5] For a thorough analysis of this group, see J. R. Commons, *Labor and Administration* (New York: Macmillan, 1973), pp. 210–264.

[6] J. S. Williams, *Labor Relations and the Law*, 3rd ed. (Boston: Little, Brown, 1965), p. 18.

Exhibit 2.1

CHARGE TO THE JURY IN THE PHILADELPHIA CORDWAINERS CASE

"What is the case before us? . . . A combination of workmen to raise their wages may be considered in a twofold point of view: one is to benefit themselves . . . , the other is to injure those who do not join their society. The rule of law condemns both. . . . [T]he rule in this case is pregnant with sound sense and all the authorities are clear on the subject. Hawkins, the greatest authority on criminal law, has laid it down, that a combination to maintain one another, carrying a particular object, whether true or false, is criminal."

Source: Condensed from 3 Commons and Gilmore 228–33, which was partially reprinted in J. S. Williams, *Labor Relations and the Law*, 3rd ed. (Boston: Little, Brown, 1965), p. 20.

Exhibit 2.2

INTERPRETATION OF THE CONSPIRACY DOCTRINE UNDER *COMMONWEALTH V. HUNT*

"The manifest intention of the association is to induce all those engaged in the same occupation to become members of it. Such a purpose is not unlawful. It would give them a power which might be exerted for useful and honorable purposes, or for dangerous and pernicious ones. If the latter were the real and actual object and susceptible of proof, it should have been specially charged. . . . In this state of things, we cannot perceive that it is criminal for men to agree to exercise their acknowledged rights in such a manner as best to subserve their own interests."

Source: 4 Metcalf 129, as contained in J. S. Williams, *Labor Relations and the Law*, 3rd ed. (Boston: Little, Brown, 1965), p. 22.

where nonmembers worked below the negotiated rate.[7] The court held the society's action was primarily to persuade nonmembers to join rather than to secure criminal ends and refused to enjoin organizing activities. However, it did not say that injunctions against other collective activities would be stopped (see Exhibit 2.2).[8]

Pre–Civil War Unions

During the first half of the 19th century, unions were faced with a number of problems, including employers who doubted their legitimacy, courts that enjoined and punished collective activity, and employment competition from increasing numbers of immigrants. But even in the face of these impediments, collective activity still occurred. Most was among skilled artisans, such as the cordwainers, but even unskilled textile workers in Massachusetts became involved.

[7] 4 Metcalf 111 (1842).

[8] Williams, *Labor Relations and the Law*, p. 22.

Newly organized workingmen's parties contributed to the election of President Andrew Jackson.[9] Following Jackson, President Van Buren issued an executive order decreasing the workday for federal employees to 10 hours. Unions in major U.S. cities successfully used strikes to secure wage increases. Union membership swelled in the early 1830s, but poor economic conditions soon tipped the scales in favor of employers, and union activity waned where membership threatened one's continued employment.

THE BIRTH OF NATIONAL UNIONS

Beginning in the 1850s, a few national trade unions formed. These early unions have all disappeared or been merged into surviving unions. Until the Civil War, unions represented certain trades or industries, a pattern that ultimately prevailed in the United States. After the Civil War, however, the first major movements were increasingly national, without craft or industry distinctions. These early movements were strongly focused on major public policy issues. Immigration posed a problem for unions because while many members were immigrants, they feared the effects that further immigration would have on wages. Many civic organizations opposed open immigration and advocated literacy tests. Trade unions adopted these positions at the end of the 1800s, partly to attain mainstream institutional legitimacy.[10]

The National Labor Union

The **National Labor Union (NLU)** was founded in 1866. Its goals were largely political and reformist rather than economic or immediate. Its leader, William Sylvis, had been a founder of the National Molders' Union in 1859. NLU goals included introduction of the eight-hour workday, establishment of consumer and producer cooperatives, reform of currency and banking laws, limitations on immigration, and establishment of a federal department of labor.

The NLU was open not only to skilled-trades workers but also to other interested and sympathetic individuals. Suffragists, particularly prominent at its national meetings, attempted to get the NLU to endorse their efforts to gain voting rights for women.

Sylvis was the backbone of the NLU. His death in 1869 and its subsequent alliance with the Greenback Party in 1872 doomed the NLU. A lack of leadership and inattention to worker problems contributed to its demise.[11] However, the first attempts to coordinate labor organizations nationally had begun—and would ultimately be successful.

[9] See F. R. Dulles, *Labor in America*, 3rd ed. (New York: Crowell, 1966), pp. 35–52.

[10] C. Collomp, "Unions, Civics, and National Identity: Organized Labor's Reaction to Immigration, 1881–1897," *Labor History*, 29 (1988), pp. 450–474.

[11] Dulles, *Labor in America*, pp. 100–113.

The Knights of Labor

The **Knights of Labor** began in Philadelphia in 1869. Its goals and membership, while different from those ultimately embodied in the U.S. labor movement, were closer to the final pattern than the NLU. It was part labor organization and part fraternal lodge. Workers were organized on a city-by-city basis across crafts. When a city assembly (the Knights' local unit) recruited enough members from a particular craft large to be self-sustaining, it was spun off.

Philosophically, the Knights of Labor was more willing than the NLU to recognize the short-term legitimacy of capitalism. The leaders of the Knights—first Uriah Stephens, then Terence Powderly—were essentially idealists who favored the use of **arbitration** rather than strikes. Employers used the philosophical opposition to strikes to their advantage. However, the rank and file were more militant than their leaders and used strikes effectively.

The Knights of Labor grew slowly, taking three years to gain enough members to establish a second assembly in Philadelphia. By 1875, district assemblies had headquarters in Reading and Pittsburgh, Pennsylvania, as well. Because it was a secret society, the Knights of Labor was in conflict with the Roman Catholic Church. Clergy believed Knights members were required to take secret oaths that might commit them to beliefs inconsistent with Roman Catholic dogma. Ultimately, negotiations between Terence Powderly and James Cardinal Gibbons led to a ruling that Roman Catholics could belong to the Knights.[12]

Depressions had taken their toll on labor unions in the 19th century, but the Knights' strength grew after one began in the early 1880s. In several railroad strikes, the Knights successfully organized workers and won its demands—a sharp contrast to the crushing defeat railroad strikers suffered in 1877. In 1885, financier Jay Gould attempted to break the union by laying off its members. Retaliating, the union struck the Wabash Railroad and refused to handle its rolling stock on other lines, forcing Gould to stop firing Knights members. The nationally publicized negotiations added impetus to organizing. By the middle of 1886, membership in the Knights of Labor reached 700,000.[13]

There was irony in the Knights' success against Jay Gould.[14] Many new members joined hoping to gain the same concessions Gould had given. But the leaders' position was oriented toward the long run rather than toward satisfying day-to-day grievances. They did not favor an incremental collective bargaining approach and firmly opposed using strikes

[12] P. Taft, *Organized Labor in American History* (New York: Harper & Row), 1964, pp. 84–89.

[13] Dulles, *Labor in America*, pp. 139–141.

[14] N. W. Chamberlain and D. E. Cullen, *The Labor Sector*, 2nd ed. (New York: McGraw-Hill, 1971), pp. 97–98.

Exhibit 2.3

THE ASCETIC TERENCE POWDERLY ON LABOR PICNICS

"I will talk at no picnics. When I speak on the labor question, I want the individual attention of my hearers, and I want that attention for at least two hours, and in that two hours I can only epitomize. At a picnic where the girls as well as the boys swill beer I cannot talk at all. . . . If it comes to my ears that I am advertised to speak at picnics . . . I will prefer charges against the offenders for holding the executive head of the Order up to ridicule."

Source: F. R. Dulles, *Labor in America: A History,* 3rd ed. (New York: Crowell, 1966), p. 136.

as weapons to pressure employers. The leaders' long-run perspective and their belief in "rational" processes for achieving ultimate objectives are typified by these quotes from Powderly and Knights of Labor publications: "You must submit to injustice at the hands of the employer in patience for a while longer," and "Do not strike, but study not only your own condition but that of your employer. Find out how much you are justly entitled to, and the tribunal of arbitration will settle the rest."[15]

Long-run goals were inconsistent with the immediate results new members sought. Differences in interests between the ascetic Powderly (see Exhibit 2.3) and the burgeoning rank and file hastened the Knights' decline. In addition, an antagonistic press increasingly linked the Knights with anarchists and radical action. Public pressure, power vested in reformist factions, and employers' unwillingness to arbitrate—all contributed to membership dropping to 75,000 by 1893. But the withering of the Knights of Labor did not end national organizations. At the height of the Knights' success, the first enduring national federation was formed.

The American Federation of Labor

The American Federation of Labor (AFL) was created in a meeting of national unions in Columbus, Ohio, in 1886.[16] It was born out of the frustration craft unionists felt about the mixing of skilled and unskilled workers in Knights of Labor assemblies and the Knights' increasingly reformist orientation. The Knights also tended toward centralization of authority, diminishing the autonomous power of individual craft unions.

Twenty-five national labor groups representing 150,000 skilled-trades workers formed the federation. The national unions maintained autonomy and control over their trades while ceding authority to the AFL to settle disputes among them.[17] During most of its history, it maintained a

[15] Ibid., p. 98.

[16] Dulles, *Labor in America*, p. 161.

[17] Ibid.

skilled-worker, or craft, orientation and an antipathy toward organizing the unskilled. The AFL concentrated on winning tangible gains by entering into collective agreements with employers. It aimed at rationalizing the workplace through labor contracts.

The early direction of the AFL was influenced by the philosophies of its first president, Samuel Gompers. As a member of the New York Cigarmakers local, he had seen radical action punished by civil authorities and had experienced the Knights of Labor's advocacy of the demands of unskilled workers. As a labor leader, these experiences led Gompers to pay close attention to the workers he represented, not necessarily the interests of all laborers. Experience also led him to take a pragmatic approach, seeking gains through bargaining rather than legislation. His long incumbency—from 1886 to 1924 except for one year—is in large part responsible for the "business" orientation of U.S. unions.

Gompers and other early leaders, such as Adolph Strasser, cemented the base on which the American trade union movement stands. They accepted the existing economic system and worked within it. They were primarily concerned with improving their members' lot. This approach is basically continued to the present day in how unions represent employees.

Taking this pragmatic, business-oriented viewpoint limited the AFL in sponsoring social reforms. It advocated legislation only when it could not bargain successfully for its objectives. The absence of an underlying ideology is best typified in Gompers's answer to a question asking what labor's goals were: "More, more, more."

Another aspect of the AFL founders' pragmatic genius was the federation's structural design that preserved the autonomy of its national union members and kept their locals subsidiary to them. This approach serves two purposes: First, the leaders' focus is toward the job problems unique to the trade they represent; second, discipline is maintained over the locals' activities. Thus a more united and rational front is presented when initiating actions or responding to management. The approach also creates the opportunity to exercise "monopoly power" by taking wages out of competition for the occupations the nationals represent. At the same time, organizing by craft conceded the fact that workers' interests were not general but fragmented.

LABOR UNREST

Bitter labor struggles marked the decades between 1870 and 1910. The period was characterized by frequent financial panics resulting in depressions, continuing adamancy by owners who refused to recognize or negotiate with unions, and intervention by government on the side of employers. Some unrest was localized and grew out of radical political action or the nationalistic solidarity of immigrant groups, but much was general to an area or industry.

In the 1870s immigrant Irish miners, having long experience with repression by English laws discriminating against Roman Catholics, struck when mine owners unilaterally cut wages below an agreed minimum. As the strike dragged on, a few diehards formed a secret organization to terrorize recalcitrant owners (known as the *Molly Maguires*—a name that originated in violent resistance in Ireland). They sabotaged mines and threatened owners and supervisors. To counter them, the mine owners hired James McParlan, a Pinkerton detective, to infiltrate the organization. After four years as a "mole," he testified in trials of accused members that resulted in 10 being hanged and another 14 jailed, ending the mine warfare.[18]

In the summer of 1877, railroads cut wages while continuing to pay high dividends to their stockholders. In the East, rail employees struck and in some instances seized railway property. In Pittsburgh, federal troops were called in to retake the property, but not before 25 people had been killed. Widespread rioting broke out. Railroad property was burned, and local business establishments were looted.[19]

In 1886, strikers and strikebreakers fought at the McCormick Harvester plant in Chicago. Police intervened, and four people were killed. A rally was held in Haymarket Square to protest the police action. As the peaceful meeting was dispersing, police arrived and ordered everyone to leave. A bomb exploded and killed one of the police. Before the carnage was over, seven more police and four workers were killed, with more than 100 injured. The riot was blamed on anarchists. Eight were arrested and charged with murder. Seven were sentenced to be hanged and the eighth imprisoned. All were pardoned six years later. Those still alive were released.[20]

Two major strikes in the 1890s helped split the labor movement while raising doubts about the power of unskilled workers to win their demands. These were the 1892 Homestead strike in the Carnegie Steel Company and the 1894 Pullman Company strike.

After Homestead workers refused to accept a company-ordered wage cut, they were locked out by Henry Frick, Carnegie's general manager. The workers correctly assumed Frick would use strikebreakers to reopen the works. To accomplish this, 300 armed Pinkerton detectives were barged up the Monongahela River behind the plant. As they neared the works, the entrenched workers opened fire, used a small cannon to try to sink the barges, and poured burning oil onto the river. After a daylong battle, the Pinkertons surrendered.

The workers' victory was short-lived. The governor ordered the militia to take over the plant, which Frick reopened with strikebreakers. The

[18] Ibid., pp. 117–118.

[19] Ibid., pp. 119–120.

[20] Ibid., pp. 123–125.

union was crushed so badly that no serious attempt was made to organize the steel mills until the 1930s.[21]

The Pullman Company produced railroad cars. Pullman workers were required to rent company-owned houses. In 1893, the company laid off half its employees, cutting wages of the rest up to 40 percent. However, rents were not reduced, and shareholders continued to receive dividends. Pullman employees attempted to get the company to adjust their economic grievances, but it refused and fired several of their leaders. The Pullman locals of the American Railway Union (ARU) reacted by striking. The company refused the union's offer to arbitrate the differences. As a result, ARU leader Eugene Debs ordered members not to handle Pullman rolling stock. Railroad employees throughout the country stopped trains and uncoupled cars manufactured by Pullman. The railroads retaliated by discharging employees found cutting out Pullman cars. But whole train crews quit and abandoned their trains if one was fired.

One management strategy led to the end of the strike. When trains were assembled, Pullman cars were connected to U.S. mail cars. If the Pullman cars were later uncoupled and the mail car was also cut out, this interfered with the mail, a federal offense. The federal government intervened by supplying federal troops and permanently enjoining interference with mail delivery and the movement of goods in interstate commerce. Debs was sent to jail for conspiracy to obstruct the mails, and the strike was broken.[22]

The failure of these industrial actions convinced one faction of the labor movement that to achieve worker goals, socialism needed to replace capitalism.[23] Revolutionary unions were spawned in the West in mining and timbering and in textiles in the East.

The Industrial Workers of the World and the Western Federation of Miners

Throughout the last 20 years of the 19th century, owners and their managers and workers became increasingly polarized. Owners hired detective agencies such as the Pinkertons to infiltrate worker organizations to gain intelligence on potential union activities. Groups of workers increasingly threatened managers in remote mining and logging towns and villages. Law enforcement was often imposed to protect owner interests against workers, especially at the state level. Workers had few assets and were often reduced to having to live in company-owned housing, with the company essentially holding their lives in thrall. Should they be discharged from work, they would also lose their residential rights. Class warfare

[21] Ibid., pp. 166–169.

[22] Ibid., pp. 171–179.

[23] See J. R. Constantine, "Eugene V. Debs: An American Paradox," *Monthly Labor Review*, 114, no. 8 (1991), pp. 30–33.

Exhibit 2.4

PREAMBLE TO THE IWW CONSTITUTION

The working class and the employing class have nothing in common. There can be no peace so long as hunger and want are found among millions of working people and the few who make up the employing class have all the good things of life.

Between these two classes a struggle must go on until the workers of the world organize as a class, take possession of the earth and the machinery of production, and abolish the wage system.

We find that the centering of management of the industries into fewer and fewer hands makes the trade unions unable to cope with the ever-growing power of the employing class. The trade unions foster a state of affairs which allows one set of workers to be pitted against another set of workers in the same industry, thereby helping defeat one another in wage wars. Moreover, the trade unions aid the employing class to mislead the workers into the belief that the working class have interests in common with their employers.

These conditions can be changed and the interest of the working class upheld only by an organization formed in such a way that all its members in any one industry, or in all industries if necessary, cease work whenever a strike or lockout is on in any department thereof, thus making an injury to one an injury to all.

Instead of the conservative motto, "A fair day's wage for a fair day's work," we must inscribe on our banner the revolutionary watchword, "Abolition of the wage system."

It is the historic mission of the working class to do away with capitalism. The army of production must be organized, not only for the everyday struggle with capitalists, but also to carry on production when capitalism shall have been overthrown. By organizing industrially we are forming the structure of the new society within the shell of the old.

seemed to be on the horizon, and from a union standpoint, its energy was embodied in new revolutionary labor unions, the Western Federation of Miners and the Industrial Workers of the World.

Just as Eugene Debs's jail term convinced him that revolutionary unionism and the abolition of capitalism were necessary, so too did the results of numerous mine strikes and wars convince "Big Bill" Haywood that miner solidarity and resistance were the answers to employer intransigence. Haywood played an active role in organizing the Western Federation of Miners (WFM), which had withdrawn from the AFL in 1897. After the long-smoldering Cripple Creek, Colorado, strike was crushed in 1904, the WFM realized it needed national support. Thus, in 1905, Haywood, Debs, and other leading socialists banded their unions together to form the **Industrial Workers of the World (IWW)** (see Exhibit 2.4).[24]

Immediately embroiled in internal political struggle, the IWW was decimated by the WFM's withdrawal in 1906, while Haywood stayed with the IWW. For his part, Haywood spent most of 1906 and 1907 as a defendant in the Frank Steunenberg assassination case. Steunenberg had

[24] Dulles, *Labor in America*, pp. 208–211.

been governor of Idaho during the second eruption of the long-festering Couer d'Alene mine wars. In the early 1890s, one eruption had been put down with the intervention of state and federal troops. Later in the decade Steunenberg became governor, running on a populist platform. This may have emboldened labor, because the mine wars resumed. As the danger of an all-out battle increased, Steunenberg petitioned President William McKinley for federal troops to put down a miners' insurrection. He had no state troops available, all of them having been federalized to serve in the Spanish-American War. McKinley obliged, and the miners' rebellion was stopped. Most of the strikers were terminated and replaced by strikebreakers. For many, this meant economic ruin.

After finishing his term, Steunenberg returned to private business in Caldwell, Idaho. There, close to Christmas 1905, he was killed by a bomb rigged to go off when he opened the front gate to his home. An intensive investigation ensued with the prosecution concluding, with the help of Pinkerton detective work, that "Big Bill" Haywood and two other labor leaders had conspired with others to kill Steunenberg for his role in crushing the miners' rebellion. In order to try them in Idaho, Haywood and his colleagues were essentially kidnapped from Denver by Pinkerton operatives led by James McParlan. The famed defense lawyer, Clarence Darrow, was brought in to defend Haywood and the others and after a lengthy trial, all were acquitted.[25]

The IWW's rhetoric was radical, but its demands were not. When involved in collective action, the IWW's demands usually related to wages and hours rather than usurping management functions.[26] Although strikes occasionally became violent, these incidents were often sparked by management actions. It must be remembered, however, that the IWW's primary goal was not to achieve better wages and working conditions but to abolish the wage system. This may be why it encountered such resistance from employers and why it was unable to build a viable union.

The most successful IWW strike involved 20,000 textile workers in 1912 in Lawrence, Massachusetts, who had suffered a wage cut. Although mostly unorganized, the workers struck, and IWW organizers took over the strike's direction. After two months, during which both sides fomented several violent incidents, worker demands were met, and the mills reopened.[27]

Despite this victory, the IWW lost a subsequent textile strike in 1913 in Paterson, New Jersey. This outcome, coupled with the advent of World War I—during which the IWW stated that its members would fight for neither side since only the capitalists would benefit—led to the IWW's

[25] For an excellent narrative of the trial and the social and political milieu of the era, see J. A. Lukas, *Big Trouble* (New York: Touchstone, a division of Simon & Schuster, 1997).

[26] J. G. Rayback, *A History of American Labor* (New York: Free Press, 1966), p. 248.

[27] Dulles, *Labor in America*, pp. 215–219.

demise. Haywood and other leaders were tried and convicted of sedition for allegedly obstructing the war effort. The IWW was effectively finished.[28]

In 1913, miners employed by John D. Rockeller's Colorado Fuel and Iron Company struck. As was often the case in mine strikes, an escalating spiral of violence ensued. Miners established a large tent colony in Ludlow, Colorado, where they lived along with their families. In April 1914, Colorado national guardsmen rode into the camp. Miners grabbed their guns and headed for the hills to divert the guardmen from their families and to defend themselves. Some of the militia pursued the miners while others strafed the camp with machine guns and later burned the tents and furnishings, indiscriminately killing dozens in the process. Public outrage followed, with a great deal of it directed at Rockefeller for his perceived hypocrisy for, on the one hand, extolling his Christian religious beliefs, while on the other, tacitly permitting violent repressive tactics.[29]

The Boycott Cases

The strike was not the only weapon labor used against employers. While local employees struck, national unions urged union members and the public to **boycott** struck or "unfair" products. Two major national boycotts to support strikes, the *Danbury Hatters* and *Bucks Stove* cases, led to sharp legal reverses for labor organizations.

In *Danbury Hatters*, the union was charged with conspiring to restrain trade in violation of the **Sherman Antitrust Act.** Under the Sherman Act, if restraint is found, actual damages can be punitively trebled. The union lost, and it appeared that its members would have to pay damages, but the AFL and the United Hatters' national organization "passed the hat" and paid the fines.[30] In *Bucks Stove*, a federal district court enjoined the boycott and held Samuel Gompers in contempt. The conspiracy doctrine specter reappeared in the application of court injunctions halting union actions. All concerted actions by unions were increasingly interpreted by federal courts as restraints on interstate commerce, and hence enjoinable and punishable.[31]

Injunctions hobbled collective actions. Their use not only ended the strikes at which they were aimed, but also reduced the willingness of workers in other situations to strike, particularly in sympathy for other strikes or in situations involving issues of workplace control.[32]

[28] Ibid., pp. 219–222.

[29] For a complete report, see U.S. Commission on Industrial Relations, *Report on the Colorado Strike* (Washington, DC: U.S. Government Printing Office, 1915).

[30] Ibid., p. 197.

[31] Rayback, *A History of American Labor*, pp. 224–226.

[32] H. J. McCammon, "'Government by Injunction': The U.S. Judiciary and Strike Action in the Late 19th and Early 20th Centuries," *Work and Occupations*, 20 (1993), pp. 174–204. See also W. E. Forbath, *Law and the Shaping of the American Labor Movement* (Cambridge, MA: Harvard University Press, 1991).

Early Legislation

Early industrywide collective actions were usually met by a two-pronged attack: adamant resistance by employers and court injunctions. To balance the power of the parties and to substitute statutory for court-made common law, Congress passed the Erdman Act in 1898, prohibiting discrimination against railroad employees based on union membership. However, in 1908 it was ruled unconstitutional as an abridgment of personal liberty and property rights.[33]

Union leaders felt the Supreme Court's application of the Sherman Act to the boycott cases hamstrung collective activity. With the election of President Woodrow Wilson and a Democratic Congress, labor expected relief to be forthcoming. In 1914, the **Clayton Act** was passed, hailed by Samuel Gompers as the "industrial Magna Carta upon which the working people will rear their structure of individual freedom."[34]

The Clayton Act removed unions from Sherman Act jurisdiction and limited the use of federal injunctions. However, enthusiasm was short-lived because the act's ambiguous wording allowed judicial interpretations that disappointed labor.[35] The Supreme Court held that, although unions could not be construed as illegal per se, their actions might still be held to restrain trade.[36] It also held that strikes terminated the normal employer-employee relationship, thereby removing the protection against injunctions for lawful employee activities.[37] Thus, the Clayton Act lost whatever teeth labor had believed it had gained.

TRADE UNION SUCCESS AND APATHY

World War I

While World War I spelled the end of the IWW, AFL unions made solid gains. During 1917, the IWW fomented numerous strikes to protest static wages as inflation grew. The National War Labor Board was established in 1918 to reduce strikes. Labor's right to organize and bargain collectively was recognized. By the end of the war, average earnings of even semiskilled union members exceeded $1,000 annually (equal to about $14,000 in 2008 dollars), and the AFL had added more than 1 million members, thus exceeding 4 million in 1919.[38]

[33] *Adair* v. *United States*, 208 U.S. 161 (1908).

[34] S. Gompers, "The Charter of Industrial Freedom," *American Federationist*, 31, no. 11 (1914), pp. 971–972.

[35] S. I. Kutler, "Labor, the Clayton Act, and the Supreme Court," *Labor History*, 3 (1962), pp. 19–38.

[36] *Duplex Printing* v. *Deering*, 254 U.S. 445 (1921).

[37] D. L. Jones, "The Enigma of the Clayton Act," *Industrial and Labor Relations Review*, 10 (1957), pp. 201–221.

[38] Dulles, *Labor in America*, pp. 226–228.

Exhibit 2.5

CHARLES M. SCHWAB, CHAIR OF THE BOARD OF BETHLEHEM STEEL, IN A SPEECH TO A CHAMBER OF COMMERCE AUDIENCE, 1918

"I believe that labor should organize in individual plants or amongst themselves for the better negotiation of labor and the protection of their own rights; but the organization and control of labor in individual plants and manufactories, to my mind, ought to be made representative of the people in those plants who know the conditions; that they ought not to be controlled by somebody from Kamchatka who knows nothing about what their conditions are."

Source: C. M. Schwab, "Capital and Labor: A Reconstruction Policy," *Annals of the American Academy of Political and Social Science*, January 1919, p. 158.

The American Plan

A variety of factors eroded labor's growth after World War I. The 1920s was a decade of relative prosperity. A decline in immigration reduced competition for jobs among unskilled workers. With the prosecution of several leaders of the IWW for sedition, management identified labor as politically extremist. Although the IWW did not represent a large portion of the labor movement, it became a symbol of the movement's danger in the public's eye. At the same time, the Bolsheviks gained power in Russia, and Americans were warned that this pattern could be duplicated in the United States if trade unions became too strong.

Against this backdrop, the **American Plan** was implemented. Employers subtly associated the union movement with foreign subversives and questioned whether it was appropriate for workers to be represented by union officials who were not employed at their plant. Employers championed the **open shop,** ostensibly to preserve the freedom of employees to refrain from joining unions. But the freedom to join was discouraged through the use of **yellow-dog contracts,** which applicants and employees were required to sign, indicating they understood union membership was grounds for discharge. As the decade wore on, yellow-dog contracts were seen increasingly as instruments of coercion, severely restricting the private rights and potential economic power of employees.[39]

Communities organized open-shop committees to protect citizens from outside labor organizers. Reinforcing the local-control–local-concern idea, many employers improved wages and working conditions in unorganized plants. Where employees began to organize, employers encouraged establishment of a company union, autonomous from a national union but not necessarily the employer (see Exhibit 2.5).[40]

[39] D. Ernst, "The Yellow-Dog and Liberal Reform, 1917–1932," *Labor History*, 30 (1989), pp. 251–274.

[40] See Chamberlain and Cullen, *Labor Sector*, pp. 109–110; and Taft, *Organized Labor*, chap. 27.

The End of an Era

The 1920s was a decade of transition for the United States. The country shifted from an agricultural to an industrial society. Mass production and the assembly line reduced skill requirements, creating an industrial rather than a craft orientation. Immigration quotas reduced the influx of impoverished potential employees. While the AFL took a stand-pat approach, some of its newer leaders began to see the importance of organizing unskilled workers.

The 1920s marked the end of the Gompers era, which spanned almost 50 years.[41] On its surface, the AFL appeared to be in decline, conserving a shrinking base. In terms of internal politics, it might be seen as a festering mass of irreconcilable factions. But the economic turmoil of the approaching Depression, combined with changes in the direction of the labor movement, signaled a sea change in U.S. public policy and labor-management relations.

INDUSTRIAL UNIONS

Until the 1930s, attempts to organize **industrial unions** were generally unsuccessful. The continuing supply of unskilled workers provided by immigration, the AFL's relative disinterest in industrial unions, and the tendency of industrially oriented unions to adopt revolutionary goals all interfered with organizing. Then changing conditions created an atmosphere favorable for industrial organizing. The Depression and new legislation that facilitated union activities helped. Established union leaders with a business-union orientation took up the industrial organizing crusade.

The Industrial Union Leadership

The leadership for industrial organizing efforts came from within the AFL. John L. Lewis and other officials of the United Mine Workers (UMW), an AFL union, spearheaded the drive over the objections of the craft unions. Lewis realized that UMW membership was eroding in a declining industry. He decided in the early 1930s the time had come to push for industrial organizing, but he was not prepared for the adamant opposition he met within the AFL. In an acrimonious debate at its 1935 convention, Lewis and "Big Bill" Hutcheson, president of the Carpenters' Union, actually came to blows (see Exhibit 2.6). The convention voted against embarking on industrial organizing. Afterward, Lewis and Philip Murray of the UMW and leaders of the Amalgamated Clothing Workers; International Ladies' Garment Workers; Typographical Union; Textile Workers; cap and millinery department of the United Hatters; Oil Field, Gas Well, and

[41] I. Yellowitz, "Samuel Gompers: A Half-Century in Labor's Front Rank," *Monthly Labor Review*, 112, no. 7 (1989), pp. 27–33.

Exhibit 2.6

LEWIS AND HUTCHESON AT THE 1935 AFL CONVENTION

The industrial union report was defeated, but the question kept recurring. Delegates from rubber, radio, mine, and mill kept urging a new policy. Their way was blocked, though, not least by the towering figure of Big Bill Hutcheson, powerful head of the Carpenters' Union. Hutcheson and Lewis had always held similar views and frequently worked together. Like Lewis, Hutcheson was a big man, 6 feet tall and 220 pounds. When a delegate raised the question of industrial unions in the rubber plants, Hutcheson raised a point of order. The question had already been settled, he contended. Lewis objected; the delegate should be heard on a problem facing his own union. "This thing of raising points of order," he added, "is rather small potatoes."

"I was raised on small potatoes," Hutcheson replied.

As Lewis returned to his seat, he paused to tell Hutcheson that the opposition was pretty small stuff. "We could have made you small," was the reply. "We could have kept you off the executive council, you crazy bastard."

Lewis swung a wild haymaker. It caught Hutcheson on the jaw; the two men grappled, crashed against a table, and fell awkwardly to the floor. President Green wildly hammered his gavel as delegates tried to separate the two heavyweights.

Source: D. F. Selvin, *The Thundering Voice of John L. Lewis* (New York: Lathrop, Lee, & Shepard, 1969), pp. 103–104.

Refining Workers; and Mine, Mill, and Smelter Workers met to form the **Committee for Industrial Organization (CIO).**[42]

Organizing the Industrial Workforce

Major efforts were begun to organize workers in the steel, textile, rubber, and auto industries. Philip Murray headed the Steel Workers Organizing Committee (SWOC), establishing 150 locals totaling over 100,000 members by the end of 1936. In early 1937, secret efforts of John L. Lewis and Myron Taylor, head of U.S. Steel, resulted in the SWOC's recognition as the bargaining agent for U.S. Steel employees. The steelworkers won an 8-hour day, a 40-hour week, and a wage increase. Other steel firms were not so readily organized. During an organizing parade at Republic Steel on Memorial Day, 1937, violence broke out, and 10 strikers were killed by Chicago police.[43]

The autoworkers were next. Despite relatively high wages pioneered by Henry Ford, jobs were tedious and fatiguing, and the companies' private police forces kept workers in line.[44] In 1936, the United Auto Workers

[42] Rayback, *History of American Labor*, pp. 348–350.

[43] Dulles, *Labor in America*, pp. 299–302.

[44] M. J. Gannon, "Entrepreneurship and Labor Relations at the Ford Motor Company," *Marquette Business Review*, Summer 1972, pp. 63–75.

Exhibit 2.7

TELEGRAM FROM SIT-DOWN STRIKERS TO GOVERNOR MURPHY

"Governor, we have decided to stay in the plant. We have no illusions about the sacrifices which the decision will entail. We fully expect that if a violent effort is made to oust us many of us will be killed and we take this means of making it known to our wives, to our children, to the people of the state of Michigan and of the country that if this result follows from the attempt to eject us you are the one who must be held responsible for our deaths."

Source: S. Fine, *Sit-Down: The General Motors Strike of 1936–1937* (Ann Arbor: University of Michigan Press, 1969), p. 278.

(UAW) sought recognition from General Motors. GM refused, but worker sentiments were so strong that "quickie" strikes resulted.[45]

In late 1936, workers at GM's Fisher body plants in Flint, Michigan, took over the plants and refused to leave. GM viewed this **sit-down strike** as criminal trespass, but the workers asserted that job rights were superior to property rights. Injunctions to oust them were ignored (see Exhibit 2.7). Michigan's governor Frank Murphy could not be persuaded to mobilize the militia to enforce the injunction. Realizing the workers could hold out, GM capitulated in February 1937, agreeing to recognize the UAW and not to discriminate against union members.[46]

This tactic was used to organize Chrysler workers as well as the glass, rubber, and textile industries. Industrial unionization had been achieved. By 1938, the CIO membership of 3.7 million exceeded membership in the older AFL by 300,000.[47]

LEGISLATION

In the 1930s, public policy toward unions shifted radically. Before the Railway Labor Act in 1926, no laws facilitated organizing or bargaining. Courts routinely enjoined unions from striking, organizing, picketing, or other activities, even if peacefully conducted. State laws limiting injunctive powers of state courts were struck down.[48]

[45] Rayback, *History of American Labor*, p. 353.

[46] S. Fine, *The General Motors Strike of 1936–1937* (Ann Arbor: University of Michigan Press, 1969).

[47] Rayback, *History of American Labor*, pp. 354–355.

[48] *Truax* v. *Corrigan*, 257 U.S. 312 (1921).

Norris-LaGuardia Act (1932)

By the time the **Norris-LaGuardia Act** was passed in 1932, Congress had recognized the legitimacy of collective bargaining. Until Norris-LaGuardia, acceptance of a collective bargaining relationship had to devolve from a voluntary employer action.

The act severely restricted the power of federal courts to issue injunctions against union activities. The act also forbade federal courts from enforcing yellow-dog contracts. Courts had previously upheld their legality.[49]

While the Norris-LaGuardia Act protected numerous previously enjoyable activities, it was a neutral policy—it did not open any right to demand that employers recognize a union of their employees. Other than the removal of the yellow-dog contract, explicit federal ground rules for employer conduct in labor-management relations still did not exist. This would change after the inauguration of President Franklin D. Roosevelt.

National Industrial Recovery Act (1933)

The National Industrial Recovery Act (NIRA), adopted in 1933, encouraged employers to band together to set prices and production quotas through industrial codes. To complete an industrial code, however, employers were required to allow employees to bargain through representatives of their own choosing, free from employer interference. However, the NIRA was ruled unconstitutional in 1935.[50]

Wagner Act (National Labor Relations Act, 1935)

As the NIRA safeguards for unions were lost, the **Wagner Act** resecured organizing rights and specified employer illegal activities. Section 7, the heart of the act, specifies the rights of employees to engage in union activities:

> Employees shall have the right to self-organization, to form, join, or assist labor organizations, to bargain collectively through representatives of their own choosing, and to engage in concerted activities, for the purpose of collective bargaining or other mutual aid or protection.

Section 8 broadly forbade interference with employees' rights to be represented, to bargain, to have their labor organizations free from employer dominance, to be protected from employment discrimination for union activity, and to be free from retaliation for accusing the employer of an unlawful (unfair) labor practice.

To investigate violations of Section 8 and to determine whether employees desired representation, the Wagner Act established the **National Labor Relations Board (NLRB),** whose major duties were to determine which, if

[49]*Hitchman Coal Co.* v. *Mitchell*, 245 U.S. 229 (1917).

[50]*Schechter Poultry Corp.* v. *United States*, 295 U.S. 495 (1935).

any, union was the employees' choice to represent them and to hear and rule on alleged unfair labor practices.

The Wagner Act also established the concept of **exclusive representation** in the agency relationship between the union and the employees. Where a majority of employees chose a union, that union would represent all employees in the unit in bargaining over issues of wages, hours, and terms and conditions of employment.

The Wagner Act did not apply to all employers and employees. Specifically exempted were those who worked for federal, state, and local governments and those subject to the Railway Labor Act. Supervisors and managers, agricultural workers, domestic employees, and family workers were also excluded from coverage.

Passage of the Wagner Act did not immediately presage a shift in U.S. labor relations. With the NIRA recently having been declared void by the Supreme Court and with Section 7 of the Wagner Act closely duplicating the NIRA section, some employers expected the courts to rule against Congress on a constitutional challenge.

EMPLOYER INTRANSIGENCE

Unions saw the Wagner Act as creating a mechanism for employees to use to gain representation. Organizing was a crucial activity, with almost half of the strikes between 1935 and 1937 undertaken to obtain recognition.

Many employers doubted the Wagner Act's constitutionality. Firms developed a variety of strategies to oppose union-organizing activities. Some fostered company unions. Differences between the AFL and the CIO were exploited.[51] Company unions received managerial support, but some gradually became relatively independent and effective as illegal domination by employers was increasingly prohibited by the NLRB.[52] Employers also used the so-called **Mohawk Valley formula,** linking unions with agitators and communists. Proponents of this strategy organized back-to-work drives during strikes, got local police to break up strikes, and aligned local interests against the focus of union activities.[53]

Congress investigated company attempts to thwart or rebuff union activities and found that companies spent almost $10 million for spying, strikebreaking, and munitions between 1933 and 1937. To prepare for potential strikes, Youngstown Sheet and Tube amassed 8 machine guns, 369 rifles, 190 shotguns, 450 revolvers, 109 gas guns, 3,000 rounds of gas,

[51] D. Nelson, "Managers and Nonunion Workers in the Rubber Industry: Union Avoidance Strategies in the 1930s," *Industrial and Labor Relations Review*, 43 (1989), pp. 41–52.

[52] S. M. Jacoby, "Reckoning with Company Unions: The Case of Thompson Products, 1934–1964," *Industrial and Labor Relations Review*, 43 (1989), pp. 19–40.

[53] Dulles, *Labor in America*, p. 278.

and almost 10,000 rounds of shotgun shells and bullets. Republic Steel allegedly possessed the largest private arsenal in the United States.[54] The Ford Motor Company had an internal police force numbering between 3,500 and 5,000 (about 1 for every 25 workers) that enforced plant rules, spied on union activity, and fomented beatings of union organizers.[55]

Constitutionality of the Wagner Act

Both sides had reasons to believe their positions were legitimate. Management had seen a long line of Supreme Court decisions adverse to labor, not the least of these the striking down of the NIRA, which was partially similar to the Wagner Act. Labor had seen sympathy for its position grow throughout the country. With President Roosevelt consolidating his position through the overwhelming electoral endorsement of the New Deal in 1936, labor believed the Court would find it difficult to invalidate the law.[56]

Opposition to the Wagner Act by employers was probably related to ideological, legal, and economic factors. Employers' creation and use of the American Plan, Mohawk Valley formula, and other devices reflected their ideological opposition to industrial unionization. Employers believed unionization would raise their labor costs. A study of the economic effects of the Wagner Act indicates the market value of companies unionized after passage of the Wagner Act decreased relative to that of nonunion firms. Thus, the reduced ability to avoid unionization following passage of the act had an economic cost for employers.[57]

The Wagner Act was ruled constitutional by the Supreme Court on April 12, 1937.[58] Earlier, the NLRB determined that Jones & Laughlin Steel had violated the act by discriminating against union members. It ordered 10 employees reinstated with back pay and told the firm to cease unfair labor practices. The appeals court had held previously that the NLRB's action was beyond the range of federal power.

In a 5–4 decision, the Court sided with the board, holding that Congress may regulate employer activities under the Constitution's commerce clause. It reaffirmed employee rights to organize and recognized Congress's authority to restrict employer activities likely to disrupt unionization. The Court ruled that manufacturing, even if conducted locally, was a process involving interstate commerce. Further, it was reasonable

[54] Ibid., pp. 277–278.

[55] See Lichtenstein, op cit., and S. Norwood, "Ford's Brass Knuckles: Harry Bennett, the Cult of Muscularity, and Anti-Labor Terror—1920–1945," *Labor History*, 37 (1996), pp. 365–391; for a history of anti-labor violence, see S. H. Norwood, *Strike-Breaking and Intimidation* (Chapel Hill: University of North Carolina Press, 2002).

[56] Taylor and Witney, *Labor Relations Law*, pp. 161–164.

[57] C. A. Olson and B. E. Becker, "The Effects of the NLRA on Stockholder Wealth in the 1930s," *Industrial and Labor Relations Review*, 44 (1990), pp. 116–129.

[58] *NLRB* v. *Jones & Laughlin Steel Corp.*, 301 U.S. 1 (1937).

for Congress to set rules and procedures governing employees' rights to organize. Finally, the Court found the board's conduct at the hearing and its orders were regular, within the act's meaning, and protected. With the Wagner Act upheld, an era of rapid industrial unionization was opened.

LABOR POWER

The CIO's momentum increased for the rest of the 1930s. Both federations raided each other's members, with employers caught in the midst. These **jurisdictional disputes** created public hostility and led to some state laws outlawing certain union activities.[59]

Although labor had been instrumental in getting its friends elected to public office in the 1930s, its ranks split in 1940 when John L. Lewis announced his support for Wendell Wilkie, the Republican candidate for president. The split originated in 1937 when Lewis had expected the Democratic administration to repay labor for its campaign assistance by providing help during the GM sit-down strike. During the strike, Lewis said:

> For six months the economic royalists represented by General Motors contributed their money and used their energy to drive [Roosevelt's] administration out of power. The administration asked labor for help, and labor gave it. The same economic royalists now have their fangs in labor. The workers of this country expect the administration to help the workers in every legal way and to support the workers in General Motors plants.[60]

President Roosevelt did nothing except urge meetings between the UAW and the company. During the strike, some of Lewis's other pronouncements were equally dramatic (see Exhibit 2.8).

The period before World War II was a time of great political ferment. Many questioned the capitalist system's ability to overcome and avoid depressions. Radical political agendas were created, with government regulation or operation of the economy proposed. However, most of the influential new industrial union leaders gave priority to trade union matters.[61] As the 1930s wore on, it became apparent that an increasingly large number of industrial union staff positions were held by communists. They did not join in President Roosevelt's support for the Allies after Germany and Russia signed a nonaggression pact and invaded and partitioned Poland in 1939.

The year 1941 was one of crisis for labor-management relations. The ambivalent stand of some industrial union leaders toward the war allowed

[59] A jurisdictional dispute occurs when two or more unions claim to (1) simultaneously represent or attempt to bargain for the same employee group or (2) simultaneously assert that their members are entitled by contract to perform a certain class of work.

[60] Rayback, *History of American Labor*, p. 368.

[61] K. Boyle, "Building the Vanguard: Walter Reuther and Radical Politics in 1936," *Labor History*, 30 (1989), pp. 433–448.

Exhibit 2.8

THE RHETORIC OF JOHN L. LEWIS

[The mid-1930s were] a time of virtual class warfare. The National Guard was called out more than a dozen times a year; strikes were broken not only by goons and ginks and company finks, in the words of the old labor song, but by tear gas and machine guns. And when a particularly disdainful Chrysler president asked for Lewis's comment in the midst of a negotiation inspired by a spontaneous sit-down at Chrysler, the six-foot-two Lewis stood up and said, "I am 99 percent of a mind to come around the table right now and wipe that damn sneer off your face." Lee Pressman, of the new CIO, later observed, "Lewis's voice at that moment was in every sense the voice of millions of unorganized workers who were being exploited by gigantic corporations. He was expressing at that instant their resentment, hostility, and their passionate desire to strike back."

. . . When F.D.R. lumped labor with management, declaring his famous "plague on both your houses" . . . Lewis intoned: "Labor, like Israel, has many sorrows. Its women weep for their fallen, and they lament for the future of the children of the race. It ill behooves one who has supped at labor's table and who has been sheltered in labor's house to curse with equal fervor and fine impartiality both labor and its adversaries when they become locked in deadly embrace."

The "sup" to which he had made reference was a $500,000 UMW contribution to F.D.R.'s 1936 campaign. Lewis was unabashed about demanding his money's worth. "Everybody says I want my pound of flesh, that I gave Roosevelt $500,000 for his 1936 campaign, and I want quid pro quo. The UMW and the CIO have paid cash on the barrel for every piece of legislation gotten. . . . Is anyone fool enough to believe for one instant that we gave this money to Roosevelt because we are spellbound by his voice?"

. . . Although Lewis was rarely photographed smiling ("That scowl is worth a million dollars," he once confided to a friend), one can see the demon gleam in his eye as he scratched out his answer (to Roosevelt's plea for a wartime no-strike pledge). "If you want to use the power of the state to restrain me, as an agent of labor, then, sir, I submit that you should use the same power to restrain my adversary in this issue, who is an agent of capital. My adversary is a rich man named Morgan, who lives in New York." Signed, in letters which ran two and a half inches tall, "Yours humbly."

Source: V. Navasky, "John L. Lewis, Union General," *Esquire*, December 1983, pp. 264–266.

employers to brand them as unpatriotic. When Philip Murray became CIO president in 1940, the stand shifted, but the label was not entirely removed. Employers refused to recognize unions, although organizing at Ford and Little Steel was finally successful. For the first time, labor's goal of "more, more, more now" was becoming intolerable to the general public. More than 4,300 strikes broke out in 1941, involving more than 8 percent of the workforce. This widespread industrial disruption would probably have been moderated by congressional action had not the attack on Pearl Harbor involved the United States in World War II.[62]

[62] Rayback, *History of American Labor*, pp. 370–373.

Exhibit 2.9

COMMENTS BY PRESIDENT ROOSEVELT ON COAL STRIKES DURING 1943

On June 23, the president issued a statement in which he said that "the action of the leaders of the United Mine Workers coal miners has been intolerable—and has rightly stirred up the anger and disapproval of the overwhelming mass of the American people."

He declared that the mines would be operated by the government under the terms of the board's directive order of June 18.

He stated that "the government had taken steps to set up the machinery for inducting into the armed services all miners subject to the Selective Service Act who absented themselves, without just cause, from work in the mines under government operation." Since the "Selective Service Act does not authorize induction of men above 45 years into the armed services, I intend to request the Congress to raise the age limit for noncombat service to 65 years. I shall make that request of the Congress so that if at any time in the future there should be a threat of interruption of work in plants, mines, or establishments owned by the government, or taken possession of by the government, the machinery will be available for prompt action."

Source: A. Suffern, "The National War Labor Board and Coal," in *The Termination Report of the National War Labor Board*, vol. 1: *Industrial Disputes and Wage Stabilization in Wartime* (Washington, DC: U.S. Government Printing Office, 1948), p. 1009.

World War II

At the outbreak of World War II, AFL, CIO, and management representatives pledged to produce together to meet the war effort. Labor pledged not to strike if a board were established to handle unresolved grievances. Even though management did not entirely concede, President Roosevelt established the National War Labor Board (NWLB). As war production rose rapidly, inflation followed. Labor demanded wage increases. The NWLB tried to maintain a policy whereby wage increases would equal changes in the cost of living. Labor objected to the check on collective bargaining and the NWLB policy on wages, but it was not changed.[63]

In 1945, notwithstanding the no-strike pledge, 4,750 strikes involved 3,470,000 workers, and 38 million worker-days were lost, exceeding the prewar high of 28.4 million days in 1937. Sporadic strikes in coal mining, led by John L. Lewis, were particularly visible. At one point, the coal mines were seized and run by Secretary of the Interior Harold Ickes (see Exhibit 2.9).[64]

The strike activity led Congress to pass the War Labor Disputes Act over President Roosevelt's veto. This act authorized the seizure of plants

[63] Taft, *Organized Labor*, pp. 546–552.

[64] Ibid., pp. 553–556.

involved in labor disputes, made strikes and lockouts in defense industries a criminal offense, required 30 days' notice to the NWLB of a pending dispute, and required the NLRB to monitor strike votes.[65]

Accommodation and innovation in bargaining was evident during World War II. Even overtly communist unions supported no-strike agreements since this aided the Soviet-American alliance in Europe.[66] In only 46 of 17,650 dispute cases before the NWLB did parties fail to reach or accept agreements. The war experience also led to a widespread acceptance of fringe benefits in lieu of wage increases. Holidays, vacations, sick leaves, and shift differentials were approved by the NWLB as part of labor contracts. Labor shortages led to the advocacy of equal employment opportunities for minorities and equal pay for men and women in the same jobs.[67]

Reconversion

As the war ended, consumers yearned for the return of durable goods. Labor looked for wage increases to offset cost-of-living increases that occurred during the war. The inevitable clash of labor and management led to the greatest incidence of strikes in U.S. history. Between August 1945 and August 1946, 4,630 strikes involved 4.9 million workers and the loss of 119.8 million worker-days (or 1.62 percent of total days available). Major strikes affected the coal, rail, auto, and steel industries. These were settled with wage increases averaging over 15 percent; and some, especially in steel, resulted in price increases as well.[68]

CHANGING THE BALANCE

The end of the war, the strikes, and the election of a more conservative Congress led to legislation to balance the power between unions and employers. The strikes of 1941, the coal problems during World War II, and the 1946 strikes stimulated legislation to expand and clarify rules applied to the practice of U.S. labor relations.

The Wagner Act had addressed only employers' unfair labor practices. The labor movement's critics argued that unions also could coerce individual employees and refuse to bargain collectively. The Wagner Act was amended and added to with the enactment of the Labor Management Relations Act of 1947, better known as **Taft-Hartley.**

[65] Ibid., p. 557.

[66] M. Torigian, "National Unity on the Waterfront: Communist Politics and the ILWU during the Second World War," *Labor History*, 30 (1989), pp. 409–432.

[67] Taft, *Organized Labor*, pp. 559–562.

[68] Ibid., pp. 563–578.

Taft-Hartley Act

Employee rights were expanded to include the right to refrain from union activities beyond membership or paying dues. Congress went further by enabling states to enact so-called **right-to-work laws** prohibiting union membership as a condition of continued employment.[69] Organized labor refers to them as "right-to-wreck" laws, enabling free riders to receive union gains applicable to an entire bargaining unit without contributing money or effort to the cause. Proponents see the laws as essential to freedom of association and protective of the right to join or not join organizations.

Union unfair labor practices were defined, recognizing the agency role the union plays for all bargaining unit members. Unions were required to bargain in good faith, and strikes to gain recognition or pressure uninvolved second parties to get at a primary employer were outlawed.

The **Federal Mediation and Conciliation Service (FMCS)** was established to aid settlement of unresolved contractual disputes. Assistance could be requested by the parties or offered directly. Provision was made for intervention in strikes likely to create a national emergency. If the president determined that a labor dispute imperiled the nation, a board of inquiry could be convened to determine the issues and positions of the parties. Provisions were included for an 80-day "cooling-off" period during which strikes were prohibited and NLRB elections on final contract proposals would be conducted.

Union officials were forbidden to accept money from employers, and employers could not offer them inducements. Secondary boycotts to force an employer to cease doing business with others (i.e., a struck or nonunion firm) were made illegal. Corporations and labor unions were forbidden to make political contributions. Federal employees were forbidden to strike.

The law tried to balance the relative power of the contenders and introduced procedures to assist the parties in solving conflicts. Because the bill represented a retreat from the protections labor had previously enjoyed, unions strongly opposed it. But business, Congress, and the public supported it. Passed by wide margins in both houses, President Truman's veto was overriden. The Taft-Hartley Act ended free-wheeling administratively initiated change by the NLRB. Rule making became subject to court review. Instead of the government promoting unionization as a counterbalance to big business, it assumed more of a referee role.[70]

[69] States passing these laws include Alabama, Arizona, Arkansas, Florida, Georgia, Idaho, Iowa, Kansas, Louisiana, Mississippi, Nebraska, Nevada, North Carolina, North Dakota, Oklahoma, South Carolina, South Dakota, Tennessee, Texas, Utah, Virginia, Wisconsin, and Wyoming.

[70] R. O'Brien, "Taking the Conservative State Seriously: Statebuilding and Restrictive Labor Practices in Postwar America," *Labor Studies Journal*, 21, no. 4 (1997), pp. 33–63.

The New Production Paradigm

The industrial upheavals accompanying the Great Depression and World War II led to a pervasive and fundamental shift in productivity regimes in the United States. Before World War II, employers institutionalized the **drive system,** in which supervisors (foremen) intensively directed and monitored the workforce and had ultimate power in hiring, firing, and pay decisions. Foremen relied on fear and orders to meet production quotas. Collective bargaining reduced their power and raised wages. Greater efficiency followed from employers' ability to hire better workers as a result of higher wages and from the fact that productivity increases provided the funding for higher wages. An era of capital-labor accords was begun that would last until the 1980s.[71]

RETRENCHMENT AND MERGER

Organized labor realized two things after Taft-Hartley. First, it would have to exert more influence in lobbying and adopt a more publicly advocative stance on labor issues. Second, the strength of management and labor had been changed by the act. The time had come to direct labor's energies toward unity. The old guard who sundered the AFL was disappearing. William Green and Philip Murray both died in 1952. Their deaths resulted in the election of a new president of the AFL, George Meany, and of the CIO, Walter Reuther. John L. Lewis's UMW was unaffiliated, thus greatly reducing the historic friction.[72]

The 1950s began a nearly 25-year period in which most large unionized employers accepted unions as legitimate representatives. Longer-term contracts were negotiated. Wage and productivity increases were closely related. Living standards and profits increased during the period. Conditions that led to the formation of the CIO—animosity from craft unionists and adamant opposition to unionization from large employers—had been mostly overcome. CIO unionists had equalized their power with the AFL, and unification became possible.[73]

Merger

The first step toward rapprochement was the ratification of a no-raid agreement in 1954. The Joint Unity Committee was established to study the feasibility of a merger. On February 9, 1955, a merger formed the combined AFL-CIO with George Meany as its president.[74]

[71] D. M. Gordon, "From the Drive System to the Capital-Labor Accord: Econometric Tests for the Transition between Productivity Regimes," *Industrial Relations*, 36 (1997), pp. 125–159.

[72] Dulles, *Labor in America*, pp. 360–372.

[73] For more information on the CIO, see R. H. Zieger, "The CIO: A Bibliographical Update and Archival Guide," *Labor History*, 31 (1990), pp. 413–440.

[74] Dulles, *Labor in America*, pp. 372–374.

Meany reendorsed Gompers's concept of "more" as it applied to a person's standard and quality of living. He reaffirmed labor's commitment to collective bargaining. He was unwilling to involve labor in management but demanded that management's stewardship be high.[75] He reiterated the business unionism approach of the U.S. union movement, while recognizing that advances for its members may lead to advances for society.

The merged AFL-CIO did not become more powerful than the two federations had been in the past. In fact, union membership as a proportion of the labor force reached its peak in 1956 at about one third. By 1964, this proportion fell to 30 percent, and membership declined by 700,000. Parts of the decline were due to less aggressive organizing, perhaps partly related to a reduction in competition for members, to better nonunion employee relations, and to the reduced relative proportion of blue-collar manufacturing workers in the labor force.

Whatever the reasons, the 1956–1965 decade was one of malaise and retreat for the labor movement.[76] Unions also gained some unwanted notoriety as congressional investigators uncovered gross malfeasance by some major national union officers.

Corruption

For two and one-half years, beginning in 1957, the American public watched televised hearings in which a parade of labor officials invoked the Fifth Amendment to avoid self-incrimination. The Teamsters Union drew the lion's share of the spotlight as witnesses disclosed that its president, Dave Beck, had converted union funds to his own use, borrowed money from employers, and received kickbacks from labor "consultants." James R. Hoffa was accused of breaking Teamster strikes and covertly running his own trucking operation. "Sweetheart" contracts with substandard benefits and guaranteed labor peace were uncovered in New York area Teamster locals operated by racketeers.

Other unions, including the Bakery and Confectionery Workers, Operating Engineers, Carpenters, and United Textile Workers, were also involved. Management contributed to the corruption by providing payoffs for sweetheart contracts that prevented other unions from organizing while the employers paid substandard rates.[77]

The publicity associated with the hearings cast a pall over the entire labor movement. By inference, all labor was corrupt. The AFL-CIO investigated internally and considered charges against the Allied Industrial Workers, Bakers, Distillers, Laundry Workers, Textile Workers, and Teamsters. The Textile Workers, Distillers, and Allied Industrial Workers agreed to mandated changes. The Bakers, Laundry Workers, and Teamsters refused and

[75] G. Meany, "What Labor Means by 'More,'" *Fortune*, 26, no. 3 (1955), pp. 92–93.

[76] Dulles, *Labor in America*, pp. 377–381.

[77] Taft, *Organized Labor*, pp. 698–704.

were expelled from the AFL-CIO in 1957.[78] Meanwhile, the congressional investigations led to legislation to reduce the likelihood of corrupt practices and to amend the Taft-Hartley Act.

Landrum-Griffin Act

The **Landrum-Griffin Act** established individual union members' rights to freedom of speech, equal voting, control of dues increases, and copies of labor agreements under which they worked. Unions were required to file periodic reports of official and financial activities and financial holdings of union officers and employees, and employers were required to report financial transactions with unions. Internal union political activities involving the election of officers and the placing of subordinate bodies under trusteeship were regulated. Recently convicted felons were barred from holding office. Extortionate picketing was prohibited.

PUBLIC SECTOR UNION GROWTH

As private sector organizing activity sank into the doldrums of the late 1950s and early 1960s, public employees became increasingly interested in unionization. In the federal service, the Taft-Hartley Act had forbidden strikes. Most state statutes forbade strikes by public employees, generally made strikers ineligible for any gains won by striking, and included summary discharge as a penalty. Concomitantly, most federal and state statutes had no mechanism for recognizing bargaining representatives.

Federal Executive Orders

In 1962, President Kennedy issued **Executive Order 10988,** a breakthrough for federal employee unions. This order enabled a majority union to bargain collectively with a government agency. Negotiations were restricted to terms and conditions of employment, not wages. Unions could not represent employees if they advocated strikes or the right to strike. Later, Executive Order 11491 established procedures for determining appropriate bargaining units, required Landrum-Griffin-type reporting by unions, granted arbitration as a final settlement procedure for grievances, specified unfair labor practices and created procedures for redressing them, and created the Federal Impasse Panel to render binding decisions when negotiations reach an impasse. This provision ameliorated the statutory no-strike provisions facing federal government employees.[79] Executive Order 11616 allowed professionals in an agency to decide whether to join a bargaining unit, allowed individuals to pursue unfair labor practice charges through grievance channels or through the assistant secretary

[78] Ibid., p. 704.

[79] Ibid., pp. 550–553.

of labor for labor-management relations, required a grievance procedure in exclusively represented units (while narrowing the range of issues allowed arbitration), and allowed some negotiating on government time.[80]

Civil Service Reform Act

Title VII of the Civil Service Reform Act of 1978 regulates labor-management relations in the federal service. The act codified the provisions written into the executive orders. It also established the **Federal Labor Relations Authority,** which acts as the federal service equivalent of the NLRB. Requirements and mechanisms for alleviating bargaining impasses and unresolved grievances under the contract are also spelled out.[81]

LABOR IN CRISIS AND TRANSITION

The AFL marked its 100th anniversary in 1982. In that century, with the exception of a one-year period, the AFL and its successor, the AFL-CIO, had only four presidents: Samuel Gompers, William Green, George Meany, and Lane Kirkland. George Meany retired from the presidency in 1979 at the age of 85 and died in 1980. Meany's service to the labor movement was great, but his passing, like the earlier passings of Green and Murray, created opportunities for rapprochement and change. After Lane Kirkland took office, the United Auto Workers and the Teamsters both reaffiliated with the AFL-CIO. However, even with this reunification, labor's numbers continued to shrink during most of the rest of the 20th century.

Rising Employer Militancy

The 1970s were not kind to the American economy, particularly to employers. During the decade there were two major oil shocks in which petroleum shortages and price increases were major influences on the economy. The Vietnam War occupied the public spotlight and contributed to inflation and dissension. Inflation became an increasing problem, with prices rising by more than 10 percent annually by the end of the decade. Unlike the case in other inflationary periods, unemployment increased as well. Major U.S. industries were under competitive attack from abroad, particularly from Japan. Autos, steel, appliance manufacturers, semiconductor producers, and other key industries were plagued with inferior goods and high labor costs.

In 1980, Ronald Reagan was elected president. Paul Volcker was the chair of the Federal Reserve Bank. During the first two years of the Reagan presidency several events occurred that helped to shape the direction of the economy to the present day. First, the Reagan administration proposed

[80] Ibid., pp. 553–555.

[81] H. B. Frazier III, "Labor-Management Relations in the Federal Government," *Labor Law Journal*, 30 (1979), pp. 131–138.

and passed a huge personal and corporate income tax cut. One of the by-products of the cut was that business expenditures became relatively more costly. Corporations had been taxed at about a 50 percent marginal rate prior to the cut, meaning that an additional dollar of expenses cut taxes by about 50 cents, thereby costing the company only 50 cents. The new marginal rate was closer to 30 percent, meaning that an additional dollar of expenses cut taxes by 30 cents, thereby costing the company 70 cents. This led to a substantial increase in the incentive to hold down costs. Second, the Federal Reserve Bank raised short-term interest rates well above 15 percent in an effort to choke off the persistent and growing inflation of the 1970s. This policy put the economy into a recession, raised unemployment to close to 10 percent, and made the dollar very expensive relative to foreign currencies, thereby stifling exports.

In order to compete in this environment, companies had to drastically cut costs. In addition, increasingly large amounts of many companies' shares were owned by large institutional investors who were becoming increasingly impatient about low financial performance. Executives were more closely monitored and more often replaced than in the past. Shareholder value became the most important criterion for them to pursue. Many companies in basic industries could no longer compete on a global basis and, as a result, shut down.[82] Others, such as the auto industry, closed inefficient plants, shed excess capacity, and cut large numbers of production workers, professionals, and managers.

Striker Replacements

Ever since the *MacKay Radio* decision,[83] the legal right of employers to replace economic strikers has been recognized. During the "labor accord" era that stretched from the late 1940s until close to the 1980s, employers seldom took advantage of that opportunity. However, a 1981 presidential decision emboldened private employers in their use of the tactic. The Professional Air Traffic Controllers Organization, which represented air traffic controllers employed by the Federal Aviation Administration, went on strike in August. President Reagan ordered them to return to work in 48 hours or face termination and the loss of ever being reemployed by the federal government. When the strikers defied the order, they were fired and replaced by military controllers until sufficient numbers of civilians had been trained to replace them.

Private employers believed that if the president was willing to replace economic strikers, they would face little deterrence from federal authorities if they adopted the same tactic. With high unemployment rates and falling real wages for blue-collar workers, replacements, in most cases, were not hard to find. One of the bitterest struggles was the negotiation

[82] See J. P. Hoerr, *And the Wolf Finally Came* (Pittsburgh: University of Pittsburgh Press, 1988).

[83] *NLRB* v. *MacKay Radio & Telegraph*, 304 U.S. 333 (1938).

between Phelps Dodge Corporation and the United Steelworkers for the copper miners in Clifton and Morenci, Arizona. The company went into the negotiations demanding deep concessions, hired replacements when workers struck, and ultimately saw the decertification and destruction of the local union as the successful end point of its strategy.[84] These setbacks put unions on the defensive—something they had not experienced since collective bargaining had been legitimized in the late 1930s. At the same time, the structure of employment was changing, with increasing proportions of the labor force involved in service occupations or in professional employment, areas in which the labor movement had no experience or little attraction for workers.

New Union Leadership

Lane Kirkland retired from the AFL-CIO presidency in 1994. John Sweeney's ascension to the presidency in 1994 was the first election of an insurgent candidate in 70 years. He ran from his position as president of the Service Employees International Union (SEIU), a union representing less skilled workers in a variety of building maintenance and medical support occupations. His platform and promise was to reenergize the union movement's organizing activities. However, his presidency did not witness an end to union decline, as low-wage jobs have been under continuing pressure from globalization and nonunion competition.

As the union movement continued to shrink following Sweeney's election, calls for more intensive and innovative organizing campaigns were made, ironically, by Andy Stern, Sweeney's successor as president of the SEIU. In frustration, Stern led a campaign to take the SEIU out of the AFL-CIO, and in 2005 the SEIU and the United Food and Commercial Workers, the Teamsters, the Carpenters, the Laborers, UNITE HERE, and the Farm Workers formed a new coalition, Change to Win, covering about 5 million members.[85] Thus, 50 years after the merger of the AFL and CIO, the labor movement was riven again. Time will tell whether competition to organize and represent workers will strengthen or sap the labor movement and whether the membership and resource base has shrunk too far to come back. At least for the time being, greater resources are being put into organizing, political action, and cooperation with labor organizations and governments in other countries than has been the case for the last half century.

Harmony within Change to Win was short-lived, however. Major differences developed within UNITE HERE, a rather strange amalgamation

[84] J. D. Rosenblum, *Copper Crucible: How the Arizona Miners' Strike of 1983 Recast Labor-Management Relations in America*, 2nd ed. (Ithaca, NY: ILR Press, 1998).

[85] For an excellent overview of Andy Stern's leadership in the SEIU, see M. Bai, "The New Boss," *New York Times Magazine*, January 30, 2005, available at www.nytimes.com/2005/01/30/magazine/30STERN.html? ex= 1264827600&en=0b1bcee9d1f4a185&ei=5088&partner=rssnyt.

of needle trades and hotel and restaurant workers, in late 2008 and early 2009. UNITE and some units of HERE split off from the remnants of HERE to form Workers United (WU), which quickly affiliated with the SEIU.[86] In the meantime, Andy Stern, the SEIU president, announced his retirement, and was succeeded in June 2010 by the election of Mary Kay Henry, who was not his personal pick.

Henry defeated Anna Burger, who is the president of Change to Win. Since Change to Win left the AFL-CIO, John Sweeney has retired and was succeeded by Ron Trumka of the Mine Workers. He's currently working to lure the SEIU back into the AFL-CIO. Thus, the top level of the labor movement is embroiled in intrigue and infighting at the very period that their national political fortunes would be best served by unity.

Summary

The following major points should be apparent in examining the early U.S. labor movement:

1. Labor organizations have been an integral part of the nation's growth at all stages.
2. Before the Great Depression, labor was faced with a hostile national environment.
3. Until Norris-LaGuardia, most of labor's activities could be—and were—enjoined by the courts when they were effective.
4. Most successful labor leaders were concerned about labor's role in representing their members' immediate concerns and refrained from advocating ideological positions.

In summary, labor encountered several hurdles in its early organization: the conspiracy doctrine, initial uplift union movements, the link with radicals, and injunctions aimed at union activities. Personalities who shaped the early American labor movement included Terence Powderly and Uriah Stephens, Samuel Gompers and Adolph Strasser, Eugene Debs and "Big Bill" Haywood.

The 1920s was a decade of retrenchment. Underneath the surface was a growing interest in industrial union organization, particularly by John L. Lewis, president of the United Mine Workers. Interest in labor legislation was growing. Then the Depression began. The 1930s saw most present labor legislation being shaped and many present-day industrial unions formed. It was a decade of turbulence, formation, and definition—and an adolescence necessary for America's labor-management relations to endure to reach adulthood and relative maturity.

[86] For an expanded explanation of the merger of UNITE HERE and its later dissolution, together with a description of its leaders, see www.prospect.org/cs/articles?article=disunite_there.

The 1930s provided the environment necessary for successful industrial unions. Both the Norris-LaGuardia and Wagner acts were passed, eliminating injunctions against most union activities and establishing collective bargaining as the preferred mode for resolving employment disputes.

The CIO was formed by dissident AFL leaders. It began by organizing efforts in primary industries, such as auto, steel, and rubber. Employers strongly resisted, but sit-down strikes and changes in public policy toward unions strengthened the CIO's efforts. By 1937, membership in the CIO was moving toward 4 million and had surpassed the AFL.

Industrial strife increased until the outbreak of World War II. The National War Labor Board was established to cope with employment problems during the wartime mobilization and to resolve disputes. Arbitration of grievances was introduced and later incorporated into collective bargaining agreements.

After the war, strikes reached unprecedented levels. In 1947, the Taft-Hartley Act, passed over President Truman's veto, provided for national emergency dispute procedures, established the Federal Mediation and Conciliation Service, and designated several union unfair labor practices. In 1959, the Landrum-Griffin Act limited the possibility of corruption in union-management relations.

The AFL and the CIO merged in 1955, but shortly after, the union movement reached its maximum growth as a share of the labor force. With the exception of the public sector, union membership has recently been declining. Major changes in employer tactics and the structure of the economy contributed to this decline. Leadership and the structure of the trade union movement has recently changed, and greater efforts are being made to organize new units. Later chapters identify the causes of these changes and their consequences for the labor movement.

Discussion Questions

1. Trace the evolution of the legal status of American unions. What activities were restricted by laws and courts? Did constraints increase or decline with time?
2. What were the major contributing causes to the failure of uplift unionism?
3. What were the advantages and disadvantages of taking a "business union" approach as opposed to advocating a labor political party?
4. Who were the leading personalities in labor relations? Which ones contributed to the definition of labor relations in the United States?
5. Who were the most effective union leaders during the 1930s and 1940s? What are your criteria for effectiveness? Would these same leaders be effective now?

Key Terms

Craft union, *27*
National union, *27*
American Federation of Labor (AFL), *27*
Congress of Industrial Organizations (CIO), *27*
Change to Win (CTW), *27*
Corporatism, *28*
Uplift unionism, *28*
Revolutionary unionism, *28*
Business unionism, *28*
Predatory unionism, *28*
Journeyman, *29*
Conspiracy doctrine, *29*
National Labor Union (NLU), *31*
Knights of Labor, *32*
Arbitration, *32*
Industrial Workers of the World (IWW), *37*
Boycott, *39*
Sherman Antitrust Act, *39*
Clayton Act, *40*
American Plan, *41*
Open shop, *41*
Yellow-dog contract, *41*
Industrial union, *42*
Committee for Industrial Organization (CIO), *43*
Sit-down strike, *44*
Norris-LaGuardia Act, *45*
Wagner Act, *45*
National Labor Relations Board (NLRB), *45*
Exclusive representation, *46*
Mohawk Valley formula, *46*
Jurisdictional dispute, *48*
Taft-Hartley, *51*
Right-to-work law, *52*
Federal Mediation and Conciliation Service (FMCS), *52*
Drive system, *53*
Landrum-Griffin Act, *55*
Executive Order 10988, *55*
Federal Labor Relations Authority, *56*

Selected Web Sites

Enter "labor history Web sites" into your search engine window. You will find university, labor union, government, and international Web sites that provide general historical information.

Employment Law and Federal Agencies

This chapter covers federal law and federal agencies that regulate employment, with particular emphasis on labor relations. The primary labor relations laws include the Railway Labor Act, Norris-LaGuardia Act, Wagner Act (as amended by Taft-Hartley and later laws), Landrum-Griffin Act, and Civil Service Reform Act. The chapter gives an overview of the statutes and major government agencies, as well as examples of the agencies' organizational structures. It also examines some of the effects of how laws are enforced by federal government agencies and how employees use protections granted by some employment laws.

In studying this chapter, keep the following questions in mind:

1. What specific types of activities are regulated?
2. In what areas have regulations been extended or retracted?
3. What employee groups are excluded or exempted from various regulations?
4. How do administrative agencies interact with employers and unions in implementing laws and regulations?

OVERVIEW

Statutory employment laws result from the interaction of the positions of a variety of interest groups in society. When a pluralistic coalition of interest groups emerges, the climate necessary for passage is created.[1] New laws or the amendment of existing laws require the bonding of interest groups around issues or agendas. As Chapter 5 will note, organized labor in the

[1] For an extended and insightful treatment of the interaction between labor organizations and the state, see R. J. Adams, "The Role of the State in Industrial Relations," in D. Lewin, O. S. Mitchell, and P. D. Sherer, eds., *Research Frontiers in Industrial Relations and Human Resources* (Madison, WI: Industrial Relations Research Association, 1992), pp. 489–523. See also W. Forbath, *Law and the Shaping of the American Labor Movement* (Cambridge, MA: Harvard University Press, 1991).

United States is politically active in advocating laws that facilitate union activities, regulate employment, and create and enhance social welfare programs.

Current laws governing organizing and collective bargaining date back to 1926 when the Railway Labor Act was enacted. Since then, five other significant pieces of legislation have followed: Norris-LaGuardia (1932), Wagner (1935), Taft-Hartley (1947), Landrum-Griffin (1959), and the Civil Service Reform Act, Title VII (1978). Each was enacted to clarify and/or constrain the roles of management and labor. Table 3.1 lists each piece of major legislation and the areas of labor relations to which it applies.

TABLE 3.1 Federal Labor Relations Laws

Law	Coverage	Major Provisions	Federal Agencies
Railway Labor Act	Private sector nonmanagerial rail and airline employees and employers	Employees may choose bargaining representatives for collective bargaining; no yellow-dog contracts; dispute settlement procedures include mediation, arbitration, and emergency boards.	National Mediation Board, National Railroad Adjustment Board
Norris-LaGuardia Act	All private sector employers and labor organizations	Outlaws injunctions for nonviolent labor union activities. Makes yellow-dog contracts unenforceable.	
Labor Management Relations Act (originally passed as Wagner Act, amended by Taft-Hartley and Landrum-Griffin Acts)	Private sector nonmanagerial and nonagricultural employees not covered by Railway Labor Act; postal workers	Employees may choose bargaining representatives for collective bargaining; both labor and management must bargain in good faith; unfair labor practices include discrimination for union activities, secondary boycotts, and refusal to bargain; national emergency dispute procedures established.	National Labor Relations Board, Federal Mediation and Conciliation Service
Landrum-Griffin Act	All private sector employers and labor organizations	Specification and guarantee of individual rights of union members. Prohibits certain management and union conduct. Requires union financial disclosures.	U.S. Department of Labor
Civil Service Reform Act, Title VII	All nonuniformed, nonmanagerial federal service employees and agencies	Employees may choose representatives for collective bargaining; bargaining rights established for noneconomic and nonstaffing issues. Requires arbitration of unresolved grievances.	Federal Labor Relations Authority

RAILWAY LABOR ACT (1926)

The **Railway Labor Act (RLA)** applies to rail and air carriers and their nonmanagerial employees. The act has five general purposes:

1. Avoiding service interruptions.
2. Eliminating any restrictions on joining a union.
3. Guaranteeing the freedom of employees in any matter of self-organization.
4. Providing for prompt dispute settlement.
5. Enabling prompt grievance settlement.

In railroads, train drivers, maintenance-of-way employees, conductors, ticket agents, shop workers, and others are covered, regardless of whether they are personally involved in moving passengers or freight. Similarly, airline pilots, cabin attendants, mechanics, reservations agents, baggage handlers, and others are covered. In 1996, the Federal Aviation Authorization Act brought air express companies, including their ground employees, under the RLA. FedEx was brought within RLA jurisdiction, but United Parcel Service (UPS) remained outside since FedEx is considered primarily an air express company while UPS is seen as primarily a ground carrier.

The RLA enables employees to choose, by majority vote, an organization to exclusively represent them for collective bargaining purposes. Under the RLA, employees within a given craft (or occupation) are entitled to be represented separately within their employers, and initial representation elections are held within a single defined occupational group. Unions or associations seeking to represent employees must be free of employer domination or assistance.

Majority representatives become the exclusive bargaining agent for the employees within the bargaining unit and are entitled to negotiate with the carrier over wages, terms, and conditions of employment. Negotiated contracts must contain a grievance procedure consistent with the requirements of the RLA.

Contract negotiations under the RLA are substantially different than under other private sector and many public sector labor laws. Under the RLA, a contract remains in effect, even after its stated amendment date, until a new agreement is reached. Before a contract can be amended, written notice must be given 30 days before the intended changes would go into effect. At this point the parties begin to negotiate activities. They may request assistance from the **National Mediation Board (NMB)** to help reach an agreement. The board may also offer its services without the request of the parties. No unilaterally imposed changes or strikes can occur (if a settlement is not reached) unless an impasse has been declared by the NMB. Only if the parties reject arbitration of their differences does

Exhibit 3.1

NORTHWEST AIRLINES–AIRCRAFT MECHANICS FRATERNAL ASSOCIATION EMERGENCY BOARD

Executive Order

Establishing an Emergency Board to Investigate a Dispute Between Northwest Airlines, Inc., and Its Employees Represented by the Aircraft Mechanics Fraternal Association.

A dispute exists between Northwest Airlines, Inc. and its employees represented by the Aircraft Mechanics Fraternal Association.

The dispute has not heretofore been adjusted under the provisions of the Railway Labor Act, as amended (45 U.S.C. 151-188) (the "Act").

In the judgment of the National Mediation Board, this dispute threatens substantially to interrupt interstate commerce to a degree that would deprive sections of the country of essential transportation service.

NOW, THEREFORE, by the authority vested in me as President by the Constitution and the laws of the United States, including sections 10 and 201 of the Act (45 U.S.C. 160 and 181), it is hereby ordered as follows:

Section 1. Establishment of Emergency Board ("Board"). There is established, effective March 12, 2001, a Board of three members to be appointed by the President to investigate this dispute. No member shall be pecuniarily or otherwise interested in any organization of airline employees or any air carrier. The Board shall perform its functions subject to the availability of funds.

Sec. 2. Report. The Board shall report to the President with respect to this dispute within 30 days of its creation.

Sec. 3. Maintaining Conditions. As provided by section 10 of the Act, from the date of the creation of the Board and for 30 days after the Board has submitted its report to the President, no change in the conditions out of which the dispute arose shall be made by the parties to the controversy, except by agreement of the parties.

Sec. 4. Record Maintenance. The records and files of the Board are records of the Office of the President and upon the Board's termination shall be maintained in the physical custody of the National Mediation Board.

Sec. 5. Expiration. The Board shall terminate upon the submission of the report provided for in sections 2 and 3 of this order.

GEORGE W. BUSH

THE WHITE HOUSE, March 9, 2001.

the NMB release them to engage in "self-help." Finally, if the president believes a work stoppage would substantially disrupt interstate commerce, an emergency board can be convened to investigate the dispute and render a report. No changes or strikes can take place until at least 30 days after the completion of an emergency board's report. Thus, relatively long periods often elapse between when negotiations start and when an agreement is reached. Presidential boards are not infrequent. President George W. Bush convened an emergency board in 2001 to deal with threatened strikes at both Northwest and United Airlines. Exhibit 3.1 covers his appointment of a board in the Northwest Airlines–Aircraft Mechanics Fraternal Association contract dispute in early 2001. (An agreement was reached before the board had completed its work.)

The **National Railroad Adjustment Board (NRAB)** and the NMB were created by the RLA. The NRAB consists of an equal number of union and management members and is empowered to settle grievances of both parties. If the board deadlocks on a grievance, it obtains a referee to hear the case and make an award. Awards are binding, and prevailing parties may sue in federal district courts to enforce the awards. In reality, most disputes are handled by Public Law Boards and Special Boards of Adjustment, which involve ad hoc arbitrators or rotating boards of neutrals who hear and rule on deadlocked dispute cases.

The NMB is composed of three members appointed by the president. It handles representation elections, mediates bargaining disputes on request, urges parties to arbitrate when mediation is unsuccessful, interprets mediated contract agreements, and appoints arbitrators if disputing parties cannot agree on one.

Compared with later acts, dispute handling under the RLA is highly detailed. Subsequent laws generally leave this up to the parties. The RLA also requires that employees be organized by craft (or occupational area), thus forcing employers to bargain with several unions often having conflicting goals. Over time, bargaining by craft has changed somewhat as mergers have formed new unions such as the United Transportation Union (UTU) and the Transportation Communications International Union (TCIU). The TCIU constitutes a merger among employees in blue- and white-collar railroad and airline occupations.

There have been differences in the way the law has been implemented in the rail and airline industries. Intracontract disputes in the airline industry are arbitrated as they are in industries covered by the NLRA. In addition, contrary to the technical wording of the law, some railway supervisors, such as yardmasters, are represented by unions.

NORRIS-LAGUARDIA ACT (1932)

The Norris-LaGuardia Act was the first law to protect the rights of unions and workers to engage in union activity. The act forbids federal courts to issue **injunctions** (orders prohibiting certain activities) against specifically described union activities and outlaws yellow-dog contracts (in which employees agree that continued employment depends on abstention from union membership or activities). These contracts had been upheld previously by the Supreme Court.[2] Since enactment, federal courts have strictly construed Norris-LaGuardia provisions.

The act recognizes that freedom to associate for collective bargaining purposes is the corollary of the collectivization of capital through incorporation. Injunctions and yellow-dog contracts interfere with freedom of association. Besides the absolute prohibition of yellow-dog contracts, injunctions against specific activities are prohibited regardless of whether

[2] *Hitchman Coal & Coke Co.* v. *Mitchell*, 245 U.S. 229 (1917).

the act is done by an individual, a group, or a union. The following cannot be enjoined:

1. Stopping or refusing to work.
2. Participating in union membership.
3. Paying or withholding strike benefits, unemployment benefits, and the like to people participating in labor disputes.
4. Providing aid or assistance for persons suing or being sued.
5. Publicizing a labor dispute in a nonviolent, nonfraudulent manner.
6. Assembling to organize.
7. Notifying anyone that any of these acts are to be performed.
8. Agreeing to engage or not engage in any of these acts.
9. Advising others to do any of these acts.

The Norris-LaGuardia Act also finally and completely laid to rest the 18th-century conspiracy doctrine. Section 5 prohibits injunctions against any of the above activities if pursued in a nonviolent manner. The effects of the *Danbury Hatters* decision (which required that union members pay boycott damages) were substantially diminished by Section 6.[3] That section mandates that an individual or labor organization may not be held accountable for unlawful acts of its leadership unless those acts were directed or ratified by the membership.

Section 7 ensures the act may not be used as a cover for violent and destructive actions. An injunction may be issued if:

1. Substantial or irreparable injury to property will occur.
2. Greater injury will be inflicted on the party requesting the injunction than the injunction would cause on the adversary.
3. No adequate legal remedy exists.
4. Authorities are either unable or unwilling to give protection.

Before an action can be enjoined, the union must have the opportunity for rebuttal. If immediate restraint is sought and there is insufficient time for an adversary hearing, the employer must deposit a bond to compensate for possible damages done to the union by the injunction. Injunctions cover only those persons or associations actually causing problems.

Section 8 restricts injunction-granting powers by requiring that requesters try to settle disputes before asking for injunctions. Section 9 forbids injunctions against all union activities in a case except allowing only those likely to lead to an injury. For example, mass picketing might be enjoined if it is violent; but the strike, payments of strike benefits, and so on could not be enjoined.

[3] *Loewe* v. *Lawlor*, 208 U.S. 274 (1908).

While the Norris-LaGuardia Act did not require that an employer recognize a union or bargain with it, it provided labor some leverage in organizing and bargaining. Labor could, henceforth, bring pressure on the employer through strikes, boycotts, and the like without worrying about federal court injunctions.

WAGNER AND TAFT-HARTLEY ACTS (AS AMENDED)

The Wagner (1935) and Taft-Hartley (1947) acts were enacted 12 years apart, with Taft-Hartley amending and extending the Wagner Act. In 1959, the Landrum-Griffin Act added amendments. In 1974, jurisdiction was extended to and special rules were enacted for private nonprofit health care organizations. The acts establish a statutory preference for using collective bargaining to resolve conflicts in the employment relationship and for roughly balancing the power of management and labor. The Wagner Act, passed during a period of relative weakness for organized labor, only spoke to employer practices. As the pendulum swung in the other direction, Taft-Hartley added union practices to the proscribed list. Finally, Landrum-Griffin aimed to fine-tune the law to match day-to-day realities.

The heart of the Wagner Act (Section 7, as amended) embodies public policy toward the individual worker and collective bargaining. It reads:

> Employees shall have the right to self-organization, to form, join, or assist labor organizations, to bargain collectively through representatives of their own choosing, and to engage in other concerted activities for the purpose of collective bargaining or other mutual aid or protection, and shall also have the right to refrain from any or all of such activities except to the extent that such right may be affected by an agreement requiring membership in a labor organization as a condition of employment as authorized in Section 8(a)(3).

Definitions

The act defines the terms *employer, employee, supervisor,* and *professional employee.*

Employer

An **employer** is an organization or a manager or supervisor acting on its behalf. However, federal, state, and local governments or any organization wholly owned by these agencies (except the U.S. Postal Service), persons subject to the RLA, and union representatives when acting as bargaining agents are excluded. Casinos owned and operated by Native American tribes that primarily employ and cater to non–Native Americans are considered employers, while other Native American–governed ventures on reservation property are not.[4] Where a person is employed by a labor supplier who provides workers for an employer, that person cannot be included in a unit of permanent employees unless the supplied employer consents.[5]

Employee

An **employee** need not be an employee of an organization in which a labor dispute occurs. For example, if firm A is struck and employees of firm B refuse to cross picket lines, even though no dispute exists with B, the workers at firm B are considered employees under the act. A person remains an employee under interpretations of the act if he or she is on strike for a contract or on strike about or fired as a result of an unfair labor practice—even if the employer does not consider the person as such—until the person is rehired or reemployed at or above a level equivalent to his or her previous job. The following groups in the private sector are not considered to be employees for organizing purposes: domestic workers, agricultural workers, independent contractors,[6] individuals employed by a spouse or parent,[7] graduate research or teaching assistants employed by private universities[8] (but not research assistants employed by private research foundations of either public or private universities),[9] or persons covered by the RLA. Undocumented workers are considered to be employees when representation questions are considered,[10] but are not entitled to reinstatement or back pay remedies where unfair labor practices have been found that involved them.[11]

Supervisor

A **supervisor** is an employee with independent authority to make personnel decisions and to administer a labor agreement. Examples of personnel decisions include hiring, firing, adjusting grievances, making work

[4] *San Manuel Indian Bingo and Casino*, 341 NLRB 1055; enforced by U.S. Circuit Court of Appeals, DC Circuit, in *San Manuel Indian Bingo and Casino* v. *NLRB*, No. 05-1392 (2007); see also A. Wermuth, "Union's Gamble Pays Off: In *San Manuel Indian Bingo and Casino*, the NLRB Breaks the Nation's Promise and Reverses Decades-Old Precedent to Assert Jurisdiction over Tribal Enterprises on Indian Reservations," *The Labor Lawyer*, 21 (2005), pp. 81–108.

[5] *H.S. Care L.L.C., d/b/a Oakwood Care Center and N&W Agency, Inc.*, 343 NLRB No. 76 (2004).

[6] *P.Q. Beef Processors, Inc.*, 231 NLRB 179 (1977).

[7] *Viele & Sons, Inc.*, 227 NLRB 284 (1977).

[8] *Brown University*, 342 NLRB 483 (2004); S. D. Pollack and D. V. Johns, "Graduate Students, Unions, and Brown University," *The Labor Lawyer*, 20 (2004), pp. 243–256.

[9] *The Research Foundation of the State University of New York Office of Sponsored Programs*, 350 NLRB 197 (2007).

[10] B. Pierce, "Are They or Aren't They? *Agri Processor* Revisits Undocumented Workers' Employee Status Under the NLRA," *Berkeley Journal of Employment and Labor Law*, 29 (2008), pp. 495–502.

[11] *Hoffman Plastic Compounds, Inc.* v. *NLRB*, 535 U.S. 137 (2002).

assignments, and deciding pay increases. A supervisor may belong to a union (although this is unlikely outside the construction or maritime industries), but groups of supervisors may not organize and bargain collectively. The supervisory definition has been broadened by two Supreme Court decisions to include as supervisors professional nurses who give work direction to nonprofessionals that involves patient care but do not have any of the other supervisory powers listed above.[12] Investors in health care facility stocks expected that these decisions would have negative effects on wages, all else equal, since share prices of companies in this industry rose abnormally in the days following the decision.[13]

Professional Employee

A **professional employee** is one whose work is intellectual in character, requiring independent judgment or discretion; whose performance cannot readily be measured in a standardized fashion; and whose skills are learned through prolonged, specialized instruction.[14] Professional employees may organize, but they may not be included in a nonprofessional unit without a majority vote of the professionals.

National Labor Relations Board

The **National Labor Relations Board (NLRB)** consists of five members appointed by the president and confirmed by the Senate. Members serve five-year terms and may be reappointed. One member, designated by the president, chairs the board. The NLRB is responsible for conducting representation elections and resolving or ruling on unfair labor practice charges.

The board may delegate its duties to a subgroup of three or more members. If a situation occurs in which there are fewer than three members who have been appointed and confirmed (or an interim appointment has not been made), the board may not render decisions.[15] It can also delegate authority to determine representation and election questions to its regional directors. The board has a general counsel responsible for investigating charges and issuing complaints. More details on the board's organization, function, and performance follow later in this chapter.

Unfair Labor Practices

The amended labor acts specify a variety of employer tactics presumed to interfere with employees' freedom of choice in being represented by

[12] *NLRB* v. *Health Care and Retirement Corp.*, 511 U.S. 571 (1994); and *NLRB* v. *Kentucky River Community Care, Inc.*, 532 U.S. 706 (2001).

[13] S. E. Abraham and P. B. Voos, "The Market's Reaction to Two Supreme Court Rulings on American Labor Law," *Journal of Labor Research*, 26 (2005), pp. 677–687.

[14] See N. A. Beales II and C. Scott, "Professionals under the Labor Management Relations Act: Lessons from the Health Care Industry," *Journal of Collective Negotiations in the Public Sector*, 24 (1995), pp. 285–300.

[15] *New Process Steel* v. *NLRB*, 560 U.S. ___ (2010).

their chosen advocates. They also specify union tactics that might coerce employees of a nonunion organization to join a union or that would interfere with a nonunion employer's ability to operate. The specified **unfair labor practices (ULPs)** are contained in Section 8; part (a) applies to employers, part (b) to unions.

Employer Unfair Labor Practices

An employer may not interfere with an employee engaging in any activity protected by Section 7. The employer may not assist or dominate a labor organization. If two unions are vying to organize a group of workers, an employer may neither recognize one to avoid dealing with the other nor express a preference for one over the other. The employer may not create a company-sponsored union and bargain with it. Employers may not create employee groups within the organization and ask them to participate in setting wages, hours, and terms and conditions of employment.

An employer may not discriminate in hiring, assignment, or other terms of employment on the basis of union membership. However, employers and unions may negotiate contract clauses requiring union membership as a condition of continued employment (a **union shop** agreement). But if such a clause is negotiated, the employer cannot discriminate against non-membership if the union discriminatorily refuses to admit an employee to membership.

Employees may not be penalized or discriminated against for charging an employer with unfair labor practices.

Finally, employers may not refuse to bargain with a union over issues of pay, hours, or other terms and conditions of employment.

Union Unfair Labor Practices

Unions may not coerce employees in the exercise of Section 7 rights, but this does not limit union internal rule making, discipline, fines, and so on. Unions cannot demand or require that an employer take action against an employee for any reason except failure to pay union dues.

Unions may not engage in—or encourage individuals to engage in—strikes or refusals to handle some type of product or work if the object is to accomplish any of the following ends:

1. Forcing an employer or self-employed person to join an employer or labor organization or to cease handling nonunion products (except in certain cases, detailed later).
2. Forcing an employer to bargain with an uncertified labor organization, that is, one whose majority status has not been established.
3. Forcing an employer to cease bargaining with a certified representative.
4. Forcing an employer to assign work to employees in a particular labor organization unless ordered to do so or previously bargained to do so.
5. Requiring excessive initiation fees for union membership.

6. Forcing an employer to pay for services not rendered.
7. Picketing an employer to force recognition of the picketing union if:
   a. The picketing group has not been certified as the employees' representative;
   b. Either no union election has taken place within the past 12 months or the picketing union requests a representation election within 30 days after picketing begins; but
   c. Nothing can prohibit a union's picketing to advise the public that an employer's employees are not unionized, provided the picketing does not interfere with pickups and deliveries.

Protected Concerted Activity

Where no evidence of threat, reprisal, or promise of benefit exists, the parties involved in collective bargaining activities are free to express views in any form.

Duty to Bargain

Unions and employers have a mutual **duty to bargain** in good faith about wages, hours, and terms and conditions of employment. Each must meet with the other when requested to negotiate an agreement, reduce it to writing, and interpret its meaning if disagreements arise. Neither is required to concede any issue to demonstrate good faith. Notifying the Federal Mediation and Conciliation Service (FMCS) is required as a condition to modify a contract. Specific and more stringent requirements are laid out for health care organizations.

Prohibited Contract Clauses

Except in the construction and apparel industries, employees and unions cannot negotiate contracts providing that particular products of certain employers will not be used. This is the so-called **hot cargo** issue. For example, a trucking union could not negotiate a contract prohibiting hauling goods manufactured by a nonunion employer. But a construction union could refuse to install nonunion goods if a contract clause had been negotiated.

Construction Employment

Contractors can make collective bargaining agreements with construction unions, even without a demonstration of majority status. The agreements may require union membership within seven days of employment and give the union an opportunity to refer members for existing job openings. These exceptions recognize the short-run nature of many construction jobs. Labor agreements may also provide for apprenticeship training requirements and may give preference in job openings to workers with greater past experience.

Health Care Picketing

A union anticipating a strike or picketing at a health care facility must notify the Federal Mediation and Conciliation Service (FMCS) 10 days in advance.

Representation Elections

The act provides that when a majority of employees in a particular unit desires representation, all employees (regardless of union membership) will be represented by the union regarding wages, hours, and terms and conditions of employment. Individuals can present their own grievances and have them adjusted if the resolution is consistent with the contract.

The NLRB determines what group of employees would constitute an appropriate unit for a representation election and subsequent bargaining. Its discretion is limited, however. First, it cannot include professional and nonprofessional employees in the same unit unless a majority of the professionals agree. Second, it cannot deny separate representation to a craft solely on the basis that it was part of a larger unit determined appropriate by the board. Third, it cannot include plant guards and other types of employees in the same unit. Also, supervisors are not employees as defined by the act; so, for example, a unit of production supervisors would be an inappropriate group for representation.

In cases of questionable union majority status, the board is authorized to hold elections (subject to certain constraints, detailed in Chapter 6). The board may also conduct elections to determine whether an existing union maintains a continuing majority status.

Unfair Labor Practice Charges and NLRB Procedures

If the board finds that an unfair labor practice (ULP) occurred, it can issue cease-and-desist orders, require back pay to make wronged persons whole, and petition a court of appeals to enforce its orders. Board activities with regard to ULPs are detailed later in this chapter.

Right-to-Work Laws

Section 14(b), one of the most controversial in the act, permits states to pass right-to-work laws. In states with these laws, employees represented by unions cannot be compelled to join a union or pay dues as a condition of continued employment. Union and **agency shop** clauses are unenforceable in these states.

Religious Objections to Union Membership in Health Care Organizations

Health care organization employees whose religious beliefs preclude membership in a union may donate a sum equal to union dues to a nonreligious charity in lieu of the dues.

Federal Mediation and Conciliation Service

The act holds that the public has an interest in maintaining stable labor relations. If conflicts between the parties interfere with stability, the government should be able and willing to offer assistance. Thus, the Federal Mediation and Conciliation Service (FMCS) was created to offer mediation services whenever disputes threaten to interrupt commerce or where they involve health care organizations. The FMCS is directed to emphasize services in contract negotiations, not grievance settlements.

National Emergency Disputes

If the president believes a labor dispute imperils the nation, a board of inquiry studies the issues surrounding the dispute. After the board submits its report, the attorney general may ask a district court to enjoin a strike or lockout. If the court agrees that the dispute threatens national security, an injunction may be issued. If an injunction is ordered, the board is reconvened and monitors the settlement process. If an agreement is not reached after 60 days, the board reports the positions of labor and management and includes management's last offer. Over the next 15 days, the NLRB holds an election among the employees to determine whether a majority favors accepting management's last offer. Five more days are taken to certify the results. At this time (or earlier, if a settlement was reached), the injunction will be discharged. If a settlement was not reached, the president forwards the report of the board, the election results, and the president's recommendations to Congress for action. Until President George W. Bush invoked the national emergency provisions in the 2002 West Coast Dock Workers strike, they had been unused since President Carter invoked them in a 1978 United Mine Workers strike.

Suits, Political Action, and Financial Relationships

Unions may sue on behalf of their members and can be sued and found liable for damages against organizational assets but not those of members. Financial dealings between an employer and a union representing its employees are forbidden. Union agents are forbidden from demanding payment for performing contractual duties. Certain regulations relating to the establishment of trust funds are also included.

Unions and corporations are forbidden to make political contributions in any elections involving the choice of federal officeholders.

Summary and Overview

The important aspects of Taft-Hartley relate to the establishment, function, and powers of the NLRB; the delineation of employer and union unfair labor practices; the promulgation of rules governing representation and certification; the creation and functions of the FMCS; and the national emergency injunction procedures. These aim at balancing the power of labor and management and stabilizing industrial relations.

Taft-Hartley was enacted the year following the largest incidence of strikes and the most time lost from work due to strikes of any year in U.S. history. Besides identifying and adding a number of union unfair labor practices, the law also specifically aimed to reduce the level of strike activity by requiring that employers and unions planning to renegotiate contracts must inform the FMCS at least 30 days before contract expiration, making FMCS services available, and creating national emergency procedures to protect the public from highly disruptive strikes in essential industries. The legislation created an environment supportive of a corporatist approach to labor-management relations that would reign until the 1970s.

LANDRUM-GRIFFIN ACT (1959)

The Landrum-Griffin Act, formally the Labor-Management Reporting and Disclosure Act (LMRDA) of 1959, resulted from congressional hearings into corrupt practices in labor-management relations. It regulates internal activities of employers and unions covered by both Taft-Hartley and the Railway Labor Act.

Bill of Rights for Union Members

Unions must provide equal rights and privileges to members in nominating, voting, participating in referenda, meetings, and so on. Each member has a right to be heard and to oppose policies of the union's leaders insofar as this does not interfere with its legal obligations. Dues, initiation fees, and assessments cannot be increased without a majority vote of approval. Members' rights to sue their unions are guaranteed as long as they have exhausted internal union procedures and are not aided by an employer or an employer association. Members of unions cannot be expelled unless due process consistent with the Bill of Rights section of the act is followed. Copies of the labor agreement between the employer and the union must be provided to every member.

Reports Required of Unions and Employers

All unions are required to file constitutions and bylaws with the secretary of labor. Unions must file annual reports detailing assets and liabilities, receipts, salaries and allowances of officers, loans made to officers or businesses, and other expenditures as prescribed by the secretary of labor. The report must also be made available to the membership. Employees covered by union contracts have little access to information on union expenditures to influence political outcomes, litigation, and the like before it is filed with the Department of Labor.[16]

[16] M. F. Masters, R. S. Atkin, and G. W. Florkowski, "An Analysis of Union Reporting Requirements under Title II of the Landrum-Griffin Act," *Labor Law Journal*, 40 (1989), pp. 713–722.

Every officer and employee (except clerical and custodial employees) must submit annual reports to the secretary of labor detailing any family income or transaction in stocks, securities, or other payments (except wages) made by a firm where the union represents employees; income or other payments from a business with substantial dealings with these firms; or any payments made by a labor consultant to such a firm.

Employers must report payments made to union officials (even if only to reimburse expenses); payments to employees to convince other employees to exercise or not exercise their rights to organize and bargain collectively; and payments to obtain information about unions or individuals involved in disputes with the employer. Employers must also report agreements with or payments to labor relations consultants to oppose union organizing campaigns.

Trusteeships

A national union may act against a local for breaching the union's constitution or bylaws. To reduce the possibility of stifling dissent, an administrative takeover or **trusteeship** of a local can be imposed only to restore democratic procedures, correct financial malfeasance or corruption, ensure performance of collective bargaining agreements, or facilitate other legitimate union functions. If a trusteeship is imposed, the national union must report the reasons for the takeover to the secretary of labor and disclose the subsidiary's financial situation. A union exercising a trusteeship cannot move assets from the subsidiary or appoint delegates to conventions from it (unless elected by secret ballot of the membership). Trustreeships are rarely imposed, but when they are it is most often to deal with corruption or financial malfeasance.

OTHER FEDERAL LAWS AND REGULATIONS

Byrnes Act (1936)

Under the Byrnes Act of 1936 it is illegal to recruit and/or transport individuals across state lines for the purpose of interfering forcefully or threateningly with peaceful picketing or the right of self-organization.

Copeland Anti-Kickback Act (1934)

The Copeland Anti-Kickback Act prohibits anyone from requiring or coercing employees on a public works construction project (or project financed by loans or grants from the federal government) to kick back part of their compensation as a condition of continued employment.

Racketeer Influenced and Corrupt Organizations Act (1970)

The Racketeer Influenced and Corrupt Organizations (RICO) Act was passed to deter corruption by requiring the forfeiture of illegal gains. Penalties treble the forfeiture amount. States have also enacted laws to reduce or eliminate corruption. In the New Jersey casino industry, the laws police employers well, but unions are more difficult to control because locals often represent workers both inside and outside casinos.[17] An analysis of corruption in New York City construction found that the work coordination necessary in construction, coupled with the unions' monopoly power to supply skilled labor, could lead to organized-crime involvement in monitoring or facilitating activities. The effect of possible corruption on union construction worker wages does not appears to be significant, however.[18]

OTHER MAJOR EMPLOYMENT LAWS

Under common law in the United States, an employer could hire or fire an employee for a good reason, a bad reason, or no reason at all.[19] Thus, at its very basis, employment is "at-will" unless a contract to the contrary has been negotiated. However, a large set of federal and state laws and their accompanying administrative regulations limit the unfettered discretion of the employer in designing and implementing the employment relationship.

Civil rights laws and regulations broadly prohibit employers from taking race, sex, color, religion, national origin, or age (being age 40 or over) into account when making employment decisions. Employers are expected to make reasonable accommodations for persons with disabilities. When men and women are employed in jobs requiring similar skill, effort, responsibility, and working conditions, differences in pay based on gender are not permitted.

Minimum wages are established by both federal and state laws and cover most employees. Employees who are not in certain defined job categories are entitled to a 50 percent pay premium for each hour beyond 40 worked in a given week. Prevailing wages for similar employment in the labor market must be paid to employees working on federal contracts. These laws are of particular interest to organized labor since they essentially take wages out of competition. To successfully bid on government contracts, a nonunion employer is required to pay wages equal to a unionized employer and therefore needs to be able to save costs on other factors or accept a lower profit. Many states also have versions of these laws that apply to contracts for construction, goods, or services with the respective

[17] B. A. Lee and J. Chelius, "Government Regulation of Union-Management Corruption: The Casino Industry Experience in New Jersey," *Industrial and Labor Relations Review*, 42 (1989), pp. 536–548.

[18] C. Ichniowski and A. Preston, "The Persistence of Organized Crime in New York City Construction: An Economic Perspective," *Industrial and Labor Relations Review*, 42 (1989), pp. 549–565.

[19] *Payne* v. *Western Atlantic Railroad*, 81 Tenn. 507 (1884).

state governments. A study of the extension of prevailing wage legislation to the construction of low-income public housing in California found that costs increased by between 9 and 37 percent, leading to a reduction of 3,100 units built per year with a given appropriation level.[20]

Social security taxes employers and employees and provides benefits for retirees, persons with disabilities, and surviving spouses and children of covered employees. The federal and state unemployment insurance program provides benefits and job-seeking services for persons who become involuntarily unemployed. The Employee Retirement Income Security Act regulates pension and benefit programs and requires that employers adequately fund established plans. Worker compensation regulations require partial income replacement and health and rehabilitation services for workers who were injured on the job.

The Patient Protection and Affordable Care Act (PPACA) of 2010 has many implications for employers, unions, and employees. Many of its provisions are not immediately effective, but will be phased in over the next 8 years. Provisions of existing collective bargaining agreements that provide for employer-paid or subsidized health care are "grandfathered" until their expiration dates (except for adding coverage for children under 26 and eliminating life-time benefit ceilings and exceptions for preexisting conditions that became effective in late 2010). Beginning in 2014, employers with 50 or more full-time employees will be required to provide specific levels of insurance or pay a penalty of $2,000 per employee. Beginning in 2018, health insurance plans that cost more than $10,200 per year for single coverage or $27,500 for family coverage will have excess costs taxed at a 40 percent rate. The likely result of PPACA is that many employers, particularly those that have labor-intensive operations, will terminate existing plans and pay the penalty.

Health and safety requirements are spelled out in the Occupational Safety and Health Act and the Mine Safety Act. Facilities are inspected by the Occupational Safety and Health Administration (OSHA) or corresponding state agencies. Evidence indicates that inspections with penalties for violations are more effective for reducing injuries than those without. The effect is greater in smaller and nonunion facilities,[21] possibly because union facilities are more likely to have joint labor-management safety committees. The Family and Medical Leave Act establishes rights for employees to take unpaid leaves to deal with family medical emergencies. Advance notification of significant layoffs is required by the Worker Adjustment and Retraining Notification Act. Table 3.2 summarizes the provisions of major federal employment laws.

[20] S. Dunn, J. M. Quigley, and L. A. Rosenthal, "The Effects of Prevailing Wage Requirements in the Cost of Low-Income Housing," *Industrial and Labor Relations Review*, 59 (2005), pp. 141–157.

[21] W. B. Gray and J. M. Mendeloff, "The Declining Effects of OSHA Inspections on Manufacturing Injuries, 1979–98," *Industrial and Labor Relations Review*, 58 (2005), pp. 571–587.

TABLE 3.2 General Federal Employment Laws

Source: Adapted from H. G. Heneman III, D. P. Schwab, J. A. Fossum, and L. D. Dyer, *Personnel/Human Resource Management*, 4th ed. (Homewood, IL: Irwin, 1989), pp. 83–88; U.S. Department of Labor Web site; U.S. Department of Justice Web site.

Law	Coverage	Major Provisions	Federal Agencies
Title VII, 1964 Civil Rights Act (as amended)	Public and private sector employers with 15 or more employees; unions	Discrimination in employment decisions is prohibited on the basis or race, sex, religion, color, and national origin.	Equal Employment Opportunity Commission (EEOC)
Age Discrimination in Employment Act (ADEA)	Persons over age 40 (except between 40 and 65 for bona fide executives)	The act prohibits discrimination in employment decisions or mandatory retirement based on age.	EEOC
Equal Pay Act (EPA)	Most employers	Differences in pay between men and women in jobs requiring substantially equal skill, effort, responsibility, and working conditions must be based on factors other than gender.	EEOC
Americans with Disabilities Act (ADA)	Employees or applicants with a mental or physical disability as defined by the ADA	Employer may not discriminate on the basis of a mental or physical disability. Employee or applicant must be able to perform the job in question with reasonable accommodations for the disability.	EEOC
Fair Labor Standards Act (FLSA)	Private sector and nonfederal public sector employers; all employees except managers, supervisors, and executives; outside salespersons and professional workers	The act mandates a minimum wage of $7.25 per hour; requires time- and-one-half pay for over 40 hours per week for covered (nonexempt) employees; and places restrictions on employment by occupation and industry for persons under age 18.	Wage and Hour Division of the Employment Standards Administration, U.S. Department of Labor
Walsh-Healy (W-H), Davis-Bacon (D-B), and Service Contracts Acts (SC)	Contractors with the federal government manufacturing or supplying goods (W-H), contract construction, or services	Employers must pay wages not less than those prevailing in the area for the type of employment used.	Same as FLSA
Social Security Act	Retirees, dependent survivors, and disabled persons who are insured by payroll taxes on their past earnings or earnings of heads of households (Railroad workers are covered by the similar Railroad Retirement Act.)	Employer and employee each pay 6.2% for retirement, survivors, and disability insurance on income up to an annually established limit and pay 1.45% each on all income for Medicare insurance. Retirees are eligible for benefits based on contribution levels beginning at age 62 and for benefits to survivors or disabled insureds and medical care benefits beginning at age 65.	Social Security Administration

(Continued)

TABLE 3.2 General Federal Employment Laws (continued)

Law	Coverage	Major Provisions	Federal Agencies
Federal Unemployment Tax Act	All employers and employees except some state and local government, domestics, farm workers, railroad workers, some nonprofit employers	Payroll tax is paid by employer (except in a few states) on defined levels of income. Levels vary across states, and rates vary across employers within states, depending on the rate and duration of layoffs from each employer. There are legislated levels of income replacement for workers who are involuntary unemployed through no fault of their own. Replacement is generally at 50% or less of regular income for a duration of 26 weeks or until new employment is secured, whichever is less.	U.S. Bureau of Employment Security, U.S. Training and Employment Service, each of the state and territorial employment security commissions
Workers' Compensation	In most states, employees of nonagricultural private sector firms except railroads	Employees are entitled to compensating benefits of up to about two-thirds of weekly wage (to a maximum limit) for work-related accidents and illnesses leading to temporary or permanent disabilities. Depending on the state law, employers make payroll-based payments to a state insurance system, purchase insurance through a private carrier, or self-insure. Insurance rates depend on the riskiness of the occupations covered and the experience rating of the insured.	Various state commissions
Employee Retirement Income Security Act (ERISA)	Private sector employers that provide pensions or insurance benefits to employees	Employers must make current payments to fund future expected liabilities. The act provides for vesting (ownership) for employees of accrued benefits after 5 years of service (generally), allows tax-free portability of pension benefits for a terminating employee, regulates fiduciaries, and requires insurance of benefits for underfunded plans.	Department of Labor, Internal Revenue Service, Pension Benefit Guaranty Corporation

Occupational Safety and Health Act	Private sector employers except domestic service employers; excludes employers covered by Federal Mine Safety Act	Employers have a general duty to provide working conditions that will not harm their employees and to meet specific standards of care as published in regulations and guidelines. Agents inspect workplaces with appropriate authorization and may issue citations calling for correction and penalties. If an employer disputes a citation, a review commission determines its appropriateness. Enforcement authority may be given to states after they have passed laws consistent with OSHA.	Occupational Safety and Health Administration (OSHA), U.S. Department of Labor; National Institute for Occupational Safety and Health; Occupational Safety and Health Review Commission
Federal Mine Safety Act	Employees in underground and surface mining operations	The act establishes procedures for identifying and eliminating exposure to toxic and other harmful materials and for inspecting mines; mandates health and safety training; and provides benefits for pneumoconiosis (black lung disease).	Mine Safety and Health Administration, U.S. Department of Labor; Federal Mine Safety and Health Review Committee
Worker Adjustment and Retraining Notification Act	Private sector employers with 100 or more employees	Employer must provide 60 days' notice of a plant closing involving 50 or more employees and 30 days' notice for mass layoffs of more than 500 employees or more than one-third of the workforce. Back-pay penalties are incurred if the notice period is inadequate.	Employment and Training Administration, U.S. Department of Labor
Family and Medical Leave Act	Employers with 50 or more employees and employees with one or more years of service (generally)	Employees may take up to 12 weeks of unpaid leave each 12-month period for care of a newborn or newly adopted baby, personal illness, or care of family member who is ill.	Wage and Hour Division, Employment Standards Administration, U.S. Department of Labor
Patient Protection and Affordable Care Act	Employers with 50 or more employees	Employment related provisions include minimum required health plan benefits, penalties for employers who do not provide insurance or whose plans are too costly for lower paid employees (beginning in 2014), and excise taxes for plans whose costs exceed legislated maximums (beginning in 2018).	U.S. Department of Health and Human Services, U.S. Department of Labor

EFFECTS OF IMPLEMENTATION OF LAWS

An intriguing analysis of labor law and labor history suggests courts have consistently interpreted new statutory law to reinforce market-oriented practices. For example, the Supreme Court, while finding the Wagner Act constitutional, reiterated management's exclusive right to make certain decisions unless it voluntarily agreed to bargain about them. Further, courts have generally permitted employer-sponsored participation plans, not finding them to be employer-dominated labor organizations.[22] Legal interpretation appears to be based on a pluralist assumption that management, labor, and government operate together, with market activities facilitated through the operation of statutory labor-management conflict resolution mechanisms.[23]

Employers are more likely to engage in actions that are later found to be unfair labor practices when there are greater differences between union and nonunion wages. The NLRB has difficulty coping with these problems because complaints cannot be processed quickly without increased staff, which must be appropriated by Congress, and the board can levy no penalties above the requirement that workers be made whole for the effects of violations.[24]

FEDERAL DEPARTMENTS AND AGENCIES

All three branches of government—legislative, executive, and judicial—are involved in labor relations. Congress writes and amends the law; the executive agencies implement and regulate within the law; and the judiciary examines the actions of the other two in light of the Constitution, the statutes, and common law. This section examines the departments and agencies concerned with labor relations functions.

Department of Labor

The Department of Labor, created in 1913, has a broad charter:

> The Department of Labor fosters and promotes the welfare of the job seekers, wage earners, and retirees of the United States by improving

[22] G. Grenier and R. L. Hogler, "Labor Law and Managerial Ideology: Employee Participation as a Social Control System," *Work and Occupations*, 18 (1991), pp. 313–333.

[23] R. L. Hogler, "Critical Labor Law, Working-Class History, and the New Industrial Relations," *Industrial Relations Law Journal,* 10 (1988), pp. 116–143; and R. L. Hogler, "Labor History and Critical Labor Law: An Interdisciplinary Approach to Workers' Control, *Labor History*, 30 (1989), pp. 185–192. For a comprehensive review and commentary on labor law and regulation, see B. E. Kaufman, ed., *Government Regulation of the Employment Relationship* (Madison, WI: Industrial Relations Research Association, 1997).

[24] R. J. Flanagan, "Compliance and Enforcement Decisions under the National Labor Relations Act," *Journal of Labor Economics*, 7 (1989), pp. 257–280.

> their working conditions, advancing their opportunities for profitable employment, protecting their retirement and health care benefits, helping employers find workers, strengthening free collective bargaining, and tracking changes in employment, prices, and other national economic measurements. In carrying out this mission, the Department administers a variety of Federal labor laws including those that guarantee workers' rights to safe and healthful working conditions; a minimum hourly wage and overtime pay; freedom from employment discrimination; unemployment insurance; and other income support.[25]

The organization of the Department of Labor is shown in Figure 3.1. Several agencies that are directly involved with employers and unions are described below.

Labor-Management Standards The Office of Labor-Management Standards administers and enforces provisions of the Landrum-Griffin and Civil Service Reform acts.

Federal Contract Compliance Programs The Office of Federal Contract Compliance Programs administers laws and regulations banning employment discrimination based on race, sex, color, religion, national origin, disability, and veterans' status for employers with federal contracts. It also administers affirmative action provisions of Executive Order 11246 and the Vietnam Era Veterans' Readjustment Act.

Wage and Hour Division The Wage and Hour Division enforces various wage and hour laws requiring minimum-wage and overtime-premium payments for covered workers. It also enforces several other laws such as the Family Medical Leave Act.

Employee Benefits Security Administration The Employee Benefits Security Administration (EBSA) develops and enforces regulations covering employee benefits programs that fall within the requirements of the Employee Retirement Income Security Act (ERISA; primarily pension, retirement, and health insurance programs). It also develops regulations supporting implementation of the Patient Protection and Affordable Care Act of 2010. The EBSA assists workers in obtaining benefits to which they are entitled, monitors plan performance, and enforces benefit protection statutes.

Workers' Compensation Programs This office administers worker compensation programs for federal employees and maritime and coal mining worker compensation laws.

Occupational Safety and Health Administration The Occupational Safety and Health Administration (OSHA) is responsible for the interpretation and enforcement of the Occupational Safety and Health Act of 1970. It investigates violations and assesses penalties through hearings held by

[25] U.S. Department of Labor, www.dol.gov, June 10, 2010.

FIGURE 3.1 **Organizational Chart of the Department of Labor**

Source: www.dol.gov/dol/aboutdol/orgchart.htm, January 28, 2011.

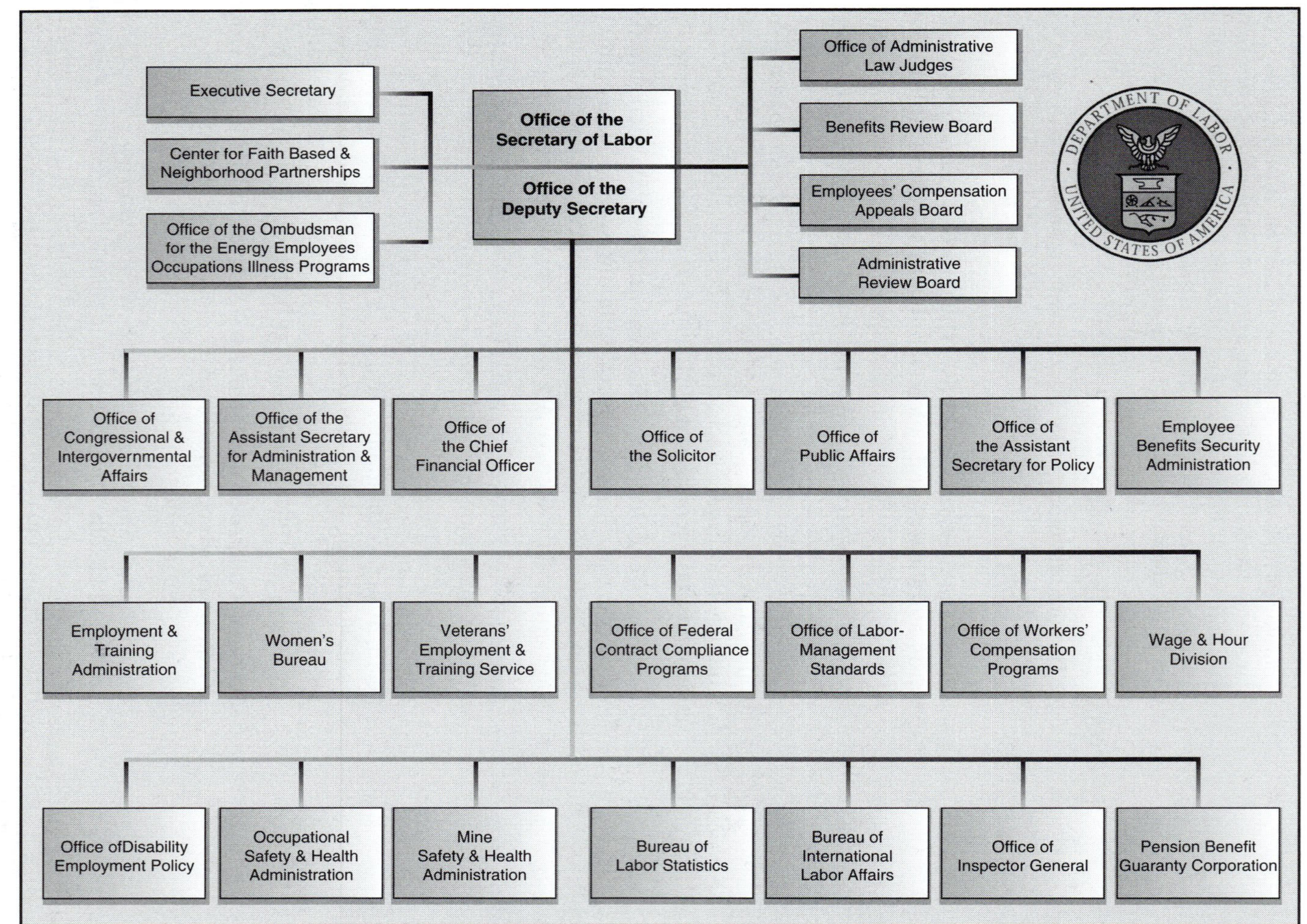

Department of Labor administrative law judges. Workers who are better educated or unionized appear to be more knowledgeable about hazards, and workers who are better protected in the exercise of their rights are more likely to refuse unsafe work.[26]

Mine Safety and Health Administration The Mine Safety and Health Administration (MSHA) enforces health and safety requirements of the Federal Mine Safety and Health Act of 1997.

Employment and Training Administration The Bureau of Apprenticeship and Training in the Employment and Training Administration (ETA) assists employers and unions in establishing high-quality skilled-trades training programs with consistent standards.

Bureau of Labor Statistics The Bureau of Labor Statistics (BLS) collects, maintains, and publishes data that interested persons use to assess the current state of the economy—nationally, regionally, or locally. It publishes the consumer price index, conducts area wage surveys, and provides unemployment data.

Bureau of International Labor Affairs The Bureau of International Labor Affairs represents the United States on multilateral trade bodies such as the General Agreement on Tariffs and Trade (GATT), the International Labor Organization (ILO), and the Organization for Economic Cooperation and Development (OECD). It also manages the labor attaché program in U.S. embassies abroad and monitors conformance with internationally recognized worker rights.

Women's Bureau The Women's Bureau focuses on the priorities of working women. Its objectives include alerting women about their rights in the workplace, proposing legislation that benefits working women, researching work aspects of concern to women, and reporting its findings to the president and Congress.

Veterans Employment and Training Service The Veterans Employment and Training Service (VETS) facilitates transitions from military service to civilian employment through training and employment search assistance. It also helps protect veterans' job-return rights following military service.

Disability Employment Policy The Office of Disability Employment Policy (ODEP) develops and influences the implementation of policies to enhance the employability of persons with disabilities.

Job Corps The Job Corps is a free education and training program to help prepare young people who have a high school education or less to prepare for a productive career.

[26] V. Walters and M. Denton, "Workers' Knowledge of Their Legal Rights and Resistance to Hazardous Work," *Relations Industrielles*, 45 (1990), pp. 531–545.

Center for Faith-Based and Neighborhood Partnerships Through cooperation with faith-based and neighborhood organizations, the Department of Labor helps develop, support, and implement programs to assist the most vulnerable and disadvantaged workers and job seekers.

Appeal Boards There are also several appeal boards within the Department of Labor that provide a forum for workers who believe they have been unfairly denied statutory benefits to which they should be entitled.

Federal Mediation and Conciliation Service

The Federal Mediation and Conciliation Service (FMCS) was established by the Taft-Hartley Act to help parties resolve labor disputes. In contract negotiation, it may mediate either through invitation or on its own motion. **Mediators** assist the parties in bargaining but have no power to impose settlements or regulate bargaining activity.

The FMCS offers preventive mediation and alternative dispute resolution programs, including problem resolution services for federal agencies as mandated by the Alternative Dispute Resolution and Negotiated Rulemaking acts of 1990. It aids local labor-management cooperation programs through grants and technical assistance enabled by the Labor-Management Cooperation Act of 1978. To foster peaceful conflict resolution of employment issues internationally, the FMCS has provided mediator training in a number of developing economies.[27]

It provides to requesting parties panels of arbitrators, who are qualified under FMCS rules, from which the parties may choose one to hear and rule on a contract dispute.

National Mediation Board

A 1934 amendment to the Railway Labor Act established the National Mediation Board (NMB). It mediates contract disputes between carriers and their unions and certifies bargaining representatives for employees. Under the RLA, unions may not strike and employers may not lock out employees unless and until the NMB has declared an impasse in negotiations and has released the parties to engage in "**self-help.**" The self-help cannot begin until 30 days after the declaration of an impasse. The NMB refers grievances to the National Railroad Adjustment Board (NRAB). The NMB may appoint a referee to assist in making NRAB awards when the panel is deadlocked. The NMB also designs and offers alternative dispute resolution training programs for employers and unions.

The NMB is also responsible for notifying the president if an unsettled, mediated dispute threatens to cripple transport in some section of the

[27] J. C. Wells, "FMCS: Past, Present, and Future," *Proceedings of the Industrial Relations Research Association*, 48 (1996), pp. 396–406.

country. The president may then appoint an emergency board to study the situation and make recommendations.

There are many fewer union certification elections since the airline and rail industries are substantially more concentrated and mature than many others. At the same time, the NMB occasionally needs to decide representation issues among large employee units created through transportation company mergers—particularly among airlines—in which the employees in one or more classes of one of the merging carriers are not unionized or are represented by different unions. In 2010, the Obama administration appointees to the NMB introduced a major change in how representation issues are decided. Prior to the change, a union was certified as a bargaining representative only if a majority of *employees* in the designated class voted for representation. Following the change, a union would win representation rights if a majority of *ballots* cast in the election favored the union.[28]

National Labor Relations Board

The NLRB was established by the Wagner Act and has jurisdiction over most for-profit employers, private for-profit and nonprofit hospitals, and the U.S. Postal Service. It determines whether employees desire union representation and whether, under federal law, unions or companies have committed unfair labor practices.

The NLRB responds to complaints or requests from unions, employees, or employers.[29] In fiscal year 2009, the board received 22,943 unfair labor practice complaints *(C cases)* and 2,912 election petitions *(R cases)* at its 51 regional, subregional, and field offices.[30] When a C case is filed, the regional office investigates. About 97 percent of C cases are closed at the regional office level. If the charge appears not to be meritorious (about 62 percent of all C cases), the charging party is asked to withdraw it or charges are dismissed. Such decisions can be appealed to the general counsel, but only about 4 percent are reversed. If the case has merit, the regional director works with the parties to try to fashion a remedy and settle the case. This succeeds in over 90 percent of cases. If the parties agree, an unresolved case may be assigned to a "settlement judge" who works with them to reach an agreement without resorting to litigation. Evidence indicates that this process is generally positively viewed by the parties if a settlement

[28] National Mediation Board, "Representation Election Procedure," *Federal Register*, 75, no. 90 (May 11, 2010), pp. 26062–26089.

[29] For complete details, see B. Garren, E. S. Fox, J. C. Truesdale, and J. A. Norris, *How to Take a Case before the National Labor Relations Board*, 7th ed. (Washington, DC: Bureau of National Affairs, 2000).

[30] *Seventy-Fourth Annual Report of the National Labor Relations Board* (Washington, DC: U.S. Government Printing Office, 2009) p. 1.

is reached.[31] Failing that, the case is heard within one to three months by an **administrative law judge.** After the judge issues a ruling, exceptions can be filed, and the case is assigned to a board member. The board must then study the case, and a three-member panel issues a ruling.[32]

If a party does not comply with an NLRB decision, the board may petition a U.S. court of appeals for enforcement. Board orders must be publicized to employees and/or union members. The board may issue cease-and-desist orders, bargaining orders, and decisions making employees whole by awarding back pay and/or reinstatement for illegal personnel actions, such as termination for union activity.

Very few initial unfair labor practice charges are ever heard by administrative law judges and passed on to the NLRB for its review. Cases that are not settled before board review are of two general types: (1) those involving a complex or unsettled issue for which there is no clear precedent, and (2) those that one party (usually management) expects to lose but in which delay of a final determination is to that party's advantage.

As noted, the five members of the NLRB are appointed for fixed terms by the president (with the consent of the Senate). Board members are individuals with expertise in labor-management relations, almost invariably attorneys, and usually members of the president's political party. To be confirmed, nominees must be knowledgeable about the law and appear fair, regardless of their political orientation. Thus, board members may be Democrats appointed by a Democratic president (Dem-Dem), Republicans appointed by a Democratic president (Rep-Dem), Democrats appointed by a Republican president (Dem-Rep), or Republicans appointed by a Republican president (Rep-Rep). Democrats may be presumed to favor labor more often when precedents are not clear, while Republicans may be expected to favor management. Board members may also be expected to pay attention to the position of the president who appointed them and, to some extent, to the makeup of Congress.

A careful study of board decisions found that in complex cases, relative to Dem-Dem members, Rep-Rep and Rep-Dem members were more likely to decide for management, while labor was favored more often during periods when Congress was more likely to favor labor's political agenda, when unemployment was high, and when unemployment was changing rapidly. In simpler cases, decisions favoring employers were more likely from Dem-Rep members, during high unemployment, and where the regional officer and administrative law judge ruled for the employer.

[31] L. Stallworth, A. Varma, and J. T. Delaney, "The NLRB's Unfair Labor Practice Settlement Program: An Empirical Analysis of Participant Satisfaction," *Dispute Resolution Journal*, 59, no. 4 (2004), pp. 22–29.

[32] D. L. Dotson, "Processing Cases at the NLRB," *Labor Law Journal,* 35 (1984), pp. 3–9; updated data from *Seventy-Fourth Annual Report of the National Labor Relations Board* (Washington, DC: U.S. Government Printing Office, 2009).

Negative factors were influential when the regional officer and administrative law judge ruled for the union and where the case occurred in a southern right-to-work state. Dem-Dems decided against the employer in almost all cases.[33] This is contrary to the conventional wisdom that Rep-Rep members are the most doctrinaire in their decisions and the most likely to disregard precedent. The general counsel's political orientation may also strongly influence outcomes because that office decides which cases should be referred to the board for decisions.

Regional staff decisions also affect how charges are handled. A review of regional board actions on unfair labor practice complaints found that refusals to issues charges were more likely when the charge was brought by an employer and where several complaints were alleged. Refusals were less likely when the charge was related to right-to-work law violations. Issuance of formal complaints was less likely when they were related to right-to-work law charges, when charges were brought by the employer, when the bargaining unit was larger, and where several violations were alleged. Voluntary settlements before issuance of a complaint were related to right-to-work laws, the number of charges by the employer, and negatively to the number of charges by the union. Voluntary settlements after issuance of a complaint were related to the number of charges by the union and negatively to the number of employer charges and the size of the bargaining unit.[34] These findings indicate that employers are less likely than unions to have the regional board issue charges or complaints, and are more likely than unions to voluntarily settle before a complaint. But if a complaint is issued, the larger the number of charges and the bigger the bargaining unit (greater potential gain from winning), the less likely the employer is to settle voluntarily.

It is unquestionably the case that the NLRB is politicized. Whenever a new president is elected from the party that was previously out of power, it is quite likely that precedents established by the outgoing administration will be modified or swept aside as new cases are brought forward to test precedents that either labor or management hopes will be overturned.[35]

NLRB decisions may alter the bargaining power between labor and management if a previously used practice is prohibited. Filing rates are influenced by the level of economic activity, and they increase for

[33] W. N. Cooke, A. K. Mishra, G. M. Spreitzer, and M. Tschirhart, "The Determinants of NLRB Decision-Making Revisited," *Industrial and Labor Relations Review*, 48 (1995), pp. 237–257.

[34] J. F. O'Connell, "The NLRB at the Grassroots," *Journal of Labor Research*, 22 (2001), pp. 761–775.

[35] For commentary on whether recent decisions have set new directions or restored established precedents, see K. R. Dolin, "Analyzing Recent Developments at the National Labor Relations Board," *Labor Law Journal*, 56 (2005), pp. 120–138; "Bush Labor Board Decisions: Pendulum Shift or Permanent Changes?" *Labor Law Journal*, 56 (2005), pp. 212–223; and W. B. Gould IV (an NLRB chair during portions of the Clinton administration), "The NLRB at Age 70: Some Reflections on the Clinton Board and the Bush II Aftermath," *Berkeley Journal of Employment and Labor Law*, 26 (2005), pp. 309–320.

both unions and managements when it appears that board composition will lead to more favorable decisions for management. Employers may increase their filings because they believe pro-management decisions may deter union tactics.[36]

Pension Benefit Guaranty Corporation

The Pension Benefit Guaranty Corporation (PBGC) is a federal agency created by ERISA with responsibility for insuring private sector **defined benefit pension plans.** A defined benefit pension plan promises retirees lifetime annuity payments based on terminal earnings and years of service with the company. Under the provisions of ERISA an employer who provides a defined benefit pension plan is required to annually set aside funds necessary to cover the expected future liabilities of the plan. The employer is also required to pay a premium to PBGC in order to provide basic benefits for retirees in the event the pension plans assets fall short of its liabilities.

Situations in which pension plans fail usually involve a failure of the plan's assets to achieve investment earnings that have been anticipated, or that the firm fails to generate sufficient revenue to continue funding the plan—through bankruptcy, for example.

LABOR LAW REFORM: A CONTINUING CONTROVERSY

Depending on which side—management or labor—is interested, calls for labor law reform are frequent. As noted in the previous discussion of the NLRB, the interpretation of the law has some degree of fluidity depending on the political orientation of the executive branch of the federal government. In general, labor favors reforms that would improve opportunities to organize and speed the process by which employees decide whether to be represented and provide a method that requires that a contract ultimately will be put in place if organizing is successful. Management favors reforms that would allow companies to implement more nonunion employee participation programs dealing with subjects that might involve wages, hours, and terms and conditions of employment—issues that are prohibited under the law in employer-sponsored programs.

In the 1990s, bills were introduced to allow the establishment of employee work teams and communications programs without violating Section 8(a)(2) of the labor acts. The pro-management so-called Team Act was passed by Congress in 1996, but vetoed by President Clinton. Ironically, there was no attempt to resurrect it during President George W. Bush's administration.

In both 2005 and 2007, an amendment to the Taft-Hartley Act was introduced that would allow the NLRB to determine majority status and certify

[36] M. Roomkin, "A Quantitative Study of Unfair Labor Practice Cases," *Industrial and Labor Relations Review*, 34 (1981), pp. 245–256.

union representation on the basis of a check of signed union authorization cards. The so-called Employee Free Choice Act (EFCA) would eliminate the need for elections and prevent managements from mounting an anti-union campaign if a majority of bargaining unit members had signed cards. Opponents of the bill stress the role of secret elections in democracies, while those in favor argue that it eliminates coercive campaigns and unnecessary delays. In 2007, the House of Representatives passed the bill, but it failed in the Senate and would most certainly have faced a presidential veto. After the Democratic presidential and congressional election sweep in the 2008 elections, passage of the EFCA was widely anticipated, especially after Senator Al Franken was finally declared the recount winner from Minnesota giving the Democrats a filibuster-proof 60–40 majority in the Senate. However, in the contentious congressional atmosphere of 2009–2010, the proposed legislation was never brought up for a vote.

The EFCA would create recognition processes closer to what exists in much of Canada, where there is substantially higher private sector union coverage. Two Canadian researchers suggest that while this type of reform may enhance organizing efforts, they will not be sufficient to revitalize unionization in the United States.[37]

Some argue that economic globalization has made increasing employment regulation a liability, and that responsiveness by employers is required to survive in an economic era the labor acts never contemplated.[38] Others argue that relatively minor changes need to be made to the labor acts to enhance competition and worker outcomes.[39] In the absence of major events like the Great Depression, World War II, or some other major economic or geopolitical crisis, it's unlikely that a significant statutory change affecting the private sector can be mobilized.[40] Given the relatively small proportion of private sector employees who are unionized, given that the Wagner Act (as amended) applies only to private sector employers and employees, given that congressional Democrats from right-to-work states run a political risk in supporting representation based on authorization card majorities, and given almost universal Republican opposition, it seems highly improbable that a circumstance would occur in which

[37] J. Godard, "Do Labor Laws Matter? The Density Decline and Convergence Thesis Revisited," *Industrial Relations*, 42 (2003), pp. 458–492; R. J. Adams, "The Employee Free Choice Act: A Reality Check," *Proceedings of the Labor and Employment Relations Association*, 58 (2006), pp. 184–189; and R. J. Adams, "The Employee Free Choice Act: A Skeptical View and Alternative," *Labor Studies Journal*, 31, no. 4 (2007), pp. 1–4.

[38] M. L. Wachter, "Labor Law Reform: One Step Forward and Two Steps Back," *Industrial Relations*, 34 (1995), pp. 382–401. See also L. Galloway and R. Vedder, "Labor Laws: Then and Now," *Journal of Labor Research*, 17 (1996), pp. 253–276.

[39] R. N. Block, "Labor Law, Economics, and Industrial Democracy: A Reconciliation," *Industrial Relations*, 34 (1995), pp. 402–416.

[40] D. J. B. Mitchell, "Discussion," *Proceedings of the Labor and Employment Relations Association*, 58 (2006), pp. 160–163.

cloture could be invoked in the Senate which would be necessary to enable its passage. Changes in labor law will inevitably occur within the areas subject to interpretation and/or regulation by the NLRB and NMB, with increasing uncertainty in labor relations regulations likely in the future. Changes can also be implemented through presidential executive orders. For example, within 10 days of taking office President Obama issued Executive Order 13496 requiring federal contractors to prominently post information in areas where workers congregate regarding how employees could seek representation for collective bargaining purposes.

Relative to the European Union (EU), workers in the United States have fewer rights to be represented in the workplace. Requirements for exclusive representation and winner-take-all elections mean that fewer workers have representation than would prefer it. Additionally, in some EU countries democratically elected works councils meet with management to discuss and/or approve or disapprove various initiatives, often involving issues that U.S. employers are not legally required to discuss. Proponents of labor law reform and industrial democracy argue that U.S. employers should be required to permit more employer representation and participation in decision making.[41]

TRADE TREATIES

Trade treaties often include provisions for minimum labor standards. These are usually included to protect jobs in high-wage countries. Developing countries seldom can afford to duplicate conditions experienced in first-world countries. Prohibitions on child labor and forced (prison) labor may be somewhat easier to enforce.[42] Area trade treaties, such as the North American Free Trade Agreement (NAFTA), offer opportunities for international cooperation by unions. To this point, however, evidence suggests they have had a greater effect on nurturing national identities rather than international development.[43]

Summary

U.S. labor law consists primarily of the Railway Labor, Norris-LaGuardia, Wagner, Taft-Hartley, and Landrum-Griffin acts. These enable collective bargaining, regulate labor and management activities, and limit intervention by the federal courts in lawful union activities.

[41] See, for example, S. Friedman and S. Wood, eds., "Employers' Unfair Advantage in the United States of America: Symposium on the Human Rights Watch Report on the State of Workers' Freedom of Association in the United States," *British Journal of Industrial Relations*, 39 (2001), pp. 585–605, and 40 (2002), pp. 113–149.

[42] C. L. Erickson & D. J. B. Mitchell, "Labor Standards in International Trade Agreements: The Current Debate," *Labor Law Journal*, 47 (1996), pp. 763–775.

[43] J. Cowie, "National Struggles in a Transnational Economy: A Critical Analysis of U.S. Labor's Campaign against NAFTA," *Labor Studies Journal*, 21, no. 4 (1997), pp. 3–32.

The legislative branch of government enacts the laws, the executive branch carries them out, and the court system tests their validity and rules on conduct within their purview.

As a cabinet department, the Department of Labor is primarily responsible for implementing human resource programs and monitoring activities. It has little direct influence on collective bargaining.

Rule-making, interpretive, and assistance agencies have major influences on employers, through either direct intervention or regulation. The FMCS and NLRB have the greatest impact on collective bargaining. The NLRB has been troubled by politicization throughout its history and by delay in ruling on unfair labor practices during the past 30 years.

Discussion Questions

1. In the absence of federal labor laws, what do you think the scope and nature of labor relations would be in the United States?
2. Are current laws strong enough to preserve individual rights in collective bargaining?
3. To what extent should the federal government have power to intervene in collective bargaining activities?
4. Should such administrative agencies as the NLRB be allowed to render administrative law decisions that can be enforced by the courts, or should an agency be required to go directly to court?
5. Are current labor laws capable of dealing with labor-management problems, or should they be abolished? If abolished, what should their replacements (if any) address?

Key Terms

Railway Labor Act (RLA), *64*
National Mediation Board (NMB), *64*
National Railroad Adjustment Board (NRAB), *65*
Injunction, *66*
Employer, *68*
Employee, *69*
Supervisor, *69*
Professional employee, *70*
National Labor Relations Board (NLRB) *70*
Unfair labor practice (ULP), *71*
Union shop, *71*
Duty to bargain, *72*
Hot cargo, *72*
Agency shop, *73*
Trusteeship, *76*
Mediator, *86*
Self-help, *86*
Administrative law judge, *88*
Defined benefit pension plans, *90*

Selected Web Sites

www.dol.gov
www.fmcs.gov
www.nlrb.gov
www.nmb.gov

Union Structure and Government

Employers and labor unions are governed differently. Employees are hired to perform tasks to accomplish employer-defined objectives. Most have little voice in choosing the objectives. These are determined by high-level managers who are monitored by owners or by boards of directors elected by shareholders or, in the case of public agencies, by their elected or appointed boards. Managers are responsible to their constituencies: a corporation's owners or shareholders or a city's voters. Union goals reflect member interests. Union leaders must be generally responsive to member desires in order to remain in office.

This chapter examines the organizational components, functions, and governance of unions and how these relate to and involve the membership. It addresses the following major questions:

1. How is the union movement organized and governed?
2. What roles do local unions, nationals, and the labor federations play?
3. How do national union organizational structures and operations differ?
4. How has the union movement changed in response to declining membership?

The U.S. labor structure has three distinct levels: the local union, the national union, and the labor federations. These are described in the following sections.

THE LOCAL UNION

The local union represents employees in day-to-day dealings with the employer. Local union jurisdictions are defined along four major dimensions: (1) the type of work performed or the industry in which it is accomplished (craft and industrial jurisdictions), (2) a specified geographic area, (3) the type of activity involved (organizing, bargaining, and so on), and (4) the level of union government applying the jurisdiction.[1] A local's constituency varies within these parameters. Many local unions operate in a specific municipality, represent workers in a single industry or trade, and frequently bargain with a single employer.

Examples include a relatively small unit (less than 100) of close-knit employees who work for a single employer, a large unit of employees from a mix of semi- or unskilled jobs who work for a single employer in one or more plants located in a single city, a skilled-trade unit whose members work for many employers and whose employment changes frequently, and a unit whose members work for many different employers in different types of jobs. Units in these examples might typify a professional local, a manufacturing company local, a building trades local, and a general local.[2]

Most local unions are chartered by and affiliated with a national union (e.g., a local union representing auto parts industry workers affiliated with the United Auto Workers). Occasionally, local unions will directly affiliate with the AFL-CIO or remain independent. Independent locals form where employees of a particular employer (often within a single plant) organize without external assistance. Some independent unions predate the Wagner Act and are adaptations of company unions originally created with employer assistance, often to avoid representation by a local established by a national union.

A local union's jurisdiction affects its size, constitution, officers, and organizational structure. A president, vice president, recording secretary, financial secretary, treasurer, and sergeant at arms, as well as trustees, are usually elected. Unless the local is large, these posts are part time and usually unpaid. Locals with over 1,000 members are likely to have full-time paid officers. Higher-level local paid union officers in larger units are generally granted leaves of absence by their employers to serve in the position. As local officers, they are responsible to their national unions and the local's members, and they also remain attached to their employer. Only about one-third of current top-level officers got their positions by defeating an incumbent. Most were elected following a retirement or were appointed. Most presidents are able to successfully endorse a successor. About half of all local presidents who are full-time officers return to bargaining-unit jobs after they leave office.[3]

Locals dealing with several employers often hire a **business agent.** Business agents ensure that contracts are being followed and refer members to available employment. They are most necessary where local

[1] J. Barbash, *American Unions: Structure, Government, and Politics* (New York: Random House, 1967).

[2] G. Strauss, "Union Democracy," in G. Strauss, D. G. Gallagher, and J. Fiorito, eds., *The State of the Unions* (Madison, WI: Industrial Relations Research Association, 1991), pp. 201–236.

[3] M. J. Goldberg, "Top Officers of Local Unions," *Labor Studies Journal*, 19, no. 4 (1995), pp. 3–23.

members work on a project basis and move between employers as work is finished on one project and becomes available on another.[4]

Two major committees operate within most locals: the **executive committee,** which is made up of the local's officers, and the grievance or **negotiation committee.** The executive committee establishes local policy; the negotiation committee reviews members' grievances and negotiates with management over grievances and contract changes. Other committees deal with organizing and membership, welfare, recreation, and political action.

At the work-unit level, **stewards** are elected or appointed. Stewards police first-line supervisors' compliance with the contract. Stewards represent grievants to the employer. They collect dues and solicit participation in union activities. Many collective bargaining contracts recognize the vulnerability of the steward's advocative position by according it **superseniority.** Stewards are then, by definition, the most senior members of the unit. They often do not have experience representing employees before they assume their positions. Union training helps them learn their responsibilities, particularly understanding the goals of the union movement, understanding the contract, and communicating with members.[5] Stewards are activists. Most are involved in other organizations outside their jobs. They average about 12 years of job experience and about 5.5 years of steward experience. About half are appointed, and only about 25 percent are opposed in elections.[6] While stewards are union activists, union leaders see their roles as being grievance handlers or representatives who operate using a rational perspective.[7] To be effective, stewards need to be well versed with regard to their legal rights and protections.[8] One local union describes the steward's role in Exhibit 4.1.

Local Union Democracy

Within the workplace, there is essentially no market for employment representation since, if there is no union, the employer unilaterally determines employment conditions without negotiating with employee subgroups (otherwise, an unlawful employer-dominated labor organization would be created) and, if a union is present, the negotiated labor agreement

[4] L. R. Sayles and G. Strauss, *The Local Union,* rev. ed. (New York: Harcourt Brace Jovanovich, 1967), pp. 2–5.

[5] B. Broadbent, "Identifying the Education Needs of Union Stewards," *Labor Studies Journal,* 14, no. 2 (1989), pp. 46–60.

[6] P. A. Roby, "Becoming Shop Stewards: Perspectives on Gender and Race in Ten Trade Unions," *Labor Studies Journal,* 20, no. 3 (1995), pp. 65–82.

[7] T. F. H. Chang, "Local Union Leaders' Conception and Ideology of Stewards' Roles," *Labor Studies Journal*, 30, no. 3 (2005), pp. 49–71.

[8] See also R. M. Schwartz, *The Legal Rights of Union Stewards*, 3rd ed. (Cambridge, MA: Work Rights Press, 1999).

Exhibit 4.1

What Is a Union Steward?

A union steward is an employee just like you. They have a job to do every day, and they answer to the same management that you do.

The key difference, though, is that a union steward has the training, the tools, and the protections to help you and other employees solve problems at work!

If you think you have a problem, then perhaps your steward can help you. He/she has been trained by the union and has special legal protections to enable them to stand up for employees when management isn't being reasonable.

The job of a union steward involves:

Representation

When you think you're in trouble. If you have a meeting with management that you believe is an investigatory interview with the possible purpose of taking disciplinary action against you, you have the right to have your union steward at the meeting. This is also known as your "Weingarten Rights."

When you have a problem that needs solving. A term you may be familiar with is "filing a grievance." A grievance is an allegation that management has violated the terms of the contract. Not every problem is a violation of the contract, and not every problem requires a grievance. Your steward may have other ways, both formal and informal, for solving problems.

Communication

Your steward will make sure to inform members about what's going on in the union—by handing out informational leaftlets, putting information on the union bulletin board, and by simply talking to people. Your steward also plays the role of feeding your ideas and issues back into the other parts of the union, such as the staff and the Executive Board.

Education

Your steward will work to make sure workers understand their rights, the contract, and any important issues the union is working on.

Organizing and Mobilizing Members

This is considered the union steward's #1 job. The strength of our union at any point in time is simply the total energy and support of the members who can be mobilized. When more members get involved, we can accomplish more—at our workplaces as well as statewide. All the other work stewards do—representation, communication, and education—is done with an eye to strengthening and increasing involvement in the union.

Source: www.seiu1984.org/onthejob/What_is_a_Union_Steward_.aspx

determines the rules that will cover all employees in a bargaining unit. One critic has argued that eliminating the exclusive representation and majority-rule requirements for unionization would create a competitive market for employee relations services. If antitrust regulations were relaxed, even for-profit organizations might decide to offer employee relations services to groups of employees across several employers.[9]

Local union governance is like municipal politics in smaller cities. Elections usually generate only moderate interest. Incumbents are usually

[9] S. Estreicher, "Deregulating Union Democracy," *Journal of Labor Research*, 21 (2000), pp. 247–264.

reelected unless the rank and file believes a critical issue has been mishandled. A local typically holds regular open business meetings. These meetings tend to be fairly mundane unless contract negotiations are approaching, and they deal mostly with reporting disbursements, communications, and pending grievances.

Only a minority of members generally attend meetings. Smaller locals and those whose members are higher skilled have higher attendance. Typical attendance rates vary between 1 and 33 percent.[10] Meetings to ratify contracts, discuss contract demands, and elect officers usually have the highest attendance rates.

Low attendance raises questions about the breadth of support and democracy of unions. Local member involvement seems low given that the union represents the members' collective bargaining interests. Local union democracy is manifested in the way factions combine into coalitions around certain issues. It is also demonstrated by contested and occasionally close elections for major offices. Local union democracy is highest in newer, small locals. Elections tend to be closer in larger units with more specialized jurisdictions, where management is not viewed as hostile and the election does not involve an incumbent.[11]

Local unions are generally relatively democratic. Pressures by members to handle grievances and improve conditions require responses by union officers. But if management is intransigent, the pressure to maintain a united front may lead to suppression of dissent.[12]

Functional Democracy

Are local unions run democratically? If democracy requires two or more relatively permanent opposition factions, the answer is generally *no*. But if democracy demands only that members have voting rights, the answer is *yes*. Local constitutions require elections of officers and limited terms. Further, the Landrum-Griffin Act requires local elections at least once every three years. Finally, under exclusive representation requirements, the union must apply the terms of the contract equally to all bargaining-unit employees.

Democratic operation requires individual commitment to union activity. While most members believe their union works to their benefit, many were not involved in its founding and may view the union primarily as their agent in employment matters. In return for dues, many members expect the union to relieve them of the effort and details involved in regulating the employment relationship. What members may want is representation in return for their dues, not participation and involvement in the union.

[10] Sayles and Strauss, *Local Union*, p. 97.

[11] J. C. Anderson, "A Comparative Analysis of Local Union Democracy," *Industrial Relations*, 17 (1978), pp. 278–295.

[12] Sayles and Strauss, *Local Union*, pp. 135–147.

FIGURE 4.1
Dual Governance in Unions

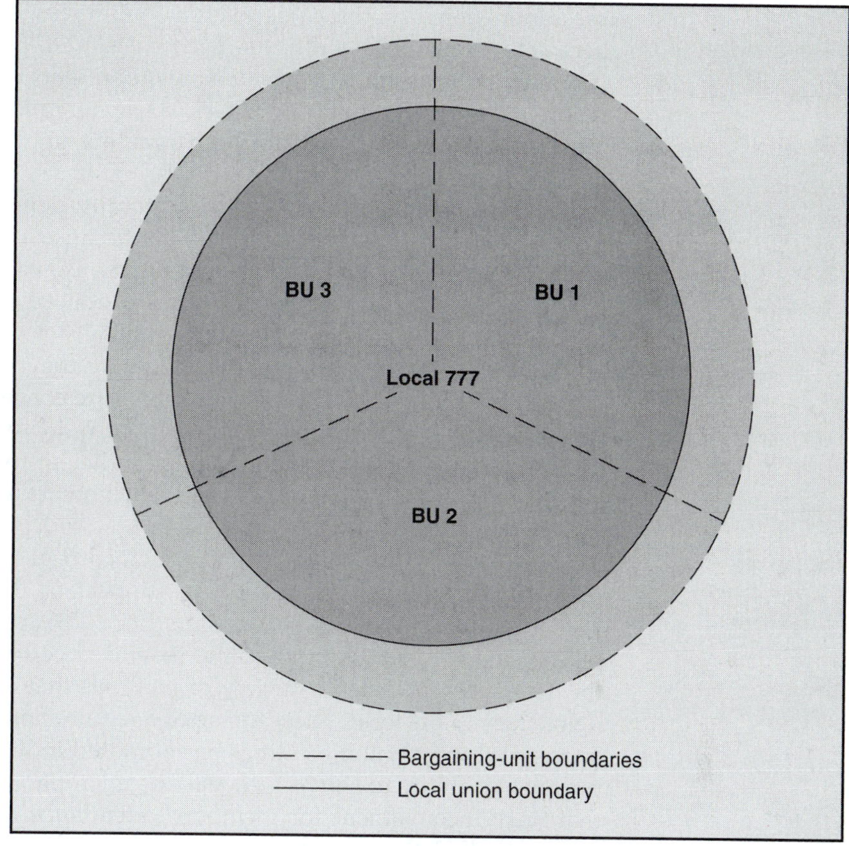

In unionized employment, an individual is simultaneously an employee and a union member. In the **functional democracy** of employment, the "parties" are the employer and the union.[13] Union members are entitled to due process under two sets of rules: (1) the local's constitution and (2) the labor contract. Each is administered by separate sets of officials—the local constitution by the executive board and the contract(s) by the negotiation committee(s). An internal check-and-balance system ensures that the contract meets union standards and is administered fairly for all bargaining-unit members.[14]

Figure 4.1 depicts the idea of **dual governance.** Assume a local includes three **bargaining units** in an **open-shop** industry. Three separate contracts

[13] N. W. Chamberlain and D. E. Cullen, *The Labor Sector,* rev. ed. (New York: McGraw-Hill, 1971), pp. 194–196.

[14] A. H. Cook, "Dual Governance in Unions: A Tool for Analysis," *Industrial and Labor Relations Review,* 15 (1962), pp. 323–349.

are administered by three negotiation committees. All local union members vote for the local's officers. Each bargaining unit's union members vote on their contracts. The shaded area represents workers who are both union and bargaining-unit members, while nonunion employees outside the local circle belong only to the bargaining unit, are represented, but have no vote for officers or on contracts.

Local unions are probably less electorally democratic than governmental units. This may not be a problem because union members generally are interested in similar types of outcomes, view the union as their agent, and evaluate it on the outcomes produced rather than the ideological stand of a faction.[15] Members generally do not feel a need to be "protected" from their union; on the contrary, they worry about management. Depending on the issue, if members are concerned about a lack of democracy, they can oust the leadership, turn down contracts, or vote to decertify. Legal safeguards are usually sufficient to require responsiveness, if not two-party democracy, and that appears to be enough for most members.

Unfortunately, there are cases in which corrupt local officers entrench themselves in power, buttressed by support or inattention from their parent national. A study of Teamsters Local 705 in Chicago, which was placed under trusteeship while the federal government was overseeing the Teamsters, revealed a variety of methods that effectively eliminated democracy in the local. These included a requirement that all questions to be raised during union meetings be submitted in writing in advance, the president's ability to shut off a speaker's microphone, and meeting times that were inconvenient for members' attendance. After these problems were remedied, the union became more militant in representing members' grievances and negotiating contracts with employers.[16] On the other hand, the executive leadership of another union in a declining labor market was paralyzed by excessive rank-and-file exercise of democratic initiatives.[17] Business agents who have responsibilities for operating hiring halls can also reduce democracy and exploit members if they play favorites in rationing job opportunities or collude with employers to provide certain members on projects.[18]

The local union is not usually an autonomous, freestanding organization. It most often owes its existence to, and almost certainly must comply

[15] Sayles and Strauss, *Local Union,* p. 141.

[16] R. Bruno, "Democratic Goods: Teamster Reform and Collective Bargaining Outcomes," *Journal of Labor Research,* 21 (2000), pp. 83–102.

[17] R. W. Hurd, "Professional Employees and Union Democracy: From Control to Chaos," *Journal of Labor Research,* 21 (2000), pp. 103–116.

[18] M. A. McCarthy, "'Why Should the Business Agents Be Bigger Than the Organization?'" *Labor Studies Journal,* 35 (2010), pp. 322–342.

with, the directives of a parent national, unless it is directly affiliated with the AFL-CIO or an independent.

Independent Local Unions

Independent local unions (ILUs) represent employees of a single employer and are not affiliated with a national or the AFL-CIO. Most ILUs were started in the 1920s under welfare capitalism or in the early 1930s following passage of the National Industrial Recovery Act (NIRA). Following the National Labor Relations Act (NLRA), many ILUs affiliated with the AFL or the CIO and some were disestablished by the National Labor Relations Board (NLRB).

ILUs might be started in the face of an organizing drive and are generally more conservative than a national affiliate. "Strong" ILUs pressure management short of striking and often threaten to affiliate with a national to put pressure on the employer. During the 1940s, ILUs often were far less racially discriminatory than nationally chartered locals.[19]

Wages of ILU members are about the same as those of employees belonging to affiliated locals.[20] ILUs may be more effective in representing local interests, but they have less bargaining power than affiliated locals that can act together during contract negotiations in multifacility operations.

NATIONAL UNIONS

National unions originally established jurisdictions over workers in specific crafts, industries, or other job territories. Many have members in Canada as well as in the United States. As noted in Chapter 2, the **(inter)national union** is historically the unit in which primary authority is vested within the union movement. Most local unions are chartered by a parent national, and many local activities are constrained or must be approved by the national body.

In 2010, there were 62 national unions with more than 10,000 members, of which 46 were affiliated with the AFL-CIO. Of approximately 15.3 million U.S. union members, a little over 8.4 million members are in nationals affiliated with the AFL-CIO. About 5.2 million belong to unions that formed the Change to Win (CTW) federation. The 30 largest unions each have more than 100,000 members. Over half of all union members belong to the four largest nationals. Large differences exist in representation rates

[19] S. M. Jacoby, "Unnatural Extinction: The Rise and Fall of the Independent Local Union," *Industrial Relations,* 40 (2001), pp. 377–404.

[20] S. M. Jacoby and A. Verma, "Enterprise Unions in the United States," *Industrial Relations,* 31 (1992), pp. 137–158.

TABLE 4.1 National Unions with More than 100,000 Members

Source: From data collected and published in C. Gifford, *Directory of U.S. Labor Organizations: 2010 Edition* (Washington, DC: Bureau of National Affairs, 2010), pp. 9–27. Membership figures were reported between 2008 and 2010.

Union	Members
National Education Association	3,235,000
Service Employees	1,857,000
State, County, and Municipal Employees	1,501,000
Teamsters	1,364,000
Food and Commercial Workers	1,320,000
Teachers	889,000
Electrical Workers	704,000
Laborers	633,000
Steel, Paper and Forestry, Rubber, Manufacturing, Energy, Allied Industrial and Service Workers	627,000
Machinists	614,000
Carpenters	511,000
Communications Workers	493,000
Operating Engineers	409,000
Auto Workers	355,000
Plumbers and Pipe Fitters	347,000
Fire Fighters	298,000
Letter Carriers	284,000
Government Employees	265,000
Postal Workers	247,000
UNITE HERE	240,000
National Postal Mail Handlers	212,000
Amalgamated Transit	192,000
Screen Actors	179,000
Sheet Metal Workers	153,000
Iron Workers	136,000
Painters	124,000
Transport Workers	120,000
Rural Letter Carriers	113,000
Theatrical Stage Employees, Moving Picture Technicians, Artists and Allied Crafts	112,000
Office and Professional Employees	110,000

between the states, with 25.2 percent unionized in New York and only 3.1 percent in North Carolina.[21] Table 4.1 lists national unions with 100,000 or more members in 2010.

Most national unions are full-time operations. Officers are full-time unionists. Departments are established and staffed with appointed and

[21] C. D. Gifford, *Directory of U.S. Labor Organizations* (Washington, DC: Bureau of National Affairs, 2010), pp. 1–4.

hired specialists. Most elect officers at their **conventions,** which are legally required to meet at least every five years. Delegates are chosen by each local and sent on a per capita basis, or they are national union officials and **field representatives.** The union convention is similar to a political convention. If the national leadership can appoint many delegates, its chances of staying in office are greatly enhanced.

National Union Goals

National unions have two major goals: (1) to organize an increasing number and share of the labor force, particularly across employers in industries within their jurisdictions, and (2) to provide representation services to enhance member well-being. These goals are obviously interrelated. Organizing success depends to an extent on the visible success the union has had in representing employees, because successful representation depends on organizing a group of employees that can exert bargaining power on the employer.

National unions formed for economic reasons. U.S. industry became more national as transportation facilities developed, and local bargaining power declined as a result. Nationals exert greater pressure on employers and assist locals during difficult periods in which they might not survive on their own. Especially during the formation of industrial unions, the national's power to negotiate similar contracts across an industry's employers enhanced gains over what could be negotiated at the local level. Support and control are thus lodged in nationals.

Union members decide whether they want continued representation by comparing contract outcomes and services received from their union with those available from alternative sources (other unions or nonunion human resource departments). Union leaders want unions to grow to enhance their power and stability and to promote bargaining power within an industry. Elected leaders and appointed full-time unionists need membership approval to retain their posts. Leaders might be expected to emphasize organizing, while members probably prefer a focus on services for present members first.

The economic environment in which organized labor participates has changed markedly over the past 30 years. Sometimes it has been more difficult for nationals than for locals to recognize the magnitude of change and the need to respond and adapt to it. Nationals often have less knowledge about actual workplace experiences than do locals, are buffered from pressures to change given their overall financial stability, and have difficulty implementing organizationwide change due to their decentralized and political nature.[22] As established manufacturing industries have pursued cost cutting through closing old facilities and opening new ones—either

[22] T. Fitzpatrick and W. Waldstein, "Challenges to Strategic Planning in International Unions," *Proceedings of the Industrial Relations Research Association,* 46 (1994), pp. 73–84.

domestically or globally—and have changed work designs to enhance productivity, there is increasing competition both between and within companies, leading to the possibility of locals competing with each other to retain work. This is a major problem for national unions in promoting solidarity and pattern bargaining.[23]

National Union Strategies and Planning

National unions vary in their interests and capabilities to adapt and innovate. A study of national unions found that planning for change was positively related to the use of environmental scanning techniques, effective structuring of management and administrative activities, and larger size, while it was negatively related to democratic structures.[24]

National unions that put more effort into planning devote more resources to organizing, participate in **corporate campaigns,** and form **political action committees (PACs).**[25] Education, budgeting, and political action are the most frequent topics of long-range planning. Support from the national's president, the use of consultants, and representing employees in the service or utility industries are related to plan implementation.[26]

National Union Jurisdictions

National unions have traditionally operated as either craft or industrial unions. Craft unions formed the AFL, and industrial unions formed the CIO. Craft and industrial jurisdictional boundaries blurred as AFL and CIO unions competed for members before their merger and as craft and industrial employment patterns changed.

Since the 1980s, organizing patterns of large U.S. nationals has taken a general union approach.[27] More than half of Teamster members work in occupations and industries with no primary relationship to transportation. The National Education Association (NEA) represents both public and private schoolteachers at primary, secondary, and postsecondary educational institutions. The United Auto Workers organizes nonteaching employees in colleges and universities, freelance writers, and legal service workers. Where employment in traditional jurisdictions declines, union leaders push for expanding jurisdictions.

[23] D. Wells, "Labour Markets, Flexible Specialization and the New Microcorporatism," *Relations Industrielles*, 56 (2001), pp. 279–304.

[24] J. T. Delaney, P. Jarley, and J. Fiorito, "Planning for Change: Determinants of Innovation in U.S. National Unions," *Industrial and Labor Relations Review*, 49 (1996), pp. 597–614.

[25] K. Stratton and R. B. Brown, "Strategic Planning in U.S. Labor Unions," *Proceedings of the Industrial Relations Research Association*, 41 (1988), pp. 523–531.

[26] Y. Reshef and K. Stratton-Devine, "Long-Range Planning in North American Unions: Preliminary Findings," *Relations Industrielles*, 48 (1993), pp. 250–265.

[27] V. G. Devinatz, "Union Organizing Trends and the Question of Postindustrial Unionism in the Early 21st Century," *Labor Law Journal*, 59 (2008), pp. 265–270.

Since the formation of Change to Win, there has been increasing competition between national unions in organizing and raiding members. The most visible and acrimonious battles have involved the Service Employees International Union (SEIU) and UNITE HERE and internicene warfare within SEIU's health care affiliates in California. UNITE HERE was formed through the merger of the needletrades (UNITE) unions with the hotel, entertainment, and restaurant workers (HERE). Disagreements between the presidents of the merging unions led the UNITE president to join the SEIU to form a new union, Workers United (WU) that began raids on UNITE HERE locals. In California, the SEIU placed its United Healthcare Workers (UHW) unit under trusteeship. Former UHW leaders formed the National Union of Healthcare Workers (NUHW) which is now locked in an organizing battle with the SEIU in California to gain representation rights for nonprofessional health care workers. In the meantime, UNITE HERE reaffiliated with the AFL-CIO and John Wilhelm, its leader, has received support from several other national union presidents, both AFL-CIO and CTW affiliates.[28]

National Structure

National unions grow and survive through organizing and maintaining their locals. Their ability to obtain and maintain membership depends on their effectiveness in dealing with environmental characteristics such as employers' resistance to unionization, changing industrial and occupational employment levels, and existing laws and regulations and their enforcement. Employment patterns result from the ultimate demand for goods and services and the quantity and quality of the labor supply. Unions have virtually no control over the former, and they have only limited control over the latter unless they provide employee training, as in the building trades.[29]

In turn, these environmental factors influence the goals of the union movement. Some of these goals can be realized internally (workplace goals) through collective bargaining, while others require public policy changes (external goals). The goals and services important to union members influence the strategies chosen and the organizational structures created to deliver them. Among the strategies, collective bargaining,

[28] As this edition was being prepared for publication, the conflict and rancor had not been resolved. There is an interesting assortment of reporting and rhetoric on the Internet about the issues and personalities involved. See http://talkingunion.wordpress.com/2009/02/10/bruce-raynor-the-missed-opportunity-of-the-unite-here-merger/ and www.huffingtonpost.com/randy-shaw/labor-movement-backs-unit_b_222933.html. For the view from the new National Union of Healthcare Workers, visit www.nuhw.org/. There are also a large number of personal story videos on YouTube related to the conflicts between the SEIU and NUHW in California.

[29] J. Fiorito, C. L. Gramm, and W. Hendricks, "Union Structural Choices," in G. Strauss, D. G. Gallagher, and J. Fiorito, eds., *The State of the Unions* (Madison, WI: Industrial Relations Research Association, 1991), pp. 103–138.

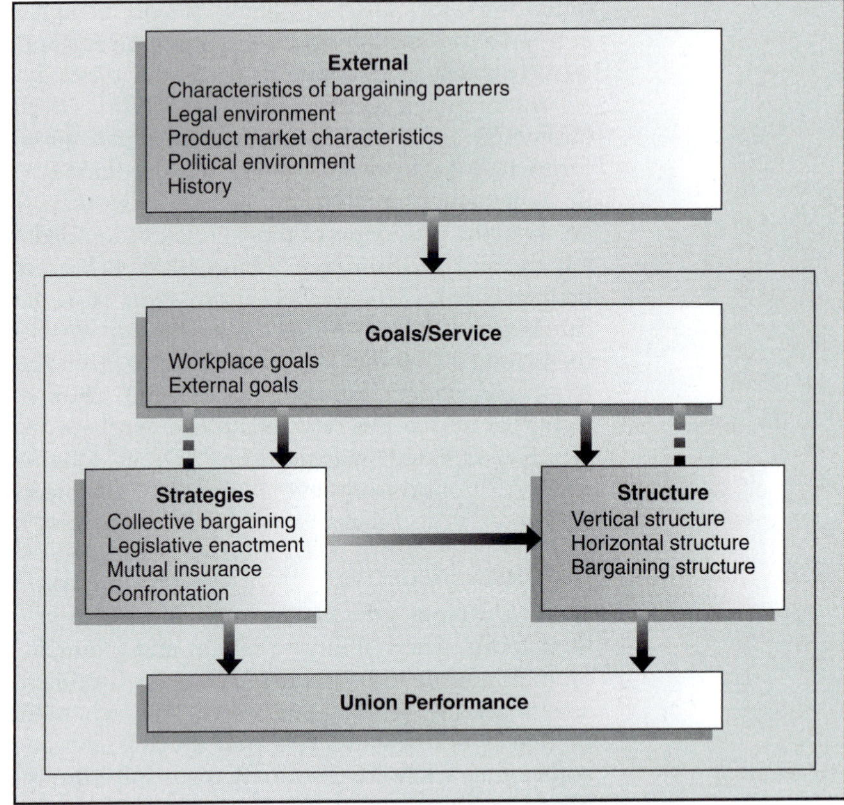

FIGURE 4.2
A Model of the Key Determinants of Union Organizational Structure

Source: J. Fiorito, C. L. Gramm, and W. E. Hendricks, "Union Structural Choices," in G. Strauss, D. G. Gallagher, and J. Fiorito, eds., The State of the Unions (Madison, WI: Industrial Relations Research Association, 1991), p. 106. Copyright © 1991 The Industrial Relations Research Association (now known as the Labor and Employment Relations Association). Champaign, IL. Reprinted by permission from the publisher.

legislative enactment, mutual insurance (the availability of aid to local unions during confrontations with employers), and confrontation (strikes, etc.) are blended to react to employer initiatives and to advance union agendas.[30] Figure 4.2 displays a model of the determinants of union organizational structures.

National union organizational structure is influenced by two factors: the service demands of members and the bargaining structures that have evolved with employers where the union represents employees. As the bargaining structures change, union organizations change with them. To demonstrate the relationships and differences between national unions, profiles of the SEIU, UAW, IBEW, Teamsters' Union, and AFSCME are presented next.

Service Employees International Union

The Service Employees International Union (SEIU) has been one of the most rapidly growing unions in the United States during the past decade.

[30] Ibid.

Its primary organizing and representation focus is on health care in hospitals, clinics, and long-term-care facilities; property services including food service, janitors, and security guards; and public services including child care workers, education workers, state and local community service workers, and mental health and disability service workers. Many SEIU locals represent primarily unskilled employees who are also often minority group members or immigrants who have no or low English language knowledge.

In addition to its representation role, the SEIU provides its members access to a broad array of financial services that might be unavailable to them normally, including a union-branded Visa credit card, financial counseling, mortgage assistance, product and service discounts, and the like. The SEIU is also very politically active in endorsing candidates, contributing financially to campaigns, enlisting volunteers for campaigning and voting, and organizing events and rallies.

The SEIU has actively promoted the development of women in both local and national union officer positions. The immediate past secretary-treasurer (Anna Burger) and current president (Mary Kay Henry) are both women.

United Auto Workers

The United Auto Workers (UAW) originally organized workers in the fabrication and assembly of autos and trucks, airplanes, construction and agricultural equipment, and associated parts suppliers. It has 730 locals. Besides its original jurisdiction, it now organizes nonprofessional workers in higher education. Since 2007, it has lost almost 300,000 members, and retired members outnumber active workers by almost 2 to 1. Prior to 1980, the domestic industry was highly concentrated (i.e., few manufacturers account for most of the production); however, both manufacturing and brand concentration has decreased markedly, with less than half of U.S. car sales belonging to U.S.-based companies. In 1980, virtually all U.S.-made automobiles were assembled by four companies: American Motors, Chrysler, Ford, and General Motors. Since then, BMW, Honda, Hyundai, Mazda, Mercedes, Mitsubishi, Nissan, and Toyota have opened U.S. assembly plants; Chrysler acquired American Motors, merged with Daimler-Benz in 1998 to form DaimlerChrysler, and was sold by DaimlerChrysler to Cerburus Capital Management in 2007, and in turn, taken through bankruptcy in 2009 and reorganized into Italian car maker, Fiat; General Motors was also taken through Chapter 11 in 2009 with the federal government becoming a majority owner until it was refloated in a November 2010 initial public offering. Through 2010, the only foreign-owned U.S. auto plants that are unionized are those that were started as joint ventures with a domestic partner. As the U.S.-based companies' share of the domestic market has declined, the proportion of auto workers represented by the UAW has also shrunk substantially. Additionally, with the passage of the North American Free Trade Agreement (NAFTA), U.S. companies opened new assembly plants in Mexico while closing older U.S. plants.

To best serve members in a consistent manner across the major manufacturers, the UAW established **national departments.** Because U.S.-based domestic automaker production facilities were virtually 100 percent unionized, these departments concentrated on representation rather than organizing activities. Figure 4.3 shows the UAW's organization at the national level.

National departments are the line portion of the organization. This is where national-local interfaces occur. Each national department has a council consisting of delegates from that department's locals. In turn, the councils form subcommittees based on common interests of the members, such as seniority and work rules. Subcommittees designate members to take part in the national negotiation council from that department.

Staff departments provide information for the national departments and assist locals through the UAW's international representatives. Besides having a "product-line" approach in its national departments, the UAW is also broken into geographic regions based on the concentration of UAW members in a given area. Regional staffs conduct organizing drives and assist remote locals or those not closely affiliated with national departments in negotiation, administration, and grievance handling. Regional staffs may also have experts in such areas as health and safety or industrial engineering.

The centralized organizational makeup of the UAW is largely a function of employer concentration of its active membership and the level at which economic bargaining occurs. However, as automakers close older, less efficient plants, local economic concessions may be traded for job security, necessitating more concern by the UAW for local bargaining issues.

International Brotherhood of Electrical Workers

The International Brotherhood of Electrical Workers (IBEW) was originally a union of skilled electricians primarily involved in contract construction. The IBEW also represents workers in electrical equipment manufacturers. Presently, it organizes and represents workers in utilities, construction, telecommunications, broadcasting, manufacturing, railroads, and government. The IBEW's locals cover relatively large geographic areas within states that reflect the high degree of mobility among construction workers as they move from project to project. The locals maintain hiring halls that allocate employment opportunities to its members.

The IBEW's organizational structure includes departments with primary responsibility for bargaining and representation in industries in which its representation is concentrated: broadcasting and recording, construction and maintenance, federal government employees, manufacturing, railroad, telecommunications, and utilities. It is also departmentalized in areas where it provides services to its members or the administrative

FIGURE 4.3 Organizational Structure of the UAW

Source: Adapted from information on www.uaw.org, August 7, 2007.

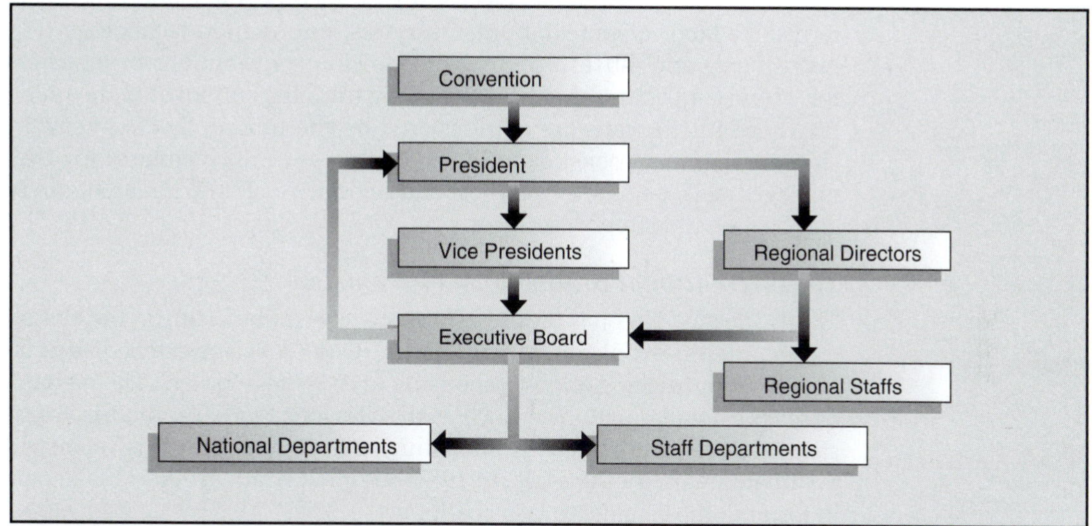

National Collective Bargaining Departments	Departments Reporting to the President	Departments Reporting to the Secretary-Treasurer	Other Departments
General Motors	Arbitration	Accounting	Conservation and Resource Development
Ford	Community Action	Auditing	Consumer Affairs
Chrysler	National CAP (Political Action)	Circulation	Organizing
Aerospace	Civil Rights	Purchasing and Supply	Recreation and Leisure-Time Activities
Agricultural Equipment	Community Services	Strike Insurance	Time Study and Engineering
Competitive Shop/ Independents, Parts and Suppliers	Education	Technical, Office and Professional	Veterans
Heavy Trucks	Government and International Affairs	Women's	
Transnationals and Joint Ventures	Health and Safety		
Technical, Office and Professional	Information Systems		
Skilled Trades	Legal		
	Legislative		
	Public Relations and Publications		
	Research		
	Research Library		
	Retired Workers		
	Social Security		

structure of the international. These include education, council of industrial relations/appeals (a jointly operated arbitration panel consisting of 6 IBEW and 6 National Electrical Contractors Association members to resolve labor disputes), human services, information technology (IT), investments and 401(k) (to grow the pension contributions of members for whom contributions either go directly from the employer to the union or where 401(k) plans are administered by the union), media, membership development, pensions and reciprocity, per capita membership (dues management), personnel, political and legislative affairs, research, safety and health, and support services.

The International Brotherhood of Teamsters

The Teamsters' Union is the closest to a general union of any in the United States. After its expulsion from the AFL-CIO in 1960, it broadened its jurisdiction from trucking and warehousing to cover all workers. The mergers of several smaller nationals, such as the Brewery Workers, into the Teamsters made it the dominant union within several industries. The Teamsters reaffiliated with the AFL-CIO in 1987, but it left again in 2005 to take part in forming the Change to Win coalition.

Given the Teamsters' early background and the local or regional nature of the trucking industry in general, bargaining and organizing are decentralized. The executive board includes the general president, the general secretary-treasurer, and 23 vice presidents. Some of the vice presidents are also international directors of Teamster area conferences. There are 21 trade divisions and departments: airline, bakery and laundry, brewery and soft drink workers, carhaul, building material and construction trade, dairy; express (DHL), food processing, graphic communications, freight, industrial trades, motion picture and theatrical trade, newspaper, magazine, and electronic media workers, parcel and small package (UPS), port, public services trade, rail, solid waste, tankhaul, trade show and convention centers, and warehouse. The national also has a number of staff departments to deliver services to members and to promote the formation of new bargaining units. Figure 4.4 depicts its organizational structure.

The Teamsters' Union has 514 local unions and 36 local joint councils. The joint councils are semiautonomous bodies that administer activities among affiliated locals. In areas where there are three or more locals, a joint council is established to coordinate activities among the locals. Each local is required to belong to a joint council and must get council permission to sign a contract or to strike. Each joint council is indirectly controlled by the executive branch. Thus, much of the grassroots organizing and representation activity is initiated or controlled at the joint council level.

The Teamsters have had a long history of difficulty with the federal government. Presidents in the 1950s and 1960s such as Dave Beck and James R. Hoffa were forced to resign for a variety of federal offenses related to using their leadership positions for personal advantage. In the 1980s, the

FIGURE 4.4 Organizational Structure of the International Brotherhood of Teamsters

Source: Reprinted with permission from Teamsters.org. Accessed at: http://www.teamsters.org/content/organizational-chart.

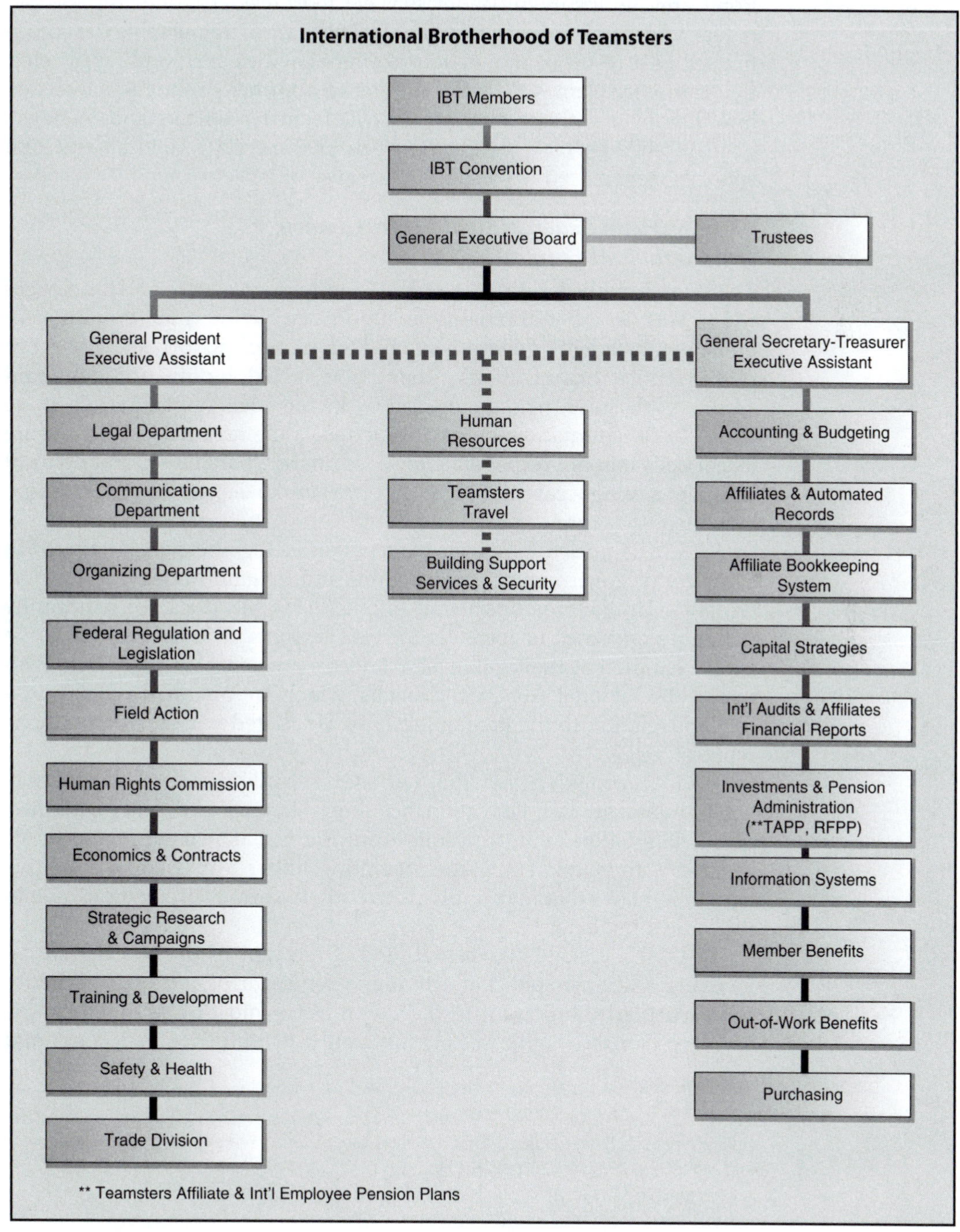

federal government imposed an external trustee following the conviction of Roy Lee Williams, then general president, for Mafia-related activities. Ron Carey, an insurgent leader, was elected president following the end of federal control. However, in late 1997 he was ruled ineligible to succeed himself as a result of money-laundering activities surrounding his election campaign. James P. Hoffa, the son of a former president, succeeded him. During the trusteeship, about 600 Teamster officers and members were expelled for racketeering. Between 1990 and 2003, 40 locals and joint councils were placed in trusteeship because of racketeering.[31]

The American Federation of State, County, and Municipal Employees

The American Federation of State, County, and Municipal Employees (AFSCME) is an industrial-type union organizing public employees outside the federal government and employees in private, nonprofit public-service organizations. The union is led by its president and secretary-treasurer, who are elected by its biennial convention. They are joined by 36 international vice presidents. At the regional level, there are 59 councils that are responsible for coordinating bargaining and political activities among locals in their regions. Figure 4.5 depicts AFSCME's organizational structure.

AFSCME's structure reflects the fact that its members are employed in a variety of governmental jurisdictions and bargain under many different laws. Unlike most industrial unions, AFSCME does not require the national's approval of local contract settlements. The decision to strike is also handled at the local level. All locals are expected to affiliate with one of the regional AFSCME councils, which are operated within jurisdictions relating to the bargaining laws associated with the occupations represented.

Services provided by the national include research, legislative, legal, organizational, educational, public relations, and other activities. AFSCME's federal nature results from the fact that its affiliated locals bargain with public employers operating under a myriad of collective bargaining laws that may apply differently to various occupations within the same jurisdiction.

AFSCME expends between 10 and 33 percent of its total budget on lobbying and other political activities.[32] Job security and pension issues are particularly important to the union. Since most of its members are employed in the public sector, the ability to influence legislators and

[31] J. B. Jacobs and D. D. Portnoi, "Administrative Criminal Law and Procedure in the Teamsters Union: What Has Been Achieved After (Nearly) Twenty Years," *Berkeley Journal of Employment and Labor Law*, 28 (2007), pp. 429–493.

[32] M. F. Masters, "AFSCME as a Political Union," *Journal of Labor Research*, 19 (1998), pp. 313–349.

FIGURE 4.5 Organizational Structure of the American Federation of State, County, and Municipal Employees

Source: Reprinted with permission from American Federation of State, County, and Municipal Employees. Accessed at: http://www.afscme.org/images/photos/afscmestructure-large.gif.

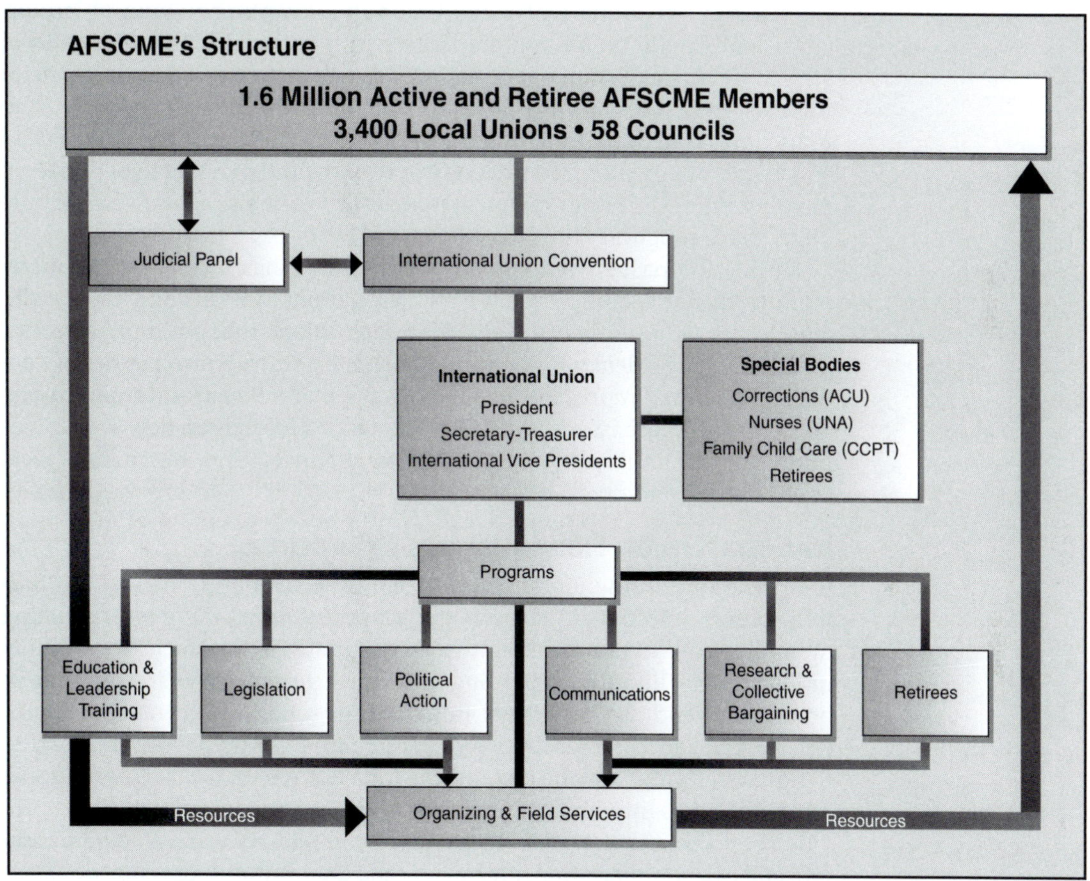

elected county and municipal officials is particularly important to its survival and growth.

National-Local Union Relationship

National unions charter locals, provide services, and usually require that locals obtain permission to ratify contracts or strike, thereby reducing the possibility of competition between locals and increasing the discipline of locals when necessary to pressure a large national employer.

Service to locals, especially from industrial unions, is provided by international representatives, who are usually individuals recruited and appointed by national union officers from local officer positions or activists interested in a union career. National unions may hire staff from other unions,[33] creating career mobility opportunities for staff experts. Large differences exist among unions in the intensity of services their professional staff members provide.[34] More intensive staff services would be expected in situations where the union is attempting to gain or protect consistent standards among employers in a given industry. The ratio of staff to members in most national unions has increased recently. Some of this has occurred naturally, as union membership has fallen faster than reductions in national staff positions. Administrative efficiency is reduced as a result, but greater staff intensity may allow the national to better serve member interests. However, increases in staff may also tend to perpetuate oligarchical practices.[35]

During the past 20 years major restructuring has taken place in many manufacturing establishments in which national unions and their affiliated locals represent employees. National unions that are more effective in helping locals deal with ongoing workplace restructuring generally are those with broad representational coverage that educate and train leaders on new workplace issues, devote resources to research on new workplace practices, use multiple communication channels, and restructure local union representation.[36]

National Union Headquarters Operations

International representatives, unlike many local union officers, are full-time union employees. Their major responsibilities involve organizing nonunion employers in industries or occupations in which the national union has an interest, providing assistance to employees interested in organizing, and assisting local unions in negotiating contracts and processing grievances. International representatives are typically assigned to regional staffs and may be responsible for a number of locals. International representatives implement consistent policies across employers, and provide expertise and presence where locals are relatively small, where local officers lack sophistication, and where the area is thinly organized.

Union clerical and professional employees frequently organize to collectively bargain with the leaders of the unions for which they work.

[33] P. F. Clark and L. S. Gray, "The Management of Human Resources in National Unions," *Proceedings of the Industrial Relations Research Association*, 44 (1992), pp. 414–423.

[34] P. F. Clark, "Organizing the Organizers: Professional Staff Unionism in the American Labor Movement," *Industrial and Labor Relations Review*, 42 (1989), pp. 584–599.

[35] P. F. Clark, "Professional Staff in American Unions: Changes, Trends, Implications," *Journal of Labor Research*, 13 (1992), pp. 381–392.

[36] A. C. Frost, "Creating and Sustaining Local Union Capabilities: The Role of the National Union," *Relations Industrielles*, 56 (2001), pp. 307–333; see also a symposium on technological effects on unions and employment in a variety of industries, *Journal of Labor Research*, 23, no. 4 (2002).

Organized staff units are most common in larger industrial unions. Some unions have strongly opposed the organization of their staff members, while others have welcomed organizing attempts. Staff unions generally bargain for the same types of employment issues that unions in general seek, but they seldom strike in support of their demands.[37]

Newly elected national union officers may discharge permanent staff employees as long as doing so doesn't interfere with the employees' roles as union members,[38] but elected union officers are protected by Title I of the Labor-Management Reporting and Disclosure Act (LMRDA) and cannot be removed for expressing dissenting opinions.[39]

Union administration has become more sophisticated as employers have increasingly opposed unionization and concession bargaining has increased. Unions rely on consultants more than they did in the past, and internal management is operated on a more businesslike basis.[40] Increasingly, national unions are adopting formal human resource and financial management practices, are less likely to require union membership as a prerequisite for hiring into staff positions, and are more likely to search for college graduates and persons with computer skills.[41]

National unions are extensive users of IT and use it most frequently for internal administration and communications to members (such as through Web sites). Unions are also increasingly using financial analysis to craft contract demands and to track organizing targets.[42] National and local unions are increasingly using IT to help develop virtual minority unions in nonunion firms, enhance democracy through online communications, provide services, and strengthen international cooperation.[43] However, unions have not been early adopters of new media technology. As the cost, availability, and ease of use continues to improve, the use of social networking technologies such as Facebook and Twitter can be

[37] Clark, "Organizing the Organizers."

[38] *Finnegan* v. *Leu*, No. 80-2150, U.S. Supreme Court, 1982.

[39] *Sheet Metal Workers International Association* v. *Lynn*, No. 86-1940, U.S. Supreme Court, 1989.

[40] For more details on union administration, see P. F. Clark and L. S. Gray, "Union Administration," in G. Strauss, D. G. Gallagher, and J. Fiorito, eds., *The State of the Unions* (Madison, WI: Industrial Relations Research Association, 1991), pp. 175–200; and J. T. Dunlop, *The Management of Labor Unions* (Lexington, MA: Lexington, 1990).

[41] P. F. Clark and L. S. Gray, "Administrative Practices in American Unions: A Longitudinal Study," *Journal of Labor Research*, 29 (2008), pp. 42–55.

[42] J. Fiorito, P. Jarley, J. T. Delaney, and R. W. Kolodinsky, "Unions and Information Technology: From Luddites to Cyberunions?" *Labor Studies Journal*, 24, no. 4 (2000), pp. 3–34; see also "Symposium: E-Voice: Information Technology and Unions," *Journal of Labor Research*, 23 (2002), pp. 171–259.

[43] W. J. Diamond and R. B. Freeman, "Will Unionism Prosper in Cyberspace? The Promise of the Internet for Employee Organization," *British Journal of Industrial Relations,* 40 (2002), pp. 569–596.

expected to be added to both national and local unions' communications tools.

National Union Governance and Politics

National union governance can be grouped into four categories: (1) governance by rule (strong adherence to constitutions in determining rights and processes), (2) governance by meetings (frequent use of meetings to determine organizational direction), (3) governance by member opposition (majority opposition controls leader direction), and (4) governance by countervailing power (limits on discretion resulting from significant ongoing organized potential opposition). Unions of the governance-by-rule type (e.g., the UAW) tend to be larger, operate in industries with a national product market, and have lower diversity in the types of workers they organize.[44]

National unions are ultimately governed by their conventions, which establish broad policies, may amend their constitutions, and frequently elect officers. Member participation in national activities depends on how convention delegates are chosen and union officers are elected. Although national unions are required by law to hold conventions and elect officers at least every five years, they differ greatly in the extent to which member involvement is sought and democratic ideals are applied to their operation.

National union democracy can be measured by the degree of control members have in the major decision-making areas unions face: contract negotiations, contract administration, service to members, union administration, and political and community activities. Members' control in each area could range from complete autocracy to consultation, veto power, or full decisional control and participation.[45] Union members' desire for democracy may be inferred through their level of participation in and their satisfaction with opportunities for involvement in union decision making. The Canadian Auto Workers have created a Public Review Board consisting of public figures who are not members of the union to hear and make binding rulings on the grievances of members regarding union governance issues.[46]

Most national unions do not have two-party systems, but a union's constitution affects the degree to which dissent may lead to a change in the union's direction. Unions electing officers on an at-large basis among all the eligible voters (either as delegates or through a general referendum) are much less likely to be responsive to factional viewpoints than

[44] P. Jarley, J. Fiorito, and J. T. Delaney, "National Union Governance: An Empirically-Grounded Systems Approach," *Journal of Labor Research*, 21 (2000), pp. 227–246.

[45] A. Hochner, K. Koziara, and S. Schmidt, "Thinking about Democracy and Participation in Unions," *Proceedings of the Industrial Relations Research Association*, 32 (1979), pp. 16–17.

[46] J. Eaton, "Union Democracy and Union Renewal: The CAW Public Review Board," *Relations Industrielles*, 61 (2006), pp. 201–222

are unions that elect executive board members on a geographic basis.[47] In the Mineworkers and the Steelworkers (both of which have changed national general presidents because of internal dissent), regionally elected executive boards have served as springboards to national campaigns. If officers are elected by convention and if the delegates to the international convention include not only those selected at a local level but also officials appointed by the incumbent, then the chance of ousting the incumbent is virtually nonexistent.[48]

Leaders of national unions generally come from union backgrounds. Their net worths are usually modest. Most have some post–high school education, but few are college graduates. Most joined unions because their employers had a union shop. Their union careers usually began in a local union position. Many had mentors, and most are very satisfied with union careers.[49]

National Unions and Public Policy

Representation aims at enhancing union members' employment outcomes through collective bargaining. Unions also serve member needs by attempting to influence public policy. Some attempts are aimed at membership interests in particular industries, while others focus on improving outcomes for all members or an identifiable subgroup across industries. Union political activity will be examined in more detail in Chapter 5.

THE AFL-CIO

From the merger of the AFL and CIO in 1955 until the disaffiliation of several major national unions to form the Change to Win coalition in 2005, the AFL-CIO was the umbrella under which the large majority of the U.S. union movement gathered. While the number of union members who are in unions that affiliate with the AFL-CIO is just over 60 percent of the total, a large majority of national unions continue to be affiliated. Since 2005, for the first time in 50 years, there is substantial competition within the union movement to determine its overall direction and mobilize working-class energies for organizing and political action.

The AFL-CIO provides an overall direction to its 57 affiliated nationals and technical assistance to individual nationals. It also has a number of directly affiliated independent local unions. To be a member of the

[47] S. Gamm, "The Election Base of National Union Executive Boards," *Industrial and Labor Relations Review*, 32 (1979), pp. 295–311.

[48] A. L. Fox II and J. C. Sikorski, *Teamster Democracy and Financial Responsibility* (Washington, DC: Professional Drivers Council for Safety and Health, 1976).

[49] P. L. Quaglieri, "The New People of Power: The Backgrounds and Careers of Top Labor Leaders," *Journal of Labor Research*, 9 (1988), pp. 271–284.

AFL-CIO, a national union must comply with the federation's Ethical Practices Code, avoid dominance by nondemocratic ideologies, and agree to resolve interunion disputes using prescribed federation procedures. Article 20 of the AFL-CIO constitution provides for internal arbitration of disputes between unions. These disputes most often involve charges of one union's attempting to organize a bargaining unit already represented by another union (raiding). Historically, there have been about 30 cases of raiding a year, and arbitrators have found violations of Article 20 in about half of these cases.[50] With the formation of Change to Win, raids may increase in the future and will not be subject to internal adjudication.

The AFL-CIO simultaneously coordinates national union interests and directs state and city central body activities. The quadrennial national convention consists of delegates who are apportioned to the convention on the basis of national union size and are elected or appointed according to their national's policy. Other delegates are sent by directly affiliated locals, state and city central bodies, and national industrial and trade departments. The convention amends the constitution, elects officers, and expresses official positions. The general board consists of the executive council, presidents of each affiliated national, and a representative from each constitutional department.

The ongoing business of the AFL-CIO is handled by the top executives, their staffs, and the constitutional departments. One set of constitutional departments—the six trade and industrial departments—relates to jurisdictional interests of the national members: building and construction trades, maritime trades, metal trades, professional employees, transportation trades, and union label and service trades. The staff portion of the organization consists of the standing committees and their equivalent departments, which include accounting; civil, human rights and women's rights; facility management; general counsel; information technology; international affairs; legislation; meetings and travel; organizing; politics; public affairs; public policy; and support services. Political activity and lobbying are major activities of the AFL-CIO. Many issues before Congress have potential direct and indirect effects on the labor movement.

THE CHANGE TO WIN COALITION

In 2005, seven national unions left the AFL-CIO to form Change to Win (CTW). The impetus for the withdrawal and formation was a belief that the AFL-CIO had an insufficient commitment to organizing unrepresented workers, particularly those in low-paying jobs, and had been unsuccessful

[50] G. W. Bohlander, "Keeping the Peace: AFL-CIO's Internal Dispute Plan, "*Dispute Resolution Journal*, 57, no. 1 (2002), pp. 21–27.

in implementing a revitalization strategy.[51] The exodus, ironically, was led by Andy Stern, the president of the Service Employees International Union—the same union from which had come Joseph Sweeney, who was the incumbent AFL-CIO president and who had run on a platform emphasizing organizing. Some cynics argue that Stern's initiative resulted from Sweeney's decision not to retire in 2005 which could have served as a springboard for Stern running for the AFL-CIO presidency.

The seven unions took 6 million members from the AFL-CIO (more than half its membership) and instantly created an energized and more militant collective. The affiliated unions included the Teamsters (IBT), Laborers (LIUNA), Service Employees (SEIU), Carpenters (UBC), Farm Workers (UFW), Food and Commercial Workers (UFCW), and UNITE HERE (the merged needletrades, textile workers, and hotel and restaurant workers). Since CTW's inception, the Laborers and UNITE HERE have returned to the AFL-CIO while the Carpenters are now unaffiliated.

The AFL-CIO has been financially and organizationally weakened by the defection of the CTW. The CTW strategic direction is strongly oriented toward organizing among workers who have not previously had effective representation, for example, janitors and maintenance workers, immigrant workers in industries that have been deunionized (e.g., meatpacking), nurses, and child care workers. CTW maintains that many potentially organizable employees will find its less adversarial approach with employers more appealing.[52]

STATE AND LOCAL CENTRAL BODIES

In addition to its departments, the AFL-CIO has a direct relationship with almost 800 state and local **central bodies.** These bodies reflect the composition of the parent AFL-CIO and the particular industrial mix of their geographic areas. The state and local centrals are directly responsible to the AFL-CIO, not to the nationals.

State and local central bodies are primarily involved in politics and lobbying. Their positions in national elections must be consistent with those of the AFL-CIO.[53] Central bodies endorse state and local candidates and testify and lobby on local and state legislative proposals. The AFL-CIO consists predominantly of affiliated nationals, while state and local

[51] A. W. Martin, "Why Does the New Labor Movement Look So Much Like the Old One? Putting the 1990s Revitalization Project in Historical Context," *Journal of Labor Research*, 27 (2006), pp. 163–185.

[52] M. F. Masters and R. Gibney, "The AFL-CIO v. CTW: The Competing Visions, Strategies, and Structures," *Journal of Labor Research*, 27 (2006), pp. 473–504; and for a pessimistic assessment, see S. Estreicher, "Disunity within the House of Labor," *Journal of Labor Research*, 27 (2006), pp. 505–511.

[53] www.aflcio.org/aboutus/thisistheaflcio/constitution/art14.cfm, August 7, 2007.

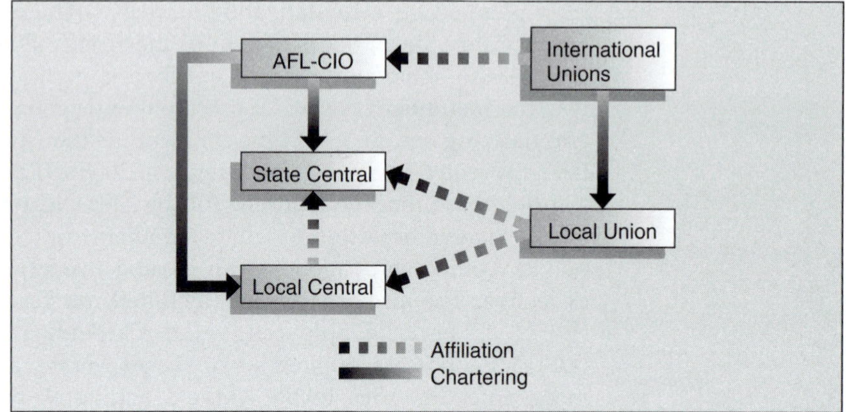

FIGURE 4.6 The Relationship of State and Local Central Bodies to the AFL-CIO

Source: Adapted from J. G. Kilpatrick and M. C. Stanley, *Handbook on Central Labor Bodies: Functions and Activities*, West Virginia University Bulletin, series 64, nos. 4–6 (October 1963), p. 5.

centrals involve local unions. Figure 4.6 shows the relationship of state and local central bodies to the AFL-CIO.

Overview of the Union Hierarchy

Power in the labor movement clearly resides in the nationals, with locals and the federation deriving their authority from the nationals. Local unions are structured to handle the day-to-day activities of the membership. Much of their effort involves policing the contract and handling grievances.

A national union could be compared with the corporate staff division of a large company where policies are developed, actions are audited to ensure conformity to policy, new businesses are launched, and advice is given to generalists in plants (or locals) on specific issues. Although the convention ultimately governs the national, many presidents have broad powers to take interim actions and to influence the delegate composition of future conventions.

The AFL-CIO is similar to a trade association, a chamber of commerce, or a national association of manufacturers. It coordinates activities among the nationals and amplifies their voices. The federation's prime functions are information, integration, and advocacy. Its greatest areas of autonomy relate to legislative and political processes.

NATIONAL UNION MERGERS

As the labor movement has shrunk and as technological change has affected the structure of employment, national unions have more frequently merged. Union mergers appear to take two forms: (1) *absorption,* in which a small or rapidly declining union becomes a part of a larger national;[54] and (2) *amalgamation,* in which two unions of roughly equal size merge to form a new union (e.g., the 1979 merger of the 500,000-member Amalgamated Meat Cutters and Butcher Workers with the 700,000-member Retail Clerks to form the United Food and Commercial Workers).[55]

Mergers involve one of three types of relationships between the merging partners: (1) *symbiotic,* in which two unions represent workers whose outputs are interdependent; (2) *commensalistic,* in which two unions competed to organize the same employees; and (3) *scale,* wherein a large union seeks to increase its efficiency or power. Symbiotic mergers prevail when unions are expanding membership, and commensalistic mergers are more common during contraction.

Mergers duplicate national union officers and services unless staffs are consolidated. Symbiotic mergers are probably the easiest because the needs of the merged membership may have little overlap. Commensalistic mergers require agreements on the role of present union officers and the fate of local unions following the merger. Mergers are eased when few integration issues exist, such as where craft identities are preserved, the regional penetration of one union is great, important historical traditions are preserved, leadership duplication problems are accommodated, and merged structures are based on strong individual union identities.[56] Union leaders see several benefits from mergers, including increased power of the merged unions, greater strategic capability, greater possibilities for growth, staff job security, and greater success possibilities for the leaders.[57] Union members favor mergers in situations where they believe a merged union will improve their employment conditions and/or the image of the union.[58]

UNION FINANCES

Union finances fall into two different categories. The first involves the day-to-day operations of the union, and the second is the fiduciary obligation of officers in some unions in the collection, trusteeship, and disbursement of pension and welfare benefits to members. The latter is usually found in craft unions or unions in which employers are too small or marginal to administer their own pension programs.

[54] C. J. Janus, "Union Mergers in the 1970s: A Look at the Reasons and Results," *Monthly Labor Review*, 102, no. 10 (1978), pp. 13–23.

[55] G. N. Chaison, "Union Growth and Union Mergers," *Industrial Relations*, 20 (1981), pp. 98–108.

[56] G. N. Chaison, "Union Mergers and the Integration of Union Governing Structures," *Journal of Labor Research*, 3 (1982), pp. 139–151.

[57] K. Stratton-Devine, "Union Merger Benefits: An Empirical Analysis," *Journal of Labor Research*, 13 (1992), pp. 133–143.

[58] K. Devine and Y. Reshef, "Union Merger Support: A Tale of Two Theories," *Relations Industrielles*, 53 (1998), pp. 517–534.

Three major sources of revenue are available to unions: dues from members; fees, fines, and assessments from members; and investment income. Dues and fees are collected at the local level. The nationals and the AFL-CIO levy a per capita tax on the locals. The current AFL-CIO per capita tax is 65 cents monthly; many nationals require locals to remit about 50 percent of dues for their operations. Dues vary widely among unions; some require a flat fee, while others scale fees to earning levels. For full-time workers, typical dues would be equal to about two to two and a half times the member's hourly pay rate per month. The parent national usually sets minimum and maximum levels, and the local can adjust within those limits. Occasionally, an assessment is added to replenish or maintain strike funds. Most unions require an initiation fee, which is often waived for workers who become members following a successful organizing drive. Initiation fees tend to be high in unions representing employees who frequently change employers, such as in construction, the performing arts, the maritime industry, and the like. In other situations, initiation fees tend to vary between about $30 and $100. Members in good standing who change unionized employers normally are not required to pay another initiation fee to their new local.

A union's ability to service the workers it represents depends, to an extent, on the dues paid by members. As noted earlier in the discussion of functional democracy, all employees who are represented are not necessarily members. In federal government employment, union shop clauses cannot be negotiated. Further, unions cannot strike. **Free riding** by nonmember federal employees approaches almost two-thirds of the number of employees represented by the American Federation of Government Employees and other federal sector unions. This has led to low solvency and the need to borrow money to cover operating expenses during certain periods. It has also probably reduced the effectiveness of the unions in bargaining and contract administration.[59]

Financial Malfeasance

The Landrum-Griffin Act, as well as state criminal codes, specifies a variety of illegal financial transactions for labor unions. In 1998, Teamsters General President Ron Carey was barred from ever holding union office again as a result of money laundering that funneled funds to his reelection campaign in 1997. In general, national unions have been free of financial transgressions by their officers. And, given the large number of local and intermediate bodies that exist, there are relatively few instances of embezzlement in these organizations. One study found that during a two-year period between 1993 and 1995, 104 persons were convicted under the federal statute prohibiting embezzlement from unions. In general, losses

[59] M. F. Masters and R. S. Atkin, "Financial and Bargaining Implications of Free Riding in the Federal Sector," *Journal of Collective Negotiations in the Public Sector*, 22 (1993), pp. 327–340.

tended to be under $25,000, the victimized unions were small in both membership and financial resources, and the perpetrators were most often male part-time officers who acted alone.[60]

A broader study of incidents of union corruption collected by the U.S. Department of Labor enumerated 1,236 incidents with costs exceeding $1.42 billion. About half of the incidents and $117 million of the losses were associated with embezzlement and other financial malfeasance. Nonfinancial corrupt practices involved denial of due process and union democracy; campaign finance; and bribery, extortion, kickbacks, and the like. The magnitude of general corruption including mob ties, racketeering, and improper political contributions totaled almost $350 million. Pension malfeasance involved 65 instances, with a cost of $945 million.[61]

Pension Administration

Pension plans are frequently administered by craft and other unions when the size of employers is small or employment is transient. Craft union dues are greater than those in industrial unions, with a portion set aside for benefits. Other unions require that employers make a per capita payment, as in the National Master Freight Agreement with the Teamsters, which required a combined health, welfare, and pension contribution of $12.39 per hour in 2008, rising to $17.39 at the end of the contract in 2013.

Administering pension programs has become an increasingly important issue for both union administrators and members. Union involvement has recently expanded with the voluntary employee benefits association (VEBA) established to handle UAW retiree health care benefits during the 2007 auto industry negotiations. More details on VEBAs will be covered in Chapter 9. The Employee Retirement Income Security Act of 1974 (ERISA) requires that pension administrators safeguard and prudently invest contributions made toward retirement. Certain investment practices, such as risky or low-interest loans, are illegal. Investments in an individual's own organization are also largely precluded. Given equivalent expected returns, however, unions may channel financing toward projects that will enhance employment of their members. For example, building trades unions may provide financing for housing projects and other activities that will require increased employment of building trades workers.

Summary

Organized labor essentially has a three-tiered structure (local, national, and federation), with power concentrated at the second level. At the local level, the most typical structure is the single-employer bargaining

[60] A. L. Bowker, "Trust Violators in the Labor Movement: A Study of Union Embezzlements," *Journal of Labor Research*, 19 (1998), pp. 571–579.

[61] A. J. Thieblot, "Perspectives on Union Corruption: Lessons from the Databases," *Journal of Labor Research*, 27 (2006), pp. 513–536.

unit. Multiemployer units are perhaps most common in the construction industry. Although the local is the workers' direct representative, members' interests in internal affairs are generally low. They appear to view the union as their employment agent and allow a cadre of activists to control its internal politics.

National unions are of two major types—craft, representing workers in a specific occupation; and industrial, representing occupations in a specific industry. National union structures, particularly the industrials, adapt to both the breadth of their constituencies and the concentration within their industries. For example, the UAW has a General Motors Department, while AFSCME has various state- or local-based councils.

Whether unions operate democratically depends on the definition of the term. Most do not have two-party systems, and many equate dissent with attempts to undermine union goals. On the other hand, local officers are elected directly, and international officials are chosen in a manner similar to a presidential nominating convention. Unions introduce democracy into the work setting by requiring a bargaining contract. Within unions, the checks and balances initiated through their constitutions and contracts increase democracy and safeguards for members.

Recently, several large unions left the AFL-CIO to form Change to Win, roughly dividing the U.S. labor movement into two large groups.

Discussion Questions

1. If you were recommending an organizational structure for a national union, what factors would you advise that it consider (industrial concentration, occupations it represents, etc.)?
2. Defend or attack the usual method of electing an international president (through local delegates and international staff members at the convention).
3. Should local unions have more control over the scope and terms of negotiated agreements, or should national unions still retain approval and veto power?
4. How should the union movement respond structurally to the increasing globalization of business?
5. What would happen to the structure of the union movement if representation were deregulated and for-profit organizations could also represent workers?
6. Are the goals of the AFL-CIO and CTW basically identical, or is the new federation a viable strategic alternative for revitalizing the labor movement?

Key Terms

Business agent, *95*
Executive committee, *96*
Negotiation committee, *96*
Stewards, *96*
Superseniority, *96*
Functional democracy, *99*
Dual governance, *99*
Bargaining units, *99*
Open shop, *99*
National union, *101*
International union, *101*
Conventions, *103*
Field representatives, *103*
Corporate campaigns, *104*
Political action committees (PACs), *104*
National departments, *108*
Central bodies, *119*
Free riding, *122*

Selected Web Sites

www.aflcio.org
www.afscme.org
www.changetowin.org
www.ibew.org
www.seiu.org
www.teamsters.org
www.uaw.org

Unions: Member and Leader Attitudes, Behaviors, and Political Activities

Chapter 4 examined the structure of the labor movement, detailing its components, offices, and activities. With unionization, wages, hours, and terms and conditions of employment are determined on a bilateral basis, and ongoing workplace governance is shared by the employer and the union.

In unionized environments, individuals are simultaneously employees and union members. Regardless of unionization status, employers have explicit expectations about employee effort and performance within their jobs. Employees ultimately are responsible for operating their union and bargaining with their employer. Member commitment and participation may vary substantially depending on the local employment environment and the governance structure of the union. This chapter examines union member participation and commitment and the role of national unions in influencing the external environment through political action. As you study this chapter, consider the following questions:

1. What factors influence the willingness of union members to participate in local union activities?
2. Can an employee be simultaneously committed to both employer and union goals?
3. What effect does union political action have on outcomes important to organized labor?
4. What factors influence the participation of women and minorities in local and national unions?

THE INDIVIDUAL AND THE LOCAL UNION

Most people who are union members joined after being hired by a unionized employer. As Chapter 10 will describe in more detail, unions usually negotiate union security clauses into collective bargaining agreements, requiring that represented employees join the union or pay an **agency fee** for representation services. In states with right-to-work laws, federal employment, and most state and local public employment, employees cannot be required to join unions if they are represented, and most often they are not required to pay agency fees.

In some occupations, unions are a major labor supply source. Where employment is transient (as in the construction and maritime industries), and when the union takes a leading role in occupational skill training (as in the building trades), entry to employment is most often through the union. In these unions, membership is not usually required to be employed by a unionized employer, but it is a prerequisite for being referred to many opportunities.

Joining, Socialization, and Leaving

As noted in Chapter 1, only about 1 in 8 employees currently works in a union-represented workplace. But research studies find that more than 6 of every 10 workers have been union members at some time during their careers, with 80 percent of this group experiencing unionization by age 26.[1] Over a career, being an employee in a unionized employer is most likely among workers who are in their forties.[2] People who are high school graduates or have completed some college are more likely to be or have been in a union job than those who dropped out of high school or completed college.[3] The lack of a high school education largely dooms someone to working in marginal occupations that lack the ability to exert bargaining power due to the large supply of potential workers given the demand, particularly at the margin. Jobs that are held by this group are not likely to be core, permanent jobs in most employers. On the other hand, people with college degrees (particularly in business, science, technology, engineering, and medicine) are part of a labor supply that is scarce relative to employers' demands, thus they are able to exert substantial individual

[1] J. W. Budd, "When Do U.S. Workers First Experience Unionization? Implications for Revitalizing the Labor Movement," *Industrial Relations*, 49 (2010), pp. 209–225; and J. E. Booth, J. W. Budd, and K. M. Munday, "First-Timers and Late-Bloomers: Youth-Adult Unionization Differences in a Cohort of the U.S. Labor Force, *Industrial and Labor Relations Review*, 64 (2010), pp. 53–73.

[2] D. G. Blanchflower, "International Patterns of Union Membership," *British Journal of Industrial Relations*, 45 (2007), pp. 1–28.

[3] Budd, op. cit.

bargaining power and/or to switch employers fairly readily if they are currently dissatisfied. Thus, unionized jobs are more readily available and hold greater appeal to those who have completed high school but are not college graduates. Employers are more interested in hiring and training people who demonstrate higher capacities to learn, and by unionizing this group can exert bargaining pressure on the employer since they would find it difficult to replace developed skills if employees were to strike.

Employers usually orient new employees to their workplaces. Most often new employees start work at the beginning of a pay period. They usually attend a group meeting at which they receive information about the company and its policies and procedures, enroll in benefit programs, and the like. Then they go to their work areas, meet their supervisors, are assigned workstations, meet their fellow employees, and begin on-the-job training. Sometimes there may be a formal training period before beginning the job. New employees are often hired in a probationary capacity, making the transition to so-called permanent employment after a training and adaptation period. While new employees in a unionized bargaining unit are covered by the labor contract from the outset, most contracts usually reserve the company's right to terminate a probationary employee for any reason without recourse to the grievance procedure.

Most collective bargaining agreements exempt probationary employees from union representation or payment of union agency fees. If there is a **union shop** agreement in the contract, new employees will be required to join immediately after the probationary period. At this point, they must pay an initiation fee and begin to pay monthly dues.

Generally, stewards enroll new members in a work unit. They explain to employees how the union represents them and how the collective bargaining agreement benefits them. Stewards make employees aware of union activities and try to get new members involved. Since the union must demonstrate majority support to represent employees, it is important for stewards to be able to spell out to present and potential members the gains the union has previously negotiated. Aspects of the contract related to protection from unilateral discipline and rationalizing job opportunities through seniority clauses reflect the operationalization of union values.[4] Personal contact by the steward in socializing new members to the union appears to be much more important than formal programs. Socialization positively influences new members' attitudes toward the union and their later commitment to the union's programs and activities.[5]

[4] P. F. Clark, C. Fullager, D. G. Gallagher, and M. E. Gordon, "Building Union Commitment among New Members: The Role of Formal and Informal Socialization," *Labor Studies Journal*, 18, no. 3 (1993), pp. 3–16.

[5] C. J. A. Fullager, D. G. Gallagher, M. E. Gordon, and P. F. Clark, "Impact of Early Socialization on Union Commitment and Participation: A Longitudinal Study, *Journal of Applied Psychology*, 80 (1995), pp. 147–157.

Where there is no union shop or required agency fee, employees do not need to pay dues to the union to receive contractual benefits. This is **free riding.** Employees who are socialized into the union or who develop feelings of union solidarity avoid free riding. Employees who are less attached to their occupations or who have less fear of arbitrary employer actions may be more willing to free ride. Those who do not believe the benefits gained through collective bargaining exceed the costs of dues and other efforts would also be less likely to join. An adversarial relationship between the union and the employer will be more likely to create a perceived need for union protection.[6] But unionized employees who perceive the labor relations in their workplaces to be adversarial are likely to decrease commitment to both the employer and the union.[7] Factors associated with higher rates of free riding (holding other factors constant) include employment in the private sector in a right-to-work state; lower earnings; employment in a white-collar occupation; higher education levels; and being younger, white, or a woman.[8]

As the economy shifts the predominance of employment increasingly toward services and there is increased diversity in the workforce, identification with traditional union goals and tactics has decreased among members in a union shop environment. Union democracy increases the perceptions of union relevance.[9]

Free riding in federal employee unions is particularly common. Federal law prohibits the inclusion of union shop or agency shop requirements in negotiated agreements. In unions that have relatively broad representation, fewer than half of the bargaining-unit members belong to the union. Only among air traffic controllers is membership greater than two-thirds of those represented.[10] Free riding diminishes the resources the union has to provide services to the employees it represents. Table 5.1 provides data

[6] S. J. Deery, R. D. Iverson, and P. J. Erwin, "Predicting Organizational and Union Commitment: The Effect of Industrial Relations Climate," *British Journal of Industrial Relations*, 32 (1994), pp. 581–598.

[7] J. B. Fuller and K. Hester, "The Effect of Labor Relations Climate on the Union Participation Process," *Journal of Labor Research*, 19 (1994), pp. 173–188.

[8] G. N. Chaison and D. G. Dhavale, "The Choice between Union Membership and Free-Rider Status," *Journal of Labor Research*, 13 (1992), pp. 355–369, although "true" free riding, where the value of benefits exceeds the costs, appears to be equal in both right-to-work and non-right-to-work states; see R. S. Sobel, "Empirical Evidence on the Union Free-Rider Problem: Do Right-to-Work Laws Matter?" *Journal of Labor Research*, 16 (1995), pp. 346–365.

[9] C. Lévesque, G. Murray, and S. Le Queux, "Union Dissatisfaction and Social Identity: Democracy as a Source of Union Revitalization," *Work and Occupations*, 32 (2005), pp. 400–422.

[10] M. F. Masters, "Federal Sector Unions: Current Status and Future Directions," *Journal of Labor Research*, 25 (2004), pp. 55–82.

TABLE 5.1 Union Membership and Free Riding in Federal Employee Unions

Source: Adapted from M. F. Masters, "Federal Sector Unions: Current Status and Future Directions," *Journal of Labor Research*, 25 (2004), pp. 64–65.

	AFGE			NFFE		
Year	Employees Represented	Members	Free Riders	Employees Represented	Members	Free Riders
1997	596,206	180,000	69.81%	123,660	16,500	86.66%
1999	578,048	191,171	66.93%	104,472	13,304	87.27%
2001	582,753	198,453	65.95%	68,539	7,528	89.02%
% change	−2.26%	10.25%	−5.53%	−44.57%	−54.38%	2.72%

Note: AFGE = American Federation of Government Employees; NFFE = National Federation of Federal Employees; NTEU = National Treasury Employees Union; and NATCA = National Air Traffic Controllers Association.

on the extent of free riding among employees represented by major federal employee unions.

In a study of the reasons that workers left their unions in situations where the bargaining relationship permitted doing so, most workers left for reasons associated with a change in job status (retired, laid off, or changed jobs), while about one-quarter left because of dissatisfaction with their union. Primary reasons for dissatisfaction had to do with a perceived lack of success in bargaining, a lack of contact from the union, and not enough effort on behalf of members. Dissatisfaction that led to the decision to leave one's present union seemed to influence attitudes of leavers toward unions in general.[11] In a situation where workers could either join or leave, a study found that joiners had lower performance appraisals, perceived procedural justice to be lower, believed the union would be instrumental in improving conditions, and had partners who were socialized into unions. Union leavers also had lower perceptions of procedural justice, but were less likely to have union representation in the workplace and had individualistic orientations.[12]

Member Participation

Union member participation involves taking part in administrative activities; attending meetings; and voting in elections, strike authorizations, and contract ratifications. One set of activities relates to the local union as an organization (e.g., attending meetings, voting in officer elections, running for office), while other activities involve the union's role as bargaining agent (e.g., voting on contract ratifications, picketing). The steward's

[11] J. Waddington, "Why Do Members Leave? The Importance of Retention to Trade Union Growth," *Labor Studies Journal*, 31, no. 3 (2006), pp. 15–38.

[12] D. M. Buttigieg, S. J. Deery, and R. D. Iverson, "An Event History Analysis of Union Joining and Leaving," *Journal of Applied Psychology*, 92 (2007), pp. 829–839.

NTEU			NATCA		
Employees Represented	**Members**	**Free Riders**	**Employees Represented**	**Members**	**Free Riders**
136,577	70,641	48.28%	14,459	10,088	30.23%
135,906	71,010	47.75%	14,771	12,020	18.62%
139,302	74,306	46.66%	18,569	12,645	31.90%
2.00%	5.19%	−3.35%	28.43%	25.35%	5.53%

TABLE 5.2
Union Orientation Categories and Proportions within Each

Source: P. Flood, T. Turner, and P. Willman, "A Segmented Model of Union Participation," Industrial Relations, 39 (2000), p. 110. Reprinted with permission from Blackwell Publishing.

Reluctant members	"I would only be a member because I have to be. I would not be in the union otherwise."	22%
Card carriers	"I don't mind being a member, but I don't have any interest in union activities."	30%
Selective activists	"Most of the time I don't get involved with the union, but I am more active on special issues."	26%
Apolitical stalwarts	"I am a loyal and active member, but I am not interested in the socialist aspects of the labor movement."	15%
Ideological activists	"I am an active member and see my involvement in the union as an extension of my political ideological beliefs."	7%

role involves both sets of activities when enrolling union members and encouraging involvement in ongoing union activities and when processing grievances and preparing for contract negotiations.

It is to the union's benefit if employees develop pro-union attitudes because these predict greater involvement in union activities and commitment to union goals. All else being equal, greater commitment increases the union's economic and political effectiveness. A study of members of a large general trade union in Ireland found that member orientation toward the union could be divided into five categories and that involvement in union activities was systematically related to which category a union member fell into.[13] Table 5.2 displays the union orientations found in the study. Less than half of the members are union activists. Table 5.3 shows the difference in participation rates associated with membership in various categories of orientation to the union. More positive

[13] P. Flood, T. Turner, and P. Willman, "A Segmented Model of Union Participation," *Industrial Relations*, 39 (2000), pp. 108–114.

TABLE 5.3 Membership Participation by Category and Activity

Source: P. Flood, T. Turner, and P. Willman, "A Segmented Model of Union Participation," Industrial Relations, 39 (2000), p. 111. Reprinted with permission from Blackwell Publishing.

	Proportion of Each Category Involved					
Union Activities	**Reluctant Members**	**Card Carriers**	**Selective Activists**	**Apolitical Stalwarts**	**Ideological Activists**	**Overall % of Members Involved**
Vote (on contracts)	71%	75%	80%	92%	88%	81%
Attend workplace meetings	13	18	25	36	46	24
Participate in electing steward	48	55	68	69	73	62
Raise grievance more than three times with steward	22	13	20	35	49	24
Speak at meetings more than three times	2	3	9	19	27	9
Attend a union annual general meeting	7	13	15	44	41	20
Canvass for the union	7	11	17	42	61	21
Mean participation*	17	19	26	41	50	

*Mean participation for all activities, excluding voting in pay ballots, for each participation category.

attitudes toward the union increase willingness to participate and, in turn, union power.

Another study found that union participation was predicted by willingness to work for the union and leadership of the member's shop steward. Willingness to work for the union was predicted by loyalty and feelings of responsibility to the union. Responsibility was predicted by union loyalty and Marxist work beliefs, while union loyalty was predicted by subjective norms about unions, the perceived instrumentality of the union in gaining important outcomes, first-year socialization into the union, and shop steward leadership. Subjective norms are the individual's beliefs about how important referents, such as friends and family, feel about unions. Participation in union activities, in turn, was associated with lower intrinsic and extrinsic job satisfaction. Marxist work beliefs also independently contributed to lower feelings of satisfaction.[14] Figure 5.1 displays the model and the relationships between components. Later research suggests that low job satisfaction predicts participation only in adversarial labor

[14] E. K. Kelloway and J. Barling, "Members' Participation in Local Union Activities: Measurement, Prediction, and Replication," *Journal of Applied Psychology*, 78 (1993), pp. 262–279.

FIGURE 5.1 Predictors of Union Participation

Source: Adapted from E. K. Kelloway and J. Barling, "Members' Participation in Local Union Activities: Measurement, Prediction, and Replication," *Journal of Applied Psychology*, 78 (1993), p. 274.

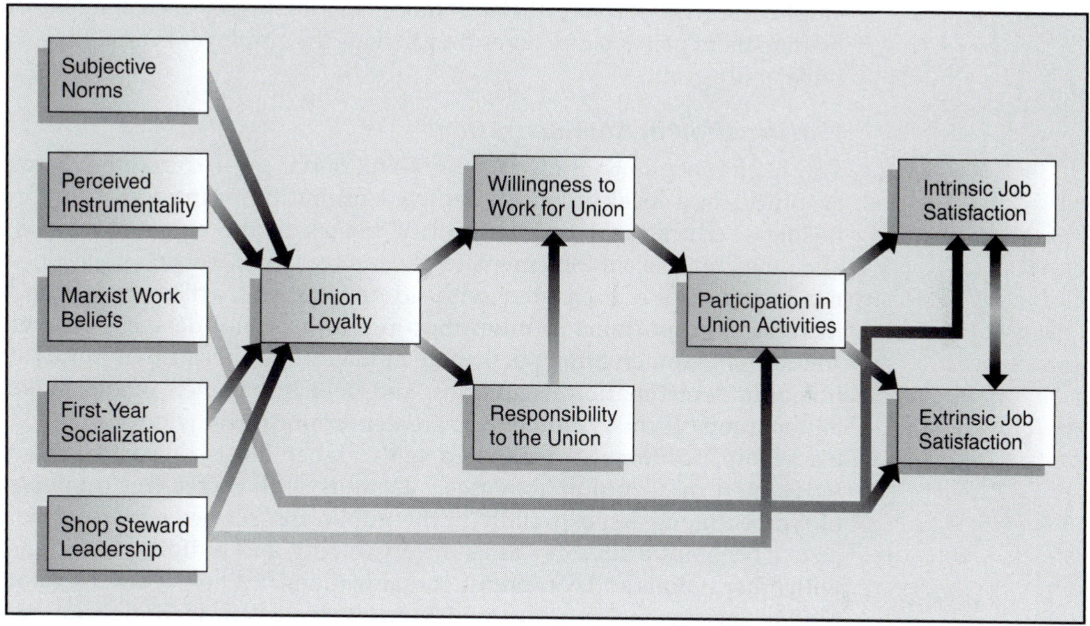

relations climates.[15] As we will discuss in Chapter 6, some components predicting participation in the union also predict a willingness to vote for the union in representation elections.

It's important to note the negative relationship between union participation and job satisfaction measures as moderated by labor relations climate. Union activists tend to be less satisfied with their employment. A poor work climate is often necessary to trigger organizing activity. Those who are most dissatisfied with their employer can be expected to put in the most effort to change the situation if quitting is not a viable option. One study of unionized schoolteachers found those who were satisfied with their jobs and participated in union activities were less likely to quit. Teachers who had low job satisfaction but who were strong participants in their union were also less likely to leave.[16] Even with low job satisfaction,

[15] Fuller and Hester, "The Effects of Labor Relations Climate on the Union Participation Process."

[16] R. D. Iverson and D. B. Currivan, "Union Participation, Job Satisfaction, and Employee Turnover: An Event-History Analysis of the Exit-Voice Hypothesis," *Industrial Relations*, 42 (2003), pp. 101–105.

continued employment is necessary to engage in local union activities; thus it's rational for a dissatisfied employee who is strongly interested in union participation not to quit. Activism is usually greater among employees who perceive that the union will be highly instrumental in helping them gain job outcomes they believe the employer is unwilling to unilaterally grant.

Participation in Administration

The likelihood that union members will serve on a committee or as an officer in a local union is predicted primarily by interest in union business, educational level, seniority, beliefs in the value of unions, and low intrinsic involvement in their jobs.[17] A member's race does not appear to be associated with administrative participation,[18] and increasing proportions of minorities in a unit do not decrease worker solidarity.[19] Women often participate at lower rates because of duties at home, underestimation of abilities, and beliefs that men would make better union officers.[20] However, a greater proportion of women in union leadership positions is associated with higher levels of participation by women in all union activities.[21] In units with increasing numbers of women members, especially in the public and service sectors, social justice becomes a stronger basis for organizing and building coalitions with other unions and community organizations.[22] Where work does not require decision making, the union is an alternate vehicle for developing and demonstrating leadership. Strong participation in union activities often stems from being raised in a union tradition and having a liberal political orientation.

Participation and Satisfaction

There is likely a U-shaped relationship between satisfaction with the union and participation in union activities, with participation being higher among members who express dissatisfaction but also higher among

[17] S. L. McShane, "The Multidimensionality of Union Participation," *Journal of Occupational Psychology*, 59 (1986), pp. 177–187.

[18] M. M. Hoyman and L. Stallworth, "Participation in Local Unions: A Comparison of Black and White Members," *Industrial and Labor Relations Review*, 40 (1987), pp. 323–335.

[19] R. Hodson, "Do Racially Mixed Work Forces Undermine Worker Solidarity and Resistance?" *Proceedings of the Industrial Relations Research Association*, 46 (1994), pp. 239–246.

[20] G. N. Chaison and P. Andiappan, "An Analysis of the Barriers to Women Becoming Local Union Officers," *Journal of Labor Research*, 10 (1989), pp. 149–162.

[21] S. Mellor, "Gender Composition and Gender Representation in Local Unions: Relationships between Women's Participation in Local Office and Women's Participation in Local Activities," *Journal of Applied Psychology*, 80 (1995), pp. 706–720.

[22] L. Briskin, "Cross-Constituency Organizing in Canadian Unions," *British Journal of Industrial Relations*, 46 (2008), pp. 221–247.

members who indicate their union is effective in achieving member goals and is interested in both intrinsic and extrinsic goals of members.[23] Local union leaders have lower job satisfaction than nonparticipating members. They also report more stress and higher ambiguity and conflict due to their union roles.[24]

Participation and Other Factors

Participation depends on a variety of environmental factors. The union's willingness to encourage democracy appears to be greater when it is not faced with a hostile employer. Political processes may be more active in larger unions, but rank-and-file participation declines for many activities. Opportunities for involvement decrease because local membership expands more rapidly than the number of local leadership positions.

As noted in Chapter 4, local union member participation in activities tends to be greater for contract and other employment issues than for union administration. Over time, participation may be decreased by bureaucratization of union activities through the administration of the contract. The contract spells out how most disputes will be handled. Negotiation committees are established within the local to decide how to deal with disputes that aren't immediately resolved. Unless committees fail to operate to the satisfaction of the rank and file, there is little need for members to be involved because the union is fulfilling its role as the employee's bargaining agent. If significant numbers of present members are replaced by new employees with different value systems, and there is no strong effort to orient them to the union, then increased participation is likely and bureaucratic structures would be deinstitutionalized.[25]

Commitment to the Union

Commitment to the union involves a psychological investment in its goals. Commitment is behaviorally reflected in participating, espousing union goals, and persuading others to join and work toward those goals. Commitment is reflected not only in the pursuit of specific local goals but also in the overall goals of the union movement.

[23] T. I. Chacko, "Member Participation in Union Activities: Perceptions of Union Priorities, Performance, and Satisfaction," *Journal of Labor Research,* 6 (1985), pp. 363–373. See also D. G. Gallagher and G. Strauss, "Union Membership Attitudes and Participation," in G. Strauss, D. G. Gallagher, and J. Fiorito, eds., *The State of the Unions* (Madison, WI: Industrial Relations Research Association, 1991), pp. 139–174.

[24] E. K. Kelloway and J. Barling, "Industrial Relations Stress and Union Activism: Costs and Benefits of Participation," *Proceedings of the Industrial Relations Research Association,* 46 (1994), pp. 442–451.

[25] V. G. Devinatz, "A Study in the Development of Trade Union Bureaucratization: The Case of UAW Local 6, 1941–1981," *Proceedings of the Industrial Relations Research Association,* 44 (1992), pp. 450–457.

Where membership is voluntary, commitment to the union is facilitated by early involvement and socialization in union activities, such as new-member orientation programs, communications to members, and continued participation by members.[26] Pro-union attitudes are a strong predictor of union commitment, which, in turn, predicts participation, but less strongly. Job satisfaction predicts commitment to the employer, which, all else being equal, predicts union commitment as well. Union instrumentality perceptions are a predictor of pro-union attitudes. Thus attitudes predict commitment and participation, and how effective the union is in accomplishing important worker goals reinforces this commitment.[27] Interactional justice perceptions—that is, how the member sees the relationships between leaders and members and how fairly "in" and "out" groups are dealt with—the effectiveness of the grievance procedure, and communications from the national union predict union support and, in turn, union commitment.[28] Figure 5.2 portrays an empirically based model of commitment.

While correlated, commitment and satisfaction are not the same construct. In the 1980s, many local unions faced major crises as plants closed or large layoffs took place. Commitment to the union was positively related to the severity of job loss, indicating an increase in cohesion during a crisis. At the same time, satisfaction with both the company and the union declined more in situations where severe job loss occurred.[29]

In employment, one might think of the employer and the union competing for employee commitment to goals and objectives. Over the last 20 years, employers have increasingly designed and implemented employee involvement programs (EIPs, covered in detail in Chapter 13) that increase employee participation in decision making in the workplace. Does workplace participation negatively affect member commitment to the union? One study indicated that attitudes toward participation did not affect union commitment. Experience with participation appeared to

[26] S. Kuruvilla, D. G. Gallagher, and K. Wetzel, "The Development of Members' Attitudes toward Their Unions: Sweden and Canada," *Industrial and Labor Relations Review*, 46 (1993), pp. 499–514.

[27] P. A. Bamberger, A. N. Kluger, and R. Suchard, "The Antecedents and Consequences of Union Commitment: A Meta Analysis," *Academy of Management Journal*, 42 (1999), pp. 304–318; and L. E. Tetrick, L. M. Shore, L. N. McClurg, and R. V. Vandenberg, "A Model of Union Participation: The Impact of Perceived Union Support, Union Instrumentality, and Union Loyalty," *Journal of Applied Psychology*, 92 (2007), pp. 820–828.

[28] J. B. Fuller, Jr., and K. Hester, "A Closer Look at the Relationship between Justice Perceptions and Union Participation," *Journal of Applied Psychology*, 86 (2001), pp. 1096–1105; and P. C. Morrow and J. C. McElroy, "Union Loyalty Antecedents: A Justice Perspective," *Journal of Labor Research*, 27 (2006), pp. 75–87.

[29] S. Mellor, "The Relationship between Membership Decline and Union Commitment: A Field Study of Local Unions in Crisis," *Journal of Applied Psychology*, 75 (1990), pp. 258–267.

FIGURE 5.2 **A Model of Union Commitment Antecedents and Consequences**

Source: Adapted from P. A. Bamberger, A. N. Kluger, and R. Suchard, "The Antecedents and Consequences of Union Commitment: A Meta-Analysis," *Academy of Management Journal*, 42 (1999), p. 307.

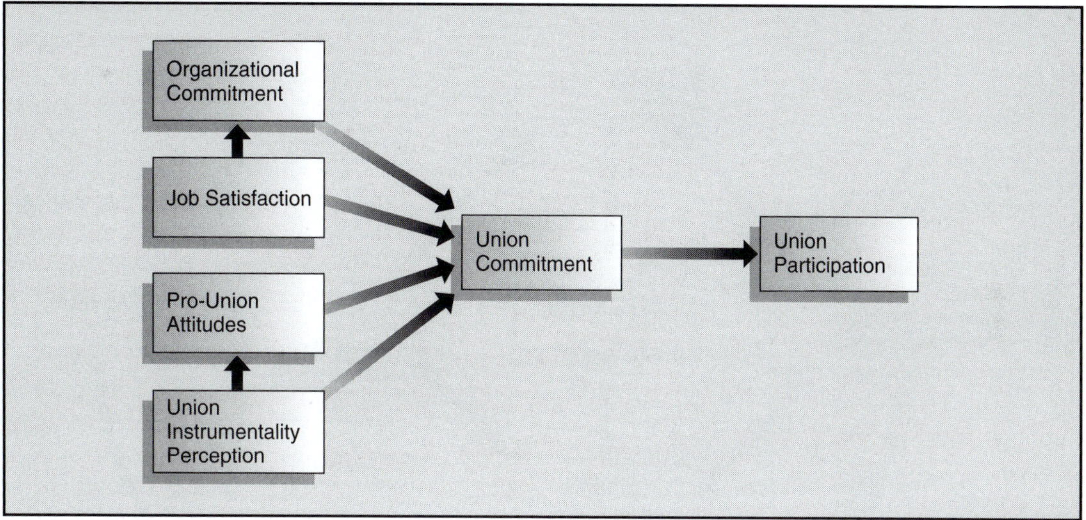

be associated with increased union commitment, but organizational and union commitment were negatively related.[30] A study of British workers across a number of employers found that the desire for unionization decreases in firms that have implemented EIPs.[31]

Dual Commitment

In unionized employment, an individual is simultaneously an employee and a union member. To which does the person owe his or her allegiance? Or can a person serve two masters? Commitment to the union and the employer has been found to be independent.[32] The suggested antecedents of **dual commitment** are shown in Figure 5.3. Dual commitment appears to be related both to individual differences[33] and to a

[30] R. C. Hoell, "How Employee Involvement Affects Union Commitment," *Journal of Labor Research*, 25 (2004), pp. 267–278.

[31] C. R. Belfield and J. S. Heywood, "Do HRM Practices Influence the Desire for Unionization? Evidence across Workers, Workplaces, and Co-Workers for Great Britain," *Journal of Labor Research*, 25 (2004), pp. 279–299.

[32] B. Bemmels, "Dual Commitment: Unique Construct or Epiphenomenon?" *Journal of Labor Research*, 16 (1995), pp. 401–422.

[33] C. V. Fukami and E. W. Larson, "Commitment to Company and Union: Parallel Models," *Journal of Applied Psychology*, 69 (1984), pp. 367–371.

FIGURE 5.3 Antecedents of Dual Commitment

Source: Adapted from B. Bemmels, "Dual Commitment: Unique Construct or Epiphenomenon?" *Journal of Labor Research*, 16 (1995), p. 405.

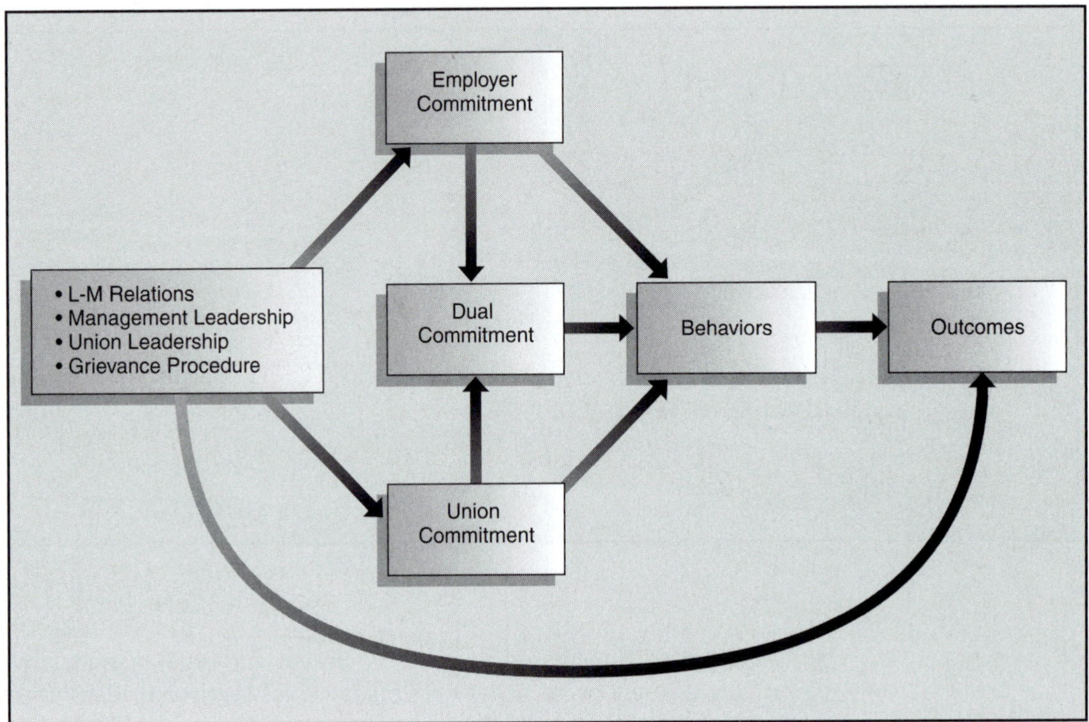

positive labor relations climate.[34] Involvement in union activities is related to higher commitment to both union and employer.[35] Commitment is also higher where employees perceive they have greater job influence and where an active, cooperative labor-management program is operating.[36] Higher commitment to employers among involved local union members should be expected, since their local union activities depend on continued local membership, which most often depends on continued employment with the represented employer.

[34] H. L. Angle and J. L. Perry, "Dual Commitment and Labor-Management Climates," *Academy of Management Journal*, 29 (1986), pp. 31–50.

[35] C. Fullager and J. Barling, "Predictors and Outcomes of Different Patterns of Organizational and Union Loyalty," *Journal of Occupational Psychology*, 64 (1991), pp. 129–144.

[36] P. D. Sherer and M. Morishima, "Roads and Roadblocks to Dual Commitment: Similar and Dissimilar Antecedents of Union and Company Commitment," *Journal of Labor Research*, 10 (1989), pp. 311–330.

Local Union Effectiveness and Member Behavior

Unions are effective if they are able to attain goals salient to their members. One study of public sector local unions identified five dimensions of union activities assumed to be associated with effectiveness: (1) member participation, (2) preparations for future negotiations, (3) involvement in political and civil activities, (4) a union mentality, and (5) the union's leadership. Holding other factors constant, political involvement in the union was related to the relative percentage of employees organized and the size of wage increases.[37]

THE INDIVIDUAL AS A UNION OFFICER

In the local union, an individual might hold an executive office such as president or secretary-treasurer, be a member of a standing committee such as the negotiating committee, or be a steward in a work unit.

Stewards

In most locals stewards are either appointed or elected. Stewards are directly responsible for advocating positions of work-group members and also responsible to higher union officers for communicating information and leaders' positions to work-unit members. Turnover is relatively high. If either the work-unit members or the leadership is dissatisfied with the steward's performance, he or she is likely to be replaced.

Stewards reduce stress in the work unit by acting as buffers between management and workers.[38] Unresolved stress is related to dissatisfaction with the union.[39] Stewards gain power by solving problems with work-unit supervisors, not from formal rights in the contract. Private sector stewards often have more power than those in the public sector because managers have more latitude to make decisions.[40]

Stewards who are interested in co-workers and committed to union goals have less role conflict between their positions as employees and union representatives than do individuals who are stewards for personal reasons.[41] Stewards in the former category are probably less worried that

[37] T. H. Hammer and D. L. Wazeter, "Dimensions of Local Union Effectiveness," *Industrial and Labor Relations Review*, 46 (1993), pp. 302–319.

[38] Y. Fried and R. B. Tiegs, "The Main Effect Model versus Buffering Model of Shop Steward Social Support: A Study of Rank-and-File Auto Workers in the U.S.A.," *Journal of Organizational Behavior*, 14 (1993), pp. 481–494.

[39] G. S. Lowe and H. C. Northcott, "Stressful Working Conditions and Union Dissatisfaction," *Relations Industrielles*, 50 (1995), pp. 420–442.

[40] P. A. Simpson, "A Preliminary Investigation of Determinants of Local Union Steward Power," *Labor Studies Journal*, 18, no. 2 (1993), pp. 51–68.

[41] J. E. Martin and R. D. Berthiaume, "Stress and the Union Steward's Role," *Journal of Occupational Behavior*, 14 (1993), pp. 433–446.

internal union politics will affect their future leadership opportunities in the union.

The local is interested in the steward's ability to adjust grievances with management, to communicate with work-unit members, and to enhance members' commitment and participation. Grassroots training for stewards influences interaction with and transmission of information to rank-and-file employees.[42] Stewards who receive training on organizational citizenship are more supportive of the union as an organization and are better able to address and support the needs of co-workers.[43]

Successfully recruiting minorities and women into steward positions in predominantly white, male-majority locals appears to require one-on-one contact, persuasion, and mentoring.[44] In turn, successful recruiting should lead to more integrated rank-and-file involvement.

Dual Commitment of Stewards

The steward's dual situation as both a full-time company employee and the work unit's employee representative for grievances against the employer is paradoxical. Is the steward committed to the union, the employer, or both? A study of about 200 stewards at one employer found about 80 percent were committed to the union, 36 percent were committed to the employer, and 12 percent were committed to neither. Union commitment was related to a perceived lack of job opportunities, a belief that the union should use grievances to punish the employer, involvement in union activities and decision making, and employment in larger establishments. Unilateral commitment to the union was predicted by low economic outcomes, perceived involvement in the union, and lack of support from the employer. Commitment to the employer was predicted by tenure; perceptions of a lack of outside job opportunities; supervisor support, promotion opportunities, and influence on the employer; and employment in smaller establishments.

Almost 30 percent of stewards were committed to the union and the employer simultaneously. Dual commitment was related to stewards' positive perceptions about the employer's supervisors, promotional opportunities, and the union's influence on the employer; positive beliefs about the union's decision-making process; a perceived lack of outside job opportunities; and beliefs that the grievance procedure is not a tool to punish supervisors. High dual commitment was predicted by involvement in

[42] J. W. Thacker and M. W. Fields, "An Evaluation of Steward Training," *Proceedings of the Industrial Relations Research Association*, 44 (1992), pp. 432–439.

[43] D. P. Skarlicki and G. P. Latham, "Increasing Citizenship Behavior within a Labor Union: A Test of Organizational Justice Theory," *Journal of Applied Psychology*, 81 (1996), pp. 161–169.

[44] P. A. Roby, "Becoming Shop Stewards: Perspectives on Gender and Race in Ten Trade Unions," *Labor Studies Journal*, 20, no. 3 (1995), pp. 65–82.

union decision making, perceived lack of outside job opportunities, influence on the employer, being a woman, and being unskilled.[45]

Local Officers

Local officers are elected by local union members. In locals with a single bargaining unit, elections are often strongly affected by collective bargaining issues. One study concludes that an incumbent local president is more likely to be reelected the higher the loyalty of local union members, the higher the confidence in the grievance procedure, the greater the satisfaction with the contract, and the better perceived the labor-management relations climate.[46] Dissatisfaction with bargaining outcomes is related to the election of insurgent candidates. Union politics are more complicated when the local negotiates several contracts. This often occurs in Railway Labor Act jurisdictions since the act requires bargaining units based on occupation. If the local represents several occupations, the numerically dominant occupation is likely to elect the officers. Where no occupation constitutes a majority, coalitions will develop depending on their perceptions of how local officers are achieving important outcomes for them.

Another situation occurs when the local union has contracts with several employers. As in the single-employer situation, if the employees of one employer constitute a majority, they are likely to elect officers from their group. On the other hand, if there are a number of bargaining units, to avoid the possibility of shifting coalitions, union officers would probably attempt to negotiate a multiemployer agreement to reduce internal political pressures, among other reasons. (We will cover multiemployer bargaining in Chapter 8.)

Differences also exist between occupational categories. Members with lower skills often form a majority. If they dominate the leadership and the negotiating committee, then the interests of skilled employees may not be addressed thoroughly. This creates internal pressure and may lead to tensions in the administration of the bargaining agreement (see the discussion of **fractional bargaining** in Chapter 14). Education and expertise help union members obtain leadership roles.[47] Thus, skilled employees may be overrepresented among the leadership relative to their numbers in the local as long as they pay attention to the bargaining interests of the majority.

[45] J. E. Martin, J. M. Magenau, and M. F. Peterson, "Variables Related to Patterns of Union Stewards' Commitment," *Journal of Labor Research*, 7 (1986), pp. 323–336.

[46] J. E. Martin and M. P. Sherman, "Voting in a Union Officer Election: Testing a Model in a Multi-Site Local," *Journal of Labor Research*, 26 (2005), pp. 281–297.

[47] See G. Strauss, "Union Democracy," in G. Strauss, D. G. Gallagher, and J. Fiorito, eds., *The State of the Unions* (Madison, WI: Industrial Relations Research Association, 1991), pp. 201–236.

Women and Minorities

As with the differences among bargaining units, identifiable subgroups within a local also may have interests in officer positions and may influence election results. In Chapter 6 we will discuss why minority group members are more interested in and likely to vote for representation. However, minorities in a local union may be underrepresented in officer positions if elections are on an at-large basis.

A study of Massachusetts local unions found that women were represented in officer positions at about the same rate as their proportion in the overall membership but that they were underrepresented as presidents or members of negotiation committees.[48] To the extent the negotiation committee influences the types of grievances pursued and decides on the issues of greatest importance in contract negotiations, women are concerned that they may not be receiving the degree of attention commensurate with their numbers in the local.[49]

Officer Commitment to the Labor Movement

Higher-level local union officers are generally granted leaves of absence from work in larger units, but they still remain attached to their employers, and they also bear responsibility to their national unions as well as to their local memberships. Local officers are committed strongly to the labor movement but are less positive about the fairness of national union elections than that of local elections. They are willing to advocate issues their national union favors, but they are more closely wedded to the traditional goals of the labor movement than to new approaches.[50]

NATIONAL UNIONS AND THEIR ENVIRONMENT

National unions are particularly interested in the environment for organizing, including the laws and regulations governing permissible activities for unions and employers, employment laws applying generally to workplaces and the administration and enforcement of those laws, and the state of the economy and the effect it has on the organizing and bargaining power of unions. One of the major vehicles for influencing all of these areas is political action, including lobbying, financial support for candidates, and assistance in election campaigns.

[48] D. Melcher, J. L. Eichstedt, S. Eriksen, and D. Clawson, "Women's Participation in Local Union Leadership: The Massachusetts Experience," *Industrial and Labor Relations Review*, 45 (1992), pp. 267–280.

[49] See also A. H. Cook, "Women and Minorities," in G. Strauss, D. G. Gallagher, and J. Fiorito, eds., *The State of the Unions* (Madison, WI: Industrial Relations Research Association, 1991), pp. 237–258.

[50] M. F. Masters, R. S. Atkin, and G. Schoenfeld, "A Survey of USWA Local Officers' Commitment-Support Attitudes," *Labor Studies Journal*, 15, no. 3 (1990), pp. 51–80.

Employment Law and Administration

Since the founding of the American Federation of Labor (AFL), the core of the American labor movement has taken a consistently business-oriented approach. As we noted in Chapter 1, its primary objectives have been to enhance the economic outcomes of its members and to create and maintain a mechanism for redressing grievances in the workplace.

The historic bargain between labor and management and the resulting laws and regulations have basically created a system in which unions have agreed to allow employers to make innovations in production while working to enhance economic outcomes for represented employees.[51] From a regulatory perspective, this means unions have been interested in creating an environment that facilitates the collectivization of labor to accomplish workplace goals. It has not intruded on the property rights of owners and managers and would be vigorously opposed by management if it did so.

Regulating Employer Decisions in the Workplace

Employers make hiring decisions without union involvement except when the union supplies workers, as in the building trades. Most unions have favored civil rights legislation requiring that employers make employment decisions without regard to race, gender, age, and national origin. At the same time, tensions may occur within national unions as the composition of the workforce changes. The leadership of national unions and the AFL-CIO tends to reflect the majority of members within each of the unions but not the proportion of members in various subgroups.

Unions have also strongly favored legislation regulating health and safety conditions, worker compensation for injuries incurred in the line of work, the payment of prevailing wages for government contract work, and unemployment insurance to compensate employees when they are involuntarily laid off. Extending these laws to all employers removes their cost from competition between employers within a given industry to some extent. However, a reduction in worker compensation and unemployment insurance costs for individuals would require lower incidences of injuries and layoffs.

The Economy

As we noted in Chapter 2, the state of the economy has historically influenced union outcomes. With the exception of the Great Depression, unions have traditionally had difficulty during economic downturns. Organizing has depended on the ability of unions to demonstrate the economic advantages they could provide to potential members. As we will note in

[51] D. Brody, "Labor's Crisis in Historical Perspective," in G. Strauss, D. G. Gallagher, and J. Fiorito, eds., *The State of the Unions* (Madison, WI: Industrial Relations Research Association, 1991), pp. 277–312.

Chapter 9, substantial evidence exists that unionization positively affects wages, but the radical restructuring that has occurred in the contemporary economy has reduced beliefs about its long-term ability to enhance job security.

To secure economic gains, either employee productivity must increase faster than wages and competitive labor costs, or employers must be able to pass labor cost increases on to consumers. With the advent of global competition, the latter is becoming increasingly difficult. Industries in which the largest wage premiums exist, relative to productivity, are potentially the most vulnerable. In addition, if workers in other locations (or countries) can immediately be made more productive by investing in more modern equipment that costs less than the future costs of expected union wages, then rational employers will send work to other locations as long as free trade is available.

Globalization and Organized Labor

One of the most important changes in the economic environment that labor unions have had to deal with is the increasing globalization of the production of goods and services. Globalization has been facilitated by a number of trade treaties (e.g., the North American Free Trade Agreement [NAFTA]), the creation and operation of the World Trade Organization (WTO) to police the imposition of tariffs higher than agreed to and the subsidization of goods and services to either maintain marginal producers or confer an export advantage, common currencies (e.g., the euro) or highly liquid currency trading markets, and the development and use of information technology to transmit data cheaply and securely.

In general, globalization is based on the premise that the prices of goods and services will fall if they are produced in the countries that have the resources to manufacture them at the highest productivity level (taking wage differences into account). So, for example, the cost of apparel and textiles has fallen in both real and nominal amounts for several years as cloth and wearing apparel have increasingly been manufactured in Southeast Asia, Africa, and the West Indies. Producers in these countries benefit by having access to broader markets that would like to take advantage of the lower prices they offer. At the same time, a large share of the U.S. textile industry has been forced out of business because it no longer can compete effectively.

Because industries tend to be concentrated where specific skills or resources are readily available, the effects of globalization are not distributed uniformly around the country. From an employment standpoint, some regions benefit and others suffer. Most of the U.S. textile industry has been located in the Carolinas and New England. The New England mills closed during the 1950s and 1960s as they became obsolete. The Carolina closings have been more recent, accompanied by frequent leveraged buyouts, wage cuts, and later bankruptcies as the price of imports continued to fall. The same scenario took place for steel workers in the rust belt (Pennsylvania, West Virginia, Ohio, Indiana, Illinois, and Wisconsin). On the other hand, employment opportunities in information technology, pharmaceuticals, finance and insurance, and entertainment increased more rapidly as export opportunities grew.

The declining industries happened to be primarily manufacturers that also were heavily unionized. The plant closings and layoffs had major effects on unionized employees. To the extent that skills were industry-specific, the closing of those industries meant that comparable job opportunities were unavailable, and workers did not have skills that matched existing employer needs. Pay levels in unionized employment are usually higher than those in comparable nonunion firms (see Chapter 9). Thus, workers were unlikely to secure a job earning nearly as much as they did before. Finally, since the industries tended to be concentrated in specific geographic regions, unemployment in those areas soared, housing values declined, and tax revenues for local infrastructure eroded.

Unions are also particularly concerned with so-called dumping by foreign manufacturers. Dumping occurs when goods are sold below their production costs. This happens most frequently in industries where there are high fixed costs, such as steel. Assume, for example, that the debt payments on a steel plant are $10 million per month. These costs are incurred whether it is operating or not. Assume further that for another $5 million in labor costs and $5 million for raw materials, the plant could produce steel that it could sell for $15 million in a given month. It would be operating at a $5 million loss, but this would be less than the $10 million loss it would incur if it shut down. Dumping increases the supply available in what is likely an already depressed market, further driving down prices and increasing the likelihood that domestic producers will not be able to survive. Where dumping is proved, tariffs are added to the price of dumped products to discourage the practice and even the playing field.

Another concern that unions have relates to labor standards. Over many decades, unions have fought for improved working conditions, particularly as they relate to health, safety, and hours of work. Foreign manufacturers in developing economies do not have these same requirements. Unions oppose the importation of goods and services that were produced in sweat shop conditions.

The labor movement has generally opposed the liberalization of trade policies, particularly where negotiated labor standards are not included in trade agreements. It has lobbied against ratification of trade treaties and directed financial resources and volunteer effort toward defeating members of Congress who support free trade initiatives. The labor movement has been largely unsuccessful to this point. The ratification and implementation of NAFTA provides a good example against which to examine union objections and efforts.

NAFTA and Organized Labor

Canada, Mexico, and the United States ratified NAFTA in 1993, substantially reducing tariffs on imports between them. NAFTA was negotiated by representatives of the three nations during the George H. W. Bush presidency and was placed on a fast-track process before he left office. President Salinas of Mexico was a strong supporter of NAFTA. Prime Minister Mulroney of Canada had earlier secured passage of a joint U.S. and Canadian pact and supported NAFTA as well. President Clinton also supported NAFTA during the 1992 campaign and after his inauguration.

Organized labor strongly opposed NAFTA. The congressional vote, in late summer 1993, was very close, with labor indicating that votes on the treaty would be considered "a litmus test" for continued labor endorsement and support. Political risks were great since Prime Minister Mulroney had resigned after the Conservative Party had been overwhelmingly defeated in Canadian elections, but NAFTA had been ratified there. Labor's position is reflected in Exhibit 5.1.

Ostensibly, labor opposed NAFTA because of a lack of environmental and employment safeguards in Mexico. Concerns were raised that a country's competitive advantage could be gained through lower costs resulting from not attending to worker welfare or implementing pollution controls. Fears regarding workers' abilities to unionize and to gain a voice in the workplace were also expressed.

A more fundamental concern had to do with the large gaps between U.S. and Canadian wages and Mexican wages. In 1990, using the United States as a base, Mexican hourly manufacturing compensation costs were only 12.5 percent of U.S. wages while Canadian wages were 7.5 percent above.[52] In labor-intensive industries, the substantial wage premium earned by U.S. and Canadian workers was seen by labor as likely to lead to a wholesale movement of jobs to Mexico. Thus, NAFTA put wages back into competition in industrial sectors where substantial success had been achieved in reducing differentials between employers.[53]

Political Action

Political action is very important to unions. As noted in Chapter 3, unions receive more favorable treatment from the National Labor Relations Board (NLRB) during Democratic administrations. Democrats in Congress are also more likely to promote legislation favored by labor unions and to appropriate funds for activities that unions support. Often, these positions

[52] U.S. Department of Labor, Bureau of Labor Statistics, *International Comparisons of Hourly Compensation Costs for Production Workers in Manufacturing*, Report 803 (Washington, DC: U.S. Government Printing Office, 1991).

[53] For positions of proponents and opponents of the treaty, and an appraisal of likely effects, see M. F. Bognanno and K. J. Ready, eds., *The North American Free Trade Agreement: Labor, Industry, and Government Perspectives* (Westport, CT: Praeger, 1993).

Exhibit 5.1

LABOR'S FRUSTRATION WITH NAFTA AND ITS FADING POLITICAL CLOUT

A month before Congress voted to ratify NAFTA, organized labor met in San Francisco to map its goals and strategies for the next two years. No political issue rose to the level of passion that labor leaders expressed about NAFTA. Calling it a litmus test of support for labor, leaders vowed to end contributions and campaign work for any member of Congress who voted to ratify the treaty. They saw it as a life or death issue that strikes at the wages and employment security of their members—particularly in manufacturing and garment making.

In November, the House of Representatives voted 234 to 200 for ratification, with 132 of 175 Republicans in favor as compared with 102 of 258 Democrats. In the Senate, the margin was greater with 27 of 55 Democrats in favor as compared with 34 of 44 Republicans (1 Democrat did not vote). Given labor's financial and grassroots support strategy, Republicans did not expect any negative effects from their votes, but Democrats had already been warned of the consequences of a "yea" vote.

What happened in the 1994 election? The Republicans swept into power (hardly a desired outcome for the labor movement) by taking 8 Democratic senate seats. Of those, 6 were in races where the Democratic incumbent was retiring. The other 2 were Democrats who had opposed NAFTA. Four Democrats who had voted for NAFTA were returned to Washington, but 4 who had voted against NAFTA lost their seats to Republicans. In the House, the Republicans scored a net gain of 54 seats. Of 102 Democrats who voted for NAFTA, 16 were defeated for reelection in 1994; 13 others did not seek reelection. Of the 156 who voted against, 19 were defeated for reelection in 1994 while an additional 8 did not seek reelection.

William H. Bywater, president of the electrical workers and organized labor's most outspoken foe of the agreement, said, "We're going to go out and defeat every congressman who votes for NAFTA."

Leaders of the big teamsters and machinists unions are saying much the same. George J. Kourpias, president of the machinists union, said he had not yet issued ultimatums against lawmakers who vote for NAFTA. "But," he added, "I can tell you, we will get no requests from our members back home to support them. They're steamed up about this." George Poulin, a machinists vice president in the Northeast who is also here, said: "Knock them off. That's our position."

Source: P. T. Kilborn, "Unions Gird for War over Trade Pact," *The New York Times*, October 4, 1993, p. A14.

are opposed by various segments of the business community. Both sides are vigorously involved in both electoral politics and lobbying.

In the current political environment, candidates for elected positions need to raise substantial amounts of money, among other things, to mount a successful campaign. Union- and corporate-based political action committees (PACs) raised and disbursed almost $500 million in support of candidates and issues in 2000. The scope of these activities during the 2000 campaign cycle was the catalyst for the Bipartisan Campaign Reform

Act (McCain-Feingold) passed in 2002. The intent of the legislation was to reduce the influence of special interests in fund-raising and last-minute attack advertising. Opponents of the legislation believed that it abridged first amendment free speech rights. In January 2010, the Supreme Court found that the BCRA violated the First Amendment and struck down the prohibition on financing issue-oriented campaign speeches by corporations and unions.[54]

Financing for political campaigns and issue-oriented campaign speech come from a variety of sources. Individuals can contribute up to a total of $115,500 over each two-year federal election cycle toward candidates and political parties at the national, state, district, and local levels. Corporations and unions can form PACs that aggregate donations from employees or members that in turn donate funds to candidates and issues. Individuals, companies, and unions can also form and/or donate money to advocacy organizations operating within the requirements of Section 527 of the Internal Revenue Code that use the funds for voter mobilization drives, issue advertising, and publicize candidates' records and/or qualifications.

In the 2010 congressional election cycle, over $1.6 billion was donated to candidates and parties, with Democrats receiving 49 percent and Republicans 46 percent of the total. About 76 percent of total contributions came from businesses (including employee contributions) with 49 percent going to Democrats and 46 percent to Republicans. Five percent of total donations came from labor groups with 74 percent allocated to Democrat and 5 percent to Republican candidates. Across all campaigns, Republican-oriented 527s spent 50.4 percent of the total of party-oriented expenditures. For congressional campaigns only, Democratic-oriented 527s spent 63 percent of the total across the party-oriented organizations.[55]

Union political action takes four basic forms: (1) financial support to candidates favoring union positions, (2) volunteer work by union members in campaigns, (3) endorsement of candidates and get-out-the-vote efforts, and (4) lobbying. Major union sources of financial support come from union PACs and union-sponsored 527 organizations. During the 2010 election campaign, the largest union-associated 527 organization expenditures were $15.5 million by the SEIU, $7.5 million by the NEA, $6.7 by the IBEW, $4.3 by the Laborers, and $3.5 by the United Food and Commercial Workers (UFCW). The majority of 527 expenditures by all types of interest groups were made to develop and air advertisements in opposition to specific candidates. Union PACs contributed $59 million to congressional candidates in 2010, with $55 million going to Democrats.[56] At the state level, unions that represent public sector employees are strong

[54] *Citizens United* v. *Federal Elections Commission*, 558 U.S. ___ (2010).

[55] Data collected by www.opensecrets.org from Federal Election Commission reports.

[56] Ibid.

financial supporters of candidates for office, particularly for incumbents who support labor's position and against incumbents who oppose labor and appear vulnerable.

In general, union members are more politically conservative than their leaders, and a substantial minority (between 20 and 40 percent) believes that unions should not be overtly involved in politics. While more politically conservative, union members also believe that their unions should have the right to use union-generated funds to support chosen political positions.[57] Given the increase in single-issue politics, labor's position is weakened by a variety of internal factions organized around these issues.[58] However, political action by public sector unions, particularly at the state and local levels, has been effective. Evidence indicates that greater political activity by public sector unions is positively related to higher public sector salary levels and more public employment jobs.[59]

Financial Support for Candidates

Union Characteristics Unions make choices about how to best deploy resources. National union political activities have increased markedly, particularly among unions representing public employers and those in which executive boards are democratically chosen.[60] Medium-sized unions spend more per capita on political action than smaller or larger unions, and spending increases as dues increase. Political spending across all labor organizations is about 4 percent of total dues. Unions representing employees in the public sector allocate the greatest proportion of dues toward political activity (e.g., American Federation of State, County, and Municipal Employees [AFSCME], 25 percent; International Association of Fire Fighters [IAFF], 17 percent; American Federation of Government Employees [AFGE] and Service Employees International Union [SEIU], 12 percent; American Federation of Teachers [AFT], 11 percent; and National Education Association [NEA], 9 percent).[61] The proportion of women in a national is also related to political activity expenditures, although evidence suggests there is less political activity than members desire.[62]

57 P. F. Clark, "Using Members' Dues for Political Purposes: The 'Paycheck Protection' Movement," *Journal of Labor Research*, 20 (1999), pp. 329–342.

58 J. T. Delaney, "The Future of Unions as Political Organizations," *Journal of Labor Research*, 12 (1991), pp. 373–387.

59 K. M. O'Brien, "Compensation, Employment, and the Political Activity of Public Employee Unions," *Journal of Labor Research*, 13 (1992), pp. 189–203.

60 M. F. Masters and J. T. Delaney, "The Causes of Union Political Involvement," *Journal of Labor Research*, 6 (1985), pp. 341–362.

61 M. F. Masters, R. Gibney, and T. J. Zagenczyk, "Worker Pay Protection: Implications for Labor's Political Spending and Voice," *Industrial Relations*, 48 (2009), pp. 557–577.

62 J. T. Delaney, J. Fiorito, and M. F. Masters, "The Effects of Union Organizational and Environmental Characteristics on Union Political Action,"*American Journal of Political Science*, 32 (1988), pp. 616–642.

In general, political contributions by rank-and-file members are quite modest. Local union officers contribute substantially more, with donations from officers with longer tenure, more education, higher income, greater willingness to support the union, and residence in a non-right-to-work law state predicting the magnitude.[63]

Candidate Characteristics Union PAC contributions and 527 activities are not evenly distributed across candidates, even when endorsements are taken into account. One factor that strongly influences the level of support is the committee assignment of Congress members. Those who are on committees with jurisdiction over labor matters receive higher contributions.[64]

Support for candidates for reelection is related directly to roll-call voting records.[65] Support appears to depend on the willingness of the organization to give, the compatibility of the candidate's ideology with that of the supporting union, the probability of the candidate's winning (with more given when the race is close), and the magnitude of the vote margin the candidate had in the last election (if an incumbent).[66] Support is related to the closeness of an incumbent's committee assignment to interests of labor, voting record, and electoral security.[67]

Endorsements and Get-Out-the-Vote Drives

Political endorsements and get-out-the-vote campaigns are valuable to candidates. Union members vote more often in general elections than do nonmembers (or their own family members), and they vote for endorsed candidates about 15 to 20 percent more often than nonmembers do. But union members do not vote more often in primaries, and about half split their votes between endorsed and unendorsed candidates.[68] The effects of union membership on voting are stronger for members with lower incomes, lower education levels, and working in situations with higher income inequality. State right-to-work laws and the lack of ability for public sector employees to bargain collectively lower these effects.

[63] M. F. Masters and R. S. Atkin, "Local Officers' Donations to a Political Action Committee," *Relations Industrielles*, 51 (1996), pp. 40–61.

[64] J. W. Endersby and M. C. Munger, "The Impact of Legislator Attributes on Union PAC Campaign Contributions," *Journal of Labor Research*, 13 (1992), pp. 79–97.

[65] G. M. Saltzman, "Congressional Voting on Labor Issues: The Role of PACs," *Industrial and Labor Relations Review*, 40 (1987), pp. 163–179.

[66] A. Wilhite and J. Theilmann, "Unions, Corporations, and Political Campaign Contributions: The 1982 House Elections," *Journal of Labor Research*, 7 (1986), pp. 175–186.

[67] K. B. Grier and M. C. Munger, "The Impact of Legislator Attributes on Interest-Group Campaign Contributions," *Journal of Labor Research*, 7 (1986), pp. 349–359.

[68] J. T. Delaney, M. F. Masters, and S. Schwochau, "Unionism and Voter Turnout," *Journal of Labor Research*, 9 (1988), pp. 221–236; and J. T. Delaney, M. F. Masters, and S. Schwochau, "Union Membership and Voting for COPE-Endorsed Candidates," *Industrial and Labor Relations Review*, 43 (1990), pp. 621–635.

Turnout is more strongly affected by unions than persuading union members to vote for endorsed candidates.[69]

When endorsements are given, organized labor almost always supports Democratic Party candidates. Some commentators argue that because of the almost exclusive endorsement and funding of Democratic candidates, labor has no leverage to demand support of its most important issues. But labor can use its power in regard to which candidates are chosen to run through its work in primary elections and party caucuses. In addition, get-out-the-vote drives depend on labor support to be effective. Labor's willingness and enthusiasm to work on these drives varies with its beliefs that the candidate will actually forward its agenda.[70]

Labor's success in mobilizing voting for endorsed candidates has increased recently. Between 1992 and 2004, union coverage in households declined from 17.7 to 14.9 percent, but the proportion of union voting households increased from 19 to 22 percent as a percentage of total voters.[71] In the 2000 presidential campaign, several local central bodies intensively worked on increasing voting in their congressional districts. Evidence indicated that the effort had some effectiveness in increasing turnout, especially in increasing voting rates among minorities and those describing themselves as members of the working class. Persons who believe there are real differences between the positions of the Democratic and Republican Parties are much more likely to vote.[72] The incremental effects of voter mobilization efforts seem to be greatest on occasional voters rather than those who frequently or never vote. Personal visits and phone calls seem to be the most successful tactics, and in a Los Angeles sample, were most effective with Latino voters.[73] Given the currently low rate of unionization, unless union political advocacy simultaneously appeals to and energizes a substantial fraction of nonunion households, it is unlikely to have significant effects on electoral outcomes.

Table 5.4 details voting of union members and nonmembers from 1952 through 2008. The data in this table indicate that union members are generally more active than nonmembers in both presidential election years and off-year elections, with higher votes in 22 of 25 elections and an average difference of about 5 percent. Union members are more likely than

[69] R. Zullo, "Union Membership and Political Inclusion," *Industrial and Labor Relations Review*, 62 (2008), pp. 22–38.

[70] T. E. Dark III, "To Reward and Punish: A Classification of Union Political Strategies," *Journal of Labor Research*, 24 (2003), pp. 457–472.

[71] R. Zullo, "Labor Council Outreach and Union Voter Turnout: A Microanalysis from the 2000 Election," *Industrial Relations*, 43 (2004), pp. 324–338.

[72] R. Zullo, "Union Cities and Voter Turnout," *Proceedings of the Labor and Employment Relations Association*, 58 (2006), pp. 193–205.

[73] J. R. Lemare, "The Interactive Effects of Labor-Led Political Mobilization and Vote Propensity on Turnout: Evidence from Five Elections," *Industrial Relations*, 49 (2010), pp. 616–639.

TABLE 5.4 Union and Nonunion Household Voting Behavior

	Union Households			Nonunion Households		
Year	Registered	Voted	% Democrat	Registered	Voted	% Democrat
1952	81	76	56	81	73	36
1954						
1956	84	76	53	81	72	36
1958		67			57	
1960	82	77	64	85	80	44
1962						
1964	88	83	83	86	76	62
1966		69			62	
1968	85	76	48	85	76	39
1970		60			59	
1972	92	75	43	90	72	33
1974		50			54	
1976	86	77	64	79	70	47
1978	76	57		71	54	
1980	82	75	51	78	71	36
1982	80	65		76	59	
1984	85	79	57	81	72	37
1986	76	55		73	52	
1988	82	75	59	80	69	44
1990	76	53		69	46	
1992	88	85	54	81	73	47
1994	86	65		74	54	
1996	90	82	68	85	71	50
1998	86	66		79	49	
2000	90	77	61	84	72	50
2002	90	62		86	63	
2004	95	90	64	88	77	46
2008	89	81	60	86	77	54

nonmembers to vote for Democratic presidential candidates. Voting in off-year elections is low by both union members and nonmembers. While the proportion of the workforce that is unionized has dropped, giving the union less voting power, the proportion of nonmembers who vote for Democratic presidential candidates has increased to somewhat offset the decline.

Lobbying

The AFL-CIO takes political positions on important employment issues such as civil rights, worker safety, and collective bargaining rights.[74] Unions also lobby for increased public spending on infrastructure projects

[74] For a comprehensive examination of these and other political representation issues, see J. Delaney and S. Schwochau, "Employee Representation through the Political Process," in B. E. Kaufman and M. M. Kleiner, eds., *Employee Representation: Alternatives and Future Directions* (Madison, WI: Industrial Relations Research Association, 1993), pp. 265–304.

accompanied by prevailing wage requirements that would boost opportunities for the employment of union members in the building trades. They also lobby to make it easier to organize workers by designating them as public employees. In Illinois, the SEIU was able to have a state agency declared the employer of record for home health care workers even though the workers are selected and managed by the client. Thus, the union has only to negotiate with the state agency and the clients become bound by the wages, terms, and conditions of employment agreed to between the agency and the union (SEIU) that has gained representation and bargaining rights.[75]

Business groups such as the Chamber of Commerce often oppose organized labor's positions.[76] Other politically oriented organizations such as the American Conservative Union and the Americans for Democratic Action (ADA) establish comprehensive agendas on a wide range of issues. Single-issue organizations such as the National Right-to-Work Committee also lobby and file amicus briefs in cases with significant possibilities of a precedent-setting decision.

Effectiveness of Activities

While unions are heavily involved in PAC and 527 activities, union members' attitudes are not monolithic and, in most cases, seem less liberal than the positions taken by their unions. Union political action appears to be more successful in influencing legislation in peripheral areas of interest (e.g., education) than in central areas of interest (e.g., labor law reform).[77] However, a study found that PAC contributions are related to votes for legislation supported by the AFL-CIO's **Committee on Political Education (COPE).** This study found other factors positively influencing pro-labor votes, including the percentage of the U.S. labor force that is unionized and the ADA rating of the senator. Factors negatively related included corporate PAC donations to the incumbent's election opponent, the percentage of the populace voting Republican in the most recent presidential election, the proportion of the labor force that is women, and being a Republican senator. Over time, increasing PAC contributions have more than offset the effect of the loss of union membership in influencing votes on legislation.[78]

[75] P. M. Mareschal, "Innovation and Adaptation: Contrasting Efforts to Organize Home Health Care Workers in Four States," *Labor Studies Journal*, 31, no. 1 (2006), pp. 25–49.

[76] D. Jacobs, "Labor and Social Legislation in the United States: Business Obstructionism and Accommodation," *Labor Studies Journal*, 23, no. 2 (1998), pp. 3–20.

[77] M. F. Masters and J. T. Delaney, "Union Political Activities: A Review of the Empirical Literature," *Industrial and Labor Relations Review*, 40 (1987), pp. 336–353.

[78] W. J. Moore, D. R. Chachere, T. D. Curtis, and D. Gordon, "The Political Influence of Unions and Corporations on COPE Votes in the U.S. Senate, 1979–1988," *Journal of Labor Research*, 16 (1995), pp. 203–221.

Use of Union Dues for Political Activity

Since the union acquires the exclusive right to represent employees and to negotiate contracts that include mandatory dues payment, members who hold political views different from those of union leaders may object to the union's allocating part of collected dues toward political activity. The Supreme Court has ruled that union members can request that their union dues be limited to the amount necessary to provide representational activities.[79] The federal government's enthusiasm for enforcing this ruling has waxed and waned depending on which party's administration was in power. In the public sector, so-called paycheck protection legislation or initiatives would require that unions get affirmative approval from each member before any portion of his or her dues be spent on political activity. In 2007, the U.S. Supreme Court ruled unanimously that Washington's law was a constitutional protection of members' First Amendment rights.[80] The movement, however, has failed to gain much political traction.

Summary

Union attention to new-member socialization leads to higher participation and commitment. Participation involves activities such as attending meetings; voting in union elections, strike authorizations, and contracting ratifications; and being a union officer. Loyalty to the union, Marxist work beliefs, and the perceived leadership of the steward influence participation. Persons who participate at higher rates are less satisfied with intrinsic and extrinsic factors of their job.

Commitment to the union is predicted by many of the same factors that influence participation. Evidence exists that members can be simultaneously committed to their unions and their employers. Studies of stewards have found that dual commitment is high when the steward had a good working relationship with the employer and believed that his or her career was strongly linked to a present employer.

Women and minorities participate at the same rate in union activities as do men and majority employees, but women are less likely found in high leadership positions. National unions are strongly involved in political activity, especially those representing employees in the public sector. While per capita support is relatively modest, legislators who are friendly to labor and who are on key committees likely to influence labor outcomes receive financial assistance. Since 1980, a majority of candidates elected to Congress have had AFL-CIO COPE endorsement. Union members vote at higher rates in general elections than does the public at large. They also are more likely to vote for Democratic candidates.

[79] *Communications Workers* v. *Beck*, 487 U.S. 735 (1988).

[80] *Davenport* v. *Washington Education Association*, 551 U.S. 177 (2007).

Discussion Questions

1. Do the predictors of union participation suggest that union leaders will likely be involved in an adversarial relationship with management?
2. How can the inclusion of women in top leadership positions in local and national unions be increased?
3. How can the facts that a majority of members of Congress are endorsed by COPE and that no significant labor law reform has been passed be reconciled?
4. Since unions represent all employees in bargaining units they have organized, should they be allowed to endorse particular candidates for office?

Key Terms

Agency fee, *127*
Union shop, *128*
Free riding, *129*
Dual commitment, *137*
Fractional bargaining, *141*
Committee on Political Education (COPE), *153*

Selected Web Sites

www.aflcio.org
www.brtable.org
www.changetowin.org
www.nam.org
www.npa1.org
www.nrtw.org
www.uschamber.com
Also try state AFL-CIO and central labor union Web sites.

Chapter **Six**

Union Organizing Campaigns

This chapter is the first of two chapters that examine how unions organize new bargaining units and how and why employers attempt to avoid being unionized. The chapter covers union organizing campaigns, the election process, and the roles of the National Labor Relations Board (NLRB) and the National Mediation Board (NMB). Chapter 7 covers employers' overall strategies for avoiding unionization and operating without unions.

Recall from Chapter 2 the long history of employer resistance to union organizing in the United States. In the mid-1930s the Wagner Act strongly facilitated and institutionalized collective bargaining as the preferred method for resolving workplace conflicts where employees chose it.

Recall also from the introductory chapters that employees become unionized only if a single union can demonstrate that a majority of employees in the unit desires representation. The concept of **exclusive representation** establishes a "winner-takes-all" outcome in representation elections. This requirement, which contributes to the adversarial relationship that exists between employers and unions, begins with an organizing campaign.

Organizing is highly adversarial and heavily regulated. Most employers actively resist. Union campaigns usually stress unfair treatment by employers, the lack of a forum for effectively voicing complaints, and the necessity of organizing to gain outcomes the employer should grant but won't without unionization. Organizing campaigns are waged intensively by both sides. The NLRB or NMB acts as a referee in the process. Where recognition disputes occur, the boards provide a forum for their settlement and rule on the permissibility of the parties' campaign conduct, if questioned. From a regulatory standpoint, this chapter focuses primarily on the NLRB's role since the preponderance of elections are conducted under its auspices.

Chapter 1 introduced some of the reasons that workers unionize. This chapter examines the flow of organizing campaigns, involvement of the labor boards, strategies and tactics used by employers and unions during election campaigns, and recent results in NLRB-monitored representation elections. Chapter 7 focuses in detail on employers' increasing interest in operating **"union-free"** and the strategies and tactics they use to avoid unionization.

In studying this chapter, consider the following questions:

1. At what points and in what ways are the labor boards involved in representation elections?
2. What strategies and tactics do employers and unions use during organizing campaigns?
3. What effects have employer campaign tactics had on union organizing success?
4. How successful are unions in organizing new units?
5. What new strategies are unions now using and how effective are they?

ORGANIZING AND UNION EFFECTIVENESS

Chapter 1 noted that unions create an opportunity through negotiated contracts for employees to have a voice in addressing workplace problems and effectively create a labor supply monopoly. Monopoly power generally leads to a union wage premium.

The ability to gain a wage premium depends on the proportion of an industry that is organized. This means that unions have a strong interest in organizing workers in industries and labor markets where nonunion competition reduces their monopoly power. However, with increasing globalization, eliminating nonunion competition is impossible.

Unions depend on members' dues to operate. More members create economies of scale. Thus the level and scope of member services are related to some extent to a union's size. Organizing new units, accreting expanded facilities, and merging with or absorbing other unions are all mechanisms used to expand membership and enhance union effectiveness. Strategies and tactics that increase the probability of success in organizing and maintaining majority status in existing units should lead to greater chances for effectiveness in bargaining and representation.

HOW ORGANIZING BEGINS

Campaigns to organize unrepresented workers begin at either the local or the national union level. National unions target specific employers or geographic areas and send professional organizers to encourage and assist local employees in unionizing. Sometimes organizers apply for jobs in the targeted firm to gain closer contact with employees. Employers cannot legally refuse to hire applicants based on union membership or concurrent union employment even if their primary purpose is to organize the workforce.[1] National union campaigns often occur if a unionized firm opens a new nonunion plant. The union representing employees in the firm's other plants campaigns to organize the new plant to maintain common employment practices across the firm. National organizing may also target nonunion firms in predominantly unionized industries. Most organizing begins at the local level when some employees decide they would be better off if they could bargain collectively with the employer.[2]

The Framework for Organizing

Organizing begins with an authorization card campaign and most often ends with the NLRB certifying the election results. Figure 6.1 presents a generalized sequence of the organizing events that will be described in the following sections. This section covers activities leading to a recognition request, petitions to the NLRB for elections, and elections in which bargaining-unit determination is uncontested. Subsequent sections examine bargaining-unit determination, the election campaign, and election certifications.

Authorization Card Campaign

An **authorization card** campaign tries to enroll employees in the union in the unit the union seeks to represent. Organizers contact employees individually to persuade them to sign cards authorizing the union to act as their agent in negotiating wages, hours, and terms and conditions of employment. Figure 6.2 shows an authorization card.

Recognition Requests

If a majority of employees the union is trying to organize signs authorization cards, the union can request recognition as the employees' bargaining agent. A union seldom requests recognition unless a substantial majority has signed because employers often question whether some workers are eligible to be represented or to vote in an election. Employers faced with a recognition request usually claim that the union's majority status is doubtful. The union may offer to have a neutral third party match the authorization card signatures with an employee list to determine whether a majority

[1] *NLRB* v. *Town & Country Electric Inc.*, 516 U.S. 85 (1995). See also M. D. Lucas, "Salting and Other Union Tactics: A Unionist's Perspective," *Journal of Labor Research*, 18 (1997), pp. 55–64.

[2] For an expanded examination of union organizing activities and permissible active management responses, see K. Bronfenbrenner, S. Friedman, R. W. Hurd, R. A. Oswald, and R. L. Seeber, eds., *Organizing to Win: New Research on Union Strategies* (Ithaca, NY: Cornell University Press, 1998); M. A. Spognardi, "Conducting a Successful Union-Free Campaign: A Primer (Part I)," *Employee Relations Law Journal*, 24, no. 2 (1998), pp. 35–42; M. A. Spognardi, "Conducting a Successful Union-Free Campaign: A Primer (Part II)," *Employee Relations Law Journal*, 24, no. 3 (1998), pp. 31–55; and J. J. Lawler, *Unionization and Deunionization: Strategy, Tactics, and Outcomes* (Columbia: University of South Carolina Press, 1990).

FIGURE 6.1 **Sequence of Organizing Events**

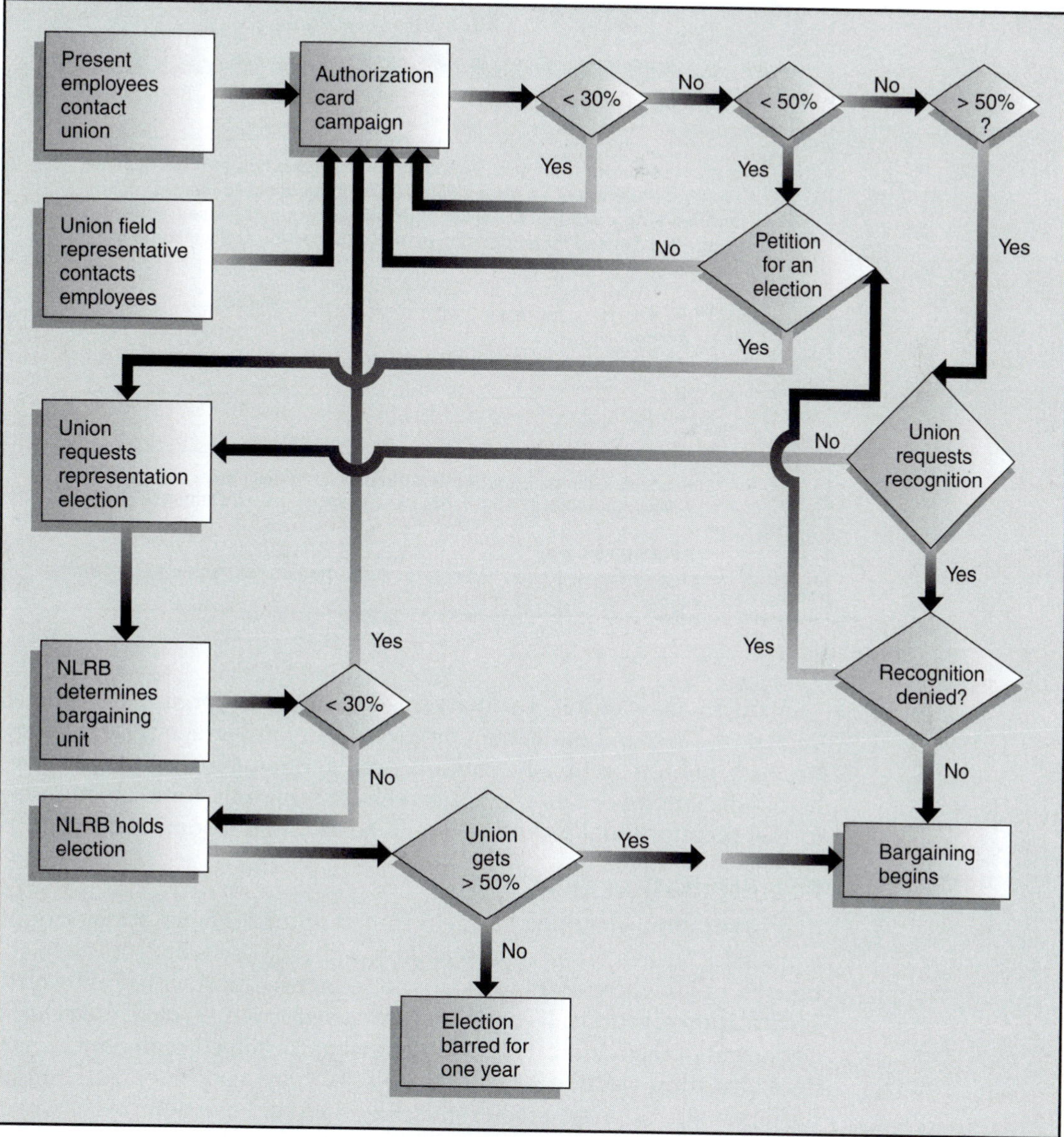

actually exists. If a majority has signed and the employer is satisfied with the appropriateness of the proposed bargaining unit, the employer can grant recognition voluntarily.[3]

[3] See J. W. Budd and P. K. Heinz, "Union Representation Elections and Labor Law Reform: Lessons from the Minneapolis Hilton," *Labor Studies Journal,* 20, no. 4 (1996), pp. 3–20, for an example of a situation in which the employer agreed ahead of time to a card check as an appropriate method for determining majority status.

FIGURE 6.2
Authorization Card

YES, I WANT THE IAM

I, the undersigned employee
(Company) ____________________

authorize the International Association of Machinists and Aerospace Workers (IAM) to act as my collective bargaining agent for wages, hours and working conditions. I agree that this card may be used either to support a demand for recognition or an NLRB election at the discretion of the union.

Name (print) ____________________ **Date** __________
Home Address ____________________ **Phone** __________
City __________ **State** __________ **Zip** __________
Job Title __________ **Dept.** __________ **Shift** __________

Sign Here X ____________________

Note: This authorization to be SIGNED and DATED in Employee's own handwriting. YOUR RIGHT TO SIGN THIS CARD IS PROTECTED BY FEDERAL LAW.

RECEIVED BY (Initial) ____________________

A union may picket an unorganized employer for up to 30 days, demanding recognition as the employees' bargaining agent. This rarely happens, but if it occurs, the employer can petition the NLRB for an election in the employee unit the union seeks to represent. If the union loses, further **recognitional picketing** would be an unfair labor practice (ULP).

Representation Elections

Representation elections are held to determine whether a majority of employees desires union representation and, if so, by which union. Elections in units where employees are not currently represented are called **certification elections.** If employees are currently represented, but at least 30 percent of them indicate they do not want continued representation, a **decertification election** is held. If a majority votes against representation, the union loses representation rights. So-called **raid elections** occur when at least 30 percent of employees indicate they would prefer a different union to represent them. Elections cannot be held if an election result was certified within the previous year. Decertification elections may not be held while a contract is in effect. Figure 6.3 shows that if interest in an election is sufficient, the union (or the employer in the absence of a demand for recognition) can petition the NLRB to hold an election to determine employees' desires. The next section traces the basic steps involved in conducting an election.

FIGURE 6.3 **Avenues to Election Petitions**

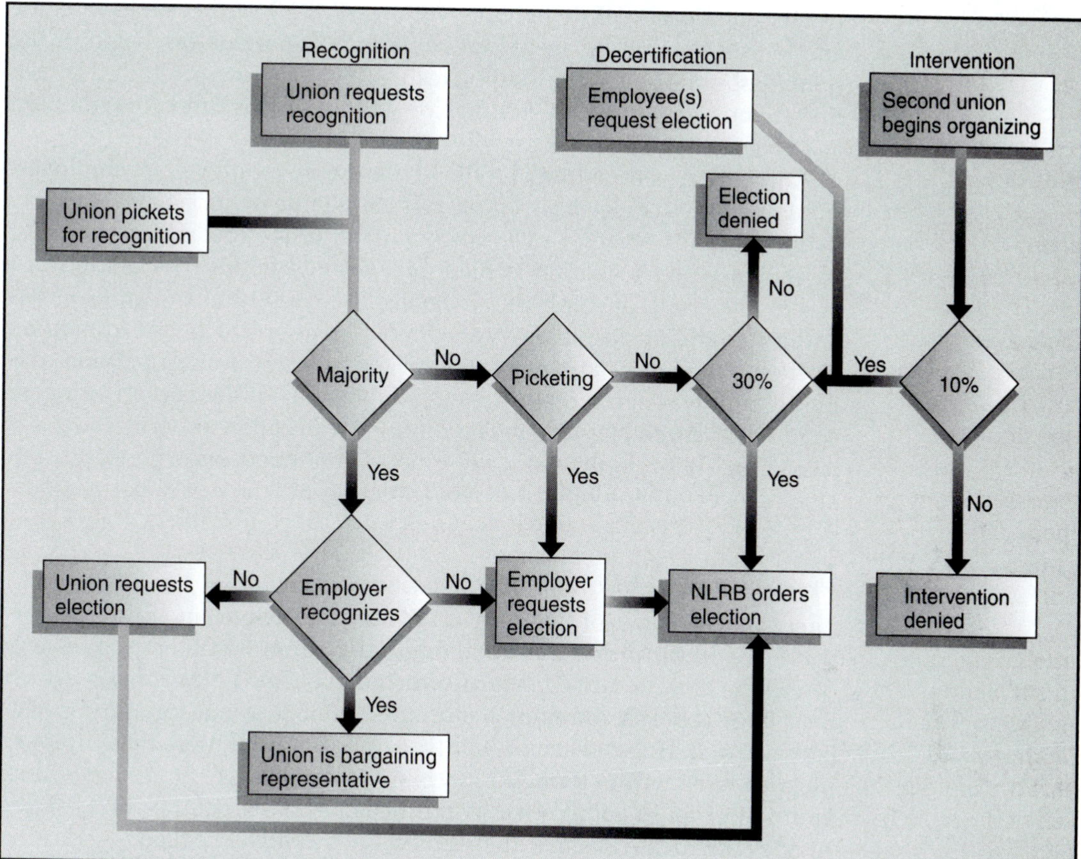

Election Petitions

The union may petition the NLRB to hold an election in the unit it is trying to organize and includes the signed authorization cards as evidence of support. The NLRB checks the signed cards against a roster of employees in the unit. If fewer than 30 percent have signed, the petition is dismissed. If more than 30 percent have signed, the union is legally within its jurisdiction, and if the employer doesn't contest the appropriateness of the proposed unit, the NLRB schedules an election. The employer frequently contests the makeup of an **appropriate bargaining unit,** requiring that the NLRB decide which employees should be included. The criteria the board uses to decide whether a proposed unit is appropriate are discussed later in this chapter.

When an appropriate bargaining unit is defined and at least 30 percent of employees in the unit have signed authorization cards, the NLRB will order an election unless the union withdraws its petition. If the union receives a majority of the eligible votes cast, the board certifies it as the employees' bargaining agent and contract negotiations can begin. If the union loses, the board certifies the results, and elections are barred in that unit for one year. In effect, certification guarantees the union or nonunion status of a bargaining unit for at least one year.[4]

An election petition may be filed by a union, employer, or employee. In certain types of elections, employers cannot file petitions because early petitions might preempt union campaign efforts. Proof of interest must be shown when a petition is filed or within 48 hours. The union must specify the group of employees it desires to represent. If an employer has had a recognition demand, it can directly petition the board to hold an election. A union or an employee can file a decertification petition asking for removal of the present bargaining agent. Under certain stringent conditions, an employer may petition for a decertification election if it has a good-faith doubt about the union's continued majority status, but an employer cannot withdraw recognition until a lack of majority status is proved.[5]

Preelection Board Involvement

There are two types of elections: (1) **consent elections,** in which the parties agree on the proposed bargaining unit and on which employees will be eligible to vote, and (2) **board-directed (petition) elections,** in which the NLRB **regional director** determines, after hearings, an appropriate bargaining unit and voter eligibility. In a petition election, the employer must provide within 7 days a so-called **Excelsior list** containing names and addresses of employees in the designated bargaining unit.[6] After 10 days but within 30 days, the election will normally be held.

The Election

The NLRB conducts the secret-ballot election. Company and union observers may challenge voter eligibility but cannot prohibit anyone from voting. After the votes are counted and challenges decided, the choice receiving a majority is declared the winner. If more than two choices (e.g., two different unions and no union) are on the ballot and none obtains an absolute majority, a runoff is held between the two highest choices. After any challenges are resolved, the regional director certifies the results. Figure 6.4 shows an NLRB election ballot.

[4] *Brooks* v. *NLRB*, 348 U.S. 96 (1954).

[5] T. C. Stamatakos and T. J. Piskorski, "*Levitz Furniture:* NLRB Rewrites the Book on Employer Efforts to Oust Incumbent Unions," *Employee Relations Law Journal*, 27 (2001), pp. 31–44.

[6] *Excelsior Underwear, Inc.*, 156 NLRB 1236 (1966).

FIGURE 6.4
Specimen NLRB Ballot

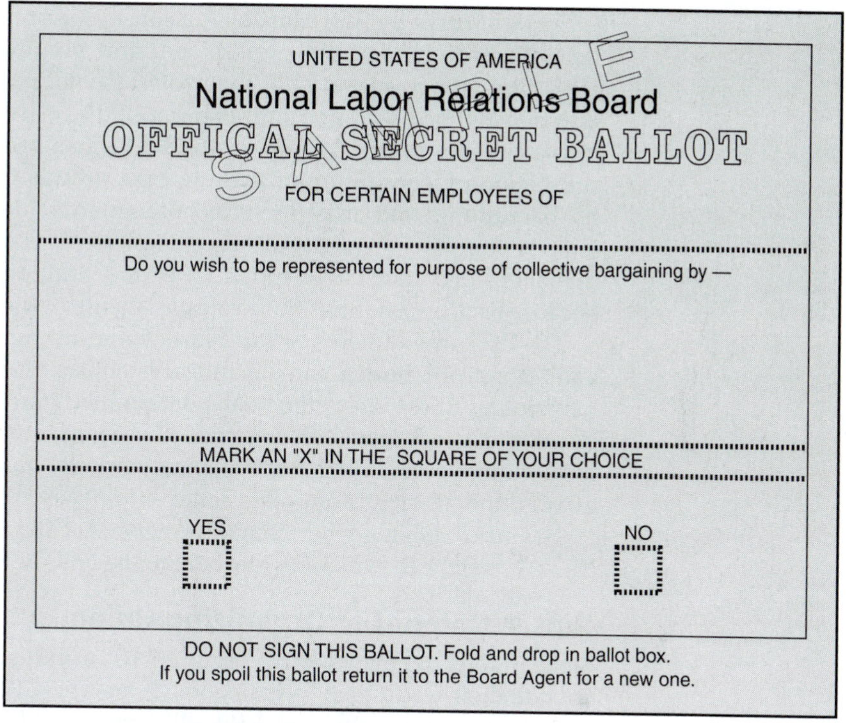
UNITED STATES OF AMERICA

National Labor Relations Board

OFFICAL SECRET BALLOT

FOR CERTAIN EMPLOYEES OF

Do you wish to be represented for purpose of collective bargaining by —

MARK AN "X" IN THE SQUARE OF YOUR CHOICE

YES

NO

DO NOT SIGN THIS BALLOT. Fold and drop in ballot box.
If you spoil this ballot return it to the Board Agent for a new one.

BARGAINING-UNIT DETERMINATION

The NLRB considers a variety of factors to determine the bargaining unit: (1) legal constraints, (2) the constitutional jurisdiction of the organizing union, (3) the union's likely success in organizing and bargaining, (4) the employer's desires to resist organizing or promote stability in the bargaining relationship, and (5) its own philosophy.

Bargaining units can differ depending on whether the focus is on organizing or contract negotiations. For example, several retail stores in a given chain may constitute an appropriate bargaining unit for representation election purposes, while for negotiating purposes, several retail stores owned by different companies may practice **multiemployer bargaining.** This chapter's discussion is concerned only with bargaining units for representation; bargaining units for negotiations are discussed in Chapter 8.

Legal Constraints

Legal constraints limit the potential scope of a bargaining unit, but within these constraints, the contending parties—labor and management—are free to jointly determine an appropriate unit. If they agree on the proposed unit, a consent election results. If they do not, the NLRB determines unit appropriateness.

Section 9(b) of the Taft-Hartley Act constrains unit determination. First, no unit can include both professional and nonprofessional employees without majority approval of the professionals. Second, a separate craft unit may not be precluded simply because the board had earlier included it in a broader group. However, the NLRB has broadly interpreted this subsection by continuing to include craft groups in larger units. Third, no bargaining unit may include both guards hired by employers to enforce company's rules and other employees. Fourth, supervisors and managers may not be included in a unit and/or bargain collectively because Section 2 defines their roles as agents of the employer.

The 1974 amendments to Taft-Hartley permitting representation in private, nonprofit health care facilities established special constraints on bargaining. In response, the board determined that separate units would be appropriate for registered nurses, physicians, other professionals, technical employees, skilled maintenance workers, business office clericals, guards, and all other nonprofessional employees.

The major difference between the Wagner Act and the Railway Labor Act (RLA) is that the RLA requires that bargaining units be formed on a craft basis.

Jurisdiction of the Organizing Union

Some unions organize certain occupations or industries. Others organize outside their traditional jurisdictions. If an AFL-CIO union is attempting to raid another affiliate, the NLRB will notify the AFL-CIO when a petition is filed to allow it to activate its internal procedures to adjudicate the problem. Problems are usually resolved because, as a condition of affiliation, unions agree to let the federation resolve internal disputes. Exhibit 6.1 provides details about a raid situation involving the SEIU (CTW) and a breakaway faction in California.

The Union's Desired Unit

Unless it seeks to represent all eligible employees within an employer, a union faces several problems in deciding which bargaining-unit configuration it desires. It must balance the unit that would be the easiest to organize against future objectives in contract negotiations. A craft union would likely seek a bargaining unit that includes only workers with relatively similar skills. Industrial unions usually seek plantwide units.

A union must be recognized before it can bargain. But organizing a unit that would have little impact on business if the union were to strike would be futile. For example, gaining a majority in a manufacturing plant custodial unit may be relatively easy, but negotiating a favorable contract would be difficult because the employer could readily subcontract the work for little incremental cost during a strike.

The union, then, has two bargaining-unit goals: (1) creating a "winnable" unit and (2) creating a unit that will have bargaining power with the employer.

Exhibit 6.1

BARE-KNUCKLED CAMPAIGNING FOR REPRESENTATION RIGHTS

Sal Rosselli and Andy Stern were powerful allies in building the power of the Service Employees International Union (SEIU) in health care organizing and bargaining. Stern was the president of the SEIU while Rosselli headed up the United Healthcare Workers–West locals in California. Rosselli had developed a reputation as an effective organizer and bare-knuckles negotiator who had won significant economic gains for his members.

In 2008, Rosselli and Stern had a falling out with Rosselli complaining that Stern's leadership style was undemocratic and centralized. In turn, Stern removed Rosselli from his position in early 2009 for financial irregularities and refusing to accept the union's transfer of 65,000 members to another local.* Rosselli and his supporters responded by forming the breakaway National Union of Healthcare Workers (NUHW) and began to organize workers whom the SEIU was targeting and raiding current SEIU units. In early 2009, NUHW presented a representation petition to the NLRB claiming an absolute majority of Kaiser Permanente workers represented by the SEIU preferred to move their representation to the NUHW. Meanwhile a federal jury found Rosselli illegally diverted over $1.5 million of dues to finance the breakaway. Campaign tactics on both sides would be equal to the most virulent management campaign against unionization. (A plethora of YouTube videos provide added details and opinions.) During the campaign, the SEIU negotiated a new contract with Kaiser which went into effect on October 1, 2010.

The big face-off came in October 2010 when 43,000 Kaiser Permanente workers had the opportunity to vote on whether to continue the SEIU as its bargaining agent or to replace it with the NUHW which would immediately provide credibility to the NUHW and position it to challenge the SEIU on a broader front. But when the results were announced, 61 percent voted to remain with the SEIU which retained its right to represent them.

* For an extended treatment of the split and inter-union disputes, see S. Greenhouse, "Union vs. Union," *New York Times*, September 14, 2010, pp. B1, B6; and the Web sites of the contenders: www.seiu-uhw.org and www.nuhw.org.

The Employer's Desired Unit

The employer often desires a unit different from, but not necessarily the opposite of, what the union wants. It prefers a unit the union is unlikely to win. If a craft union is organizing, the employer would favor a plant-wide unit. If unskilled workers are the most interested and they are a majority of the workforce, the employer may seek to exclude craft groups. Figure 6.5 shows why management might argue for a smaller unit than the union desires. Assume in this case that 60 percent of production and maintenance employees favor representation, while only 40 percent of other occupations would vote for the union. If the election were held in the union's desired unit and all employees voted, the union would win by 860 to 790. If management were able to exclude other employee groups, only the production and maintenance employees would be unionized.

FIGURE 6.5
Conflicting Unit Desires

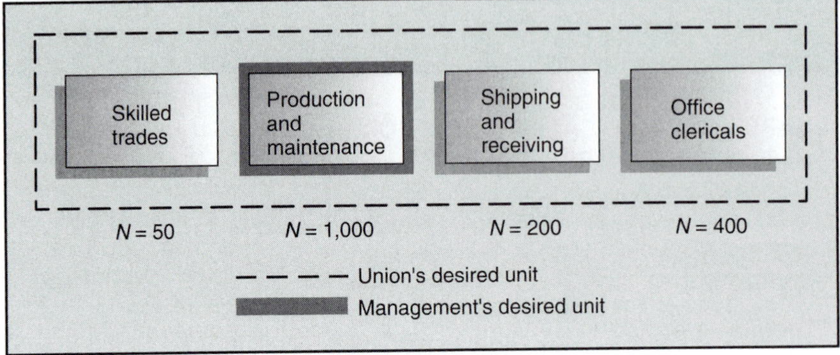

The employer also would like a unit configured to minimize union bargaining power if the union wins. Thus, the employer might desire functionally independent units, which would allow continued operations if a strike occurred. But it would also like to avoid fragmented units, which would decrease bargaining power if different contract expiration dates enable unions to threaten a sequence of strikes.

NLRB Policy

In general, if the petitioned unit is deemed to be appropriate by the NLRB, then that would be the election unit. Otherwise the board would consider alternatives proposed by the parties or it would propose an alternative.[7] In determining appropriateness, the board considers carefully the **community of interests** of the employees in the proposed unit.[8] Factors that would establish a community of interests would include:

1. *Degree of functional integration.* This refers to the extent to which all potentially includable employees are required to provide the company's output. For example, in the *Borden Co.* decision the board recognized that although 20 different facilities with varying human resource policies were involved in the seemingly independent processes of manufacturing (3) and distributing (17) ice cream, an appropriate unit would contain all 20 plants because of the interrelationships among facilities necessary to market the final product.[9]
2. *Common supervision.* If employees in two or more different occupations worked under common supervision, a unit including only one of the occupations would probably be inappropriate.

[7] *Boeing Co.*, 337 NLRB 152 (2001).

[8] www.nlrb.gov/nlrb/legal/manuals/RCase_Outline/law12.pdf.

[9] *Borden Co., Hutchinson Ice Cream Div.*, 89 NLRB 227 (1950).

3. *The nature of employee skills and functions.* Employees at a particular facility may have differences in job duties, but similar levels of skills (e.g., unskilled employees who perform a variety of different but simple jobs) and be considered as an appropriate group for organizing.
4. *Interchangability and degree of contact among employees.* If employees transfer frequently across plants or offices, their community of interest may be similar, leading the board to designate a multiplant unit.
5. *Work situs.* Employees who work within the same location are presumed to have a greater community of interests than those who do not, although this would not be dispositive in determining appropriateness.
6. *General working conditions.* An appropriate unit could be determined even if there were some existing difference in work rules, pay practices, and other procedures that were applied to the group of employees in the requested unit.
7. *Fringe benefits.* Differences in pay rates or benefits would not necessarily lead to a unit being found to be inappropriate.
8. *Extent of organization.* After these factors have been analyzed, the board may consider the degree to which organizing has occurred in a proposed unit, although this is not considered the prime factor. The Supreme Court has ruled that the board could consider it because Section 9(c)(5) of the Taft-Hartley Act requires that the board consider allowing employees the fullest freedom to exercise their rights.[10]

Many of these factors are related. For example, common supervision is more likely to occur within a single work site, and general working conditions would also be more likely to be similar, thus increasing the likelihood of a finding of a community of interests. Thus the board's determination frequently rests on several factors.

Craft Severance

The term **craft severance** means that a group of employees with a substantially different community of interests is allowed to establish a separate unit. Craft severance can occur during initial unit determination or when a group of employees votes to leave their bargaining unit. Severance is easier during initial organizing.

The NLRB will allow craft severance only when the following conditions are present: (1) a high degree of skill or functional differentiation between groups and a tradition of separate representation; (2) a short bargaining history in the present unit and a low degree of likely disruption if severance is granted; (3) a distinct separateness in the established unit among members of the proposed unit; (4) a different collective bargaining history in the industry; (5) low integration in production; and (6) a high

[10] *NLRB* v. *Metropolitan Life Insurance Co.*, 380 U.S. 438 (1965).

degree of experience as a representative for the craft of the union desiring severance.[11] Craft severance has been allowed in cases where a recognizable difference exists in the communities of interest and there is no prior contrary bargaining history.[12]

What Factors Are Used?

Except in health care, no administrative rules apply. The board determines bargaining-unit appropriateness on a case-by-case basis. For severance, the overriding factor is bargaining history, buttressed by functional integration in an employer's operation. For representation, community of interest and functional integration are important. The workers' community of interest is affected by the production process, transfer policies, geographic proximity, and administrative decision making.

There are few judicial precedents, and bargaining-unit determinations are unappealable because they are not final orders. If an employer believed the board's determination was wrong, it would refuse to bargain if it lost the election and the board would seek enforcement of its order in the courts. In most cases, the courts leave board unit orders undisturbed.

Other Issues in Unit Determination

Organizational structures change over time. What was initially an appropriate unit may not be appropriate now. Major factors involved in the ongoing definition of a unit include new facilities and acquisitions, reorganization, job reclassification, sale to another firm, or joint employment.

Accretion

Accretion occurs when a new facility is added to the bargaining unit or when an existing union in an employer wins representation rights for employees previously represented by another union. The NLRB generally applies the same criteria to accretion as it applies to initial unit determination. However, the board gives extra weight to the desires of employees in the unit subject to accretion.[13]

Reorganization and Reclassification

An employer occasionally reclassifies jobs or reorganizes administrative units. These changes might make a previously defined bargaining unit inappropriate, and the parties may redefine the unit by consent. Failing

[11] *Mallinckrodt Chemical Works*, 162 NLRB 387 (1966).

[12] *E. I. duPont de Nemours & Co.*, 162 NLRB 413 (1966), and *Anheuser-Busch, Inc.*, 170 NLRB No. 5 (1968).

[13] Compare *Consolidated Edison Co.*, 48 LRRM 1539 (1961), where no accretion to an established unit was permitted but a distinct unit was ordered, with *Textile, Inc.*, 46 LRRM 1264 (1960) and *Special Machine & Engineering Inc.*, 124 LRRM 1219 (1987), where accretion occurred, and *Honeywell, Inc., Semiconductor Division*, 140 LRRM 1147 (1992), where no accretion was allowed due to employee desires.

this, the employer would have to refuse to bargain, and the union would have to file a ULP charge for the board to reexamine appropriateness.

Successor Organizations

A firm that acquires or merges with another firm assumes existing contractual obligations.[14] Where ownership changes but operations continue unchanged, the new owner must recognize the union but does not need to honor the existing contract.[15] Where operations continue but, because of layoffs and/or new hires, the union lacks a majority, the employer has no obligation to honor a contract.[16] When a closed firm is reopened by new owners, the bargaining relationship continues if a majority of the employees worked for the former company and were in a represented unit.[17]

Joint Employers

Occasionally a group of employees has two employers. If an employment agency supplies temporary employees to another and both can fire, discipline, change wages, and so on, then they are joint employers. An appropriate bargaining unit can include temporary joint employees, regardless of whether the employer that hires and pays them consents.[18] Agency employees have tried unsuccessfully to organize in Microsoft and Amazon.com. Even if successful, they would face the possibility that the units in which they work would be sold. They have had some success in being legally classified as company employees for benefit purposes.[19]

The Railway Labor Act and Airline Mergers

The last decade has seen a substantial amount of consolidation among domestic air carriers, together with the formation of supporting regional carriers that contract with the major airlines to provide service on routes with fewer passengers per flight. Recently, two major mergers have had a substantial effect on union representation in the airline industry—Delta's takeover of Northwest and the merger of Continental into United.

Except for its pilots, Delta's employees were not represented by unions, while virtually all of Northwest's organizable employees were represented.

[14] *John Wiley & Sons, Inc.* v. *Livingston*, 376 U.S. 543 (1964).

[15] *NLRB* v. *Burns International Security Services,* 406 U.S. 272 (1972).

[16] *Howard Johnson Co., Inc.* v. *Detroit Local Joint Executive Board, Hotel and Restaurant Employees & Bartenders International Union, AFL-CIO*, 417 U.S. 249 (1974).

[17] *Fall River Dyeing and Finishing Corp.* v. *NLRB*, 482 U.S. 27 (1987); see also R. F. Mace, "The Supreme Court's Labor Law Successorship Doctrine after *Fall River Dyeing*," *Labor Law Journal,* 39 (1988), pp. 102–109.

[18] *M. B. Sturgis, Inc.*, 331 NLRB 173 (2000).

[19] D. D. van Jaarsveld, "Collective Representation among High-Tech Workers at Microsoft and Beyond: Lessons from WashTech/CWA," *Industrial Relations,* 43 (2004), pp. 364–385; see also *Vizcaino* v. *Microsoft Corp.*, 173 F.3d 713 (9th Cir. 1999).

A majority of employees in all occupations were Delta employees before the merger, so unless unions representing Northwest employees could retain their strength among that group and convince a substantial number of Delta employees that they would be better off unionized, all employees might become unrepresented following NMB-supervised elections. All merged employee groups involved in elections voted against union representation.

For Continental and United, with the exception of the pilots, major groups of employees are represented by different unions in the merger partners. In order to realize synergistic savings, the airline will want to see representation consolidations in the future. This may take some time, however, since in a 2005 merger of America West with U.S. Airways there are still separate bargaining representatives for similar types of employees.

THE ORGANIZING CAMPAIGN

Organizing campaigns are highly contentious. Increasingly, unions and employers fight bitterly over the future of the employment relationship for the targeted work group. The discussion to this point has focused on the overall framework and basic rules for determining whether a majority of employees wants union representation. The campaign has many of the characteristics of a political campaign. This section examines the actual practices of unions and employers during organizing campaigns and provides examples of how the parties, particularly employers, bend the rules to gain an advantage in influencing the outcome of the campaign.

The usual catalyst for a campaign is employees' frustration about their wages and benefits or their inability to influence outcomes in the workplace. It's also possible that a national union that organizes similar types of employers identifies the employer as a ripe target for organizing. In the latter case, the national union needs to size up the organizing climate, including the economic and political climate; evidence of union interest or activity by employees; likely community attitudes or support; and the demographic characteristics of the potential unit. If a decision is made to pursue organizing, a strategy is developed. As soon as management becomes aware of any organizing activity, it also develops a strategy to thwart the activity.[20] Figure 6.6 presents a theoretical model of the organizing and certification election process.

Unionization aims to permanently change the employment relationship by institutionalizing collective bargaining as the method through which managers and employees deal with each other about future wages, hours, and terms and conditions of employment. For the union, organizing is an ongoing process. The campaign aims not only to secure a majority who

[20] K. Bronfenbrenner, "The Role of Union Strategies in NLRB Certification Elections," *Industrial and Labor Relations Review*, 50 (1997), pp. 195–212.

FIGURE 6.6 **Theoretical Model of the Certification Election Process**

Source: K. Bronfenbrenner, "The Role of Union Strategies in NLRB Certification Elections," *Industrial and Labor Relations Review,* 50 (1997), p. 197.

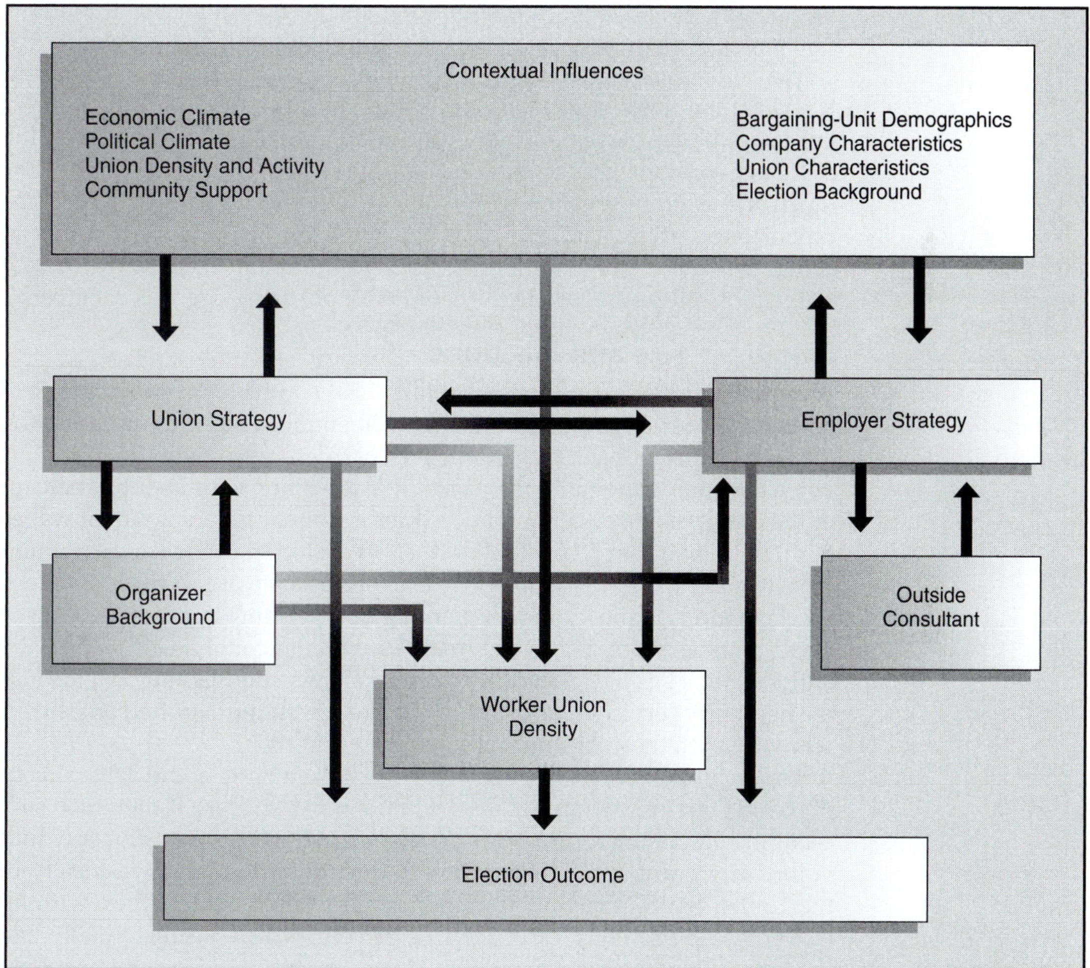

will vote for representation but also to develop an identification with the union and solidarity among employees so that they will be willing collectively to threaten or resist the employer when their interests are at stake.

The union needs to convince those who didn't initially sign authorization cards that it can and will improve their employment outcomes. Employees who are hired after unionization need to be recruited to join and to be socialized to better understand and support the union's goals. To be successful, the union must negotiate an initial contract that improves the conditions that led to organizing. A permanent support organization must be established within the unit to address member concerns and challenge management when workers' rights have been abridged.

If unionized, many decisions that managers previously implemented unilaterally would require consultation and negotiation with the union. The national union with which the local affiliates will likely pressure the employer to operate much more like unionized competitors in its industry. It's likely the union will focus on improving wages and benefits beyond the level the employer and other nonunion employers offer. Given the economic consequences of unionization, the employer needs to decide how much and what types of effort it will invest in the campaign to defeat the unionization drive. And, if it loses, the employer must decide whether to accept the outcome or to implement evasive and intransigent tactics to frustrate union efforts and erode the confidence of bargaining-unit members.

Employer Size and Elections

For more than 20 years, over half of all NLRB-conducted certification elections have been in units with less than 30 employees. Assuming that the average unit size is 20, that employees earn an average of $15 per hour when the organizing campaign starts, that the union wins about 50 percent of the elections, that average union dues are equal to two hours of wages per month, and that 50 percent of dues are remitted to the national union with which the local is affiliated, the expected increase in dues revenues for the national from conducting an organizing campaign in one of these small units is about $1,800 per year. To remain economically viable, the national must be able to amortize its organizing expenses and provide half the necessary services a unit would require (given the expected 50 percent win rate) with these revenues.

For an employee, the cost of union dues is equal to about 1.15 percent of pay (24 out of 2,080 straight-time paid hours per year). If the union succeeds in negotiating future contracts that exceed what the employer would voluntarily grant, the return on union dues is quite high. Historically in the United States, the wage premium paid to union employees, with all else equal, is usually greater than 10 percent, which is substantially less than the cost of the dues that support the structure necessary to negotiate the increase and provide other bargaining-agent services to employees.

Very few elections take place in private sector establishments with 500 or more employees. In 2009, the NLRB conducted 18 elections in units of 500 or more, and unions won 15 of those elections. The average size of these units is close to 1,150. If pay and dues remission are as described above for small units, the expected annual return to an organizing campaign for the national union would be $103,500. However, there are fewer large units available to organize than in the past.[21]

[21] H. S. Farber, "Union Success in Representation Elections: Why Does Unit Size Matter?" *Industrial and Labor Relations Review,* 54 (2001), pp. 329–348.

Economic returns from union representation are substantially greater than costs of organizing for employees in most industries. The cost of organizing an additional worker is roughly equal to the annual earnings increase of covered workers.[22] Thus, unions recoup their investment through dues, and employees receive an increasing and continuing wage premium compared to nonunion employees.

General Organizing Campaign Rules

Through their rulings on ULP cases, the NLRB and courts have established guidelines of permissible conduct for unions and employers in organizing campaigns. If either violates the rules, a ULP may be found and some redress ordered, which may include rehiring fired employees with back pay, rerunning an election, or imposing a bargaining order if the violations were egregious.

No-Distribution or No-Solicitation Rules

Most employers prohibit solicitations by any organization on company property or on company time. These rules prohibit labor organizers from gaining easy access to employees because legally they can be barred from access like representatives of other organizations. Organizing is more difficult if workers must be contacted off the job, especially if their residences are widely dispersed.

No-solicitation rules do not apply to employees. Employee organizers can solicit fellow workers on company premises (during nonworking time) unless it's clearly shown that solicitation interferes with production.[23] Nonemployee organizers (e.g., international union field representatives) can, in most instances, be barred from soliciting on company property.[24] Thus, early in-plant support is necessary for a drive to be successful.

Organizers may gain access to clerical and technical employees through employers' e-mail systems. Within the company, it is much easier for employees to contact and solicit others (and it is also easier for the employer to trace their actions). Employers can restrict computer and e-mail system use to working time, thereby making all internally developed e-mail communications related to organizing a violation subject to disciplinary action.[25] Employees generally have the right to send personal messages to

[22] P. B. Voos, "Union Organizing: Costs and Benefits," *Industrial and Labor Relations Review*, 37 (1983), pp. 576–591.

[23] *Republic Aviation Corp.* v. *NLRB*; and *NLRB* v. *LeTourneau Co.*, 324 U.S. 793 (1945).

[24] *NLRB* v. *Babcock and Wilcox Co.;* v. *Seamprufe, Inc.;* and *Ranco, Inc.* v. *NLRB*, 351 U.S. 105 (1956).

[25] D. V. Yager and T. S. Threlkeld, "Workplace Cyberspace—Going Where No Board Has Gone Before," *Employee Relations Law Journal*, 25, no. 2 (1999), pp. 53–70; see also J. M. Hunter, "The NLRA at 70: Employer E-Mail and Communication Policies and the National Labor Relations Act," *Labor Law Journal*, 56 (2005), pp. 196–202.

each other, but employers have the right to block incoming e-mail.[26] While the issue is not settled, an employer would likely commit a ULP if it permitted employees to solicit for other purposes on the employer's e-mail system, but forbid union soliciting.[27]

Organizers may solicit on company property if reasonable access to employees is unavailable, as in remote operations such as logging, or where workers live in a company town.[28] But organizers may not solicit on quasi-public property, such as shopping mall courts or parking lots.[29] Employers reduce soliciting opportunities by requiring that employees leave working areas and plants at the end of their shifts. Employer property rights generally receive precedence over the rights of employees to solicit when the two sets of rights are in conflict.[30]

Communications

Employees can be required to attend meetings on company premises during working hours to hear presentations opposing the union.[31] However, if solicitation is barred during nonworking time (as in a retail establishment), the union may be entitled to equal access.[32]

Employers cannot promise employees new benefits if the union loses, but they can point out that if the union is certified, present levels of wages and benefits will be subject to negotiation.[33] If extraneous racial propaganda is used in campaigns, it is likely a rerun will be ordered if objections are filed.[34] However, there is no requirement generally that campaign rhetoric be truthful, although the board has switched its position on this

[26] S. S. Robfogel, " Electronic Communication and the NLRA: Union Access and Employer Rights," *Labor Lawyer,* 16 (2000), pp. 231–252.

[27] C. N. O'Brien, "Employer E-Mail Policies and the National Labor Relations Act: D.C. Circuit Bounces *Register-Guard* Back to the Obama Board on Discriminatory Enforcement Issue, *Labor Law Journal*, 61 (2010), pp. 5–14.

[28] *Marsh* v. *Alabama*, 326 U.S. 501 (1946); *Lechmere Inc.* v. *NLRB*, 502 U.S. 527 (1992).

[29] *Central Hardware Co.* v. *NLRB*, 407 U.S. 539 (1972); and *Hudgens* v. *NLRB*, 424 U.S. 507 (1976).

[30] R. N. Block, B. W. Wolkinson, and J. W. Kuhn, "Some Are More Equal than Others: The Relative Status of Employers, Unions, and Employees in the Law of Union Organizing," *Industrial Relations Law Journal*, 10 (1988), pp. 220–240; see also A. Story, "Employer Speech, Union Representation Elections, and the First Amendment," *Berkeley Journal of Employment and Labor Law*, 16 (1995), pp. 356–457.

[31] *Livingston Shirt Corp.*, 107 NLRB 400 (1953).

[32] *May Department Stores Co.*, 136 NLRB 797 (1962).

[33] One commentator argues that employers' First Amendment rights are abridged by prohibiting campaign promises of future benefits for voting against representation. See P. J. Caldwell, "Campaign Promises in NLRB Elections: Advancing Employer Speech through Political Elections Law and the First Amendment," *Labor Law Journal*, 56 (2005), pp. 239–259.

[34] N. A. Beadles and C. M. Lowery, "Union Elections Involving Racial Propaganda: The *Sewell* and *Bancroft* Standards," *Labor Law Journal*, 42 (1991), pp. 418–424.

several times.[35] Voters tend to decide their positions early in the campaign; thus, truth or falsity may have little effect during the waning days.[36]

The 24-Hour Rule

Because it would be impossible for a union or an employer to rebut a last-minute campaign statement, employers or unions cannot hold a captive-audience presentation during the 24 hours directly preceding an election.[37]

Interrogation

Employer interrogation of employees during a campaign would probably be legal only if used to test a claim of majority status,[38] but it would be unfair if (1) the employer has been hostile toward unions, (2) information is likely to be used against a particular individual, (3) the questioner is a high-level manager, (4) the interrogation is done in an intimidating manner, or (5) the respondents are fearful.[39]

Surveillance

Employers routinely operate a variety of surveillance equipment to track the security of their premises. If videotaping is used to record protected concerted activity, such as organizing by employees during break times in nonwork areas, this would be a ULP.[40]

Union Strategy and Tactics

Organizing campaigns have three distinct sequential goals: (1) obtaining signed authorization cards from a majority in the unit the union seeks to represent; (2) obtaining voluntary recognition based on a card count or a board-directed election; and (3) achieving the negotiation, ratification, and implementation of a first contract.

Obtaining a majority requires that employees sign an authorization card for an organizer. For this to happen, the organizer must contact employees, convince them that unionization is to their benefit, and indicate what strategy the union has to prevent the employer from retaliating against union adherents. While Section 7 of the Taft-Hartley Act forbids

[35] Beginning with *Hollywood Ceramics Co.*, 140 NLRB 221 (1962), which required truthfulness; adopting *Shopping Kart Food Markets, Inc.*, 229 NLRB 190 (1977), which did not; shifting to *General Knit of California, Inc.*, 239 NLRB 101 (1978), which did; and concluding with *Midland National Life*, 263 NLRB No. 24 (1982), which did not.

[36] J. M. Walker and J. J. Lawler, "Union Campaign Activities and Voter Preferences," *Journal of Labor Research*, 7 (1986), pp. 19–40.

[37] *Peerless Plywood,* 107 NLRB 427 (1953).

[38] *Blue Flash Express Co.*, 109 NLRB 591 (1954).

[39] *Bourne v. NLRB*, 322 F. 2d 47 (1964).

[40] J. A. Mello, "Salts, Lies and Videotape: Union Organizing Efforts and Management's Response," *Labor Law Journal*, 55 (2004), pp. 42–52.

employers and unions to interfere with employees' rights to join or not join a union, employers frequently retaliate against activists.

Organizing needs to gain the support of workers and also may need to proactively blunt management's campaign or potential retaliation. Where the employer is a significant economic entity in the local area, **community action** is an important adjunct.[41] When the employer is not particularly dependent on the local community, but is well known to the public or can be linked to other organizations that are, the union may also undertake a **corporate campaign** to inform the public and pressure the employer to conduct a fair campaign.

Over the past 15 years, new organizing strategies have been developed by national unions of the AFL-CIO. Traditional campaigns make heavy use of handbilling, letters to employees in the unit, and mass recruiting meetings. Less often these are supplemented with community action, corporate campaigns, and negotiating for recognition (most often in the building trades).[42] The new strategies use national union representatives who are trained in organizing and a developed internal cadre to wage an intensive one-to-one rank-and-file campaign.[43]

Campaigns establish individual contacts through home visits, small-group meetings, and one-to-one solicitation on the job site during non-working times. Campaigns stress themes related to fairness, dignity, and justice and often downplay, but do not ignore, economic issues.

As the campaign gains momentum, an internal organizing committee is established. Solidarity days are scheduled on which signed-up members wear union buttons and/or T-shirts to work to signal their strength. A negotiating committee may also be established to define what specific outcomes are important to obtain in a first contract. This both personalizes the campaign to the unit and gets workers to realize that winning the campaign is necessary before desired bargaining outcomes can be attained.[44]

Most campaigns still use traditional strategies. Only one-third use resource coordination and community action. Corporate campaigns are used about one-quarter of the time, and negotiating with employers for preferential hiring is used least often.[45] Table 6.1 indicates the organizing tactics used in a sample of elections. In campaigns, unions have one advantage over management because they can suggest positive changes unionization would bring, but employers may not legally communicate future benefits that would result from an organizing failure.

[41] See R. Bussel, "Taking on 'Big Chicken': The Delmarva Poultry Justice Alliance," *Labor Studies Journal*, 28, no. 2 (2003), pp. 1–24.

[42] R. B. Peterson, T. W. Lee, and B. Finnegan, "Strategies and Tactics in Union Organizing Campaigns," *Industrial Relations*, 31 (1992), pp. 370–381.

[43] Bronfenbrenner, "The Role of Union Strategies in NLRB Certification Elections."

[44] Ibid.

[45] Peterson et al., "Strategies and Tactics."

TABLE 6.1
Percentage Use of Various Union Organizing Tactics

Source: Adapted from R. B. Peterson, T. W. Lee, and B. Finnegan, "Strategies and Tactics in Union Organizing Campaigns," *Industrial Relations*, 31 (1992), p. 375.

Tactic	%
Traditional:	
Handbilling	77%
Mailing letters	100
Holding meetings	100
Signing authorization cards	100
Corporate campaigns:	
Attacking source of finance	30
Action of stockholders	10
Confronting employers on antiunion stands	33
Isolating employers	7
Conducting boycotts	6
Using private intelligence	22
Negotiating:	
Neutrality pledge language	7
Accretion agreements	6
Preferential transfers	4
Preferential hiring language	33
Coordinating resources with other unions	35
Working closely with community leaders to facilitate community acceptance of union	33

Studies indicate grievance handling, job security, and economics are important issues. Differences in treatment across employee groups and decreases in influence in the workplace are often catalysts for organizing. Restructuring related to health care reform has been perceived by nurses to negatively affect patient care and reduce their decision-making ability. Unless they perceived they had administrative support to cope with reorganization, intentions to vote for unionization increased.[46]

A match between the demographic characteristics of the target unit for organizing and the organizers increases success rates, particularly in units predominantly populated by women and/or minorities.[47] If the bargaining unit is predominantly female, face-to-face organizing tactics

[46] P. F. Clark, D. A. Clark, D. V. Day, and D. G. Shea, "Healthcare Reform and the Workplace Experience of Nurses: Implications for Patient Care and Union Organizing," *Industrial and Labor Relations Review*, 55 (2001), pp. 133–148.

[47] K. Bronfenbrenner, "Organizing Women: The Nature and Process of Union-Organizing Efforts among U.S. Women Workers since the Mid-1990s," *Work and Occupations*, 32 (2005), pp. 441–463.

are more successful and advancement and technical training issues are more salient.[48] Organizing campaigns aimed at college and university faculty members are more successful if they stress rational calculations of what unionization could offer rather than stressing trade union solidarity or values.[49] Minority group members are significantly more likely to favor unionizing.[50] Younger employees are less likely to vote for unions. This, however, is apparently not directly age-related but rather due to a lack of experience with employment and unions. Union representation may be seen as an "experience good."[51] Women organizers and organizers for the Service Employees International Union (SEIU) focus more on participation in the workplace, women's issues, and union consciousness in their campaigns.[52] Exhibit 6.2 portrays information from the SEIU's "Janitors for Justice" campaign in Los Angeles that sought to build Latino solidarity.[53]

Beliefs about unions and the opinions of others salient to the future influence voting behavior. A "big labor" perception reduces the willingness to vote for representation, but beliefs that unions are instrumental for gaining positive employment outcomes leads to voting for representation.[54] Personal contact is associated with election success for unions.[55] Voters are influenced by co-worker and family member attitudes toward unionization but not generally by supervisors or managers. Among pharmacists the intention to vote for a union was predicted by prior union experience, being in a union household, and beliefs that the union would

[48] M. L. Lynn and J. Brister, "Trends in Union Organizing Issues and Tactics," *Industrial Relations*, 28 (1989), pp. 104–113.

[49] V. G. Devinatz, "Reflections of a Rank-and-File Faculty Union Organizer at a Public University," *Journal of Collective Negotiations*, 30 (2003), pp. 209–221.

[50] S. M. Hills and G. DeSouza, "Women's Intentions to Vote for Union Certification across Time," *Labor Studies Journal*, 21, no. 4 (1997), pp. 64–80.

[51] A. Bryson, R. Gomez, M. Gunderson, and N. Meltz, "Youth-Adult Differences in the Demand for Unionization: Are American, British, and Canadian Workers All That Different?" *Journal of Labor Research*, 26 (2005), pp. 155–167.

[52] M. Crain, "Gender and Union Organizing," *Industrial and Labor Relations Review*, 47 (1994), pp. 227–248.

[53] C. D. R. Cameron, "Forming More Perfect Unions: What Organizing Success among Latino Workers in Southern California Means for the Future of the American Labor Movement," *Labor Studies Journal*, 25, no. 1 (2000), pp. 45–65; see also J. J. Chun, "Public Dramas and the Politics of Justice: Comparison of Janitors' Union Struggles in South Korea and the United States," *Work and Occupations*, 32 (2005), pp. 486–503.

[54] H. Park, P. P. McHugh, and M. M. Bodah, "Revisiting General and Specific Union Beliefs: The Union-Voting Intentions of Professionals," *Industrial Relations*, 45 (2006), pp. 270–289.

[55] D. M. Savino and N. S. Bruning, "Decertification Strategies and Tactics: Management and Union Perspectives," *Labor Law Journal*, 43 (1992), pp. 201–210.

Exhibit 6.2

Janitors for Justice 2001 Campaign

JUSTICE FOR JANITORS 2001
An international campaign for justice

About Justice for Janitors

Justice for Janitors is a 16-year-old campaign that began in 1985 in Denver, Colorado. The campaign is about hard-working janitors uniting for fair working conditions with support from our communities.

Last year, 100,000 SEIU (Service Employees International Union) janitors in 16 cities across the U.S. made a committment to coordinate their efforts so that janitors could secure a living wage and win health insurance and full-time work. They also vowed to help other janitors win a voice on the job by joining together in a union. Check out our victories!

As part of our campaign, janitors and community supporters demonstrate every June 15th—Justice for Janitors Day—to call attention to our fight for the American Dream.

Justice for Janitors Day was established after janitors in Los Angeles were beaten by police during a peaceful demonstration against the cleaning contractor ISS, on June 15, 1990. The public outrage that generated from this incident resulted in ISS agreeing to recognize L.A. janitors in a union.

In remembrance of that day, SEIU janitors and supporters take action every June 15th in cities nationwide and in countries around the world.

Source: www.justiceforjanitors.org/j4j/about/

improve the professional environment.[56] These influences, combined with beliefs about the union's instrumentality for achieving employment goals, predict actual votes very well.[57]

[56] P. P. McHugh and M. M. Bodah, "Challenges to Professionalism and Union Voting Intentions: The Case of Pharmacists," *Journal of Labor Research*, 23 (2002), pp. 659–271.

[57] B. R. Montgomery, "The Influences of Attitudes and Normative Pressures on Voting Decisions in a Union Certification Election," *Industrial and Labor Relations Review*, 42 (1989), pp. 262–279.

Factors Related to Union Success in Organizing

Union campaign success within industries is affected by firm size, capital intensity, the ratio of labor to total costs, and extremes in profitability. In general, large, unprofitable firms are most vulnerable.[58] Unless there are salient local issues, even well-orchestrated organizing drives are likely to fail, as did efforts to organize several state Blue Cross–Blue Shield insurers.[59]

An analysis of 261 elections found that union wins were predicted by the percentage of authorization card signers, holding solidarity days (buttons and T-shirts), establishing a bargaining committee before the election, and focusing on fairness and justice issues. Teamsters-led drives were significantly less successful. Success was lower in larger units and where the election unit was different from the petition unit. Delay was positively related to success in one-on-one style campaigns. Unemployment and union density were positively related, as was unionization in other units in the same company. Company profitability and a preexisting, quality-of-work-life program were negatively related. Units in which wages were low, workers were younger, and the majority of employees were women and/or minorities were more likely to unionize. Finally, campaigns were more successful when organizers were based in a national union and had one to five years of rank-and-file experience.[60]

Unions that use innovative methods, specialize in representing specific employee groups, and do not have centralized control have more organizing success.[61] Unions that are decentralized and take advantage of information technology are more successful.[62] Unaffiliated locals are more successful in organizing than AFL-CIO unions.[63] In the nonhospital health care industry, unions win more often in for-profit units; when organized by the United Food and Commercial Workers (UFCW) union, American Nurses Association, or an independent; in smaller units; and where the employees are professionals.[64] The SEIU succeeded in organizing child

[58] C. L. Maranto, "Corporate Characteristics and Union Organizing," *Industrial Relations*, 27 (1988), pp. 352–370.

[59] H. R. Northrup, "The AFL-CIO Blue Cross–Blue Shield Campaign: A Study of Organizational Failure," *Industrial and Labor Relations Review*, 43 (1990), pp. 525–541.

[60] K. Bronfenbrenner, "The Role of Union Strategies in NLRB Certification Elections."

[61] J. Fiorito, P. Jarley, and J. T. Delaney, "National Union Effectiveness in Organizing: Measures and Influences," *Industrial and Labor Relations Review*, 48 (1995), pp. 613–635.

[62] J. Fiorito, P. Jarley, and J. T. Delaney, "Information Technology, U.S. Union Organizing and Union Effectiveness," *British Journal of Industrial Relations*, 40 (2002), pp. 627–658.

[63] M. H. Sandver and K. J. Ready, "Trends in and Determinants of Outcomes in Multi-Union Certification Elections," *Journal of Labor Research*, 19 (1998), pp. 165–172; and V. G. Devinatz and D. P. Rich, "Information, Disinformation, and Union Success in Certification and Decertification Elections," *Journal of Labor Research*, 17 (1996), pp. 199–210.

[64] C. Scott, A. Seers, and R. Culpepper, "Determinants of Union Election Outcomes in the Non-Hospital Health Care Industry," *Journal of Labor Research*, 17 (1996), pp. 701–715.

care workers in Illinois using nontraditional approaches that bypassed NLRB-supervised elections,[65] and it succeeded with home health care workers in California by identifying employers and working with both caregivers and consumers to improve the quality of both employment and care.[66] Organizing immigrant workers has often begun through community organizing efforts that escalate to include a drive for unionization.[67] Immigrants with language and/or document deficiencies are much less likely to hold public sector jobs, hence less likely and perhaps more difficult to unionize.[68]

Union organizers do not expect that all campaigns will be successful on the first attempt. If there is a substantial union vote that fails to achieve a majority and if the turnover rate is relatively low, the union can rely on an established cadre to work on subsequent campaigns. In these situations, the union's future campaigns focus on tracking whether management fulfilled postelection promises that it made to address employee problems.[69]

Neutrality Pledges and Card Check Agreements

Where not all units of an employer are already organized, unions try to negotiate neutrality pledges into the collective bargaining agreement. These pledges require that the employer agree not to oppose future organizing drives by the union within the company. Card check agreements may also be negotiated for units that are not currently unionized. Neutrality agreements have been negotiated between the Communications Workers (CWA) and the major land-line phone companies, except CenturyLink, and the CWA has card check agreements with AT&T and Verizon.[70] UNITE HERE has a neutrality pledge agreement with both Hilton and Starwood hotel chains.[71]

Card check agreements substantially increase the probability of organizing success. The effect is considerably greater than that of neutrality

[65] F. P. Brooks, "New Turf for Organizing: Family Child Care Providers," *Labor Studies Journal*, 29, no. 4 (2004), pp. 37–44.

[66] L. Delp and K. Quan, "Homecare Worker Organizing in California: An Analysis of a Successful Strategy," *Labor Studies Journal*, 27, no. 1 (2002), pp. 1–24. See also P. M. Mareschal, "Innovation and Adaptation: Contrasting Efforts to Organize Home Care Workers in Four States," *Labor Studies Journal*, 31, no. 1 (2006), pp. 25–49.

[67] J. Gabriel, "*Si, Se Peude*: Organizing Latino Immigrant Workers in South Omaha's Meatpacking Industry," *Journal of Labor Research*, 29 (2008), pp. 6–87.

[68] R. Milkman, "Labor Organizing among Mexican-Born Workers in the United States," *Labor Studies Journal*, 32, no. 1 (2007), pp. 96–112.

[69] Lawler, *Unionization and Deunionization*, pp. 23–24.

[70] J. Keefe and R. Batt, "Telecommunications: Collective Bargaining in an Era of Industry Reconsolidation," in P. F. Clark, J. T. Delaney, and A. C. Frost, eds., *Collective Bargaining in the Private Sector* (Champaign, IL: Industrial Relations Research Association, 2002), pp. 263–310.

[71] R. W. Hurd, "U.S. Labor 2006: Strategic Developments across the Divide," *Journal of Labor Research*, 28 (2007), pp. 313–325.

pledges because a card check would never be sought before the union held a majority. With a neutrality pledge, bargaining-unit determination might still be an issue and an election would be held.[72] One study comparing U.S. and Canadian organizing campaigns found that about 3 to 5 percent of the difference in unionization between the two countries can be accounted for by the greater prevalence of card checks leading to voluntary recognition in Canada.[73] In British Columbia, organizing law first permitted card majorities to be sufficient for recognition. Later, elections were required, and union organizing success declined by 19 percent. When card check evidence was reinstituted as sufficient, success rebounded by 19 percent.[74] Requiring an election instead of allowing card checks enables the employer to orchestrate an opposition campaign. Management frequently argues that permitting recognition through card checks may increase potential coercion by organizers. However, a survey of workers who had experience with card check and election situations felt that employers were more coercive than union organizers or co-workers.[75]

Management Strategy and Tactics

Management plans strategy and tactics both at corporate offices and at the site where organizing is occurring. Except in the public sector or where neutrality pledges have been given, management strongly resists organizing. Advisers are sent out at the first sign of union activity. Major firms have specific goals for repelling or containing union organizing efforts.[76]

Many organizations conduct attitude surveys and ask supervisors to keep alert for signs of potential organizing activity. When organizing occurs, consultants are often hired to assist managers in conducting an anti-union campaign.[77] Uncovering union activity in a covert manner, restricting solicitations, waging an intense campaign, and opposing a consent election reduce union win rates.[78] If an election petition is filed,

[72] A. E. Eaton and J. Kriesky, "Union Organizing under Neutrality and Card Check Agreements," *Industrial and Labor Relations Review*, 55 (2001), pp. 42–59.

[73] S. Johnson, "The Impact of Mandatory Votes on the Canada-U.S. Union Density Gap: A Note," *Industrial Relations*, 43 (2004), pp. 356–363.

[74] C. Riddell, "Union Certification Success under Voting versus Card-Check Procedures: Evidence from British Columbia, 1978–98," *Industrial and Labor Relations Review*, 57 (2004), pp. 493–517.

[75] A. E. Eaton and J. Kriesky, "NLRB Elections versus Card Check Campaigns: Results of a Worker Survey," *Industrial and Labor Relations Review*, 62 (2009), pp. 157–172.

[76] A. Freedman, *Managing Labor Relations* (New York: Conference Board, 1979), p. 33; and A. Freedman, *The New Look in Wage Policy and Employee Relations* (New York: Conference Board, 1985), pp. 5–6.

[77] B. E. Kaufman and P. E. Stephan, "The Role of Management Attorneys in Union Organizing Campaigns," *Journal of Labor Research*, 16 (1995), pp. 439–455.

[78] K. F. Murrman and A. A. Porter, "Employer Campaign Tactics and NLRB Election Outcomes: Some Preliminary Evidence," *Proceedings of the Industrial Relations Research Association*, 35 (1982), pp. 67–72.

management almost always contests the proposed bargaining unit to gain time to mount an intensive opposition campaign. Delay in conducting an election is strongly associated with union losses.[79]

Management campaigns paint unions as outsiders that are less concerned than the employer about employee welfare. They also argue that unionization may not improve conditions and that employees will lose the right to deal individually with employers on employment conditions. Management communicates directly with employees and their families to oppose the union. Employers hold mass meetings, small-group discussions with management specialists, and individual interviews giving information on present (not anticipated) company human resource programs.[80] Supervisors, a group that communicates daily with rank-and-file employees, need extensive briefings on the company's position and how to avoid ULPs.

Undecided employees tend to vote for the company rather than the union.[81] Unless employees make an effort to gain exposure to the union's position, they will have heard much more from management during the campaign.

Management uses tactics that give early warnings of organizing and combine outside consultants, strong inside involvement, and delays.[82] One study found that union win rates decreased when employers increased wages (illegal), made promises about future changes (illegal), held frequent captive-audience meetings, and sent several letters to employees during the campaign. But union tactics were about three times as influential as management tactics.[83]

Some employers, particularly those with low wages and poor working conditions,[84] purposely commit ULPs to blunt organizing drives. In 2001 the Supreme Court enforced an NLRB finding against Beverly Enterprises barring it from intimidating employees attempting to organize. The nursing home operator, in a campaign orchestrated by top management, was

[79] C. Riddell, "The Causal Effect of Election Delay on Union Win Rates: Instrumental Variable Estimates from Two Natural Experiments," *Industrial Relations*, 49 (2010), pp. 371–386.

[80] For an overview and incidents involving consultants for both sides, see *Labor Relations Consultants: Issues, Trends, and Controversies* (Washington, DC: Bureau of National Affairs, 1985).

[81] J. Getman, S. Goldberg, and J. B. Herman, *Union Representation Elections: Law and Reality* (New York: Russell Sage Foundation, 1976), pp. 100–108.

[82] Murrman and Porter, "Employer Campaign Tactics and NLRB Election Outcomes"; J. Lawler, "Labor-Management Consultants in Union Organizing Campaigns: Do They Make a Difference?" *Proceedings of the Industrial Relations Research Association*, 34 (1981), pp. 374–380; and J. J. Lawler, "Union Growth and Decline: The Impact of Employer and Union Tactics," *Journal of Occupational Psychology*, 59 (1986), pp. 217–230.

[83] Bronfenbrenner, "The Role of Union Strategies in NLRB Certification Elections."

[84] R. B. Freeman and M. M. Kleiner, "Employer Behavior in the Face of Union Organizing Drives," *Industrial and Labor Relations Review*, 43 (1990), pp. 351–365.

found to have committed 240 ULPs in 54 facilities across 18 states.[85] The cost of back pay to employees for rehiring fired union activists was far less than the potential costs of negotiated wage increases if the union won. Employer ULPs occur most often in industries where unionization is prevalent and where the labor acts have been violated previously.[86] Consequences are slight. Discrimination against union activists decreases union organizing success by about 17 percent.[87] Employees who perceived that their employers committed ULPs in campaigns were less likely to vote for representation than those who had not, other things being equal.[88] Employers involved in multiple campaigns increase their likelihood of committing ULPs.[89] ULP charges by unions have increased substantially since 1970, and at the same time, union election success and the number of elections have fallen. The intensity of management campaigns has continued to increase while organizing activity has decreased. Estimates indicate that management spends $500 or more per person in a proposed bargaining unit to finance its campaign to oppose unionization.[90] For an employee with compensation costs of $30,000 per year, this is substantially less than the likely negotiated pay increase in a first contract.

THE ROLE OF THE NLRB

The NLRB conducts the election and certifies the results. If there are ULP charges, it must decide whether they occurred and interfered with employees' Taft-Hartley Section 7 rights to freely choose. The NLRB's position is that an election should "provide a laboratory in which an experiment may be conducted, under conditions as nearly ideal as possible, to determine the uninhibited desires of the employees."[91]

Election Certifications

After the election, ballots are counted to determine whether any alternative received a majority. If no objections or unfair campaign charges are

[85] P. F. Clark, "Health Care: A Growing Role for Collective Bargaining," in P. F. Clark, J. T. Delaney, and A. C. Frost, eds., *Collective Bargaining in the Private Sector* (Champaign, IL: Industrial Relations Research Association, 2002), pp. 91–135.

[86] M. M. Kleiner, "Unionism and Employer Discrimination: Analysis of 8(a)(3) Violations," *Industrial Relations*, 23 (1984), pp. 234–243.

[87] W. N. Cooke, "The Rising Toll of Discrimination against Union Activists," *Industrial Relations*, 24 (1985), pp. 421–442.

[88] T. J. Keaveny, J. Rosse, and J. A. Fossum, "Campaign Tactics and Certification Election Outcomes," unpublished manuscript (Milwaukee, WI: Marquette University, 1989).

[89] J. Lawler, *Unionization and Deunionization*, pp. 76–77.

[90] M. M. Kleiner, "Intensity of Management Resistance: Understanding the Decline of Unionization in the Private Sector," *Journal of Labor Research*, 22 (2001), pp. 519–540.

[91] *General Shoe Corp.*, 77 NLRB 127 (1948).

filed, the NLRB certifies the results. If a union won, it becomes the employees' exclusive representative and can begin contract negotiations. If it lost, and challenges are unsuccessful, then an **election bar** takes effect, barring elections for one year. Even if a winning union loses its majority within the year, the board won't permit a new election. The Supreme Court has ruled that certification is equivalent to an elected term in office, even if the official's constituents no longer support him or her.[92] If the union lost the election, the employer cannot legally take action against its supporters because they have, under Section 7, the right to attempt to organize.

Setting Aside Elections

If challenges are filed and the board finds the activity interfered with the employees' abilities to make a reasoned choice, the election will be set aside and rerun. If the violations are trivial, the board certifies the results.

Bargaining Orders

In some cases, the board considers an employer's **totality of conduct;** that is, was an employer's overall conduct so coercive that it eroded a preelection majority? For example, assume that a majority of employees sign authorization cards and attend union meetings and that the employer interrogates employees, threatens cutbacks and possible plant closings, or indicates that it would never agree to bargaining demands even if the union won. If the union loses and the board finds employer conduct undermined an actual union majority, it issues a **bargaining order,** requiring the employer to recognize and negotiate with the union. The remedial approach is imposed because the union would have won if not for the employer's illegal conduct.[93] Following the Supreme Court's decision in the *Gissel* case, circuit courts have generally enforced so-called *Gissel* orders only where there is clear evidence that a majority of employees favored the union at some point during the campaign, that the majority was undermined as a direct consequence of the employer's actions, and that a rerun could not redress the problems. About half of NLRB *Gissel*-type orders are enforced by circuit courts.[94]

The Impact of Board Remedies

Unions win rerun elections less frequently than they win initial elections. This is consistent with evidence that intensive employer campaigns

[92] *Brooks* v. *NLRB*, 348 U.S. 96 (1954).

[93] *NLRB* v. *Gissel Packing Co.*, 395 U.S. 575 (1969); for a case in which the NLRB issued a bargaining order where no majority had been demonstrated but where the employer's behavior was seen as preventing its establishment, see G. R. Salem, "Nonmajority Bargaining Orders: A Prospective View in Light of *United Dairy Farmers*," *Labor Law Journal*, 32 (1981), pp. 145–157.

[94] P. J. Leff, "Failing to Give the Board Its Due: The Lack of Deference Afforded by the Appellate Courts in *Gissel* Bargaining Order Cases," *Labor Lawyer,* 18 (2002), pp. 93–120.

TABLE 6.2
Union Win Rate by Unit Size, Fiscal 2009

Size of Unit	Number Eligible	Total Elections	% Won by Union
<10	2,273	367	65.9%
10 to 19	5,018	318	56.9
20 to 29	5,087	197	60.4
30 to 39	3,910	115	64.3
40 to 49	4,801	108	65.7
50 to 69	7,987	133	66.2
70 to 99	10,079	118	66.1
100 to 149	12,604	103	66.0
150 to 199	7,474	46	69.6
200 to 299	11,359	54	57.4
300 to 499	9,671	26	57.7
500 to 999	6,910	14	78.6
1,000 and over	7,795	5	80.0

reduce union win rates. However, delays in conducting a rerun appear to operate in the union's favor.[95] Bargaining orders do not necessarily lead to a contract. An examination of a large number of *Gissel*-type cases found that in only 39 percent were unions able to achieve a contract. Success in getting a contract is apparently independent of unit size, extent of organization, or type of employer violation.[96]

Besides reruns or bargaining orders, the NLRB can issue cease-and-desist orders for ULPs during organizing drives. If employees were fired for union activity, their reinstatement will be ordered with back pay and interest to cover the difference between actual earnings and wages they would have earned after the unlawful discipline. However, if employers fire undocumented workers for organizing, the Supreme Court has ruled that they are not entitled to back pay because they were never legally entitled to work.[97]

Election Outcomes

In 2009, 78,736 persons voted in 1,651 NLRB-conducted representation elections. Of these, 1,338 were requested by unions, employees, or employers in initial representation (labeled RC and RM cases by the NLRB), and 269 were filed by employees seeking decertification (RD cases). Table 6.2

[95] M. Mayfield and J. Mayfield, "NLRB Election Delays: Do They Make a Difference?" *Labor Law Journal*, 50 (1999), pp. 53–57.

[96] B. W. Wolkinson, N. B. Hanslowe, and S. Sperka, "The Remedial Efficacy of *Gissel* Bargaining Orders," *Industrial Relations Law Journal*, 10 (1989), pp. 509–530.

[97] *Hoffman Plastic Compounds, Inc.* v. *NLRB*, 535 U.S. 137 (2002).

shows the size of bargaining units, number of employees eligible to vote, total elections, and percentage of elections won by unions in 2009. Over half of these elections were conducted in units of less than 30 employees. Unions won about 63.2 percent of all elections. Union win rates are higher in white-collar units, and independent unions win more frequently than unions affiliated with the AFL-CIO.

Other Types of Representation Changes

After certification, some events might lead an employer to doubt whether the union continues to have a majority. Low membership, little bargaining activity, lack of interest by national union representatives, and significant workforce changes could contribute to this doubt. In small units, a national union may abandon the local if there are difficult relations with the members. If there have been strikes, the employer might have replaced the strikers. Even though the unit consists of new employees, the employer cannot presume replacements oppose the union. An employer may withdraw recognition only if there is clear-cut evidence that the union has actually lost its majority.[98] However, if an employer has a good-faith doubt about majority status, it may request a decertification election.[99]

If an election bar does not exist and no contract is in force, another union could supplant the current bargaining representative. So-called raid elections require showings of interest similar to initial representation elections. Incumbent unions win raid elections more often when there is higher unemployment, in large units, and the local is affiliated with a national union.[100]

Contextual Characteristics Related to Election Results

Union Characteristics

Unaffiliated unions win more often than AFL-CIO unions. They may be more in tune with workplace interests.[101] Larger and more democratic unions win more often. Direct benefits to members and relatively lower dues enhance organizing success for white-collar employees but make no difference for blue-collar workers.[102] Teamsters win fewer elections.

[98] *Allentown Mack Sales & Serv.* v. *NLRB*, 522 U.S. 359 (1998).

[99] Stamatakos and Piskorski, "*Levitz Furniture*: NLRB Rewrites the Book on Employer Efforts to Oust Incumbent Unions."

[100] E. Arnold, C. Scott, and J. Rasp, "The Determinants of Incumbent Union Victory in Raid Elections," *Labor Law Journal*, 43 (1992), pp. 221–228.

[101] V. G. Devinatz and D. P. Rich, "Representation Types and Union Success in Certification Elections," *Journal of Labor Research*, 14 (1993), pp. 85–92.

[102] C. L. Maranto and J. Fiorito, "The Effect of Union Characteristics on the Outcome of NLRB Certification Elections," *Industrial and Labor Relations Review*, 40 (1987), pp. 225–239.

Environmental Characteristics

Organizing is easier in units where employees are in relatively homogeneous skill groups. If job-duty changes increase the skill mix, lower organizing success can be expected.[103] State right-to-work laws appear to damage the credibility of organized labor. Organizing attempts decrease about 50 percent in the first five years after their passage and an additional 25 percent over the next five years. Membership is reduced between 5 and 10 percent.[104]

Preferences for unionism among private sector and public sector employees differ. In the private sector, preferences are associated with beliefs that the union will be instrumental for workplace changes, the union's image, job dissatisfaction, and beliefs that the employer will not positively change the workplace. Public sector employees are most influenced by the union's image and the employer's inability to positively change the workplace. Public sector employees respond more positively to job security themes during a campaign than do those in the private sector.[105] Registered nurses who were employed by health care providers involved in mergers or restructurings perceived a reduction in the attention paid to health care and their interest in increased unionization.[106]

Worker Characteristics

Most representation election voting models focus on attitudes and characteristics predicting an intent to vote and the relationship between intent and actual voting.[107] Studies of race and ethnic characteristics find that only African Americans have a stronger preference for representation.[108] In a South Florida study, African Americans had more favorable attitudes toward unions than did whites, who, in turn, had more favorable attitudes than Hispanics. Women were more willing to vote for unions

[103] R. S. Demsetz, "Voting Behavior in Union Representation Elections: The Influence of Skill Homogeneity and Skill Group Size," *Industrial and Labor Relations Review*, 47 (1993), pp. 99–113.

[104] D. T. Ellwood and G. Fine, "The Impact of Right-to-Work Laws on Union Organizing," *Journal of Political Economy*, 95 (1987), pp. 250–273.

[105] J. Fiorito, L. P. Stepina, and D. P. Bozeman, "Explaining the Unionism Gap: Public-Private Sector Difference in Preferences for Unionization," *Journal of Labor Research*, 17 (1996), pp. 463–478.

[106] P. F. Clark, D. A. Clark, D. Day, and D. Shea, "Health Care Reform's Impact on Hospitals: Implications for Union Organizing," *Proceedings of the Industrial Relations Research Association*, 51 (1999), pp. 61–67.

[107] For a comprehensive summary and analysis of this research, see H. N. Wheeler and J. A. McClendon, "The Individual Decision to Unionize," in G. Strauss, D. G. Gallagher, and J. Fiorito, eds., *The State of the Unions* (Madison, WI: Industrial Relations Research Association, 1991), pp. 47–84.

[108] G. DeFreitas, "Unionization among Racial and Ethnic Minorities," *Industrial and Labor Relations Review*, 46 (1992), pp. 284–301.

than men.[109] Recent immigrants unionize at about the same rate as other new entrants to the labor force.[110] Family values and work beliefs predict attitudes toward unions, with people whose families were union members and who have Marxist and/or humanistic work beliefs having a stronger interest in joining a union.[111]

FIRST CONTRACTS

If a union wins a representation election, it still can face formidable barriers in bargaining with the employer. Before bargaining can begin, the NLRB has to certify the election results. Employers may object to a variety of campaign irregularities and, if the election was close, the eligibility of some voters. If objections are raised, some time will elapse until the board issues a ruling. During the delay, the company may take a number of employee relations actions that indicate it will take a tough stance toward the union. In addition, it may discipline union activists, thereby committing ULPs and reducing long-run interests in remaining unionized. If the union is faced with an intransigent management strategy, it will need to use substantial energy and resources to combat the employer.[112]

For its part, the union needs to shift its tactics from an organizing to a negotiating mode. Organizing is highly adversarial, while negotiating requires that the parties, especially the union, start from the position that gaining agreement on a contract is a primary goal. If a national union assisted in organizing, this may be the point at which a new representative—one not involved in organizing—is brought in to assist the new local.[113] Newly organized local members are usually inexperienced in negotiating and need training and assistance from the national. An unaffiliated local often has difficulty learning how to negotiate, but this weakness may be offset by greater worker involvement in its organization and operation.

An employer may also undermine the union during the bargaining process. It might refuse to bargain on technical grounds such as the

[109] R. Silverblatt and R. J. Amann, "Race, Ethnicity, Union Attitudes, and Voting Predilections," *Industrial Relations*, 30 (1991), pp. 271–285.

[110] E. Funkhouser, "Do Immigrants Have Lower Unionization Propensities than Natives?" *Industrial Relations*, 32 (1993), pp. 248–261.

[111] J. Barling, E. K. Kelloway, and E. H. Bremermann, "Preemployment Predictors of Union Attitudes: The Role of Family Socialization and Work Beliefs," *Journal of Applied Psychology*, 76 (1991), pp. 725–731.

[112] W. N. Cooke, "Failure to Negotiate First Contracts," *Industrial and Labor Relations Review*, 38 (1985), pp. 163–178; and W. N. Cooke, "The Rising Toll of Discrimination against Union Activists."

[113] T. F. Reed, "Securing a Union Contract: Impact of the Union Organizer," *Industrial Relations*, 32 (1993), pp. 188–203.

appropriateness of the bargaining unit. This will require NLRB intervention and a bargaining order. It also might bargain in a defiant or evasive manner by making it difficult for the union to get information about the employer's situation and starting with an offer that includes conditions and wages lower than those presently implemented.[114]

A particularly egregious example of attempting to thwart organizing and bargaining is represented by the S. Lichtenberg case. After organizing failures in 1966 and 1971, the Amalgamated Clothing and Textile Workers (ACTWU) finally organized the rural Georgia curtain maker in 1988. The ACTWU tied the organizing effort to community concerns. The unit was 90 percent African American women. After losing the representation election, the company delayed the start of negotiations and fired employees who were union leaders. The NLRB ordered reinstatement with back pay. The ACTWU provided training on leadership and collective action, particularly following certification. A corporate campaign alerted Kmart and JCPenney, two major S. Lichtenberg customers, about unionization issues and also tied in civil rights issues. A first contract was finally negotiated in 1991. The company continued to fight the union by hiring replacements, and it attempted to decertify during a strike in 1994.[115]

If the employer can forestall reaching an agreement for at least one year after initial certification, employees could (with sufficient interest) petition for a decertification election. It is also possible that the union could fail to enroll a majority of workers as union members and conclude that interest in representation is waning. It might, in unusual circumstances, abandon the negotiations and walk away from the situation. A study of union organizing drives found that only one out of seven election petitions resulted in a contract within a year. Campaigns in which unions filed ULP charges were 30 percent less likely to result in a contract.[116]

Evidence suggests that newly organized employers have been taking a harder line in negotiating first contracts, especially since there are few real penalties the NLRB can implement for refusing to bargain. Where a management is particularly intransigent, community action and/or corporate campaigns may be the only effective strategy the union can use to buttress its attempts to win an initial contract. A study of FMCS-assisted negotiations found that in about a quarter of cases, managements and unions failed to reach agreement on a first contract.[117]

[114] R. W. Hurd, "Union-Free Bargaining Strategies and First Contract Failures," *Proceedings of the Industrial Relations Research Association*, 48 (1996), pp. 145–152.

[115] R. Bussel, "Southern Organizing in the Post-Civil Rights Era: The Case of S. Lichtenberg," *Industrial and Labor Relations Review*, 52 (1999), pp. 528–538.

[116] J.-P. Ferguson, "The Eyes of the Needles: A Sequential Model of Union Organizing Drives, 1999–2004," *Industrial and Labor Relations Review*, 62 (2008), pp. 3–21.

[117] J. Cutcher-Gershenfeld and T. A. Kochan, "Taking Stock: Collective Bargaining at the Turn of the Century," *Industrial and Labor Relations Review*, 58 (2004), pp. 3–26.

Summary

Organizing is an intense process involving unions, employers, and the NLRB. The union's goal is to organize a majority of employees, the employer seeks to avoid unionization, and the NLRB's role is to provide employees with the opportunity to make a free choice about whether to be represented or to remain unorganized.

A union organizing campaign can be started by employees or by union organizers. Components of the campaign include the signing of authorization cards, demands for recognition, election petitions, determining an appropriate bargaining unit, the election campaign, the election, and NLRB certification of the results.

The organizing campaign includes communications from the union and employer, attempts by the union to contact every potential voter, mass meetings, small-group meetings with supervisors, and development of union committees in preparation for bargaining. Employers usually have an advantage in accessing employees to present their campaign positions.

Recent results show that unions improve their chances for success where organizers with rank-and-file work experience conduct a person-to-person grassroots campaign that emphasizes fairness, voice, and equity issues. Employers usually campaign intensively against unionization and often commit ULPs in the process. The penalties for ULPs include, among other things, restoration of discharged employees with back pay, election reruns, or bargaining orders. Increasingly, corporate campaigns are used as an adjunct to local organizing in influencing employer resistance to organizing.

Unions win almost two-thirds of all contested elections. A large share of elections are conducted in units with fewer than 30 employees. Even if a union wins an election, there are several difficulties it must overcome to successfully negotiate a first contract.

Discussion Questions

1. To what extent should the NLRB get involved in determining bargaining units? Shouldn't the vote be in the unit preferred by the employees?
2. Should union organizers have more or less access to employees in organizing campaigns than they have now?
3. Should the NLRB require union organizer access to the workplace as a quid pro quo for an employer demanding an election rather than agreeing to a card check, thereby gaining a delay in the outcome?
4. Do employers have an unfair tactical advantage in union organizing situations?
5. Is an adversarial relationship necessary for successful organizing and permanent unionization of an employer's establishment?

Key Terms

Exclusive representation, *156*
Union-free, *157*
Authorization card, *158*
Recognitional picketing, *160*
Representation election, *160*
Certification election, *160*
Decertification election, *160*
Raid election, *160*
Appropriate bargaining unit, *161*
Consent election, *162*
Board-directed (petition) election, *162*
Regional director, *162*
Excelsior list, *162*
Multiemployer bargaining, *163*
Community of interests, *166*
Craft severance, *167*
Accretion, *168*
Community action, *176*
Corporate campaign, *176*
Election bar, *185*
Totality of conduct, *185*
Bargaining order, *185*

Web Sites

www.aflcio.org
www.changetowin.org
www.laboreducator.org
www.nlrb.gov
www.nrtw.org
www.nuhw.org
www.seiu.org

Case: *GMFC Custom Conveyer Division*

Last year, General Materials and Fabrication Corporation (GMFC) acquired a manufacturer of custom-built conveyer equipment used in the freight forwarding industry. The nonunion plant, renamed the Custom Conveyer Division (CCD), employs about 120 production employees, 3 supervisors, a general supervisor, a production manager, 2 engineers, 3 office clericals, and a plant manager. The production employees are in five semi-skilled job classifications: fabricator, welder, prepper, painter, and assembler.

The fabricators convert raw material, such as steel plates and tubes, into parts using presses, sheers, numerical-control cutting equipment, and the like. Welders take the fabricated parts and create frames for conveyer subassemblies. They also weld sheet metal into complex slides and chutes. Preppers clean welding slag, grind welds, degrease welded assemblies, and perform other cleaning activities necessary before painting. Painters spray paint assemblies using a variety of paints and painting equipment, taking special care not to paint areas where additional parts will be attached. Assemblers, working in teams, use the welded subassemblies and fabricated parts (purchased parts such as rollers, chains, sprockets, belts, motors, and switches) to assemble the equipment and test its operation. Then the assemblers travel to the installation site to combine the subassemblies and test the completed custom installation.

The plant is located in Cumberland, a small rural city of about 2,500. All employees are hired from about a 20-mile radius around the plant. The starting wage for all classifications is $12 per hour, with an increase to $12.50 after a 60-day probationary period. Wages increase to a maximum of $14 per hour in three 50-cent increases at six-month intervals. About 75 percent of the employees are earning the maximum hourly rate. CCD pays for comprehensive health insurance for all employees and provides for 80 percent of the cost of dependent coverage. Turnover is very low, averaging about 5 percent per year from all causes. Two other plants in Cumberland hire employees with the same types of skills and pay a starting wage of $11 per hour. Most of GMFC's employees have been hired from those plants.

The plant earned over $1.25 million after taxes last year on gross revenues of $9 million. Sales have been increasing about 20 percent per year recently. Total labor costs last year were $4.5 million. Materials cost $1.5 million. Facility maintenance was $0.5 million and depreciation on the plant and equipment equaled $0.75 million. Taxes totaled $0.5 million. Labor and material costs are variable. Maintenance and depreciation are fixed for the next year since about 20 percent of the plant's capacity is unused. If expansion continues, there is enough space on the current property to double the plant size at a cost of about $10 million. The local labor market can provide workers with the required entry-level skills if the operations were to double over the next four years. Five other competitors manufacture this type of equipment, but GMFC-CCD has established a reputation for high quality and low cost, and its market share is expanding. Because most of the conveyer systems are used in airports and warehouse operations in large cities, transportation is required for each unit shipped. GMFC paid about $16.5 million for the operation when it was purchased last year.

UNION ORGANIZING

The district director of the United Steelworkers in the region in which Cumberland is located wants to increase the number of members in the district. He received an e-mail today from

Dave Neumeier, an employee of GMFC-CCD, who is a former Steelworker member. Dave suggested that CCD was ripe for organizing given the difference in wages between CCD and GMFC's main Central City operation. He said some of the preppers were dissatisfied, too, because their work was much more repetitive and dirtier than the other jobs but the pay was the same.

The district director assigned two of his newest organizers, Rebecca Shea and Rick Anderson, to attempt to organize the plant. Rebecca just graduated from the state university with a bachelor's in labor studies. Rick was a welder for a heavy-equipment manufacturer. The district director has given them a copy of the GMFC contract that's currently in force (see the mock negotiating exercise at the end of Chapter 11). Rebecca and Rick have been instructed to try to get jobs at the plant and begin organizing internally. If that's not possible, they are to contact Neumeier and get names and addresses of employees. In either event, they need to formulate a strategy for organizing.

MANAGEMENT

James Holroyd, the plant manager, has just held his weekly supervisors meeting. A supervisor, Steve Christian, said a new employee who just moved to the area, Dave Neumeier, has a Steelworkers local sticker on the inside of his toolbox. While there has been no union activity at CCD, Holroyd was told by GMFC top management to make sure the operation remained nonunion. While work has been steady lately, a layoff is possible in two months if new orders aren't received.

The plant has a generous recreational program for employees, with a party every quarter; sponsored bowling, softball, and flag football teams; and an extensive DVD library for free use by employees.

PROBLEM

If you have a union organizer role, develop a strategy for organizing this plant. Consider such things as the authorization card campaign, contacts with employees, campaign literature, comparisons you want employees to make, bargaining-unit determination, coping with delays, and potential ULP charges.

If you have a management role, develop a strategy to maintain a nonunion employment situation. How would you determine whether an organizing threat is likely? Create employee communications, supervisory training programs, and the like. Consider how you would respond to potentially untruthful campaign literature. How will you deal with Dave Neumeier if he starts to encourage employees to unionize?

Chapter Seven

Union Avoidance: Rationale, Strategies, and Practices

Chapter 6 examined union organizing campaigns. The chapter covered the flow of events associated with a campaign, union strategies and tactics, management responses, the roles of the National Labor Relations Board (NLRB) and the National Mediation Board (NMB), and the factors influencing election outcomes. At several points, the chapter emphasized that, except in isolated instances, most employers strongly resist organizing drives.

In this chapter we explore in greater depth the reasons for employers' resistance, strategies that employers are using to create and maintain a "union-free" employment environment, tactics that they use to prevent union success in organizing, the role of decertifications in deunionizing partially unionized employers, and the effects of organizational and job structuring on limiting unionization within employers.

As you study this chapter, consider the following questions:

1. Are employers increasing or decreasing their opposition to unions in the current era? What evidence is there to support your position?
2. What are the economic effects of initial unionization on the employer?
3. What factors are related to an employer avoiding unionization?
4. If an employer faces an organizing campaign, what strategies and tactics are included in a typical employer response?
5. What is a decertification election, and how does it differ from other NLRB elections?

HISTORICAL OVERVIEW

The business and labor history of the United States, going back to the Philadelphia Cordwainers, is replete with examples of employer resistance to unionization. The fundamental differences in philosophies, goals, and values of capitalists and trade unionists make this resistance inevitable and make employer accommodation after unionization sometimes difficult.

Capitalistic and Trade Union Philosophies

Capitalists (either entrepreneurs or investor-owned corporations) use their resources to create mechanisms (productive processes) that will enable them to develop and sell goods and services in the marketplace at prices great enough to yield a higher return than that from other alternative investments. Employees are hired to produce the output. Employees are generally free to leave at any time, and capitalists would like to have the freedom to hire or terminate them, individually or collectively, as necessary to achieve their business purposes. Capitalists assume the risk that they will not be able to realize a positive yield from their investments and ideas. If they fail, their investments will be diminished or lost. They also expect that if they are successful in the marketplace (i.e., their returns are greater than they might realize through riskless investment) they will be able to retain their profits as a reward for taking the risk.

Trade unionists believe that wealth is ultimately created by the workers who produce the products or deliver the services to the consumer. In cases where the firm is successful in the market (i.e., it makes a profit), unions attribute a large measure of the success to the efforts of employees. Their actions are seen as ultimately adding the value to the inputs that make the products and services attractive in the market. From a union perspective, these gains need to be shared with the employees. While employers would like complete freedom to hire, fire, and assign workers to jobs, unions see employees as becoming increasingly invested in their jobs with their employers. Job property rights are established over time and employers should be constrained in the types of decisions they can make about employees as employees accrue seniority and firm-specific skills. Unions also believe that employees should have a role in determining the rules that will be used to decide how profits and productivity gains will be distributed and how the workplace will be governed. Employees are seen as investing a substantial part of their lives in employment, often with a particular employer. As such, they are entitled to a role in determining how the social system in which they are involved should be operated.

Employer Resistance before World War II

As noted in Chapter 2, employers engaged in a variety of strategies and tactics to avoid unionization or to reduce its power. They used security forces to police the workforce, forcibly kept out organizers, or ferreted out internal union activists or sympathizers from the late 1800s to World War II. These types of tactics were particularly prevalent in steel and auto production plants.

Employer resistance was greatest and most successful where workers were essentially unskilled, where employers controlled entry to occupations, and where an employer was the dominant business in a given location. The organization of the workplace gave a great deal of power to foremen (supervisors) in the direction, control, and discipline of the workforce. The ability of an employee to retain a position depended to a large extent on whether he or she pleased the supervisor. This approach has been labeled the "drive system," and it held sway in manufacturing for most of the first third of the 20th century.[1]

During the 1920s and 1930s, employers implemented their own versions of "community action" plans—the American Plan and the Mohawk Valley formula. Both of these sought to link labor unions with interests outside the community—especially with foreign ideologies. The Mohawk Valley formula, in particular, mobilized community leaders and police against organizing and strikes. Both plans stressed the need for workers to be able to refrain from joining unions and to be able to deal directly with their employers rather than through outside agents. Where unionization seemed unavoidable, employers worked with sympathetic employees to help establish so-called **company unions** that would not be affiliated with a larger international and would be less militant and more familiar and sympathetic with the employer's situation.[2] The passage of the Wagner Act, however, made employee organizations that were established and assisted by employers illegal.

The Corporatist Period

From the late 1940s through the middle to late 1970s, large U.S. employers and unions moved through a period during which unions were essentially conceded a permanent role in a tripartite employment environment involving employers, unions, and the government as reflected in public policy toward employment. Laws and regulations favored collective bargaining as the method for dealing with industrial disputes. Productivity rose at a steady rate, and wage increases could be financed without substantial inflationary pressure until the late 1960s and 1970s.

However, the demand shock of the Vietnam War and the oil supply shocks of the 1970s and their effects on inflation, together with the

[1] D. M. Gordon, "From the Drive System to the Capital-Labor Accord: Econometric Tests for the Transition between Productivity Regimes," *Industrial Relations*, 36 (1997), pp. 125–159.

[2] S. M. Jacoby, "Reckoning with Company Unions: The Case of Thompson Products, 1934–1964," *Industrial and Labor Relations Review*, 43 (1989), pp. 19–40; and D. Nelson, "Managers and Nonunion Workers in the Rubber Industry: Union Avoidance Strategies in the 1930s," *Industrial and Labor Relations Review*, 43 (1989), pp. 41–52.

beginnings of economic globalization, led employers to increasingly resist wage increases and additional unionization. At the same time, the rate of productivity gains in the United States declined substantially, and the economies of Japan and Western Europe were beginning, for the first time, to outstrip major segments of U.S. manufacturers. Economic returns to shareholders had gone flat in the early 1970s, and the U.S. economy was stagnating in low productivity, inflation, and uncompetitiveness in an increasingly global economy.

Union-Free Employment

Employers in newer or more rapidly growing industries such as information technology, financial products and services, discount retailing, and personal services either had never been unionized to any extent or were experiencing many new entrants who were not unionized. Employers in established industries like autos and steel were heavily unionized and faced substantial economic problems. New companies entering the steel industry, for example, created so-called mini-mills that could produce low-end commodity products at substantially cheaper prices with much lower investments and lower-wage nonunion employees.

To gain flexibility in the design of work and employee assignments, and to reduce wage levels, employers embarked on a variety of union-free strategies (detailed later in this chapter). These strategies were aimed at avoiding unionization in nonunion facilities and at reducing or eliminating unionization in the others. This approach represented a shift in management strategy from trying to secure the "best bargain" to practicing "union avoidance."[3] The initiative was aided during the Reagan administration by a shift in public policy away from the corporatist approach and toward labor and management having greater freedom to use whatever legal tactics each wanted to use to achieve its objectives. Some argue that the scales were tipped to the extent that previously illegal tactics were either reinterpreted to be legal or overlooked as administrative oversight was reduced.[4]

THE ECONOMIC RATIONALE

Chapter 1 noted that unions introduced voice and monopoly power into the workplace. For employers, the introduction of monopoly power leads to decreased profitability. As Chapter 9 will note, unionized workers' wages are significantly higher than those of nonunion workers in virtually every industry. The ability of unions to increase wages through monopoly

[3] A. Freedman, *Managing Labor Relations* (New York: Conference Board, 1979).

[4] W. B. Gould, IV, *Agenda for Reform: The Future of Employment Relationships and the Law* (Cambridge, MA: MIT Press, 1993), pp. 11–62.

power is one of the leading reasons that employers oppose unions. All else being equal, shareholder value declines since higher wages reduce profits, leading to lower share prices.

Inflexible Rules

Chapter 10 will discuss how unionization changes the policies and practices employers can use to promote, transfer, and lay off employees. Over time, various work rules and production standards are also established. These rules and standards have the potential to negatively influence productivity because they reduce the employer's ability to include merit as a criterion in making personnel decisions and they reduce flexibility in adapting to change by applying restrictive work rules.

Profitability

Unionized firms are less profitable than nonunion firms and less profitable subsequent to unionization.[5] Decreased profitability may occur as a result of employers' extending negotiated wage and benefit increases to nonrepresented employees to avoid further unionization. While productivity increases have been found following unionization for represented employees, this may not carry over to nonunion employees who also received increased pay.[6]

Shareholder Value

Shareholder returns are reduced following unionization. A study tracking organizing success after the passage of the Wagner Act in the 1930s found that organized firms had about a 20 percent lower rate of return to shareholders than did firms remaining nonunion.[7] Firms involved in organizing drives and whose securities are publicly traded experience a reduction in share prices when an election petition is filed,[8] a reduction of about 4 percent following a successful campaign, and a 1.3 percent reduction even if the union lost.[9] The latter probably occurs because, whether they win or lose, firms facing union activity increase wages more than those that don't.[10] If unionization leads to lower shareholder returns, other things

[5] R. B. Freeman and J. L. Medoff, *What Do Unions Do?* (New York: Basic Books, 1984), pp. 181–190.

[6] B. E. Becker and C. A. Olson, "Unions and Firm Profits," *Industrial Relations*, 31 (1992), pp. 395–415.

[7] C. A. Olson and B. E. Becker, "The Effects of the NLRA on Stockholder Wealth in the 1930s," *Industrial and Labor Relations Review*, 44 (1986), pp. 116–129.

[8] S. G. Bronars and D. R. Deere, "Union Representation Elections and Firm Profitability," *Industrial Relations*, 29 (1990), pp. 15–37.

[9] R. S. Ruback and M. B. Zimmerman, "Unionization and Profitability: Evidence from the Capital Market," *Journal of Political Economy*, 92 (1984), pp. 1134–1157.

[10] R. B. Freeman and M. M. Kleiner, "Impact of New Unionization on Wages and Working Conditions," *Journal of Labor Economics*, 8 (1990), pp. S8–S25.

equal, as the agents of shareholders, top managers could be expected to try to reduce unionization in their firms, particularly if a substantial proportion of their compensation is in the form of stock options.[11] On the other hand, lower returns in unionized firms are accompanied by lower risk in that security prices are less volatile, perhaps reflecting increased risk sharing by employees through layoff procedures, and the fact that wage rates are fixed during the duration of the contract.[12] CEOs of unionized firms are paid 19 percent less on average, all else being equal, with less risk-based compensation.[13]

Company Investment Decisions

Employers reduce their historical rates of investment in newly unionized facilities. The reduction is equal to what would occur if the corporate income tax rate were increased by 33 percent.[14] U.S. employers invest less in and are less likely to locate operations in developed economies that have greater amounts of employment regulation or that impose terms of collective agreements negotiated elsewhere, or resist unionization more strongly than do firms that are headquartered in Europe or Japan. In Korea, compared to Korean-owned companies and compared to the United States, European-owned firms were significantly more likely to be unionized. In Taiwan, compared to U.S.-owned firms, being Japanese-owned was positively related to being unionized.[15]

Industrial Structure

Evidence suggests that productivity differences between union and nonunion employers are greatest in construction, where unionized workers have higher skills than nonunion workers. Relatively speaking, in service industries, unionized worker quality is lower than that of their nonunion counterparts. The service sector is expanding relative to the size of the manufacturing and construction sector. To the extent that lower unionized service worker quality translates into lower productivity, greater resistance to unionization should be seen in the service sector. Additionally, labor is a larger share of total costs in the service sector, so the effects of a given wage

[11] This and other issues are discussed and analyzed in B. E. Becker and C. A. Olson, "Labor Relations and Firm Performance," in M. M. Kleiner, R. N. Block, M. Roomkin, and S. W. Salsburg, eds., *Human Resources and the Performance of the Firm* (Madison, WI: Industrial Relations Research Association, 1987), pp. 43–86.

[12] B. E. Becker and C. A. Olson, "Unionization and Shareholder Interests," *Industrial and Labor Relations Review*, 42 (1989), pp. 246–261.

[13] K. Banning and T. Chiles, "Trade-Offs in the Labor Union CEO Compensation Relationship," *Journal of Labor Research*, 28 (2007), pp. 347–357.

[14] B. C. Fallick and K. A. Hassett, "Investment and Union Certification," *Journal of Labor Economics*, 17 (1999), pp. 570–582.

[15] P. Feuille, J. Lawler, J. Bae, and S. J. Chen, "Unionization Determinants of Multinational Firms," *Proceedings of the Industrial Relations Research Association*, 51 (1999), pp. 101–109.

increase following unionization would have greater impact. The service sector's secular relative growth rate could be a primary contributor to the increased resistance of employers in general to union organizing.

UNION-FREE APPROACHES

A union-free organization is one that is entirely unorganized in its U.S. operations. Many companies fit this label, but among very large companies, they are more likely to be in the financial services industry.

A study of large nonunion organizations identified two types of firms operating without unions—doctrinaire and philosophy-laden. A **doctrinaire organization** explicitly desires to operate without unions and implements human resource policies it believes will lead employees to resist them. Its human resource policies frequently mimic what unions have won in similar organizations through collective bargaining—for example, paying wages equal to or exceeding what unions have negotiated in that industry.[16] Thus, its practices are essentially a substitute for unionization. A **philosophy-laden** company has no unions, but the lack of organizing is because of the organization's employee relations climate. Management engages in human resource practices it believes are right.[17] Many of these firms are included in lists of "most admired" employers or "best places to work." They are essentially invulnerable to unionization because their employment practices are more attractive to their employees than those unions typically advocate and are able to negotiate. The policies are evidently congruent with employee desires because union organizing activities in these firms are practically nonexistent. We will examine these two approaches and explore the human resource policies of each.

Environmental Factors Associated with Union Avoidance

A variety of environmental factors is associated with union avoidance, some of which employers consider when making locational choices. Union penetration is highest in the Northeast and Midwest and lowest in the South and rural areas. Employers may locate in lightly unionized areas for two reasons. First, employers may believe employees in areas where unions have relatively little membership may be less willing to join unions. Mixed evidence exists on this point, as discussed in Chapters 1 and 6. Second, plants located in areas without unions don't provide opportunities that would enable employees to compare economic benefits provided

[16] D. G. Taras, "Managerial Intentions and Wage Determination in the Canadian Petroleum Industry," *Industrial Relations*, 36 (1997), pp. 178–205; see also W. Lewchuk and D. Wells, "When Corporations Substitute for Adversarial Unions: Labour Markets and Human Resource Management at Magna," *Relations Industrielles*, 61 (2006), pp. 639–665.

[17] F. K. Foulkes, *Personnel Policies in Large Nonunion Companies* (Englewood Cliffs, NJ: Prentice Hall, 1980), pp. 45–57.

by union and nonunion organizations, and as a result, employees may not be motivated to organize for economic reasons. This assumption rests on the belief that employees will choose local plants as a logical comparison, instead of other plants in the industry. However, the evidence suggests that justice, fairness, and dignity issues are more salient than economics for successful organizing.[18]

Employers may associate plant size as a factor to use in avoiding unions. While very large plants are more difficult to organize, employers may also believe that the type of human resource management they would prefer is difficult to implement in a large plant. Thus, the trend appears to be toward locating plants in labor markets that are able to support medium-size operations and planning that they will generally not exceed 500 employees unless returns to scale are large. One problem with smaller plants is that they may not be optimally productive given the appropriate capital–labor mix.[19] Plants also should not be smaller than 200 employees because a union can capitalize quickly on an issue in a smaller plant and because the plant population may be relatively homogeneous, enabling quicker and more nearly uniform agreement among employees on whether to be represented.

Differences also exist among and within industries. Industries with a large proportion of white-collar workers, such as finance, are less likely to be unionized. But within industries, some firms have not been organized, while others are completely unionized. In construction, relatively new organizations remain nonunion by guaranteeing employment during usual layoff periods and by implementing human resource policies on an organizationwide basis. Newly incorporated, technically oriented industries also have had a relatively low level of unionization, even when located in traditionally highly unionized areas. Some of this is probably due to employment security resulting from rapid growth and abundant alternative employment opportunities, while other aspects of resistance to organization may be related to progressive employee relations policies and practices. Further, many of these firms locate manufacturing facilities offshore, in lower-wage areas far from their technical facilities, or they outsource production.

Wage Policies

Large nonunion organizations generally try to lead the market in their pay levels. They try to anticipate what unions will gain at the bargaining table and provide pay increases equal to or exceeding that level, awarding them before unions gain theirs. Nonunion organizations may also

[18] K. Bronfenbrenner, "The Role of Union Strategies in NLRB Certification Elections," *Industrial and Labor Relations Review*, 50 (1997), pp. 195–212.

[19] M. Milkman and M. Mitchell, "Union Influence on Plant Size," *Journal of Labor Research*, 16 (1995), pp. 319–329.

implement merit pay policies, using performance measures to differentiate pay increases. They communicate pay and benefit levels and practices to employees.[20] More recently, companies may implement skill-based pay programs to support new organizational structures stressing team designs. Additionally, increasing numbers of companies are considering or implementing profit-sharing or gainsharing programs.

To accomplish these wage goals, an organization's pay must compare favorably with others.[21] Location in a growing industry with relatively high profits or a position as market leader in the industry should enable an organization to maintain its ability to pay. In turn, a high-paying employer may have an advantage in recruiting and retaining more productive high-quality employees who are motivated to retain their high-paying jobs.[22]

If a philosophy-laden organization considers employee preferences as it is expected to do, then benefit levels in nonunion employers should closely lead those in unionized employers because they might be expected to react quickly to changing needs associated with changing age and gender mixes in their workforces.

Nonwage Policies

Unionized employers generally have lower turnover rates and higher rates of internal promotion and transfer than nonunion employers. If an employer sought to emulate the conditions employees desire, it would have a rationalized internal labor market with high levels of information on job opportunities available to employees.

Large nonunion firms generally have formalized job-posting systems, with clearly communicated and unambiguous promotion criteria that emphasize seniority and skills as well as development opportunities so that employees can develop the skills necessary to take advantage of openings that are likely to occur.[23]

Philosophy-laden firms have generally taken a career-oriented approach toward employment. Full-time nonprobationary employees are assumed to be likely to spend their entire careers with the organization. Thus, nonunion firms frequently require longer probationary periods or hire substantial numbers of part-time employees to provide a buffer for permanent employees during periods of fluctuating product demand.[24] They also provide substantial amounts of targeted training and development programs to continuously upgrade skills and prepare employees to perform well in expanded job roles.

[20] Foulkes, *Personnel Policies in Large Nonunion Companies*, pp. 158–163.

[21] Ibid., pp. 165–167.

[22] J. Yellen, "Efficiency Wage Models of Unemployment," *American Economic Review*, 74, no. 2 (1984), pp. 200–205.

[23] Foulkes, *Personnel Policies in Large Nonunion Companies*, pp. 123–145.

[24] Ibid., pp. 99–122.

Human Resource Expenditures

In unionized employers, union representation and the negotiated contract take the place of many human resource programs devised by nonunion employers. Management has less need to attend closely to employee desires because doing so is the union's responsibility and the contract spells out how employee relations will be handled. Staffing and development needs are handled through on-the-job training, and employees are retained through union wage premiums, negotiated seniority clauses, and the employees' initial and continuing interest in being represented.

Nonunion employers have higher human resource expenditures, and more human resource workers are involved in employee relations. Pay is more closely linked to individual, group, and organizational performance, with opportunities for high performance to result in higher pay than in comparable unionized employers. Development activities are emphasized. Supervisory support for problem solving is offered through the human resource department instead of the grievance system.

Employment Security

Union members have the rules for determining their employment security spelled out in the contract. Almost always, increasing competitive-status seniority is associated with greater rights to continued employment in a present job or another job for which an employee is qualified. Recently, these rights have been of lower value where employers have opted to close entire facilities, but even there, entitlements to transfers and severance pay are often spelled out in contracts and benefit levels increase with seniority.

Employees in nonunion companies have their employment rights determined by their employers. Unless otherwise provided, it's legally assumed an employee is hired at the will of the employer and can be terminated for a good reason, a bad reason, or no reason at all, as long as the termination is not for a reason prohibited by employment law. However, courts have increasingly narrowed employers' rights to terminate at will, particularly where employers are judged to have acted in bad faith.[25] Even where employers have contracts with employees, and where a discharge could lead to a breach-of-contract suit, employers may be vulnerable to heavier tort damages for bad-faith behavior associated with a discharge.[26]

In the reciprocal employment relationship, employees may come to feel that an implied contract exists between them and their employer. When employees invest in developing skills for their present employer and apply conscientious effort, they see themselves as producing benefits

[25] E. C. Wesman and D. C. Eischen, "Due Process," in J. A. Fossum and J. Mattson, eds., *Employee and Labor Relations*, SHRM-BNA Series, vol. 4 (Washington, DC: Bureau of National Affairs, 1990), p. 117.

[26] M. J. Keppler, "Nonunion Grievance Procedures: Union Avoidance Technique or Union Organizing Opportunity," *Labor Law Journal*, 41 (1990), pp. 557–562.

for the employer. In turn, employees may build expectations of long-term employment in return for effort and loyalty.[27]

Nonunion employers use a variety of methods to enhance employment security for at least some employees. Given the need for flexibility in the workforce, more employers are subcontracting or allocating jobs that need relatively little training about the employer's specific mode of operation to supplemental or complementary workforces of temporary employees. Frequently, these employees are hired on a contract basis for a particular term—usually a year or less. These employees are explicitly told they have no employment security guarantee beyond the period for which they are hired. When faced with a need for major employment reductions, employers have increasingly implemented expanded separation incentives, redeployment to other facilities with or without retraining, training programs for new occupational assignments, expanded personal leaves, and work-sharing programs that involve cuts in salary and hours to save jobs or to provide incentives for those willing to terminate employment.[28]

Employee "Voice" Systems

Lower turnover in unionized situations (detailed in Chapter 10) might be related to the fact that union employees have an opportunity to voice their needs for change through the grievance and negotiation processes. Where these mechanisms are absent, employees who desire change may be able to achieve it only by "voting with their feet."[29]

In unionized organizations, employees are able to exercise their voice on immediate issues through grievance procedures and on long-term issues through participation in negotiation committees. Employees who have the greatest disagreements with an organization's operations might be expected to be most involved in union activities at the employer level.

In nonunion employers, employees have no contractual entitlement to redress grievances or to have a voice in how the organization should be run. Some nonunion organizations, particularly those with philosophy-laden backgrounds, have constructed elaborate systems that enable employees to voice complaints and get action on them.[30]

A model system enables an employee to communicate directly with his or her company's chief executive officer, who has a department that directly investigates causes of complaints and reports its findings.

[27] J. A. Fossum, "Employee Relations," in J. A. Fossum and J. Mattson, eds., *Employee and Labor Relations*, SHRM-BNA Series, vol. 4 (Washington, DC: Bureau of National Affairs, 1990), pp. 12–14.

[28] F. K. Foulkes, "Employment Security: Developments in the Nonunion Sector," *Proceedings of the Industrial Relations Research Association*, 41 (1988), pp. 411–417.

[29] A. O. Hirschman, *Exit, Voice, and Loyalty* (Cambridge, MA: Harvard University Press, 1970).

[30] For an overview, see R. Bernbeim, *Nonunion Complaint Systems: A Corporate Appraisal* (New York: Conference Board, 1980).

Exhibit 7.1

THE OPEN-DOOR POLICY

The Open-Door Policy is deeply ingrained in [the company's] history. This policy is a reflection of our belief in respect for the individual. It is also based on the principle that every person has a right to appeal the actions of those who are immediately over him in authority. It provides a procedure for assuring fair and individual treatment for every employee.

Should you have a problem which you believe the company can help solve, discuss it with your immediate manager or your location's personnel manager or, in the field, with the manager of your location. You will find that a frank talk with your manager is usually the easiest and most effective way to deal with the problem.

Second, if the matter is still not resolved, or is of such a nature you prefer not to discuss it with your immediate manager or location personnel manager, you should go to your local general manager, regional manager, president or general manager of your division or subsidiary, whichever is appropriate.

Third, if you feel that you have not received a satisfactory answer, you may cover the matter by mail, or personally, with the Chairman of the Board.

Source: Fred K. Foulkes, *Personnel Policies in Large Nonunion Companies* (Englewood Cliffs, NJ: Prentice Hall, 1980), p. 300.

The employee's superiors may be the focus of the investigation, but the employee is not identified, and no reprisals may be made against the person who filed the complaint. Exhibit 7.1 is a commentary on how one of these systems works.

To reduce potential employee cynicism about management's commitment to neutral grievance procedures, IBM operates a system that allows employees with complaints to have direct anonymous access to high-level management. When complaints are received, investigations are required, and the remedial action to be taken, if any, is communicated back to the grievant. Follow-up is monitored by high-level management.

These so-called **open-door policies** vary substantially in their real access to higher-level managers—in terms of the types of complaints or questions that can be taken up and also the degree to which employees must first contact lower-level supervisors and managers before higher-level managers will review a complaint.[31]

Another innovative approach is creating an employee review board to act as an impartial group to resolve outstanding grievances. Where this approach is used, a review board of randomly chosen employees or persons at the same relative organizational level as the grievant hears the evidence and renders a binding decision for the employer and the grievant.

[31] D. M. McCabe, "Corporate Nonunion Grievance Procedures: Open Door Policies—A Procedural Analysis," *Labor Law Journal*, 41 (1990), pp. 551–556.

Employees may have concerns about due process. For due process to operate, a procedure must necessarily include an objective investigator and decision maker who has the power to make a binding decision for both an employee and the employer.[32] Unless the employee believes the employer's procedures allow a valid appeal, the employee may prefer to take an employment grievance to court as a tort issue.[33] Nonunion procedures in the public sector are relatively similar to union grievance procedures. Peer review panels are sometimes included. Their effectiveness is related to employees' use of them, training in their operation, assistance by management in processing complaints and obtaining information for grievants, full and fair hearings, and an explanation of the decision.[34]

Some large nonunion organizations also periodically conduct attitude surveys for early identification of potentially troublesome areas. Such problem areas might include certain employee groups or certain employee relations policies such as advancement, pay, or development opportunities. Given that attitudes may be precursors of subsequent behaviors, the diagnosis of potential problems allows management to conduct remedial activities to eliminate potential areas of contention.

Grievance procedures introduce justice systems to the workplace. *Justice* can be defined in several ways: distributive (methods used to decide relative shares of an outcome), procedural (methods used to determine how decisions are reached), and interactional (methods used to communicate). Perceptions of organizational justice are influenced by all three, but procedural justice is the strongest, followed by interactional and distributive. Employee input in the process and independence of decision makers are important components of all three justice types.[35]

In some organizations, supervisors and managers are evaluated by their subordinates as well as by other performance indicators. They are expected to maintain a work environment leading to positive employee attitudes as measured by periodic surveys. When attitude surveys point out a problem, they may be required to devise action plans to eliminate difficulties.

Nonunion employers that operate in competitive environments are particularly interested in managing conflicts in their organizations. A conflict that leads to a dispute or the possible violation of an employment law or regulation will occupy considerable management time and incur expense and uncertainty until a settlement is reached. Litigation consumes

[32] D. W. Ewing, *Justice on the Job: Resolving Grievances in the Nonunion Workplace* (Boston: Harvard University Press, 1989).

[33] Keppler, "Nonunion Grievance Procedures."

[34] G. W. Bohlander and K. Behringer, "Public Sector Nonunion Complaint Procedures: Current Research," *Labor Law Journal*, 41 (1990), pp. 563–567.

[35] D. Blancero, "Nonunion Grievance Systems: Perceptions of Fairness," *Proceedings on the Industrial Relations Research Association*, 44 (1992), pp. 458–464.

resources and polarizes positions within the organization. Increasingly, employers are developing preventive methods to diagnose potential employment disputes at an early point and to train employees and supervisors to recognize and avoid situations that create unnecessary disputes.[36]

About half of nonunion firms have grievance procedures. These firms have higher proportions of managers and professional employees, are larger, value human resource management, do not have unionized employees, and are not in a high-technology industry. Some grievance procedures include binding arbitration if a grievance is unresolved. Characteristics associated with third-party resolution include union avoidance strategies, being a smaller firm, low assets per employee, not being in manufacturing, and being a high-tech firm.[37]

Where nonunion grievance procedures exist, rates are higher when peer review and/or nonunion arbitration is used for deciding cases. If managers are included in the final phase of the resolution process, grievance rates are lower, probably due to cynicism regarding the fairness of the process. Grievance rates are lower in team-based and high-performance work organizations.[38]

Other Innovative Techniques

Some organizations hold mass meetings between employees and top-management officials to get a sense of possible problems. One approach involves meetings between top managers and groups of lower-level employees to present current problems. This "deep-sensing" approach may give top managers a better reading on the pulse of employee morale, and employees in turn might expect more action on their problems.

Another approach, called *vertical staff meetings,* includes about a dozen employees from various levels who are picked at random to meet with the division's president at a monthly meeting. The president follows up on the problems disclosed by the attendees and reports to the participants.[39]

[36] D. B. Lipsky and R. L. Seeber, "Dispute Resolution in the Changing Workplace," *Proceedings of the Industrial Relations Research Association*, 54 (2004), pp. 30–40.

[37] J. T. Delaney and P. Feuille, "The Determinants of Nonunion Grievance and Arbitration Procedures," *Proceedings of the Industrial Relations Research Association*, 44 (1992), pp. 529–538.

[38] A. J. S. Colvin, "The Dual Transformation of Workplace Dispute Resolution," *Industrial Relations*, 43 (2003), pp. 712–735.

[39] For additional perspectives on employee voice, see T. A. Mahoney and M. R. Watson, "Evolving Modes of Work Force Governance: An Evaluation," in B. E. Kaufman and M. M. Kleiner, eds., *Employee Representation: Alternatives and Future Directions* (Madison, WI: Industrial Relations Research Association, 1993), pp. 135–168. For an overview of recent research on nonunion grievance procedures, see R. B. Peterson, "The Union and Nonunion Grievance System," in D. Lewin, O. S. Mitchell, and P. D. Sherer, eds., *Research Frontiers in Industrial Relations and Human Resources* (Madison, WI: Industrial Relations Research Association, 1992), pp. 131–162.

Employer/Employee Committees

Employers have formed various types of management-employee committees. Quality circles are one example. Others involve employees' making recommendations to management regarding hiring, personnel assignments, hours, terms and conditions of employment, and other similar issues, which are the subject of collective bargaining in unionized employers.

The Taft-Hartley Act forbids dominance of a labor organization by an employer. The *Electromation* decision narrows an employer's ability to broadly ask employees to consider employment issues.[40] Involvement of employees in nonmandatory bargaining issues is unlikely to lead to successful charges of employer dominance.

Employee participation in some of these committees may be similar to collecting attitude survey data from a sample of the plant population and using these data as a representation of overall employee attitude. It also enables both groups to enrich their understanding of what each perceives as problems in the workplace and their causes.

In Canada, company unions are permitted, and there has been a long history of nonunion employee representation in Imperial Oil. The Joint Industrial Council (JIC) in Imperial dealt with a variety of workplace issues, including wages and benefits. However, when employee JIC members perceived they were losing influence in decision making on employment issues, they organized a union with the former JIC representatives as the new union's officers.[41] Canadian firms with nonunion representation plans that stray far from offering union-type wages and benefits usually end up becoming organized.[42]

Prior to being banned by the Wagner Act, a number of company unions were created, mostly during the 1920s. These were formed with the assistance of management and were operated at the enterprise level. Their outlawing by the Wagner Act was related to the conclusion that they lacked independence and had a compromised ability to represent worker interests. A recent analysis of company unions suggests, however, that they often enhance worker outcomes and generally benefit both employees and employers.[43]

Developing Practices in Nonunion Employee Relations

Increasingly, companies have explicit union avoidance policies and tailor human resource practices to support these goals. Several differences between companies with an explicit union avoidance policy and those

[40] *Electromation, Inc.*, 309 NLRB No. 163 (1992).

[41] D. G. Taras and J. Copping, "The Transition from Formal Nonunion Representation to Unionization: A Contemporary Case," *Industrial and Labor Relations Review*, 52 (1998), pp. 22–44.

[42] D. G. Taras, "Evolution of Nonunion Employee Representation in Canada," *Journal of Labor Research*, 20 (1999), pp. 31–52.

[43] B. E. Kaufman, "The Case for the Company Union," *Labor History*, 41 (2000), pp. 321–350.

TABLE 7.1
Company Practices among Nonunion Employees

Source: A. Freedman, *The New Look in Wage Policy and Employee Relations* (New York: Conference Board, 1985), p. 17. Reprinted by permission of the Conference Board Review.

Company Initiative	Number of Companies in Which: Managers Are Encouraged to Develop or Sustain	Practice Exists
Information-related:		
Employees are given information about competitive or economic conditions of plant or business		431
Employees track their group's quality or productivity performance		264*
Participation-related:		
Employee participation programs (quality circles, quality-of-work-life programs)	364*	
Autonomous work teams	107*	
Employees meet in small work groups to discuss production or quality		340*
Compensation-related:		
Profit-sharing, gainsharing, or bonus programs for nonexempt employees	191	
Employees receive productivity or other gainsharing bonuses		121
"Payment for knowledge" compensation systems	107	
All-salaried compensation systems	173	
Miscellaneous:		
Formal complaint or grievance system	378*	
Work sharing instead of layoffs	176*	
Flextime or other flexible work schedules	162	

*Statistically significant relationship with a company preference for union avoidance, at 0.05 or better.

without one include providing more information to employees regarding their work group's productivity, more work-group discussion of quality or productivity issues, more encouragement of participation mechanisms, such as quality circles and autonomous work teams, work sharing in preference to layoffs, and the development and operation of formal complaint systems.[44] Table 7.1 shows the number of positive responses toward a variety of human resource practices among a sample of large employers.

Besides differences in communication and participation, new nonunion and traditional unionized employers differ in the way the workplace is organized. To increase flexibility, employers have substantially reduced the number of job classifications. In many situations, employees are organized into teams, and the team is responsible not only for production but also for maintenance of its equipment. The team may have only one or two

[44] A. Freedman, *The New Look in Wage Policy and Employee Relations* (New York: Conference Board, 1985), pp. 16–20.

TABLE 7.2
Employer Influence, Contextual Control, and Monitoring Tactics

Source: Adapted from J. J. Lawler, *Unionization and Deunionization: Strategies, Tactics, and Outcomes* (Columbia: University of South Carolina Press, 1990), pp. 120–121.

Objective	Employer Activities
Influence	Orientation programs
	Quality circles (especially blue collar)
	MBO (management by objectives) (especially for white-collar and professional employees)
	Information sharing
	Attitude surveys
	Structuring of group interaction
	Empathetic management style
Contextual control	Plant location
	Small plant size
	Outsourcing and use of flexible employment arrangements
	Employee screening
	Supervisor selection and training
	Influential HRM department
	Desirable working conditions
	High wages, good fringe benefits
	Job security
	Career advancement opportunities
	Grievance program
	Restrictions on workplace solicitations by union supporters
Monitoring	Attitude surveys
	Surveillance
	Reports from operatives and management loyalists
	Review of employee complaints
	Review of personnel records

different jobs, which are defined on the basis of skill level rather than the functional specialty of the job holder.[45]

PREVENTIVE PROGRAMS

In an effort to avoid being organized, employers design programs aimed at influencing employees to identify with management and the goals and culture of the organization, controlling contextual attributes that unions typically argue they can improve, and monitoring attitudes and behaviors of employees to gain early evidence of any changes or situations that might encourage organizing.[46] Table 7.2 lists several initiatives management implements in each of these areas.

Some of the activities under contextual control and monitoring may be traded off or be used with increased emphasis. For example, intensive

[45] T. A. Kochan, H. C. Katz, and R. B. McKersie, *The Transformation of American Industrial Relations* (New York: Basic Books, 1986), pp. 81–108.

[46] J. J. Lawler, *Unionization and Deunionization: Strategies, Tactics, and Outcomes* (Columbia: University of South Carolina Press, 1990), pp. 118–128.

employee screening may be implemented to reduce the need for later surveillance and to create a workforce with more company-oriented attitudes.[47] Some activities within contextual control may also be exchanged. For example, high wages and good fringe benefits vary depending on the locations being compared. If labor costs are an issue, the firm may decide to locate in a lower-wage area and then pay at rates exceeding the competition. In any case, implementing these activities requires a more intensive employee relations/human resource management effort than it would in a unionized setting. The employer needs to determine that the long-term benefits exceed the costs.

MANAGEMENT CAMPAIGN TACTICS IN REPRESENTATION ELECTIONS

Campaign tactics depend to an extent on the size and sophistication of the employer. Smaller employers or units based in more remote locations often rely on labor relations consultants or attorneys to assist in organizing and implementing the campaign. As we noted in Chapter 6, the use of consultants has a negative effect on union success rates. As in preventive processes, employers may implement a variety of influence, contextual control, and monitoring activities to reduce the chances of the organizing union's gaining recognition.[48] Table 7.3 lists the activities frequently used by employers. Table 7.4 shows the frequency of a variety of common employer campaign themes that were used in a sample of 201 elections.

Management often uses a variety of consultants in opposing unionization once an organizing campaign begins. Consultants may include attorneys, campaign advisers, advocates of positive labor relations, security services that provide investigation resources, trade and industry associations that provide expertise gained from previous campaigns, advocacy groups that oppose unions in general, and educational institutions that might provide union avoidance information.[49] Consultants use particularly sophisticated approaches to blunt organizing attempts. They attempt to mimic the characteristics of organizers by matching their demographic makeup for contacts with employees. Firms hire former union officers to provide better intelligence on how to communicate during a campaign and also to blunt the idea that unionization is the preferred path

[47] G. M. Saltzman, "Job Applicant Screening by a Japanese Transplant: A Union-Avoidance Tactic," *Industrial and Labor Relations Review*, 49 (1995), pp. 88–104.

[48] Lawler, *Unionization and Deunionization*, pp. 139–160.

[49] Ibid., p. 90.

TABLE 7.3
Employer Election Campaign Tactics

Source: Adapted from J. J. Lawler, *Unionization and Deunionization: Strategies, Tactics, and Outcomes* (Columbia: University of South Carolina Press, 1990), pp. 141–142.

Objective	Employer Activities
Influence	Captive audience speeches
	Small-group and individual meetings
	Letters, posters, handbills, and other written communications
	Threats and/or inducements
	Films, slide shows
Contextual control	External:
	Use of regulatory agency procedures
	Election delays
	Linkages with community institutions (banks, police, newspapers, churches, etc.)
	Intraunit:
	Supervisor training
	Discriminatory treatment of union supporters
	Short-term improvement in wages and working conditions
	Establish or support employee anti-union committee
	Refuse workplace access to union organizers
	Restrict workplace solicitations by union supporters
	Excelsior-list misreporting
	Neutrality agreements
Monitoring	Attitude surveys
	Surveillance
	Interrogation
	Reports from operatives and management loyalists

TABLE 7.4
Relative Frequencies of Common Employer Campaign Themes

Source: Adapted from J. J. Lawler, *Unionization and Deunionization: Strategies, Tactics, and Outcomes* (Columbia: University of South Carolina Press, 1990), pp. 149.

Campaign Theme	Frequency (%)
Bargaining impact themes	66%
Strikes may occur	40
High union dues	33
Potential for fines and assessments by the union	24
Unions cannot guarantee any changes	14
Possible plant closing	14
Bargaining may actually reduce wages, benefits, etc.	5
Antiunion themes	35
Union will interfere with good worker-management relations	7
Union dominated by outsiders	13
Union has failed elsewhere	6
Union is corrupt	9
Union is radical or leftist	6
Union will subject workers to rules	6
Unionism is inconsistent with employee and community values	1
Pro-company themes	20
Management is a friend to workers	7
Workers already enjoy high wages and/or good working conditions	9
Give company another chance	8

to advancement. Industrial psychologists have developed and deployed attitude surveys to identify union "hotspots" and improve the ability of managers to screen out applicants with union sympathies. If an organizing campaign is underway, security companies are retained who have experience in organizing campaigns. Many of their operatives are former military personnel or retired police officers. Surveillance activities are mounted to identify any potential sabotage of employer property or other union activity that would not be permitted by labor laws.[50]

Several tactics, such as improving wages, hours, and terms and conditions of employment or treating union supporters in a discriminatory manner, are unfair labor practices (ULPs). Evidence indicates that an aggressive campaign that includes unfair labor practices is associated with management victories.[51] Since the costs of committing an unfair labor practice are very low for employers relative to the costs of unions winning elections, this actually reinforces employer choices to commit them. Extensive advice on how to conduct a legal campaign in opposition to a union is readily available.[52]

The lower an employer's wage is relative to others in its industry, the greater management's resistance will be. Employer resistance increases more rapidly with differentials than do employee desires for unionization.[53] An active union avoidance strategy for new facilities decreases the likelihood of organizing from about 15 to 1 percent.[54]

DECERTIFICATIONS

Once certified, unions face periodic risks in continuing as the bargaining agent. A majority may vote to oust the union after the election bar ends if no contract is in effect. Decertification occurs more often in small units that lack local leadership and have low member involvement in union activities, a higher frequency of strikes, a high turnover of represented

[50] J. Logan, "The Union Avoidance Industry in the United States," *British Journal of Industrial Relations*, 44 (2006), pp. 651–675.

[51] W. T. Dickens, "The Effect of Company Campaigns on Certification Elections: Law and Reality Once Again," *Industrial and Labor Relations Review*, 36 (1983), pp. 560–575.

[52] See, for example, M. A. Spognardi, "Conducting a Successful Union-Free Campaign: A Primer (Part I)," *Employee Relations Law Journal*, 24, no. 2 (1998), pp. 35–52; and Part II, 24, no. 3 (1998), pp. 31–55.

[53] R. B. Freeman, "The Effect of the Union Wage Differential on Management Opposition and Union Organizing Success," *American Economic Review*, 76, no. 2 (1986), pp. 92–96.

[54] T. A. Kochan, R. B. McKersie, and J. Chalykoff, "The Effects of Corporate Strategy and Workplace Innovations on Union Representation," *Industrial and Labor Relations Review*, 39 (1986), pp. 487–501; see also J. J. Lawler and R. West, "Impact of Union-Avoidance Strategy in Representation Elections," *Industrial Relations*, 24 (1985), pp. 406–420.

employees, low union density in the industry, and affiliation with a large national union.[55]

Since the 1950s and 1960s, decertification elections have increased from 5 percent of all elections to between 12 and 25 percent. Decertifications are strongly related to macroeconomic measures, institutional changes reflected in increasing ULPs, relative reductions in social spending as unemployment increases, and a Republican administration in office.[56]

JOB STRUCTURING

Employers and unions may be involved in a continual battle about whether jobs fall within the jurisdiction of the bargaining unit. At the time that an election is held, the NLRB defines what jobs and what employees are within the bargaining unit. As noted, the law requires that professionals affirmatively agree to be part of a bargaining unit before they can be included. If the nature of the work design is changed radically and skill requirements are increased, the employer may argue that the jobs required to perform the work are no longer a part of the bargaining unit as it was defined at election time. If, at the same time, low-skilled jobs are outsourced, the bargaining unit is gradually hollowed out by job design changes, and bargaining power is lost.

Summary

Differences between capitalistic and trade union philosophies related to the operation of the workplace cause inevitable conflicts. Employers have long resisted attempts to unionize, with industrial-type unions having little success in organizing workers until passage of the Wagner Act. Following a "corporatist" period of about 30 years after World War II, in which management generally conceded a legitimate role for labor, employers took a harder line against organizing and bargaining beginning in the late 1970s. Currently, many employers have a union-free employment goal and implement strategies to avoid new organization and to eliminate current unionization in their firms.

Unionization has a variety of economic effects on employers. In general, productivity of unionized workers is higher than that of nonunion workers in manufacturing and construction but not in the service sector. Union members earn a substantial pay premium. Where unions have

[55] See J. C. Anderson, G. Busman, and C. A. O'Reilly III, "What Factors Influence the Outcome of Union Decertification Elections?" *Monthly Labor Review*, 102, no. 11 (1979), pp. 23–31; and D. A. Ahlburg and J. B. Dworkin, "The Influence of Macroeconomic Variables on the Probability of Union Decertification," *Journal of Labor Research*, 5 (1984), pp. 13–28.

[56] E. A. Nilsson, "The Growth of Union Decertification: A Test of Two Nonnested Theories," *Industrial Relations*, 36 (1997), pp. 324–348.

negotiated wage and benefit improvements, employers generally pass these along to unorganized workers as well. Thus, the cost of unionization is not fully related to unionized workers only. Studies of stock price changes associated with unionization and deunionization generally find that share prices fall at a higher-than-expected rate when unionization or attempts to unionize occur.

Employers implement a variety of practices in an attempt to remain union-free. Employers adopting a philosophy-laden approach create an employment relationship that fits a particular culture and manner of treating employees. As a result, employees see their situations as being, in most respects, as good as or better than what they would be able to negotiate if they were represented. In other, more traditional approaches, employers may purposely implement a set of employment practices that closely mimic a unionized environment, thereby reducing the likelihood that issues would arise to lead to unionization.

Some of the areas on which nonunion employers focus in their avoidance of unionization include plant location decisions, wage and benefit policies, staffing practices, and employee grievance systems.

Preventive programs involve attitude surveys, surveillance, employee communications, and supervisor training. If an organizing attempt takes place, intensive communications, hiring consultants, and procedural delays are often implemented. If the union wins recognition, the employer may take an intransigent approach to bargaining an initial contract.

Decertifications are an increasing proportion of NLRB-conducted elections. These must be initiated by employees during a period in which a contract is not in effect.

Discussion Questions

1. Is the increasing resistance of employers to unionization a new phenomenon or simply a return to the historic relationship that has existed between unions and managements in the United States?
2. Would you expect a stronger anti-union response from an employer in manufacturing or an employer in a service industry?
3. In today's increasingly competitive employment environment, would you expect to find many (or any) employers taking a philosophy-laden approach?
4. Should public policy change in some way so that unions that win representation rights have a guarantee that they will be able to negotiate a first contract?

Key Terms

Company union, *197*
Doctrinaire organization, *201*
Philosophy-laden, *201*

Case: *Locating the New Recreational Vehicle Plant*

GMFC is planning to expand its U.S. operations by building a new plant that will employ about 500 production workers. This new plant will manufacture motorized recreational equipment, including all-terrain vehicles, personal watercraft, and snowmobiles. The equipment will assemble mechanical components produced in other GMFC operations or purchased from suppliers. The new plant will fabricate fiberglass body parts and complete the final assembly process.

GMFC would like to operate the new plant union-free. It's likely that the United Auto Workers (UAW), and perhaps other internationals, will attempt to organize the workforce within a year after start-up. You are a member of a planning committee for the new plant. Your primary area of responsibility involves issues related to potential unionization and labor costs. What advice would you provide to the company on size, location, staffing, wages and benefits, and other employee relations issues that would help GMFC keep the new plant union-free and competitive?

The Environment for Bargaining

Organizing campaigns focus on the individual employer and union trying to organize a bargaining unit. While organizing is in progress, both parties concentrate on the question at hand—whether the employees desire representation. If employees vote to be represented, the employer and the union must bargain within the realities of the environment in which they operate. Environmental aspects influencing bargaining include the degree of competition in the employer's product market, the employer's financial condition, the employer's capital-labor mix, the bargaining-issue interests of the union, the effects of unionization on the employer's relationship with the labor market, and any laws and regulations related to the industry in which the employer operates and the fact that it is now unionized.

This chapter explores the economic environment in which collective bargaining occurs, the influence of the economic environment and the bargaining structure on bargaining power, and bargaining structures that unions and managements design. The chapter begins a four-chapter segment on bargaining issues and negotiations. Chapter 9 focuses on wage and benefit issues and evidence related to the effects of unions in these areas. Chapter 10 concentrates on nonwage issues and union members' perceptions of their unions' effectiveness. Chapter 11 covers the organizational structures in which employers and unions negotiate, important employer and union bargaining goals, the negotiation process, and the identification and quantification of contract costs.

In studying this chapter, consider the following questions:

1. How does the degree of competition within the product market influence the bargaining behavior of the parties?
2. What effect does unionization have on the wage and employment decisions of employers?
3. What influences do laws and regulations have on collective bargaining?
4. How does the globalization of certain markets affect employers and unions?

5. What joint decisions do employers and unions make in their bargaining relationship to attempt to insulate themselves from market conditions?
6. How do economic conditions, product market concentration, and bargaining structure influence bargaining power?

THE LEGAL AND POLITICAL STRUCTURE

Chapter 2 introduced the notion that, in some nations, labor relations is dealt with in a corporatist fashion. Under a corporatist regime, employers, unions, and governments are all actors in the evolving employment relationship. Prior to the passage of the Railway Labor Act (RLA) and the Wagner Act, with the exception of emergency periods such as World War I and severe labor unrest in the late 19th century, employers and unions used their sheer bargaining power to deal with each other without government involvement or intervention. In most cases, this meant employers were able to exercise substantially more power and rely on property rights to essentially crush unions except where employees controlled access to the acquisition of skills.

In 1926, the Railway Labor Act injected the federal government into transportation negotiations in the form of the National Mediation Board (NMB). In situations where employers and unions could not agree on how an industrial conflict was to be resolved, the NMB could assist, emergency boards could be convened, and ultimately Congress was empowered to impose solutions when the parties were unable to do so on their own.

In 1936 the Wagner Act established collective bargaining as the preferred method for resolving labor disputes in situations in which a majority of employees favored it. Unlike the Railway Labor Act, the Wagner Act did not create laws and regulations for dealing with impasses, but rather listed a set of prohibited practices for employers and left it up to the parties to negotiate a solution, taking into account their relative bargaining power.

After the large number of strikes that occurred immediately before and after World War II, the Taft-Hartley Act shifted the negotiating environment toward a more corporatist perspective by establishing the Federal Mediation and Conciliation Service (FMCS) to help parties reach agreement in difficult situations, legislating rules for so-called national emergency disputes that would temporarily enjoin strikes and require fact finding, and defining a set of union unfair labor practices to balance those that employers were forbidden to use.

Section 8(d) of the Labor Management Relations (Taft-Hartley) Act of 1947 sets forth in one sentence the essence of collective bargaining in the United States:

> For the purposes of this section, to bargain collectively is the performance of the mutual obligation of the employer and representative of the employees to meet at reasonable times and confer in good faith with

respect to wages, hours, and terms and conditions of employment, or the negotiation of an agreement, or any question arising thereunder, and the execution of a written contract incorporating any agreement reached if requested by either party, but such obligation does not compel either party to agree to a proposal or require the making of a concession.

This broad definition affects both the process and the issues. For example, regarding process, what does "good faith" mean? Regarding issues, what do "wages, hours, and other terms and conditions of employment" signify? Unions, employers, the National Labor Relations Board (NLRB), and the courts have all grappled with these questions. Novel demands and bargaining tactics have been challenged to determine whether they conform to the statute. Chapters 11, 12, 14, and 15 examine **good-faith bargaining** and its impact on process. Chapters 9 and 10 examine "wages, hours, and other terms and conditions of employment" issues.

Bargaining issues can be divided into three legal categories: mandatory, permissive, and prohibited. **Mandatory bargaining issues** deal with wages, hours, and other terms and conditions of employment. Wages and hours are straightforward, dealing with economics and work schedules, but the concept "terms and conditions of employment" is amorphous. A reasonable test of whether an issue is within this area is whether the practice would have a direct and immediate effect on union members' jobs and is strongly determined by labor cost factors.[1] Examples are a plant closing or a reassignment of work between job groups. **Permissive bargaining issues** do not require a response because they have no direct impact on management or labor costs. A demand by a union to have a say in the establishment of company product prices would be permissive. **Prohibited bargaining issues** are statutorily outlawed, such as demands that employers use only union-produced goods. Another distinction between mandatory and permissive issues is that neither party may go to **impasse** (refuse to agree on a contract) over a permissive issue. Figure 8.1 describes tests used to distinguish between mandatory and permissive issues.

The labeling of issues as mandatory and permissive affects their appearance in contracts. Permissive issues are not included as frequently where the distinction is imposed. Union bargaining power increases the likelihood of dealing with permissive issues in the contract.[2]

Regulation of Employment

In addition to laws, regulations, and administrative agencies established to support collective bargaining as a method for resolving industrial disputes, other laws have been enacted to regulate wages and hours, prohibit

[1] J. T. Delaney, D. Sockell, and J. Brockner, "Bargaining Effects of the Mandatory-Permissive Distinction," *Industrial Relations*, 27 (1988), pp. 21–36.

[2] J. T. Delaney and D. Sockell, "The Mandatory-Permissive Distinction and Collective Bargaining Outcomes," *Industrial and Labor Relations Review*, 42 (1989), pp. 566–583.

FIGURE 8.1 How Mandatory (M) or Permissive (P) Bargaining Status Is Determined

Source: J. T. Delaney, D. Sockell, and J. Brockner, "Bargaining Effect of the Mandatory-Permissive Distinction," *Industrial Relations*, 27 (1988), p. 24. Reprinted with permission from Blackwell Publishing.

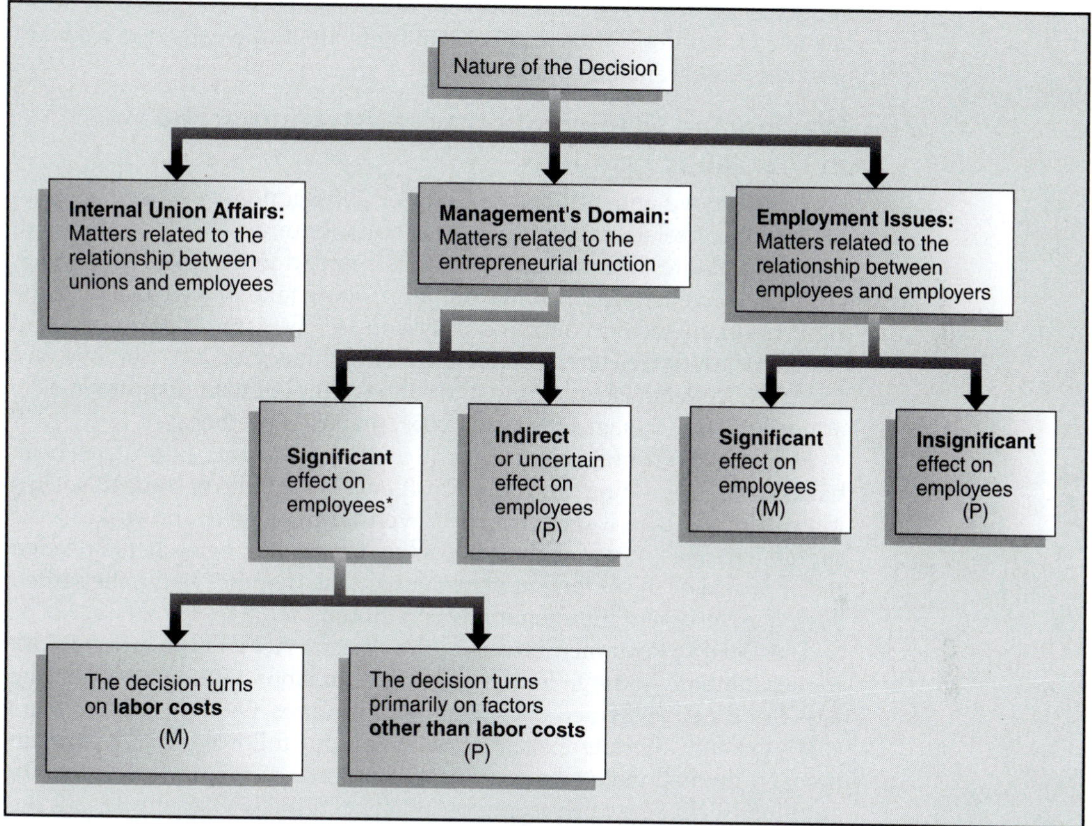

*The duty to engage in effects-bargaining typically attaches to such issues.

child labor, provide employment-based social welfare payments, prohibit discrimination in employment, promote health and safety in the workplace, and regulate private pension and benefit programs.

With the exception of worker compensation laws, which were passed during the 1900s and 1910s, and the 1926 Railway Labor Act, the Wagner Act preceded or was contemporaneous with most of the other non-civil-rights statutory employment laws. The enactment of all these laws was supported by organized labor. Some dealt with issues that unions were unable to win at the bargaining table, but at the same time, their passage and effective enforcement may have decreased the perceived need among employees to unionize.

To some degree, the extension of laws and regulations into broad areas of employment practices establishes a quasi-corporatist relationship between the government and employers, and it involves unions as well where they represent employees. Where unions are present, the laws and regulations establish a base on which gains can be negotiated. Ironically, legislation favored by unions that protects employees or applicants and regulates aspects of the employment relationship, when passed, reduces the need for unionization and bargaining to attain the ends that were not previously guaranteed by law.

Waxing and Waning of Corporatist Approaches in U.S. Labor Relations

As noted above and detailed in Chapter 2, federal government involvement in labor relations has varied substantially throughout the history of the United States. During all periods, as detailed in Chapters 2, 3, and 6, courts have generally held that property rights take precedence over the right to organize and collectively bargain. At the same time, courts and statutory law increasingly endorsed the legitimacy of labor unions and the role of collective bargaining in resolving employment disputes in situations in which this was the employees' preferred method.

Federal government involvement in labor relations was at its peak between the beginning of World War II and the middle of the 1970s. During World War II all wages and prices were administered, and strikes were prohibited. This meant that all collective bargaining agreements needed the approval of the federal government and all disputes had to be settled even if government intervention was required.

The Taft-Hartley amendments to the Wagner Act laid the groundwork for substantially more federal involvement in labor relations through the FMCS and national emergency dispute procedures. Over the next 20 years (1947 through the late 1960s), presidents who followed Harry Truman invoked the national emergency procedure on a number of occasions. In addition, it became fairly common practice in major disputes to call the parties to Washington to "jawbone" them into agreeing on an appropriate settlement. Federal government involvement probably moderated some extreme positions of the parties in a number of disputes, but it also dampened the bargaining power that the more powerful side held going into the negotiations.

This corporatist approach worked reasonably well during a period in which productivity was growing at an annual rate of about 3 percent and inflation was in check. However, by the end of the 1960s, inflation started to rise rapidly and with it came an increase in wage demands. Increasing uncertainty led negotiators to take more extreme positions. In addition, unions were not particularly willing to adhere to wage-increase ceilings promulgated by the Nixon administration, given the uncertain inflation environment.

While it was not then readily apparent, the growing globalization of the economy was becoming more apparent as a result of the Arab oil embargo of 1972 to 1973. Increasingly, the U.S. economy was becoming more tightly linked with the rest of the world, and the value of the dollar and the relative desirability of U.S. goods and services at home and abroad depended on their quality and cost.

The declining corporatist regime essentially ended with the inauguration of Ronald Reagan as president. The federal government reduced its regulatory profile and a more laissez-faire approach to labor relations was permitted. Employers had already begun to take a harder line on economic negotiations and to actively avoid unionization.[3] The unionized proportion of the labor force had been falling for 30 years. As a result, the political imperative to intervene on labor's behalf had declined. When President Reagan fired and replaced striking federal air traffic controllers, private sector employers were emboldened to take a harder line in bargaining.

While there have been both Democratic and Republican presidents over the past 30 years, there haven't been major differences in the federal government's approach to labor relations. The laissez-faire approach has prevailed in the sector covered by the Taft-Hartley Act. While the NLRB members appointed by various presidents have frequently switched their interpretations of the law, mostly related to issues of representation, no new legislation has been enacted that has altered the bargaining power of either of the parties. As long as the parties comply with the most basic legal requirements, they are essentially free to slug it out in the collective bargaining arena. As succeeding chapters will note, this also means that there is substantially more decentralization and variation in how labor relations are practiced than existed during the earlier corporatist period.

PUBLIC POLICY AND INDUSTRIAL ORGANIZATION

Since the passage of the Sherman Antitrust Act in 1890, public policy has limited industrial concentration and collusive activities between producers in a single industry. Excessive industrial concentration is not defined in the statute or by the courts, but it is dealt with by the Federal Trade Commission on a case-by-case basis. On the other hand, price fixing and other collusive activities have been vigorously prosecuted when discovered, and persons or organizations that have been harmed by them have been entitled to recover treble damages.

The growth and maturation of most industries seem to follow a general pattern. During an industry's infancy, production is labor-intensive. Product characteristics are relatively diverse. As consumer preferences are revealed, some producers go out of business because their products do not meet consumers' needs. As production methods become standardized, capital and cheaper labor are substituted for skilled craft work, and more efficient producers lower prices to gain market share, thus driving

[3] See A. Freedman, *Managing Labor Relations* (New York: Conference Board, 1979).

marginal producers from the industry. Over time, an industry becomes dominated by relatively few firms, and the less dominant either mimic the leader or occupy niches in which the leader chooses not to produce. For example, the microcomputer industry had hundreds of manufacturers and software development companies in the early 1980s producing equipment and programs that were largely incompatible with one another. Apple gained an early lead, and IBM realized that it needed a product in the rapidly growing market. The PC was developed for that market and used an Intel processor and an operating system developed by Microsoft. These became the standards for the industry. New manufacturing and sales models were developed (e.g., by Dell), and a variety of applications were increasingly produced by a smaller subset of software firms. By the late 1980s, the industry was substantially consolidated. The introduction and promotion of freely available LINUX operating systems and JAVA software are attempts to reduce the Microsoft-Intel control of the computing market.

COMPETITION AND CONCENTRATION IN MARKETS

In the classic economic model, a competitive market includes many producers that sell similar products. Consumers have good information about product attributes and prices. Producers that sell at prices above the market will not be able to remain in business. The demand for goods and services in this type of market is highly *elastic,* meaning that if a producer decreases its prices, buyers will quickly shift toward purchases from this low-price firm. The reverse would happen to producers that did not respond to the decrease. In a competitive market, if a producer does not quickly match a drop in the market price, it will be unable to sell enough to remain in business.

A concentrated market is one with relatively few producers. Probably the best example is the commercial aircraft industry with only two companies producing intercontinental airliners—Airbus Industries and Boeing. The investment necessary to enter the industry, in both financial and production competence terms, creates an almost insurmountable barrier to entry.

In a competitive industry there are many small producers. Organizing one company gives the union virtually no bargaining power on wages. Since there would be a great deal of effort necessary to unionize the industry, unions don't focus on competitive industry companies unless they are concentrated geographically or the employees in the company request assistance. With regard to geographic concentration, this usually involves a set of local service providers such as janitorial services, security services, or hotels. Here the service is provided in the locality where the employees reside.

In concentrated industries, it's important for the union to organize most or all employers and to bargain with them on the same time schedule. In this way, all employers will encounter the same demands and will be less resistant because at least part of any negotiated wage increases can be passed on to consumers through simultaneous price increases. With globalization, this has been increasingly difficult because unions operate nationally, while product competition is international.

A firm may also gain competitive advantage through patents. Companies in the pharmaceutical and information technology industries often earn higher profits from their monopoly positions as patent owners, either through higher prices for the patented products they produce or through license fees paid by other producers to use the patented attribute.

REGULATION AND DEREGULATION

Regulation of certain industries has existed in the United States for over a century. The Interstate Commerce Act was passed in 1887 to regulate interstate rail freight rates. Congress intended to reduce or eliminate price discrimination between small and large shippers and to maintain an incentive for transportation companies to provide service to rural areas. Other industries that have had services and charges regulated include communications, banking, petroleum products and natural gas, electrical utilities, interstate trucking, and airlines. But over the past several years, federal regulation in many of these areas has been reduced or eliminated. The initial result has been the elimination of monopolies and the restoration of price competition.

Deregulation enabled new companies to enter and created competition in wages between union and nonunion sectors of the industries. Until now, wages and employment have been most affected by deregulation in trucking, air carriers, and telecommunications. Airline deregulation had relatively little initial effect on mechanics' pay, but pilots' salaries fell between 3 and 11 percent, and salaries of flight attendants dropped from 11 to 18 percent.[4] Mechanics would have alternative employment opportunities in their occupation in other industries, an advantage not enjoyed by pilots and flight attendants. Following deregulation in the trucking industry, coverage of truckers by the National Master Freight Agreement negotiated by the Teamsters and Trucking Management Inc. fell by two-thirds. Wages fell by 27 percent, and return on equity for unionized trucking companies fell by 22 percent between 1977 and 1990 due to decreases in freight shipping rates.[5] The effects of deregulation continue to occur in other industries. Exhibit 8.1 contains information about how a union used the fact that its employer was in a regulated industry to guarantee jobs in a proposed merger.

[4] D. Card, "Deregulation and Labor Earnings in the Airline Industry," in J. Peoples, ed., *Regulatory Reform and Labor Markets* (Boston: Kluwer, 1998), pp. 183–229.

[5] M. H. Belzer, "Collective Bargaining after Deregulation: Do the Teamsters Still Count?" *Industrial and Labor Relations Review*, 48 (1995), pp. 636–655.

Exhibit 8.1

QWEST UNIONS SAY THEY WON'T BLOCK TAKEOVER

A settlement between Qwest and its [Minnesota-based] labor unions over jobs and severance has removed one major barrier to the $10.6 billion acquisition of [Denver-based Qwest,] Minnesota's largest telephone company[,] by Louisiana-based CenturyLink.

In the settlement, the Communications Workers of America [(CWA)] and the International Brotherhood of Electrical Workers [(IBEW)] agreed to drop their opposition to the Qwest acquisition and CenturyLink agreed to maintain approximately the current Qwest ratio of union workers to management employees for 30 months after the acquisition closed.

In addition, CenturyLink agreed to not close any Qwest call centers staffed by union employees before May 2012. CenturyLink also would provide enhanced severance benefits for Qwest union workers if they are laid off before October 2012.

Qwest has about 3,300 employees in Minnesota, including 2,100 union employees.

Source: Excerpted from Steve Alexander, "Qwest Unions Say They Won't Block Takeover" *Star Tribune* (Minneapolis, MN), October 26, 2010, pp. D1.

GLOBAL COMPETITION

Many U.S. industries encounter formidable foreign competition. Steel is an example. Because it is essentially a commodity, production and shipping cost differences cannot be passed on to buyers. Certain fixed costs for plants and equipment, incurred whether the company is operating or not, lead producers during periods of lower demand to sell steel at a loss for a short time rather than shut down a plant. Where excess capacity exists in the short run, foreign firms may "dump" steel in the United States at prices below their costs. Services can also be dumped. In 2002, President Bush imposed steel tariffs that were ruled in 2004 to be in violation of World Trade Organization (WTO) agreements. Exhibit 8.2 tells about the imposition of tariffs on Chinese-produced tires by the Obama administration. The political power of unions appears to influence the imposition of tariffs since industries with higher union coverage are more likely to have them levied against competitive goods produced offshore.[6]

In the auto industry, American producers encountered global competition in the mid-1970s as a result of increased fuel prices following the formation of OPEC. Fuel efficiency became a more important criterion in purchase decisions. Increased consumer attention to quality also began to

[6] M. J. Slaughter, "Globalization and Declining Unionization in the United States," *Industrial Relations*, 46 (2007), pp. 329–346.

Exhibit 8.2

OBAMA ADMINISTRATION ORDERS TARIFF ON CHINESE TIRE IMPORTS

WASHINGTON, D.C.—Following an announcement by the White House, United States Trade Representative Ron Kirk released the following statement today on the U.S. decision to impose remedies under Section 421 of the 1974 Trade Act to stop a harmful surge of imports into the U.S. of Chinese tires for passenger cars and light trucks. Following what the ITC determined was a surge, production of similar products in the U.S. dropped, domestic tire plants closed, and Americans lost their jobs. Today's steps are designed to level the playing field for American workers in the tire market.

The three-year remedies, consisting of an additional tariff of 35 percent ad valorem in the first year, 30 percent ad valorem in the second, and 25 percent ad valorem in the third year, are being imposed after a finding by the United States International Trade Commission that a harmful surge of imports of Chinese tires disrupted the U.S. market for those products. President Obama also announced today that Trade Adjustment Assistance will be targeted to help affected workers, industries, and communities immediately, while tariff changes take effect.

"When China came in to the WTO, the U.S. negotiated the ability to impose remedies in situations just like this one," said Kirk. "This Administration is doing what is necessary to enforce trade agreements on behalf of American workers and manufacturers. Enforcing trade laws is key to maintaining an open and free trading system.

"These remedies are a necessary response to the harm done to U.S. workers and businesses, designed to achieve the objective of curbing what the ITC determined was a harmful surge of Chinese tires into the U.S. market," said Kirk. "China is America's second largest trading partner, and the health and strength of our relationship are very important to both countries. We consulted with China as allowed for under the WTO. This decision has been based carefully on America's rights under WTO rules, namely China's accession agreement, and on sound economic calculations."

Source: "Kirk: White House Fulfilling Trade Enforcement Pledge With Announcement of Remedies in Chinese Tire Case," Press Release, Office of the United States Trade Representative, Executive Office of the President, September 2009.

dominate purchase decisions within various price ranges. Differences in labor costs across producing countries led to price advantages for producers in some nations. These differences include variations in both wages and labor productivity. Relative costs also increase or decrease depending on the exchange rate between the dollar and foreign currencies.

When these types of changes occur, the elasticity of demand for a particular firm's products increases substantially because the industry is no longer concentrated. Wage increases cannot be as easily passed through. Auto union wage and benefit concessions that began in the 1980s and continued through the 2007 bargaining round were partly due to labor costs (combined with other costs) that would not permit U.S. manufacturers to operate at a profit given competitive pricing of products in the industry. After short-run reductions in wages (labor) and parts suppliers' prices (materials), some obsolete plants (capital) were shut down to reduce the cost content of new vehicles. Even with these changes, the economic crisis that began in 2008 decreased domestic auto sales so severely that excess capacity, legacy health and pension obligations, and relatively high wages forced both General Motors and Chrysler into Chapter 11 bankruptcy proceedings. (These effects will be discussed in more detail in Chapter 9.)

Both unskilled and skilled services are also affected by global competition. Improvements in information technology, communications, and transportation have all affected the demand for domestic labor in various jobs and industries. Given the substantial reductions in global communications costs, call centers can be operated from countries that have sufficient numbers of English-speaking workers available in their labor markets at wages below the U.S. wages. Back-office operations of banks and financial service companies can be performed more efficiently in other parts of the world where normal working hours occur while it is nighttime here. Computer programming and other more sophisticated project work can also be offshored. Heavy maintenance work on commercial airliners can be performed in East Asia at much lower hourly rates than those in the United States, reducing substantially the demand for domestically based mechanics. All of these alternatives reduce union bargaining power for representatives of these types of employees.

Global competition in basic industries has decreased the wages and employment of domestic workers.[7] Domestic producers are moving some labor-intensive operations to countries with lower labor costs. On the other hand, German automobile manufacturers such as Daimler (Mercedes) and BMW opened plants in the United States and began buying auto producers in lower-wage European countries such as Great Britain. Changes enabled by the North American Free Trade Agreement were opposed by unions because they threatened some high-wage jobs.

LABOR FORCE DEMOGRAPHICS AND EMPLOYER GROWTH

The composition of the labor force affects the productivity and labor costs of employers. In general, worker productivity improves with experience, and experience is gained over time—thus, age and experience are inextricably linked. Pay also generally increases with experience, particularly if the experience is translated into observable performance having increasing economic value. As worker productivity increases with experience, fewer workers are required to produce a given level of output. As employers gain experience with production methods, refinements are made that improve productivity.

[7] R. B. Freeman, "Are Your Wages Set in Beijing?" *Journal of Economic Perspectives*, 9, no. 3 (1995), pp. 15–32.

As Chapter 9 will note, collective bargaining agreements include very complex pay arrangements. In addition to the amounts of pay associated with hours of work and jobs to which people are assigned, other forms of compensation (benefits) such as health insurance, pension plans, and a variety of types of paid time off are also negotiated. The costs of many of these benefits depend on the demographic makeup of the workforce. In addition, they are influenced by factors outside the control of both labor and management. Health and pension costs are related to the age distribution of the workforce covered by a labor agreement, but they also are linked to the prices of medical and financial services, which are largely determined outside the control of the bargainers. Additionally, new requirements that will be put into place between 2010 and 2018 by federal health care legislation will have an effect on employers' costs and limitations of unions' abilities to bargain for certain types and levels of benefits and coverages. As a population ages, it is inevitable that health care costs will increase on a relative basis. As new inventions and treatments are introduced that have greater efficacy for good medical outcomes, a substantially inelastic demand results, with employers bearing the bulk of the escalating costs. In turn, employers put pressure on unions to agree to co-pays, reduced coverage, elimination of coverage for retired workers, and other concessions.

For an employer that has a contract requiring benefit coverage for retired workers, if the proportion of retired to active workers increases, the employer's relative costs will increase even if the per-person cost of benefits does not. This means that an employer in a mature or declining industry will find its per-employee labor costs escalating more rapidly as its size decreases, potentially accelerating the decline. Legacy costs are especially important to companies that face global competition.

CHANGES IN CONSUMER DEMAND

Since the 1950s, in developed economies there has been a secular shift in consumer demand from goods toward services. Some of the shift is due to satisfaction of basic material needs, and some is due to the aging of the population. To the extent that unions have been concentrated in manufacturing, construction, and mining industries, their relative employment has decreased. To the extent that employers are increasing the service side of their businesses, there is increasing resistance to the spread of unionization within the firm.

The range of skills required by changing consumer demands has increased. There are more jobs with both low and high skills than in the past. Low-skill jobs seldom command very high wages, and the return on investment from organizing them has usually been low. On the other end, increasing skill levels have moved a larger share of jobs into the professional arena—an area that unions generally have had a hard time organizing. Each of these factors has reduced the bargaining power of unions over the last 20 years.

EMPLOYER INTERESTS

As noted in Chapter 4, private sector firms are ultimately answerable to their shareholders. Labor is hired to accomplish organizational objectives. Shareholders seek a higher risk-adjusted return than other investments offer, which means a firm's original purpose may no longer be the one by which investors can best realize their objectives. To meet investor objectives, management seeks to maximize profits in its present operations and to shift investment from areas with declining returns to those where improvement is anticipated, with the greatest amount of flexibility possible. Firms might be expected to leave previous markets and enter new ones as the environment changes the rates of return for various industries. Mergers and acquisitions reflect the mobility of capital. If a firm is not making an acceptable return on its equity, a lower-earning division can be sold, forcing unions to deal with successor owners. Part of an organization can also be spun off, as General Motors did with its parts-producing operations in creating Delphi Corporation and as Ford did in creating Visteon. After Delphi was spun off, its cost structure, together with declining auto production following 9/11, led the company to seek protection under Chapter 11 of the Bankruptcy Code in 2005. Following its own bankruptcy in 2009, General Motors strategically reacquired some Delphi operations in 2010 in order to assure itself of needed parts as production was increased. Exhibit 8.3 provides details.

Labor as a Derived Demand

Labor is necessary to produce and sell products and services. Total sales depend on aggregate consumer purchases. Thus, the demand for labor is derived, with the level of employment influenced by the elasticity of demand for the employer's products. The derived demand for labor is more inelastic if (1) a given type of labor is essential in the production of the final products, (2) the market demand for the final products is inelastic, (3) the cost of labor is a small part of the total product cost, and (4) the supply of materials and/or capital is inelastic.[8] These situations indicate skilled trades in relatively small bargaining units where substitutes are not readily obtainable and where price has little influence over sales and would be least likely to cause employers to resist a demand for wage increases.

When an employer is a relatively small factor in a labor market and/or when there is substantial unemployment, its supply of labor is likely

[8] A. Marshall, *Principles of Economics*, 8th ed. (New York: Macmillan, 1920).

Exhibit 8.3

GM TALKS CONCESSIONS FOR REACQUIRED FORMER DELPHI PLANTS

Even as it talks of the need to ramp up production at several U.S. assembly plants, General Motors Corp. is sending another message to the handful of former Delphi Inc. plants it "reacquired" as part of Delphi's departure from bankruptcy: costs have to be reduced.

The *Detroit News* reports today GM is seeking wage concessions from the United Auto Workers union workers who staff the components plants. The gambit likely was inevitable: GM spent billions to purchase the plants when Delphi exited its protracted bankruptcy late last year in order to assure the orderly delivery of vital parts—but GM reportedly is seeking to sell many, if not all of the facilities. The company already announced earlier this month it is selling the Nexsteer steering-components plant in Saginaw, MI.

The report that GM wants to reduce labor costs hardly is a surprise, then, as it brings these plants—and the thinking that originally created Delphi—full circle.

Prior to Delphi's inception, these plants were GM-owned facilities burdened by the same high labor costs as GM assembly plants. Delphi was created by GM in 1999 to spin off the plants under the aegis of an independent company in order to remove their typically money-losing operations from GM's balance sheet.

The strategy was an effective accounting ploy, but did not change the baseline problem: the plants largely were unprofitable.

. . . Labor concessions at the plants may improve their attractiveness to new investment, but GM likely still will find them a difficult sell in what currently remains a problematic auto industry and fluid investment environment. In effect, if Delphi could not operate the facilities profitably, the chances for a new owner to do so are not promising, irrespective of new labor-cost reductions.

Source: B. Visnic, "GM Talks Concession for Reacquired Former Delphia Plants," *Edmunds Auto Observer*, January 19, 2010, www.autoobserver.com/2010/01/gm-talks-concessions-for-reacquired-former-delphi-plants.html.

to be quite elastic, and hiring more employees has little effect on wage rates. But if several employers hire the same type of labor simultaneously and/or unemployment is low, a wage increase will be necessary to obtain a larger supply. Employers are likely to be able to pass on the cost of a wage increase if they are in a noncompetitive product market, because a price increase will not greatly reduce quantities sold if product demand is inelastic.

Employers often view labor from a short-run perspective. When more employees are needed, they can be hired; when fewer are needed, they can be laid off. The amount of labor hired would be determined by the price of output, the elasticity of demand, and the firm's productivity given its capital equipment. Economic theory suggests workers will be added until the added value of the additional output no longer exceeds the wage. The value of the output produced by hiring an additional worker (the amount of the product times the price) is called the **marginal revenue product**. If the demand curve shifts, its elasticity changes and employers would need more or fewer workers. Unions are interested in reducing employers' ability to lay off employees in response to demand reductions and to create rules for how layoffs would be implemented if they were necessary.

In the short run, the marginal product of additional labor declines because the employer is using a fixed amount of capital. For example, a university contains a fixed number of classrooms. At some point, hiring additional faculty would not lead to more classes being taught because there would be no place to teach them. Consider another alternative—the online university. In this case, the marginal product of additional labor would not decline nearly as rapidly since capital costs are much less. Greater enrollment would require adding some additional administrative staff and record-keeping equipment, but classrooms would not be an issue. The declining marginal product of labor means labor demand is somewhat inelastic (downward-sloping), even though demand for the company's product might be very elastic. In concentrated industries, the demand for a firm's product is never completely elastic because each firm is a large proportion of the industry and each firm's products have some unique characteristics. Therefore, the labor demand is less elastic than it is in the competitive situation because marginal revenue at the point where market demand intersects the labor supply price would be less than the price of labor. Figure 8.2 gives examples of employment change comparisons in competitive and concentrated situations.

FIGURE 8.2
Effects of Product Market Concentration on Employment When Demand Changes

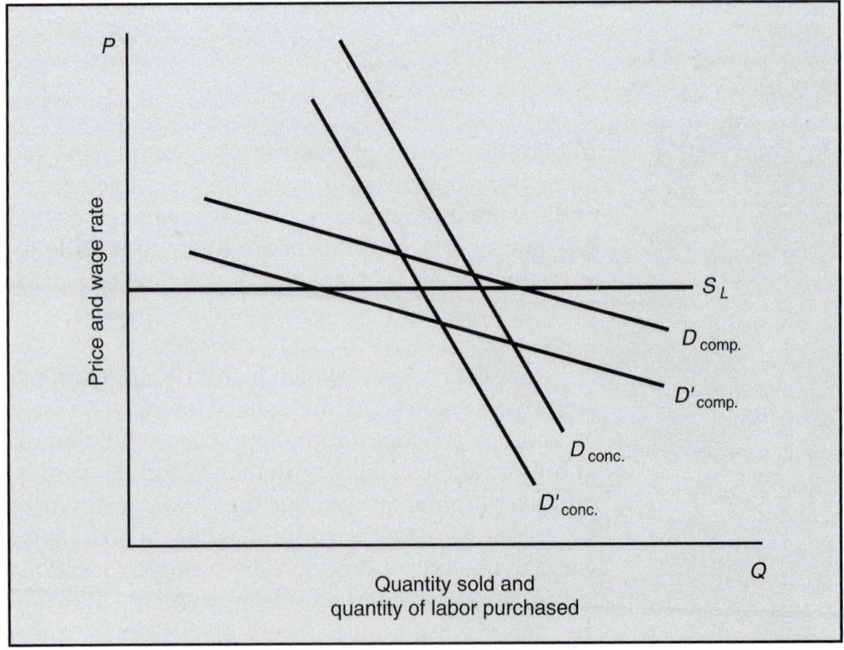

Labor-Capital Substitution

Labor and capital are required to produce products and services. Besides being interested in moving in and out of product and service markets quickly, employers also would like to change the capital-labor mix as the relative costs of the two change. Consider the airlines' methods for passenger check-in for flights. Until recently, a passenger went to the airline's ticket counter at the airport and presented a paper ticket to the airline's agent. The agent identified the customer; verified information on the ticket; entered data using a CRT terminal; accepted, weighed, and tagged baggage; and printed a boarding pass. Airlines now use electronic tickets, have installed self-service touch-screen check-in terminals, and also have Web-based options for check-in. A customer without baggage to check can check in using the Internet, print a boarding pass, and then go directly to the airport gate without contact with an agent. If there are bags to check, the customer can use the self-service terminal to check in and print baggage tags and boarding passes. An unskilled employee verifies identification and attaches the baggage tags.

Once the initial investment is made in programming the airline's computer to handle reservations and check-in procedures and the terminals are purchased, maintenance costs are quite small. The airline has made several substitutions. Several ticket agents are replaced by terminals and a few lower-skilled baggage handlers. Ongoing ticket agent effort is replaced by the one-time efforts of systems information technology specialists and a low level of ongoing system and hardware maintenance and upgrades.

One of the technological changes that has had the biggest effect on employment and wages is the introduction of containerization in international trade.[9] Instead of having ships packed and loaded in ports, manufacturers can now load containers at their factories, transport them to ports, and have entire containers loaded onto ships using high-capacity cranes. Employment of longshore and stevedore workers has decreased substantially around the world at the same time that shipping volumes have ballooned.[10]

Employers would like to make adjustments whenever a different combination of factors would improve returns. Changes in the use of capital are generally based on relatively long-term payoffs. To the extent that labor contracts fix wages and restrict layoffs, the use and costs of labor are not changeable in the short term, leaving the employer with what it believes is a suboptimal combination. If negotiations result in increased wages, the employer can be expected to reduce the use of labor and potentially increase the use of capital. Figure 8.3 shows a graphical example of

[9] M. Levinson, *The Box: How the Shipping Container Made the World Smaller and the World Economy Bigger* (Princeton, NJ: Princeton University Press, 2006).

[10] P. J. Turnbull and V. J. Wass, "Defending Dock Workers—Globalization and Labor Relations in the World's Ports," *Industrial Relations*, 46 (2007), pp. 582–612.

FIGURE 8.3
Capital-Labor Trade-Offs When Wages Increase

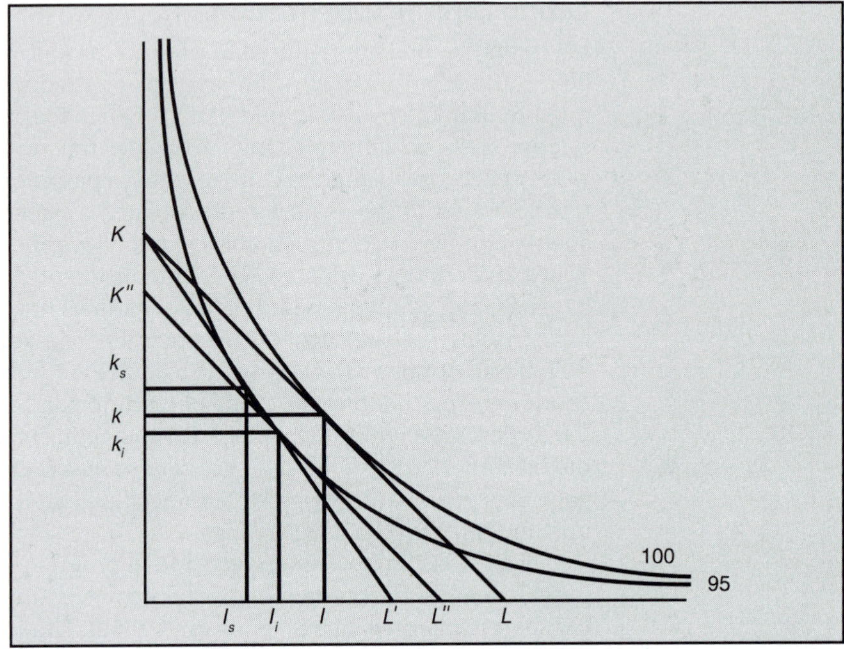

the type of adjustments an employer would make over a period of time following a wage settlement that increased wages while the price of capital remained constant.

Assume the cost of capital (*K*) is graphed on the vertical axis and labor (*L*) on the horizontal axis. The points *K* and *L* represent the amounts of each that can be purchased with a budget of a given size. The straight line connecting *K* and *L* (*KL*) is a *budget line* representing all combinations of capital and labor that can be purchased with this budget amount. The arc labeled *100* is an *isoquant* representing all combinations of labor and capital that could be combined to produce 100 units of output. The lowest point on this arc is the most efficient combination of labor and capital necessary to produce this level of output. In this example the arc contacts the budget line at this most efficient point. The corresponding points on the *K* and *L* axes are *k* and *l*. No other combination of labor and capital could produce 100 units of output with the current budget.

If labor's wage increases while the cost of capital remains constant, the amount of labor that can be purchased with this budget decreases. The new budget line (*KL'*) lies below the old budget line at all points except *K* (purchase only capital). No part of the line contacts the 100-unit-output isoquant. Thus the employer's *real income* has declined since it can't purchase as much as before for the same amount of money. If it maintained the same budget, it would have to lower production to a level at which the budget line contacted a lower isoquant, say, 95. The point of tangency between *KL′* and the 95-unit isoquant determines the new most efficient use of each input, k_s, l_s.

If the employer had produced 95 units with the previous labor-capital price relationship (*K″L″*), the most efficient point on the 95-unit-output isoquant would be k_i, l_i. The decrease from l to l_i and k to k_i is the *income effect,* reflecting the real income decrease for the employer. The move from k_i, l_i to k_s, l_s is the *substitution effect,* representing the shift from labor toward capital to achieve the most efficient combination given the present real budget.

Labor Markets

One of the outcomes of unionization is that the union acquires monopoly power over the labor supply. It doesn't actually supply the labor, but the contract fixes its price. Unions are most attracted to employers that have power to influence prices in the product market and/or wages in the labor market because these are most able to pay higher wages. A contracted wage elasticizes the labor supply at the negotiated rate.

Figure 8.4 demonstrates what happens to an employer that is a monopsonist (single purchaser of labor in a given market) following unionization. In the preunionization situation the *marginal revenue product (MRP)* curve reflects the declining productivity of added labor. The *S* curve represents the labor supply curve in the market. Since the firm is a monopsonist, this is its supply curve. The **marginal supply curve** *MS* represents the additional cost associated with expanding the workforce. For example, if one worker could be hired at $10 but the wage would need to increase to $11 before a second would take the job, the cost (marginal supply) of adding the second worker is $11 + $1 increase for the previously hired worker, or $12. The firm will hire no more workers than would be necessary to profit maximize *(MS = MRP)*. This would be equal to *E* measured at its intersection with the *S* curve. *W* would be the wage necessary to hire *E* workers.

Depending on its **bargaining power**, the union could negotiate a wage at any level up to the intersection of *MS* and *MRP*. Any increase beyond *W* would reduce the employer's profits, but the employer would also now be able to expand employment (if needed) out to *E′* without incurring greater costs than the negotiated wage for each additional worker. Unionization has transferred some level of profits into wages, but it has also increased the ability of the employer to respond to increases in demand with an elastic labor supply.

In some situations (described below), the union deals with several employers in a highly competitive industry. As long as the consumer demand for the goods and services produced by the industry is quite inelastic, a wage increase will not have major effects on employment because consumers will not purchase much less as prices rise to absorb the wage increase.

FIGURE 8.4
Monopsony Wage and Employment Decisions

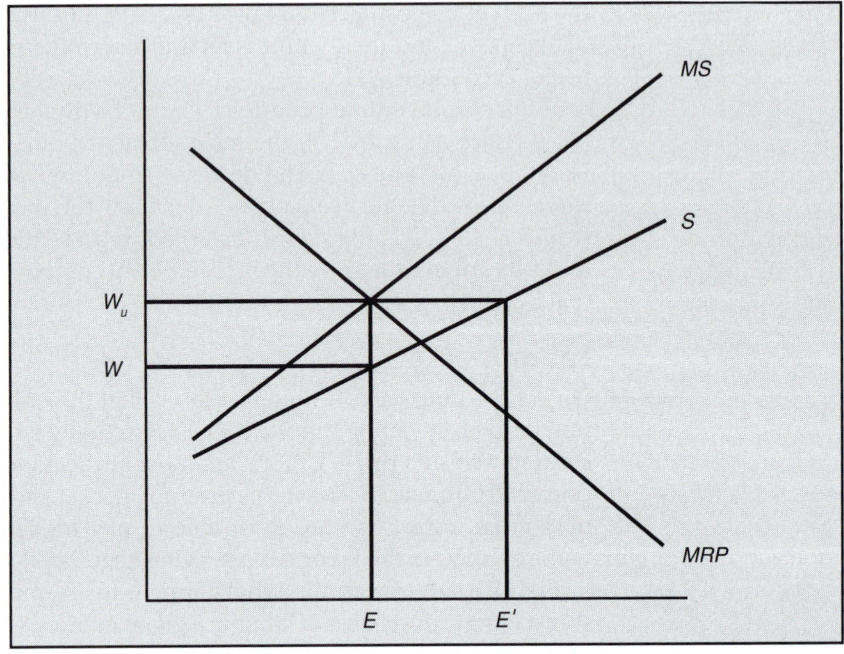

EMPLOYEE INTERESTS

Employee interests differ from those of employers. Employers are interested in accomplishing the organization's objective, which in the private sector is to maximize long-term profits. Employees want to maximize the long-term return to their investment in skills and the effort they exert in employment. Investors diversify their risks across a portfolio, while employees are generally unable to diversify their employment risks because they are tied to a single occupation. To the extent that employees invest in skills specific to their current employer, their long-term returns depend on job security and the employer's ability and willingness to pay.

A variety of job outcomes are important to employees. Union members want more influence in the workplace, cooperation from management, and union representation.[11] They are also interested in pay and job security. Their interests probably vary with the nature of the current employment environment. For example, when layoffs are rising, job security is more important than wage and fringe benefit improvements.

[11] R. B. Freeman and J. Rogers, *What Workers Want* (Ithaca, NY: Cornell University Press, 1999), pp. 39–64.

Employees' interests often can be met in their employment, but where they are not and when employees do not have other opportunities, forming a union can create bargaining power by monopolizing the internal labor supply.

UNION INTERESTS

Employees unionize to obtain outcomes that they believe they are unable to obtain as individuals. Member desires have a major impact on union bargaining goals. It has been suggested that contract demands reflect the preferences of the "median voter" in a unit,[12] thus requiring that the contract be acceptable to at least a majority to be ratified. Local union officers are often elected by a single bargaining unit. Bargaining success directly influences their ability to be reelected. Where local unions service several bargaining units, local officers might be less concerned about the content of individual contracts.

Unions demonstrate their effectiveness by negotiating contracts that improve employment conditions for their members, attract new members, and organize additional units. As an institution, the union desires security as the employees' representative through negotiated union shop agreements.

Two major goals of unions are higher wages and more members.[13] Labor is presumed to prefer both, but in dealing with employers, unions often make trade-offs between them. If wages increase relative to competitors, an employer must reduce employment (membership). For wages to increase, productivity must grow at least at the same rate. However, a national union might be willing to sacrifice a small fraction of employment in a unit to gain higher wages that will increase its organizing leverage in nonunion units with increasingly lower relative wages.

BARGAINING POWER

Bargaining power can be conceptualized as "my cost of disagreeing on your terms relative to my cost of agreeing on your terms."[14] For example, a grocer in a highly competitive market may find that agreeing to a wage demand will eliminate its profit margin and eventually force it out of business. Thus, it would object to a union wage proposal. The employees would likely pressure the union to lower its demands unless strike

[12] M. D. White, "The Intra-Unit Wage Structure and Unions: A Median Voter Model," *Industrial and Labor Relations Review*, 35 (1982), pp. 565–577.

[13] A. M. Carter, *Theory of Wages and Employment* (Homewood, IL: Irwin, 1959), pp. 88–94.

[14] N. W. Chamberlain and D. E. Cullen, *The Labor Sector*, 2nd ed. (New York: McGraw-Hill, 1971), p. 227.

benefits were equivalent to present wages or equivalent alternative employment were available. On the other hand, an employer that sells products in a less-than-competitive market may accept a relatively large wage demand because the costs can be largely passed on to consumers, and it might forgo substantial lost profits or permanently reduced market share if it had to endure a long strike.

The elasticity of demand for products has a major effect on bargaining power. Union bargaining power is enhanced when the employer has a monopoly in the product or service market because the demand for its output is relatively more inelastic than it would be in a competitive market. For example, consumers in a remote community with only one food store would be at its mercy. As prices increased, they might buy less of each food group, but total revenues would continue to rise with lower volume because the community would need to eat.

Unionization elasticizes the labor supply at the contract wage, as long as the wage is above the competitive market wage. When unions are able to organize an employer in a purely competitive industry, negotiating a wage increase (other things being equal) will necessarily lead to a reduction in employment as the employer will be forced to replace labor with capital or to cut back on employment in the short term to remain profitable. Thus, it is to the union's benefit to cooperate in creating a more inelastic demand curve in the employer's product market.

A grocery clerks' union in the remote food store example should be able to gain a large wage increase because the cost can be passed through to the store's customers. But how might the union gain a wage increase in a large city with hundreds of food stores? By bargaining in a unit that includes all stores, each store will pay the same wage increase and will attempt to pass the increase through to consumers simultaneously. No store with the same capital-labor mix would gain a competitive advantage. Less motivation would exist for any single store to resist a wage increase because all stores would encounter the same wage outcomes, leading to relatively little impact on the volume of sales if the market demand curve is relatively inelastic. To gain bargaining power, the union encourages the formation of a multiemployer bargaining unit, and the employers usually find this to be in their interest because no one is placed at a competitive disadvantage when contracted wages increase as long as there are no new nonunion entrants. There generally need to be high barriers to new nonunion firms entering the market to be able to sustain a multiemployer unit.

Ability to Continue Operations (or Take a Strike)

In addition to being affected by demand and supply characteristics of the product market in which a firm operates, employer bargaining power is enhanced substantially by its ability to take a strike. Many conditions influence this ability, including timing, perishability of the product, technology, availability of replacement employees, and competition.

Timing

A strike will have less impact on an employer if it comes during off-peak periods. Facetiously, a strike of Santa Clauses on December 26 wouldn't faze an employer. If timing cannot be controlled, it frequently can be neutralized by the company by having large inventories or accelerating deliveries to customers prior to a strike. However, this strategy has become less viable as employers have increasingly implemented just-in-time inventory systems.

Perishability of the Product

A food processor would be at a relative disadvantage if a strike occurred at the point when fruits or vegetables ripened for packing. There is a short window during which the produce must be processed, or it will spoil. Similarly, struck transportation carriers would lose quasi-perishable goods, such as business travel, permanently because the scheduled time to take the flight will not recur for the customer.

Technology

If a firm is capital-intensive, frequently it can continue to operate by using supervisors in production roles. For example, oil refiners and telecommunications providers frequently can operate for a considerable time period, if struck, given their high levels of automation.

Availability of Replacements

Strike replacements might come from either of two sources. First, and most possible in capital-intensive firms, supervisors may be able to perform enough of the duties of strikers to maintain operations. Second, the looser the labor market and the lower the jobs' skill level, the easier it will be for an employer to hire and use replacements effectively. In several recent instances, hiring replacements or the threat of hiring them has influenced negotiations.

Multiple Locations and Staggered Contracts

An employer with several plants producing the same product and having different contract expiration dates can continue to produce a large fraction of normal output in nonstruck plants.

Integrated Facilities

When output from one plant is necessary for production in several others, there is more bargaining power in the supplier plant. This situation frequently occurs in the auto industry at plants producing parts like electrical equipment or radiators for all vehicles in a manufacturer's line. Problems associated with strikes in supplier facilities have become more critical as manufacturers have moved toward just-in-time parts deliveries.

Lack of Substitutes

Ability to take a strike increases if no adequate substitutes for the organization's outputs are available. Revenues are not irretrievably lost; they are only postponed until the firm is in production. Public education is an example of this type of product or service.

Union Bargaining Power

Just as employer bargaining power is enhanced by its ability to take a strike, union bargaining power is increased by its ability to impose costs with a strike. Union wage gains in bargaining are higher where significant barriers to entry exist for new employers, industrial concentration is high, and foreign competition is low. Within the industry, high union coverage by a dominant union also facilitates bargaining power.[15] Union bargaining power has decreased significantly in the past 30 years as barriers to entry have decreased through mergers and acquisitions that have been facilitated by substantial expansions of investment banking operations. With increased globalization, industrial concentration has fallen, decreasing the ability of employers to pass wage increases to customers.

Union bargaining power increases when it exerts some control over the external labor supply or occupational practices and where rights and benefits are portable between employers and the occupation establishes performance standards and disciplinary procedures.[16]

BARGAINING STRUCTURES

The election unit is not necessarily the unit in which bargaining occurs. The parties may decide a larger negotiating unit would be mutually beneficial. This section explores variations in bargaining-unit structures presently used for negotiating contracts.

Bargaining structures for negotiation often aggregate employer units, either collecting numbers of small employers that operate in the same industry in a given region or lumping together various geographically separated plants or units of a single employer. Less often, unions representing employees within a single employer have coordinated bargaining. Bargaining units larger than election size occasionally bargain over wage issues only and leave nonwage issues for local determination.

Since the decline of corporatist approaches to bargaining, there has been an increase in the decentralization of bargaining, with a greater likelihood than in the past that economic issues will be negotiated at the local level. Given differences in the relative efficiency of plants across a company and

[15] L. Mishel, "The Structural Determinants of Union Bargaining Power," *Industrial and Labor Relations Review*, 40 (1986), pp. 90–104.

[16] D. S. Cobble, "Organizing the Postindustrial Work Force: Lessons from the History of Waitress Unionism," *Industrial and Labor Relations Review*, 44 (1991), pp. 419–436.

choices that companies can make about future investments, tailoring a contract to fit a particular location is becoming increasingly important. From a local union's perspective, job security issues are often more salient than the national union's economic goals, and the local may wish to make certain economic agreements or concessions with the employer that are in the interests of its members but that go against the interests of the national. Decentralization of bargaining increases management control because employers can pressure local groups to accept concessions in return for agreeing not to close plants in a local area.[17] Some employers have introduced so-called high-performance work organization concepts in their workplaces. Among other things, these concepts include self-managed work teams and lean production methods. Competition between and within companies is increased by paying greater attention to productivity and quality. Bargaining interests increase at the local level to maintain employment levels. Workers gain somewhat more control at the local level because they are more involved in making decisions about the production process within their work teams.[18]

Gaining and preserving bargaining power is very important to both parties. Consider an automobile producer with a number of different types of production facilities. One might produce engines, another transmissions, and a third cooling and air-conditioning systems, and three others are final assembly plants. If the company had its way, it would probably want four different bargaining units: one would include the components plants and the other three would each cover a single assembly plant. The reasoning would be that a closure of one of the parts plants would soon shut down all three assembly plants, but the reverse is not possible. The company would want to require that all the component plants agree to a strike before it could occur. The union would probably prefer the reverse from a strictly bargaining-power viewpoint. The company and union will probably agree to negotiate all economics in one unit because the union wants to avoid the political problems of different settlements in each plant and the company wants to avoid being whipsawed by the possibility of strikes at each of the three supplier plants.

In examining bargaining structures, we will first explore aggregations of employer units, followed by the union side, including public policy issues influencing the structure of the negotiating relationship.

Multiemployer Bargaining

In a given geographic area, many industries consist of large numbers of relatively small employers. Examples include contract construction, the garment industry, and retail and wholesale trade. Within an industry, the

[17] F. Traxler, "Bargaining (De)centralization, Macroeconomic Performance and Control over the Employment Relationship," *British Journal of Industrial Relations*, 41 (2003), pp. 1–27.

[18] D. Wells, "Labour Markets, Flexible Specialization and the New Microcorporatism," *Relations Industrielles*, 56 (2001), pp. 279–304.

FIGURE 8.5
Effect of a Wage Increase for a Single Employer in a Competitive Product Market

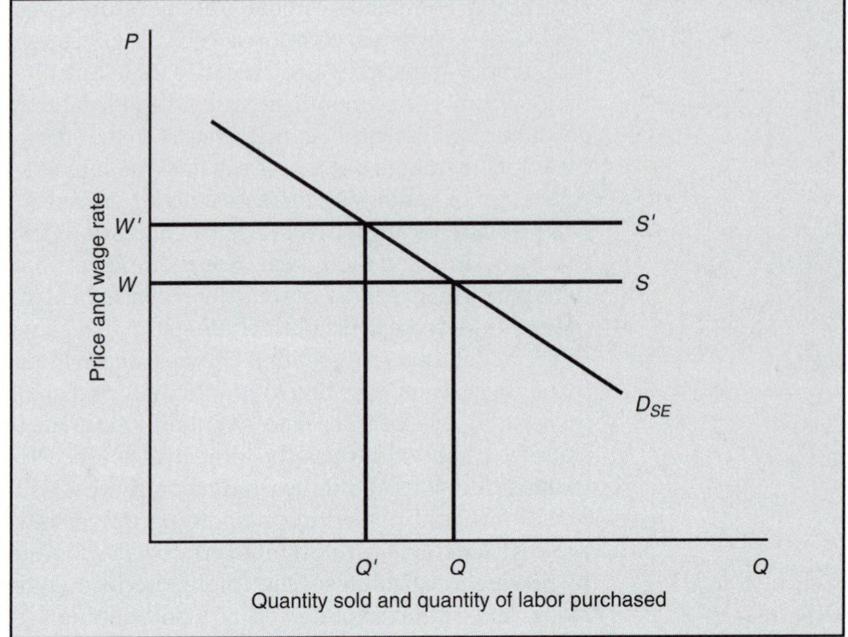

issues leading to unionization likely will be relatively common across employers, and one union is often the bargaining agent for most of the employees in the local industry.

These employers often compete for sales in a local market. Since all employers in the local industries (e.g., grocers) offer essentially similar goods and services, the demand for each employer's products is highly elastic (price-sensitive). Thus, a wage increase would be difficult to pass on to customers. To remain competitive after a wage increase, an employer must cut back on its use of labor and also produce less. Figure 8.5 shows why this result occurs.

For the union, besides the political risks associated with job loss, employer differences in willingness to grant wage increases will result in a varied wage pattern in the area, and members in units where wage increases are lower may become dissatisfied with their representation. Employers will also be more motivated to compete on the basis of labor cost differences.

To reduce these problems and to gain the monopolist's advantage in passing wage increases on to consumers, employers and unions frequently form **multiemployer bargaining units**. In a multiemployer unit, a single set of negotiators speaks for all employers, and the negotiated wage applies to all members of the bargaining association. The contract expires at the same time for all, so everyone faces the same economic

FIGURE 8.6
Effect of a Wage Increase for a Multiemployer Bargaining Unit

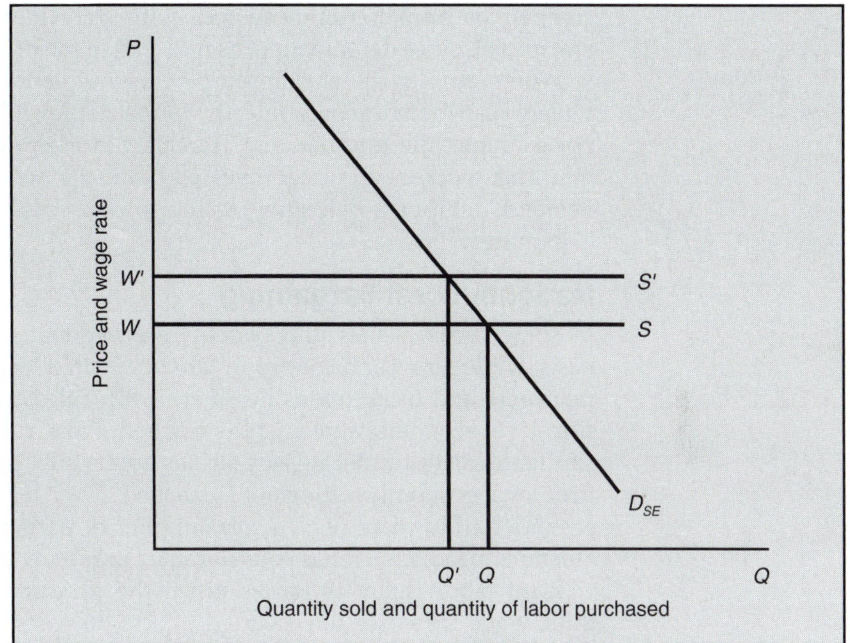

risk of strikes. Each employer faces a product and service demand curve essentially equivalent to the market demand curve because wage-related costs will be passed on by all members simultaneously. Figure 8.6 shows the effects of a wage increase in a multiemployer bargaining unit. If the market demand for the employers' goods and services is quite inelastic, most of the wage increases can be passed through with relatively minimal effects on employment.

The most successful multiemployer bargaining occurs when employers have roughly comparable nonlabor costs, all employers are unionized, and new firms have a relatively high cost of entry. If so, employers in the bargaining unit would probably not be differentially affected by a wage increase, nor would the union have to compete against nonunion labor.

Industrywide Bargaining

While most multiemployer bargaining is done within a relatively small geographic area, it also occurs on an industrywide basis when products or services are essentially commodities. In trucking, major unionized interstate truckers are represented by an employers' association that bargains with the Teamsters Union, resulting in the National Master Freight Agreement. However, maintaining an **industrywide bargaining** structure is a perilous proposition. As more employers are included, their sizes and abilities to take strikes become dissimilar. In trucking, employers face significant competition from nonunion sources, with union bargaining power in general decline since deregulation, as reflected in major wage concessions.[19]

Where employees change employers frequently and employers are widely distributed geographically, industrial-level bargaining can occur. For example, the International Transport Workers Federation represents maritime workers and negotiates pay rates for workers on "flag of convenience" shippers belonging to the International Maritime Employers Committee.[20]

National/Local Bargaining

In some firms, wages and benefits are negotiated on a companywide basis, while terms and conditions are negotiated locally. Most often, plant managers and local unions negotiate work rules and other items after a firm-level economic agreement is reached. Work rules may be negotiated simultaneously, but local-issue strikes are usually prohibited until after a firm-level economic settlement is reached. If the local represents employees in a critical plant (e.g., a sole supplier of parts necessary for all final assembly products), it has considerable bargaining power.

Plant labor intensity varies given the production technology used; thus, wage increases have varied effects on costs across plants. In one plant, a wage increase may push costs over revenues, leading to its closing. Employees in that local might lose their jobs due to a national increase. Economic settlements involving concessions are more often being negotiated at the plant level, especially when problems vary among plants. When both parties perceive contract difficulties to be related to local problems, or when the union expects to get trade-offs for concessions, organizationwide bargaining is more prevalent.[21]

Wide-Area and Multicraft Bargaining

In construction, bargaining is traditionally conducted locally. In most instances, crafts bargained separately with employers. Decentralized negotiations led to many strikes as a result of cross-craft comparisons. Increasingly, construction employers and unions use wide-area and multicraft bargaining. These configurations involve several craft unions in a given geographic market. If unions have strong national leaders, this arrangement is likely to be successful because it solidifies their positions through the use of politically appointed regional staffs to assist in bargaining. At the same time, internal politics at the local level has become more difficult, because

[19] M. Belzer, "Trucking: Collective Bargaining Takes a Rocky Road," in P. F. Clark, J. T. Delaney, and A. C. Frost, eds., *Collective Bargaining in the Private Sector* (Champaign, IL: Industrial Relations Research Association, 2002), pp. 311–342.

[20] N. Lillie, "Global Collective Bargaining on Flag of Convenience Shipping," *British Journal of Industrial Relations*, 42 (2004), pp. 47–67.

[21] P. Cappelli, "Concession Bargaining and the National Economy," *Proceedings of the Industrial Relations Research Association*, 35 (1982), pp. 362–371.

the rank and file may pressure local leaders to match other settlements instead of concentrating on smoothing the bargaining process.[22] Increased competition from nonunion contractors has encouraged a more stable labor relations climate in the unionized construction sector. A major factor in successfully bidding on projects is a record of finishing on time and within budgets. Project labor agreements involving the general contractor, its various subcontractors, and craft union representatives help to guarantee labor costs and eliminate work stoppages.

Pattern Bargaining

In highly concentrated industries, the dominant union chooses a major employer as a bargaining target. Negotiations are concentrated on this target firm, which is struck if agreement is not reached. When agreement is reached, the union moves on to the remaining firms in turn and usually quickly concludes an agreement along the lines of the initial bargain. **Pattern bargaining** has occurred frequently in companies in highly unionized concentrated industries.[23] Pattern bargaining was practiced in the auto industry for many years before the recent GM and Chrysler bankruptcies led to renegotiated contracts that are less favorable than the one covering Ford workers. Airlines tend toward pattern bargaining. Airlines negotiate agreements on an occupational basis and at widely spaced intervals both within and across the unionized sector. Airline negotiations pay particular attention to competitive labor rates since fares are set on a highly competitive basis, and negotiated rates—both up and down—track closely with recent competitive settlements in other unionized carriers. While pattern bargaining is not strictly a structural type, it represents a form of quasi-industrywide bargaining.

Some say pattern bargaining broke down during the 1980s due to major variations in plant efficiency levels among employers with several plants and between old and new plants in areas with low unionization. Managers responsible for bargaining increasingly cited firm profitability and labor cost measures as more important than industry wage patterns in their bargaining stances.[24] Unions, on the other hand, want to maintain a pattern to avoid internal political problems and to serve as a base for launching demands for wage increases.[25] Moving away from a pattern

[22] P. T. Hartmann and W. H. Franke, "The Changing Bargaining Structure in Construction: Wide-Area and Multicraft Bargaining," *Industrial and Labor Relations Review*, 34 (1980), pp. 170–184.

[23] For detailed examinations of the history and present bargaining structures in these (and other) industries, see H. C. Katz, "Automobiles," in D. B. Lipsky and C. B. Donn, eds., *Collective Bargaining in American Industry* (Lexington, MA: Lexington Books, 1987), pp. 13–54, 79–102.

[24] A. Freedman, *The New Look in Wage Policy and Employee Relations* (New York: Conference Board, 1985), p. 9.

[25] P. Cappelli, "Collective Bargaining," in J. A. Fossum, ed., *Employee and Labor Relations*, SHRM-BNA Series, vol. 4 (Washington, DC: Bureau of National Affairs, 1990), pp. 191–193.

results in more variance in wages across employers. However, evidence suggests that variance decreased between 1977 and 1983, a period during which substantial concessions were granted by unions.[26] By the later 1980s, the UAW was able to reestablish patterns within industries in which it represented employees, with the exception of aerospace and agricultural equipment.[27] Internal politics within the UAW help to reinforce pattern bargaining. Political factions coalesce around differences in settlements, serving as a strong motivation for union officers to maintain a pattern to remain in office.[28]

How, can these differences be resolved? First, during the late 1970s, inflation increased rapidly at the same time that labor contracts ran for multiyear periods. Thus, newly negotiated contracts established new patterns at the same time inflation led to large variances. Second, during the 1980s, waves of concessions occurred within fairly short periods, resulting in low wage variance as companies and unions bargained down to lower wage levels. However, large differences existed in other contract provisions such as early retirement, job security, union-management participation, and profit sharing.[29]

Pattern bargaining has made a comeback in the office cleaning industry in Los Angeles following the successful organizing by the Justice for Janitors campaign of the Service Employees. While no formal multiemployer arrangement has been established, the possibility of strikes against employers that refused to accept the pattern, and the relative ease with which customers could switch cleaning services, enhanced the development of pattern settlements.[30]

Conglomerates and Multinationals

A conglomerate is a business operating in several distinct industries. For example, a firm may operate a fast-food chain, sell data processing services, manufacture agricultural chemicals, and produce household appliances. Bargaining differs from that of a firm specializing in a single industry. The conglomerate often bargains with several unions and has contracts with different expirations. By its nature, a conglomerate has high bargaining power. No part of its business is large relative to others, and its

[26] K. J. Ready, "Is Pattern Bargaining Dead?" *Industrial and Labor Relations Review*, 43 (1990), pp. 272–279.

[27] C. L. Erickson, "A Re-Interpretation of Pattern Bargaining," *Industrial and Labor Relations Review*, 49 (1996), pp. 615–634.

[28] J. W. Budd, "The Internal Union Political Imperative for UAW Pattern Bargaining," *Journal of Labor Research*, 16 (1995), pp. 43–55.

[29] J. P. Hoerr, *And the Wolf Finally Came* (Pittsburgh, PA: University of Pittsburgh Press, 1988), pp. 474–476.

[30] C. L. Erickson, C. L. Fisk, D. J. B. Mitchell, and K. Wong, "Justice for Janitors in Los Angeles: Lessons from Three Rounds of Negotiations," *British Journal of Industrial Relations*, 40 (2002), pp. 543–567.

parts do not depend on each other for components or processes. Thus, it could afford to take a long strike at any subsidiary.[31] If a conglomerate is struck, unions gain less than they would in firms operating in a single industry.[32] On the other hand, conglomerates do not usually perform as well as firms that concentrate in one or a few industries since management must be much more sophisticated to understand the nuances of each.

Conglomerates have evolved substantially over the past 40 years. There are fewer publicly traded conglomerates than in the past, and where they exist, they tend to actively acquire and sell units depending on future prospects and performance relative to other units in the industries in which they participate. Thus, managers in each business unit face strong pressure to perform and would likely resist economic pressures from unions to avoid having their units sold. Private equity has also created conglomerates, often consisting of businesses that have relatively uncompetitive cost structures. Generally, the goal of these firms is to reduce costs, improve performance, and refloat the businesses through initial public offerings (IPOs) as independent companies. As a successor organization (see Chapter 6), the business must negotiate with the union representing its employees (if there is one), but it does not need to continue the current agreement. Bargaining power can be substantial in situations like these.

Multinational organizations have great bargaining power because unions representing U.S. employees do not represent offshore employees. Thus, the firm can offset high U.S. bargaining power by diversifying production across a set of countries in which it has markets or from which the labor and additional transportation costs would be less than the costs in the United States. Evidence indicates that location decisions are more strongly related to the potential market size of a host country than to its wage levels or industrial relations environment.[33]

Coordinated Bargaining

Coordinated bargaining occurs where two or more national unions represent employees of a single major employer. In coordinated bargaining, unions seek comparable agreements with common expiration dates. Each agrees that others can sit in on bargaining and make suggestions to the other unions' negotiators. The largest continuing example of coordinated bargaining involves General Electric and a coalition of unions led by the

[31] C. Craypo, "Collective Bargaining in the Conglomerate, Multinational Firm," *Industrial and Labor Relations Review*, 29 (1975), pp. 3–25.

[32] D. C. Rose, "Are Strikes Less Effective in Conglomerate Firms?" *Industrial and Labor Relations Review*, 45 (1991), pp. 131–44.

[33] M. F. Bognanno, M. P. Keane, and D. Yang, "The Influence of Wages and Industrial Relations Environments on the Production Location Decisions of U.S. Multinational Corporations," *Industrial and Labor Relations Review*, 58 (2005), pp. 171–200.

Exhibit 8.4

COORDINATED BARGAINING IN GE

What Is the CBC?

The GE Coordinated Bargaining Committee (CBC) is comprised of 13 unions that represent GE workers. These are the UE, IUE-CWA, IBEW, UAW, IAM, USWA, SMW, IBT, UA, NABET, IFPTE, IBFO, and AFTRA. Of all the unions in the CBC only two—the UE and IUE-CWA—have national agreements (as opposed to local contracts) with General Electric. The CBC is a way for the unions that represent GE workers to coordinate their work on behalf of their members. It allows the different unions to exchange information systematically, to coordinate their bargaining proposals, and to work together to win the best possible contract settlements from GE.

It is important to remember that the CBC does not negotiate with GE *per se* and does not have a union contract with GE. Each union negotiates its own contract.

The CBC operates by consensus among the various unions. The CBC does not make any decisions that are binding on the unions involved. Each union maintains its independence and its right, if it chooses, to do something different from what the other unions in the CBC decide to do. However, the CBC ensures that all unions at least know what the others are doing with regard to the negotiations. During the past several sets of negotiations with GE, it has in fact worked out that the UE, the IUE-CWA, and other unions have concluded the negotiations by making the same recommendations to their members.

How the CBC Works

- ***The Steering Committee*** is composed of one representative from each union in the CBC. The CBC Steering Committee is the body with primary responsibility for coordinating the work of the CBC and the member unions.
- ***Contract Proposals:*** Prior to the start of negotiations, each CBC union has the opportunity at one or more subcommittee meetings, to discuss contract proposals. Each union, in their separate negotiations with GE, is free to submit whatever proposals their members want, but through the CBC we try to achieve unity on the key bargaining issues. A union that feels strongly about a particular bargaining goal will try to convince the other unions to adopt it as a proposal so that the union will face GE as a united front on the issue.
- ***Negotiations:*** During the national negotiations, only the UE and IUE-CWA National Agreements are actually being formally negotiated. However, the other unions send representatives as a sign of unity, and they are given input into the discussions because the UE and IUE-CWA national settlements set the pattern for what the other unions will receive in their local negotiations. For several years all CBC unions have insisted, and GE has agreed, that the basic settlement with the UE and IUE-CWA be extended to all other CBC unions whose contracts expire at or near the same time as the two national contracts.

Source: Excerpted from www.ueunion.org/unity2007_barghist.html.

Electronic Workers and United Electrical Workers. Exhibit 8.4 provides information about the unions involved in the coalition and the coordination involved in bargaining with GE.

More recently, the Communications Workers and the Electrical Workers along with some smaller unions have started **coalition bargaining** with the agreement of Verizon Corporation. This arrangement increases union bargaining power but is also accompanied by an increased willingness to try innovative solutions to employment problems during a period of rapid technological change in the telecommunications industry.[34]

Craft Units within an Employer

In railroads and airlines, the Railway Labor Act requires that bargaining units be organized on a craft basis. This means employers with organized employees will have to bargain with several unions. Not all of the unions have equivalent bargaining power because the employer may continue to operate if particular unions strike (and others are willing to cross their picket lines). In the airlines, with the outsourcing of heavy maintenance work, only pilots have the power to inflict substantial economic costs by striking.

Centralization and Decentralization in Bargaining

Increased competition poses problems for both unions and employers not only in structuring the bargaining relationship between the parties but also within organizations. For employers, the uniqueness of particular plant and work-group issues and the shifting of responsibilities for profitability to business units has reduced the involvement of corporate staffs and other industrial relations professionals in bargaining and administering the contract. With the focus moving from a corporate to a business-unit perspective, unions have lost leverage on economic issues.[35]

Tension may exist between a national union and its locals. The degree of control nationals exert is reflected in the degree to which locals must allow national participation in negotiations, permissions to strike, and vetoes over negotiated agreements. Control may extend to process and/or content issues in bargaining. As noted above, unions must be able to reduce competition with both nonunion and union workers to improve conditions. Nonunion competition is reduced through extending organizing, while union competition is reduced by requiring equivalent pattern agreements. Locals may not have adequate information to negotiate competitive agreements. The national can provide a means for gathering and disseminating information across a wide number of units.[36]

[34] J. Keefe and R. Batt, "Telecommunications: Collective Bargaining in an Era of Industry Reconsolidation," in P. F. Clark, J. T. Delaney, and A. C. Frost, eds., *Collective Bargaining in the Private Sector* (Champaign, IL: Industrial Relations Research Association, 2002), pp. 263–310.

[35] H. C. Katz, "The Decentralization of Collective Bargaining: A Literature Review and Comparative Analysis," *Industrial and Labor Relations Review*, 47 (1993), pp. 3–22.

[36] W. E. Hendricks, C. L. Gramm, and J. Fiorito, "Centralization of Bargaining Decisions in American Unions," *Industrial Relations*, 32 (1993), pp. 367–390.

Changes in Industrial Bargaining Structures and Outcomes

Major changes have occurred in bargaining structures in several industries that have been heavily organized in the past and have undergone major changes over the past two decades.[37]

In addition to the public sector, there are a few industries or locations in which a larger share of employees has been organized recently. Professional sports is highly organized, with baseball and basketball players exercising significant bargaining strength.[38] Growing unionization in health care and the consolidation of health care providers has led to the greater use of organizationwide bargaining structures and, in some cases, multiemployer bargaining, although there also have been cases of breakups of multiemployer groups as excess capacity has developed among providers in a given geographic area.[39] The Las Vegas hotel industry has become highly organized, while Reno hospitality employers are essentially nonunion. Wages and benefits in Las Vegas are up to 40 percent higher than those in Reno. Unionization has a major effect on this difference since nonunion workers in other Las Vegas industries earn no premium over their counterparts in Reno.[40]

In most industries that have been under economic siege during the last 30 years, bargaining structures have tended to become decentralized, particularly in steel, tires, and trucking. In telecommunications, overcapacity and declining worker productivity have been problematic. Jobs are being restructured out of the bargaining unit and into management and professional jobs. Union coverage at AT&T shrank by 55 percent from 1984 through 1992, and the ratio of managers to nonmanagers increased from 1:4 to 1:3.[41] In addition, existing hard-wired communications companies are acquiring or starting wireless and broadband companies and strongly

[37] See P. F. Clark, J. T. Delaney, and A. C. Frost, eds., *Collective Bargaining in the Private Sector* (Champaign, IL: Industrial Relations Research Association, 2002), pp. 263–310.

[38] J. B. Dworkin and R. A. Posthuma, "Professional Sports: Collective Bargaining in the Spotlight," in P. F. Clark, J. T. Delaney, and A. C. Frost, eds., *Collective Bargaining in the Private Sector* (Champaign, IL: Industrial Relations Research Association, 2002), pp. 217–262.

[39] P. F. Clark, "Health Care: A Growing Role for Collective Bargaining," in P. F. Clark, J. T. Delaney, and A. C. Frost, eds., *Collective Bargaining in the Private Sector* (Champaign, IL: Industrial Relations Research Association, 2002), pp. 91–136.

[40] C. J. Waddoups and V. H. Eade, "Hotels and Casinos: Collective Bargaining during a Decade of Expansion," in P. F. Clark, J. T. Delaney, and A. C. Frost, eds., *Collective Bargaining in the Private Sector* (Champaign, IL: Industrial Relations Research Association, 2002), pp. 137–178. This paper points out, among other things, that in casinos operated by Native Americans, there is no legal right to organize and bargain due to tribal sovereignty.

[41] J. Keefe and K. Boroff, "Telecommunications Labor-Management after Divestiture," in P. F. Clark, J. T. Delaney, and A. C. Frost, eds., *Collective Bargaining in the Private Sector* (Champaign, IL: Industrial Relations Research Association, 2002), pp. 303–372.

resisting organizing or accretion in these units. However, recently the Communications Workers has been able to get some of the major local operators to remain neutral in organizing campaigns and/or allow card checks for recognition in their wireless business units. These concessions were extracted by the union in return for agreeing to support rate-increase requests to state regulators.[42]

Unionization in the construction industry has declined from 50 to 25 percent as employers have increasingly established nonunion subsidiaries ("double-breasting"). Union power is also decreased when employers escape previously negotiated prehire agreements. Unions have responded by "salting" union organizers in nonunion contractors to encourage unionization.[43]

Public Policy and Court Decisions

The NLRB permits coordinated and coalition bargaining,[44] and it required General Electric to bargain with a negotiating committee representing several unions as long as each union represented GE employees. Outside representatives could not vote on offers but could observe and comment. Unions have also been permitted to demand common contract expiration dates among employers in a single industry.[45]

At its most elemental level, a bargaining unit is what labor and management say it is. This is a seeming tautology, but as we noted in Chapter 6, the NLRB ordered consent elections in companies where labor and management did not dispute the makeup of the bargaining unit for representation purposes, and no prohibited employees were included. But once they are past the representation stage, the parties are free to make the bargaining unit more (but not less) inclusive in negotiations; this may lead to novel bargaining structures to accommodate peculiarities of the unions, firms, or industries involved.

The expansion of a bargaining unit results only from the voluntary agreement of the parties. In a case where a union charged a company with refusing to bargain when it would not consider a companywide fringe benefit program, the NLRB held that only the local units are certified and any expanded unit would have to be by mutual agreement.[46]

Where employers and unions have negotiated a multiemployer unit, the NLRB and the courts have generally held that employers cannot

[42] Ibid.

[43] S. G. Allen, "Developments in Collective Bargaining in Construction in the 1980s and 1990s," in P. B. Voos, ed., *Contemporary Collective Bargaining in the Private Sector* (Madison, WI: Industrial Relations Research Association, 1994), pp. 411–446.

[44] *General Electric Co.*, 173 NLRB 46 (1968).

[45] *AFL-CIO Joint Negotiating Committee for Phelps-Dodge* v. *NLRB*, 3rd Circuit Court of Appeals, No. 19199, 1972, p. 313.

[46] *Oil, Chemical, and Atomic Workers* v. *NLRB*, 84 LRRM 2581, 2nd Circuit Court of Appeals, 1973.

FIGURE 8.7 Bargaining Patterns

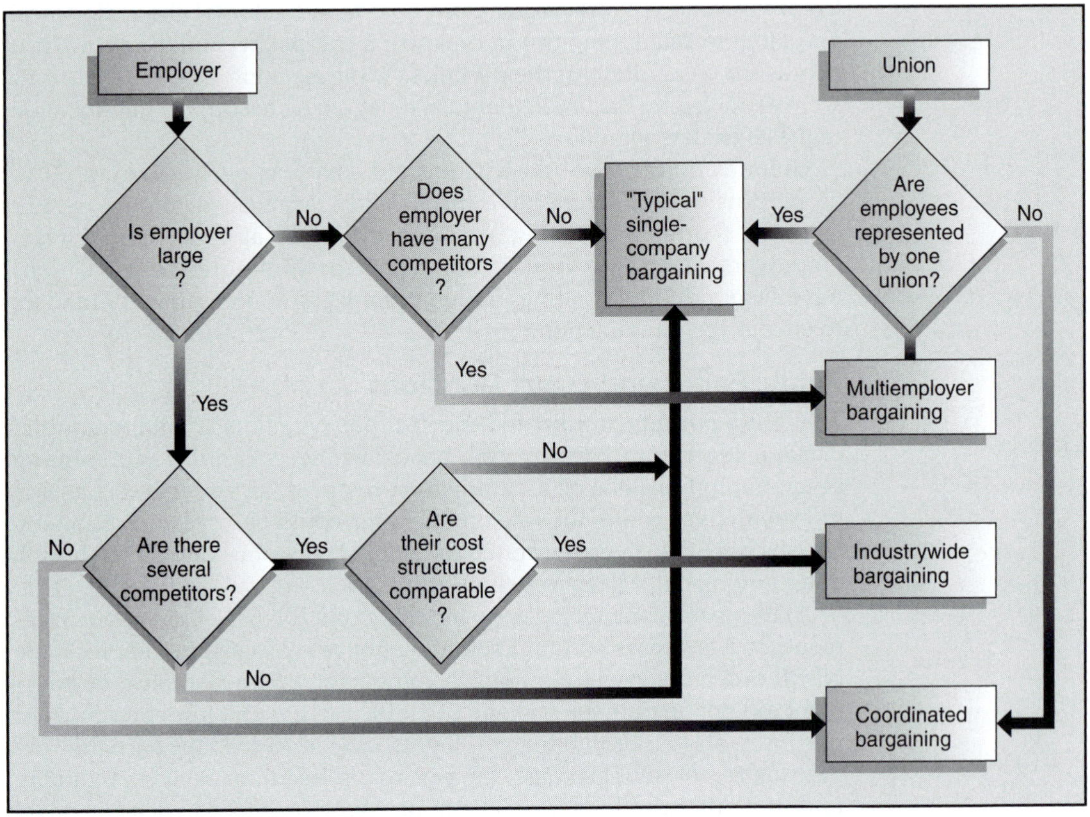

Employer
Is employer large ?
No
Does employer have many competitors ?
No
"Typical" single-company bargaining
Yes
Union
Are employees represented by one union?
No
Yes
Multiemployer bargaining
Yes
No
Are there several competitors?
Yes
Are their cost structures comparable ?
Yes
Industrywide bargaining
No
No
Coordinated bargaining

unilaterally withdraw from the unit during negotiations without the union's consent, even if a bargaining impasse has been reached. The U.S. Supreme Court did not see impasses as unusual in bargaining or sufficiently destructive of group bargaining to allow the withdrawal of unit members.[47] Figure 8.7 represents a flowchart that predicts the type of bargaining structures that could evolve in the special situations discussed.

Influence of Bargaining Power and Structure

Bargaining structures can influence bargaining power, and the relative effects for both unions and managements can be altered by the structures they agree to use. Chapters 9 and 10 examine a variety of bargaining issues. Just as the inelasticity of demand for labor influences the degree to which management can grant wage increases, so the inelasticity of demand related to any of the separate demands of labor will influence the outcome of the bargaining relationship. The employer is much more likely

[47] *Bonanno Linen Service* v. *NLRB*, 454 U.S. 404 (1982).

FIGURE 8.8 **A Conceptual Framework for the Determinants of Bargaining Outcomes**

Source: Adapted from J. T. Delaney and D. Sockell, "The Mandatory-Permissive Distinction and Collective Bargaining Outcomes," *Industrial and Labor Relations Review*, 42 (1989), p. 571.

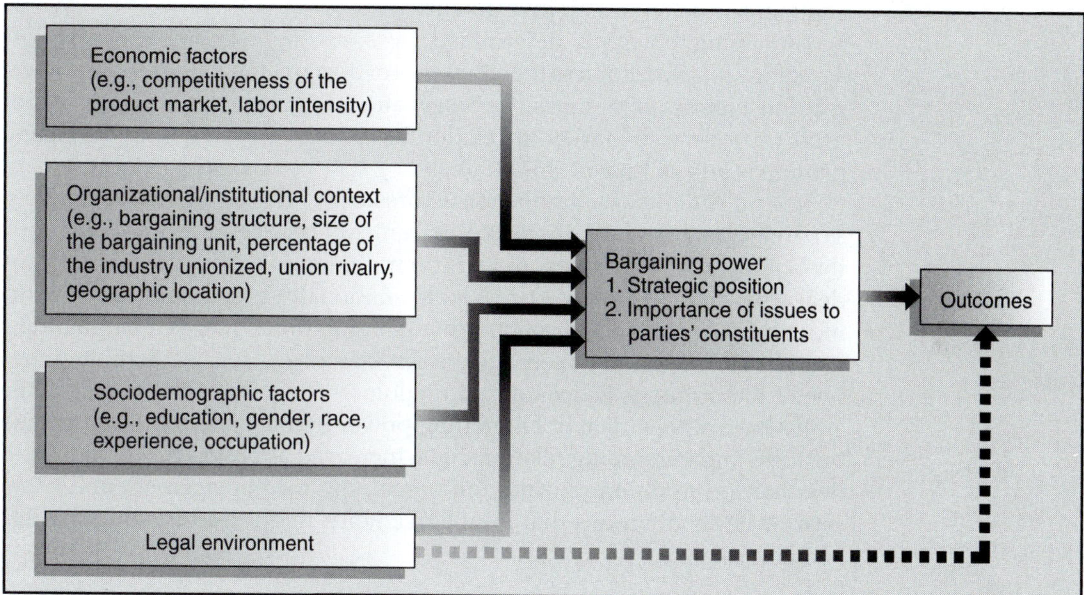

to grant in total a demand expected to have relatively little effect on overall costs than one that will broadly affect outcomes. This is one reason pension benefits and health care have grown from small-cost to large-cost items in the labor contract. Figure 8.8 is a helpful diagram of several of the variables that shape bargaining power and its effect on bargaining outcomes.

Summary

Labor, capital, and raw materials combine to produce products or services. Employers generally adjust labor and raw material inputs in the short term and capital in the long term. Labor is a derived demand depending on the level of consumers' demands for the firm's goods and services. The elasticity of this demand influences wages and employment. In the United States, legislation prohibits employers from creating product or service market monopolies; thus, employers compete regarding the costs of their products and attempt to reduce labor costs. Deregulation and foreign competition have recently increased the elasticity of consumer demand for products and have allowed competition by lower-cost forms of labor—nonunion and foreign. This situation has led to concessions by unionized employees in industries affected by these changes.

Employers generally create strategies that allow them to concentrate in product and service markets with the greatest returns on investment.

Where necessary, they want to be able to substitute capital for labor if its efficiency is higher. Employees, concerned about gaining a return on their investment in training and employment, require job security and wages commensurate with their investment.

Bargaining power is determined by assessing whether the costs of agreeing are greater or less than the costs of disagreeing. Bargaining-power relationships are sometimes purposely altered to create more power in the product or service market in relation to consumers. Multiemployer bargaining is an example of this strategy.

Several different bargaining structures exist. The election unit may be expanded as the result of mutual agreements between the employer and the union. Small employers often form multiemployer bargaining units to deal with a single union. Occasionally, nationally based employers form industrywide units to bargain with a national union. Pattern bargaining, in which one company's settlements serve as a basis for negotiating in the rest of the industry, is declining. Conglomerates and multinationals generally have a great deal of bargaining power because of their fragmented business and bargaining relationships. Increased attention to competitiveness has led to decentralization in bargaining for management and concern by national unions that local agreements might lead to whipsawing and concessions.

Discussion Questions

1. What effect does a lower elasticity of demand have on the wage and employment outcomes for the employer and the union?
2. How is bargaining power influenced by deregulation and foreign competition? Who is most affected by these changes—labor or management?
3. Why are employers less likely to approve coalition bargaining than unions are to approve multiemployer bargaining?
4. How do technological changes affect the relative bargaining power of the parties?

Key Terms

Good-faith bargaining, *220*
Mandatory bargaining issues, *220*
Permissive bargaining issues, *220*
Prohibited bargaining issues, *220*
Impasse, *220*
Marginal revenue product, *231*
Marginal supply curve, *235*
Bargaining power, *235*
Bargaining structure, *240*
Multiemployer bargaining units, *242*
Industrywide bargaining, *243*
Pattern bargaining, *245*
Coordinated bargaining, *247*
Coalition bargaining, *248*

Case: *Material Handling Equipment Association Bargaining Group*

GMFC is a charter member of the Material Handling Equipment Association (MHEA). The organization was started in the late 1940s and now includes 30 members producing over 95 percent of all domestic material handling equipment. Presently, these manufacturers produce 70 percent of the material handling equipment sold in the United States. About 80 percent of the association's total production is for the domestic market. Primary foreign markets are in Europe and Latin America, with increasing marketing emphasis in Eastern Europe.

All members are unionized, to some extent, with the proportions of production jobs organized ranging from 25 to 100 percent. GMFC is 80 percent unionized. Most companies bargain with the Steelworkers, the Auto Workers, or the Machinists. Some variations exist between contracts within employers and across employers in the association.

Unions have been particularly interested in negotiating relatively similar contracts across employers and national-level agreements within employers.

The MHEA industrial relations executives recently studied the possibility of industrywide bargaining. Coincidentally, since they were proposing a merger, the major unions representing MHEA employees explored potential coalition bargaining arrangements.

Taking either a management or a union role, formulate arguments for or against (1) industrywide bargaining with each separate union, (2) industrywide bargaining with coalition bargaining representing employees, (3) bargaining at the local level on all issues with the union that happens to represent the employees.

Chapter Nine

Wage and Benefit Issues in Bargaining

Wages are always a major issue in bargaining. Management is concerned with wage and benefit issues because its ability to compete depends to some extent on its labor costs. Firms producing equivalent output with lower labor costs will have higher profits and be better able to operate during downturns.

Both labor and management are concerned with the overall level of pay and also with how pay rates and pay increases are determined for different jobs and about the mix of wages and benefits paid to employees.

This chapter examines the components of union wage demands, bargaining on specific aspects of the pay program, the effects unions have on pay levels in both union and nonunion organizations, and the prevalence of wage and benefit issues in contracts.

As you study this chapter, consider the following issues and questions:

1. What are the strongest current arguments unions and/or managements use in the proposal or defense of present or future wages and benefits?
2. What effect do wages and benefits have on the economic performance of the employer and on nonunion employees of the same or other employers?
3. How does the form of wages influence employer and employee outcomes?
4. How does the system for allocating salary increases differ in union and nonunion organizations?
5. How does the usual structuring of union wage and benefit demands alter the structure of wage differentials in an organization over time?

UNION AND EMPLOYER INTERESTS

The union movement has always argued that wealth is ultimately created by labor, in all its forms, and that the distribution of income is excessively unequal. While not denying employers' rights to a return on investment, unions would not agree that profit maximization should be a firm's primary goal. Unionization aims to increase the power of workers to increase their share of the firm's revenue.

Private sector employers are ultimately interested in maximizing shareholder value. They would also prefer the greatest possible flexibility in structuring their operations, including the mobility of capital. They would like to manage pay programs to minimize labor costs and obtain the most output per dollar.

In the next sections we will examine the background of union wage demands and the components of the pay program.

COMPONENTS OF WAGE DEMANDS

In framing its wage demands, the union relies on three major criteria: (1) equity within and across employers, (2) the company's ability to pay, and (3) its members' standards of living. These criteria suggest that unions make a number of comparisons in formulating wage demands.

Equity

With regard to equity, unions want wages for jobs they represent to exceed, or at least be consistent with, those of equivalent nonunion jobs in the firm. They also expect equivalence in insurance benefits across jobs because personal risks are not related to job or salary level. Unions attend to bargains forged in other industries, but because of global competition and deregulation, upward pattern bargaining across industries has declined. Unions also want uniformity in wage rates for the same jobs in different locations of the same company. For example, an auto assembly worker at Ford's Kansas City, Missouri assembly plant earns the same rate as another on a similar job in Wayne, Michigan. These patterns within a single employer are eroding, however, as plant-level negotiations often lead to concessions in older, less efficient plants to avoid shutdowns and the resulting loss of jobs.

Income inequality is also a component of the equity demand. Unequal distributions exist where different workers in different jobs earn different pay. From a union standpoint, excessive inequality would be related to income differences between production workers, professionals, and executives that are larger than members can justify. For the union, inequality suggests there may be an opportunity to redistribute income from higher- to lower-level jobs. Income inequality has increased substantially since 1980.

Exhibit 9.1

DOUGLAS FRASER RECALLS WALTER REUTHER'S POSITION ON CONCESSIONS

Fraser . . . urge[d] a change in union behavior, in speeches to UAW groups. There were always critics present who challenged him, invoking Reuther's name as the final authority.

Fraser told me about one such meeting when I visited him in 1985. . . . "I went into one lion's den last week, a union meeting," Fraser said, "and there was this old Commie there who I knew would raise that precise issue, 'Reuther spinning in his grave.'" Fraser chuckled and rummaged in a desk drawer. He pulled out a mimeographed text of a speech.

So I brought this along and read it:

> All industries and all companies within an industry do not enjoy the same economic advantages and profit ratios. We cannot blind ourselves to this fact at the bargaining table. As an employer prospers, we expect a fair share, and if he faces hard times, we expect to cooperate. . . . Our basic philosophy toward the employers we meet at the bargaining table is that we have a great deal more in common than we have in conflict, and that instead of waging a struggle to divide up scarcity, we have to find ways of cooperating to create abundance and then intelligently find a way of sharing that abundance.

Fraser showed me the first page of the text. It was an address delivered by Walter P. Reuther in 1964 at the University of Virginia.

Source: John P. Hoerr, *And the Wolf Finally Came* (Pittsburgh, PA: University of Pittsburgh Press, 1988), p. 195.

Some of this can be attributed to occupational changes, but reduced union coverage is a major contributor to increased inequality.[1] Union coverage is an important factor because inequality has decreased in the public sector over the same period as public sector union coverage increased.[2]

Ability to Pay

While **ability to pay** takes two forms, the primary argument relates to a firm's profitability. When profits are increasing, unions expect to receive pay increases. They resist accepting reduced pay when profits decline, but they may concede when employers have incurred substantial losses and job losses for union members would be the alternative. Some critics within unions have condemned concessions, arguing that past labor leaders would not have accepted them. Exhibit 9.1 recalls one of longtime UAW president Walter Reuther's speeches, as told by Douglas Fraser, the UAW president during initial auto concessions in the early 1980s.

[1] J. DiNardo and T. Lemieux, "Diverging Male Inequality in the United States and Canada, 1981–1988: Do Institutions Explain the Difference?" *Industrial and Labor Relations Review*, 50 (1997), pp. 629–651; and N. M. Fortin and T. Lemieux, "Institutional Changes and Rising Wage Inequality: Is There a Linkage?" *Journal of Economic Perspectives*, 11, no. 2 (1997), pp. 75–96.

[2] M. A. Asher and R. H. DeFina, "The Impact of Changing Union Density on Earnings Inequality: Evidence from the Private and Public Sectors," *Journal of Labor Research*, 18 (1997), pp. 425–437.

TABLE 9.1
Cost Comparisons for Labor- and Capital-Intensive Firms

	Labor-Intensive Firm	Capital-Intensive Firm
Material cost	$ 500,000	$ 500,000
Capital cost	100,000	400,000
Labor cost	400,000	100,000
Total cost	$1,000,000	$1,000,000
Cost of 10% wage increase	40,000	10,000
Net total cost	$1,040,000	$1,010,000

Ability to pay is also related to the proportion of labor costs in a company's total costs. Generally, unions believe that the lower a firm's labor intensity (i.e., the lower the share of costs going to labor), the greater its ability to pay. This assumption is based on the relatively lower elasticity of the derived demand for labor in capital-intensive firms. Table 9.1 illustrates the effects of wage increases on the costs of labor- and capital-intensive firms.

Standard of Living

The **standard-of-living** component takes on two meanings. One involves the purchasing power of employees' pay (real wages). If prices increase by 10 percent for the things an average worker buys but wages rise only 6 percent over the same period, real wages have eroded by 4 percent. Where negotiated, a **cost-of-living adjustment (COLA)** is intended to maintain parity between wages and prices over time. The inclusion of COLAs influences the prevalence of other contract provisions. During the 1990s, Canadian contracts with COLAs also had longer durations, had lower base wage increases, and were more likely to include performance-based pay provisions.[3]

Standard-of-living issues also arise with unions' beliefs that their members' purchasing power needs to be improved so that they can enjoy higher qualities of goods and services. Some comparison or equity aspects are included here, but the comparison is with society in general, not with a specific work group.

Figure 9.1 presents the wage demand components just discussed. Equity is related to both internal and external comparisons, ability to pay is related to profits and labor intensity, and standard of living is related to real wages and absolute improvement. Although equity issues were discussed first, none of these pay issues is, a priori, more important than another.

PAY PROGRAMS

Collective bargaining alters the status quo in pay administration by substituting a negotiated contract for management's unilaterally determined practices. A useful way to understand pay programs is to divide decisions

[3] O. Azfar, "Innovation in Labor Contracts: On the Adoption of Profit Sharing in Canadian Labor Contracts," *Industrial Relations*, 39 (2000), pp. 313–335.

FIGURE 9.1 **Wage Demand Components**

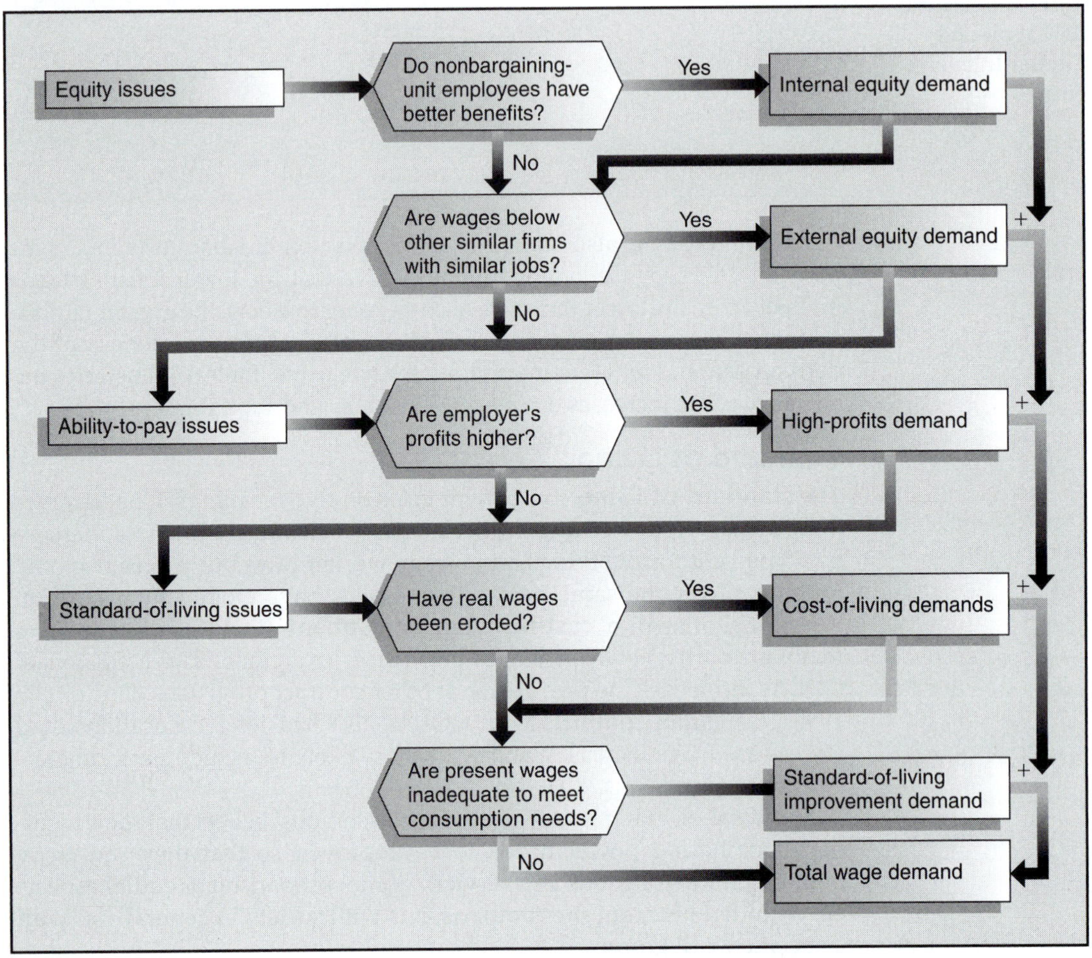

about them into four major components: pay level, pay structure, pay form, and pay system.[4] **Pay level** refers to how an employer's average pay rates for jobs compare with other employer's rates. **Pay structure** consists of the sets of wage rates the employer applies to different jobs and the ranges of wage rates possible within specific jobs in the organization. **Pay form** is the method by which compensation is received; it includes cash, insurance payments, deferred income, preferential discounts, payments in kind, and recreational and entertainment programs. **Pay system** refers to the methods used to determine how much each individual will earn

[4] H. G. Heneman III and D. P. Schwab, "Work and Rewards Theory," in D. Yoder and H. G. Heneman, Jr., eds., *ASPA Handbook of Personnel and Industrial Relations* (Washington, DC: Bureau of National Affairs, 1979), pp. 6-1–6-2.

within a job. The system might be based on piece rates, other productivity or performance indexes, skill level, time worked, seniority with the organization, or other factors. Union and management approaches to these pay program components are covered in the following sections.

Pay Level

The basic components associated with pay-level changes are those shown in Figure 9.1: ability to pay, equity, and standard of living.

Ability to Pay

A variety of considerations influence ability to pay. The general level of business activity influences profits. When the economy is strong and unemployment is low, wage demands increase and the incidence of strikes to support bargaining demands rises. Employers that have relatively capital-intensive production processes or that bargain with several relatively small units do not have the incentive to avoid large wage increases that labor-intensive firms have. The ability to pay is usually an issue raised by the union, but employers experiencing reduced profits (or losses) or changes in their industries' competitive level argue for pay reductions. Pay-level comparisons become more difficult to make as pay form becomes more complex.

Employers are interested in reducing the fixed proportion of pay. Employees may also be interested in making pay flexible if doing so leads to more job security. Profit sharing has been increasingly negotiated into contracts as a quid pro quo for concessions. For example, auto workers have significant opportunities for profit sharing if their firms do well. If profits are down or losses occur, a lower level of pay enables the employer to retain more employees.

In attempting to reduce the rate of growth in employees' base wage levels, firms have offered lump-sum bonuses for agreeing on a contract. For example, assume the union seeks a 4 percent pay increase for employees earning about $40,000 annually. If the employer pays a $2,000 (5 percent) lump-sum bonus instead, it may be saving money because the base for future increases remains at $40,000 and no additional benefits are paid on the $2,000. If the proportion of wage-tied nonstatutory benefits is greater than 20 percent, the employer saves in the first year.

Equity

Achieving equity across employees in a given industry is important for unions because it has the effect of taking wages out of competition. All employers pay essentially the same, so advantages must be earned through more marketable products or greater productive efficiency.

Some have argued that major national unions respond to the bargaining success of their counterparts. To remain competitive with other unions in organizing and representation, trade union leaders will need to obtain settlements equivalent to or better than others recently wrung from management. Major settlements are presumed to be key-comparison or pattern-setting agreements; however, wage imitation is likely to be decreased by (1) differences between industries in which employers operate, (2) differences in the ability to pay within these industries, and (3) the time between pattern setting and later settlements.[5] As competition has increased in many industries, management bargainers have increasingly emphasized company productivity trends and profit levels and deemphasized industry patterns and settlements in other industries.[6]

Standard of Living

Inflation increases the importance unions place on maintaining a standard of living. The inclusion of COLAs increased rapidly during the 1970s when inflation was high and employers were interested in longer contracts. However, the escalation of wages in response to inflation is usually lower than the measured inflation rates.[7] Since the 1980s, firms increasingly made the deferral, modification, or elimination of COLAs a major concession bargaining objective.[8]

Where COLAs exist, pay levels within the contract period are tied to changes in the consumer price index (CPI). Contracts usually provide for quarterly payments based on the difference between the CPI at the time the contract became effective and the index level at the end of the current quarter. As an example, assume that a contract effective January 1, 2012, provides for a base wage of $15.00 per hour and a COLA of 2 cents for each 0.25-point increase in the CPI. If the CPI increases 3 points by December 31, 2012, then employees would receive a lump-sum payment of 24 cents for each hour worked during the following quarter.

A very important COLA consideration is whether increases are incorporated into the base wage. Unions prefer to include them in the base before the current contract expires because, if inflation were high, an extremely large increase would be needed to bring the base up to a real-income standard equivalent to that earned at the end of the expiring contract.

Pay Structure

The pay structure is the pattern of wage rates for jobs within the organization. Within the bargaining unit, the union negotiates these rates with management. Pay differentials may be negotiated on a job-by-job basis or may result from using a negotiated job evaluation system. Job-by-job

[5] D. J. B. Mitchell, *Unions, Wages, and Inflation* (Washington, DC: Brookings Institution, 1980), p. 50.

[6] A. Freedman, *A New Look in Wage Policy and Employee Relations* (New York: Conference Board, 1985), pp. 7–12.

[7] Mitchell, *Unions, Wages, and Inflation*, pp. 48–50.

[8] Freedman, *A New Look in Wage Policy and Employee Relations*, pp. 10–12.

negotiations often create difficulties over time because the original job structure established a hierarchy of jobs separated by specific pay differentials. Bargaining often results in across-the-board pay increases of equal magnitude for all bargaining-unit jobs. While absolute wage differentials are maintained, relative differences shrink, causing wage compression. For example, two jobs with original pay rates of $7.50 and $15.00 per hour have a 50 percent differential. Over time, across-the-board increases of $7.50 per hour shrink the relative differential to 33 percent. Establishing rates for new jobs during the contract and determining rates for jobs where no external comparisons exist also cause problems. Job evaluation methods help employers and unions deal with these problems.

Job Evaluation

Job evaluation determines the relative position of jobs within a pay structure. The procedure has several steps and requires decision-making rules that must be negotiated. In general, job evaluation includes the following steps: (1) The jobs to be evaluated must be specified (usually jobs covered by the contract); (2) jobs must be analyzed to determine the behaviors required and/or the traits or skills necessary to perform each job; (3) of the behaviors or traits identified, those that vary across jobs and are agreed to be of value to the employer are grouped into compensable factors; (4) for evaluation purposes, each factor is clearly defined, and different degrees of involvement for each factor are determined; (5) point values are assigned to factors and degrees within a factor; (6) job evaluation manuals used to apply the method are written; (7) all jobs are rated.[9] Table 9.2 is an example of identified factors, point assignments, and degree levels within factors. Figure 9.2 is a specimen of the types of definitions assigned to factors and degrees within a factor.

Job evaluation involves either (1) using a union-management committee to determine compensable factors and the degree to which they are required in bargaining-unit jobs or (2) negotiating the points to be applied to evaluations completed by management. Advantages associated with a well-designed and well-administered job evaluation system include reduction of compression in wage differentials if increases are given as a percentage of the total points assigned to the job and the ease with which a new job can be slotted into an existing pay structure. The primary disadvantage is that the union and management must initially agree on the identification, definition, and point assignments associated with compensable factors.

Grade Structures

Often organizations will divide jobs into several different grades to reflect differences in the skill levels required and also to create a promotional ladder that employees may climb during their careers with the company.

[9] For more information on job evaluation techniques, see G. T. Milkovich, J. M. Newman, and B. Gerhart, *Compensation*, 10th ed. (Burr Ridge, IL: McGraw-Hill/Irwin, 2011).

TABLE 9.2 **Points Assigned to Factors and Degrees**

Source: H. Zollitsch and A. Langsner, *Wage and Salary Administration*, 2nd ed. (Cincinnati: South-Western Publishing, 1970), p. 186.

		Degrees and Points						
	Percent	1st Degree	2nd Degree	3rd Degree	4th Degree	5th Degree	6th Degree	Weight (%)
Skill	50%							
1. Education and job knowledge		12 points	24 points	36 points	48 points	60 points	72 points	12%
2. Experience and training		24	48	72	96	120	144	24
3. Initiative and ingenuity		14	28	42	56	70	84	14
Effort	15							
4. Physical demand		10	20	30	40	50	60	10
5. Mental and/or visual demand		5	10	15	20	25	30	5
Responsibility	20							
6. Equipment or tools		6	12	18	24	30	36	6
7. Material or product		7	14	21	28	35	42	7
8. Safety of others		3	6	9	12	15	18	3
9. Work of others		4	8	12	16	20	24	4
Job conditions	15							
10. Working conditions		10	20	30	40	50	60	10
11. Unavoidable hazards		5	10	15	20	25	30	5
Total	100%	100%	100%	100%	100%	100%	100%	100%

An employer would be more likely to implement this type of approach if most of the jobs were filled from within and there was a substantial need for training and experience within the company to perform well in the jobs.

Several characteristics of grade structures must be negotiated. First, the parties would need to decide how many grades would be in the structure. Second, they would have to decide which jobs to assign to which grades. Third, they would have to determine differences in pay between grades. And fourth, they would have to decide the minimum and maximum pay rates an employee could earn within a pay grade. There could also be separate structures for production, maintenance, and skilled-trades workers within a facility. Figure 9.3 displays an example of a grade structure that might be implemented in a production environment.

Skill-Based Pay

Most pay structures in unionized settings base pay differences on employees' grades and job classifications. **Skill-based pay (SBP)** ties pay to the skills employees have acquired. An inexperienced employee is hired at a starting rate. As the employee learns prescribed skills, pay is increased.

FIGURE 9.2
Definition of Factor and Degrees within Factor

Source: G. T. Milkovich and J. M. Newman, *Compensation*, 4th ed. (Homewood, IL: Irwin, 1993), p. 137. Reprinted with permission of the McGraw-Hill Companies, Inc.

1. Knowledge

This factor measures the knowledge or equivalent training required to perform the position duties.

1st Degree

Use of reading and writing, adding and subtracting of whole numbers; following of instructions; use of fixed gauges, direct reading instruments, and similar devices; where interpretation is not required.

2nd Degree

Use of addition, subtraction, multiplication, and division of numbers including decimals and fractions; simple use of formulas, charts, tables, drawings, specifications, schedules, wiring diagrams; use of adjustable measuring instruments; checking of reports, forms, records, and comparable data; where interpretation is required.

3rd Degree

Use of mathematics together with the use of complicated drawings, specifications, charts, tables; various types of precision measuring instruments. Equivalent to one to three years' applied trades training in a particular or specialized occupation.

4th Degree

Use of advanced trades mathematics, together with the use of complicated drawings, specifications, charts, tables, handbook formulas; all varieties of precision measuring instruments. Equivalent to complete accredited apprenticeship in a recognized trade, craft, or occupation; or equivalent to a two-year technical college education.

5th Degree

Use of higher mathematics involved in the application of engineering principles and the performance of related practical operations, together with a comprehensive knowledge of the theories and practices of mechanical, electrical, chemical, civil, or like engineering field. Equivalent to complete four-year technical college or university education.

Relatively few job classifications exist, and employees can be moved between assignments based on the employer's needs. This pay plan combines structural (job or task relationships) and system (pay changes based on individual behavior or skills) aspects. The practice supports team-based production, which blurs job boundaries, and thus is not found in many unionized plants. Figure 9.4 represents paths of progression in an SBP plan. Where SBP plans exist in unionized settings, they were usually implemented before representation.[10]

Lane-and-Step Plans

In the unionized public sector, lane-and-step plans are often implemented for jobs in which increased education and experience are assumed to be related to productivity or performance differences. They are particularly prevalent in unionized primary, secondary, and nonresearch university

[10] T. A. Kochan, H. C. Katz, and R. B. McKersie, *The Transformation of American Industrial Relations* (New York: Basic Books, 1986), p. 158.

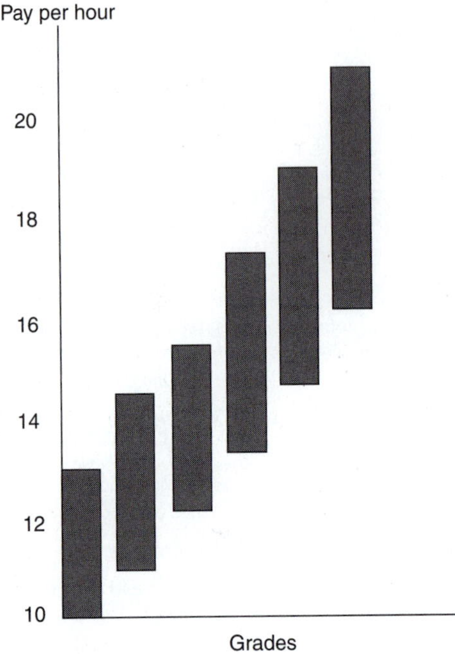

FIGURE 9.3
Example of a Grade Structure

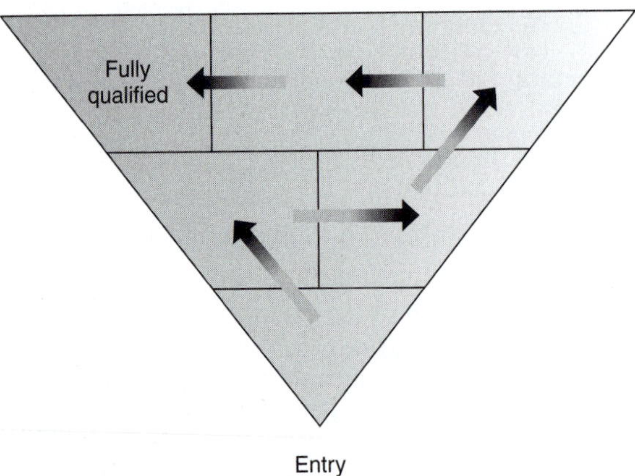

FIGURE 9.4
Skill-Based Pay Plan Skill Blocks and Progression

teaching occupations. In a lane-and-step system, pay rates are based on length of service in the organization and the highest amount of education completed. The negotiated lane and step serves as an indicator of the trade-offs that exist between accumulating experience and acquiring additional education if an employee wants to improve his or her pay. Figure 9.5 is an example of the lane-and-step agreement in the contract between Special School District 1 (Minneapolis, MN) and the Minneapolis Federation of Teachers (AFT).

FIGURE 9.5 Example of Lane-and-Step Schedule

Lane Step	II BA	III BA+15	IV BA+30	Va BA+45	Vb MA	VIa BA+60	VIb MA+15	VII MA+30
1	29,521	30,179	30,824	32,051	32,051	32,997	32,997	33,939
2	30,930	31,456	32,282	33,700	33,700	34,692	34,692	35,684
3	32,567	33,033	33,891	35,550	35,550	36,566	36,566	37,488
4	34,478	34,788	35,684	37,286	37,286	38,575	38,575	39,598
5	36,066	36,579	37,535	39,002	39,002	40,301	40,301	41,403
6	37,881	38,478	39,431	41,186	41,186	42,631	42,631	43,539
7	39,849	40,445	41,450	43,637	43,637	44,806	44,806	45,773
8	44,363	45,033	45,281	45,879	45,879	47,049	47,049	48,267
9			48,614	49,079	49,079	50,093	50,093	51,337
10				53,783	53,783	54,979	54,979	55,232
11					55,695		58,392	59,421
15	45,363	46,033	49,614	54,783	56,695	55,979	59,392	60,421
20	46,863	47,533	51,114	56,283	58,195	57,479	60,892	61,921
25	48,363	49,033	52,614	57,783	59,695	62,392	62,392	63,421
30	49,363	50,033	53,614	58,783	60,695	63,392	63,392	64,421

Two-Tier Pay Plans

Two-tier pay plans lower wage costs through a decreased starting rate for new hires. Two types of two-tier pay plans exist. One starts new employees at a lower rate and requires that they put in more time than present employees to reach top rates. The other creates a permanent differential under which new hires will never earn the current top rate. Employers benefit most if turnover is high or the company plans to expand. The rate of change is most rapid when retirement rates are also increasing. Both the employer and the union might expect problems when lower-tier employment levels begin to exceed half of the total. Successful implementation of these plans requires careful employee communications and assurances that job security will be enhanced.[11]

Two-tier pay plans are more prevalent in unionized firms and have usually been negotiated without significant management concessions.[12] In the airline industry, two-tier plans were usually installed in the absence of financial distress or market share shifts and were frequently negotiated following other union concessions. Airlines justified two-tier plans as aligning their pay rates more closely to comparable jobs in the market for persons with equivalent skill levels.[13] In the 2007 auto negotiations, the companies won the right to start new employees in noncore jobs at lower

[11] Ibid., pp. 132, 170.

[12] S. M. Jacoby and D. J. B. Mitchell, "Management Attitudes toward Two-Tier Pay Plans," *Journal of Labor Research*, 7 (1986), pp. 221–237.

[13] D. J. Walsh, "Accounting for the Proliferation of Two-Tier Wage Settlements in the U.S. Airline Industry, 1983–1986," *Industrial and Labor Relations Review*, 42 (1988), pp. 50–62.

pay rates than current employees receive in return for limited job security guarantees. The effects of two-tier pay plans on firm performance are mixed, with slightly positive effects on shareholder value.[14]

Unless many new employees are hired, the union shouldn't incur severe political problems from new members for some time. Management may face problems, in that employees doing equal work receive unequal pay. Employees in two-tier pay plans can compare their pay among themselves or with employees in other organizations. As pay tends to fall behind what other employers pay, dissatisfaction results. Dissatisfaction may also occur if employees compare their outcomes given effort unfavorably with others in the firm.[15]

Pay Form

Pay components not received in cash are received as either insurance or deferred compensation. Insurance typically includes hospital and medical coverage, life, disability, and dental benefits. It may also include retiree health benefits, particularly if employees are eligible to retire before qualifying for Medicare coverage at age 65. Deferred compensation usually involves pension benefits. Noncash wage forms have advantages and disadvantages. For the employee, the benefit of the form depends partly on usage. Employees with dependents need life and family health care insurance more than those without dependents. Employer-purchased insurance benefits and pension contributions are not currently taxable income. Pension contributions are not taxed until the employee uses them after retiring. Some benefits, such as holidays or vacations, are paid in cash at the employee's rate and are regularly taxable.

Employers are increasingly concerned about the form of pay for all employees because contracts often specify the amounts of insurance coverage rather than the amount of employer contributions. Unorganized employees often hope the union successfully negotiates for benefit improvements that might obligate management to provide the same for them. Health care, pensions, and retiree health care benefits have been the most contentious items in contract negotiations since the beginning of the 2000 decade. There is substantially more complexity and uncertainty surrounding benefits than there is for cash compensation. In addition, for at least the past decade the rate of increase in the cost of benefits has been much greater and much less controllable than that for cash compensation. The following sections will go into specific detail about the types of benefits that are negotiated and how employer costs are incurred.

[14] S. L. Thomas and M. M. Kleiner, "The Effect of Two-Tier Collective Bargaining Agreements on Shareholder Equity," *Industrial and Labor Relations Review*, 45 (1992), pp. 339–351.

[15] R. T. Lee and J. E. Martin, "Internal and External Referents as Predictors of Pay Satisfaction among Employees of a Two-Tier Wage Setting," *Journal of Occupational Psychology*, 64 (1991), pp. 57–66.

Wage- and Person-Tied Benefits

The costs of some benefits (e.g., vacations and holidays) and statutory payments (social security and Medicare payroll taxes) are essentially a function of wages. The cost of each of these is directly proportional to the wage each employee earns. Assume that two employees in different jobs earn different rates. Employee A earns $18 per hour, and employee B earns $15 per hour. A's pay is 20 percent higher than B's. When both are off work on Memorial Day, B will be paid $120 (8 × $15) and A will be paid $144, 20 percent more than B. If a union and employer negotiate a new contract that increases wages by 3 percent, the cost of any benefit that is wage-tied will increase by exactly the same proportion.

Some other benefits such as health insurance are person-tied; that is, the cost to the employer is linked to the number of employees, not the level of their pay. Consider the two employees in the example above. If both employees are single without dependents, the costs of their health insurance premiums are the same. If one is single without dependents and the other has dependents, then the one with the dependents has a higher premium cost—irrespective of their pay rates. Health insurance issues are discussed below.

Other benefits are tied to a combination of person and wage characteristics. For example, disability and life insurance usually provide payments based on an employee's rate of pay when a claim is filed, and premium costs increase with wages but also are dependent on the age and gender of the employee, with premiums for older employees and men higher than those for younger employees and women earning the same wages. Pension plans also blend wage and person characteristics in their determination. Their administration is very complex and will be explained below.

Health Insurance

Rising health care costs have been an increasing problem for employers; employees; unions; members of the public; and federal, state, and local governments. Between 1983 and 2010, data from the consumer price index (CPI) indicate that health care cost inflation was 77 percent higher than the overall rate. For this period, average wages increased by about 14.5 percent more than inflation, while the cost of employer-provided health care benefits increased 2.4 times more rapidly than wages.[16] In 2011, it was expected that large and midsize employers that provide health care benefits would incur an average annual cost of $10,730 per employee.[17] Currently, health

[16] This figure was calculated using data from the consumer price index (U [Urban worker]) and the employment cost index published by the Bureau of Labor Statistics of the U.S. Department of Labor and the Annual Average Wage Index published by the Social Security Administration of the U.S. Department of Health and Human Services.

[17] "Employer Health Care Costs Expected to Rise by 8.2% in 2011, Towers Watson Survey Finds," Towers Watson Press Release, September 15, 2010, http://finance.yahoo.com/news/Employer-Health-Care-Costs-bw-2834601793.html?x=0&.v=1.

care services and products account for more than 16 percent of the gross domestic product of the United States. Even if health care inflation were to be contained, the aging of the baby boom cohort will inexorably increase the footprint of the health care sector over the next 20 to 30 years.

Health care benefit costs are a concern for all employers that include the benefit as part of their pay programs. They are also of particular concern to both employers and unions involved in collective bargaining relationships. From an employer standpoint, the increasing magnitude of health care costs and the uncertainty surrounding their annual rate of change make it difficult to control and predict future labor costs. Since health care benefits are a person-based benefit, if health care costs increase faster than wages, employers will become increasingly reluctant to hire additional employees, all else being equal. Given employers' desires for certainty or predictability in costs during the term of a contract, they would prefer to include a specific amount of premiums to be paid per employee in each year of the contract, shifting the risk of possible premium increases beyond the negotiated amount to the employees.

In practice, most large employers that offer health care benefits to employees do not purchase health insurance, but rather self-insure, since the cost of health care, like wages, is a usual cost of doing business. They usually do contract with insurers to administer their programs. Insurers interact with providers to ensure that payment is not made for services that are not included in the plan and to direct employee patients to low-cost and high-quality services. Insurers handle the paperwork involved in the plan and bill the company for covered services. If billings exceed what the employer anticipated, it will essentially experience a health care "insurance premium" increase as a result.

If an employer provides a specific package of health care benefits, and if the costs increase faster than wages, labor costs will escalate more rapidly than expected during the term of a multiyear collective bargaining agreement (CBA). Table 9.3 details what might happen to costs over the course of a contract. The example in Table 9.3 shows that a health insurance program costing $7,800 per employee per year decreases in cost per hour as the number of hours worked increases since it is person- not wage-tied. Assume a new contract is negotiated in an environment where a 10 percent ($65.00) monthly premium increase is anticipated but where the possible increase might be 15 percent ($97.50). The contract also includes a 2 percent base pay increase. Assume that there are three groups of workers, all of whom earn the same hourly pay rate, who are entitled to health care coverage. One group works a standard 40-hour week, another works a 32-hour week, and the third works a 48-hour week (with 8 hours paid at a 50 percent premium). In this example the health care cost increase should increasingly motivate the employer to eliminate part-time workers and replace them with overtime since the hourly cost is less.

TABLE 9.3 **Cost per Employee for Wage and Health Care Increases**

	Present Rate	Total Cost/Year	Cost per Hour	Increase Offered	Projected Cost	Cost per Hour	Possible Cost	Cost per Hour
Full-time (2,080 hours/year)								
Pay per hour	15.00	31,200	15.00	0.30	31,824	15.30	31,824	15.30
Health insurance per month	650.00	7,800	3.75	65.00	8,580	4.13	8,970	4.31
Totals and averages		39,000	18.75		40,404	19.43	40,794	19.61
Part-time (1,664 hours/year)								
Pay per hour	15.00	24,960	15.00	0.30	25,459	15.30	25,459	15.30
Health insurance per month	650.00	7,800	4.69	65.00	8,580	5.16	8,970	5.39
Totals and averages		32,760	19.69		34,039	20.46	34,429	20.69
Overtime (2,496 hours/year)								
Pay per hour	15.00	40,560	16.25	0.30	41,371	16.58	41,371	16.58
Health insurance per month	650.00	7,800	3.13	65.00	8,580	3.44	8,970	3.59
Totals and averages		48,360	19.38		49,951	20.01	50,341	20.17

Because federal wage and hour laws require that employees who are not in a supervisory or managerial, professional, or outside sales position, or who are paid by the hour receive a 50 percent premium for working more than 40 hours per week, an employer would generally reduce costs by hiring new employees when more work is needed. However, if person-tied benefits such as insurance and paid time off exceed 50 percent of base pay, an employer would prefer overtime unless the contract requires a higher premium. The total amount of person- and wage-tied benefits is estimated to be 30.4 percent of total compensation (about 44 cents for every $1 of cash compensation).[18] Thus, increasing person-tied benefits restricts new hiring. Even if benefits are below 50 percent, if costs incidental to hiring and benefits exceed the overtime premium, employers will resist new hiring.[19]

Health care cost containment has increased in importance for both parties. Managements have sought to negotiate contribution limits rather than pay for coverage, or at least to require deductibles or co-payments, and/or move plans to managed care providers. Unions have strongly resisted and either have threatened to strike or actually did strike to sustain current levels of health care coverage.

[18] Bureau of Labor Statistics, U.S. Department of Labor, "Employer Costs for Employee Compensation—June 2010," Economic News Release, September 8, 2010.

[19] J. A. Fossum, "Hire or Schedule Overtime? A Formula for Minimizing Labor Costs," *Compensation Review*, 1, no. 2 (1969), pp. 14–22.

Patient Protection and Affordable Care Act of 2010 (PPACA—Obama-Care) The PPACA was signed into law by President Obama on March 23, 2010. The signing date is important because provisions of the law began to take effect six months later on September 23, 2010. Additional provisions will become effective on succeeding anniversaries through 2018. Going forward, the PPACA substantially changes the health care environment and the latitude that management and labor has in crafting worker health care coverage. Several of the provisions that took effect in 2010 resulted in immediate cost increases for employers that offer health care plans. Other provisions that become effective in 2014 may lead to additional employer-borne costs or could provide an incentive for employers to drop or negotiate to drop health care coverage and pay the consequent penalties instead. Table 9.4 contains a summary of the major provisions in the act.

The PPACA permits current collectively bargained plans limited "grandfathered" status. Provisions related to dependent eligibility for insurance, annual limits, and elimination of waiting periods for preexisting conditions must be added, even to grandfathered plans. It appears that the legislation will make it difficult for a plan to remain grandfathered and there may be little benefit to trying to remain in that status. Both management and union representatives should be aware of the future changes that are required. Management in particular may need to negotiate provisions enabling the health care benefit provisions in the contract to be reopened for further negotiations as changes are mandated and as regulations shift. Requirements for affordability that become effective in 2014 may provide a floor from which unions can negotiate while the Cadillac tax imposed in 2018 will impose a benefit ceiling, especially if cost escalation continues at its recent rate.

Pension Plans

In companies that offer pension plans, one or more of several types might be offered. These include **defined benefit pension plans, defined contribution pension plans**, and tax-advantaged **salary reduction plans** that may include a matching contribution from the employer. Table 9.5 describes basic features of each of these plans.

Before the 1970s, most company-sponsored pensions were defined benefit plans. Pension payments to retirees were made from their current revenues. As the number of retirees relative to the number of active employees increased, and as life expectancies were growing longer, expenses for pensions increased much more rapidly than other labor costs. As liabilities increased, and as some companies encountered financial difficulties, defaulting on promised pension payments began to occur. As a result, legislation to regulate private sector pension and insurance benefit plans was developed, introduced, and passed in 1974.

Pension plans are regulated by the Employee Retirement Income Security Act (ERISA) of 1974. The law does not require that an employer

TABLE 9.4 Major Provisions of PPACA Affecting Employers

Source: Information developed from "PPACA Interactive Timeline," *Employee Benefit News*, http://ebn.benefitnews.com/health-care-reform/timeline.html, November 20, 2010.

2010
Employers must provide reasonable break times for mothers of children under the age of 1 to express breast milk.
A federal program was established to reimburse companies for 80 percent of health care costs between \$15,000 and \$80,000 per year incurred for a retired employee between the ages of 55 and 64. Total reimbursement available from the program is \$5 billion between 2010 and 2014 when the program expires.
Annual limits on health care benefit payments per individual may not be less than \$750,000.
Insured plans must establish internal and external appeal processes.
Health care plans that offer dependent coverage must allow dependent children under age 26 to be covered unless he or she is eligible for coverage in another employer-sponsored plan.
Lifetime limits on coverage for essential health services are eliminated.
For children under age 19, exclusion for preexisting conditions is prohibited.
Coverage for certain defined preventive services must be provided on a no-cost basis.
Insurers whose loss ratio is less than 85 percent of premiums must offer a rebate.
2011
Annual limits on health care benefit payments per individual may not be less than \$1,250,000.
Class Act provides a voluntary federal long-term care insurance program. Employers may automatically enroll employees in the plan subject to an opt-out choice.
2012
Annual limits on health care benefit payments per individual may not be less than \$2,000,000.
Employer must provide a uniform summary of health care benefits consistent with U.S. Department of Health and Human Services (HHS) guidelines on enrollment or reenrollment.
\$1 per enrollee tax to fund research on comparative health care outcomes.
2013
Research tax increases to \$2 per enrollee (sunsets in 2019).
Annual allocations to flexible spending accounts by employees capped at \$2,500.
FICA tax raised by 0.9 percent for single individuals earning more than \$200,000 or households earning more than \$250,000 annually.
Employer must notify employees about the availability of insurance exchanges and the possibility that a federal subsidy might be available to them.
2014
Annual limits eliminated.
Employers with 50 or more employees that do not offer coverage must pay a \$2,000 fee for the 31st and each succeeding employee for every full-time employee who receives financial assistance through an exchange. Employers that do offer coverage and whose employees receive assistance through an exchange due to unaffordability must pay the lessor of \$3,000 per employee or \$2,000 for the 31st and each succeeding employee.
Plan participants must be allowed to participate in clinical trials of new treatments.
An annual out-of-pocket limit for participants is implemented.
Plans must offer affordable coverage to all employees who work 30 or more hours per week.
Large employers must offer affordable plans that meet minimum-value standards or risk penalty. Coverage is deemed "unaffordable" if its cost exceeds 9.5 percent of household income or does not pay at least 60 percent of allowable costs.
Employers may have to provide vouchers equal to the cost of their insurance to employees whose income is less than 400 percent of the federal poverty level and whose health care premiums cost between 8 and 9.8 percent of

(Continued)

TABLE 9.4 **Major Provisions of PPACA Affecting Employers (continued)**

household income to buy insurance through an exchange. If coverage can be purchased for less than the value of the voucher, the employee can keep the difference without penalty. This section was repealed by the final 2011 budget bill passed and signed into law in April 2011.

Small employers (fewer than 100 employees) may offer coverage or purchase coverage through exchanges (virtual marketplaces for purchasing insurance).

Plan must pay out at least 60 percent of actuarial value.

No one can be excluded from coverage due to a preexisting condition.

Plans must cover a list of "essential health benefits" as defined by the HHS.

2017

Large employers (100 or more employees) may offer coverage or purchase coverage through exchanges.

2018

"Cadillac" tax of 40 percent imposed on value of coverage exceeding $10,200 for single persons and $27,500 for family coverage (indexed for inflation). Tax is paid by employer/insurer. Employee contributions to health savings accounts and flexible spending accounts are included in the coverage value.

TABLE 9.5 **Main Features of Types of Pension Plans**

	Defined Benefit	Defined Contribution	Salary Reduction [401(k), 403(b)]
Funding	Annual actuarially determined contribution to fiduciary to fund anticipated future liabilities. Amount depends on expected life expectancy of present and future retirees, level of benefits accrued, anticipated retirement dates, anticipated lengths of service at retirement, and rates of return on investment of pension funds.	(a) Money purchase plan in which company contributes a fixed percentage of pay annually to an employee's account. (b) Profit-sharing plan in which a fixed percentage of profit is allocated to each employee in proportion to his or her proportion of total employee pay in that employee group.	Employee elects to contribute some proportion of pretax income to his or her retirement account. Amounts may be matched or multiplied by employer up to a statutory maximum.
Retirement benefit formula and level	At retirement, a monthly payment during the retiree's lifetime based on terminal salary and length of service, e. g.,average of last 3 years' pay × years of service ×.02. May be adjustable for inflation and may be a supplement to social security to a defined maximum amount.	A lump sum at retirement equal to contributions and accrued investment returns. May be transferrable to an individual retirement account (IRA) and/or be used to purchase an annuity to provide lifetime payments.	A lump sum at retirement equal to contributions and accrued investment returns. May be transferrable to an individual retirement account (IRA) and/or be used to purchase an annuity to provide lifetime payments.
Investment options	Employer's fiduciary decides where to invest funds.	Employer's fiduciary decides where to invest funds, or employee is given a menu of choices.	Investment in shares of employer and/or a choice of investment funds managed by a fiduciary.
Who bears investment risk?	Employer	Employee	Employee

offer a pension plan, but where one exists, the employer must comply with several rules (which will be detailed shortly). ERISA obligates that employers with pension plans must allow all employees aged 21 and over to participate. As employees accrue service, their accrued benefits become vested (owned) after five years. If they quit after that point, their employer must allow them to make a tax-free transfer of the funds to an IRA. If the employer has a defined benefit plan, it must make an annual actuarially based contribution that will cover the expected future retirement costs. This is to ensure that if the company fails, the accrued pension benefits will nevertheless be paid. Employer contributions must be turned over to a financial trustee (fiduciary) whose responsibility is to invest them for the benefit of the future retirees. Not more than 10 percent of the plan's assets can be invested in the employer's stocks or bonds. If a company files a bankruptcy petition, it may, under certain circumstances, abrogate its pension obligations, although its previous contributions would continue to remain in the plan. It can also choose to terminate a fully funded plan. If it does, it provides a payment equal to the amount of pension that would be provided at retirement if the employee were to have the current salary and length of service at retirement. The employee would then roll this sum over into an IRA to avoid taxability of the payment. However, it's unlikely that a union would agree, in negotiations, to allow an employer to terminate an existing plan.

Before ERISA, companies that had defined benefit plans almost never funded them with an amount equivalent to future liabilities. The law allowed employers 40 years (until 2014) to fully fund an underfunded plan. For many large companies in mature industries, this meant that the relative size of a company's retiree population could easily become larger than its active population, and the amounts necessary to fully fund the plan would become an increasing amount of compensation expenses. To the extent that companies with these plans also needed to reduce their workforces (as in autos and steel), one of the typical methods was to offer earlier retirement to long-service employees. These employees retired at younger-than-projected ages—putting even more pressure on retirement funding.

Virtually no employer has begun a traditional defined benefit pension plan since ERISA was passed. Currently, employers typically choose 401(k) plans in the private sector and 403(b) plans in the public sector. Neither of these obligates the employer to make any payment or to continue a payment at a particular level, thus substantially reducing the risks associated with traditional pension plans. There is also no guaranteed benefit—the employee bears the investment risk. Thus the plan is, by definition, continuously fully funded. Pension reform legislation passed in 2006 increases incentives for employers to offer 401(k) plans and to terminate defined benefit plans. Under the new provisions, firms must account for the value of securities that the firm holds to offset future liabilities. To the extent that the value fluctuates with financial market volatility, the changes will distort perceptions of the firm's operating results since fluctuations will fall through to the bottom line.

Public Sector Defined Benefit Plans In general, the pension plan options that are available in the public sector are the same as in the private sector, with one significant exception: In virtually all states, there are at least some public sector employees who are not included in the social security system because they are enrolled in a state plan that provides benefits to meet or exceed what is available from social security. While the same types of retirement plans exist in both the private and public sector, public sector employers are more likely to offer defined benefit than defined contribution plans as their primary retirement plan.

As noted above, ERISA requires private sector employers to maintain pension funding at levels necessary to cover the expected future liabilities of their defined benefit plans. There is no similar requirement for public sector plans. Funding levels for public sector pension plans are ultimately determined by the legislative body (state, city, school board, etc.) that is responsible for the public sector unit that operates the pension plan. During the recent financial crisis that began in October 2008, it became apparent that many public pension plans were severely underfunded.[20] At some point, the legislatures (and taxpayers) will either need to reallocate funds from other purposes to pension payments or to increase taxes to meet the obligations. Unlike the private sector, where an employer that becomes insolvent can declare bankruptcy and restructure debt, states do not have nor need to have that option. States have sovereign immunity from suits. Thus, creditors have no recourse if the state fails to meet its obligations unless the state permits itself to be sued. Depending on whether state pensions are constitutionally protected, future payouts may encounter some risk. Municipal pension plans would be at risk in a bankruptcy filing, which is permitted under the U.S. bankruptcy code.

Many public sector employers also offer retiree health care benefits. The underfunding in these plans is even more severe (as a proportion of future liabilities) than for the pension plans.

Voluntary Employee Benefits Associations

Some private sector employers continue to provide health care for retirees, particularly for the period between their retirement (if below age 65) and when they reach eligibility for Medicare at age 65. The plans may also continue to provide supplemental health care insurance beyond Medicare after that point. In situations where a company has a large group of retirees relative to the size of the active workforce, the cost of health care benefits

[20] The Pew Center on the States, *The Trillion Dollar Gap: Underfunded State Retirement Systems and the Road to Reform*, Washington, DC: Pew Charitable Trust, 2010.

escalates rapidly. This problem is what led the U.S. domestic automobile manufacturers to negotiate the formation of a **voluntary employee benefits association (VEBA)** with the UAW in their 2007 contract. In return for a one-time payment to fund the VEBA, the auto manufacturers transferred their liability for providing and administering medical care for retirees to the UAW, which has created an independent trust fund to manage the benefits. Going forward, the management of the trust has the responsibility of operating the plan for the benefit of the UAW's General Motors, Ford, and Chrysler retiree members.

When GM filed for Chapter 11 bankruptcy in 2009, the company was reorganized with a new set of shareholders: the U.S. Treasury with 60 percent, the UAW-VEBA with 17.5 percent, the governments of Canada and Ontario with 12.5 percent, and bondholders with 10 percent. In the 2010 General Motors initial public offering (IPO), the UAW-VEBA reduced its stake to 10.7 percent by selling 102.3 million shares. It used the proceeds to invest in other financial assets to reduce its investment concentration risk. Ironically, for UAW retirees the investment performance of the VEBA will determine whether their benefit levels will be preserved.

Other Benefits

As Table 9.15 at the end of this chapter notes, a large variety of benefits might be included in a CBA. Typically life and disability insurance would be included. Vacations, holidays, sick leave, bereavement leave, jury duty leave, and other paid and nonpaid time off would be specified. Other types of benefits might include newborn care, family care, tax-free dependent care reimbursement accounts, resources and referrals for professional family care, adoption assistance, and flexible hours.

Benefits and Demographics

Many contracts increase benefits as seniority accrues. For example, amounts of vacation are often linked to years of service. With longer average service, a workforce will receive more paid time off, increasing the cost of time worked, other things being equal. If pay increases with seniority, this introduces a multiplicative effect on the cost of vacations. Health care costs are associated with age and gender. Under CBAs, employment discrimination, and tax laws, if employers provide benefits they cannot differentiate entitlements based on age, gender, or job level. Many employers self-insure, while others purchase health insurance from an indemnity provider or contract with a health maintenance organization. In any event, the costs of health care are closely associated with the health events the workforce experiences. Figure 9.6 is a rough approximation of the actuarial distribution of health care costs for men and women at various age levels. Note that health care costs for women are higher until about age 55; then men's annual health care costs cross and exceed women's for the rest of their lives. The age and gender composition of the workforce directly

FIGURE 9.6
Actuarially Based Monthly Health Care Costs Related to Age and Gender, 2010 Data

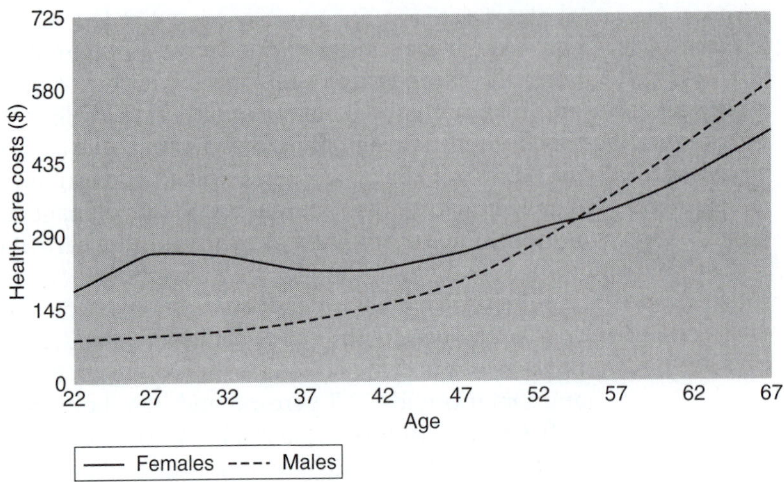

affects the costs of health care for the employer. All else equal, companies in more mature, stable, or declining industries are likely to have higher health care costs because of the older average age of their workforces.

Because negotiated contracts often link benefits and promotions to seniority, turnover of more senior employees is reduced in unionized firms; at the same time, older applicants are less likely to look for a union job because they would be unlikely to accrue enough seniority to acquire the major benefits that seniority confers under the contract. Seniority and turnover issues will be covered in substantial detail in Chapter 10.

Pay System

The pay system consists of the methods used to decide pay for each employee. All methods for bargaining-unit employees will be specified in the contract. In this section, we identify many of the negotiated arrangements for individual employee pay changes.

Membership

Contracts often provide some forms of compensation simply for membership in the organization. Many employee-tied benefits (e.g., health, life, and disability insurance) are based on membership. They are usually unrelated to the number of hours worked in a given month, as long as the employee was active during a designated period.

Seniority

Several pay system features are related to seniority. **Benefit status seniority** refers to entitlements that individuals accrue from continued employment. Many pay systems provide for step pay increases based on length of service within a job or grade level. These increases usually have a cap because a certain pay range is assigned to a given job.

If the pay structure includes steps based on length of service within a given grade, then tenure influences an individual's pay. Such types of methods are common in teacher contracts.

Tenure may entitle employees to use accrued benefits such as retirement. Some contracts allow employees to retire after a defined length of service (e.g., 30 years), rather than at a specific age. Auto workers pioneered these benefits in the private sector; in the public sector, they are most prevalent in the uniformed services.

Time Worked

Most contracts base pay on how much time is worked and when it is worked. Wages are calculated on an hourly basis in these cases. In addition, the level of wages frequently depends on the amount of time worked during a given period (overtime) and the time of day during which the work is accomplished (shift differentials).

Merit

Merit pay plans link pay increases to employers' evaluations of employee performance. Unions usually strongly resist them. An employer could insist on including a merit pay plan in a new contract. However, it cannot unilaterally implement a plan if a new contract cannot be negotiated unless it provides the union an opportunity to consult on the criteria used to determine timing and amount of the pay increases.[21]

Productive Efficiency (Piece Rates)

These incentive plans have a bargained base output level, above which employees receive extra compensation. Depending on the plan, these additions are on a straight-line, increasing, or decreasing basis as production increases.

Negotiating an appropriate base is often difficult, and grievances frequently occur when employees are transferred to jobs where they lack sufficient experience to exceed the standard. Circumstances beyond the employees' control can intrude, reducing chances to achieve high output (e.g., poorly fitting components on an assembly job).

Gainsharing Plans

Gainsharing plans pay bonuses to groups of employees whose productivity exceeds an established standard. At the same time, profits also generally increase. This section details a number of widely implemented plans.

The Scanlon Plan The **Scanlon plan** was born in the late 1930s in a struggling steel mill. With no profits and employees demanding higher wages

[21] L. M. Goodman, "Merit Pay Proposals and Related Compensation Plans—*Detroit Typographical Union* v. *NLRB* and *McClatchy Newspapers* Revisited," *Labor Lawyer*, 18 (2002), pp. 1–14.

TABLE 9.6
Simple Labor Formula

Sales	$ 98,000
Returned goods	− 3,000
Net sales	$ 95,000
Inventory	+ 5,000
Production value	$100,000
Labor bill:	
Wages	$ 16,000
Salaries	8,000
Vacations and holidays	1,800
Insurance	1,700
Pensions	500
Unemployment	500
FICA	+ 1,500
Total labor bill	$ 30,000
Ratio	0.30

Source: C. F. Frost, J. H. Wakeley, and R. A. Ruh, *The Scanlon Plan for Organizational Development: Identity, Participation, and Equity* (East Lansing: Michigan State University Press, 1974), p. 103. Reprinted with permission.

and better working conditions, their union leader, Joseph Scanlon, saw that gaining the demands would force the company's closure. To meet the company's profit goals and the union's economic demands, he proposed that the parties work together to increase productivity, to which a wage bonus would be linked. Two underlying foundations are participation by all employees and equity in reward distribution.[22]

The participation system is based on a recognition that abilities are widely distributed in the organization and that change in the organization's environment is inevitable. Because change occurs and employees at all levels may have solutions to problems or suggestions to improve productivity, the system includes an open suggestion procedure. Suggestions are evaluated and acted on by joint worker-management committees, which make recommendations up the line. Figure 9.7 details a typical committee structure and its actions.

A suggestion is evaluated by a work unit's **production committee**. If a suggestion has merit and can be implemented in the unit, the production committee can implement it. If the suggestion is questionable or has wide impact, it is sent to a **screening committee** (consisting of executives and employee representatives) for evaluation and possible implementation.

The screening committee is also responsible for determining the bonus to be paid each month or quarter. The bonus is calculated by comparing the usual share of product costs attributed to labor against the most recent actual costs. For example, if each $1 of sales has traditionally required 30 cents' worth of labor, then any improvement, to say 29 or 25 cents, would represent a productivity improvement. Table 9.6 represents a simple formula in which labor costs are 30 percent of the total production value.

[22] C. F. Frost, J. H. Wakeley, and R. A. Ruh, *The Scanlon Plan for Organization Development: Identity, Participation, and Equity* (East Lansing: Michigan State University Press, 1974), pp. 5–26.

FIGURE 9.7 Scanlon Plan Production Committee

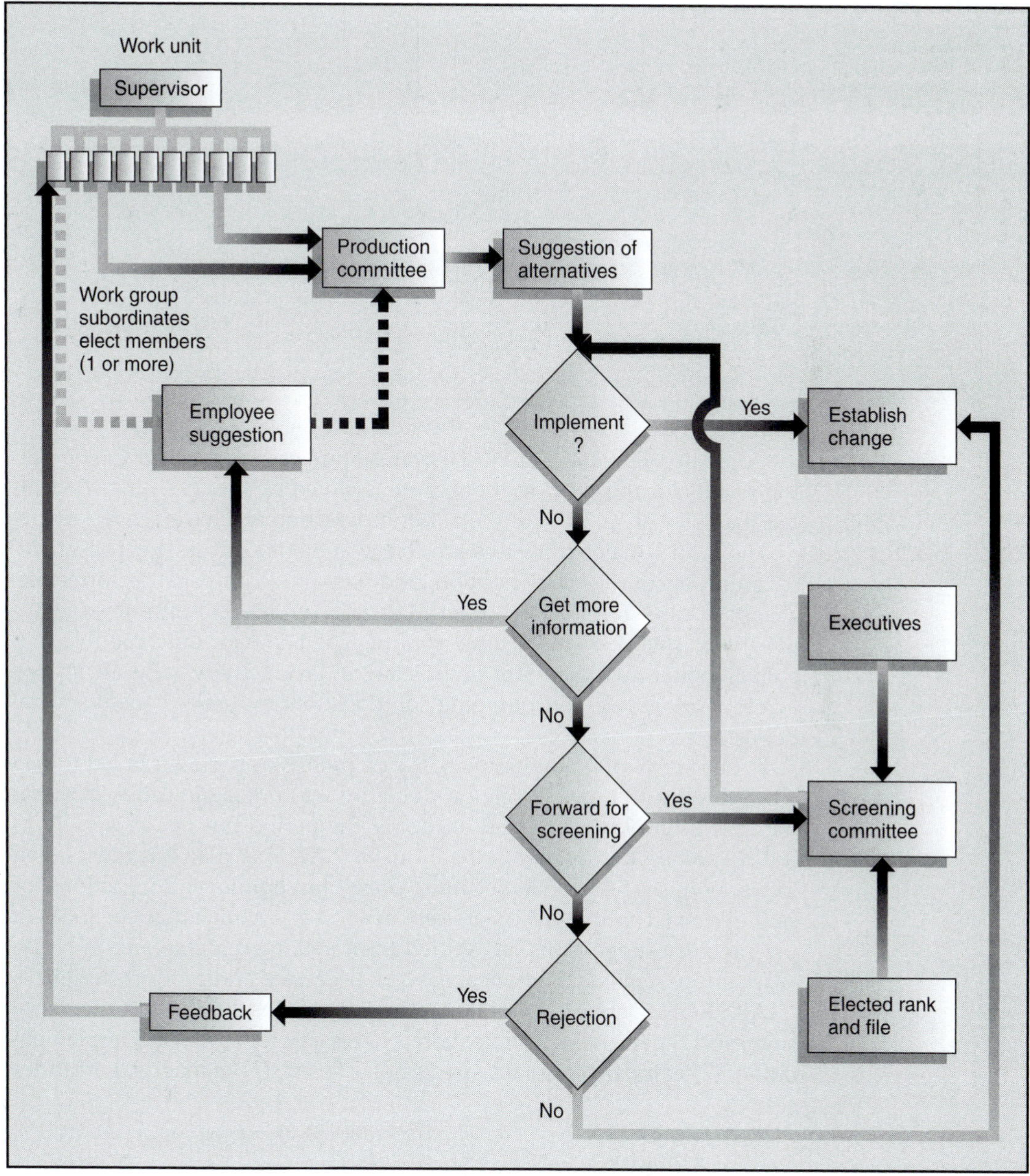

TABLE 9.7
Bonus Report

Source: Modified from C. F. Frost, J. H. Wakeley, and R. A. Ruh, *The Scanlon Plan for Organizational Development: Identity, Participation, and Equity* (East Lansing: Michigan State University Press, 1974), p. 15.

a. Scanlon ratio	0.40/1.00
b. Value of production	$100,000
c. Expected costs (*a* × *b*)	40,000
d. Actual costs	30,000
e. Bonus pool (*c* – *d*)	10,000
f. Share to company—20% (*e* × 0.20)	2,000
g. Share to employees—80% (adjusted pool) (*e* × 0.80)	8,000
h. Share for future deficits—25% of adjusted pool (*g* × 0.25)	2,000
i. Pool for immediate distribution (*g* – *h*)	6,000
j. Bonus for each employee* as a percentage of pay for the production period (*i* ÷ *d*)	20%

The June pay record might look like this for a typical employee:

Name	Monthly Pay for June	Bonus Percent	Bonus	Total Pay
Mary Smith	$900	20%	$180	$1,080

*This example assumes all employees are participating in the plan at the time this bonus is paid; for example, there has been no turnover, and no employees are in their initial 30-, 60-, or 90-day trial periods.

Companywide and individual bonuses are calculated after the operating results for the previous period are received by the screening committee. Table 9.7 gives an example of a company and an employee report.

The plan's major purposes are to reward both parties for productivity gains, encourage participation, and tie pay to company performance. The plan aims to reduce labor input for a given level of output—a factor over which workers have some control. The behavior-outcome relationship is higher than that with profit sharing. Productivity gains are shared across work groups, encouraging solutions that mutually benefit several departments.

In one study of a Scanlon plan, over a nine-year period it failed to pay a bonus only 13 times. While productivity was not significantly better, it increased. Employment decreased over the period but not as rapidly as it did at others companies in the industry.[23] Another plan has often failed to pay bonuses because of declining prices, but employee suggestions for savings have continued to increase.[24] In another organization, the focus of productivity suggestions has shifted from making material and in-house work improvements to improving work processes and product design.[25]

Although comparing Scanlon plan results has limitations, evidence suggests (1) perceived participation is necessary for successful implementation, (2) company or plant size is not a factor, (3) managerial attitudes

[23] C. S. Miller and M. Schuster, "A Decade's Experience with the Scanlon Plan: A Case Study," *Journal of Occupational Behavior*, 8 (1987), pp. 167–174.

[24] G. Pearlstein, "Preston Trucking Drives for Productivity," *Labor-Management Cooperation Brief*, No. 13, U.S. Department of Labor, Bureau of Labor-Management Relations and Cooperative Programs, 1988.

[25] J. B. Arthur and L. Aiman-Smith, "Gainsharing as Organizational Learning: An Analysis of Employee Suggestions over Time," *Proceedings of the Industrial Relations Research Association*, 48 (1996), pp. 270–277.

TABLE 9.8
Rucker Plan Bonus Calculation

Historic labor input percentage	45%
Employees' share	50%
Value of production	$1,000,000
Materials and supplies	550,000
Outside purchases, nonlabor costs	125,000
Value added (VA)	325,000
Allowed labor costs (VA ×.45)	146,250
Actual labor costs	134,500
Bonus pool	11,750
Employee share	5,875
Participating payroll	117,500
Bonus percentage	5%

toward the plan predict its success, (4) successful implementation takes considerable time, (5) plans are more successful where expectations are high but realistic, (6) a high-level executive must lead implementation for it to be successful, and (7) the type of production technology is not related to success or failure.[26]

The Rucker Plan The **Rucker plan** has some participative elements of the Scanlon plan, but management names an idea coordinator to handle suggestions. Bonuses are calculated by determining the historical value added by direct labor. Any improvement in value added will earn a bonus. Employees may receive bonuses based on output increases, lower scrap rates, and other subcontracting or material savings. However, if costs increased while productivity also increases, bonuses may not be paid. A Rucker plan might be suggested for an employer not ready to participate to the degree a Scanlon plan requires, but it may be difficult to negotiate in a contract.[27] Table 9.8 is an example of how Rucker plan bonus pools are calculated.

Impro-Share **Impro-Share** ties pay to improved productivity. While consultative management is suggested, employee participation is minimal except that a bonus committee is responsible for determining some aspects of the bonus formula. The bonus formula is somewhat complex, but the result subtracts the actual hours employees work from the "base value earned hours" of their output. If the result is positive, the employees' share (say, 50 percent) is divided by the actual number of hours worked to obtain a bonus percentage. For example, if an employee worked 1,000 hours during a period, and base value earned hours were 1,100 with a 50 percent share, the bonus would be 5 percent. Table 9.9 shows how the Impro-Share bonus is determined.

[26] J. K. White, "The Scanlon Plan: Causes and Correlates of Success," *Academy of Management Journal*, 23 (1979), pp. 292–312.

[27] M. Schuster, *Union-Management Cooperation: Structure, Process, and Impact* (Kalamazoo, MI: W. E. Upjohn Institute for Employment Research, 1984).

TABLE 9.9
Calculation of Impro-Share Bonus

Base Productivity Factor Calculation:

$$\frac{\text{Direct labor hours + indirect labor hours}}{\text{Direct labor hours}}$$

Example:
40 direct labor employees
20 indirect labor employees
40 hours per week

$$\frac{40(40) + 20(40)}{40(40)} = 1.5$$

Work-Hour Standard:

$$\frac{\text{Total production work hours}}{\text{Units produced}}$$

Example:

Direct employees	20
Hours per employee	40
Pieces produced	1,000
Total hours	800
Hours per piece	0.8

Bonus Calculation:

Units produced	1,100
Allowed hours	0.8
Base productivity factor	1.5
Impro-Share base (units × allowed hours × BPF)	1,320
Base hours	1,320
Actual hours	1,200
Gained hours	120
Pay per hour	$10.00
Employee share	0.50

Bonus:

$$\frac{\text{Pay per hour} \times \text{gained hours} \times \text{employee share}}{\text{Actual hours}}$$

$$\frac{10 \times 120 \times 0.5}{1{,}200} = \$\,0.50$$

Impro-Share allows employers to direct incentives toward specific jobs or groups and decreases competitors' abilities to determine wage costs based on bonus formulas. However, employees have difficulty calculating what they will receive.[28] A study of Impro-Share plans in both union and nonunion environments found that productivity increased an average of 8 percent the first year after the plan's introduction. By the third year, productivity was up an average of 17.5 percent. Much of the gains can be attributed to reductions in defects and downtime. Larger workplaces had

[28] Ibid.

TABLE 9.10 **Characteristics of Major Gainsharing Programs**

Source: Adapted from D. O. Kim, "The Characteristics of Gainsharing Plans in North America: A Congruence Perspective," *Journal of Labor Research*, 26 (2005), p. 467.

	Scanlon Plan	Multicost Scanlon Plan	Rucker Plan	Impro-Share Plan
Formula base for bonus	Payroll / Sales value of production	Payroll, material, overhead / Sales value of production	Payroll / Value added	Actual hours / Standard labor hours
Typical employee share	75% of gain	75% of gain	50% of gain	50% of gain
Information needed	Payroll, value of production	Payroll, value of production, material cost, overhead, and other costs	Payroll, value of production, material cost	Time standards and production levels
Expertise needed	Basic accounting	Advanced accounting	Intermediate accounting	Industrial engineering and extensive accounting
Employee vote in implementation decision	Yes	Yes	Yes (optional)	Usually no
Suggestion system	Formal	Formal	Formal	Not part of plan but may be added
Employee involvement	Screening and production committees	Screening and production committees	Screening and production committees (optional but often used)	Productivity team (optional)

lower rates of improvement, suggesting "free riding" is less of a problem in smaller plants.[29] Table 9.10 details the features of the major gainsharing plans.

Profit Sharing

To make labor costs more flexible, employers have proposed and implemented **profit-sharing plans** when workers agree to forgo base wage increases. The employee's total pay is based on both job level and employer profitability. The size of an employee's bonus depends on his or her proportion of total pay in the unit, the size of the employer's profit, and the agreed-on formula for determining the size of the pool to share. Table 9.11 shows how a profit-sharing formula would work.

The sizes of profit-share bonuses bear little relationship to individual employee effort or performance. They are strongly influenced by the state of the economy and product design decisions made by executives, managers, and engineers.

Profit sharing makes compensation more flexible. During economic downturns, pay goes down as profits fall, potentially reducing the need to

[29] R. T. Kaufman, "The Effects of Improshare on Productivity," *Industrial and Labor Relations Review*, 45 (1992), pp. 311–322.

TABLE 9.11
Example of a Profit-Sharing Formula

Measure	Amount
Assets	$5,000,000
Participating payroll (total pay for employees in plan)	5,000,000
Profits (after taxes)	1,250,000
Expected rate of return on assets (15%)	750,000
Profits to share (profits minus expected return)	500,000
Employees' share (20% of profits to share in this plan)	100,000
Profit-sharing bonus (employees, share/payroll)	2%

lay off employees. Some evidence exists that as unemployment increases, firms with profit sharing are less likely to lay off employees.[30]

Time Not Worked

Employees receive pay when not at work for a variety of reasons such as holidays, vacations, sick leave, and jury duty. Supplementary unemployment benefits (SUB) are paid during layoffs under some contracts. SUB adds payments from a trust fund to top up unemployment insurance benefits. The addition enables workers to maintain income close to regular straight-time wages. If layoffs are large and of long duration, benefit payments may exceed the trust fund balance, and SUB ends until the funds are rebuilt.

UNION EFFECTS ON PAY

Unionization fixes wages for the unionized employer. High levels of unionization and pattern bargaining within an industry decrease competition among employers. This section examines union influences on wages and variables that either magnify or moderate that influence.

Union Effects on Pay Levels

The general conclusion from studies of the effects of unionization are that the wages of represented employees are significantly higher than the wages of employees in similar nonunion employers, with a recent study finding a 21.5 percent differential.[31] This section will examine differences in the effects of unions by industry, occupation, individual employee demographic characteristics, employer characteristics, changes over time (including differences in concession levels), union organizing effects, the state of the economy, legal effects, and union spillover effects.

[30] D. L. Kruse, "Profit-Sharing and Employment Variability: Microeconomic Evidence on the Weitzman Theory," *Industrial and Labor Relations Review*, 44 (1991), pp. 437–453.

[31] O. Eren, "Measuring the Union-Nonunion Wage Gap Using Propensity Score Matching," *Industrial Relations*, 46 (2007), pp. 766–780.

TABLE 9.12
Average Union Wage Premium and Trend in Premium by Industry

Source: Adapted from B. Bratsberg and J. F. Ragan, Jr., "Changes in the Union Wage Premium by Industry," *Industrial and Labor Relations Review*, 56 (2002), p. 81.

Industry	Percent Premium	Trend
Construction	31.6%	–
Printing	29.4	–
Trucking	27.5	–
Other transport	27.4	
Air transportation	25.7	
Retail trade	23.6	–
Tobacco	16.8	
Food products	15.6	–
Transportation equipment	15.0	+
Lumber	14.8	
Rubber	13.9	
Stone, clay, and glass	13.8	
Wholesale trade	13.4	
Services	13.3	–
Railroads	13.0	+
Paper	12.1	+
Fabricated metal	12.1	
Utilities	11.8	
Miscellaneous manufacturing	11.7	+
Leather	10.2	+
Communications	9.2	+
Primary metal	9.1	
Industrial metal	9.0	
Furniture	7.6	
Electronic equipment	7.0	+
Mining	6.9	–
Apparel	6.4	–
Finance	5.9	–
Petroleum	4.0	+
Chemicals	2.7	+
Textiles	2.1	
Instruments	1.9	

Industrial Effects

Union workers are paid better than nonunion workers, on average, in virtually every industry where organized labor exists.[32] Table 9.12 details the range of differentials. If a firm or industry has developed specific assets (methods or processes) that require specific skills to operate, unions are able to bargain larger-than-normal increases.[33] Specific assets are more likely to be created in concentrated industries and larger firms. Wage premiums do not come without a cost to labor, however. Industries having

[32] B. Bratsberg and J. F. Ragan, Jr., "Changes in the Union Wage Premium by Industry," *Industrial and Labor Relations Review*, 56 (2002), pp. 65–83.

[33] J. K. Cavanaugh, "Asset-Specific Investment and Unionized Labor," *Industrial Relations*, 37 (1998), pp. 35–50.

TABLE 9.13
Union Wage Differentials in Percent by Subgroup

Source: D. G. Blanchflower and A. Bryson "What Effect Do Unions Have on Wages Now and Would Freeman and Medoff Be Surprised?" *Journal of Labor Research,* 25 (2004), p. 388. Reprinted with kind permission of Springer Science and Business Media.

	1974–1979	1996–2001
Men	19%	17%
Women	22	13
Ages 16–24	32	19
Ages 25–44	17	16
Ages 45–54	13	14
Ages >= 55	19	16
Northeast	14	11
Central	20	15
South	24	19
West	23	22
< High school	33	26
High school	19	21
College 1–3 years	17	15
College 4 years	4	3
Whites	21	16
Nonwhites	22	19
Tenure 0–3 years	20	20
Tenure 4–10 years	16	15
Tenure 11–15 years	10	11
Tenure 16+ years	17	8
Manual	30	21
Nonmanual	15	4
Manufacturing	16	10
Construction	49	39
Services	34	16
Private sector	21	17

the highest union wage premiums had the greatest employment decreases during the 1970s.[34]

Individual Effects

Unions have greater effects for employees who have less education and shorter tenure and who are nonwhite, younger or older than the average worker, male, a resident of a southern state, a transport operative, or a laborer as compared to other members of their groups who are not unionized.[35] Table 9.13 shows union wage differentials across a number of demographic groups and compares recent differentials with those of the mid-1970s.

[34] P. D. Linneman, M. L. Wachter, and W. H. Carter, "Evaluating the Evidence on Union Wages and Employment," *Industrial and Labor Relations Review*, 44 (1990), pp. 34–53.

[35] R. B. Freeman and J. L. Medoff, *What Do Unions Do?* (New York: Basic Books, 1984), p. 49; see also, P. V. Wunnava and N. O. Peled, "Union Wage Premiums by Gender and Race: Evidence from PSID 1980–1992," *Journal of Labor Research*, 20 (1999), pp. 415–423; S. M. Donohue and J. W. Heywood, "Unionization and Nonunion Wage Patterns: Do Low-Wage Workers Gain the Most?" *Journal of Labor Research*, 21 (2000), pp. 489–502; and D. G. Blanchflower and A. Bryson, "What Effect Do Unions Have on Wages Now and Would Freeman and Medoff Be Surprised?" *Journal of Labor Research*, 25 (2004), pp. 383–414.

Wage-Level Difference Effects over Time

A large set of studies of the union-nonunion wage gap concluded that the average gap is about 10 percent; narrowing occurs during periods of expansion and widening during periods of high unemployment as a result of the rigidities of contracts.[36] From 1971 to 1999 union wage premiums declined slightly, while variation among union wages decreased.[37] Recently, differentials have fallen somewhat, but unionized males have retained their advantage while the differential for women has declined.[38] Evidence from Canadian contracts demonstrates pervasive avoidance of nominal wage cuts and greater real-wage rigidity during periods of low inflation relative to nonunion firms.[39]

Union wage premiums have not declined as a result of negotiated concessions.[40] Real-wage concessions did not occur in the early 1980s. Inflation abated faster than nominal wages.[41] Concessions were more frequently negotiated in small, high-paying firms with lower union coverage. A history of layoffs and poor stock performance also increased their likelihood.[42] Real concessions have been negotiated in several industries since 2000, but this has not eroded differentials substantially, indicating that unions retain bargaining power for the current members. At the same time, evidence indicates that union success in influencing both wage and employment outcomes peaked in the 1950s and 1960s and the union movement's current well-being is similar to what existed in the 1920s.[43]

Union Organizing Effects

Across worker subgroups, becoming unionized, remaining unionized, or becoming employed in unionized organizations is associated with higher wages.[44] The presence or increase of unionization influences occupational

[36] S. P. Jarrell and T. D. Stanley, "A Meta-Analysis of the Union-Nonunion Wage Gap," *Industrial and Labor Relations Review*, 44 (1990), pp. 54–67.

[37] Bratsberg and Ragan, "Changes in the Union Wage Premium by Industry."

[38] M. L. Blackburn, "Are Union Wage Differentials in the United States Falling?" *Industrial Relations*, 47 (2008), pp. 390–418.

[39] L. N. Christofides and T. Stengos, "Wage Rigidity in Canadian Collective Bargaining Agreements," *Industrial and Labor Relations Review*, 56 (2003), pp. 429–448.

[40] M. E. Haggerty and D. E. Leigh, "The Impact of Union Wage Concessions on Wage Premiums," *Industrial Relations*, 32 (1993), pp. 111–123.

[41] J. W. Budd, "Union Wage Concessions in the 1980s: Adding Realism to Nominalism," *Proceedings of the Industrial Relations Research Association*, 58 (1996), pp. 311–318.

[42] L. A. Bell, "Union Wage Concessions in the 1980s: The Importance of Firm-Specific Factors," *Industrial and Labor Relations Review*, 48 (1995), pp. 258–275.

[43] J. Pencavel, "How Successful Have Trade Unions Been? A Utility-Based Indicator of Union Well-Being," *Industrial and Labor Relations Review*, 62 (2009), pp. 147–156.

[44] Freeman and Medoff, *What Do Unions Do?* pp. 46–47; and S. Raphael, "Estimating the Union Earnings Effect Using a Sample of Displaced Workers," *Industrial and Labor Relations Review*, 53 (2000), pp. 503–521.

wages within a local market. One study found that an increase in union density of 10 percent is associated with 2 percent higher wages for unionized grocery workers and about 0.68 percent more for nonunion workers.[45] Unionization may occur because of employees' dissatisfaction with low wages compared to the wages at other employers or of other workers in their community. Thus, unions also can raise wages from a below-average level to a level equivalent with others.[46] A study of firms facing organizing drives found that in the year subsequent to the drive, pay levels were higher than those of a control group facing no union activity. The study also found that firms in which organizing activity occurred had pay levels lower than comparative levels before the drive began. The premium following unionization was nowhere near the level found between union and nonunion firms, in general, with initial contract demands focusing more heavily on issues of workplace democracy.[47]

Declines in union coverage, at least in the construction industry, were not associated with reductions in the union wage differential.[48]

The Effects of Economic Conditions

For both unionized and nonunion workers the inverse relationship between unemployment and wages became more pronounced in the early 1980s.[49] Global competition influences union pay premiums. For every 10 percent increase in market share gained by imports in an industry, the differential narrowed about 2 percent. Unions are less likely to seek high increases in domestic industries with heavy import competition.[50] In the short run, union wages are insensitive to changes in the unemployment rate compared to wages in the nonunion sector.[51]

Legal Factors

In states with right-to-work laws, employees cannot be required to belong to a union as a condition of continued employment. For union members, right-to-work laws or strong campaign activity for such laws is associated

[45] R. C. Johansson and J. S. Coggins, "Union Density Effects in the Supermarket Industry," *Journal of Labor Research*, 23 (2002), pp. 673–684.

[46] See O. Ashenfelter and G. E. Johnson, "Unionism, Relative Wages, and Labor Quality in U.S. Manufacturing Industries," *American Economic Review*, 62 (1972), pp. 488–507.

[47] R. B. Freeman and M. M. Kleiner, "The Impact of New Unionization on Wages and Working Conditions," *Journal of Labor Economics*, 8 (1990), pp. S8–S25.

[48] D. Belman and P. B. Voos, "Union Wages and Union Decline: Evidence from the Construction Industry," *Industrial and Labor Relations Review*, 60 (2006), pp. 67–87.

[49] J. W. Budd and Y. Nho, "Testing for a Structural Change in U.S. Wage Determination," *Industrial Relations*, 36 (1997), pp. 160–177.

[50] R. J. Cebula and U. Nair-Reichert, "Union Rent Seeking and Import Competition in U.S. Manufacturing," *Journal of Labor Research*, 21 (2000), pp. 477–488.

[51] P. V. Wunnava and A. A. Okunade, "Countercyclical Union Wage Premiums? Evidence for the 1980s," *Journal of Labor Research*, 17 (1996), pp. 289–296.

with lower wages.[52] State prevailing-wage laws require that construction employers pay all employees the prevailing wage for public sector construction projects, whether they are union members or not. Where states have repealed these laws, construction worker wages have dropped slightly, but the wages of unionized workers have decreased significantly and there has been a decrease in the black-nonblack wage differential.[53]

Union Spillovers

Union wage increases lead to nonunion increases, but the reverse is not true. High unemployment dampens spillovers, while increasing inflation raises them. Union-union spillovers are also found, suggesting that pattern bargaining influences union settlements. Wages for hotel workers in nonunion hotels in cities where hotel work is heavily unionized are substantially higher than wages in less heavily unionized cities.[54] Political and equity issues promote spillovers over and above market forces.[55] Nonunion wage changes do not appear to have any subsequent effects on union wage levels.[56]

Summary of the Evidence

An extensive recent study of union wage differentials reached the following conclusions:

1. The private sector wage premium is lower today than it was in the 1970s.
2. The union wage premium is countercyclical.
3. There is evidence of a secular decline in the private sector union wage premium.
4. There remains big variation in the premium across workers.
5. State-level union wage premia vary less than occupation- and industry-level premia.
6. Union workers remain better able than nonunion workers to resist employer efforts to reduce wages when market conditions are unfavorable.
7. Public sector wage effects are large and similar to those in the private sector.[57]

[52] W. J. Wessels, "Economic Effects of Right-to-Work Laws," *Journal of Labor Research*, 2 (1981), pp. 55–75.

[53] D. P. Kessler and L. F. Katz, "Prevailing Wage Laws and Construction Labor Markets," *Industrial and Labor Relations Review*, 54 (2001), pp. 259–274.

[54] C. J. Waddoups, "Union-Nonunion Wage Differentials in the U.S. Hotel Industry," *Proceedings of the Industrial Relations Research Association*, 51 (1999), pp. 161–168.

[55] J. W. Budd, "Institutional and Market Determinants of Wage Spillovers: Evidence from UAW Pattern Bargaining," *Industrial Relations*, 36 (1997), pp. 97–116.

[56] S. Vroman, "The Direction of Wage Spillovers in Manufacturing," *Industrial and Labor Relations Review*, 36 (1992), pp. 102–112.

[57] Blanchflower and Bryson, "What Effect Do Unions Have on Wages," pp. 406–407.

Union Effects on Pay Structures and Inequality

Compared with nonunion firms in the same industries, pay for workers in the same jobs is more equal in unionized firms. In a national sample of employees, those who moved from nonunion to union employment had more equal wages, while for those who made opposite moves, the reverse was true. The results are consistent with negotiating contracts that focus on the desires of the median voter and put together coalitions that are best served by settlements that reduce variance in wage increases. They are also consistent with the reduction or elimination of individual factors on wage increases. But the median-voter model can also explain steeper wage structures. In school districts with strong community support for schools, there was a relatively strong relationship between length of service, amount of education, and pay for schoolteachers where a majority of teachers had relatively long service.[58]

Wage compression is increased by across-the-board wage increases. The average decrease in dispersions attributed to unionization is about 22 percent.[59] Most bargaining-unit employees benefit economically from unionization, but a study across the income distribution in Canada finds that employees whose earnings are in the lowest four quintiles gain from unionization, but the top quintile loses.[60] A study of the effects of organizing among Canadian child care workers found that unionization increased wages for lower-level employees by about 15 percent, but the increases were far less for those in skilled positions unless they were a majority of the bargaining unit.[61] Figure 9.8 shows differences between hypothetical union and nonunion wage dispersions.

The decrease in union coverage in the United States over the past 55 years has been accompanied by an increase in wage inequality. About 15 percent of the total change can be attributed to lower unionization independent of changes in the occupational and industrial structure.[62] Similar increases have occurred in Canada and Great Britain as unionization has decreased. Right-to-work laws are also associated with greater inequality in income distributions.[63]

[58] L. Babcock and J. Engberg, "Bargaining Unit Composition and the Returns to Education and Tenure," *Industrial and Labor Relations Review*, 52 (1999), pp. 163–178.

[59] R. B. Freeman, "Union Wage Practices and Wage Dispersion within Establishments," *Industrial and Labor Relations Review*, 34 (1982), pp. 489–509.

[60] R. P. Chaykowski and G. A. Slotsve, "Earnings Inequality and Unions in Canada," *British Journal of Industrial Relations*, 40 (2002), pp. 493–519.

[61] G. Cleveland, M. Gunderson, and D. Hyatt, "Union Effects in Low-Wage Services: Evidence from Canadian Childcare," *Industrial and Labor Relations Review*, 56 (2003), pp. 295–305.

[62] D. Card, "The Effect of Unions on Wage Inequality in the U.S. Labor Market," *Industrial and Labor Relations Review*, 54 (2001), pp. 296–315; D. C. Card, T. Lemieux, and W. C. Riddell, "Unions and Wage Inequality," *Journal of Labor Research*, 25 (2004), pp. 519–562.

[63] M. Nieswiadomy, D. J. Slottje, and K. Hayes, "The Impact of Unionization, Right-to-Work Laws, and Female Labor Force Participation on Earnings Inequality across States," *Journal of Labor Research*, 12 (1991), pp. 185–195.

FIGURE 9.8
Differences in Wage Levels and Dispersions between Unionized and Nonunion Employers

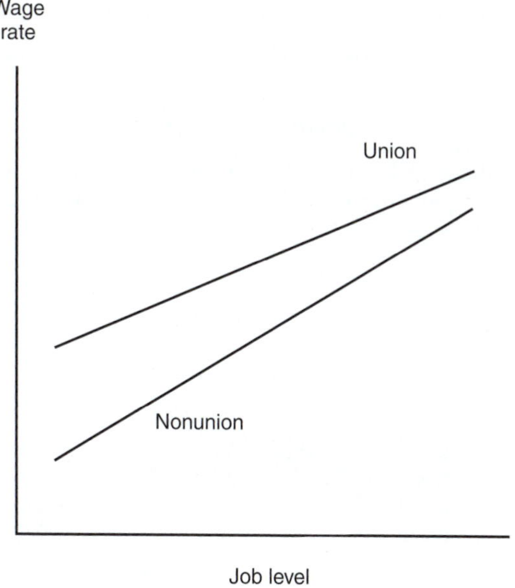

Union Effects on Pay Form

Differences between unionized and nonunion employees are perhaps greatest when benefits are considered. Union members are about 25 percent more likely than nonunion employees to be covered by an employer-provided health insurance plan and about 30 percent more likely to participate in an employer-sponsored pension program.[64]

Union members prefer larger proportions of their pay as benefits. Employers prefer a lower proportion. Unions have the greatest impact on small or low-wage employers, and they most greatly influence the costs of insurance, followed by vacations and holidays, overtime premiums, and pensions. Compared to nonunion situations, unions have the greatest relative influence on pensions—possibly reflecting the returns to seniority included in most contracts—followed by insurance and vacations and holidays. Unions have a negative effect on the use of overtime (but not premium rates), sick leave, and bonuses.[65] A comparison of private sector unionized and nonunion workers in 2004 found that unionized workers receive about $5.00 per hour more on average ($8.51 vs. $3.52) in non-statutory benefits and about $10.00 more per hour in total compensation.[66]

[64] J. W. Budd, "Non-Wage Forms of Compensation," *Journal of Labor Research*, 25 (2004), pp. 597–622.

[65] R. B. Freeman, "The Effect of Unionism on Fringe Benefits," *Industrial and Labor Relations Review*, 34 (1981), pp. 489–509.

[66] J. W. Budd, "The Effect of Unions on Employee Benefits: Updated Employer Expenditure Results," *Journal of Labor Research*, 26 (2005), pp. 669–676.

TABLE 9.14 **Union-Nonunion Differences in the Private Sector Total Compensation Package, 2004**

Source: Adapted from J. W. Budd, "The Effect of Unions on Employee Benefits: Updated Employer Expenditure Results," *Journal of Labor Research*, 26 (2005), p. 671.

	Union		Nonunion	
	Share of Total Compensation	Percent with the Benefit	Share of Total Compensation	Percent with the Benefit
Total compensation per hour	1.000 [$32.13]		1.000 [$22.01]	
Straight-time hourly wage	0.644		0.741	
Benefits, total	0.356		0.259	
Benefits, mandated	0.091	100.0	0.099	100.0
Benefits, voluntary	0.265	99.7	0.160	96.4
Health insurance	0.102	96.0	0.060	68.5
Defined benefit retirement	0.044	76.4	0.007	16.2
Defined contribution retirement	0.012	50.9	0.014	56.3
Life and disability insurance	0.006	91.3	0.004	63.7
Vacation	0.034	91.1	0.025	77.2
Holidays	0.023	90.4	0.018	77.4
Sick leave	0.009	68.5	0.006	58.3
Overtime premiums	0.021	87.0	0.011	53.2
Shift differentials	0.006	49.6	0.002	12.6
Nonproduction bonuses	0.005	36.2	0.010	41.7
Other	0.006	80.9	0.003	53.6

Table 9.14 shows amounts and fractions of pay associated with wages and various benefits for both unionized and nonunion workers.

Pension wealth is substantially greater among unionized employees than comparable nonunion employees. Differences appear greatest for collectively bargained plans having higher initial benefits, earlier retirement opportunities, and larger postretirement increases in benefits.[67] In states with prevailing-wage laws for public works, construction worker pension benefits were substantially higher, perhaps reflecting employer preferences for trading benefits for wages that would be subject to payroll taxes.[68]

Union Effects on Pay Systems

Little is known about how unions specifically influence pay systems, and existing data are based on the industry level. Unionized employers are much more likely to determine pay increases using easily identifiable criteria and automatic progression and are less likely to have merit reviews or other forms of individual determinations. Union jobs are more repetitive, have more measurable performance criteria, and need to apply incentive

[67] S. G. Allen and R. L. Clark, "Unions, Pension Wealth, and Age-Compensation Profiles," *Industrial and Labor Relations Review*, 39 (1986), pp. 502–517.

[68] J. S. Petersen, "Health Care and Pension Benefits for Construction Workers: The Role of Prevailing Wage Laws," *Industrial Relations*, 39 (2000), pp. 246–264.

pay less because performance monitoring is easier.[69] In general, incentive- and performance-based pay programs are used less often in unionized settings.[70]

UNION EFFECTS ON FIRM PERFORMANCE

Unionization and the usually resulting seniority rules change employees' orientations toward long-term employment and the benefits accruing with seniority. We will explore the effect of unionization on mobility and turnover in Chapter 10, but unionized employees are older and more experienced, other things equal, than their nonunion counterparts. Estimates indicate that human capital per worker (knowledge, skills, and abilities related to the job) is about 6 percent higher in unionized settings.[71]

Productivity

Because the evidence suggests that a unionized workforce increases wage costs, compared to unorganized firms in the same industries, a unionized firm should be at a competitive disadvantage, other things being equal. But these other things are not all equal. Industry-level studies have found unionized establishments to be 24 percent more productive on average than nonunion establishments. If the extent of unionization in the industry is considered, the productivity effect increases to 30 percent. Unionization also apparently has an impact on worker quality within the establishment as measured by experience, training, schooling, and the like. Evidence indicates that production worker quality in union establishments is 11 percent higher, while nonproduction worker quality is lower by 8 percent.[72]

Within industries, unionization appears to have differential effects. Research on construction industry productivity found that unionized workers on private sector projects were up to 51 percent more productive than their nonunion counterparts. The differentials decreased markedly in public sector construction projects, however.[73] Some of this difference may be due to prevailing-wage legislation that applies to federal and many state projects, generally requiring that the union wage in an area be applied to all workers when bids are made, thereby eliminating any wage advantage

[69] J. Garen, "Unions, Incentive Systems, and Job Design," *Journal of Labor Research*, 20 (1999), pp. 589–604.

[70] A. Verma, "What Do Unions Do to the Workplace? Union Effects on Management and HRM Policies," *Journal of Labor Research*, 26 (2005), pp. 415–449.

[71] R. B. Freeman and J. L. Medoff, "The Impact of Collective Bargaining: Illusion or Reality?" in J. Stieber, R. B. McKersie, and D. Q. Mills, eds., *U.S. Industrial Relations, 1950–1980: A Critical Assessment* (Madison, WI: Industrial Relations Research Association, 1981), pp. 47–98.

[72] Ibid.

[73] S. G. Allen "Further Evidence on Union Efficiency in Construction," *Industrial Relations*, 27 (1988), pp. 232–240.

for nonunion contractors. In education, student achievement was negatively affected by unionization among public school teachers through increased use of administrators and reductions in instruction time, but student achievement was positively influenced through increased preparation time, teacher experience, and smaller student-teacher ratios.[74] In hospitals and nursing homes, productivity was higher in unionized establishments in the private sector, but little difference was noted in the public sector.[75] While not a direct measure of productivity, a study of California hospitals found that, other things being equal, the mortality rate of heart attack victims was 5.5 percent lower in hospitals where registered nurses were unionized.[76] A study in the auto parts industry found little difference in productivity levels between organized and unorganized establishments, and failure to account for firms that may have gone out of business may upwardly bias the union effects on productivity.[77]

Decreases in profitability may occur as a result of employers' extending wage increases to nonrepresented employees to avoid further unionization. While productivity increases have been found following unionization for represented employees, this may not carry over to nonunion employees who received increased pay.[78]

Higher turnover in nonunion organizations may explain productivity differences (covered in Chapter 10). If experience is related to skill levels, unionized firms have higher skill levels, leading to greater productivity. Because union contracts reduce the wage dispersion within jobs in firms, employees may believe seniority-based pay systems reduce competition between workers and make them more willing to share job information and train new employees.

Organizational Investment and Growth Decisions

Since unionization generally leads to wage premiums, unless productivity increases as rapidly as labor costs, labor becomes more expensive relative to capital. Production technologies shift somewhat, moving away from least-cost combinations.[79]

[74] R. W. Eberts, "Union Effects on Teacher Productivity," *Industrial and Labor Relations Review*, 37 (1984), pp. 346–358.

[75] S. G. Allen, "The Effect of Unionism on Productivity in Privately and Publicly Owned Hospitals and Nursing Homes," *Journal of Labor Research*, 7 (1986), pp. 59–68.

[76] M. Ash and J. A. Seago, "The Effect of Registered Nurses' Unions on Heart Attack Mortality," *Industrial and Labor Relations Review*, 57 (2004), pp. 422–442.

[77] R. S. Kaufman and R. T. Kaufman, "Union Effects on Productivity, Personnel Practices, and Survival in the Automotive Parts Industry," *Journal of Labor Research*, 8 (1987), pp. 333–350.

[78] B. E. Becker and C. A. Olson, "Unions and Firm Profits," *Industrial Relations*, 31 (1992), pp. 395–415.

[79] R. W. Eberts, "Unionization and Cost of Production: Compensation, Productivity, and Factor-Use Effects," *Journal of Labor Economics*, 9 (1991), pp. 171–185.

Unionized firms invest about 20 percent less in physical capital and have lower research and development budgets compared to equivalent nonunion firms.[80] This is probably related to reduced returns to investment associated with higher labor costs in unionized firms. At the same time, unionization leads to increased capital intensity as the labor-capital price relationship changes following unionization.[81]

Evidence indicates that employment growth rates in unionized plants are about 3 to 4 percent lower on average than the rates in comparable nonunion plants.[82] A Canadian study found that private sector unionization reduced employment growth by about 2.2 percent per year.[83] A U.S.-based study found that employment growth following recession was lower in states with high rates of unionization.[84] Unionization is associated with lower flexibility in responding to market changes, with fixed benefit costs the primary reason.[85]

Profitability and Returns to Shareholders

Wage concessions in airlines during the 1980s and 1990s were related to share price increases. Concessions in one airline were seen as advantageous from a profitability standpoint since shares in other airlines dropped on the announcement. Prior to deregulation, investors responded positively to increases for flight attendants but negatively to cuts for mechanics. Following deregulation, cuts for flight attendants, clericals, and pilots were positive, reflecting the general unavailability of alternative opportunities for these occupations.[86]

Takeovers of unionized firms result in higher shareholder return (41 percent) compared with takeovers of nonunion employers. Wage concessions following acquisition of unionized firms have averaged about 8 percent, or half of the union premium.[87]

[80] B. T. Hirsch, "Firm Investment Behavior and Collective Bargaining Strategy," *Industrial Relations*, 31 (1992), pp. 95–121.

[81] S. G. Bronars, D. R. Deere, and J. S. Tracy, "The Effects of Unions on Firm Behavior: An Empirical Analysis Using Firm-Level Data," *Industrial Relations*, 33 (1994), pp. 426–451.

[82] J. S. Leonard, "Unions and Employment Growth," *Industrial Relations*, 31 (1992), pp. 80–94; and R. J. Long, "The Effect of Unionization on Employment Growth of Canadian Companies," *Industrial and Labor Relations Review*, 46 (1992), pp. 691–703.

[83] S. Walsworth, "Unions and Employment Growth: The Canadian Experience," *Industrial Relations*, 49 (2010), pp. 142–156.

[84] R. Krol and S. Svorny, "Unions and Employment Growth: Evidence from State Economic Recoveries," *Journal of Labor Research*, 28 (2007), pp. 525–535.

[85] E. Magnani and D. Prentice, "Did Lower Unionization in the United States Result in More Flexible Industries?" *Industrial and Labor Relations Review*, 63 (2010), pp. 662–680.

[86] S. L. Thomas, D. Officer, and N. B. Johnson, "The Capital Market Response to Wage Negotiations in the Airlines," *Industrial Relations*, 34 (1995), pp. 203–217.

[87] B. E. Becker, "Union Rents as a Source of Takeover Gains among Target Shareholders," *Industrial and Labor Relations Review*, 49 (1995), pp. 3–19.

TABLE 9.15
Contract Clauses Primarily Related to Pay Program Implementation

Pay Form	Insurance:	Accidental death and dismemberment
		Alcohol and drug abuse treatment
		Comprehensive medical insurance
		Dental care
		Disability, short-term
		Disability, long-term
		Health care continuation
		Hospitalization
		Legal assistance
		Life
		Major medical
		Medical-related insurance
		Miscellaneous medical expenses
		Optical care
		Physician visits
		Prescription drugs
		Retiree health care
		Sickness and accident
		Surgical
	Pensions:	Defined benefit plan
		Defined contribution plan
		Early retirement
		Employer contribution matches
		Salary reduction plan
		Vesting requirements
Pay Level		Cost-of-living adjustments (COLAs)
		Deferred increases
		Hiring rates
		Shift differentials
		Wage reopeners
Pay Structure		Job classification procedures
		Land-and-step plans
		Skills-based pay
		Two-tier structures
		Work progression
Pay System	Incentive plans:	Gainsharing plans
		Piece-rate systems
		Profit-sharing plans
	Income maintenance:	Call-in pay
		Severance pay
		Supplementary unemployment benefits
		Termination pay
		Lump-sum payments

An analysis of a large number of research studies found that unions depress profits by an average of 6 percent in the United States.[88] Unionization has not been found to have any consistent effects on firm insolvency. The rates of union and nonunion plant closures in manufacturing are about equal. While profitability is lower in unionized firms, insolvency may be related to management's failure to convey sufficient relevant information for the union to be able to make a saving concession.[89]

WAGE CLAUSES FOUND IN CONTRACTS

Employers and unions negotiate a large variety of wage-related clauses into contracts. Table 9.15 displays major types of wage and benefit clauses as they relate to pay level, structure, form, and system characteristics.

Summary

Wage demands are central to every contract negotiation. In forming their bargaining positions, unions are often concerned with equity among employee groups, the ability of the firm to pay an increase, and the change in its members' standard of living since the last negotiation.

Pay programs, whether negotiated in contracts or formulated by the employer, address issues related to the level of pay in relation to the market, the structure of pay rates for jobs within the organization, the form in which pay is delivered as wages or benefits, and the system used to determine individual entitlements to varied pay treatment. A variety of concerns are subject to negotiation, with unions stressing equality and ability-to-pay issues and management favoring pay programs that positively influence productive employee behavior. Managements have also been increasingly interested in lowering base pay levels and in making a larger proportion of pay flexible and responsive to changes in economic conditions.

Evidence indicates that unionization is associated with significantly higher pay levels. Pay structures tend to be somewhat flatter than those in nonunion organizations, with a larger proportion of pay given in benefits. CBAs generally contain fewer contingencies surrounding pay increases and have a larger proportion of pay in the form of deferred compensation.

Evidence indicates organized companies are more productive and less profitable than nonunion companies. Productivity differences in favor of unionized employers appear confined to blue-collar occupations and the private sector. Unionization is also generally associated with lower shareholder returns.

[88] H. Doucouliagos and P. Laroche, "Unions and Profits: A Meta-Regression Analysis," *Industrial Relations*, 48 (2009), pp. 146–184.

[89] R. B. Freeman and M. M. Kleiner, "Do Unions Make Enterprises Insolvent," *Industrial and Labor Relations Review*, 52 (1999), pp. 510–527.

Discussion Questions

1. What are the costs and benefits for management of allowing the union to decide how the economic package should be divided?
2. What demands would most likely be advocated by union leaders interested in obtaining contract ratification?
3. What information would you use to make predictions about the economic demands and probable settlement for a particular union-management negotiation?
4. What are the economic benefits of union membership to employees, and to what extent can these benefits be increased before employers face problems?
5. What are the trade-offs among increased wages for unions, productivity effects, and profitability effects on organizations?

Key Terms

Ability to pay, *258*
Standard of living, *259*
Cost-of-living adjustment (COLA), *259*
Pay level, *260*
Pay structure, *260*
Pay form, *260*
Pay system, *260*
Job evaluation, *263*
Skill-based pay (SBP), *264*
Two-tier pay plan, *267*
Defined benefit pension plan, *272*
Defined contribution pension plan, *272*
Salary reduction plan, *272*
Voluntary employee benefits association (VEBA), *277*
Benefit status seniority, *278*
Scanlon plan, *279*
Production committee, *280*
Screening committee, *280*
Rucker plan, *283*
Impro-Share, *283*
Profit-sharing plan, *285*

Web Sites

www.iir.berkeley.edu/library/contracts
www.bls.gov/cba/home.htm

Case: *Health Care Bargaining and the PPACA*

GMFC is a multidivisional company with over 50,000 employees. Given its size, it has chosen to self-insure its health care coverage and subcontracted administration to Vesuvius Health Care (VHC), one of the five largest health insurance companies in the United States. In addition to paying claims, VHC is also the gatekeeper on what procedures are covered by the plan and negotiating payment levels with major health care providers. Prior to the effective date of various PPACA provisions, the GMFC health care plan had a lifetime benefit limit of $2 million per covered employee or dependent and offered coverage to dependents up through the age of 22 if enrolled in a full-time degree program. The PPACA has required GMFC to change its coverage to accommodate new benefit and age limit requirements, adding some cost to the company for the current plan.

Looking forward, GMFC wants to make sure that its coverage includes the essential health benefits required by PPACA, but is concerned with the rate of health care cost inflation.

Local 384 is looking toward 2018 and is concerned that the company may abandon the plan because it might be vulnerable to the Cadillac tax.

GMFC is considering dropping health care coverage after 2014 and paying the federal penalties instead. This would leave employees in a situation where they would need to purchase insurance from one of the virtual exchanges. If GMFC were to do this, Local 384 would demand a large wage increase to offset the reduction in contributions from the company. In any event, there would be significant labor relations problems associated with a drastic change like this.

Assuming that these issues will be a major one in the upcoming negotiations, prepare either a union or a management position on the issue of future health care benefits in GMFC, recognizing that the employer will be decreasingly able to compete if total compensation costs continue to increase and regulatory mandates become more cumbersome.

Nonwage Issues in Bargaining

Wage and nonwage issues are not completely separable. Both have economic consequences for the employer. For example, provisions relating to hours of work frequently specify when overtime premiums begin. This chapter considers issues associated with hours and terms and conditions of employment and then examines the effects of unions on nonwage outcomes for employees and employers.

Nonwage issues are important to both union members and employers. For employers, the length of the contract, the design of work, and the scope of management rights clauses are important. For union members, job security provisions (particularly those related to promotions and layoffs), grievance procedures, and work schedules are important. To secure its representation rights, the union would like employees to be required to join the union. How promotions and layoffs are handled influences outcomes that are important to each party.

As you study this chapter, consider the following questions:

1. What effects do federal regulations and contract provisions have on management decision making as it relates to scheduling work?
2. How do discipline and discharge procedures operate, and what procedures are available for employees to redress improper discipline by management?
3. How do job classification and job design affect the employment relationship?
4. What effect do seniority clauses have on employee behavior?
5. What impact does collective bargaining appear to have on the job satisfaction of represented employees?

NONWAGE PROVISIONS OF CURRENT CONTRACTS

Certain types of nonwage contract clauses appear in a relatively large proportion of collective bargaining agreements. Table 10.1 displays nonwage subjects that are often included in collective bargaining agreements.

TABLE 10.1
Basic Nonwage Clauses in Contracts, 1995

Source: Compiled from *Collective Bargaining Negotiation and Contracts* (Washington, DC: Bureau of National Affairs, 1995).

Clause	Clause
Contract term:	Bumping permitted:
One year	Manufacturing contracts
Two years	Non manufacturing contracts
Three years	Leaves of absence:
Four years or more	Personal
Contract reopeners	Union
Automatic renewal	Maternity
Discipline and discharge:	Family
General grounds for discharge	Paternity, child care, or adoption
Specific grounds for discharge	Funeral
Grievance and arbitration:	Civic
Steps specified	Paid sick
Arbitration as final step	Unpaid sick
Hours and overtime:	Military
Daily work schedules	Management and union rights:
Weekly work schedules	Management rights statement
Overtime premiums	Restrictions on management
Daily overtime premiums	Subcontracting
Sixth-day premiums	Supervisory work
Seventh-day premiums	Technological change restrictions
Pyramiding of overtime prohibited	Plant shutdowns or relocations
Distribution of overtime work	In-plant union representation
Acceptance of overtime	Union access to plant
Restrictions on overtime	Union bulletin boards
Weekend premiums	Union right to information
Lunch, rest, and cleanup	Union activity on company time
Waiting time	Union-management cooperation
Standby time	Seniority:
Travel time	Probationary periods at hire
Voting time	Loss of seniority
Holidays:	Seniority lists
None specified	As factor in promotions
Less than 7	As factor in transfers
7, 7½	Status of supervisors
8, 8½	Strikes and lockouts:
9, 9½	Unconditional pledges (strikes)
10, 10½	Unconditional pledges (lockouts)
11, 11½	Limitation on union liability
12 or more	Penalties for strikers
Eligibility for holiday pay	Picket line observance

(Continued)

TABLE 10.1 Basic Nonwage Clauses in Contracts, 1995 (continued)

Clause	Clause
Layoff, rehiring, and work sharing:	Union security:
Seniority as criterion	Union shop
Seniority as sole factor	Modified union shop
Notice to employees as required:	Agency shop
No minimum	Maintenance of membership
1–2 days	Hiring provisions
3–4 days	Dues checkoff
5–6 days	Vacations:
7 or more	3 weeks or more
	4 weeks or more
	5 weeks or more
	6 weeks or more
	Based on service
	Work requirement for eligibility
	Vacation scheduling by management
	Working conditions and safety:
	Occupational safety and health
	Hazardous work acceptance
	Safety and health committees
	Safety equipment provided
	Guarantees against discrimination:
	Guarantees mentioned
	EEO pledges

UNION AND MANAGEMENT GOALS FOR NONWAGE ISSUES

Chapter 9 suggested that unions are concerned with equity, ability to pay, and standards of living in formulating wage demands and have simultaneous economic and job security goals. Employers are expected to resist demands that create uncertainty about their likely future costs or that interfere with their ability to be flexible or to respond to changes in their operating environment through the introduction of new production technologies.

Unions want to maintain the representational role they won during organizing. This means that they will want newly created jobs placed within the union's jurisdiction. They also want to emphasize job security and the use of **seniority** as the primary criterion for determining entitlements to promotions and avoiding layoffs.

DESIGN OF WORK

Work design involves determining what tasks, duties, and responsibilities (TDRs) are bundled together and assigned to a particular employee. Usually, several employees will have virtually similar TDRs assigned to them—in other words, they are assigned to positions in the same job. Jobs can be characterized as narrow or broad. Narrow jobs have a relatively small number of duties assigned to them, broad jobs a relatively large number. Jobs can also be defined in terms of their depth. Relatively deep jobs require sophisticated skills, while the skills for shallow jobs are relatively simple to acquire and use. The design of work is very important to both employers and unions and has evolved substantially over time.

Work Design History

Prior to the industrial revolution, virtually all products were produced by a single individual. This meant that production was highly labor-intensive and that any complex product required very high skills. The industrial revolution introduced machinery into the production process. Products could be produced at a lower price, and as a result, demand increased. As the amount of goods sold increased, job specialization was implemented and skill requirements dropped quickly.

Taylorism

Near the beginning of the 20th century, interest in efficiency increased. Industrial engineering was in its infancy. Frederick Taylor introduced "scientific management" to design work in the most efficient way possible given the capital equipment in use. Efficiency was promoted by narrowing jobs and concentrating on how to make repetitive operations more automatic and less fatiguing. Little or no attention was paid to psychological reactions to work design, and except for training on how to be more efficient in the current job, little was included on how to develop employees for higher-level jobs. The work design also included a hierarchical organizational and supervisory structure in which rank-and-file workers had no say in the workplace.

Fordism

Henry Ford's work design transformed the automobile industry in the early decades of the 20th century. His production technology enabled the mass production of complex products. Major innovations included the development of close manufacturing tolerances, which allowed interchangeable parts, and the introduction of the assembly line, which required that employees perform relatively few steps in the production process. The latter innovation substantially deskilled jobs in automobile (and other) manufacturing. As a result, Ford, and others who imitated this technology, could focus primarily on hiring for motivation rather than ability, since few skills were required to perform the work.

Ford introduced a darker aspect to the Tayloristic assembly-line approach—an internal security force to monitor employee effort and to quickly identify pockets of malcontents in the workforce. As the decades went by, this security force increased in size and used particularly brutal tactics to deter unionization.[1]

The Drive System

The drive system developed concurrently with Taylorism and Fordism. Under the drive system, the production floor was controlled by foremen (supervisors). Foremen had unlimited authority to govern the workplace. They decided who was hired, who was fired, how employees were to be paid, and how the work was to be done. Employees had no voice and depended on their relationship with their foreman for their continued livelihood.

The work design aspects of Taylorism, combined with the internal security force of Fordism and the monarchic influence of the foreman under the drive system, ultimately intensified the interests of unskilled workers in unionization.

The Corporatist Environment

Following World War II, a 30-year corporatist environment developed. For most large organizations, this meant that the design of work was collectively bargained. Specific jobs were established, and promotion structures were defined. Most large firms employed work designs that required firm-specific skills. These skills led to enhanced production quality and/or efficiency. Jobs were relatively narrow, but employee experience enhanced productivity. Employees could look forward to jobs with lower physical requirements, as they were able to bid into them with increasing seniority. Wage rates were associated with specific jobs so that if a person was temporarily transferred to a job with higher levels of responsibilities, the wage rate would change for as long as the person was in that job. Supervisory control was substantially checked by the union compared to the drive system, but rank-and-file employees had little or no responsibility for workplace decision making. This design worked quite well during a period of relative price stability and little global competition.

Workplace Transformation

Employers are frequently faced with a need to change how work is accomplished. The causes of the need for change may come from outside the organization (exogenous change) including changes in competitive products and services, the state of the economy, or changes in laws and regulations; or they may be caused by factors within the organization (endogenous) such as the introduction of a new technology, an innovation in products or services, or changing goals and objectives of new managers. Exogenous changes accelerated in the late 1970s and early 1980s,

[1] For more details, see N. Lichtenstein, *The Most Dangerous Man in Detroit: A History of Walter Reuther and the UAW* (Charlottesville: University of Virginia Press, 1995).

beginning a transformation in American workplaces that continues to the present.[2] Changes included removing several layers of management, thereby increasing the importance of production worker decision-making skills, increasing attention to quality, reducing the amount of material and in-process inventory to free up working capital, creating teams of broadly skilled workers that would be able to adapt quickly to changing product volume and mix, and reducing staffing levels to enhance efficiency.

With this transformation, unions faced demands for radical work design and work rule changes. Unions generally resisted these changes without increases in job security guarantees. Successful changes often required reorienting the labor-management relationship toward a more cooperative approach (detailed in Chapter 13) and incorporating productivity-based gainsharing programs (as described in Chapter 9).

In order to remain competitive in a global economy, manufacturing employers have been particularly interested in reducing the number of distinct job classifications in both production and maintenance to gain flexibility in staffing and avoid idle time during maintenance operations due to narrow job jurisdictions. Broader capability requirements in broader job classifications reduce the need for supervision. Managers believe unions' resistance to change will be higher where technological change requires negotiation.[3] Unions, however, will generally accept technological change as long as bread-and-butter issues are protected.[4] Auto industry evidence indicates a reduction in job classifications is associated with a reduction in the supervision required, small improvements in the quality of output, and a small increase in total labor hours required for an equivalent level of output.[5]

Taken together, these changes in organizational and work design are components of so-called high-performance work organizations (HPWO). Firms that implement HPWOs have higher productivity and financial performance and higher wage levels.[6] Companies that had introduced HPWOs by 1992 had more layoffs by 1997 than those without HPWOs. Unions reduced the incidence of layoffs; however, a variety of innovations such as teams, quality circles, and total quality management were all

[2] See T. A. Kochan, H. C. Katz, and R. B. McKersie, *The Transformation of American Industrial Relations* (New York: Basic Books, 1986).

[3] B. Bemmels and Y. Reshef, "Manufacturing Employees and Technological Change," *Journal of Labor Research*, 12 (1992), pp. 231–246.

[4] U. E. Gattiker and D. Paulson, "Unions and New Office Technology," *Relations Industrielles*, 54 (1999), pp. 245–276.

[5] J. H. Keefe and H. C. Katz, "Job Classifications and Plant Performance in the Auto Industry," *Industrial Relations*, 29 (1990), pp. 111–118.

[6] J. Godard, "Unions, Work Practices, and Wages under Different Institutional Environments: The Case of Canada and England," *Industrial and Labor Relations Review*, 60 (2007), pp. 457–476.

associated with increased layoffs. The layoffs that occurred tended to be selective because total employment continued to grow. Fewer contingent workers were used, and flatter organizational structures had been implemented.[7] Where teamwork has been implemented, the role of supervisors changes to training and facilitation while workers gain substantial discretion and control over their work. Their satisfaction increases and their jobs become more secure, while supervisors experience the opposite.[8]

In return for job security guarantees, employers negotiated team-oriented production designs, where workers are responsible for several tasks and can be assigned to a variety of jobs. "Cell-manufacturing" techniques require substantially more knowledge and skill in tracking inventories, measuring quality, and determining how production activities will be undertaken. This approach requires that employees have higher skill levels, thereby potentially decreasing their interest in unionization as the lines between professional and production employees are blurred.[9] At the same time, unionized blue-collar employees have an increased likelihood of receiving off-the-job training.[10]

The telecommunications industry has been undergoing continuous exogenously driven change for over 20 years. These changes include the court-ordered breakup of the AT&T wireline monopoly, competitors' development of virtual networks, the switch from analog to digital technologies, the introduction and spread of wireless telephony, the increasing capacity of hardwire and wireless broadband transmission, and the increasing substitutability of the Internet for proprietary communication methods. All of these introduced radical changes in the types of skills needed by employees to install, operate, and repair the evolving systems.

When new technology is introduced, union-represented jobs are more likely to be deskilled if management is successful in designating the jobs that are to be outside the bargaining unit. Contractual seniority requirements may entitle jobs to employees who are not the most able to fully operate new equipment. Management is particularly unwilling to include jobs requiring programming within the bargaining unit when new technology is installed.[11] In telecommunications, the reclassification of

[7] P. Osterman, "Work Reorganization in an Era of Restructuring: Trends in Diffusion and Effects on Employee Welfare," *Industrial and Labor Relations Review*, 53 (2000), pp. 179–196.

[8] R. Batt, "Who Benefits from Teams? Comparing Workers, Supervisors, and Managers," *Industrial Relations*, 43 (2004), pp. 183–212.

[9] K. Knauss and M. Matuszak, "Responding to Technological Innovations: Unions and Cell Manufacturing," *Labor Studies Journal*, 17, no. 1 (1992), pp. 29–48.

[10] P. Osterman, "Skill, Training, and Work Organization in American Establishments," *Industrial Relations*, 34 (1995), pp. 125–146.

[11] M. R. Kelley, "Unionization and Job Design under Programmable Automation," *Industrial Relations*, 28 (1989), pp. 174–187.

positions from bargaining unit to either professional or managerial categories has reduced the proportion of the workforce that is unionizable from about 75 to 40 percent. In situations where rapid change occurs, employers may prefer to stop doing certain types of work and outsource it. In one case, union militancy, including pressuring regulatory bodies not to grant requested rate increases, persuaded one major telecommunications company to restructure bargaining-unit jobs to include more high-performance work practices rather than outsource them.[12] Slightly less than 30 percent of the workforce is currently organized.[13]

Some work rule changes try to increase efficiency by using equipment more fully than it had been (as in the case of Teamster drivers previously hauling less-than-full loads).[14] Other work rule changes increase flexibility through greater skills and management's ability to assign employees to an increasingly wide variety of tasks. However, unionized employers are generally less able to use flexible staffing arrangements (part-time and temporary workers), but their ability to subcontract is generally not affected. In turn, the ability to subcontract has a generally positive effect on core bargaining-unit workers' wages. Job flexibility contributes to job security and enables the employer to specialize in markets for new products.[15] Labor flexibility is greater in companies without unions, but flexibility in the use of other inputs is higher in unionized firms.[16]

Work rules reserving certain responsibilities to certain jobs reduce efficiency, but they may preserve employment levels. One study of the construction industry found that restrictive work rules increase labor costs by about 5 percent. However, building trade unions appear willing to give up 5 percent in wages to increase staffing levels by 3 percent.[17] In construction it's important to note that the union supplies labor in the unionized sector since employees are referred from the union hiring hall. Thus, it's to the median voter's interest to concede wages to get more employment since most work is for a relatively short period with a single contractor, followed by a return to the union for the next referral.

[12] M. Ramirez, F. Guy, and D. Beale, "Contested Resources: Unions, Employers, and the Adoption of New Work Practices in U.S. and U.K. Telecommunications," *British Journal of Industrial Relations*, 45 (2007), pp. 495–517.

[13] J. H. Keefe, "The Future of Work and Labor Organizations on Telecommunications Networks," *Proceedings of the Industrial Relations Research Association*, 51 (1999), pp. 227–236.

[14] Kochan et al., *Transformation of American Industrial Relations*, pp. 117–118.

[15] C. L. Gramm and J. F. Schnell, "The Use of Flexible Staffing Arrangements in Core Production Jobs," *Industrial and Labor Relations Review*, 54 (2001), pp. 245–258.

[16] E. Magnani and D. Prentice, "Unionization and Input Flexibility in U.S. Manufacturing, 1973–1996," *Industrial and Labor Relations Review*, 59 (2006), pp. 386–407.

[17] S. G. Allen, "Union Work Rules and Efficiency in the Building Trades," *Journal of Labor Economics*, 4 (1986), pp. 212–242.

HOURS OF WORK

Setting hours of work is a mandatory bargaining issue and is regulated by federal and state wage and hour laws. Union campaigns for shorter work hours have been a priority since the early 1800s, with the National Labor Union proposing an eight-hour day after the Civil War. The federal government regulated work hours for civil servants during President Van Buren's administration and imposed overtime penalties for private sector employers beginning in the 1930s.

Federal Wage and Hour Laws

In 1937, the **Fair Labor Standards Act (FLSA)** was enacted to regulate wages, hours, and working conditions of private sector employers involved in interstate commerce. Briefly, the legislation requires that employees who are not in supervisory roles, outside sales positions, or jobs requiring independent discretion using complex knowledge must be paid a 50 percent premium over their regular pay rates for more than 40 hours per week. This premium requirement covers all employees whose work is of a routine nature or requires close supervision and direction. Employees who are entitled to an overtime premium are often referred to as **nonexempt** employees, while those who are not entitled are called **exempt** employees. The legislation also established a minimum wage and prohibits persons under age 16 or 18 from working in specific occupations or industries.

Congress had previously enacted the **Davis-Bacon** and **Walsh-Healy** acts, which required overtime premiums after 40 hours per week for employees in the same types of jobs as are covered by the FLSA and payment of wages equal to those paid in the local area or industry for the jobs to which they were assigned if employees were doing government contract construction work or producing manufactured goods for the federal government. These laws, enacted during the Depression, were intended to stimulate expanded employment and take wages out of competition for federal government work. Employers would save by hiring more employees rather than by having existing employees work overtime.

In 2004, the Department of Labor issued new administrative rules increasing the amounts that employees must earn to be exempt from overtime, regardless of job characteristics, and relaxed the regulations regarding what types of training and job activities would lead to an employee being classified as exempt. No jobs requiring supervision or primarily manual work changed classifications, but some nursing jobs requiring that position holders supervise teams did become exempt. As before, any job that was paid on an hourly basis, regardless of job duties, continued to qualify for overtime (be classified as nonexempt).

Collective Bargaining and Work Schedules

Unions have continually favored reducing the workweek and workday. A 40-hour week is typical in most contracts, and employers strongly resist further reductions. Unionized workers work fewer hours than nonunion workers in more heavily unionized sectors of the economy, but full-time schedules are more likely in unionized sectors,[18] although mandatory overtime in some unionized sectors, particularly in the auto, health care, and telecommunications industries, has been the subject of intense negotiations and strikes. Exhibit 10.1 is an example of the Communications Workers' position in the 2000 Verizon strike in which it won restrictions on mandatory overtime.

Entitlements to and Restrictions on Overtime

Contracts usually specify rules for assigning overtime. Overtime is often rotated among workers based on seniority, balancing hours in the work group before returning to the senior worker to begin a new cycle. Some contracts allow employees to refuse more than a specified number of overtime hours per week. Employees who have not met this threshold would be subject to discipline for refusing to work scheduled overtime. Unions representing registered nurses have sometimes been able to negotiate restrictions on mandatory overtime into collective bargaining agreements and have also been able to gain legislative support for restricting overtime in some states.[19]

Shift Assignments and Differentials

In firms where continuous-flow operations are most efficient (such as chemical manufacturers and refiners) or where product demand levels and heavy plant investment justify multishift operations, contracts specify work schedule assignment rules. Seniority generally governs entitlement to shift preference among employees with similar types of skills. Shifts may also rotate. For example, an intact shift might work from midnight to 8 a.m. for four weeks, rotate to the 8 a.m. to 4 p.m. shift for four weeks, and then rotate to the 4 p.m. to midnight shift for four weeks.

Alternative Work Schedules

A variety of alternative work schedules have been designed to meet employee's desires and employer requirements. Most have been implemented in nonunion organizations, and most have expanded daily work hours and shortened the number of days in the workweek.[20]

[18] J. S. Earle and J. Pencavel, "Hours of Work and Trade Unionism," *Journal of Labor Economics*, 8 (1990), pp. S150–S174.

[19] P. F. Clark and D. A. Clark, "Union Strategies for Improving Patient Care: The Key to Nurse Unionism," *Labor Studies Journal*, 31, no. 1 (2006), pp. 51–70.

[20] For a complete summary of these innovations, see J. L. Pierce, J. W. Newstrom, R. B. Dunham, and A. E. Barber, *Alternative Work Schedules* (Boston: Allyn & Bacon, 1989).

Exhibit 10.1

WHY WE MAY GO ON STRIKE AGAINST BELL ATLANTIC (VERIZON) BECAUSE STRESS AND OVERTIME ARE MAKING US SICK

There are not enough employees to meet the exploding demand for Bell Atlantic's new services. For you, that means long waits for installations, changes, repairs, or questions about your bill.

For workers, it means forced overtime, even when we have kids to pick up from day care or other obligations. It means work speed-ups, unfair discipline, and lousy training. It means we can't give you the good service we'd like to because we're pressured to move too quickly from one customer to the next. And as Bell Atlantic turns up the stress and pressure, the chance for errors goes up as well.

Source: Communications Workers of America Web site content available during August 2000.

Unions often oppose long-workday schedules because they have stressed fatigue, safety, and long-term health impacts in arguing for shorter days. But worker satisfaction improves and fatigue does not appear to be a problem even in strenuous occupations.[21] Where employees want to work fewer days and off-job demands in a given day are not great, compressed workweeks may benefit both employers and employees. The union must be aware of member preferences. In one case, a union opposing compressed work schedules was threatened with decertification if it did not go along with the schedule change.[22]

Paid Time Off

Paid time off includes holidays, vacations, and defined leave periods. Paid time off is relatively straightforward, although management may restrict entitlements or use. For example, employees must normally work the days before and after a holiday to receive holiday pay. Employers may also restrict vacation schedules. If operations are highly integrated and insufficient numbers of employees are available to continue in the absence of vacationing workers, management usually sets aside a period for vacations and shuts down. Other organizations may require that vacations be taken during slack periods. Flextime is becoming more important to many employees and can be expected to increase in importance in future negotiations.

[21] H. R. Northrup, "The Twelve-Hour Shift in the North American Mini-Steel Industry," *Journal of Labor Economics*, 12 (1991), pp. 261–278.

[22] H. R. Northrup, J. T. Wilson, and K. M. Rose, "The Twelve-Hour Shift in the Petroleum and Chemical Industries," *Industrial and Labor Relations Review*, 32 (1979), pp. 312–326.

LENGTH OF CONTRACTS

Most contracts exceed one year in length, with most being three or four years. Some provide for wage reopeners during the agreement, especially when COLAs are not included. Employers try to avoid one-year contracts because they believe short contracts lead to more strikes and contract administration problems, lower employee morale, and higher and more unpredictable labor costs.[23] Longer-term contracts are more difficult to negotiate, especially if economic environments are changing. Renegotiating long-term contracts was found to be harder when global competition is great; where capacity utilization, the firm's product prices, and the number of vacant positions substantially vary during the contract period; where buyer or seller concentration in the industry is high among larger employers; and during periods of high inflation.[24] Contract durations have increased independently of many of these factors to provide greater certainty for both labor and management.[25] Most contracts have automatic renewal provisions if not renegotiated. Recall that contracts covered by the Railway Labor Act do not have expiration dates but rather have dates at which they are amendable. Negotiations begin at that point rather than needing to be concluded by that date.

UNION AND MANAGEMENT RIGHTS

Contracts specify the union's representation rights. Most relate to the number of union stewards or representatives permitted within the bargaining unit, their rights to access employees in various plant areas, the amount of time off available for union representation activities and who is responsible for compensating this time, office space, access to bulletin boards, and access of nonemployee union officials to the workplace.

In most contracts management reserves the right to act in areas not constrained by the agreement. Typical reserved rights include the right to subcontract work that could be performed by the bargaining unit,[26]

[23] S. M. Jacoby and D. J. B. Mitchell, "Employer Preferences for Long-Term Union Contracts," *Journal of Labor Research*, 5 (1984), pp. 215–228.

[24] J. M. Cousineau and R. Lacroix, "Imperfect Information and Strikes: An Analysis of Canadian Experience, 1967–82," *Industrial and Labor Relations Review*, 39 (1986), pp. 377–387.

[25] K. J. Murphy, "Determinants of Contract Duration in Collective Bargaining Agreements," *Industrial and Labor Relations Review*, 45 (1992), pp. 352–365.

[26] The Supreme Court decision in *Fibreboard Paper Products* v. *NLRB*, 379 U.S. 203 (1964), requires bargaining by management if a union requests when subcontracting is being considered, unless the union has expressly waived its right in this area; however, this rule has been relaxed somewhat by *First National Maintenance* v. *NLRB*, 107 LRRM 2705 (U.S. Supreme Court, 1981), and later by the NLRB when it held that removal of union work to another facility of the company would be permissible if bargaining has reached an impasse [*Milwaukee Spring Div. of Illinois Coil Spring Co.*, 115 LRRM 1065 (1984), enforced by the U.S. Court of Appeals, District of Columbia Circuit, 119 LRRM 2801 (1985)], or for a legitimate business reason if there were no antiunion animus [*Otis Elevator Co.*, 115 LRRM 1281 (1984)].

to assign bargaining-unit work to supervisors in emergencies or to train new employees, to introduce technological changes to improve efficiency, and to determine criteria for plant shutdowns or relocations.[27] When management does not reserve these rights, the union is entitled to bargain during the course of the contract if changes involving job security occur. For example, if a plant closure would result in layoffs, the absence of a clause leaving this determination to management requires bargaining on its effects if the union requests it.

Outsourcing some part of an operation to another employer increasingly concerns unions since it threatens job security and leads to pressure for concessions, particularly if the new source is a lower-wage nonunion operation. Unions are also concerned with an employer's selling or spinning off part of its operations to another company or establishing a new firm. In these instances, the new owner or firm is often more able to reduce wages and/or employment.

Management rights clauses specify rights to direct the workforce, establish production levels, and frame appropriate company rules and policies. Establishing rules and procedures and directing the workforce form a base for clauses relating to discipline and discharge.

DISCIPLINE AND DISCHARGE

Most contracts specify that employees can be discharged or disciplined for just cause. Some reasons are spelled out in the contract, and others relate to violations of rules the employer may promulgate under power retained in a management rights clause.

Specific grounds in discipline and discharge clauses most often cover intoxication, dishonesty or theft, incompetence or failure to meet work standards, insubordination, unauthorized absence, misconduct, failure to obey safety rules, violations of leave provisions, or general violations of company rules.[28] Committing a violation does not necessarily mean an offender will be automatically discharged but rather means that he or she will be subject to discipline. However, an employer must be consistent in the way discipline is imposed to successfully defend its disciplinary actions against grievances.

Discipline and discharge clauses also spell out the due process procedures necessary before discipline can be imposed. Renegotiation of a

[27] Unless the basic nature of the operation is changed, relocation is a mandatory subject of bargaining. See C. J. Griffin, Jr., and M. A. Jones, "Work Relocations—The Changing Rules Represent a Victory for Organized Labor," *Employee Relations Law Journal*, 17 (1991), pp. 389–404.

[28] For more details, see *Collective Bargaining Negotiations and Contract* (Washington, DC: Bureau of National Affairs, updated as necessary), tab sec. 40.

long-term contract frequently requires that disciplinary action records from before a certain point be removed from employees' files.

Employees are expected to follow the directions of their supervisors and to carry out their job duties. There may be situations in which employees believe that an assignment is not within the duties of their jobs or that an assignment is unsafe. An employee runs a risk of being disciplined for insubordination for failing to carry out a job direction. Employers, however, must be careful to avoid disciplining a group of employees who protest a supervisory direction because this would likely be determined to be "protected concerted activity." Discipline might constitute an unfair labor practice.

GRIEVANCE AND ARBITRATION

Grievance procedures are a high-priority bargaining issue for unions because they allow employees to object to unilateral management action during the term of the agreement. For example, assume an employee believes a supervisor unjustly suspended him or her for a work rule violation. Without a grievance procedure, no review of the supervisor's action would be possible. Grievance procedures are also useful to management because the aggrieved employee is expected to use this forum when an alleged violation occurs, rather than refusing a work assignment or walking off the job.

Grievance procedures usually specify who receives a grievance, the right of employees to representation at various steps in the process, the path a grievance follows if it cannot be resolved by the parties when it is filed, and the time limits at each step before some action is required. Chapter 14 will discuss grievance procedures in considerable detail.

Most contracts specify that when parties cannot agree on the disposition of a grievance, a neutral third party will arbitrate the dispute and render a decision binding on both parties. The contract specifies how an arbitrator is selected, how arbitrators are paid, the powers of the arbitrator, and the length of time an arbitrator has to render a decision. Arbitration of contract interpretation disputes will be covered in Chapter 15.

High grievance rates are associated with decreased productivity. While low morale might be a hypothesized cause, productivity decreases also occur because employees and supervisors are involved in grievance processing rather than production.[29] Where production rates and methods change, grievance rates might be influenced. For example, in a long-term study of an aircraft manufacturer, the level of planned production and an increase in the variety of production methods to be used, which would cause frequent job classification changes, were both associated with higher

[29] C. Ichniowski, "The Effects of Management Practices on Productivity," *Industrial and Labor Relations Review*, 40 (1986), pp. 75–89.

grievance rates.[30] Thus, grievance rates may reduce productivity and follow from higher productivity requirements.

STRIKES AND LOCKOUTS

Pledges by unions and managements to avoid strikes and lockouts while the agreement is in force appear in most contracts. Managements frequently demand a no-strike agreement in return for arbitrating unresolved grievances. Unions usually do not give up the right to strike during the contract if management refuses to comply with an arbitration award. Some work stoppages are permitted by contracts, including refusing to cross picket lines of other unions striking the same employer and performing struck work. Some contracts reserve the right to strike over work rule changes during the contract's duration.

Many contracts require that if unauthorized work stoppages **(wildcat strikes)** occur, the union will disavow the strike and urge employees to return to work. If employees continue a wildcat strike, many contracts specifically permit these employees to be discharged.

UNION SECURITY

Because the union is the exclusive representative of employees in the bargaining unit, the union would like employees to be required to join and pay dues for the representational services the union renders on their behalf. Different levels of **union security** may be negotiated. Except in states with right-to-work laws, contracts may contain agency or union-shop clauses. The following are definitions of various forms of union security:

1. **Closed shop** requires that employers hire only union members. Although this requirement is illegal, a contract clause can require that the employer offer the union an opportunity to fill vacant assignments. These arrangements occur most frequently in the construction, entertainment, and maritime industries, where many employers are relatively small and have relatively short-term demands for certain occupations.
2. **Union shop** requires that any bargaining-unit employee employed with the firm for a specific time (not less than 30 days, or 7 days in construction) must become a union member (to the extent of paying dues) as a condition of continued employment.

30 M. M. Kleiner, G. Nickelsburg, and A. Pilarski, "Monitoring, Grievances, and Plant Performance," *Industrial Relations*, 34 (1990), p. 89.

3. **Modified union shop** requires that any bargaining-unit employee who was hired after a date specified in the agreement must become a union member within a specific time as a condition of continued employment.
4. **Agency shop** requires that any bargaining-unit employee who is not a union member must pay a service fee to the union for its representation activities.
5. **Maintenance of membership** requires that any bargaining-unit employee who becomes a union member must remain one as a condition of continued employment as long as the contract remains in effect (but members can legally resign and retain employment).[31]

Contracts often include a **dues checkoff** in which employers deduct union dues from members' pay and forward the amount directly to the union. The process generally benefits all parties. First, it avoids workplace disruptions involved in collection. Second, it insulates employees from union disciplinary action for nonpayment of dues. Third, it ensures a smooth cash flow for the local union's financial operations.

Unions usually bargain for the highest form of union security attainable, but some might argue that a union or agency shop is not in the individual member's best interest. If union membership were not compulsory, those who joined or remained members would make sure that the union accomplished important ends efficiently. State right-to-work laws enable a preliminary test of whether union membership is influenced by the efficiency of the local union, because individuals can choose whether to join. One study found that the costs of a local's operation were lower in right-to-work states but that no differences in dues levels, provision of benefits or services, compensation of union officers, or profitability of investments existed.[32] Right-to-work laws increase **free riding** (union representation without paying dues) by about 8 percent. Of the employees who freeride, about 30 percent appear to do so because union membership cannot be required, while the other 70 percent would not work in an establishment where union membership was compulsory.[33] Right-to-work laws have a significantly negative effect on union density in the private sector.[34] Some evidence shows that the proportion of union members in the bargaining unit influences the union's bargaining power because wage levels increase with higher membership.[35]

[31] *Pattern Maker's League of North America* v. *NLRB*, 473 U.S. 95 (1985).

[32] J. T. Bennett and M. H. Johnson, "The Impact of Right-to-Work Laws on the Economic Behavior of Local Unions—A Property Rights Perspective," *Journal of Labor Research*, 1 (1980), pp. 1–28.

[33] R. S. Sobel, "Empirical Evidence on the Union Free-Rider Problem: Do Right-to-Work Laws Matter?" *Journal of Labor Research*, 16 (1995), pp. 346–365.

[34] J. C. Davis and J. H. Huston, "Right-to-Work Laws and Union Density: New Evidence from Micro Data," *Journal of Labor Research*, 16 (1995), pp. 223–234.

[35] S. Christenson and D. Maki, "The Wage Effect of Compulsory Union Membership," *Industrial and Labor Relations Review*, 37 (1983), pp. 230–238.

WORKING CONDITIONS AND SAFETY

Working conditions and safety clauses deal with the provision of safety equipment, the right to refuse hazardous work, and the creation of management-union safety committees. Many health and safety collective bargaining concerns have been superseded by the Occupational Safety and Health Act (OSH Act). Unions may negotiate higher standards than what the act requires.[36] Unions have an additional effect beyond the OSH Act, however. In construction, unionized worksites are visited by OSHA inspectors more often, maintain a higher level of safety, and have higher penalties for violations.[37] A British study found that safety committees appointed by the union rather than management were more effective in reducing accidents.[38]

In one health and safety study, petrochemical workers perceived greater risk from, and worried more about exposure to, dangerous carcinogens if they were union members or contract workers and had low job control. Regarding concerns about explosions, risk perceptions were related to job demands and being a contract worker, but not a union worker. Contract workers felt their union had less influence on workplace safety than core employees did for their union.[39]

Employers have also taken initiatives in the health and safety area with programs aimed at detecting and reducing substance abuse. Many employers have adopted prehire drug screening programs, over which unions have no control because applicants do not have representation rights. Unions and employers may potentially clash about bargaining over and administration of periodic or random drug tests, with unions arguing the tests constitute an invasion of privacy and may not be supported by just cause, while employers argue they are entitled to control the operation of the workplace and need to operate as safely as possible.[40]

[36] For an extended overview of occupational safety and health issues, see H. G. Heneman, III, D. P. Schwab, J. A. Fossum, and L. D. Dyer, *Personnel/Human Resource Management*, 4th ed. (Homewood, IL: Irwin, 1990).

[37] D. Weil, "Building Safety: The Role of Construction Unions in the Enforcement of OSHA," *Journal of Labor Research*, 13 (1992), pp. 121–132.

[38] B. Reilly, P. Paci, and P. Holl, "Unions, Safety Committees, and Workplace Injuries," *British Journal of Industrial Relations*, 33 (1995), pp. 275–288.

[39] J. E. Baugher and J. T. Roberts, "Perceptions and Worry about Hazards at Work: Unions, Contract Maintenance, and Job Control in the U.S. Petrochemical Industry," *Industrial Relations*, 38 (1999), pp. 522–541.

[40] For more details, see E. C. Wesman and D. E. Eischen, "Due Process," in J. A. Fossum, ed., *Employee and Labor Relations*, SHRM-BNA Series, vol. 4 (Washington, DC: Bureau of National Affairs, 1990), pp. 96–100.

SENIORITY AND JOB SECURITY

Seniority issues cut across several of the economic and noneconomic bargaining issues. Seniority may entitle employees to higher pay levels or to overtime, preferences on vacation periods, lengths of vacations, eligibility for promotions and transfers, and insulation against layoffs. Seniority provisions have been shown to positively influence the pay level of blue-collar workers represented by unions.[41]

A distinction must be made between benefit- and competitive-status seniorities. **Benefit-status seniority** is related to entitlement to organizationwide or bargaining-unit-wide benefits established in the contract. For example, if the contract specifies that vacation length depends on seniority, then the date of hire (as adjusted by any layoffs or leaves) establishes a benefit status. Most contracts base benefit entitlements on an employee's total length of employment since being hired.

Competitive-status seniority relates to entitlement to bid on promotions and transfers and to avoid layoffs. Benefit- and competitive-status seniorities occasionally overlap, but competitive-status seniority is usually accumulated within a job or department. Assume that an employee with five years' total service who currently works in an assembly job bids on an inspection job. Competitive-status seniority among the inspectors would begin as of the date of the job change. If a subsequent layoff occurred in which employees with four or fewer years of service on the job were furloughed, this inspector would be laid off. The inspector's benefit-status seniority would be five years, but his or her competitive-status seniority would begin only from the date that he or she obtained the inspector job. Competitive-status seniority is more likely to be companywide than departmentwide when the employer is small and capital-intensive, there is a single-employer bargaining unit, and the production technology requires that the employer provide substantial training.[42]

Layoff Procedures

Layoffs are usually in inverse order of seniority, protecting the most senior worker for the longest period. Many contracts specify layoffs on the basis of departmental seniority; some permit **bumping**, whereby a senior employee is entitled to displace a junior employee in another department or job as long as the senior employee is qualified for it. In almost 60 percent of the contracts surveyed in a recent sample, seniority was the sole provision for determining layoff or job retention rights during cutbacks.[43]

[41] K. G. Abraham and H. S. Farber, "Returns to Seniority in Union and Nonunion Jobs: A New Look at the Evidence," *Industrial and Labor Relations Review*, 42 (1988), pp. 3–19.

[42] J. F. Schnell, "An Ordered Choice Model of Promotion Rules," *Journal of Labor Research*, 8 (1987), pp. 159–178.

[43] *Collective Bargaining Negotiation and Contracts* (Washington, DC: Bureau of National Affairs, updated as necessary), tab sec. 60.

In another 30 percent of the contracts, seniority was the determining factor if the individual was qualified for the remaining jobs.

Promotions and Transfers

The Collective Bargaining and Negotiating Contracts survey found that seniority is less frequently a criterion for promotions and transfers than for layoffs. In about half of contracts, seniority is the sole or determining factor for promotions if qualifications are essentially equal. For transfers, seniority is also a sole or determining factor in half of the contracts.[44]

Depending on the contract, seniority for someone promoted out of the bargaining unit (e.g., to first-line supervision) may continue to be accumulated, frozen, or lost after time. Employers usually desire clauses protecting accumulated seniority for supervisors because rank-and-file employees may be more willing to vie for promotions where risks of job loss are less if they fail or if employment is later reduced.

Time Away from Work

Contracts usually provide for holidays, vacations, rest periods, and leaves. Each year the average unionized employee enjoys one more paid holiday than the national average.

Contracts also include provisions related to paid breaks, lunches, changing and cleanup, and other periods in which no production work occurs but employees are compensated.

Most vacation clauses link entitlement to length of service, with some contracts allowing five weeks or more, usually after 20 or more years of service. Employers experience higher vacation costs for senior employees because of both the greater time away from work and the higher pay that senior employees are likely to be earning.

A variety of situations in which paid or unpaid leave will be granted are also included. Paid leaves often include time for funerals of close relatives, sick leave, and jury duty. Unpaid leaves are available for civic responsibilities (such as elected office), union work (such as local president), and family leave (over and above that required by law).

EFFECTS OF UNIONS ON NONWAGE OUTCOMES

Unions influence nonwage outcomes for both employers and employees, predominantly in hiring, promotions, transfers, turnover, and retirement. Employee satisfaction is also related to union membership. This section explores research on the effects of unions on these types of nonwage outcomes.

[44] Ibid., tab sec. 68.

FIGURE 10.1 Union Effects on Hiring Practices

Source: M. J. Koch and G. Hundley, "The Effects of Unionism on Recruitment and Selection Methods," *Industrial Relations*, 36 (1997), p. 352. Reprinted with permission from Blackwell Publishing.

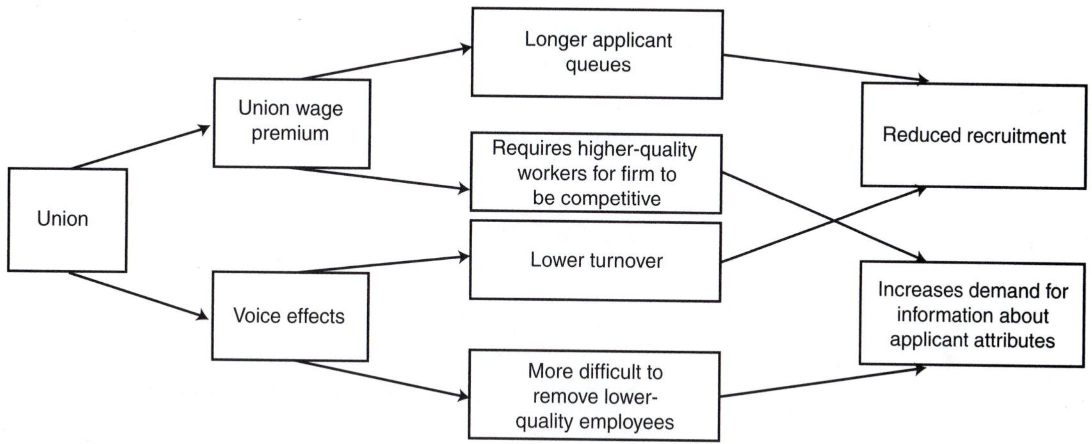

Union Influences on Hiring

Lower-skilled workers prefer union jobs; thus for lower-skilled jobs, a unionized employer will have a larger pool from which to select. Applicants who do not obtain union employment when they are young see union jobs as less attractive as time passes because promotion opportunities are at least partially related to seniority.[45] Among the unemployed, those with higher pay requirements, women, minorities, and former union members are more likely to wait for a union job opening, but this tendency is inversely related to unemployment levels and the duration of individual unemployment.[46] Unionized employers use fewer recruiting sources and methods, probably because of the availability of more applicants from chosen sources. However, this increases the number of selection hurdles, primarily because the likelihood of an employee quitting is lower and the ability to discharge unsatisfactory workers is decreased. Figure 10.1 shows a model suggesting why these differences occur.[47]

Minorities are a higher proportion of new hires in unionized as compared to nonunion organizations.[48]

Employers that actively avoid unionization may attempt to screen out prounion applicants. This practice, while rare, violates the Taft-Hartley

[45] J. S. Abowd and H. S. Farber, "Job Queues and the Union Status of Workers," *Industrial and Labor Relations Review*, 36 (1983), pp. 354–367.

[46] J. S. Heywood, "Who Queues for a Union Job?" *Industrial Relations*, 29 (1990), pp. 119–127.

[47] M. J. Koch and G. Hundley, "The Effects of Unionism on Recruitment and Selection Methods," *Industrial Relations*, 36 (1997), pp. 349–370.

[48] J. S. Leonard, "The Effect of Unions on the Employment of Blacks, Hispanics, and Women," *Industrial and Labor Relations Review*, 39 (1985), pp. 115–132.

Act. Unfair labor practice charges are most likely to be upheld when the employer is involved in an organizing campaign or is openly hostile to the union or when the applicant is applying for a skilled position.[49]

Promotions, Transfers, and Turnover

Most contracts specify the methods for filling vacant positions requiring promotions or transfers. In nonunion organizations, unless policy or custom dictates otherwise, the employer may use any legal criterion for filling jobs.

Turnover in nonunion organizations is greater than that in unionized employers with equivalent jobs. Chapter 6 suggested that a relatively stable workforce is necessary for a successful organizing campaign. A plausible explanation for lower turnover following unionization would be the stable base preceding it. But employers with represented workforces are no more likely than other employers to hire innately stable applicants.[50] Lower turnover is probably related to union wage premiums of about 3 to 8 percent for taking a unionized job, while losses from leaving one are about 7 to 11 percent.[51]

Contract provisions requiring that promotion and transfer decisions be based on seniority may explain union-nonunion differences in quit rates. The greater the weight given to seniority in job assignments, the lower the turnover rates.[52] Collective bargaining also provides employees with a voice in how the organization is managed. Grievance procedures and contract negotiations provide a vehicle for changing the work environment. Without collective bargaining, employees must quit to escape unsatisfactory conditions.[53]

When nonunion employees have grievances, unless their employers have established grievance procedures, the employee must accept the employer's unilateral action or quit (assuming the action was not unlawful). In unionized employers, employees are entitled to due process, and grievances might be allowed. Lags in the grievance process will extend tenure until a grievance is finally decided against the employee.

[49] T. L. Leap, W. H. Hendrix, R. S. Cantell, and G. S. Taylor, "Discrimination against Prounion Job Applicants," *Industrial Relations*, 29 (1990), pp. 469–478.

[50] R. B. Freeman, "The Effect of Unionism on Worker Attachment to Firms," *Journal of Labor Research*, 1 (1980), pp. 29–61.

[51] J. D. Cunningham and E. Donovan, "Patterns of Union Membership and Relative Wages," *Journal of Labor Research*, 7 (1986), pp. 127–144; and P. Kuhn and A. Sweetman, "Wage Loss Following Displacement: The Role of Union Coverage," *Industrial and Labor Relations Review*, 51 (1998), pp. 384–400.

[52] R. N. Block, "The Impact of Seniority Provisions on the Manufacturing Quit Rate," *Industrial and Labor Relations Review*, 31 (1978), pp. 474–488.

[53] R. B. Freeman, "Individual Mobility and Union Voice in the Labor Market," *American Economic Review*, 67 (1976), pp. 361–368; see also J. T. Addison and C. R. Belfield, "Union Voice," *Journal of Labor Research*, 25 (2004), pp. 563–596.

Other inducements to stay in a unionized firm relate to expected progress in the next round of negotiations and perceptions about the likelihood of vacancies for which the individual can qualify through seniority.[54]

Unionization does not change layoff and discharge likelihoods, but laid-off unionized employees are much more likely to return when recalled than nonunion employees.[55] Compared to nonunion employees, unionized employees are more likely to be recalled from layoffs but are less likely to find a new job if permanently separated.[56] Unionized employees are 23 percent more likely to receive unemployment insurance benefits when laid off as compared to similar nonunion workers.[57] In the absence of supplemental unemployment benefit packages, unionized employers should have a cost advantage—recall that costs are lower because of fewer vacancies and new employees need less training. Management can "store" labor for future demand at relatively minimal costs.[58]

Seniority provisions may also result from management attention toward the interests of senior bargaining-unit members (they are much more likely to be represented on negotiating committees than are junior members) and away from the impact of the external labor market on the establishment of employment policy. Thus, where cost differences are not significant and the experience of senior employees is related to productivity, negotiated seniority clauses may benefit both the employer and longer-tenure employees. Bargaining-unit members are probably more willing to ratify contracts with significant benefits for seniority because many of them are likely to have more seniority if turnover in union situations is less. Unionized employees may also anticipate achieving these benefits in later years.

If seniority clauses actually create opportunities for senior employees, over time unionized employees should have more internal job changes than nonunion employees. One study found that quit rates for white union members were substantially below those of nonunion employees and that transfer and promotion rates were significantly higher. Almost all union members who had been with the same employer for more than 10 years had made at least one internal job change. Education was negatively related to a bargaining-unit promotion but positively related to a promotion out of the bargaining unit. Promotions were more likely with more seniority in unionized situations, while they were less likely in nonunion employment. Unlike the nonunion situations in which women were less

[54] Freeman, "Effect of Unionism on Worker Attachment to Firms."

[55] Ibid.

[56] T. L. Idson and R. G. Valletta, "Seniority, Sectoral Decline, and Employee Retention: An Analysis of Layoff Unemployment Spells," *Journal of Labor Economics*, 14 (1996), pp. 654–676.

[57] J. W. Budd and B. P. McCall, "The Effect of Unions on the Receipt of Unemployment Insurance Benefits," *Industrial and Labor Relations Review*, 50 (1997), pp. 478–492.

[58] J. L. Medoff, "Layoffs and Alternatives under Trade Unions in U.S. Manufacturing," *American Economic Review*, 70 (1979), pp. 380–395.

likely to receive promotions, gender made no differences in situations where employees were represented.[59] Interests in career flexibility within the employer were found to be higher among unionized employees.[60]

Retirement Programs

Many contracts establish a minimum service requirement for full retirement benefits. Early retirees would want health care continued because they would not be eligible for social security retirement benefits until age 62 and Medicare until age 65. Chapter 9 detailed problems in funding retiree health care programs in mature and/or shrinking industries.

The Age Discrimination in Employment Act prohibits negotiating a mandatory retirement age. However, mandatory retirement may be required in situations where age has been ruled to be a bona fide occupational qualification, as is the case for airline pilots and police officers.

Early retirement decisions appear to be strongly influenced by the retiree's economic expectations and general health. The better the expectations and the worse the health, the more likely the individual is to retire early.[61] Married men plan to retire earlier when they expect larger pensions from both private and public sources, when their pensions have a known benefit level, when they are homeowners, when they have earned relatively higher wages, and when they are in poorer health.[62] Union members have greater predictability in benefits because a larger share is covered by defined benefit pension plans.[63]

As benefit levels increase and as retirement decisions cover a range of time periods rather than a particular date, greater retirement planning by individuals and organizations is probable. Some contracts provide pension benefits that, when combined with social security and tax advantages, impose a cash penalty on an employee who continues to work after becoming eligible for social security.

Job Satisfaction

Union effects on job satisfaction are not clear-cut. Chapter 6 noted dissatisfaction was a significant predictor of pro-union voting in organizing

[59] C. A. Olson and C. J. Berger, "The Relationship between Seniority, Ability, and the Promotion of Union and Nonunion Workers," in D. B. Lipsky and J. M. Douglas, eds., *Advances in Industrial and Labor Relations* (Greenwich, CT: JAI Press, 1983), pp. 91–129.

[60] K. E. Boroff and K. W. Ketkar, "Investigating Career Flexibility among Union-Represented Employees," *Proceedings of the Industrial Relations Research Association*, 46 (1994), pp. 268–278.

[61] R. Barfield and J. Morgan, *Early Retirement: The Decision and the Experience* (Ann Arbor: Survey Research Center, University of Michigan, 1969).

[62] A. Hall and T. R. Johnson, "The Determinants of Planned Retirement," *Industrial and Labor Relations Review*, 33 (1980), pp. 241–254.

[63] J. Stewart, "The Retirement Behavior of Workers Covered by Union and Nonunion Pension Plans," *Journal of Labor Research*, 18 (1997), pp. 121–136.

campaigns.[64] Receiving the benefits a union might gain is expected to increase job satisfaction, but a large-scale, cross-sectional study found that job satisfaction was lower among union members than nonunion employees when other variables were held constant.[65]

Job satisfaction increases for union members whose jobs change as the result of a transfer or promotion but not leaving the previous employer. The reverse was found for nonunion employees: Their satisfaction increased with turnover[66] and did not change as the result of internal job movements.[67]

A cross-sectional study found that job satisfaction among unionized employees was somewhat lower than it was among nonunion employees, but results varied when facets of satisfaction were compared. Union members were more satisfied with their pay, valued it more, and received more pay than nonunion employees. Promotion satisfaction was also greater, largely because union members place lower value on promotions than other outcomes. This result can be partially accounted for by relatively lower pay differences between job levels in unionized work. Union members were less satisfied with supervisors and co-workers, especially with regard to supervisory behavior. They were also less satisfied with their jobs, which generally had less varied tasks than those of nonunion employees.[68] Unions influenced the satisfaction of employees toward supervisors and the job by pointing out potential sources of problems the union will help employees solve. However, within bargaining units, one study found no differences between union members and nonmembers on job satisfaction or intentions to quit.[69]

Unionization in nursing homes influenced perceptions of job quality among employees. Other factors related to positive perceptions included being a skilled-care-provider facility, being owned by a chain, having a

[64] J. G. Getman, S. B. Goldberg, and J. B. Herman, *Union Representation Elections: Law and Reality* (New York: Russell Sage Foundation, 1976), pp. 53–57.

[65] R. B. Freeman, "Job Satisfaction as an Economic Variable," *American Economic Review*, 69, no. 2 (1978), pp. 135–141.

[66] Olson and Berger, "Relationship between Seniority, Ability, and Promotion."

[67] B. Artz, "The Impact of Union Experience on Job Satisfaction," *Industrial Relations*, 49 (2010), pp. 387–405.

[68] C. J. Berger, C. A. Olson, and J. W. Boudreau, "Effects of Unions on Job Satisfaction: The Role of Work-Related Values and Perceived Rewards," *Organizational Behavior and Human Performance*, 32 (1983), pp. 289–324; for additional confirmatory evidence, see S. Schwochau, "Union Effects on Job Attitudes," *Industrial and Labor Relations Review*, 40 (1987), pp. 209–234; for a comprehensive review, see T. H. Hammer and A. Avgar, "The Impact of Unions on Job Satisfaction, Organizational Commitment, and Turnover," *Journal of Labor Research*, 26 (2005), pp. 241–266.

[69] M. E. Gordon and A. S. DeNisi, "A Re-Examination of the Relationship between Union Membership and Job Satisfaction," *Industrial and Labor Relations Review*, 48 (1995), pp. 222–236.

religious or ethnic affiliation, having private pay patients, and having trained administrators.[70]

Finally, the strength of the union reduces fears that an employer might be able to increase work effort through threats.[71] At the same time, the degree of unionization appears positively related to job satisfaction and the willingness to cooperate, be productive, and reduce waste.[72]

Summary

Nonwage issues in contracts are related primarily to hours of work, lengths of contracts, management rights, union security, and seniority provisions. All of these have economic consequences for the employer and represented employees.

Work-hour issues relate to establishing the length of the workday, entitlements to overtime, shift assignments, and the number of days worked during given periods. Evidence suggests that employers may prefer innovative schedules with fewer days and longer hours in some operations.

Management rights clauses spell out areas in which management exercises decision-making control. Management also establishes rights to make and enforce reasonable rules. Grievance and arbitration clauses provide due process rules for situations in which bargaining-unit members disagree with management's interpretation and operation of the contract.

Union security clauses provide requirements related to dues payment and union membership. Union shops require that all bargaining-unit members belong to the union, while agency shop agreements require that nonmembers pay dues.

Seniority can be broken down into competitive- and benefit-status seniority. Competitive-status seniority relates to entitlements to jobs, while benefit-status seniority refers to compensation benefits.

Lower-skilled workers, particularly younger applicants, prefer union jobs since seniority is a factor in promotions in most union settings. Promotions and transfers occur more often in unionized settings, and turnover is lower. Job satisfaction among union members is about equivalent to that among nonunion employees, but there are differences in the levels of satisfaction for different aspects of the employment relationship.

[70] L. W. Hunter, "What Determines Job Quality in Nursing Homes?" *Industrial and Labor Relations Review*, 53 (2000), pp. 463–481.

[71] F. Green and S. McIntosh, "Union Power, Cost of Job Loss, and Workers' Effort," *Industrial and Labor Relations Review*, 51 (1998), pp. 363–383.

[72] M. Kizilos and Y. Reshef, "The Effects of Workplace Unionization on Worker Responses to HRM Innovation," *Journal of Labor Research*, 18 (1997), pp. 641–656.

Discussion Questions

1. Is it to an employer's advantage to enjoy the lower turnover rates that unionization seems to include?
2. Why are union officials likely to oppose flexible work hours and other innovative work schedules?
3. What potential problems and benefits are likely with early or flexible retirement programs?
4. Should either unions or managements be concerned with the apparently small effect of higher economic outcomes on overall union member satisfaction?

Key Terms

Seniority, *304*
Fair Labor Standards Act (FLSA), *310*
Nonexempt, *310*
Exempt, *310*
Davis-Bacon Act, *310*
Walsh-Healy Act, *310*
Management rights clause, *314*
Grievance procedures, *315*
Wildcat strikes, *316*
Union security, *316*
Closed shop, *316*
Union shop, *316*
Modified union shop, *317*
Agency shop, *317*
Maintenance of membership, *317*
Dues checkoff, *317*
Free riding, *317*
Benefit-status seniority, *319*
Competitive-status seniority, *319*
Bumping, *319*

Case: *GMFC Attitude Survey*

GFMC is a member of the Heritage Group, a consortium of employers with personnel research departments that participate in employment studies and share information. All members agreed this year to administer the same attitude surveys to their employees and relate the measures to variables such as turnover and productivity. To gain union cooperation in Central City, GMFC agreed to share the results of the survey and the broader study with Local 384. In return, Local 384 urged members to complete the surveys they received.

When comparative information became available, the results shown in the table were sent to Central City.

If you were a union or management representative, what would you make of the results? What impact might this have on the potential for negotiations in the next round of contract talks?

	Satisfaction Percentile	
	Central City	Total
Pay	53	50
Promotions	36	50
Work itself	62	50
Supervisors	27	50
Co-workers	86	50
	Turnover Percentile	
Rate per 100	18	50

Contract Negotiations

The negotiation of a labor contract is critically important to both parties. The agreement governs their relationship for a defined time period. For the employer, the contract has cost impacts and constrains management decision making. For the union, it spells out union members' rights and returns from their employment relationship.

Why does a contract emerge in the form that it does? How do the parties prepare for bargaining? What influences do the rank and file or the various functional areas within an organization have on the demands made in the negotiations? How does each group organize for bargaining? What constitutes success or failure in negotiations? What sequence of activities usually occurs during negotiations?

In this chapter we first examine the activities preceding the negotiations from both union and management perspectives. Then we look at the theory and tactics of the negotiating process and the steps necessary for agreement and ratification. Finally, we examine management's assessment of bargaining.

As you read this chapter, consider the following questions:

1. How do both management and the union prepare for negotiations?
2. How are negotiating teams constituted for bargaining?
3. What processes are involved in negotiations?
4. How are agreements reached, and what processes are necessary to obtain approval by the union rank and file for ratification?

Except for initial contracts and financial exigencies, negotiations are triggered by a preagreed date for renegotiations and the law. The Taft-Hartley Act requires that the party desiring modification give at least 60 days' notice before any terms can be changed. Under the Railway Labor Act, a party must indicate it wants to modify the agreement. However, regardless of the amendment date, the existing contract remains in effect until a new one is agreed on, and strikes cannot occur until 30 days after the National Mediation Board (NMB) has declared an impasse.

Figure 11.1 portrays a general sequence of activities in the bargaining process. The diagram lays out the basic prenegotiation activities, the proposals and responses in bargaining, and the possible outcomes of

FIGURE 11.1 Bargaining Process Events

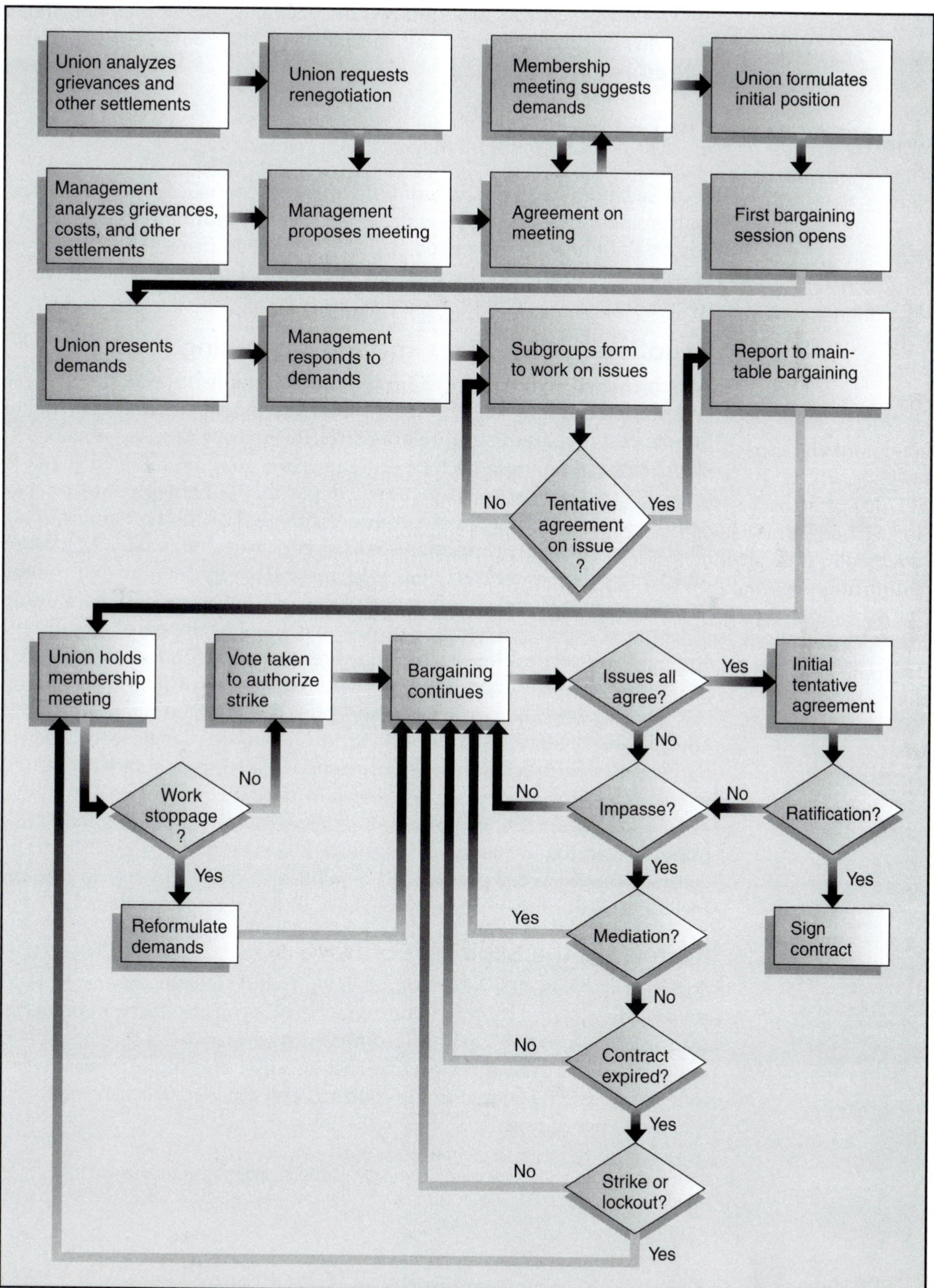

bargaining, together with settlement procedures. Both parties have an idea how they would like a new contract to be shaped. Either they have taken positions during an organizing campaign or they have had experience with an existing agreement.

MANAGEMENT PREPARATION

Because labor is a large share of total operating costs for most employers, management must be well aware of the cost implications of contract proposals. Both heavily organized and less organized firms should be aware of contract implications because benefits won at the bargaining table are frequently passed on to unorganized employees.

Negotiation Objectives and the Bargaining Team

The chief executive officer (CEO) ultimately establishes economic targets and needed changes with advice from the top management team. The top human resource/industrial relations (HRIR) executive is responsible for coordinating preparations for bargaining and may be the lead management negotiator. Various functional departments help prepare for bargaining and want to see certain issues pursued at the bargaining table. Production managers are interested in work rules and costs. Marketing managers want a contract that will minimize production disruptions. Accounting personnel supply many of the cost figures used for bargaining.

Contract objectives should support the goals of the employer at both strategic and tactical levels. Top management needs to forecast carefully the competitive environment that it will face in the future. It needs to lay out the strategic choices it faces and how the possible alternatives will affect its use of all types of labor. Tactically, it should plan how to structure the negotiation process in ways necessary to achieve a contract that will enable it to prosper across a variety of different competitive situations.[1] Within the organization, it needs to consider contract clauses that could possibly lead to production disruptions. If cost certainty is important, the contract should avoid person-tied benefits and cost-of-living clauses and include gainsharing, profit sharing, and/or piece-rate pay plans.

Reviewing the Expiring Contract

Top management, the labor relations staff, and first-line supervisors all review the expiring contract. The review centers on contract language that contributed to cost or operating difficulties during the contract, areas in which frequent grievances occurred, the results of arbitration cases, current practices not covered in the contract, and other contract supplements that affect operations.

[1] See E. G. Fisher, "Can Strikes Pay for Management? Pro Sports' Major Turnarounds," *Relations Industrielles*, 62 (2007), pp. 3–30.

Preparing Data for Negotiations

Necessary pay and benefit data include relevant comparisons, such as rates paid within the industry, local labor market rates for occupations covered by the agreement, settlements gained by unions known as pattern setters, and changes in the cost of living since the last negotiations.

Employee demographics such as seniority, age, sex, job classification, and shift are important. Because entitlement to many benefits is tied to seniority, a workforce with an increasing number of senior workers will incur higher benefit costs, even without a negotiated increase in benefit levels. For example, if vacations increase from two to three weeks after five years of service, a workforce that has 200 employees with three years of seniority at the beginning of a three-year agreement would have 200 employees with six years of seniority at the end, assuming there is no turnover. This change would mean an increase of 200 weeks of vacation by the end of the agreement. The employer will be paying for 200 unworked weeks and may need to hire five more employees to make up for the lost production. Knowing how many employees are on each shift enables employers to calculate shift differential costs.

Internal economic data, such as benefit costs, participation in discretionary benefit plans (recreation, etc.), overall earnings levels, and the amount and cost of overtime, are important. Information on competitive overall earning levels is important because some employee groups may feel underpaid when they actually are not. For example, skilled-trades employees in industrial plants earn less per hour than their counterparts in contract construction, but they are laid off less frequently because of weather or lack of work and thus may have higher annual gross earnings.

Knowledge of the union's negotiation and ratification procedure is also important. The bargaining team needs to know how the union signals concessions and drops demands during the process. If the union negotiator is new, information on his or her negotiating style is important. The time necessary for ratification and whether the union usually works after contract expiration are important from a deadline standpoint.

The employer's current level of operations and anticipated future changes are important in assessing bargaining power on certain issues. For example, if little inventory is available and customer orders have increased recently, but there are several competitive sources available for similar products and services, then a strike might be disastrous. The increasing use of just-in-time inventories and other sophisticated supply-chain management methods has increased bargaining power for unions since operations could not normally continue if a strike occurred.

Identification of Probable Union Demands

Using information from grievances under the expiring contract and feedback from first-line supervisors, management may be able to assess the likelihood of certain demands and the union's likely tenacity during bargaining. In large companies with national-level negotiations, attention to union bargaining conventions should inform management about the issues to which the union has committed itself. Other pattern settlements should offer clues to management.

Costing the Contract

As noted in Chapter 9, the level and type of wage and benefit changes specified in the contract have a definite cost impact for the employer. To make rational choices among possible demands and to counteroffer with an acceptable package that minimizes its costs, management must accurately cost contract demands.

Management can use a variety of costing methods of varying sophistication. An example of a relatively simple approach highlighting many of the issues is portrayed in Table 11.1. This example shows some of the important dynamics in long-term contracts. Costs for wages may increase at different rates than do costs for paid time off or insurance benefits. In general, the costs of insurance to cover certain events, such as medical care, are outside the employer's control unless the employer has negotiated a fixed dollar amount of insurance to be purchased.

The implications of certain contract terms are not straightforward and must be examined closely to capture real-cost impacts.[2] First, the "**roll-up**," or amount by which overtime and wage-tied benefits are increased by changes in the base rate, must be tracked. Second, overtime premiums greater than those required by law should cause the firm to consider whether overtime is controllable and whether labor cost increases can be passed on to customers. Third, vacation costs need to be examined critically. For example, vacations for maintenance employees may be essentially costless if work can be postponed until vacations are over, but production employees' vacations may require scheduling overtime, thereby increasing vacation costs by the premium rate, or hiring an equivalent number of full-time employees. Fourth, relief time may cost more if it is broken up into short periods. Some time may be necessary to begin the break and then return to work. This slippage may require adding more employees to sustain production volume.[3]

Benefits costing is not straightforward. Pension costs may depend not only on a defined contribution rate (e.g., 5 percent of base wages) but also on quit rates, vesting (personal ownership of benefits) rules, and pay rates at the time of retirement. For example, if the contract vests contributions after five years of service but only 20 percent of employees ever accrue

[2] M. H. Granof, *How to Cost Your Labor Contract* (Washington, DC: Bureau of National Affairs, 1973).

[3] Ibid., pp. 55–56.

TABLE 11.1 Costing Changes in Contract Terms

	Current	Demand	Year 1	Demand	Year 2	Demand	Year 3
Direct payroll—annual cost per employee:							
Average straight-time pay per hour	$15.00	$0.75	$15.75	$0.60	$16.35	$0.50	$16.85
Working days per year (52 wks. × 5 days)	260		260		260		260
Paid time off (days per year):	48.85		48.85		49.85		52.35
Holidays	9.00		9.00	10.000	10.00		10.00
Vacation days	15.00		15.00		15.00	17.5	17.50
Sick leave days	5.00		5.00		5.00		5.00
Breaks (30 min. per day for days at work)	14.44		14.44		14.44		14.44
Paid time off for union activities	5.42		5.42		5.42		5.42
Average days worked per year	211.15		211.15		210.15		207.65
Pay for time worked:							
Straight-time pay (working days × 8 × avg. s-t pay)	27,720		29,106		30,215		31,139
2nd shift differential per hour	0.225	0.236	0.236	0.245	0.245	0.253	0.253
Shift differential (30% of employees × straight-time pay)	140		147		153		158
Overtime (50% standard FLSA rate × 100 hr. per employee)	753		791		821		846
Overtime (100% holiday rate × 8 hr.)	121		127		131		135
Total average pay per employee	28,734		30,171		31,320		32,278
Average pay per hour worked	17.01		17.86		18.63		19.43
Increase over current level			1,437		2,586		3,544
Percent increase over current level			5.00%		9.00%		12.33%
Statutorially required taxes and insurance:							
Social security and medicare taxes, 7.65%	2,198		2,308		2,396		2,469
Unemployment tax (2.5% × $7,000)**	175		175		175		175
Workers' compensation (3.2% × total straight-time pay)***	887		931		967		996
Total average statutory payments per employee	3,260		3,414		3,538		3,641
Increase over current level			154		278		381
Percent increase over current level			4.73%		8.52%		11.67%
Cost of negotiated benefits:							
Insurance (company contribution):*							
Health	5,000		*5,625*		*6,328*		*7,119*
Dental	520		*546*		*573*		*602*
Optical	0	250	250		250	500	500
Prescription drugs	1,000		*1,100*		*1,210*		*1,331*
Life	120		*126*		*131*		*135*
Short-term disability	250		*263*		*274*		*286*
Long-term disability	120		*126*		*131*		*135*
Total insurance costs	7,010		8,036		8,897		10,107
Cost per hour worked	4.15		4.76		5.29		6.08

(Continued)

TABLE 11.1 **Costing Changes in Contract Terms (continued)**

	Current	Demand	Year 1	Demand	Year 2	Demand	Year 3
Increase over current level			1,026		1,887		3,097
Percent increase over current level			14.63%		26.92%		44.18%
Pension—3% straight-time earnings match	832		873		906		934
Pay for time not worked:							
Holidays	1,080		1,134		1,308		1,348
Vacation days	1,800		1,890		1,962		2,359
Sick leave days	600		630		654		674
Breaks (30 min. per day for days at work)	1,733		1,819		1,888		1,946
Paid time off for union activities	650		683		709		730
Total pay for time not worked	5,863		6,156		6,521		7,057
Cost per hour worked	3.47		3.64		3.88		4.25
Increase over current level			293		658		1,195
Percent increase over current level			5.00%		11.23%		20.38%
Total statutory and negotiated benefits	16,964		18,479		19,862		21,740
Increase over current level			1,514		2,898		4,775
Percent increase over current level			8.93%		17.08%		28.15%
Cost of benefits as a percent of pay for time worked	59.04%		61.25%		63.42%		67.35%
Total pay and benefits per employee	45,699		48,650		51,182		54,018
Increase over current level			2,951		5,484		8,319
Percent increase over current level			6.46%		11.27%		16.25%
Expected productivity improvement		2.50%		2.50%		2.50%	
Adjusted labor cost	45,699		47,463		49,934		52,700
Labor cost per unit increase			3.86%		9.27%		15.32%

*Benefit costs in italics represent anticipated increases in insurance premiums due to inflation or demographic changes in the unit.
**Unemployment insurance rate shown is an example for this table only. Rates and tax base differ between employers depending on layoff experience and state location.
***Worker's compensation rate and base is an example for this table only. Rates and bases vary depending on state law and work-related injury rates experienced by a particular employer.

five years, pension costs would be far less than the 5 percent of base wages. Health insurance usually provides a certain level of benefits (e.g., 80 percent of the first $5,000 of medical expenses and 100 percent above $5,000 annually). Unfortunately, employers have little control over the premium charged for the benefits. Thus, they can only estimate future costs.[4]

Employers need to evaluate salary-increase costs closely over the duration of the contract. For example, given interest rates and the total amounts paid, agreeing to increases of 50 cents, 50 cents, and 75 cents over a three-year agreement might cost the company less than 90 cents, 40 cents, and 30 cents. In the former case, the total increase is $1.75, while in the latter it is $1.60. But in the former case, an employee would earn 50 cents per hour more for three years ($1.50), 50 cents more for two years ($1.00), and 75 cents more for one year—a total of $3.25 more over the contract period. In the latter case, the employee would get 90 cents more for three years ($2.70), 40 cents for two years ($0.80), and 30 cents for one year—a total of $3.80. But postponing increases to give a larger total increase during the agreement raises the base wage rate for subsequent negotiations.[5] Management should also consider the costs of wages and benefits that will be granted to nonunion employees to preserve wage differentials and equity.

A detailed example of costing contract demands is included with the negotiating exercise at the end of this chapter. The method used for costing must enable management to calculate the effects of various union proposals quickly and provide an accurate estimate of their costs.

Bargaining Books

A **bargaining book** is a cross-referenced file that enables negotiators to quickly determine what contract clauses would be affected by a demand. It contains a history of specific contract terms and a code to indicate a proposal's relative importance to management. Many bargaining books are tied to spreadsheets so that answers to "what if" questions can be calculated quickly. Following is information likely to be included for each clause:

1. The history and text of the particular clause as it was negotiated in successive contracts.
2. Comparisons of the company's experience to those experiences of other companies in the industry, including comments on similarities and differences.
3. Company experiences both in operation and in grievances.
4. Legal issues, including both National Labor Relations Board (NLRB) determinations and judicial decisions.

[4] Ibid., pp. 60–69.

[5] Ibid., pp. 83–126.

TABLE 11.2 Management Planning for Contract Negotiations

Source: A. Freedman, *Managing Labor Relations* (New York: Conference Board, 1979), p. 24. Copyright © The Conference Board, 1979, used by permission.

	8 to 12 Months before Contract Expires	4 to 8 Months	1 to 4 Months before Commencement of Negotiations	During Negotiations	Postnegotiations
Local unit management	1. Assigns responsibility for community surveys estimating union demands and employee attitude. 2. Assesses the total corporate community and union compensation/benefits plans. 3. Assesses union/employee motivation and goals for impending negotiations.	1. Division management, corporate E.R., and corporate insurance project alternative benefit proposals that are to be designed and costed. 2. Continues all steps in the planning process.	1. Secures division approval of strategy, negotiating plans, and cost estimates.	1. Continues negotiations, clears significant cost variances from plan with division management. 2. Integrates benefit negotiations with all other items. 3. Secures agreement in accordance with plan. 4. Agrees with union on method and expense to inform employees of new contract terms.	1. Evaluates previous negotiations against plan within 30 days. 2. Assigns responsibilities for the planning process to integrate with the division's plans. 3. Identifies tentative objectives for next contract. 4. Completes wage/benefit adjustment form.
Division headquarters management	1. Ensures local unit is preparing for negotiations. 2. Plans, through annual financial plan, projected impact of inventory buildup, possible settlement costs, etc. 3. Identifies internal responsibilities and relationships (corporate, law, E.R., insurance, benefits, etc.).	1. Coordinates the development of strategy and negotiating plan, consulting with corporate employee relations and benefits. 2. Develops with local management, corporate E.R., and insurance projected alternative benefit proposals that are to be designed and costed.	1. Approves negotiating plan strategy. 2. Clears benefit and corporate policy variances from plan with corporate employee relations. 3. Communicates progress to senior management and corporate employee relations.	1. Provides, in addition to those points in "1 to 4 Months" column, identification of end position, and supports local negotiators in maintaining this position.	1. Evaluates all aspects of the previous negotiations within 45 days. 2. Identifies and communicates all long-range needs to executive management and corporate employee relations.

	4. Keeps corporate employee relations informed.	3. Makes broad judgment of impact on company and expected proposals in relation to division and corporate goals, strategy, and plans. 4. Evaluates plans to control costs and deviations from plan/strategy.	4. Approves cost variances from plan. 5. Identifies strike issues.		3. Integrates planning process in the division growth plan.
Corporate employee relations	1. Advises division and local management of union's national position on economics, benefits, and other issues. 2. Counsels on any anticipated conflict with corporate policy, other divisions, etc. 3. Provides available historical information pertinent to planning.	1. Assists division, local management, and corporate insurance in projecting and preparing alternative benefit proposals that are to be designed and costed. 2. Keeps division and local unit informed of any external developments having impact on its planning.	1. Consults with division on strategy and plans; available for on-the-scene assistance or to consult with international union officers; recommends corporate point of view on issues. 2. Approves all variances from corporate personnel policy and benefit plan proposals. 3. Ensures that all issues are resolved at the required levels.	1. Provides same as "1 to 4 Months" column. 2. Identifies to division management potential problems having corporate impact; if necessary, advises corporate management of unresolved major issues.	1. Counsels with union and/or unit management on negotiating experiences and/or evaluation of new contract. 2. Informs other units of results. 3. Initiates needed objectives for study, policy change, or corporate decision.
Corporate law department	1. Counsels on request.	1. Counsels on request and reviews current contract as required. 2. Approves benefit plan drafts to ensure legal compliance.	1. Counsels and drafts contract language on request. 2. Makes counsel available to review contract language before signing.	1. Provides same as "1 to 4 Months" column.	1. Reviews new contracts for possible problems; advises division and corporate employee relations.

5. Points the company would like to have changed, differentiated into minimum, maximum, and intermediate possibilities.
6. Changes the union may have previously demanded, the union's justification for these demands, and arguments management used to rebut them.
7. Data and exhibits, including cost and supporting analysis.
8. Progress in the current negotiation, together with drafts of various company proposals.[6]

Strike Preparation

As noted, anticipating vulnerability to a strike may substantially improve management's bargaining power. The employer also needs to plan how it will handle a potentially disruptive situation, particularly if it expects to continue operations.

The employer balances the costs and benefits of operating during a strike. If it operates, labor relations will undoubtedly be troublesome after a contract is negotiated, particularly if replacements have been hired. Additional security may be required, and picket-line observation will be important. Suppliers, customers, and government agencies will require notification if a strike occurs. For important customers, alternative methods of supply—including supply through competitors—may be necessary. Management views a credible threat to replace strikers as increasing bargaining power, but it may not have a major effect on outcomes.[7]

Strategy and Logistics

Finally, management must construct the strategies it will use to move toward an agreement. Management must decide who has the power to make concessions and what the final positions are beyond which it will not go.

A place to hold bargaining meetings must be arranged. If meetings will be held away from the employer's premises, cost-sharing questions must be resolved before negotiations start. The union will probably prefer a neutral site, given evidence (explored later in this chapter) that the employer takes a tougher bargaining stance on its home ground. Table 11.2 shows management time frames and functions involved in preparations for negotiations.

[6] M. S. Ryder, C. M. Rehmus, and S. Cohen, *Management Preparation for Bargaining* (Homewood, IL: Dow Jones–Irwin, 1966), pp. 65–66.

[7] J. W. Budd and W. E. Pritchett, "Does the Banning of Permanent Strike Replacements Affect Bargaining Power?" *Proceedings of the Industrial Relations Research Association*, 46 (1994), pp. 370–378.

UNION PREPARATION

To an extent, union preparations parallel management's, with important distinctions. Traditionally, unions see contract negotiations as an opportunity to improve their outcomes. Politically, leaders are expected to gain ground or face membership problems. The union may not be as well prepared to respond to possible management demands as management is to respond to union demands, especially if the national union is not involved in the negotiations.

National-Level Activities

National union research departments track contract settlements. The employer's ability to improve pay and benefits is assessed. Some unions retain financial analysts to parse financial information to determine whether the company's future financial condition matches what management negotiators claim. This is particularly important when management is demanding concessions. Unions that negotiate later than others within an industry are able to learn from other settlements what positions employers have taken with regard to various demands. This information helps to better estimate final settlement positions and avoid strikes.[8] The ability of union members to take strikes is assessed. The union's strike fund balance and the state of members' personal savings are important considerations when the union assesses its bargaining power. The national must also consider the target company's ability to withstand a strike and its vulnerability to competition.

If the negotiations involve many units of a single company or are conducted on an industrywide basis, the national is usually responsible for negotiating economic issues. National-level bargaining teams usually consist of national officers and officers of some key locals. The inclusion of senior members, who are paid more, leads to better-negotiated wage outcomes.[9]

Before negotiations begin, the national union may call a **bargaining convention** at which local delegates hear the national's plans for bargaining and propose their own issues. The convention has two major purposes. First, grassroots issues are raised for inclusion in the bargaining agenda. Second, the union's leadership has a forum for publicly committing itself to certain bargaining positions. Commitment to issues strengthens the union's bargaining power, because conceding later at the bargaining table will be more difficult. The union is also interested in homogenizing attitudes of members around the salience of important issues and heightening

[8] P. Kuhn and W. Gu, "Learning in Sequential Wage Negotiations: Theory and Evidence," *Journal of Labor Economics*, 17 (1999), pp. 109–140.

[9] M. Conlin and T. Furusawa, "Strategic Delegation and Delay in Negotiations over the Bargaining Agenda," *Journal of Labor Economics*, 18 (2000), pp. 55–73.

adversarial attitudes.[10] A study of teacher union members found that attitudes were less varied during negotiation years compared to "off" years. Attitudes toward pay and management declined, while attitudes related to teaching were unchanged.[11]

Local-Level Preparations

At the local level, the negotiating committee is usually elected with the other officers and has responsibility for negotiating contracts and processing grievances. The committee identifies contract clauses (e.g., allocation of overtime) susceptible to more than one interpretation or viewed as inequitable by the membership. Locals are also served by the national union's field representatives. As a result, members learn about settlements reached by other locals. They also learn which issues the national considers critically important to include in all contracts.

The employer's financial performance is known if the employer's shares are publicly traded, and this information may help the union to gauge the level of its economic demands. However, in firms that operate in several industries (e.g., General Electric is involved in power plant equipment, home appliances, medical electronics, financial services, and other industries), the relative contributions of each division are difficult to separate. The union knows the perishability of the employer's products, its competition, and its ability to operate during a strike. It is also aware of industry trends to move production offshore, move to another region of the country, or substitute capital for labor when high economic demands are won. Small bargaining units and independent unions are less likely to reach an impasse, possibly because of better ongoing knowledge of their counterparts, and they have less of a need to achieve a national pattern.[12]

Local unions hold membership meetings before the negotiations to inform the membership about important issues and to solicit more input. These meetings also help determine local members' commitment to bargaining issues in case a strike is called.

After negotiations are under way, the union usually calls another membership meeting. The negotiating committee reports on progress and requests authorization to call a strike if necessary. Overwhelming approval is usually given. A strike vote does not mean a strike will occur but rather gives bargainers the authority to call one after the contract expires.

[10] R. A. Friedman, *Front Stage, Back Stage: The Dramatic Structure of Labor Negotiations* (Cambridge, MA: MIT Press, 1994), pp. 27–45.

[11] M. A. Griffin, P. E. Tesluk, and R. R. Jacobs, "Bargaining Cycles and Work-Related Attitudes: Evidence for Threat-Rigidity Effects," *Academy of Management Journal,* 38 (1995), pp. 1709–1725. See also J. W. Budd, "The Internal Union Political Imperative for UAW Pattern Bargaining," *Journal of Labor Economics*, 16 (1995), pp. 43–55.

[12] R. Hebdon, D. Hyatt, and M. Mazerolle, "Implications for Small Bargaining Units and Enterprise Unions on Bargaining Disputes: A Look into the Future?" *Relations Industrielles*, 54 (1999), pp. 503–526.

NEGOTIATION REQUESTS

Section 8(d) of the Taft-Hartley Act requires that the party wanting to renegotiate the contract (usually the union) must notify the other party of its intention and offer to bargain a new agreement. Notice must come at least 60 days before the end of the contract if the requesting party intends to terminate the agreement at that time.

Employers usually propose a time—often not immediate—and place for negotiations to begin. Often this means initial demands are not made until 30 days or less before the contract expires. After notice is served, both parties start final bargaining preparations.

WHAT IS BARGAINING?

Bargaining, at a basic level, is the communication by two parties of the terms they require to consummate a transaction and the subsequent acceptance or rejection of the terms by both. *Negotiation* is the set of techniques parties use to influence the terms of the ultimate settlement.[13]

Bargaining is required because the parties have a conflict of interest on issues that jointly affect them. They must decide how to divide resources and other intangible issues in which they have joint interests. Negotiation requires the presentation of positions, their evaluation by the other party, and counterproposals. The process requires a sequential rather than a simultaneous mode because each party must have time to evaluate the other's proposals before responding.[14] Bargaining processes that involve proposals and counterproposals have higher expected payoffs than ones that involve making a proposal that is followed only by an acceptance or rejection.[15] Following is a description of bargaining or negotiating from an economic perspective:[16]

1. Negotiation occurs if both parties believe they will benefit by agreeing. The employer benefits by continuing to operate, and the union benefits by meeting member needs.
2. Concessions made during negotiations are voluntary. Concessions, in number and degree, may be influenced by the size of the demands and

[13] C. M. Stevens, *Strategy and Collective Bargaining Negotiations* (New York: McGraw-Hill, 1963), pp. 2–4.

[14] J. Z. Rubin and B. R. Brown, *Social Psychology of Bargaining and Negotiation* (New York: Academic Press, 1975), pp. 2–18.

[15] S. Blount and R. P. Larrick, "Framing the Game: Examining Frame Choice in Bargaining," *Organizational Behavior and Human Decision Processes*, 81 (2000), pp. 43–71.

[16] J. G. Cross, *The Economics of Bargaining* (New York: Basic Books, 1969), pp. 4–6.

the opponent's beliefs about the demander's willingness to concede, but any movements made are still voluntary.[17]

3. Negotiations are seen as productive. They may disclose areas of agreement or alternatives not previously considered by either party.
4. Negotiations as used in labor-management relations are characterized by verbal and/or written demands and concessions.
5. The bargaining process requires competition before the benefits available accrue to the parties involved in the bargaining.

A behavioral definition of the collective bargaining process includes the following:[18]

1. Collective bargaining includes some issues that generate conflict between the parties and others that require collaboration to accommodate the separate interests of both.
2. Attitudes and feelings play a part in the outcome of negotiations over and above what results from the bargainers' rationally defined attributes. Further, the bargainers do not come together only for this negotiation but must maintain an ongoing relationship. Thus, the results of the negotiations affect the long-term nature of the bargaining relationship.
3. The bargainers are often acting on behalf of others rather than for their own ends. They are representing constituents who evaluate their performance and may affect their tenure as negotiators.

Collective bargaining results because either labor or management is unwilling to agree to the other's total agenda. The following basic rules appear to govern the bargaining process:[19]

Rule 1 states that an impending contract expiration is necessary for the commencement of bargaining. During the course of the agreement, the parties have essentially agreed not to bargain, so the anticipated expiration allows the renewal of bargaining.

Rule 2 states that the initial bargaining demand should be large. Even though both parties are fairly certain the initial positions are substantially different from what each is willing to settle for, the large initial demand creates room for bargaining and allows relatively large concessions when the time is right.

Rule 3 explains that the negotiating agenda is determined by the initial demands and counterproposals. In other words, the issues initially raised by the parties constitute the focus of the bargaining.

[17] F. Zeuthen, *Problems of Monopoly and Economic Warfare* (Boston: Routledge and Kegan Paul, 1930).

[18] R. E. Walton and R. B. McKersie, *A Behavioral Theory of Labor Negotiations* (New York: McGraw-Hill, 1965), pp. 3–4.

[19] Stevens, *Strategy and Collective Bargaining Negotiations*, pp. 27–56.

Additions to the initial agenda are seldom made, and offers made in regard to these items can rarely be retracted.

Rule 4 precludes strikes or lockouts before a certain time and requires that notice be given if a strike is possible after this point.

Rule 5 provides that negotiations terminate when an agreement is reached. This rule may contain a requirement that unresolved issues be arbitrated or operations continued to preclude an emergency while an agreement is reached.

Rule 6 requires that the parties negotiate in good faith. To do this, the parties must respond to each other's demands and take no unilateral action to change the existing conditions before the end of negotiations.

Thus, bargaining involves parties that have a mutual interest in reaching agreement on a variety of issues. Negotiators are agents for others who stand to have their positions altered as a result of bargaining. Personal characteristics of bargainers, as well as the power of the parties they represent, are likely to influence the outcome. The union has strong interests in a continuing relationship, while management often has no intrinsic interest in its continuation.

BEHAVIORAL THEORIES OF LABOR NEGOTIATIONS

Distributive Bargaining

Bargaining includes four behavioral components. **Distributive bargaining** occurs when the parties disagree on an issue and when its settlement will involve a loss for one party and a gain for the other.[20] Assume the union wants a 60-cent hourly increase, and the parties ultimately settle for 30 cents. The 30-cent increase is a gain to labor and a loss to the company, which is not to say the loss is greater than the company expected. The company may have believed a settlement for anything less than 35 cents would be better than it expected. Distributive bargaining simply means some resource is in fixed supply, and one party's gain of that resource is the other party's loss.

Because distributive bargaining involves the division of outcomes on a bargaining issue, much of the negotiation process involves providing the opponent with information on the importance of a particular position, the likelihood of future movement on that position, and possible trade-offs that might be made for a concession. Through bargaining, each side may pick up cues as to where the other is willing to settle. An important part of this process is identifying the commitment a bargainer attaches to a position. One bargaining strategy would be to demand most of what

[20] Walton and McKersie, *A Behavioral Theory of Labor Negotiations*, p. 4.

would constitute an acceptable outcome and then threaten the other party with a strike if the demand is rejected. Evidence from bargaining experiments suggests, however, that fairness in outcomes is incorporated into bargainers' sequences of offers.[21] Table 11.3 portrays various management and union commitment statements and analyzes them as to their finality, specificity, and consequences for ignoring them.

Integrative Bargaining

Integrative bargaining is used when the parties face a common problem.[22] For example, a company may be experiencing high employee turnover which also leads to an erosion in union membership with union stewards needing to spend a great deal of time recruiting new members. Both parties would be motivated to work together to solve their joint problem.

Integrative bargaining occurs when employers and unions accommodate each other's needs without cost or through simultaneous gains. Integrative bargaining frequently involves employers' desires to improve flexibility and unions' desires for increased job security.[23] Some attention is currently being paid to so-called **mutual-gains bargaining.** This is an example of integrative bargaining in which the parties approach the negotiations with the idea that when it's concluded, both sides will have benefited.

Attitudinal Structuring

Attitudinal structuring refers to activities parties use to increase cooperation, hostility, trust, and/or respect.[24] Changed attitudes are expected to change predispositions to act. Relationship patterns will affect or follow one party's action toward the other, beliefs about legitimacy, level of trust, and degree of friendliness.[25] The predominant patterns of these attitudinal dimensions (shown in Figure 11.2) fall within the categories of conflict, containment-aggression, accommodation, cooperation, and collusion.

Conflict occurs when each party seeks to destroy the other's base. Neither acknowledges the legitimacy of the other, and each pursues activities to interfere with the other's existence. Containment-aggression involves demonstrating a high degree of militancy while recognizing the other's right to exist. Accommodation occurs when each party accords the other a legitimate role and allows the other to represent its position as a legitimate interest. Cooperation occurs when each party sees the other's position as legitimate and when common issues are of simultaneous concern to both parties. Collusion takes place when both parties join to subvert the goals of

[21] J. Ochs and A. E. Roth, "An Experimental Study of Sequential Bargaining," *American Economic Review*, 79 (1989), pp. 355–384.

[22] Walton and McKersie, *A Behavioral Theory of Labor Negotiations*, p. 5.

[23] Ibid., pp. 129 ff.

[24] Ibid., p. 5.

[25] Ibid., pp. 184–180.

TABLE 11.3 **Interpretive Comments about the Degree of Firmness in Statements of Commitments**

Source: B. M. Selekman, S. K. Selekman, and S. H. Fuller, *Problems in Labor Relations*, 2nd ed. (New York: McGraw-Hill, 1958), pp. 221, 226, 233. Material from these pages used in formulating table by R. E. Walton and R. B. McKersie in *A Behavioral Theory of Labor Negotiations* (New York: McGraw-Hill, 1965), pp. 96, 97.

(1) Statement of Commitment	(2) Degree of Finality of Commitment to a Position	(3) Degree of Specificity of That Position	(4) Consequences or Implications Associated with a Position (the threat)
From a negotiation involving a middle-size manufacturing plant in 1953: "We have looked very seriously and must present this [10-cent package] as our final offer."	The statement "must present this as our final offer" is not as strong as "this is our final offer." The strength of the word *final* is somewhat hedged by the more tentative phrase "must present this as."	The reference to the "10-cent package" was fairly specific.	No reference to the consequences. What the other party is expected to associate with the company's position would depend on the company's reputation or other confirming tactics. It would seem to imply that the company is ready to take a strike.
A union replied later, "The membership disagreed" with the company's economic proposal. "The present contract will not extend beyond 12:00 tonight."	Significantly, the membership was reported as only having "disagreed"; it did not "reject."	Reference to "economic proposal" is not specific. Hence the degree of disagreement is unclear.	By stating "the present contract will not extend," they *do not* state that there would be a strike. And in the particular context it was not clear that they would strike.
From the public statements regarding the 1955 negotiations between the UAW and the Ford Motor Company: Henry Ford II suggested alternative ways of achieving security "without piecemeal experimenting with dangerous mechanisms or guinea pig industries." This was a statement of opposition to the union's GAW proposal.	The statement contained no hint about the finality of his commitment of opposition.	The phrase "piecemeal experimenting . . ." clearly avoided reference to just what was objected to.	There were no references to the consequences associated with ultimate failure to agree.

(Continued)

TABLE 11.3 Interpretive Comments about the Degree of Firmness in Statements of Commitments (continued)

(1) Statement of Commitment	(2) Degree of Finality of Commitment to a Position	(3) Degree of Specificity of That Position	(4) Consequences or Implications Associated with a Position (the threat)
From the transcripts of a negotiation in the oil industry: Management stated, "If you say now or never or else [on a wage increase demanded by the union], I would say go ahead; we are prepared to take the consequences."	This was an explicit, binding commitment.	The company's position was also clear in this instance—it was not prepared to make any concession on the issue at hand.	The company was indicating its readiness for a work stoppage.
Later the union spokesman replied, "My advice to your employees will be not to become a party to any agreement which binds them to present wages."	What the union leader's advice will be is final. It says nothing about the finality of that position of the party, however.	The advice "not to become a party to any agreement which binds them to present wages" is hardly specific. Any increase would meet the test of this statement. In fact, even a reopening clause would avoid "binding the union to present wages."	Although at first glance this statement seems to commit the union to a wage increase "or else," it leaves the union the option of continuing with no contract and with signing a contract that has a way of adjusting wages in the future. The context did nothing to clarify just what consequences were to be associated with the union's position.
"I don't believe that they [the rest of the union committee] can recommend acceptance" of the company's offer.	"I don't believe" is more tentative than "I know they cannot."	"I don't believe that they can recommend acceptance" leaves unanswered whether the union committee would recommend that the membership not accept the offer or merely make no recommendation. Moreover, the reference is only to the company's *offer as it now stands.*	Not specified here, but the union had begun to refer to economic sanctions.

FIGURE 11.2 **Attitudinal Components of the Relationship Patterns**

Source: R. E. Walton and R. B. McKersie, *A Behavioral Theory of Labor Negotiations* (New York: McGraw-Hill, 1965), p. 189.

Attitudinal Dimensions	Pattern of Relationship				
	Conflict	**Containment-Aggression**	**Accommodation**	**Cooperation**	**Collusion**
Motivational orientation and action tendencies toward other	Competitive tendencies to destroy or weaken		Individualistic hands-off policy	Cooperative tendencies to assist or preserve	
Beliefs about legitimacy of other	Denial of legitimacy	Grudging acknowledgment	Acceptance of status quo	Complete legitimacy	Not applicable
Level of trust in conducting affairs	Extreme distrust	Distrust	Limited trust	Extended trust	Trust based on mutual blackmail potential
Degree of friendliness	Hate	Antagonism	Neutralism—courteousness	Friendliness	Intimacy—"sweetheart relationship"

the parties they represent; for example, when management covertly assists a union in organizing in return for a nonmilitant stance on bargaining.[26]

Attitudes toward bargaining have polarized since the 1970s. Almost 20 percent of a sample of large U.S. manufacturing employers adopt strategies beyond containment-aggression with a goal of eliminating unions. Conversely, almost one-third have adopted a cooperative approach, emphasizing joint union-management programs, while another one-third mix containment-aggression and cooperation strategies. Union-busting tactics were linked to companies with lower financial performance, while cooperation was related to companies with higher performance. In both cases, however, employers closed union facilities and opened new non-union plants.[27] One study of managerial stances toward labor relations found that tougher approaches were related to low sympathy for union goals, larger plant size, low capital intensity, low market share, and educational requirements for the job.[28]

Intraorganizational Bargaining

Intraorganizational bargaining is the process for achieving agreement within one of the bargaining groups.[29] For example, a management

[26] Ibid., pp. 186–188.

[27] D. G. Meyer and W. N. Cooke, "U.S. Labour Relations in Transition: Emerging Strategies and Company Performance," *British Journal of Industrial Relations*, 31 (1992), pp. 531–552.

[28] J. Godard, "Whither Strategic Choice? Do Managerial IR Ideologies Matter?" *Industrial Relations*, 36 (1997), pp. 206–228.

[29] Walton and McKersie, *A Behavioral Theory of Labor Negotiations*, p. 5.

bargainer might convince the management team that a 40-cent raise is necessary to avoid a strike, although management had determined previously that the union would likely settle for 35 cents. Intraorganizational bargaining also comprises the activities union negotiators engage in to sell an agreement to the membership.

The union negotiators must be able to sell an agreement to members once it has been reached. To do this, the team has to balance competing needs of subgroups within the union. One tactic is estimating some reasonable range of contract outcomes to members. Suggesting that excessive demands could damage the bargaining relations (see "Attitudinal Structuring," above) can help moderate initial demands. Difficulties in gaining agreement among negotiators within a team reduces or eliminates the opportunity to engage in mutual-gains bargaining.[30]

BARGAINERS AND THE BARGAINING ENVIRONMENT

As the behavioral theory noted, negotiation outcomes are likely to be influenced by the attributes of the parties and the context of the negotiations. Since the negotiations are complex and take place over a relatively extended time period, the parties need to be sophisticated about the manner in which they conduct negotiations and the characteristics of the participants.

Attributes of the Parties

Research has found that a variety of attitudes toward bargaining and gender differences influence outcomes. From the standpoint of attitudes toward bargaining, negotiators with prosocial values prefer to pursue a cooperative approach to bargaining, while competitive-social-value bargainers favor gains over losses.[31] This suggests that if the parties are engaged in distributive bargaining, using competitive bargainers will be to their advantage, while if integrative bargaining is desired, prosocial-value bargainers will be more likely to achieve an acceptable bargain. Straightforwardness in a bargainer is associated with a greater willingness to concede where bargaining power for the bargainer is high, but if bargaining power is equal low straightforwardness is associated with greater concessions.[32] Bargainers' aspiration levels influence outcomes,

[30] R. B. McKersie, T. Sharpe, T. A. Kochan, A. E. Eaton, G. Strauss, M. Morgenstern, "Bargaining Theory Meets Interest-Based Negotiations: A Case Study," *Industrial Relations*, 47 (2008), pp. 66–96.

[31] C. K. W. DeBreu and T. L. Boles, "Share and Share Alike or Winner Take All? The Influence of Social Value Orientation upon Choice and Recall of Negotiation Heuristics," *Organizational Behavior and Human Decision Processes*, 76 (1998), pp. 253–276.

[32] D. S. DeRue, D. E. Conlon, H. Moon, and H. W. Willaby, "When Is Straightforwardness a Liability in Negotiations? The Role of Integrative Potential and Structural Power," *Journal of Applied Psychology*, 94 (2009), pp. 1032–1047.

and expectations of settlement improve chances of reaching an agreement. However, differences in expectancies may lead to impasses where settlements could otherwise have been reached.[33]

The interaction of interpersonal orientation, motivational orientation, and power affects the bargaining relationship. Interpersonal orientation reflects responsiveness to others—reacting to, being interested in, and appreciating variations in another's behavior.[34] Motivational orientation pertains to whether bargaining interests are individual (seeking only the party's own interest), competitive (seeking to better an opponent), or cooperative (seeking positive outcomes of interest to both parties).[35] Power involves the range of bargaining outcomes through which the other party may be moved.[36] Power is low when the negotiator has few alternatives if an agreement is not reached.[37]

Given these individual differences and contextual variables, bargaining effectiveness should be greatest when interpersonal orientation is high, motivational orientation is cooperative, and power is equal and low.[38] The interaction of these variables may have no effect on how the parties structure their negotiating teams. Much of the structuring must depend on the goals of the party (e.g., breaking ground on productivity issues requires cooperation) and on beliefs about the tactics an opponent may use (e.g., assigning low-interpersonal-orientation bargainers to a team). The evidence regarding the interaction of individual differences and their effect on negotiation outcomes is mixed.[39]

An analysis of a large number of studies of male-female differences in negotiating behavior found that women are slightly less competitive bargainers than men, except in so-called tit-for-tat situations, in which they become more competitive.[40] Another large-scale analysis of bargaining studies found that men tend to negotiate slightly better outcomes than women.[41] A study of collective bargaining negotiations found that male

[33] S. B. White and M. A. Neale, "The Role of Negotiator Aspirations and Settlement Expectancies in Bargaining Outcomes," *Organizational Behavior and Human Decision Processes*, 57 (1994), pp. 303–317.

[34] Rubin and Brown, *Social Psychology of Bargaining and Negotiation*, p. 158.

[35] Ibid., p. 198.

[36] Ibid., p. 213.

[37] R. L. Pinkley, "Impact of Knowledge Regarding Alternatives to Settlement in Dyadic Negotiations: Whose Knowledge Counts?" *Journal of Applied Psychology*, 80 (1995), pp. 403–417.

[38] Rubin and Brown, *Social Psychology of Bargaining and Negotiation*, pp. 256–257.

[39] L. Thompson, "Negotiation Behavior and Outcomes: Empirical Evidence and Theoretical Issues," *Psychological Bulletin*, 108 (1990), pp. 515–532.

[40] A. E. Walters, A. F. Stuhlmacher, and L. L. Meyer, "Gender and Negotiator Competitiveness: A Meta-Analysis," *Organizational Behavior and Human Decision Processes*, 76 (1998), pp. 1–29.

[41] A. F. Stuhlmacher and A. E. Walters, "Gender Differences in Negotiation Outcomes: A Meta-Analysis," *Personnel Psychology*, 52 (1999), pp. 653–678.

negotiating teams were more likely to reach agreement. Curiously, female managers preferred **interest-based bargaining** (a form of mutual-gains bargaining), while female union negotiators preferred to avoid using it.[42]

The Process of Negotiation

Labor negotiations are seldom conducted privately. While the general public and most management and union constituents are excluded, the negotiating teams witness the bargainers' behavior. Bargaining with an audience makes concessions more difficult. Difficulty increases if the bargainer is highly loyal to the group or if the group is strongly committed to the bargaining issue. If the other party interprets a concession as a sign of weakness, retaliation is likely in subsequent negotiations.[43] Bargainers can use two tactics to overcome these problems. First, to increase an opponent's willingness to concede, the bargainer should respond to the opponent's concession in another important area or should indicate that a major concession required hard bargaining. Second, the negotiator should realize public commitment to an issue reduces the degree to which objective data can modify the position. But the skilled negotiator is aware that public commitment may be a tactic to justify support for an issue not really viewed as important.

Bargaining, by definition, involves a situation in which the goals of the negotiators are mostly in conflict. Because of this basic level of disagreement, escalating conflict is always a potential problem. Where the parties attack each other in negotiations, the responses tend to become increasingly extreme. When this occurs, an extreme distributive outcome is more likely. Lack of reciprocation or reciprocating in a noncontentious manner to a conflictual attack reduces the likelihood of a conflict spiral. A bargainer who responds to escalating conflict by labeling the process as ineffectual can also reduce conflict spirals.[44]

It's important to remember that the union is the employees' bargaining *agent*. Members expect that their bargainer will be an expert negotiator. The lead negotiator is usually a national union representative, an experienced local negotiator, or an attorney hired by the local. The top HRIR executive, attorney, or trade association representative represents management. The lead negotiator is responsible for structuring interactions within the negotiating team and coordinating communications between its members. The lead must project a hard public line to maintain the commitment of constituents but also be willing and able to concede to reach an agreement.[45]

[42] J. Cutcher-Gershenfeld, "The Social Contract at the Bargaining Table: Evidence from a National Survey of Labor and Management Negotiators," *Proceedings of the Industrial Relations Research Association*, 51, no. 2 (1999), pp. 214–222.

[43] Rubin and Brown, *Social Psychology of Bargaining and Negotiation*, pp. 43–54.

[44] J. M. Brett, D. L. Shapiro, and A. E. Lytle, "Breaking the Bonds of Reciprocity in Negotiations," *Academy of Management Journal*, 41 (1998), pp. 410–424.

[45] R. A. Friedman, *Front Stage, Back Stage*, pp. 47–112.

When there are several negotiators on each side, some act as information brokers during negotiations while others broker trust. As bargaining deadlines approach, roles of these negotiators blur, while gatekeeper and group representative roles become more distinct.[46]

Unless each party's initial demands are acceptable to the other, one or both must concede to reach an agreement. A problem occurs in offering concessions, however, since an offered concession may be reduced in value in the eyes of the recipient once it has been made. To avoid this problem, parties should be aware of the priority of demands so that the concession is perceived as having the highest value.[47] Alternatively, a concession costing a certain amount might be made and the opponent offered the choice of the area to which the concession will be applied.

The bargaining environment, perceptions of the bargainers, and complexity of the negotiations all influence outcomes. Conducting the negotiations in a neutral environment is important because a party is less willing to make concessions on its home ground. Thus, unions should avoid bargaining at the plant. The perceived characteristics of the opponent are also important. If a party perceives the opponent as nondeferring, then it will not seek concessions as vigorously. As more issues are injected into bargaining, **logrolling** (trading blocks of apparently dissimilar issues, such as a union shop for a work rule change) occurs frequently. Also, a sequence of offers, counteroffers, and issue settlement will result from bargaining on numerous issues.[48] Where several bargaining issues exist, simultaneously considering the issues is more likely to produce an agreement than following a sequential approach.[49]

Perceived fairness depends on the perspective of the offer's recipient. Bargaining experiments have found situations in which both sides submit offers they believe are fair and would result in settlement but a settlement does not occur because the opposing party does not perceive the offer as fair.[50] Offers that are labeled as "fair" but are offered without additional information often contain lower terms.[51]

[46] R. A. Friedman and J. Polodny, "Differentiation of Boundary Spanning Roles: Labor Negotiations and Implications for Role Conflict," *Administrative Science Quarterly*, 37 (1992), pp. 28–47.

[47] M. A. Neale and M. H. Bazerman, *Cognition and Reality in Negotiation* (New York: Free Press, 1991), pp. 75–77.

[48] Rubin and Brown, *Social Psychology of Bargaining and Negotiation*, pp. 130–156.

[49] L. R. Weingart, R. J. Bennett, and J. M Brett, "The Impact of Consideration of Issues and Motivational Orientation on Group Negotiation Process and Outcomes," *Journal of Applied Psychology*, 78 (1993), pp. 504–517.

[50] L. Babcock, G. Loewenstein, S. Issacharoff, and C. Camerer, "Biased Judgments of Fairness in Bargaining," *American Economic Review*, 85 (1995), pp. 1337–1343; and L. Babcock and G. Loewenstein, "Explaining Bargaining Impasse: The Role of Self-Serving Biases," *Journal of Economic Perspectives*, 11, no. 2 (1997), pp. 109–126.

[51] M. M. Pillutla and J. K. Murnighan, "Being Fair or Appearing Fair: Strategic Behavior in Ultimatum Bargaining," *Academy of Management Journal*, 38 (1995), pp. 1408–1426.

The types and levels of concessions convey information about each party's true position. For example, several concessions on a given issue followed by no subsequent movement could signal that a party has reached its resistance point. A retreat toward an original position may signal that a party is toughening its stance. Concessions appearing to reward the requester's behavior may increase cooperation between the parties and may strengthen the role of an attractive counterpart to the requester's constituency.[52] When parties are having difficulty achieving a settlement, shifting the focus from *how* to achieve a settlement to *why* a settlement is necessary appears to make the parties more amenable to movement.[53]

Bluffing

Bluffing has been studied extensively. In most negotiations, neither party expects to win its initial demands, and the other knows the demands exceed the expected settlement.

Bluffing is valuable because if one party stated a final position first, there can be no exploration of ways to reach an agreement. Bluffing allows a bargainer to test the firmness of an opponent's demands without a full commitment to a settlement and provides an opportunity to learn about the opponent's expectations.[54]

If bluffing is used to gain information, the union is likely to make a more extreme initial demand, because it has less financial information than does management. An examination of contract settlements between the Tennessee Valley Authority and its unions showed that agreements on economic issues are more often closer to employer than union proposals. However, if management is pressured by outside forces, settlements tend to be closer to the union's positions.[55] The union runs a risk if it makes very high demands, because these may increase management's cost expectations and lead to a strike over points the union would likely be willing to concede.[56]

Perceptions of Bargainers

Through the bargaining experience, negotiators form perceptions about their opponents' relative bargaining power and likely willingness to concede. A bargainer would have high strategic power if (1) agreement is

[52] Rubin and Brown, *Social Psychology of Bargaining and Negotiation*, pp. 276–278.

[53] J. F. Brett, G. B. Northcraft, and R. L. Pinkley, "Stairways to Heaven: An Interlocking Self-Regulation Model of Negotiation," *Academy of Management Review*, 24 (1999), pp. 435–451.

[54] Cross, *Economics of Bargaining*, pp. 169–180.

[55] R. C. Bowlby and W. R. Schriver, "Bluffing and the 'Split-the-Difference' Theory of Wage Bargaining," *Industrial and Labor Relations Review*, 32 (1979), pp. 161–171.

[56] H. S. Farber, "The Determinants of Union Wage Demands: Some Preliminary Empirical Evidence," *Proceedings of the Industrial Relations Research Association*, 30 (1977), pp. 303–310.

less advantageous for the bargainer than for the opponent, (2) more ways exist to satisfy the bargainer's needs than the opponent's needs, (3) more credible threats can be made by the bargainer than by the opponent, (4) maintaining the relationship is more important to the opponent, and (5) the opponent is under heavier time pressure.[57]

Within this framework, an example of condition 1 is an employer with a large backlog of orders. The company might be more motivated to settle because large profits would be lost by not doing so. The union faces relatively little pressure because it believes lost wages would be made up with overtime after a strike. As an example of condition 2, an employer struck in one of many plants producing the same output would have a distinct bargaining advantage. Condition 3 involves beliefs that threatened actions will be taken. It reinforces the idea that a strike may have value for future bargaining situations. In condition 4, unions are expected to be more responsive because the bargaining process is necessary to maintain the relationship. Finally, condition 5 involves employers that deal in perishable goods, such as food producers and air travel (holiday travel lost because of strikes), and thus are under greater pressure to settle on the union's terms.

The Roles of the Actors in Negotiations

An analysis of the dramatic characteristics of labor negotiations suggests "front-stage" activities are directed at different audiences—the lead negotiator is performing for the negotiating team, and team members are performing for each other and their constituencies. The show aims to demonstrate adherence and effort toward bargaining goals.[58] Figure 11.3 diagrams the acting and audiences.

One tactic, used particularly by management, limits participation of those likely to take militant stances or be unwilling to modify positions as bargaining continues. This gives the negotiator greater freedom to respond during the bargaining process.[59]

In the later stages of bargaining, lead negotiators may conduct private sidebar conferences to convey information about each party's willingness to concede, the relative importance of issues, and the like. The ability to productively use sidebars requires a climate of trust between the negotiators.[60]

Negotiators are concerned with their reputations after the agreement is reached. A settlement may help or hinder a negotiator's career, depending on the outcome and the degree to which he or she is associated with it.

[57] J. M. Magenau and D. G. Pruitt, "The Social Psychology of Bargaining: A Theoretical Synthesis 1," in G. M. Stephenson and C. J. Brotherton, eds., *Industrial Relations: A Social Psychological Approach* (New York: Wiley, 1979), pp. 197–199.

[58] Friedman, *Front Stage, Back Stage*, pp. 85–99.

[59] Ibid., pp. 281–340.

[60] Ibid., pp. 94–97.

FIGURE 11.3
Audience Structure for Main-Table Negotiations

Source: R. A. Friedman, *Front Stage, Back Stage, The Dramatic Structure of Labor Negotiations* (Cambridge, MA: MIT Press, 1994), p. 86.

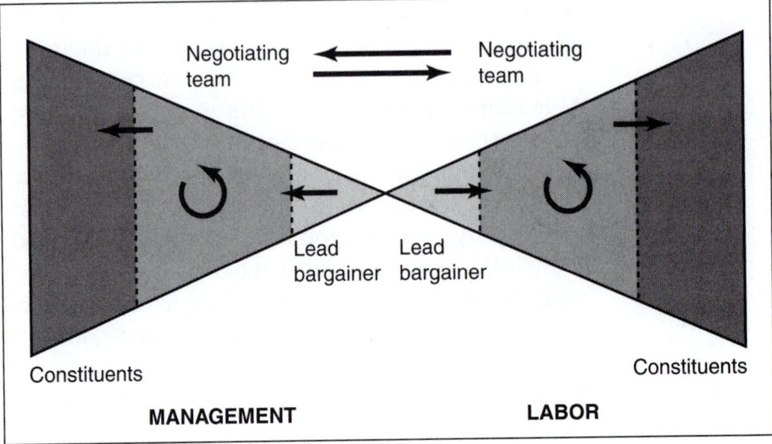

Negotiators who have particular information may control the direction of the negotiations and have greater effects on their outcome.[61]

CONTRACT NEGOTIATIONS

In this section we examine activities involved in bargaining a new contract. Activities include tactics, information requirements, and union and employer requirements for agreements. Labor laws require that the parties meet at reasonable times and places and bargain in good faith over issues involving wages, hours, and terms and conditions of employment.

Initial Presentations

Although not legally required to do so, the party requesting changes in its favor presents its demands first. Thus, the union presents demands when seeking improvements and management when seeking concessions. At this presentation, the initiating side specifies all areas of the contract in which changes are desired. This session also allows the union to present all grievances or positions developed through the membership meetings. The union does not expect to gain all of these changes, but as a political organization it has an obligation to state the positions of individual members. It also creates new bargaining positions that alert management to expect more vigorous future demands in these areas.

The responding party may choose not to reply to demands at the opening session. When it responds, its offer is usually different from what it would be willing to settle for. If management adheres to or refuses to move

[61] K. L. Valley, S. B. White, M. A. Neale, and M. H. Bazerman, "Agents as Information Brokers: The Effects of Information Disclosure on Negotiated Outcomes," *Organizational Behavior and Human Decision Processes*, 51 (1992), pp. 220–236.

past its original position, it must provide information, if asked by the union, to support any positions based on an inability to pay.[62]

Bargaining on Specific Issues

If the issues are complex, the negotiating committee and company representatives frequently divide themselves into subcommittees to negotiate specific issues. For example, contract language on work standards may be handled by a subgroup of production employees or union stewards and production supervisors. Usually the subgroups do not have the authority to finalize issues they discuss, because these may form part of a trade-off package, but they may bring tentative agreements or positions back to the main table for consideration.

At the main table, issues not forming part of a combined package or being used as trade-offs may be initialed by the parties as finalized for the ultimate agreement. Thus, the final settlement is not necessarily a coalescence on all issues simultaneously but rather a completion of negotiations on final areas in which disagreement exists.

In most negotiations, nonwage issues—union security clauses, seniority provisions, work rules, and the like—are decided first. Wage and benefit issues are often settled as a package near the end of negotiations. As noted earlier in discussing the certainty of outcomes and the potential costs of package characteristics, management must consider wages and benefits carefully.

Tactics in Distributive Bargaining

Each party enters the negotiations with certain positions it hopes to win. Management has an economic position it wants to protect. The union has specific wage and benefit demands it perceives as achievable. Bargaining is the process by which each party tries to influence the perceptions of the other to adopt its positions as a final outcome.

The following represents the types of approaches the parties use to influence the resistance points of their opponents through information transmission:

> "I do not think you really feel that strongly about the issues you have introduced."
>
> "I believe that a strike will cost you considerably more than you are willing to admit."
>
> "I believe a strike will cost me almost nothing in spite of your statements to the contrary."
>
> "I feel very strongly about this issue regardless of what you say."[63]

[62] *NLRB* v. *Truitt Mfg. Co.*, 351 U.S. 149 (1956).

[63] Walton and McKersie, *A Behavioral Theory of Labor Negotiations*, p. 60.

Certain tactics may be used during negotiations to assess the actual point at which an opponent would prefer to settle. Addressing questions to various members of the negotiating team may gain, through their responses, an overall flavor of the most important issues. To highlight the importance of a particular issue, the party proposing the issue may provide detailed information to clearly establish its position. For example, a firm faced with a large wage demand may provide detailed data on the wage costs of its competition and its inability to pass increases through to its customers.

In one tactic, a party tries to get its opponent to see that the opponent's demands will not result in as positive an outcome as it expects. For example, the union may see a demand for more paid time off as a way to increase employment, but the company may show that increased costs will result in replacing existing workers with robots.

Committing to a Position

Committing to a position can be a powerful bargaining tool. If the opposition perceives no more movement will be made on a specific issue, it may then concede to the offered point if within its settlement range. Three components of a position signaling commitment are: finality (communication indicating no further movement will be made), specificity (the clarity of the position), and the consequences (the contingent outcomes, such as a strike, that will occur if the demand is not accepted as proposed).[64]

Several tactics may signal commitment to the opposition. Most relate to the issue of consequences. For example, a strike authorization vote signals union commitment. A company preparing to close operations or refusing to accept new orders signals it is prepared to call the union's bluff. Consider the 1981 Federal Aviation Administration–Professional Air Traffic Controllers Organization dispute in which President Reagan indicated the government would not bargain during a strike (finality) and that all strikers must return to work within 48 hours (specificity) or be permanently severed from federal employment (consequences).

Deadlines

Negotiations are seldom settled until close to a deadline.[65] There are two reasons for this. First, the more time available, the more information that might be disclosed to lead to a better final solution. Second, the constituents of the bargainers may believe that settlement before the deadline constitutes poor effort and that their position could have been improved.[66]

[64] Ibid., p. 93.

[65] A. E. Roth, J. K. Murnighan, and F. Schoumaker, "The Deadline Effect in Bargaining: Some Experimental Evidence," *American Economic Review*, 78 (1988), pp. 806–823.

[66] B. P. McCall, "Interest Arbitration and the Incentive to Bargain: A Principal-Agent Approach," *Journal of Conflict Resolution*, 34 (1990), pp. 151–167.

The presence of a deadline increases the rate of concessions.[67] The deadline effect may help explain why negotiations under Taft-Hartley jurisdiction usually take substantially less time than Railway Labor Act negotiations.

Settlements and Ratifications

When the negotiators agree on a new contract, the union team still has responsibilities to fulfill before the final agreement is signed. In most unions, two hurdles remain to be cleared before the tentative agreement becomes permanent. First, the international union must approve the agreement. This ensures that a local will not negotiate an agreement substantially inferior to other contracts in the international or other unions. Second, most unions require a referendum among the bargaining unit's membership to ratify the contract. To do this, the bargaining team conducts a membership meeting and explains the contract gains won in negotiations. The team then generally recommends settlement, and the members vote to accept or reject.

If the negotiating committee recommends acceptance, the membership nearly always votes to ratify. However, some exceptions occur. Reasons for contract rejections include an inability to alter positions through bargaining, final positions outside the opponent's settlement range, hostile relationships between the parties, poor coordination in bargaining, or a failure to estimate correctly the priorities of the membership.[68] A study of a specific contract ratification found votes for approval were more likely to come from union members who were satisfied with their pay, believed they had few alternative employment options, were positively disposed toward the quality of the union's representation, and had lower job satisfaction.[69] Intense communication between union officers and rank-and-file members together with a few contract changes that were more appealing to the median voter within a unit led to the ratification of a contract that was initially rejected.[70]

When the negotiating committee unqualifiedly recommends ratification but the contract is rejected, union negotiators are placed in a precarious position. Management may question whether they are in touch with their constituents. During the negotiations, management may have conceded on issues of seeming importance to union bargainers but of questionable relevance to members. The negotiating committee also may

[67] S. G. S. Lim and J. K. Murnighan, "Phases, Deadlines, and the Bargaining Process," *Organizational Behavior and Human Decision Processes*, 58 (1994), pp. 153–171.

[68] D. R. Burke and L. Rubin, "Is Contract Rejection a Major Collective Bargaining Problem?" *Industrial and Labor Relations Review*, 26 (1973), pp. 820–833.

[69] J. E. Martin and R. D. Berthiaume, "Predicting the Outcome of a Contract Ratification Vote," *Academy of Management Journal*, 38 (1995), pp. 916–928.

[70] J. E. Martin, "An Individual Level Study of Contract Ratification Support," *Industrial Relations*, 47 (2008), pp. 102–107.

have difficulty selling a subsequent settlement to the membership because its credibility was undermined by the earlier rejection.

Sometimes, management questions whether the bargaining committee is representing the true wishes of the membership. Management bargainers may suggest a package be submitted to the membership for ratification. The company may not insist that the union take a proposal to its members for a vote because this is not a mandatory bargaining issue.[71] If union negotiators are reasonably certain a proposal that management wants put to a vote will be rejected, it might strengthen its bargaining position by taking the proposal to the bargaining unit and having it voted down.

Nonagreement

Occasionally the parties may fail to reach an agreement, either before or after the contract expires. A variety of activities may then occur, including mediation, strikes, lockouts, replacements, management's implementation of its last offer, and arbitration. Impasses lead to very complex issues, which will be detailed in Chapter 12.

THE BARGAINING ENVIRONMENT AND OUTCOMES

During the 1980s when companies requested concessions, unions responded most frequently by asking for greater job security, limits on **subcontracting**, or some form of profit-sharing or **gainsharing** program. They were most successful in obtaining job security and gainsharing but very unsuccessful in limiting subcontracting.[72] Table 11.4 shows perceptions of factors that unions and managements felt heavily influenced negotiations in 1996 and 1999.

Increasingly, bargainers have been urged to pursue integrative solutions using interest-based bargaining methods. One study examined factors related to negotiations that resulted in contracts with one of more of the following innovations: new pay systems (pay for knowledge, gainsharing, or profit sharing), worker input into managerial decisions, team-based work systems, joint committees, or any combination of two or more of these. For new pay systems, the degree of international competition, threats to replace workers, and brainstorming sessions were significantly related to their implementation. For worker input in management decisions, first contracts, interest-based bargaining training, and brainstorming sessions were positively related, while male union bargainers were negatively associated with these innovations. For team-based work systems, the need for flexibility and brainstorming sessions were positively related, but being in the service sector was negatively related. More than

[71] *NLRB* v. *Wooster Division of Borg Warner Corp.*, 356 U.S. 342 (1958).

[72] A. Freedman, *The New Look in Wage Policy and Employee Relations* (New York: Conference Board, 1985), pp. 10–15.

TABLE 11.4
Union and Management Perceptions of Factors "Heavily Influencing" Collective Bargaining Contract Negotiations

Source: J. Cutcher-Gershenfeld and T. A. Kochan, "Taking Stock: Collective Bargaining at the Turn of the Century," *Industrial and Labor Relations Review,* 58 (2004), p. 17. © Cornell University.

	Union		Management	
Factors Influencing Bargaining	**1996**	**1999**	**1996**	**1999**
Competitive Pressure				
Domestic competition	22%	12%	22%	23%
International competition	8	11	4	6
Flexibility/Capability Pressure				
Work rule flexibility	20	15	15	19
Pressure to upgrade skills	5	7	4	5
New technology	6	5	2	4
Trust				
Low trust	28	20	14	10
Employment Fear				
Fear of job loss	24	17	12	10
Threat of plant closing	8	7	5	5
Fear of movement to nonunion operation	4	4	1	1

one innovation was positively related to a first contract, international competition, the need for flexibility, threats to replace workers, interest-based bargaining training, and brainstorming sessions.[73] This study seems to indicate that interest-based bargaining may be spurred by credible threats as long as it doesn't lead to a premature hardening of positions. The threats and information that makes them credible may force a consideration of innovations.

Companies that are vulnerable to strikes or that have been struck in the past are more likely to settle above their wage targets. This trend lends credence to the suggestion that striking may constitute an investment in bargaining power for the union. Companies emphasizing union containment goals as well as bargaining goals are more likely to achieve their targets.[74] However, success in bargaining cannot necessarily be attributed to a hard-line approach because a heavily unionized firm cannot readily have a credible containment policy. Containment may be related to relatively small proportions of employees being unionized, which, in turn, increases bargaining leverage. Conservative accounting practices, such as the use of last-in, first-out (LIFO) inventory valuation and accelerated depreciation practices, were related to more success in obtaining concessions from unions.[75]

[73] J. Cutcher-Gershenfeld and T. A. Kochan, "Taking Stock: Collective Bargaining at the Turn of the Century," *Industrial and Labor Relations Review*, 58 (2004), pp. 3–26.

[74] Freedman, *Managing Labor Relations*, p. 48.

[75] R. D. Mautz, Jr., and F. M. Richardson, "Employer Financial Information and Wage Bargaining: Issues and Evidence," *Labor Studies Journal*, 1, no. 3 (1992), pp. 35–52.

An extensive study of smaller unionized Michigan firms examined negotiations between 1987 and 1991. Only about one-third of settlements were achieved through traditional bargaining. The rest were either highly contentious or cooperative. Fully one-sixth were not settled within a week after the old contract expired. Long delays were associated with unilateral imposition of a new contract by management. For contracts that involved multiple rounds of concessions, wages were reduced first and benefits second, with few promises of increased job security. Open warfare preceded a transition from traditional to either highly contentious or cooperative bargaining relationships. Strikes tended to speed settlements but could be used successfully only by unions with reasonable levels of bargaining power.[76]

Firms with higher amounts of asset-specific investments had lower bargaining power. Unions captured a larger portion of profits through wage increases in these situations. In the long run, high union density lowers investment and employment growth.[77]

Summary

Managements prepare for bargaining by gathering internal and comparative data, including employee distributions by job, seniority, shift, and so forth. Other data relate to wage increases in other negotiations, local labor market rates, and so on. Many different functional departments obtain information and help in formulating a management negotiating position. Contract terms that may be renegotiated must be costed to assess their relative financial impact on the employer. Bargaining books assist in negotiations.

Unions prepare for bargaining by determining what issues are important to their members. The political nature of unions requires that they pay attention to the interests of major employee groups. National-level preparation involves collecting and analyzing data, while local-level preparation formulates bargaining positions and involves members in forming a negotiating team.

Bargaining occurs in situations where both parties expect the act of bargaining to improve their positions. One side may expect an improvement in benefits, while the other gains certainty in outcomes through the contracting process. Attributes of the bargaining situation and the personalities of the parties involved influence outcomes. Bluffing appears to be important because it allows the parties to explore the significance of and

[76] J. Cutcher-Gershenfeld, P. McHugh, and D. Power, "Collective Bargaining in Small Firms: Preliminary Evidence of Fundamental Change," *Industrial and Labor Relations Review*, 49 (1995), pp. 195–212.

[77] J. K. Cavanaugh, "Asset-Specific Investment and Unionized Labor," *Industrial Relations*, 37 (1998), pp. 35–50.

reasons behind demands without initially stating positions they might want to retreat from later.

Collective bargaining is suggested to have four components: distributive bargaining (one party's gain is the other's loss), integrative bargaining (a settlement improves both parties' positions), attitudinal structuring (attempts to create atmospheres likely to obtain desired concessions), and intraorganizational bargaining (the parties try to convince constituents within their own organizations to change positions).

Bargaining usually begins with the party seeking a change presenting its positions. Changes are handled sequentially, although logrolling occurs on occasion. Following a tentative agreement, the union's members must ratify it. Failure to ratify appears related primarily to difficulties in attitudinal structuring and intraorganizational bargaining.

Discussion Questions

1. To what extent should management allow the union to select the components of an economic package in a contract negotiation?
2. What balance should exist between local-level and national-level influences in negotiations? Should this balance differ by bargaining issue?
3. How could an opponent in bargaining overcome what appears to be a strong commitment to an issue by its opposite member?
4. What strategies should management use in bargaining when a settlement that was unanimously recommended by the union's bargaining team is rejected?
5. Why would it be harder for heavily unionized organizations to settle on their bargaining targets than for those with a small proportion of unionized employees?
6. What attitudinal structuring and intraorganizational bargaining tactics would be different for integrative as compared to distributive bargaining?

Key Terms

Roll-up, *332*
Bargaining book, *335*
Bargaining convention, *339*
Distributive bargaining, *343*
Integrative bargaining, *344*
Mutual-gains bargaining, *344*
Attitudinal structuring, *344*
Intraorganizational bargaining, *347*
Interest-based bargaining, *350*
Logrolling, *351*
Subcontracting, *358*
Gainsharing, *358*
Across-the-board, *365*

Mock Negotiating Exercise

This negotiating exercise will help you develop an appreciation of and insight into the principles and problems of collective bargaining. Using information covered to this point in the text, you will act as a member of a union or management bargaining team in formulating strategies and tactics for negotiations. Following a more detailed approach to contract costing and instructions, the exercise presents a copy of the expiring contract between General Materials & Fabrication Company (GMFC) and Local 384 of the United Steelworkers of America.

A. CONTRACT COSTING

Contract costing is not straightforward. The cost changes often depend on changes in employee seniority, the way increased vacations are handled, and similar issues not directly associated with the amount of an hourly wage increase. A costing example will be created so that you can see the effects. Assume a bargaining unit containing 100 employees will renegotiate its contract. Five pay grades presently have pay rates, given length of service in the organization, as shown in Table MN.1.

The 100 employees are distributed by grade and seniority, as shown in Table MN.2.

Table MN.3 shows the historic turnover rates (proportion of employees who quit or retire in a given year) of bargaining-unit employees by grade and seniority level.

TABLE MN.1
Pay Rates

	Seniority				
Grade	**< 1 yr.**	**1–2 yr.**	**3–5 yr.**	**6–10 yr.**	**> 10 yr.**
1	8.50	9.00	9.50	9.50	9.50
2	9.50	10.00	10.50	11.00	11.00
3	10.50	11.00	11.50	12.00	12.50
4	11.50	12.00	12.50	13.00	13.50
5	12.50	13.00	13.50	14.00	14.50

TABLE MN.2
Employment Levels

	Seniority					
Grade	**< 1 yr.**	**1–2 yr.**	**3–5 yr.**	**6–10 yr.**	**> 10 yr.**	**Total**
1	8	2				10
2	2	4	14			20
3		5	15	20	5	45
4			3	6	6	15
5				2	8	10
Total	10	11	32	28	19	100

TABLE MN.3
Turnover Rates by Grade and Seniority

Grade	Seniority				
	< 1 yr.	1–2 yr.	3–5 yr.	6–10 yr.	> 10 yr.
1	0.25	0.10	0.10	0.10	0.10
2	0.10	0.05	0.05	0.00	0.00
3	0.05	0.05	0.05	0.00	0.02
4	0.00	0.00	0.00	0.00	0.03
5	0.00	0.00	0.00	0.00	0.10

The employer's retirement plan provides for full vesting of benefits at five years of service. Employees who quit before accruing five years of service forfeit their accrued benefits. The plan is fully funded to provide pensions for present employees, taking anticipated turnover into account. The retirement program provides that employees will receive an equivalent of 5 percent of their gross pay (regular and overtime) contributed to their pension funds.

The health care program provides hospital and medical coverage paid by the employer. Twenty-five of the employees are single and without dependents. The other 75 have families, but of these, 5 are families in which both the husband and the wife are employed by this company, so premiums need not be paid for both. Health care premiums are $300 per month for single employees and $700 per month for those with dependents. Premiums are expected to increase 10 percent next year for both single and family policies.

Under the contract, overtime is apportioned (within grade) on the basis of seniority, with each employee entitled to five hours of overtime before the next junior employee in that grade is entitled. After all employees within the grade have received overtime, the cycle is repeated. During the last year, overtime was available in the following number of hours by grade: grade 1—520 hours, grade 2—840, grade 3—1,640, grade 4—1,020, and grade 5—780. The overtime premium for all these hours was 50 percent. Table MN.4 shows the average number of hours of overtime per employee by seniority and grade level during the past year.

All employees receive nine paid holidays and three paid sick days each year. The average employee takes two sick days, regardless of grade or

TABLE MN.4
Hours of Overtime

Grade	Seniority					
	< 1 yr.	1–2 yr.	3–5 yr.	6–10 yr.	> 10 yr.	Total
1	51.25	55.00				520
2	40.00	40.00	42.86			840
3		35.00	35.00	37.00	40.00	1,640
4			65.00	67.50	70.00	1,020
5				75.00	78.75	780

TABLE MN.5
Average Wage Cost per Employee

Grade	Seniority				
	< 1 yr.	1–2 yr.	3–5 yr.	6–10 yr.	> 10 yr.
1	18,333	19,463	19,760	19,760	19,760
2	20,330	21,400	22,515	22,880	22,880
3	21,840	23,458	24,524	25,626	26,750
4	23,920	24,960	27,219	28,356	29,498
5	26,000	27,040	28,080	30,695	31,873

seniority levels. Vacations are tied to length of service. Employees with less than one year of service do not accrue vacation time. Those with 1 to 2 years are entitled to one week; 3 to 5 years, two weeks; 6 to 10 years, three weeks; and more than 10 years, four weeks.

All employees are presently working on one shift, and all have two paid break periods of 10 minutes in the morning and afternoon.

Table MN.5 shows the average wage cost per employee by grade and seniority level under the expiring contract. It is calculated by multiplying the wage rate by 2,080 (the number of hours in a normal work year) plus the number of overtime hours from the appropriate cell in Table MN.4 times 1.5 (to account for the overtime premium rate).

Social security and Medicare tax rates total 7.65 percent. Assume that unemployment insurance is 4 percent on the first $10,000 of earnings and that workers' compensation insurance premiums are 2.2 percent of total payroll. With pensions vesting in five years, the pension contribution for people with less than six years of service must be multiplied by the likelihood that they will remain for that period to get the total contribution required. Table MN.6 is a matrix of probabilities of an employee remaining long enough to receive vested benefits.

Present pension costs by grade and seniority (number of employees times wage cost times retention factor) are shown in Table MN.7.

Present wage costs (straight time and overtime at time and a half) are obtained by multiplying the cells in Table MN.2 by corresponding cells in Table MN.5. The results are shown in Table MN.8.

TABLE MN.6
Pension Vesting Probabilities

Grade	Seniority				
	< 1 yr.	1–2 yr.	3–5 yr.	6–10 yr.	> 10 yr.
1	0.61	0.81	0.90	1.00	1.00
2	0.81	0.90	0.95	1.00	1.00
3	0.86	0.90	0.95	1.00	1.00
4	1.00	1.00	1.00	1.00	1.00
5	1.00	1.00	1.00	1.00	1.00

TABLE MN.7
Total Pension Costs*

	Seniority					
Grade	< 1 yr.	1–2 yr.	3–5 yr.	6–10 yr.	> 10 yr.	Total
1	4,455	1,576	0	0	0	6,031
2	1,651	3,863	14,973	0	0	20,487
3	0	5,293	17,473	25,626	6,688	55,079
4	0	0	4,083	8,507	8,849	21,439
5	0	0	0	3,070	12,749	15,819
Total	6,106	10,732	36,528	37,202	28,286	118,855

*All amounts rounded to nearest dollar.

TABLE MN.8
Total Wage Costs*

	Seniority					
Grade	< 1 yr.	1–2 yr.	3–5 yr.	6–10 yr.	> 10 yr.	Total
1	146,668	38,925	0	0	0	185,593
2	40,660	85,600	315,211	0	0	441,471
3	0	117,288	367,856	512,520	133,750	1,131,414
4	0	0	81,656	170,138	176,985	428,779
5	0	0	0	61,390	254,983	316,373
Total	187,328	241,813	764,723	744,048	565,718	2,503,628

*All amounts rounded to nearest dollar.

The total labor costs in the last year of the expiring contract were:

Wages	\$2,503,628
Pension contributions	118,855
Social Security (0.0765 × wages)	191,528
Unemployment insurance (0.04 × \$10,000 × number of employees)	40,000
Worker's compensation (0.022 × wages)	55,080
Health insurance (25 singles × \$300 × 12 months)	90,000
Health insurance (75 families × \$700 × 12 months)	630,000
(Less health insurance for 5 husband-wife duplications)	(42,000)
Total	\$3,587,091

For the coming year, assume the following set of contract demands:

1. A 50-cent **across-the-board** wage increase.
2. Ten cents additional per grade from grade 2 on.
3. A 6 percent pension contribution.
4. One week additional vacation for all employees with more than five years of service.

Assume that turnover rates will be the same next year, all terminees and retirees are replaced at grade 1, and present employees are promoted to fill their vacancies. Five will be lost: grade 1, < 1 year—2; grade 2, 3 to 5 years—1; grade 3, 3 to 5 years—1; and grade 5, >10 years—1. Employees will also increase one year in seniority. Assume that employees within seniority groups are relatively evenly distributed and those promoted are most often the most senior person applying, but in only two-thirds of cases is the most senior person eligible. The vacation demand will result in the company losing 56 weeks of work. Assume that an additional employee must be hired at grade 1 to make up for 42 weeks of the loss and the other 14 weeks must be worked as overtime, evenly distributed among employees in grades 3 to 5 according to seniority rules. This results in 560 additional hours, with 200 hours apportioned to grade 5 and 180 each to grades 3 and 4. At the end of the contract year, the grade and seniority matrix (after turnover) could look as shown in Table MN.9.

Table MN.10 shows the seniority level and distribution of employees after promotions have been made and new hires added.

If the union wins its demands, the new wage rates would be as shown in Table MN.11.

Overtime for the coming year (assuming it is the same as last year except for additional hours necessary if the vacation demand is won) is shown in Table MN.12.

Table MN.13 shows the average wage cost per employee for straight time and overtime, given the proposed demands.

Multiplying Table MN.10 by Table MN.13 yields the total wage cost (less benefits) under the new contract. The results are shown in Table MN.14.

Multiplying turnover probability (Table MN.6) by total wages in Table MN.14 gives the pension costs under the new contract as 6 percent. These are shown in Table MN.15.

TABLE MN.9
Remaining Employees

	Seniority					
Grade	< 1 yr.	1–2 yr.	3–5 yr.	6–10 yr.	> 10 yr.	Total
1	6	2	0	0	0	8
2	2	4	13	0	0	19
3	0	5	14	20	5	44
4	0	0	3	6	6	15
5	0	0	0	2	7	9
Total	8	11	30	28	18	95

TABLE MN.10
Seniority Levels with Promotions and New Hires

	Seniority					
Grade	< 1 yr.	1–2 yr.	3–5 yr.	6–10 yr.	> 10 yr.	Total
1	6	5	0	0	0	11
2	0	6	12	2	0	20
3	0	2	12	23	8	45
4	0	0	2	6	7	15
5	0	0	0	2	8	10
Total	6	13	26	33	23	101

TABLE MN.11
Postnegotiation Pay Rates

	Seniority				
Grade	< 1 yr.	1–2 yr.	3–5 yr.	6–10 yr.	> 10 yr.
1	9.00	9.50	10.00	10.00	10.00
2	10.10	10.60	11.10	11.60	11.60
3	11.20	11.70	12.20	12.70	13.20
4	12.30	12.80	13.30	13.80	14.30
5	13.40	13.90	14.40	14.90	15.40

TABLE MN.12
Postnegotiation Overtime Distribution

	Seniority					
Grade	< 1 yr.	1–2 yr.	3–5 yr.	6–10 yr.	> 10 yr.	Total
1	45.00	50.00				520
2		40.00	42.50	45.00		840
3		40.00	40.00	40.00	42.50	1,820
4			80.00	80.00	80.00	1,200
5				95.00	98.75	980

TABLE MN.13
Postnegotiation Wage Cost per Employee

	Seniority				
Grade	< 1 yr.	1–2 yr.	3–5 yr.	6–10 yr.	> 10 yr.
1	19,328	20,473	20,800	20,800	20,800
2	21,008	22,684	23,796	24,911	24,128
3	23,296	25,038	26,108	27,178	28,298
4	25,584	26,624	29,260	30,360	31,460
5	27,872	28,912	29,952	33,115	34,313

TABLE MN.14
Postnegotiation Total Wage Cost*

	Seniority					
Grade	< 1 yr.	1–2 yr.	3–5 yr.	6–10 yr.	> 10 yr.	Total
1	115,965	102,363	0	0	0	218,328
2	0	136,104	285,548	49,822	0	471,474
3	0	50,076	313,296	625,094	226,380	1,214,846
4	0	0	58,520	182,160	220,220	460,900
5	0	0	0	66,231	274,505	340,736
Total	115,965	288,543	657,364	923,307	721,105	2,706,283

*All amounts rounded to nearest dollar.

TABLE MN.15
Postnegotiation Total Pension Costs*

	Seniority					
Grade	< 1 yr.	1–2 yr.	3–5 yr.	6–10 yr.	> 10 yr.	Total
1	4,227	4,975	0	0	0	9,202
2	0	7,370	16,276	2,989	0	26,636
3	0	2,712	17,858	37,506	13,583	71,658
4	0	0	3,511	10,930	13,213	27,654
5	0	0	0	3,974	16,470	20,444
Total	4,227	15,056	37,645	55,398	43,266	155,593

*All amounts rounded to nearest dollar.

TABLE MN.16
Postnegotiation Wage Increases (%)

	Seniority				
Grade	< 1 yr.	1–2 yr.	3–5 yr.	6–10 yr.	> 10 yr.
1	5.9	5.6	5.3	5.3	5.3
2	6.3	6.0	5.7	5.5	5.5
3	6.7	6.4	6.1	5.8	5.6
4	7.0	6.7	6.4	6.2	5.9
5	7.2	6.9	6.7	6.4	6.2

Pension costs increase by $37,078 (or 31 percent more) because of increased seniority, which leads to a greater likelihood of staying, combined with the 20 percent increase in contribution rates. Following are the total costs in the first year of a new contract:

Wages	$2,706,283
Pension contributions	155,933
Social security	207,031
Unemployment insurance (101 × 4% × 10,000)	40,400
Worker's compensation (2.2% of payroll)	59,538
Health insurance (26 singles @ $333 per month)	103,896
Health insurance (75 families @ 777 per month)	699,300
(Less health insurance for 5 husband-wife duplications)	(46,620)
Total	$3,925,761

Under the proposed new contract, total labor costs would increase by 9.4 percent, even though average straight-time percentage wage increases would rise between 5.3 and 7.2 percent by grade and seniority level, as shown in Table MN.16.

B. APPROACH

Assume the GMFC–Local 384 contract is due to expire soon and the union has made a timely notification to management that it desires renegotiation. It is your responsibility to negotiate a new contract. Following are the demands of both labor and management and supplemental information that will help in choosing contract demands.

C. DEMANDS

The union may formulate its demands from the following set, including all items from *a* through *d* and choosing any four from *e* through *k:*

a. A general wage increase of 5 percent of base wages per hour as of March 1 of each year during each year of the contract. If the contract length exceeds two years, wage negotiations may be reopened before the beginning of the third year and every second following year thereafter.

b. The company will neither subcontract work the bargaining unit is capable of performing nor close the plant or move any of the plant's operations during the life of the agreement.

c. The company will train bargaining-unit members to operate and maintain computer technology used in the production process, and all production technician jobs will be included in the bargaining unit.

d. Implementation of a cost-of-living adjustment (COLA) based on 7 cents per hour for each 1-point increase in the consumer price index. COLA payments will be calculated based on revised U.S. Department of Labor Bureau of Labor Statistics data for urban workers and paid at the first pay day in the third month of each succeeding quarter.

e. The company will implement a prescription drug benefit that will pay the full cost of generic drug prescriptions and 80 percent of proprietary drug prescriptions.

f. The first Tuesday after the first Monday in November will be a paid holiday in even-numbered years in order to permit employees to more conveniently exercise their rights to vote in federal elections.

g. Vacation accumulation will be increased by 0.02 hour per straight-time hour worked for employees with 20 or more years of service.

h. The company's 401(k) match will be increased from up to 3 percent to up to 5 percent of gross pay for employees contributing to the plan and will contribute 2 percent to the account of all other employees, including those who do not make individual contributions.

i. A union shop clause will be implemented, with membership required after 60 days of employment.

j. Double pay will be given for all overtime after nine hours in a day and for all Sunday or holiday work.

k. Mandatory overtime cannot exceed 10 hours in any given week.

The company's offers and demands will be formulated from the following list. All demands between *a* and *d* will be included in the offer, and any four demands between *e* and *k* may be included:

a. The length of the agreement shall be six years.

b. Wage increases of a 2 percent lump sum when the contract is ratified, a 2 percent lump sum on March 1 of the second year, a 2.5 percent lump sum on March 1 of the third year, a 2 percent base wage increase on March 1 of the fourth year, and a 2.5 percent base wage increase on March 1 of the fifth and sixth years.

c. Employees will be required to pay for 20 percent of single or family health care insurance premiums as provided by the contract.

d. The supplementary unemployment benefit will be discontinued.

e. Persons promoted to supervisory positions will continue to accrue seniority within the bargaining unit after their promotion and retain bumping rights back into the bargaining unit if an economic reduction in force among supervisors is implemented.

f. The annual increase in the employer's contribution to the employee health care benefit will be limited to the percentage wage increase negotiated.

g. Employees may not refuse Saturday overtime and/or up to two hours of overtime per day, including Saturday.

h. Bargaining-unit members who elect to join the union must maintain membership during the life of the agreement. With each contract expiration, individuals who have been members will be free to withdraw during the first week of the subsequent agreement.

i. The losing party in arbitration shall be responsible for paying the arbitrator's fee for hearing the case and rendering an award.

j. A wellness program that will include counseling and prevention programs to address high-risk behaviors such as poor dietary habits, smoking, and lack of exercise that detrimentally affect health will be offered. Any employee who does not participate must pay a 25 percent surcharge on his or her required health care contributions.

D. ORGANIZATION FOR NEGOTIATIONS

Each labor team will be headed by a chief negotiator. One member of the labor team should assume the role of international representative. Team sizes should be not less than three nor more than eight. Each management team will be headed by the plant labor relations director and may include managers from other functional areas—manufacturing, accounting, shipping, and so forth. Management team sizes should be about the same as labor team sizes.

Before negotiations, each team should:

1. Construct its demand or offer package, and identify the relative priority of the issues being included.
2. Identify issues it would be willing to trade off.
3. Develop bargaining books tying demands to provisions in the present contract. Identify for each demand a desired settlement position, an expected settlement position, and a maximum concession position before bargaining.
4. Cost the provisions of the contract that would be changed. (Both parties should do this.)
5. Identify and develop strategies and tactics to be used during the negotiations. Structure the roles of each member.

E. NEGOTIATIONS

1. At the first bargaining session, labor and management shall first agree on an agenda and order of presentation. If a mutually satisfactory agenda cannot be achieved, the following may be used:
   a. Each demand or offer will be presented separately, with the other party responding. Normally, where both sides will make offers on the same issue, the union will present its demand first.
   b. All demands will be presented and responded to before any concession is made.
2. As you begin to bargain, you should remember that once a concession is made, it is very difficult to retract it. Thus, carefully consider changes in your positions before announcing them.
3. During the process, it is often beneficial to suspend face-to-face negotiations and hold a caucus of your bargaining group to consider a demand or concession.
4. As you negotiate, consider the impact the bargaining outcomes you attain will have on the bargaining relationship after the contract is signed. Is this a concession the other side can live with?
5. After the contract is agreed to, management must determine the final cost impact of the agreement, and the union must develop a strategy for gaining rank-and-file ratification.

F. ADDITIONAL INFORMATION

1. The terms of the contract may have some cost impact outside the bargaining unit because improved benefits are usually passed on to nonunion, white-collar workers.
2. Over the last contract, the average amount of overtime per year was distributed as shown in Table MN.17.
3. The bargaining unit has experienced a declining population for 30 years. At the end of 1980 the bargaining unit totaled 1,208, the largest ever achieved. As the result of layoffs during several recessions, continued improvements in productivity, and the introduction of computer-assisted manufacturing equipment, output could be maintained and/or increased with a decreasing or steady population. In 1992, the company offered an early retirement program with substantial incentives for senior workers. This provided an opportunity for the company to hire a new employee cohort for the first time in several years. Between 1999 and 2001, the company installed a substantial amount of computer-controlled production equipment. This has increased productivity substantially. The jobs that are involved with installing, operating, and maintaining the equipment have been filled primarily with professionals

TABLE MN.17
Average Overtime Hours Worked and Paid per Employee under the Expiring Agreement

	Production			Nonproduction		
	2009	**2010**	**2011**	**2009**	**2010**	**2011**
Saturday hours	0	0	10	0	0	10
Weekday hours	0	6	10	0	2	2
Holiday hours	0	0	0	0	0	0
Sunday hours	0	0	0	0	0	0
Total overtime hours	0	0	20	0	2	12
Paid overtime hours	0	9	30	0	3	18
Paid straight-time hours	1,760	2,080	2,080	1,840	2,080	2,080
Total paid hours	1,760	2,089	2,110	1,840	2,083	2,098

TABLE MN.18
Bargaining-Unit Population by Seniority Level, as of January 1, 2012

Years of Seniority	Number of Employees	Cumulative Number	Turnover Rate (%)
40	2	2	10.0
39	29	31	10.0
38	61	92	8.0
37	49	141	6.0
36	63	204	4.0
35	16	220	2.0
34	41	261	2.0
33	61	322	2.0
32	47	369	2.0
31	13	382	1.0
30	43	425	1.0
29	2	427	1.0
28	5	432	1.0
27	0	432	1.0
26	0	432	1.0
25	5	437	1.0
24	6	443	1.0
23	2	445	1.0
22	4	449	1.0
21	5	454	1.0
20	4	458	1.0
19	0	458	1.0
18	0	458	1.0
17	8	466	1.0
16	16	482	1.0
15	27	509	1.0
14	20	529	1.0
13	8	537	1.0
12	3	540	1.0
11	1	541	1.0
10	2	543	1.0
9	0	543	1.5
8	0	543	2.0
7	14	557	2.5
6	0	557	3.0
5	0	557	4.0
4	0	557	5.0
3	0	557	6.0
2	0	557	8.0
1	2	559	10.0
<1	6	565	20.0

and technicians who have been assigned to the production director's staff. Due to the economic crisis that became acute in fall 2008, the entire plant was shut down for February and the first four weeks of March 2009 because of a lack of orders. When it reopened, 20 percent of production and 10 percent of nonproduction employees were not immediately called back. In September 2009, half of those laid off were recalled. Everyone who had less than four years' seniority was permanently laid off and given a severance payment equal to 10 percent of annual straight-time pay for their classification for each year of service from hire until the February layoff date. This payment was based on a special agreement between the union and the company negotiated in August 2009 that was concluded as a condition of the recall. The present seniority list (as of January 1, 2012) is shown in Table MN.18. Turnover includes quits, retirements, promotions, and transfers out of the bargaining unit. Most bargaining-unit employees continue to work beyond 30 years of service.

4. The Central City plant was built 60 years ago and was expanded repeatedly between 1972 and 1975. No expansion is planned presently for the Central City facility. The company has similar U.S. and foreign operations. One relatively new plant in the Sun Belt is unorganized. Across the company, about 75 percent of production employees are represented, all by the Steelworkers.
5. Presently, 538 bargaining-unit members belong to the union.
6. The average arbitration case cost the company and the union $8,175 each during the last contract. Arbitrators heard 8 cases and ruled for the company on 6.
7. Table MN.19 gives a distribution of bargaining-unit employees by job and seniority.
8. Productivity changes over the past five years have been as follows: 2004—up 3.5 percent, 2005—up 2.5 percent, 2006—up 1.5 percent, 2007—up 3 percent, 2008—up 2.5 percent. Over the past five years, product price changes were up 0.8 percent in 2004, up 1.2 percent in 2005, down 0.5 percent in 2006, up 1.8 percent in 2007, up 2.5 percent in 2008, up 3.2 percent in 2009, up 1.1 percent in 2010, and up 0.3 percent in 2011. The equivalent number of units shipped in each of the past five years was up 6.3 percent in 2004, up 3.7 percent in 2005, up 2.7 percent in 2006, down 1.2 percent in 2007, down 3.9 percent in 2008, down 11.5 percent in 2009, up 4.9 percent in 2010, and up 7.7 percent in 2011.
9. You should consider changes in the costs of health benefits, social security, and other wage-tied benefits, as well as changes in the consumer price index (if applicable) when costing contract terms.
10. About two-thirds of employees with 20 or more years of service have chronic health conditions that required prescription drugs (e.g., high cholesterol, high blood pressure, and type II diabetes).

TABLE MN.19 Seniority Level by Job Classification, as of January 1, 2012

	Years of Seniority																																									
Job Title	**<1**	**1**	**2**	**3**	**4**	**5**	**6**	**7**	**8**	**9**	**10**	**11**	**12**	**13**	**14**	**15**	**16**	**17**	**18**	**19**	**20**	**21**	**22**	**23**	**24**	**25**	**26**	**27**	**28**	**29**	**30**	**31**	**32**	**33**	**34**	**35**	**36**	**37**	**38**	**39**	**40**	**Total**
Assembler 1	4	2	0	0	0	0	0	13	0	0	2	1	3	6	18	11	0	0	0	0	0	0	0	0	0	0	0	0	0	0	0	0	0	0	0	0	0	0	0	0	0	60
Assembler 2	0	0	0	0	0	0	0	0	0	0	0	0	0	0	0	13	11	6	0	0	3	4	3	2	6	5	0	0	5	0	39	12	40	51	0	0	0	0	0	0	0	200
Assembler 3	0	0	0	0	0	0	0	0	0	0	0	0	0	0	0	0	0	0	0	0	0	0	0	0	0	0	0	0	0	0	0	0	0	0	33	11	45	40	46	23	2	200
Skilled production 1	0	0	0	0	0	0	0	0	0	0	0	0	0	0	0	0	2	0	0	0	0	0	0	0	0	0	0	0	0	1	2	0	0	4	2	1	4	1	1	0	0	18
Skilled production 2	0	0	0	0	0	0	0	0	0	0	0	0	0	0	0	0	0	0	0	0	0	0	0	0	0	0	0	0	0	0	0	1	0	1	2	0	3	2	3	2	0	14
Skilled production 3	0	0	0	0	0	0	0	0	0	0	0	0	0	0	0	0	0	0	0	0	0	0	0	0	0	0	0	0	0	0	1	0	3	2	2	1	2	2	4	3	0	20
Skilled maintenance 1	0	0	0	0	0	0	0	0	0	0	0	0	0	0	0	0	1	0	0	0	0	0	0	0	0	0	0	0	0	0	0	0	2	0	0	1	0	0	0	0	0	4
Skilled maintenance 2	0	0	0	0	0	0	0	0	0	0	0	0	0	0	0	0	0	0	0	0	0	0	0	0	0	0	0	0	0	0	0	0	1	0	0	0	2	2	2	0	0	7
Skilled maintenance 3	0	0	0	0	0	0	0	0	0	0	0	0	0	0	0	0	0	0	0	0	0	0	0	0	0	0	0	0	0	1	0	0	1	0	0	0	2	1	3	1	0	9
Material handling and production support	1	0	0	0	0	0	0	0	0	0	0	0	0	1	2	2	2	1	0	0	1	0	1	0	0	0	0	0	0	0	1	0	0	3	1	0	3	0	1	0	0	20
Maintenance	1	0	0	0	0	0	0	1	0	0	0	0	0	1	0	1	0	1	0	0	0	1	0	0	0	0	0	0	0	0	0	0	0	0	1	2	2	1	1	0	0	13
Total	6	2	0	0	0	0	0	14	0	0	2	1	3	8	20	27	16	8	0	0	4	5	4	2	6	5	0	0	5	2	43	13	47	61	41	16	63	49	61	29	2	565

11. For wage-comparison and producer price index change purposes, GMFC operations are in North American Industry Classification System (NAICS) code 33312 (Construction Machinery and Equipment). Costs of energy and intermediate goods used in production have been much more volatile than the prices of finished goods during the past several years.
12. Recent selected financial information for this location is shown in Table MN.20. Economic value added is difference between net income earned during the year and the current market interest rate for corporate long-term debt multiplied by the total amount of liabilities and capital (net income minus long-term interest rate times liabilities and capital).

TABLE MN.20
Selected Financial Information for This Location—Income Statement, Balance Sheet, and Employment and Performance Data (Financial Data in $ thousands)

	2007	2008	2009	2010	2011
Income Statement					
Net sales	266,053	247,806	212,409	220,618	236,942
Materials	157,663	171,490	132,060	147,437	156,856
Depreciation	3,954	3,391	2,826	2,647	2,560
Compensation	56,087	51,239	39,187	44,195	43,814
Interest expense	1,929	1,728	1,296	1,083	975
Income from operations	46,420	19,958	37,040	25,256	32,737
Profit sharing	4,642	1,996	3,704	2,526	3,274
Net income from operations	41,778	17,962	33,336	22,731	29,464
General, selling, and administrative expenses	19,102	18,825	15,299	16,024	18,519
Taxable income	22,676	–863	18,037	6,707	10,945
Provision for taxes	8,390	–319	6,674	2,481	4,050
Net income	14,286	–544	11,363	4,225	6,895
Balance Sheet					
Assets					
Current assets	70,296	64,941	63,279	67,743	71,024
Plant and equipment (less accumulated depreciation)	20,346	16,955	15,879	15,358	12,798
Total assets	90,642	81,896	79,158	83,101	83,822
Liabilities and capital					
Current liabilities	52,651	46,734	34,690	36,260	31,639
Long-term debt	22,858	20,572	18,515	16,663	14,997
Retained earnings	15,133	14,589	25,953	30,178	37,073
Total liabilities and capital	90,642	81,896	79,158	83,101	83,709
Total number of employees at year end	905	829	738	722	721
Bargaining-unit employees at year end	715	653	588	571	565
Return on assets	**15.76%**	**–0.66%**	**14.36%**	**5.08%**	**8.23%**
Economic value added	**8,213**	**–5,130**	**6,851**	**–595**	**1,789**

AGREEMENT

between

GENERAL MANUFACTURING & FABRICATION COMPANY

CENTRAL CITY, INDIANA,

and

LOCAL 384, UNITED STEELWORKERS OF AMERICA

AFL-CIO

Effective March 1, 2009

CONTENTS

Article 1.	Purpose	378
Article 2.	Recognition	378
Article 3.	Checkoff of Union Dues	378
Article 4.	Management	379
Article 5.	Representation	379
Article 6.	Hours	379
Article 7.	Wages	381
Article 8.	Seniority	384
Article 9.	Grievance Procedure and No-Strike Agreement	388
Article 10.	Vacations	389
Article 11.	Leaves for Illness and Family Emergencies	390
Article 12.	General	392
Article 13.	Renewal	397
Appendix	Classified Base Rates	398

ARTICLE 1. PURPOSE

1.01 It is the intent and purpose of the parties hereto that this Agreement will promote and improve industrial and economic relations between the employees and the COMPANY, and to set forth herein a basic agreement covering rates of pay, hours of work, and other conditions of employment to be observed by the parties and to ensure the peaceful settlement of disputes and to prevent stoppages of work.

ARTICLE 2. RECOGNITION

2.01 The COMPANY recognizes Local Union No. 384, United Steelworkers of America, AFL-CIO, as the exclusive bargaining agent for all hourly paid employees designated in the bargaining unit by the National Labor Relations Board for the Central City plant and warehouses, which includes all production and maintenance employees including machine shop employees and receiving department and warehouse employees but excluding boiler room employees, clerical employees, watchpersons, guards, assistant supervisors, supervisors, and any other supervisory employees with authority to hire, promote, discharge, discipline, or otherwise effect changes in the status of employees or effectively recommend such action.

2.02 Any employee who is a member of the UNION on the effective date of this Agreement shall, as a condition of employment, maintain his/her membership in the UNION to the extent of paying membership dues.

2.03 Any employee who on the effective date of this Agreement is not a member of the UNION shall not be required to become a member of the UNION but shall be required to pay an amount equal to the UNION's regular monthly dues. Any such employee, however, who during the life of the Agreement joins the UNION must remain a member as provided in Section 2.02.

ARTICLE 3. CHECKOFF OF UNION DUES

3.01 Upon individual authorization from members, monthly UNION DUES in an amount to be determined by the UNION shall be deducted by the COMPANY from each member's first pay in each month. Such sums shall be forwarded by the COMPANY to the financial secretary of the UNION before the 15th day of the month.

ARTICLE 4. MANAGEMENT

4.01 The UNION and its members recognize that the successful and efficient operation of the business is the responsibility of management and that management of the plant and the direction of the working force is the responsibility of the COMPANY, provided, in carrying out these management functions, the COMPANY does not violate the terms of this Agreement.

4.02 The COMPANY retains the sole right to discipline and discharge employees for cause, provided that in the exercise of this right it will not act wrongfully or unjustly or in violation of the terms of this Agreement.

ARTICLE 5. REPRESENTATION

5.01 The UNION shall designate a UNION COMMITTEE of no more than 10 members who shall represent the UNION in meetings with the COMPANY, with no more than 7 employees actively working in the plant as members of the committee.

5.02 The COMPANY agrees that during meetings held with management members of the UNION required to attend shall be paid at their regular hourly base rate for all time lost from their regularly assigned work schedule.

ARTICLE 6. HOURS

6.01 ***Work Day*** A day starts at the beginning of the first shift and ends at the close of the third shift. The first shift is any shift that starts after midnight. Normally the first shift starts at 7:00 a.m. or 8:00 a.m. Present shift schedules will continue unless changes are mutually agreed to by the COMPANY and the UNION.

6.02 ***Payroll Week*** The payroll week starts at the beginning of the first shift on Monday and ends at the end of the third shift on Sunday.

6.03 ***Daily Overtime*** Time and one half shall be paid for all hours worked in excess of eight in any one day.

6.04 ***Weekly Overtime*** Time and one half shall be paid for all hours worked in excess of 40 in any one payroll week for which overtime has not been earned on any other basis.

6.05 ***Saturday Work*** Time and one half shall be paid for work performed on Saturday between the hours of 7:00 a.m. or 8:00 a.m. Saturday to 7:00 a.m. or 8:00 a.m. on Sunday.

6.06 *Sunday Work* Double time shall be paid for work performed on Sunday between the hours of 7:00 a.m. or 8:00 a.m. Sunday to 7:00 a.m. or 8:00 a.m. Monday.

6.07 *Consecutive Hours over 8* Time and one half shall be paid for all hours worked over 8 but less than 12.

6.08 *Consecutive Hours over 12* Double time shall be paid for all consecutive hours worked over 12.

6.09 *Distribution of Overtime* Overtime shall be distributed on an equitable basis within the department in a manner to be decided by the supervision and the UNION representatives in that department, giving consideration to seniority and ability to perform the work. Refused overtime hours shall be credited as overtime hours worked for purposes of distributing overtime.

6.10 *Limits on Mandatory Overtime* Employees may be required to work for no more than 12 hours during any 24-hour period. Employees who have worked at least 10 hours of overtime during the current payroll week will be permitted to refuse additional overtime work during that payroll week.

6.11 *Shift Premium*

a. A shift premium of 30 cents per hour will be paid to all employees for all hours worked on a particular day if 50 percent or more of the hours worked on that day fall between the hours of 3:00 p.m. and 11:00 p.m.

b. A shift premium of 40 cents per hour will be paid to all employees for all hours worked on a particular day if 50 percent or more of the hours worked on that day fall between the hours of 11:00 p.m. and 7:00 a.m.

6.12 *Holidays*

a. After completion of the probationary period an hourly employee not working on the holiday will be granted holiday benefit consisting of eight hours' straight-time pay at his or her regular hourly base rate on the following holidays:

New Year's Day	Thanksgiving
Memorial Day	Christmas
Independence Day	December 24
Labor Day	December 31
Floating holiday	

b. Double time in addition to the holiday pay, as stated in Section 6.12a, will be paid for all hours worked on the above holidays.

c. The floating holiday will be designated by the COMPANY. The UNION will be notified at least 90 days prior to the day set by the COMPANY.

d. A holiday starts at the beginning of the first shift and ends at the close of the third shift. When one of these holidays falls on Sunday, the holiday shall be observed on Monday. When one of these holidays falls on Saturday, the holiday shall be observed on Friday.

e. To be eligible, the employee must be at work on the day for which he or she is scheduled prior to the holiday and following the holiday unless absence is established for any of the following reasons:

1. Unavoidable absence caused by sickness or injury.
2. Emergencies in the immediate family.
3. Regularly scheduled vacation. The holiday will not count against vacation.
4. Any other justifiable absence previously approved by his or her supervisor.

ARTICLE 7. WAGES

7.01 *Skill-Based Pay Plan* Effective March 1, 1997, a skill-based pay plan will be implemented. Pay will be based on employees' demonstrated skills. Skill blocks associated with ability to perform work in five job categories will be defined jointly by the COMPANY and the UNION. The five categories are assembler, skilled production, skilled maintenance, material handling and production support, and maintenance. In the assembler, skilled production, and skilled maintenance categories, there are three levels in each requiring significantly increasing skill levels. In the material handling and production support and maintenance categories, there is a single level.

a. ***Assembly Category*** The skills associated with the former Assembler grades 1, 2, and 3 will constitute those required to perform as an Assembler, level 1. All employees currently assigned to these grades will be initially qualified as Assembler, level 1. The skills associated with the former Assembler grades 4, 5, and 6 will constitute those required to perform as an Assembler, level 2. All employees currently assigned to these grades will be initially qualified as Assembler, level 2. The skills associated with the former Assembler grades 7, 8, 9, and 10 will constitute those required to perform as an Assembler, level 3. All employees currently assigned to these grades will be initially qualified as Assembler, level 3.

b. ***Skilled Production Category*** The skills associated with the following jobs will be associated with skilled production, level 3: tool and model maker, tool and die maker, jig grinder operator, machinist, welder, and precision grinder. The skills associated with the following jobs will be associated with skilled production, level 2: layout and setup worker, painter, profile mill operator, machinist trainee, capital assembly worker, and weldment finisher. The skills associated with the following jobs will be associated with skilled production, level 1: metal fabricator, grinder operator, milling machine operator, lathe operator, head assembly worker, developmental assembler, experimental assembler, and assembler.

c. ***Skilled Maintenance Category*** The skills associated with the following jobs will be associated with skilled maintenance, level 3: systems control technician, measurement and control technician, instrument maintenance technician, electrician, refrigeration and air conditioning mechanic, steamfitter, development electronics technician, millwright mechanic, maintenance mechanic, and millwright. The skills associated with the following jobs will be associated with skilled maintenance, level 2: none. The skills associated with the following jobs will be associated with skilled maintenance, level 1: cabinet maker, locksmith, specialist, oiler, and trades helper.

d. ***Material Handling and Production Support*** The skills associated with the following jobs are associated with the material handling and production support skill set: steelroom handler, head stockroom clerk, yard worker, stock service worker, truck driver, tool crib attendant, stockroom clerk, waste hauler, and yard laborer.

e. ***Maintenance*** The skills associated with the following jobs are associated with the maintenance skill set: air conditioning cleaner and janitor.

7.02 ***Skill Level Rates*** Skill level rates effective March 1, 2009, as shown in the appendix, shall be continued without change during the duration of this agreement.

7.03 ***Certification of Qualifications*** All employees will be given skill tests each March 1 to determine their current skill levels. If employees pass the next higher level skill test, they will be promoted to that level (not more than one level per year). If employees fail a test at their current level, level 1 employees have one year to requalify or be terminated. Level 2 or above retain their current pay rates for one year and then will be demoted if they don't qualify on the next test. There is no fixed number of openings at any level. When employees qualify, they will be advanced at the rate of one level per year or less. Certification tests will be developed jointly by the COMPANY and the UNION and will be administered jointly annually on March 1 by the COMPANY and UNION. For its part, the COMPANY will offer not less than 30 hours of skill training scheduled during normal working hours annually to employees who request it.

7.04 ***Promotional Increases*** When an employee is promoted to a higher level, he or she will receive the classified rate for the job the first Monday on or after his or her promotion.

7.05 ***Temporary Transfers between Departments*** When in the interest of effective and economical operation or as a means of deferring layoffs it is desirable to transfer employees temporarily from one department to another, such temporary transfers may be made for a maximum period of four weeks, if mutually agreeable to both the COMPANY and the UNION. Wherever possible, departmental seniority will be given due consideration in determining employees to be transferred. The UNION agrees to cooperate with the COMPANY in arranging such temporary interdepartment transfers. The COMPANY agrees not to request temporary interdepartment transfers except in the interests of efficient and economical operation or as a means of deferring layoff.

7.06 ***Employee Reporting and No Work Available*** Employees reporting for work according to their regularly assigned work schedules without being notified in advance not to report and work is not available shall be allowed a minimum of four hours' pay at the employees' regular straight-time hourly base rate except in cases beyond the control of the COMPANY.

7.07 ***Call-In Pay*** Employees who have been recalled to work after they have completed their regularly scheduled shift and have left the plant shall be given a minimum of four hours' work if they so desire. If four hours' work is not available, the employee shall be paid the hours worked according to the wage and premium pay policy, and the remainder of the four hours not worked shall be paid at the employee's regular straight-time hourly rate.

7.08 ***Jury Duty*** The COMPANY agrees to pay the difference between jury duty pay and the employee's straight-time hourly base rate earnings when the employee is called for jury duty. When called, the employee will be scheduled to work on the first shift whenever possible. The employee shall be required to report for work whenever he or she is able to work four consecutive hours or more of the first shift.

7.09 Effective March 1, 1982, 10 percent of profits (net income from operations before provision for income taxes) generated by the plant for the calendar year ending on December 31, 1982, and continuing thereafter on December 31 of each calendar year will be divided among members of the bargaining unit. Each employee will receive an amount equal to his or her hours worked divided by the total number of hours worked by the bargaining unit during the calendar year times the profit proportion (if any). Profit-sharing payments will be made not later than March 31 of the following year for distributions earned for the preceding calendar year.

ARTICLE 8. SENIORITY

8.01 ***Plant Seniority*** Plant seniority shall be determined from the employee's earliest date of continuous employment with the COMPANY and shall apply to divisional and plant layoffs and plant recalls after layoff.

8.02 ***Departmental Seniority*** Departmental seniority shall be determined from the employee's earliest date of continuous employment in the department and shall apply to promotions, demotions, and reductions in force within the department.

8.03 ***Termination of Seniority*** Seniority shall terminate for the following reasons:

- **a.** Voluntary resignation.
- **b.** Discharge for proper cause.
- **c.** Absence for three successive working days without notice, unless satisfactory reason is given.
- **d.** Failure to report to work after layoff within five working days after being notified by registered letter (return receipt requested) at the employee's last available address, unless satisfactory reason is given. A copy of the written offer shall be sent to the UNION.

8.04 ***Employees on Layoff***

- **a.** Employees who are or shall be laid off due to lack of work and later reemployed shall retain their seniority as of the time of the layoff but will not accumulate seniority during the layoff period. If an employee after the first six months of layoff declines to return to work when contacted by the production personnel office regarding an opening, his or her seniority rights shall be terminated.
- **b.** Employees shall be given three working days' notice of impending layoff from the plant or three days' pay in lieu thereof.

8.05 ***Probationary Employees***

- **a.** A new employee shall be on probation without seniority for 40 days actually worked after date of employment by the COMPANY, during which period the COMPANY shall determine the employee's ability to perform satisfactorily the duties and requirements of the work. Layoff or discharge of an employee during such probationary period shall not be subject to the grievance procedure.
- **b.** Upon satisfactorily completing the probationary period, the employee will be placed on the department's seniority list, and his or her departmental seniority shall date from the beginning of the probationary period. If an employee is transferred to another department during his or her probationary period, his or her departmental seniority shall date back to the date of transfer to the new department upon completion of the probationary period.

8.06 *Transfers*

a. When an employee leaves his or her department to accept a job in another department, his or her seniority rights in the department that he or she left shall not be forfeited for a period of 90 days. If the employee chooses to return to his or her home department (home department is where he or she has recall and return rights) within 90 days from the date of such transfer, he or she shall be returned to his or her former job not later than the third Monday following his or her request. If he or she requests transfer to another department within 12 months of his or her return to his or her home department, he or she shall, upon being transferred, forfeit all departmental seniority rights.

b. If an employee signs a plant posting and during the 90-day period in that job signs another plant posting, he or she has the original 90 days to return to his or her home department but has no right of return to the second department he or she left.

8.07 *Layoffs*

a. *Departmental* When the number of employees in a department is reduced, layoffs shall be made on the basis of departmental seniority, providing those remaining are qualified to perform the work.

b. *Divisional* The employee ultimately laid off from a department shall be entitled to bump into the department of the least senior employee in the plant on the basis of plant seniority, provided he or she has the necessary qualifications to perform the job to which he or she is assigned. In multiple reductions involving the displacement of employees in the department in which reduction is taking place, the employees with the most departmental seniority of those on the original reduction schedule will be retained in the department, providing employees in the reducing department do not have sufficient plant seniority to allow them to remain in the plant. Others reduced from the department will be assigned to one or two shifts according to plant seniority. Upon notification to the production personnel department, special shift requests will be given consideration.

c. *Plant* The employee laid off from his or her division shall be entitled to bump into the department of the least senior employee in the plant, providing the claiming employee has the necessary qualifications to perform the job to which he or she is assigned and has more than six months of plant seniority to his or her credit. In case any of the jobs vacated by the least senior employees in the plant are on a one- or two-shift basis as opposed to the ordinary three-shift basis, the employees being laid off from a division who have the most plant seniority shall automatically be given these one- or two-shift jobs.

Upon notification to the production personnel department, special shift requests will be given consideration.

d. The employee so transferred shall accept, according to his or her seniority, the position vacated to make room for him or her. The supervisor shall have the right to place the crew as he or she sees fit on jobs carrying the same classified rate in all cases of emergencies and vacancies, taking into account the most efficient utilization of his or her working force.

e. When a classification is eliminated, the employee(s) occupying that classification may exercise his or her seniority to claim any classification within the department to which his or her seniority entitles him or her. The employee(s) then affected will follow the normal layoff procedure.

8.08 *Recall after Layoff*

a. When it is necessary to employ additional employees, employees laid off due to lack of work will be recalled in order of their plant seniority, providing they are qualified to handle the jobs, before new employees are hired.

b. When an employee is recalled after layoff for a job in another department and accepts, he or she will retain his or her home departmental seniority until such time as he or she declines an opportunity to return to his or her home department, subject to Section 8.06. If a laid-off employee declines, he or she shall remain on recall to his or her home department for a period not to exceed six months after layoff date. If, during the six months' period, the employee wishes to be considered for an opening in another department, he or she may do so by notifying the production personnel office. Thereafter, he or she must return to work when offered employment by the COMPANY or his or her seniority will be terminated.

8.09 *Leaves of Absence*

a. Members of the UNION, not to exceed two in number at any one time, shall be granted leaves of absence for the duration of this Agreement to work directly for the local UNION. It is further agreed that four additional leaves shall be granted to any employees of the COMPANY covered by this Agreement who have been or who may in the future be elected to or appointed to a full-time office in the international union or the state federation of labor, AFL-CIO, providing that such leaves do not exceed the duration of this Agreement. Upon being relieved of their official union positions, they will be entitled to full seniority rights as though they had been employed by the COMPANY continuously.

b. Employees, not to exceed 1 percent of the UNION's membership, who are members of the UNION when delegated or elected to attend a UNION convention or conference shall be granted such leaves of absence as may be necessary, providing reasonable notice is given the COMPANY.

c. Any employee elected to or appointed to any federal, state, or city public office shall be granted a leave of absence during the period he or she is actively engaged in such service.

d. ***Maternity Leave***

1. An employee who becomes pregnant will be granted a leave of absence upon request at any time during pregnancy and extending for three months after the birth of the child. Where leave of absence is taken, such employee shall not lose seniority that was acquired before the beginning of such leave of absence.
2. All employees placed on maternity leave of absence shall have their seniority dates adjusted upon their return by an amount of time equal to the number of days absent prior to and after the birth of the child.

8.10 ***Supervisory and Other Salaried Positions***

a. It is recognized that all supervisory employees are representatives of management and the assignment of their duties, promotions, demotions, and transfers is the responsibility of the COMPANY and cannot be determined on the basis of seniority.

b. Hourly employees promoted to a supervisory position shall accumulate seniority until such a time that he or she holds a supervisory position continuously for six months. After six continuous months his or her seniority in the bargaining unit shall be frozen as of the date of promotion. If later reduced to an hourly job, he or she shall be assigned to the skill class to which his or her accumulated or frozen seniority entitles him or her in the department that he or she left to become a supervisor. Supervisors who are reduced will be required to certify at a given skill level within their classifications not later than 18 months following reduction. No supervisor as herein defined shall have posting privileges until 30 days following his or her reassignment to an hourly production job. In return for protecting an employee's seniority while he or she is in a supervisory position as well as allowing him or her the right to claim a job in the bargaining unit if reduced from his or her supervisory position, supervisors who are reduced to hourly jobs shall become members of the UNION within 30 days.

c. Supervisory and other salaried employees will not perform the work of hourly production employees except in cases of emergency.

ARTICLE 9. GRIEVANCE PROCEDURE AND NO-STRIKE AGREEMENT

9.01 *Departmental Representatives* The UNION may designate representatives for each section on each shift and in each department for the purpose of handling grievances that may arise in that department. The UNION will inform the human resources department in writing as to the names of the authorized representatives. Should differences arise as to the intent and application of the provisions of this Agreement, there shall be no strike, lockout, slowdown, or work stoppage of any kind, and the controversy shall be settled in accordance with the following grievance procedures:

9.02 *Grievances*

Step 1. The employee and the departmental steward, if the employee desires, shall take the matter up with his or her supervisor. If no settlement is reached in Step 1 within two working days, the grievance shall be reduced to writing on the form provided for that purpose.

Step 2. The written grievance shall be presented to the supervisor or the general supervisor and a copy sent to the human resources department. Within two working days after receipt of the grievance, the general supervisor shall hold a meeting, unless mutually agreed otherwise, with the supervisor, the employee, and the departmental steward and the chief steward.

Step 3. If no settlement is reached in Step 2, the written grievance shall be presented to the departmental superintendent, who shall hold a meeting within five working days of the original receipt of the grievance in Step 2 unless mutually agreed otherwise. Those in attendance shall normally be the departmental superintendent, the general supervisor, the supervisor, the employee, the chief steward, departmental steward, a member of the human resources department, the president of the UNION or his or her representative, and the divisional committee person.

Step 4. If no settlement is reached in Step 3, the UNION COMMITTEE and a national representative of the UNION shall meet with the MANAGEMENT COMMITTEE for the purpose of settling the matter.

Step 5. If no settlement is reached in Step 4, the matter shall be referred to an arbitrator. A representative of the UNION shall meet within five working days with a representative of the COMPANY for the purpose of selecting an arbitrator. If an arbitrator cannot be agreed upon within five working days after Step 4, a request for a list of arbitrators shall be sent to the Federal Mediation and Conciliation Service. Upon obtaining the list, an arbitrator shall be selected within five working days. Prior to arbitration, a representative of the UNION shall meet with a representative of the COMPANY to reduce to writing wherever possible the actual issue to be arbitrated. The decision of the arbitrator shall be final and binding on all parties. The salary, if any, of the arbitrator and any necessary expense incident to the arbitration shall be paid jointly by the COMPANY and the UNION.

9.03 In order to ensure the prompt settlement of grievances as close to their source as possible, it is mutually agreed that the above steps will be followed strictly in the order listed and no step shall be used until all previous steps have been exhausted. A settlement reached between the COMPANY and the UNION in any step of this procedure shall terminate the grievance and shall be final and binding on both parties.

9.04 The arbitrator shall not have authority to modify, change, or amend any of the terms or provisions of the Agreement or to add to or delete from the Agreement.

9.05 The UNION will not cause or permit its members to cause or take part in any sit-down, stay-in, or slowdown in any plant of the COMPANY or any curtailment of work or restriction of production or interference with the operations of the COMPANY.

9.06 The UNION will not cause or permit its members to cause or take part in any strike of any of the COMPANY's operations, except where the strike has been fully authorized as provided in the constitution of the international union.

ARTICLE 10. VACATIONS

10.01 *Vacation Time Accumulation*

a. For employees with less than 36 months of credited service, vacation time will be accumulated at the rate of 0.02 hour for each straight-time hour worked.

b. For employees with 36 or more months but less than 120 months of credited service, vacation time will be accumulated at the rate of 0.04 hour for each straight-time hour worked.

c. For employees with 120 or more months but less than 180 months of credited service, vacation time will be accumulated at the rate of 0.06 hour for each straight-time hour worked.

d. For employees with 180 or more months but less than 300 months of credited service, vacation time will be accumulated at the rate of 0.08 hour for each straight-time hour worked.

e. For employees with 300 or more months of credited service, vacation time will be accumulated at the rate of 0.10 hour for each straight-time hour worked.

10.02 Use of accrued vacation time shall be granted at such times of the year as the COMPANY finds most suitable, considering both the wishes of the employee according to plant seniority and the requirements of plant operations.

10.03 One week of vacation pay shall consist of 40 hours' pay at the employee's regular straight-time hourly base rate.

10.04 Unused vacations may be accumulated across years, however, the time accrued will be discounted each year by the average percent increase of the bargaining-unit hourly wage. For example, if 20 days are accumulated and unused and there is a 5 percent increase, the accumulated days will be reduced to 19.

10.05 If a holiday recognized within this Agreement falls within an employee's vacation period, he or she shall be granted an extra day of vacation, provided the employee is eligible for holiday pay on that holiday.

10.06 Employees who are laid off will be continued at their regular straight-time hourly wage until their accumulated vacation is exhausted. Seniority will continue to be accrued over the length of the accumulated vacation. Employees on layoff status who continue to be paid their accumulated vacation wages are ineligible to apply for unemployment benefits or to receive supplementary unemployment benefits until their vacation pay is exhausted.

10.07 Employees who terminate their employment for any reason are entitled to receive the value of their accumulated vacation at their straight-time hourly wage rate in their final pay.

ARTICLE 11. LEAVES FOR ILLNESS AND FAMILY EMERGENCIES

11.01 *Personal Injury or Illness* Employees shall be entitled to five working days' sick leave (40 hours' straight-time pay at the employee's regular hourly base rate) in any one calendar year. Such benefits, not to exceed 8 hours in any day, will apply only to time lost from scheduled work for reasons of personal illness or injury except that no benefits will be paid for the first two scheduled working days of any period of such absence for any employee with less than five (5) years of credited service.

11.02 *Accumulation* Sick leave benefits unused in any year of the plan may be accumulated for possible use in the next two years. When fourth-year benefits become available, the unused benefits from the first year automatically cancel and so on for each succeeding year. Order of sick leave usage is, first, the current year's benefits and second, the oldest year's benefits. Employees out sick before January 1 whose absence due to that illness extends through January 1 will first use those benefits that were available at the commencement of the absence.

11.03 *Waiting period* There shall be no waiting period for the first five days (40 hours) of sick leave usage in a benefit year. However, no benefits shall be payable for the first normally scheduled working day in any period of absence commencing thereafter.

11.04 *Definitions*

a. Unavoidable absence is defined as follows:

1. Unavoidable absence caused by sickness or injury.
2. Emergencies in the immediate family.

b. Immediate family shall consist of the following with no exceptions:

Spouse	Son	Sister
Mother	Daughter	Mother-in-law
Father	Brother	Father-in-law

In addition, the death of the employee's grandfather or grandmother will be recognized as an emergency in the immediate family to the extent of allowing one day's benefit, provided it is necessary that he or she be absent.

11.05 *Hospitalization and Convalescence*

a. A 15-year hourly employee will receive straight-time pay at his or her regular hourly base rate for time lost due to hospitalization in a recognized hospital or convalescence thereafter that occurs during the first 40 hours he or she is scheduled to work in any week not to exceed 8 hours in any day. The total amount of such allowance will not exceed 80 hours in any one year, calculated from year to year. Benefits provided in this paragraph will not apply to days of unavoidable absence for which benefits are paid under the provisions of Section 11.04.

b. A 25-year hourly employee will receive straight-time pay at his or her regular hourly base rate for time lost due to hospitalization in a recognized hospital or convalescence thereafter that occurs during the first 40 hours he or she is scheduled to work in any week not to exceed 8 hours in any day. The total amount of such allowance will not exceed 160 hours (an additional 80 hours to [a] above) in any one year, calculated from year to year. Benefits provided in this paragraph will not apply to days of unavoidable absence for which benefits are paid under the provisions of Section 11.04 above.

11.06 In order to obtain these benefits, the employee shall, if required, furnish his or her supervisor satisfactory reason for absence.

11.07 The COMPANY and the UNION agree to cooperate in preventing and correcting abuses of these benefits.

ARTICLE 12. GENERAL

12.01 ***Bulletin Boards*** The COMPANY shall provide bulletin boards that may be used by the UNION for posting notices approved by the industrial relations manager or someone designated by him or her and restricted to:

a. Notices of UNION recreational and social affairs.

b. Notices of UNION elections.

c. Notices of UNION appointments and results of UNION elections.

d. Notices of UNION meetings.

e. And other notices mutually agreed to.

12.02 ***Relief Periods***

a. Relief periods of 25 minutes for every eight-hour work period will be on COMPANY time at such times in each department as will be most beneficial to the employees and the COMPANY. A lunch period on COMPANY time and premises may be substituted for relief period, provided the total time allowed for lunch and relief period in an eight-hour work period does not exceed 25 minutes.

b. Employees leaving the COMPANY premises for lunch during their shifts must clock out and will not be paid for the time they are away.

c. The relief and lunch periods in each department will be determined by the department supervisors and the UNION stewards, considering both the wishes of the employees and the requirements of efficient departmental operations.

12.03 All benefits now in effect and not specifically mentioned in this Agreement affecting all hourly paid employees of the COMPANY shall not be terminated for the duration of this Agreement.

12.04 ***Sickness and Accident*** The COMPANY agrees to maintain its current sickness and accident insurance plans, as amended, effective December 1, 1985. Benefits begin one month after the sickness and accident initially occurred and continue for six months. Benefits will be equal to 60 percent of the employee's straight-time wage at the time of the sickness or accident.

12.05 ***Long-Term Disability Plan*** Subject to the provisions and qualifications of the long-term disability plan, there will be available monthly income benefits commencing after 26 weeks of continuous disability and continuing until recovery or death but not beyond the normal retirement date. The monthly amount will be $25 per $1,000 on the first $20,000 of group life insurance.

12.06 ***Group Life Insurance***

a. The COMPANY will pay for the first $20,000 of group life insurance available to employees. Employees will have the option of purchasing an additional amount of insurance in accordance with their earnings class schedule.

b. The present permanent and total disability benefit is replaced by a disability waiver-of-premium provision under which coverage will be continued during periods of total disability, while long-term disability payments are being made, but reduced each month by the amount of the long-term disability benefit. Reductions will cease when the amount of insurance in force is equal to the greater of (a) 25 percent of the original amount or (b) the employee's postretirement life amount calculated as of the date of commencement of long-term disability payments. Coverage will be reduced to the latter amount at the earlier of (a) normal retirement age or (b) commencement of any employee retirement income.

12.07 *Retirement Income Plan*

a. The COMPANY will sponsor a 401(k) retirement plan to be administered by Commonwealth National Bank, Central City, Indiana. Any employee may participate in the plan. Employees may make pretax contributions in any amount permitted by current federal tax statutes. For employees who choose to participate, the COMPANY will match 60 percent of contributions up to a maximum of 3 percent of gross pay in any given calendar year. From a menu of choices provided by the plan trustee, employees may allocate how contributions will be invested.

b. The COMPANY will provide for 100 percent vesting of its contributions after five (5) years' service. All individual employee contributions and earnings (losses) are the exclusive property of contributing employee.

c. Contributions and any investment income earned on them that are forfeited by employees who terminate prior to the vesting of pension benefits will be returned to the COMPANY. If an employee terminates in a situation in which the value of the investments attributable to employer contributions are in a loss status, the terminating employee is not responsible for paying the difference between the contributions and the forfeited amount.

d. The UNION acknowledges that neither the COMPANY nor the PLAN ADMINISTRATOR has a fiduciary responsibility to employees as a result of its contributions to or administration of the 401(k) plan. Both the UNION and the COMPANY strongly urge plan participants to seek and utilize professional financial advice before deciding how to allocate plan contributions to various investment options.

12.08 ***Health Care Plan*** For the first $2,500 in medical costs incurred by an employee and his or her family each calendar year, the COMPANY will pay 80 percent of the cost when provided by a Preferred Provider Organization (PPO) approved by the employer. If the employee chooses care from another provider, the employer will pay 80 percent of the cost of the treatment as determined by the PPO fee schedule. For coverage beyond the first $2,500, the COMPANY will contract with Indiana Blue Cross–Blue Shield to provide hospitalization and medical insurance for all employees and their family members residing at home (except children over 21). The COMPANY will pay 90 percent of the premiums necessary to provide full coverage of necessary and approved surgical, medical, and hospital care under Blue Cross–Blue Shield fee schedules when performed by a participating doctor in a participating hospital according to procedures approved by Indiana Blue Cross–Blue Shield. The lifetime liability limit under the Blue Cross–Blue Shield contract for any insured or his/her dependents is $1,500,000.

12.09 Departmental agreements between COMPANY and UNION representatives shall not supersede provisions contained in this Agreement should controversies arise. In no case, however, shall any retroactive adjustment be made if and when such a departmental agreement is canceled. Wherever possible, the UNION shall receive a copy of the agreement.

12.10 ***Optical Care Insurance*** The company will self-insure optical care for bargaining-unit members. The company will provide for one eye exam per year for each employee and his or her dependents as provided by the company's PPO. Examinations conducted by other providers will be reimbursed up to $15 per employee and/or dependent per year. The company will pay for one pair of standard prescription glasses every other year for employees and/or their dependents whose vision prescriptions are measured by the employer's PPO. Eyeware is dispensed by the employer's PPO. If eyeware is not dispensed by the PPO, the employer will reimburse up to $100 per employee and/or dependent every two years. In odd-numbered years of this agreement, employees with birth years ending in odd numbers will be eligible for new prescription eyeware; in even-numbered years, employees with even-numbered birth years will be eligible. Employees must submit claims not later than three months after expenses are incurred to Employee Benefits Coordinators, Inc., the COMPANY'S payment coordinator. Forms for requesting payment are available in the production personnel office.

12.11 ***Safety***

a. The COMPANY will make reasonable provisions for the safety and health of the employees of the plant during the hours of their employment. Such protective devices and other safety equipment as the COMPANY may deem necessary to protect employees from injury properly shall be provided by the COMPANY without cost to the employees. The supervisor in each department will arrange for this equipment.

b. Gloves and uniforms required on such jobs and in such departments as the COMPANY may deem necessary shall be furnished and maintained by the COMPANY.

c. The UNION agrees in order to protect the employees from injury and to protect the facilities of the plant that it will cooperate to the fullest extent in seeing that the rules and regulations are followed and that it will lend its wholehearted support to the safety program of the COMPANY.

d. Rotating UNION departmental representatives chosen by the UNION will participate in periodic safety inspections conducted by departmental supervision and safety staff.

e. The COMPANY agrees that it will give full consideration to all suggestions from its employees or their representatives in matters pertaining to safety and health, including proper heating and ventilation, and if these suggestions are determined to be sound, steps will be taken to put them into effect.

f. It shall be considered a regular part of each employee's regular work to attend such safety meetings as may be scheduled by the COMPANY. Hours spent at safety meetings will be compensated for as hours worked.

g. It is understood that the COMPANY shall not be required to provide work for employees suffering from compensable or other injuries; the COMPANY, however, will offer regular work that may be available to such employees, provided that they can perform all duties of the job.

12.12 Other than for the recall provisions of the Agreement and the privileges accorded an employee under the COMPANY group insurance plans, employees on layoff shall not be entitled to the benefits of this Agreement except eligibility to continue in the health care plan at the employee's expense consistent with the requirements of federal COBRA regulations.

12.13 ***Supplementary Unemployment Benefit Plan***

a. ***Objective*** To provide a greater measure of income protection during periods of unemployment for all eligible employees by supplementing state unemployment benefit payments.

b. ***Principles***

1. To provide income protection for permanent full-time employees as mentioned in (a) above.

2. To preserve the necessary differential between amount received while unemployed and straight-time weekly earnings while working so as to provide an incentive for the unemployed to become employed. This differential is defined to be 65 percent of straight-time weekly earnings less any normal deductions that are not of the savings variety.
3. The COMPANY will pay the difference between 65 percent of straight-time weekly earnings less normal deductions and the state unemployment benefit for which the employee qualifies. In the event the state benefit check is reduced because of ineligibility, the SUB payment will be reduced in the same proportion. The straight-time weekly earnings will be based on the week of layoff. The number of weeks an employee qualifies for depends on length of service.

c. *Eligibility*
   1. Permanent, full-time employees covered under this Agreement.
   2. Five years or more of service.
   3. On layoff from the COMPANY as per seniority provisions in the UNION-MANAGEMENT Agreement and with the following conditions present:
      a. Be able and available for work.
      b. Maintain an active and continuing search for work.
      c. Register and maintain constant contact with the State Employment Office.
      d. Accept referral by the COMPANY to other employers in the area and accept resulting employment offers if deemed suitable under terms of the existing state system.
      e. Layoff not due to a strike, slowdown, work stoppage, or concerted action.
      f. Layoff not due to a labor dispute with the COMPANY or labor picketing conducted on the COMPANY premises that interferes with the COMPANY's operations.
      g. Layoff not due to voluntary quit.
      h. Layoff not due to disciplinary suspensions or discharges.
      i. Layoff not due to leaves of absence.
   4. Weeks of eligibility.
      0–5 years' service credit—0 weeks of SUB.
      5–26 years' service credit—1 week of SUB for each full year of service credit.
      26 or more years' service credit—26 weeks of SUB.

d. ***Reinstatement*** When an employee has received any benefits for which he or she is eligible under this plan as per the schedule, he or she will have his or her full benefits reinstated after 6 months of continuous service.

e. ***To Obtain Benefits*** To obtain benefits, the employee must initiate the claim by preparing the necessary forms and presenting his or her state unemployment check weekly to the personnel office for verification and process of claim.

12.14 The COMPANY will contract with Delta Dental Plan to provide full coverage for preventive dental care and basic restorations up to a limit of $200 annually. The plan will also provide for a lifetime orthodontic benefit of $2,000 for each employee and/or his or her spouse and children when a Delta Dental Plan dentist determines that orthodontia is necessary to prevent higher costs of future dental treatments if left uncorrected.

12.15 In the event any section or any article of this Agreement shall be found to be illegal or inoperable by any government authority of competent jurisdiction, the balance of the Agreement shall remain in full force and effect.

12.16 ***Nondiscrimination Agreement***

a. The COMPANY and the UNION agree that the provisions of this agreement shall apply to all employees covered by the Agreement without discrimination, and in carrying out their respective obligations, it will not discriminate against any employee on account of race, color, national origin, age, sex, or religion.

b. In an effort to make the grievance procedure a more effective instrument for the handling of any claims of discrimination, special effort shall be made by the representatives of each party to raise such claims where they exist and at as early a stage in the grievance procedure as possible. If not earlier, a claim of discrimination shall be stated at least in the third-step proceedings. The grievance and arbitration procedure shall be the exclusive contractual procedure for remedying discrimination claims.

ARTICLE 13. RENEWAL

13.01 This Agreement shall become effective as of March 1, 2009, and shall continue in full force and effect until 11:59 p.m., February 29, 2012, and thereafter from year to year unless written notice to modify, amend, or terminate this Agreement is served by either party 60 days prior to the expiration of this Agreement, stating in full all changes desired.

13.02 After receipt of such notice by either party, both parties shall meet for the purpose of negotiating a new agreement within 30 days from the date of service of said notice, unless the time is extended by mutual agreement.

APPENDIX Classified Base Rates

Job Title	Rate	Job Title	Rate
Assembler, level 1	16.75	Skilled maintenance, level 1	17.52
Assembler, level 2	19.03	Skilled maintenance, level 2	19.79
Assembler, level 3	21.32	Skilled maintenance, level 3	22.09
Skilled production, level 1	18.28	Mat'l hand. & prod. support	17.52
Skilled production, level 2	20.56	Maintenance	14.46
Skilled production, level 3	22.83		

Chapter Twelve

Impasses and Their Resolution

Negotiations don't always yield an agreement. If you're buying a car and the dealer won't accept the highest offer you are willing to make, there is no sale. The same happens in collective bargaining when employers and unions can't agree on contract terms. The failure to reach agreement is called an *impasse*. Unlike a car purchase, unions aren't free to find new employers to deal with, and employers must still be willing to negotiate with their employees' representatives.

Most negotiations do not result in an impasse. The parties usually find a common ground for settlement without strikes or third-party interventions. Data from 2009 show that less than 0.005 percent of the time available for work was lost to strikes.[1]

This chapter examines the causes of impasses in the private sector, tactics used to resolve them, and interventions of third parties. Public sector impasses and their resolution are generally more complex and often applicable only to certain occupational classifications. These are covered in Chapter 16.

In reading this chapter, you should focus attention on these issues:

1. What actions can labor and management legally take after an impasse is reached?
2. What is involved in third-party interventions?
3. What tactics are used by employers and unions when impasses are reached?
4. What are the effects of strikes on employers?

IMPASSE DEFINITION

A bargaining **impasse** occurs when the parties are unable to reach an agreement. It may result from nonoverlapping settlement ranges—the least the union is willing to take is more than the most the employer is

[1] www.bls.gov/news.release/wkstp.nr0.htm.

willing to offer—or may occur when one or both parties are unable or unwilling to communicate enough information about possible settlements for an agreement to be reached. The first type is more difficult to overcome because doing so requires that at least one party adjust its settlement range to reach a solution. The second type may be helped by mediation.

Under the Taft-Hartley Act, if the parties are at an impasse and the contract has expired, in most circumstances the union is free to strike and the employer is free to lock out employees. The process is much more complicated under the Railway Labor Act (RLA). There, one or both of the parties must petition the National Mediation Board (NMB) to declare an impasse. At that point, if the parties have refused voluntary arbitration, and if the NMB declares an impasse, they enter into a 30-day cooling-off period, during which they can continue to negotiate. At the end of the 30 days, the NMB decides whether to permit strikes or lockouts or allow the employer to unilaterally impose a contract. It might also recommend referral to a presidential emergency board. If such a board is established, it would deliberate for 30 days and propose a recommended settlement, followed by another 30-day cooling-off period. If the parties have still not reached an agreement, they are released to engage in self-help.[2]

THIRD-PARTY INVOLVEMENT

Third-party involvement includes mediation, fact-finding, and arbitration. In most non-RLA negotiations (except private sector health care), parties must both agree before any third-party involvement can occur. The only major exception involves national emergency disputes under the Taft-Hartley Act, in which outside fact-finding is required. Because most public sector employees are prohibited from striking, third parties are used more frequently. Third-party interventions in the public sector are covered in Chapter 16.

MEDIATION

In **mediation,** a neutral third party tries to assist the parties to reach an agreement. Procedures are tailored to the situation and aimed at opening communications and identifying settlement cues the parties may have missed.

While some parties use mediation before an impasse, a mediator most often deals with parties that are unable to agree on their own, are at an

[2] See A. von Nordenflycht and T. A. Kochan, "Labor Contract Negotiations in the Airline Industry," *Monthly Labor Review*, 126, no. 7 (2003), pp. 18–28 for detailed information about the number of impasses and the length of negotiations often seen in the domestic airline industry under the RLA.

impasse, and have broken off negotiations. The mediator may have trouble not only in getting a settlement but also in restarting bargaining. To show strength, both sides may refuse to propose a bargaining session; if one appears willing to reopen bargaining, the other might interpret this as weakness or as a willingness to concede.

The mediator must ultimately get the parties face to face to reach a settlement, but the mediator may meet with the parties several times just to assess possibilities of movement. Moving to the mediator's office may strengthen his or her hand in the process. Parties need to communicate and negotiate but not with an intensity that leads them to harden their positions.[3]

Bargainers are rewarded by their constituencies for getting the best possible deal. To an extent, reaching an impasse indicates they have represented their positions vigorously. Mediators are rewarded for gaining agreements. Their concern is not what either party achieves; thus, they are unlikely to influence the direction of the outcome.[4]

The mediator must keep communications open and move the parties toward settlement, if possible. To assess settlement possibilities, the mediator may try out hypothetical settlements to gauge the parties' reactions. Evidence indicates that the parties are at least as able as the mediator to recognize the major issues in the negotiation and the likely outcome.[5] However, they may not be able to reach an agreement because of an inability to explore potential settlements without assistance. The relative rigidity of a party's position must be determined so that the mediator knows on what issues the party is willing to compromise. As a strike deadline looms, the mediator communicates the likelihood of a strike, possible settlement packages, and costs of striking versus settling on the current proposal.[6]

Mediator Behavior and Outcomes

Because mediators operate in a crisis atmosphere, they must have a special mix of experience, talents, and behaviors. They usually take one of two approaches. In the first, the mediator tries to create an acceptable package by obtaining the facts in dispute and the parties' settlement priorities. With this information, the mediator attempts to "make a deal" that both parties

[3] W. E. Simkin, *Mediation and the Dynamics of Collective Bargaining* (Washington, DC: Bureau of National Affairs, 1971).

[4] M. H. Bazerman, M. A. Neale, K. L. Valley, E. J. Zajac, and Y. M. Kim, "The Effect of Agents and Mediators on Negotiation Outcomes," *Organizational Behavior and Human Decision Processes*, 53 (1992), pp. 55–73.

[5] A. Zumbolo, "Expert Judgment in the Mediation of Collective Bargaining Disputes," *Proceedings of the Industrial Relations Research Association*, 56 (2004), pp. 202–207.

[6] For a detailed guide on how a mediator organizes and conducts a mediated negotiation, see. P. D. Roose, "Process, Strategy, and Tactics in Labor-Management Mediation," *Dispute Resolution Journal*, 58, no. 4 (2003), pp. 24–33.

can accept. In the second, through information exchanges between the parties to help them establish priorities and prepare negotiating proposals, mediators orchestrate how the parties build their settlement.[7] Deal makers are less likely than orchestrators to get agreements.[8]

Mediation involves establishing a working relationship between the parties, improving the negotiating climate by facilitating communications and using single-party caucuses, addressing issues, and applying pressure for settlement.[9] Mediation facilitates settlement by (1) reducing hostility through focusing on bargaining objectives; (2) enhancing understanding of the opponent's position; (3) adjusting negotiating formats through chairing, subcommittee creation, and the like; (4) assuming the risk in exploring new solutions; (5) affecting perceptions regarding costs of conflict; and (6) contributing to face-saving facilitating concessions.[10] Table 12.1 shows a set of mediator behaviors and how they can be grouped into clusters. A study of the effects of mediator behavior on the likelihood and quality of a dispute settlement found that contextual, facilitating, and maneuvering behaviors were all positively related while reflexive behaviors were negatively related.[11]

Other influences on mediator behavior and bargaining outcomes involve dispute intensity and mediator activities. Intense disputes reduce the likelihood of mediated settlements, particularly when the employer is unable to pay the increase demanded. When negotiations have broken down, mediators who act aggressively achieve settlements more frequently.[12] Impasses involving a first contract, dislike between key negotiators, conflict within management or union teams, union strength, pattern bargaining, and an inability to pay are more often resolved by intensive mediation. Intense mediation involves the parties being willing to discuss their true feelings before the meeting and to discuss real costs of the proposed packages.

A study examining reactions of managements and unions to mediated settlements found that management believed mediator expertise and

[7] D. M. Kolb, "Strategy and the Tactics of Mediation," *Human Relations*, 36 (1983), pp. 247–268.

[8] D. M. Kolb, "Roles Mediators Play: Contrasts and Comparisons in State and Federal Mediation Practice," *Industrial Relations*, 20 (1981), pp. 1–17.

[9] K. Kressel and D. G. Pruitt, "Conclusion: A Research Perspective on the Mediation of Social Conflict," in K. Kressel, and D. G. Pruitt, and associates, eds., *Mediation Research* (San Francisco: Jossey-Bass, 1989), pp. 394–435.

[10] A. Karim and R. Pegnetter, "Mediator Strategies and Qualities and Mediation Effectiveness," *Industrial Relations*, 22 (1983), pp. 105–114.

[11] R. Martinez-Pecino, L. Munduate, F. J. Medina, M. C. Euwema, "Effectiveness of Mediation Strategies in Collective Bargaining," *Industrial Relations*, 47 (2008), pp. 480–495.

[12] T. A. Kochan and T. Jick, "A Theory of the Public Sector Mediation Process," *Journal of Conflict Resolution*, 22 (1978), pp. 209–241.

TABLE 12.1
Mediator Tactics and Behaviors

Sources: P. J. D. Carnevale and R. Pegnetter, "The Selection of Mediator Tactics in Public Sector Disputes: A Contingency Analysis," *Journal of Social Issues* 41, no. 2 (1985), p. 73; and M. E. McLaughlin, P. Carnevale, and R. G. Lim, "Professional Mediators' Judgments of Mediation Tactics: Multidimensional Scaling and Cluster Analysis," *Journal of Applied Psychology*, 76 (1991), p. 471.

Reflexive	Try to gain their trust/confidence. Develop rapport with them. Attempt to speak their language. Avoid taking sides in important issues. Express pleasure at their progress. Use humor to lighten the atmosphere. Let them blow off steam in front of me. Control their expression of hostility.
Facilitating	*Face saving:* Suggest proposals to help avoid appearance of defeat. Help save face. Take responsibility for their concessions. *Constituency:* Suggest review of needs with constituency. Help them deal with problems with constituents. *Bridging:* Clarify the needs of the other party. Argue their case to the other party. Assure them that the other party is being honest.
Maneuvering	*Make suggestions:* Suggest a particular settlement. Make substantive suggestions for compromise. Suggest trade-offs among the issues. Discuss other settlements. *Pressing:* Express displeasure at their progress. Press them hard to make compromise. Point out costs of disagreement. Tell them the next impasse step is no better. Try to change their expectations. Tell them their position is unrealistic. *Agenda implementation:* Keep negotiations focused on the issues. Control the timing or pace of negotiations. Keep the parties at the table and negotiating. Use late hours, long mediation. Call for frequent caucuses.
Contextual	*Agenda structuring:* Attempt to simplify agenda. Have them prioritize the issues. Attempt to settle simple issues first. Teach them impasse procedures.

impartiality increased the likelihood of settlements, while the union attributed settlements to mediator neutrality and persistence. Mediation strategies most often cited by management as facilitating settlement included discussions of costs of disagreement, suggestions of face-saving proposals, and gains in the parties' trust. Unions said changing expectations and devising an improved negotiating framework hastened settlement.[13] Another study found that a skillful mediator can focus on both the bargaining environment and the specific issues in the negotiations at hand. Such mediators were more successful in gaining agreements by emphasizing a collaborative orientation. Hostility between the parties substantially reduced the possibility of an agreement.[14]

Although mediation is an art, mediator behaviors and dispute type or intensity can be classified; thus, an appropriate style of mediation can be selected to match the intensity of the dispute to exert the greatest likelihood of a settlement. Alternatively, mediators whose styles best fit the impasse could be assigned to the case.[15]

Mediator Backgrounds and Training

Almost all FMCS mediators have previous experience as either management or union negotiators or neutrals in labor relations disputes, they are most often over 45, and many have long experience in the FMCS.[16] This mixture of backgrounds and the independence of the FMCS were ensured by its first director, Cyrus Ching.[17] Exhibit 12.1 displays the toughness and impartiality he established for the FMCS.

A newly appointed mediator generally begins with a two-week training program in Washington and then is sent to a regional office to learn procedures and work with experienced mediators. By the end of the first year, a first case has been assigned. Summaries and specialized training supplement experience as the mediator is assigned to increasingly complex cases.

Mediator Activity

The Taft-Hartley Act requires that parties notify the FMCS 30 days before the expiration of a contract when negotiations are under way and an agreement has not been reached. Table 12.2 shows notifications and caseloads for the FMCS during fiscal years 2006 to 2009. The FMCS was involved in 37 percent of negotiations in bargaining units with more than 1,000 members.

[13] P. F. Gerhart and J. E. Drotning, "Dispute Settlement and the Intensity of Mediation," *Industrial Relations*, 19 (1980), pp. 352–359.

[14] P. M. Mareschal, "What Makes Mediation Work? Mediators' Perspectives on Resolving Disputes," *Industrial Relations*, 44 (2005), pp. 509–517.

[15] See J. Webb, "Behavioral Studies of Third-Party Intervention," in G. M. Stephenson and C. J. Brotherton, eds., *Industrial Relations: A Social Psychological Approach* (New York: Wiley, 1979), pp. 309–331; and J. A. Wall, Jr., "Mediation: A Categorical Analysis and a Proposed Framework for Future Research," *Academy of Management Proceedings*, 40 (1980), pp. 298–302.

[16] Simkin, *Mediation and the Dynamics of Collective Bargaining*, pp. 57–69. More recent work suggests the pattern hasn't changed. See Kolb, "Roles Mediators Play."

[17] A. H. Raskin, "Cyrus S. Ching: Pioneer in Industrial Peacemaking," *Monthly Labor Review*, 112, no. 8 (1989), pp. 22–35.

Exhibit 12.1

CYRUS CHING AND THE 1949 STEEL NEGOTIATIONS

In 1949, when the United Steelworkers and the large steel producers were approaching the showdown over employer-subsidized pensions, Ching felt the only way to avert a strike was through appointment of a presidential fact-finding board. Truman, whose early experiences with labor in the White House made him reluctant ever to get back into the middle of a major industrial confrontation, was cool to the idea. . . . Philip Murray assured Ching that his union would keep its members at work if the companies agreed to appear before the fact finders. Ching anticipated no difficulty on that score, because any recommendations made by the panel would not be binding.

The board of directors of U.S. Steel proved wary, however, and the rest of the industry held off, awaiting "Big Steel's" response. The first word from the board was a telegram to Truman raising questions about the function of the fact finders. Ching regarded all of these inquiries as legitimate, and he had a telegram designed to overcome U.S. Steel's apprehensions sent over the president's signature. The company directors came back with a second telegram to Truman, raising further questions, and Ching was called to the White House for a decision on what the government's next step should be. Ching advised Truman not to answer the wire, but instead to empower the FMCS chief to call Benjamin Fairless, the company's chairman, and tell him he was speaking in the president's name. Given a green light by Truman to proceed, Ching was blunt in his conversation with Fairless the next day.

"My conversation is going to be very short this morning," Ching said. "Number one, I want to tell you that you can't bargain with the president of the United States and, number two, will you send an answer, yes or no, this morning. Either you will or you won't, no more exchanging of telegrams." Fairless gasped, "You're quite plainspoken this morning," he said. "Yes, I intended to be. And that is the message I'm giving you from the president in answer to your telegram." That conversation ended the holdout and the fact-finding panel began its vain effort to head off a strike.

Source: A. H. Raskin, "Cyrus S. Ching: Pioneer in Industrial Peacemaking," *Monthly Labor Review* 112, no. 8 (1989), pp. 33–34.

TABLE 12.2 Mediation Services Program Data

Source: Adapted from *FMCS 2009 Annual Report*, p. 6, available at www.fmcs.gov.

	FY 2006	FY 2007	FY 2008	FY 2009
Assigned cases	15,072	14,663	14,308	13,887
Mediated cases	5,484	5,329	4,836	4,767
Activity rate	29%	31%	29%	30%
Percentage of mediated cases settled	86%	86%	87%	86%
Activity rate in bargaining units with more than 1,000 members	45%	51%	38%	37%

Most cases do not require the intervention of mediators. Data from the FMCS Annual Report series show that mediation is used more often when first contracts are being negotiated and when the term of the contract is for three years. Thus, negotiator inexperience and/or the permanency of the agreement appear to inhibit agreement without outside assistance.

Mediation is one third-party intervention method. It is an active process for keeping the parties together using a neutral approach. Mediation helps the parties settle on their own terms when they have been unable to do so without assistance.

FACT-FINDING

Fact-finding has a long history in U.S. labor relations. In the 19th century, it was used to fix blame on one party rather than finding the underlying causes of the dispute.[18] In present-day fact-finding, a neutral party studies the issues in dispute and publishes a recommendation for settlement.[19] Parties may decide to adopt the published findings or return to bargaining.

Fact-finding has been used primarily in Taft-Hartley emergency disputes (in which it has been relatively ineffectual) and in railroad and airline disputes when the president has created emergency boards under the RLA.[20] The use of RLA emergency boards has declined, and Taft-Hartley injunctions were unused between 1971 and 2002. However, in early 2001, President George W. Bush established an emergency board the weekend before a 30-day cooling-off period imposed by the NMB was to expire in the Aircraft Mechanics Fraternal Association–Northwest Airlines contract negotiations, which otherwise would have allowed the union to strike if no settlement was reached. The airline and the mechanics settled the dispute before the fact-finders were due to deliver their report. In 2002, President Bush halted a West Coast longshore worker strike with a Taft-Hartley injunction. Before a fact-finding report could be prepared, a mediated settlement was reached.

Fact-Finding and the Issues

Private sector fact-finders are not very successful on distributive bargaining issues. They make recommendations but do not personally facilitate bargaining. Neither party may grant legitimacy to an outsider in determining or recommending what either is entitled to. On the other hand, RLA emergency board fact-finders have had some success in integrative

[18] T. J. McDermott, "Fact-Finding Boards in Labor Disputes," *Labor Law Journal*, 11 (1960), pp. 285–304.

[19] C. M. Rehmus, "The Fact-Finder's Role," *Proceedings of the Inaugural Convention of the Society of Professionals in Dispute Resolution*, 1973, pp. 34–44.

[20] Rehmus, "Fact-Finder's Role," pp. 35–36.

bargaining areas. In the rail industry, new technology raised job security issues for unions and survival issues for managements. The parties can implement solutions proposed by neutrals without as much resistance from constituents. Thus, fact-finders facilitate integrative bargaining through the proposal of solutions and encourage intraorganizational bargaining by legitimizing positions the principal negotiators may be willing to raise but see as unacceptable to the memberships.

INTEREST ARBITRATION

Interest arbitration is frequently used in the public sector. Arbitration differs substantially from mediation and fact-finding. While mediation assists the parties to reach their own settlement, arbitration hears the positions of both and decides on binding settlement terms. While fact-finding recommends a settlement, arbitration dictates it.

There are two classes of labor arbitration—interest and rights. **Interest arbitration** deals with situations in which the parties have an interest in the terms of the agreement because the contract will specify future rights. **Rights arbitration** involves the interpretation of an existing contract to determine which party is entitled to a certain outcome or to take a certain action.[21]

In the United States, interest arbitration was used by the National War Labor Board during World War II and has been imposed on railroads by Congress on a number of occasions since the 1960s. Interest arbitration is offered by the NMB in impasses before the parties are released to engage in "self-help" (strikes and lockouts). If the Employee Free Choice Act (as it was introduced in 2009) were to become law, arbitration would be required if negotiations to reach a first contract were at an impasse.

The government may also pressure a settlement without resorting to statutory processes. As Exhibit 12.2 details, during the Northwest Airlines–Air Line Pilots Association strike of 1998, Bruce Lindsey, counsel to the president, and Secretary of Transportation Rodney Slater joined NMB chairwoman Maggie Jacobsen to arm-twist the parties into reaching an agreement.

REVIEW OF THIRD-PARTY INVOLVEMENTS

Of the three methods of third-party involvements, only arbitration guarantees resolution. However, interest arbitration has been avoided in the private sector. Fact-finding also has a relatively checkered past. When used, it has been imposed on the parties, which are free to ignore its

[21] *Elgin, Joliet, & Eastern Railway Co.* v. *Burley*, 325 U.S. 71 (1945).

Exhibit 12.2

FEDERAL GOVERNMENT ARM-TWISTING

When the Northwest Airlines pilots strike ended Saturday and the gags were lifted on union officials, they spoke in respectful tones about the role White House deputy counsel Bruce Lindsey and other government officials played in ending the biggest walkout of pilots in aviation history.

"It helps when you've got the president's pager number," said Mark Innerbichler, one of 17 voting members on the Master Executive Council of the Northwest Air Line Pilots Association (ALPA).

Innerbichler and other union leaders were briefed Saturday on the government's "arm-twisting" campaign before they ratified the proposed four-year agreement, ending the 15-day strike by 6,200 Northwest pilots.

In the end, the company and union compromised on pre-strike contract proposals that contained serious differences.

In coaxing the settlement, Lindsey overtly threatened ALPA and Northwest negotiators with White House intervention if they didn't each soften their positions and craft an agreement of their own, Innerbichler said.

At that point in the talks, neither side wanted a Presidential Emergency Board, which would have ordered the pilots back to work.

The company feared that the board would be stacked with arbitrators sympathetic to labor, and the union clung to its original worry that White House interference would set a dangerous precedent for labor groups throughout the airline industry.

"[Lindsey] looked at the clock, and he said, 'In one hour I'm going to pick up the phone. The executive order is already written because I wrote it myself before I left Washington,'" Innerbichler said.

He said Lindsey, working in tandem with National Mediation Board Chairwoman Maggie Jacobsen and federal mediator Jack Kane, backed up his words Thursday morning by packing his suitcases and threatening to leave. By about 1 p.m., ALPA and Northwest negotiators agreed on a proposed pact that would end the strike. Only then did Lindsey return to Washington. He never commented publicly about his role in the settlement and he avoided the press during his visit to the Twin Cities.

Source: Excerpted from T. Kennedy, "Clinton Aide Lindsey Was Pivotal in Ending Strike, Both Sides Say," *Star Tribune* (Minneapolis, MN), September 14, 1998. Reprinted with permission.

recommendations. Actually, fact-finding doesn't involve facts, only values associated with the possible positions taken on outcomes in the dispute. Mediation is neutral in that it requires that the parties bargain their own terms. It has been relatively successful in keeping parties at the table, given the FMCS caseload and success rate reported earlier.

Sometimes at impasse mediation has been refused, and mediation and fact-finding don't always break impasses. Then strikes, lockouts, or other pressuring activities occur. Strikes pressure employers to settle on union terms. Lockouts or hiring replacements are attempts to get unions to settle on employer terms. We will examine their use, effectiveness, and legality next.

STRIKES

The four major types of strikes have one thing in common: the employees refuse to work. An **economic strike** is called after a contract expires and usually after there is an impasse to pressure the employer to settle on the union's terms. In this type of strike, the union believes the strike's costs (both economic and political) will be less to it than to the employer, and that the benefits to the union from achieving its demands are greater than the strike's costs. An economic strike can be called over any mandatory bargaining issue. But if a union goes to impasse over a permissive issue, it commits an unfair labor practice (ULP).[22]

Unfair labor practice strikes protest employer labor law violations. If an employer violates the law, the employees' right to strike in protest and to be reinstated at its end is absolutely protected by the NLRB and the courts. A **wildcat strike** is an unauthorized stoppage during the contract. Employees may be disciplined if the strike breaches a no-strike clause. A **sympathy strike** occurs when one union strikes to support another union's strike. Such strikes occur where more than one union represents employees in a single establishment or where several plants have separate contracts. The union's right to support another union is guaranteed by the Norris-LaGuardia Act, even if its contract contains a no-strike clause and provides for arbitration of unresolved grievances,[23] unless it's clear that the no-strike clause prohibits sympathy strikes.[24]

If the parties bargain in good faith to an impasse, an economic strike ensues, and both parties refuse to move further, the gulf would be permanent. The employer has the right to implement its last offer if the contract has expired, but employees are also free to strike. If employees continue striking, the employer would need to hire new employees to remain in business. It is legal to replace economic strikers and resume operations.[25] But replacements would be in the bargaining unit represented by the striking union as long as it is certified.

Strike Votes and Going Out

Unions usually take strike authorization votes during negotiations to strengthen their bargaining positions. This doesn't mean a strike will occur, only that the union may go on strike after the contract expires. A local union usually needs the national's approval to strike. If it strikes without

[22] *Detroit Resilient Floor Decorators Union*, 136 NLRB 756 (1962).

[23] *Buffalo Forge Co.* v. *United Steelworkers of American, AFL-CIO*, 92 LRRM 3032 (U.S. Supreme Court, 1976).

[24] *John Morrell Co.* v. *UFCW, Local 304A*, U.S. Court of Appeals, 8th Circuit, 1990, 135 LRRM 2233.

[25] *NLRB* v. *MacKay Radio & Telegraph*, 304 U.S. 333 (1938).

approval, the local and its officers may be disciplined, the international may place the local under trusteeship, or strike benefits may not be paid.

If an impasse occurs and a strike has been authorized, union negotiators decide whether to strike or continue to work under terms of the expired contract. Continuations occur more often than strikes. Strikes are more likely if unemployment rates have decreased recently and/or employees in the bargaining unit have suffered a drop in their real wages.[26]

Unions usually require that members participate in strike activities, such as picketing, to receive strike benefits, and they may discipline members who refuse to strike. A strike may increase the cohesiveness and solidarity of the union. UAW members involved in contract negotiations in 1976 and 1977 were surveyed four times. During the talks, Ford was struck, but GM and Chrysler were not. While on strike, Ford employees' attitudes toward their international union and its leaders were more positive than they were before the strike and more positive than those of fellow union members at GM and Chrysler.[27]

Observers often believe that strikes occur because of a failure to communicate enough information about likely settlement ranges. However, strikes are also the collective voice of employees to show employers that workers need not continually comply. A study of Canadian strikes found that the rigidity of management practices and internal union politics influence union members' willingness to strike and the strike's subsequent length.[28] The willingness of individual union members to strike is increased by perceptions that the current employment relationship is unfair or unjust and among members who have a stronger collectivist orientation to work.[29] A study of Temple University faculty members whose union voted to reject a contract offer and three days later voted not to comply with an injunction to end a strike found that votes against the contract offer were predicted by low job satisfaction, low commitment to the employer, perceived instrumentality of the strike, being a woman, and not being in an engineering or hard science department. Votes to defy the injunction were related to low pay satisfaction, commitment to the union, strike support within the member's department, and perceived instrumentality of the strike. Predictors of militant activity included commitment to the union, strike support within the member's department,

[26] P. C. Cramton and J. S. Tracy, "Strikes and Holdouts in Wage Bargaining: Theory and Data," *American Economic Review*, 82 (1992), pp. 100–121.

[27] R. Stagner and B. Eflal, "Internal Union Dynamics during a Strike: A Quasi-Experimental Study," *Journal of Applied Psychology*, 67 (1982), pp. 37–44.

[28] J. Godard, "Strikes as Collective Voice: A Behavioral Analysis of Strike Activity," *Industrial and Labor Relations Review*, 46 (1992), pp. 161–175.

[29] D. M. Buttigieg, S. J. Deery, and R. D. Iverson, "Union Mobilization: A Consideration of the Factors Affecting the Willingness of Union Members to Take Industrial Action," *British Journal of Industrial Relations*, 46 (2008), pp. 248–267.

perceived instrumentality of the strike, comfort with demonstrative or confrontational forms of militancy, and being in upper professorial ranks (not assistants or instructors, so probably insulated by tenure).[30]

Strikes are a powerful weapon with strong social overtones. There are mixed reactions to strikes, largely dependent on social status, irrespective of union membership. People having a higher social status generally disapprove of strikes and coercive picketing, while persons in lower social status groups are more likely to approve militant action.[31] Members of the public who have stronger prounion attitudes and who believe that management's contract offer is unfair are more likely to support strikers and strike activities like refusing to cross picket lines.

Picketing

Picketing is one of the most noticeable union activities. In picketing, the union informs the public about the dispute and appeals to others to stop doing business with the employer during the dispute. Federal courts may not enjoin picketing unless there is a clear and present danger to life or property. States may not restrict peaceful picketing because it is protected by the First Amendment.[32] However, some restrictions are imposed on **recognitional picketing** under Landrum-Griffin.

To be protected from employer reprisals, employees must publicize that they are involved in a labor dispute when they picket or inform the public about the employer or its products and services.[33] Picket lines are aimed at influencing or persuading others not to engage in business transactions with the picketed employer. Business transactions include buying from, supplying to, working for, and the like. Picket lines are also aimed at maintaining solidarity of union by discouraging members who do not necessarily favor the strike from returning to work. As long as picket-line behavior could not be reasonably construed to be coercive or intimidating toward others, destructive to property, or interfering with the completion of business transactions, it would not be enjoinable or an unfair labor practice.[34] The site and manner of the picketing are also of concern, because the union can be accused of illegal secondary activity in certain instances. The next sections examine various types of picketing. Legal picketing is not

[30] J. A. McClendon and B. Klaas, "Determinants of Strike-Related Militancy: An Analysis of a University Faculty Strike," *Industrial and Labor Relations Review*, 46 (1993), pp. 560–573.

[31] G. M. Saltzman, "The Impact of Social Class on Attitudes toward Strikes: A Four Country Study," *Labor Studies Journal*, 22, no. 3 (1997), pp. 28–56.

[32] *Thornhill* v. *Alabama*, 310 U.S. 88 (1940).

[33] *NLRB* v. *Local Union, 1229, International Brotherhood of Electrical Workers*, 346 U.S. 464 (1953).

[34] For an analysis of the consequences of violence to picket-line perpetrators, see D. M. Partridge, "Violence and Strikers' Rights to Reinstatement: Two Decades' Experience under *Clear Pine Mouldings*," *Employee Relations Law Journal*, 35, no. 2 (2009), pp. 52–68.

necessarily associated with strikes; it may also involve informational and recognitional activities.

Picket lines inform other unions' members of the dispute and ask that they not cross. They also aim at deterring their members from working. Differences exist in union members' potential willingness to honor picket lines, however. Those who have less positive attitudes toward the union and who are earning lower wages than average are less willing to strike as long and more willing to cross picket lines.[35] Where represented employees cross picket lines, the union's bargaining power is decreased because their crossing increases the employer's ability to operate. In one situation, crossing behavior after a strike authorization vote was taken was positively related to a "no" vote for the authorization, satisfaction with management, and perceived hardship and was negatively related to union commitment and co-worker social support. Crossing a picket line after a contract rejection was positively associated with a vote to accept and negatively associated with union commitment and co-worker social support.[36]

Common Situs Picketing

The place where picketing occurs may affect secondary employers. This is important in construction, where a primary contractor and subcontractors work together on a common site. Each uses different trades; may or may not be unionized; and may have different wages, terms, and expiration dates in contracts. If unions strike in sympathy with a primary dispute, even if it involves only one contractor, a whole site may be shut down.

A *primary employer* is one involved in a dispute, and a *neutral employer* is one affected by the picketing activity of the primary's employees. The laws governing **common situs picketing** in construction were established in the *Denver Building Trades Council* cases.[37] Picketing began when it was learned the primary contractor on the site had employed a nonunion subcontractor. The picketing was aimed at forcing the general contractor to drop the subcontractor. When picketing began, all other union workers refused to cross the picket line. The primary contractor maintained the dispute was with the subcontractor and general picketing of the site was an illegal **secondary boycott** designed to force neutral employers not to do business with the subcontractor. The court's ruling forbids construction unions to picket sites to force a primary employer to cease doing business with a nonunion subcontractor. The usual practice at construction sites is to establish reserved gates for each employer. Primary-dispute pickets may then patrol only their employer's gate.

[35] M. H. LeRoy, "Multivariate Analysis of Unionized Employees' Propensity to Cross Their Union's Picket Lines," *Journal of Labor Research*, 13 (1992), pp. 285–292.

[36] B. S. Klaas and J. A. McClendon, "Crossing the Line: The Determinants of Picket Line Crossing during a Faculty Strike," *Journal of Labor Research*, 16 (1995), pp. 331–346.

[37] *NLRB* v. *Denver Building Trades Council*, 341 U.S. 675 (1951).

Ambulatory Site

Sometimes the objects of a strike move from place to place, such as a ship being struck by a seafarers union. In one case, when the ship was moved to dry dock for repairs, the union tried to picket next to the ship. Dry dock managers refused to allow this, and a picket line was set up at the entrance to the dock. Such picketing was ruled legal if (1) the object is currently on the secondary employer's site, (2) the primary employer continues to engage in its normal business, (3) the picketing is reasonably close to the strike object, and (4) the picketing discloses the dispute is with the struck employer and not the site owner.[38]

Multiple-Use Sites

Multiple-use sites, such as shopping malls, include several employers. There it is difficult to picket a primary employer without disrupting secondary businesses. The struck employer has usually leased the site from another company that owns the shopping mall. The Supreme Court has held that peaceful picketing to inform the public about a dispute must not interfere with other stores or the shopping mall owner.[39] Since it is difficult to legally picket a multiple-use site, unions have switched to using billboards, banners, and inflatable rats and parking them just off the premises but in a prominent place for potential customers to view them.[40] Figure 12.1 is an example of how inflatable rats are used in labor disputes.

Slowdowns

Unions have increasingly turned to slowdowns to put pressure on employers. A slowdown most often involves **working to rules**. Employees refuse to perform tasks outside their job descriptions, follow procedures to the letter, and refuse overtime. Because they are complying with the contract and company work rules, they can seldom be disciplined.[41] An example of a slowdown or work-to-rule activity was the Air Line Pilots Association's refusal to fly overtime at United Airlines in the summer of 2000 until a new contract was negotiated. Exhibit 12.3 details the effects.

Another example of a disruption short of a strike was the CHAOS (create havoc around our system) tactic used by America West Airlines's flight

[38] *Sailor's Union of the Pacific (Moore Dry Dock Co.),* 92 NLRB 547 (1950).

[39] *Edward J. DeBartolo Corp.* v. *Florida Gulf Coast Building and Construction Trades Council and NLRB*, U.S. Supreme Court, No. 86-1461 (1988).

[40] For an analysis of the developing law on whether this constitutes picketing or protected free speech, see T. F. Ryan and K. M. Davis, "Banners, Rats, and Other Inflatable Toys: Do They Constitute Picket Activity? Do They Violate Section 8(B)(4)?" *The Labor Lawyer*, 20 (2004), pp. 137–154.

[41] "Labor's Shift: Finding Strikes Harder to Win, More Unions Turn to Slowdowns," *The Wall Street Journal*, May 22, 1987, pp. 1, 6; see also a publication for union members, *The Inside Game: Winning with Workplace Strategies* (Washington, DC: Industrial Union Department, AFL-CIO, 1987).

FIGURE 12.1
Strike Rat

Source: http://tyronemalone.blogspot.com/2007/11/strike-rat-takes-out-jack-bauer.html. Photo from the public domain.

attendants. They would inform management immediately before a flight that they were striking (a protected concerted activity), and then, when the flight was canceled, they would immediately abandon the strike and request reinstatement. If they were refused reinstatement, this would be a potential ULP.[42] Flight attendants at Northwest Airlines also threatened to use this technique in 2006 when the airline was seeking to abrogate their contract during Chapter 11 bankruptcy proceedings.

Corporate Campaigns

In a **corporate campaign**, the union exerts pressure where the employer might be vulnerable to support a collective bargaining objective. A corporate campaign first explores the company's business activity to uncover possible regulatory violations recorded by government agencies, such as the Environmental Protection Agency or Occupational Safety and Health Administration. The campaign also finds which other corporations are closely linked as suppliers, customers, financial backers, and the like. Corporate investigations will also include detailed analyses of the firm's publicly reported financial data.

The second phase involves publicizing items detrimental to the employer's interests that support the union's demands. The campaign tries to get outsiders to pressure the employer to settle with the union on terms beneficial to the employees. Some of the activities may be undertaken to motivate consumer boycotts.[43] A corporate campaign successfully forced the

[42] S. Estreicher and R. Siegel, "Partial Strikes under the Railway Labor Act: The Need for a Doctrine of Unprotected Concerted Activity," *Labor Lawyer*, 18 (2002), pp. 15–25.

[43] H. Datz, L. Geffner, J. M. McLaughlin, and S. Kellock, "Economic Warfare in the 1980s: Strikes, Lockouts, Boycotts, and Corporate Campaigns," *Industrial Relations Law Journal*, 9 (1987), pp. 82–115.

Exhibit 12.3

WORKING TO RULES TO PRESSURE EMPLOYERS

The Chicago Transit Authority (CTA) bus drivers' union threatened a "working to rules" slowdown to pressure the CTA to limit demands for concessions during their 2010 contract negotiations. Drivers would adhere strictly to CPA operating rules not to exceed 35 miles per hour, to require that all passengers be seated or standing securely before proceeding, and not proceeding through already green lights after picking up passengers.

Capistrano (California) Unified School District teachers staged a one-week work slowdown in January 2010 to protest a 10 percent wage cut. Their union encouraged them to stop doing any work not required by their labor agreement, including taking work home, returning parent calls at night, and voluntary tutoring of students during lunch or after school. The slowdown was aimed at demonstrating to parents the uncompensated non-contractual extra work that teachers willingly provide.

After their contract expired in April 2000, an overwhelming proportion of United Airlines pilots refused to work overtime causing delays and cancellations of up to 200 flights per day.

Sources: Adapted from J. Byrne, "CTA Bus Drivers Threaten Work Slowdown," *Chicago Tribune*, February 14, 2010; S. Martindale, *OCRegister.com*, January 21, 2010; and D. Barboza, "United Airlines Cancels More Flights," *New York Times*, August 9, 2000, p. C18.

J. P. Stevens Company to negotiate a first contract with the Clothing and Textile Workers, which had won representation rights several years earlier.

Coordinated Campaigns

Coordinated campaigns simultaneously pressure the employer on several fronts, occurring instead of a strike or in reaction to a lockout. Such campaigns may pursue legislative investigations of company practices. They may also encourage tracing shipments of company goods to other firms, particularly if the struck company is a supplier, and then indicating that using the goods will be publicized. If there is international financial involvement, unions may seek cooperation from unions in other countries to pressure investors.[44] Exhibit 12.4 explains how the tactic was developed and used in the Ravenswood Aluminum Corporation lockout (which was controlled by the then-fugitive financier, Marc Rich, who was later pardoned by President Clinton just before leaving office in 2001).

Employer Responses to Strikes

Various responses are available to employers when struck; such responses generally fall into three categories: (1) shut down the affected area, (2) continue operating, or (3) contract out work for the duration. Each response has its own consequences and can cause retaliatory action.

[44] T. Juravich and K. Bronfenbrenner, *Ravenswood: The Steelworkers' Victory and the Revival of American Labor* (Ithaca, NY: Cornell University Press/ILR Press, 1998).

Exhibit 12.4

COORDINATED CAMPAIGN ACTION

Their first action [in Switzerland] was a press conference outside [Marc] Rich headquarters in Zug. The Swiss metalworkers had publicized the event, which was well attended. Throughout the crowd signs could be spotted declaring solidarity of Swiss trade unionists with the "American Aluminum Workers." Uehlein and Chapman described the lockout, the NLRB complaint, the OSHA charges, and the connection between Rich and Ravenswood. Uehlein declared, "If we did not believe in the relationship between Ravenswood and Marc Rich, we would not have come to Zug. . . ."

Then Dan Stidham, after introducing himself as "A union man all my life," told the crowd what Emmett Boyle, Marc Rich, and the lockout meant to the workers and their community. He ended his remarks:

> But we won't go away, and neither will all the people around Ravenswood who are supporting us. They don't like scabs any more than we do. And they don't like absentee owners lining their own pockets at the expense of the standard of living of entire communities. And that's what's happening. Without paychecks, we've had to struggle to support our families. We're not buying all the things we need, and small businesses, ones that we've patronized for years, are really hurting. They're having to cut back, too, and lay off workers. But RAC doesn't care. Not as long as it can sell aluminum and hire scabs. That's why we're here, to get some help from our union brothers and sisters in Europe, so we can help our union brothers and sisters back home.

Source: T. Juravich and K. Bronfenbrenner, *Ravenswood: The Steelworkers' Victory and the Revival of American Labor* (Ithaca, NY: Cornell University Press/ILR Press, 1998), p. 116.

Shutdowns

Shutdowns avoid highly negative consequences for future labor relations. But if there is a shutdown, production revenues are lost, and competitors may gear up to take over the lost production, a consequence that could permanently reduce the struck company's market share. If a firm is a sole supplier, its customers may encourage others to enter the market as alternative sources. In addition, during periods of high demand, the firm may lose its suppliers as they fill orders from more reliable customers. For employers who have implemented a labor-intensive production technology, this might be their only realistic decision.

Continued Operations

Continued operations may be accomplished by two strategies. Neither is relished by the union, but the second will almost certainly lead to militant action. The first is to continue to operate using supervisors and other nonproduction workers, which is feasible if the firm is not labor intensive and if maintenance demands are not high. Automated and

Exhibit 12.5

WHAT IS A SCAB?

After God had finished the rattlesnake, the toad, and the vampire, He had some awful substance left with which He made a scab. A scab is a two-legged animal with a corkscrew soul, a water-logged brain, and a combination backbone made of jelly and glue. Where others have hearts, he carries a tumor of rotten principles.

When a scab comes down the street, men turn their backs, and angels weep in heaven, and the devil shuts the gates of hell to keep him out. No man has a right to scab as long as there is a pool of water deep enough to drown his body in, or a rope long enough to hang his carcass with. Judas Iscariot was a gentleman compared with a scab. For betraying his Master, he had character enough to hang himself. A scab hasn't!

Esau sold his birthright for a mess of pottage. Judas Iscariot sold his Savior for 30 pieces of silver. Benedict Arnold sold his country for a promise of a commission in the British Army. The modern strikebreaker sells his birthright, his country, his wife, his children, and his fellow men for an unfulfilled promise from his employer, trust, or corporation.

Esau was traitor to himself. Judas Iscariot was a traitor to his God. Benedict Arnold was a traitor to his country.

A strikebreaker is a traitor to his God, his country, his family, and his class!

Source: P. S. Foner, *Jack London, American Rebel* (New York: Citadel Press, 1947), pp. 57–58.

continuous-flow operations, such as in the chemical industry, fall into this category. If this strategy is used, supervisor-employee relations may be strained after the strike because the supervisors' work may have enabled the company to prolong the strike. Evidence indicates that employers in most industries are able to continue operating without using permanent replacements.[45]

The second strategy is to hire strike replacements. Because this jeopardizes strikers' jobs, violence is likely. If a company can hire replacements, it substantially reduces union bargaining power. However, strike replacements face a difficult situation. They are reviled by strikers as scabs (see Exhibit 12.5 for a definition almost invariably used when replacements are hired), and, due to low seniority, they may be vulnerable to layoff when a new contract is signed. However, if the employer can operate for a year without an end to the strike, new employees could vote to decertify the union. Violence often occurs when employers continue operations with supervisors or replacement workers. Major examples include the New York Daily News, Detroit Free Press–Detroit News, and Phelps-Dodge strikes.

[45] C. L. Gramm, "Empirical Evidence on Political Arguments Relating to Replacement Worker Legislation, *Labor Law Journal*, 42 (1991), pp. 491–496.

Strike Replacements and Public Policy

Since the *Mackay* decision, employers have been free to hire replacements for economic strikers. The frequency of replacing strikers is low, but it increased between 1975 and 1990.[46] With the increased threat or use of replacements, unions lobbied for legislation to prohibit replacing economic strikers. Most Canadian provinces prohibit strike replacements. Employers argue that eliminating the threat of replacements would substantially reduce their bargaining power, but one study of the effects of the laws in Canada, where they vary across provinces, indicates they have little effect on the economic outcomes in bargaining.[47] However, another study found that laws forbidding strike replacements are associated with 2 percent higher wage settlements per year, all else being equal. The probability of a strike also increased from about 15 to almost 27 percent.[48] Another Canadian study found that strike duration was increased from 48 days without replacements to 280 days with them.[49] In Canada, enactment of provincial laws banning strike replacements and allowing workers to refuse to handle struck work resulted in employers reducing the rate of business investment to a level about equal to what would be experienced in a recession.[50]

Employers run some legal and operating risks using replacements. The NLRB finds unfair labor practices in most strikes where replacements are used.[51] If the ULPs involve a refusal to bargain, the employer may face potentially large back-pay liabilities.[52] Where employers continue operations using nonproduction workers or hiring replacements, higher injury rates follow, with higher workers's compensation insurance rates likely.[53] A case study of the Detroit Newspaper Association strike that began in

[46] M. H. LeRoy, "Regulating Employer Use of Permanent Strike Replacements: Empirical Analysis of NLRB and RLA Strikes 1935–1991," *Berkeley Journal of Employment and Labor Law*, 16 (1995), pp. 169–208.

[47] J. W. Budd, "Canadian Strike Replacement Legislation and Collective Bargaining: Lessons for the United States," *Industrial Relations*, 35 (1996), pp. 245–260.

[48] P. Cramton, M. Gunderson, and J. Tracy, "Impacts of Strike Replacement Bans in Canada," *Labor Law Journal*, 50 (1999), pp. 173–179.

[49] H. C. Jain and P. Singh, "The Effects of the Use of Strike Replacements on Strike Duration in Canada," *Labor Law Journal*, 50 (1999), pp. 180–186.

[50] J. W. Budd and Y. Wang, "Labor Policy and Investment: Evidence from Canada," *Industrial and Labor Relations Review*, 57 (2004), pp. 386–401.

[51] M. H. LeRoy, "The Changing Character of Strikes Involving Permanent Strike Replacements," *Journal of Labor Research*, 16 (1995), pp. 423–438.

[52] Juravich and Bronfenbrenner, *Ravenswood*. In this case the NLRB found that the company owed $120 million in back pay (about $70,000 per worker). Had the finding been implemented, the company would have been forced out of business. As part of the contract settlement, the union agreed to a substantial reduction in the back-pay award.

[53] W. D. Allen, "How Strikes Influence Work-Injury Duration: Evidence from the State of New York," *Proceedings of the Industrial Relations Research Association*, 46 (1994), pp. 306–314.

1995 chronicles how meticulously thorough strike preparations and lack of solidarity among union members enabled an employer to continue operations with replacements and hamstring the union with successful unfair labor practices charges related to picket-line violence and intimidation.[54]

Contracting Out

Strikes have serious consequences for employers with major customers whose businesses require output on a fixed schedule, particularly if competitors offer the same services. One strategy is to arrange for a competitor to temporarily handle the work.

On its face, this seems foolproof—there are no problems with strikebreakers and the union, and customers get their work done on time—however, it's not. If the subcontractor is unionized, its employees legally can refuse to perform the work when a struck employer has initiated the order. Such refusals are allowed under the so-called **ally doctrine**.

For example, a printing firm responsible for providing Sunday supplements to newspapers was struck by its employees. To maintain its ability to meet the weekly schedule, it subcontracted the work to another firm. When the second firm's employees learned why they were doing the work, they refused to perform it. The first employer charged this was a secondary boycott, but the NLRB reasoned the dispute became primary through the handling of the struck work for the primary employer.[55]

Health care providers are granted an exception to the ally doctrine. Sick patients can't wait for care until a strike ends. Hospitals accepting patients from struck hospitals cannot risk an extension of the strike to them. Section 8(b)(4) of the Taft-Hartley Act was amended to allow a limited exemption to the ally doctrine for health care providers. If one hospital is struck and another supplies an occasional technician to assist, no ally relationship is established. But if shifts of nurses were provided by a group of hospitals, they would become allies. Thus, the magnitude of assistance is the determining factor in whether struck work can be refused.

Rights of Economic Strikers

If replacements are hired, strikers may still get their jobs back. First, if they offer unilaterally to return and if their jobs or others they qualify for are unfilled, refusing to rehire them is a ULP since strikes are protected by Section 7 of the Taft-Hartley Act. Second, if employees ask for reinstatement at the strike's end, they are entitled to their jobs, if open, or to preference in hiring when positions become open.[56] Employers may give job preferences to replacements or employees who crossed the picket line before the end

[54] J. A. Taylor, "The Detroit Newspaper Strike: A Template for Employers Preparing for and Operating during a Labor Strike," *Labor Law Journal*, 59 (2008), pp. 166–189.

[55] *Blackhawk Engraving Co.*, 219 NLRB 169 (1975).

[56] *NLRB* v. *Fleetwood Trailer Co., Inc.*, 389 U.S. 375 (1967).

TABLE 12.3
Work Stoppages Involving 1,000 or More Workers, 1948–2009

Source: www.bls.gov/news.release/wkstp.nr0.htm.

Year	Number of Strikes	Workers Involved (000)	Person-Days Idle (000)	Percent of Total Days Available
1948	243	1,435	26,127	0.22
1953	437	1,623	18,130	0.14
1958	332	1,587	17,900	0.13
1963	181	512	10,020	0.07
1968	392	1,855	35,367	0.20
1973	317	1,400	16,260	0.08
1978	219	1,006	23,774	0.11
1983	81	909	17,461	0.08
1988	40	118	4,381	0.02
1993	35	182	3,981	0.01
1998	34	387	5,116	0.02
2003	14	129	4,091	0.01
2008	17	171	3,344	0.01
2009	5	13	124	<0.005

of the strike.[57] They are not required to reinstate employees who commit sabotage and picket-line violence. But discharges must be for cause, and the grievance procedure would be available for hearing disputes over these discharges.

Evidence on the Incidence, Duration, and Effects of Strikes

Strikes are popularly viewed as counterproductive. Those not directly involved might be inconvenienced, and often a winner is not apparent. Companies' profits are eroded by lost sales, and workers lose income that takes years to make up even if the strike gains higher wages than the employer's last prestrike offer. But striking or taking a threatened strike may be a long-term investment. If a union never supports its demands with militant action, the employer may doubt the credibility of its threats. A short strike may be a relatively low-cost investment in gaining large future demands. From an employer standpoint, taking a strike may be necessary for gaining agreement to introduce new work methods or for lowering expectations.[58]

The number and length of strikes have fallen sharply since the end of the 1970s. In 2009, as compared with 1953, there were 1.1 percent as many strikes in large employers and about 0.7 percent as many days lost due to strikes. Compared with 1983, there were only 6 percent as many strikes and only 0.7 percent as many days lost. The incidence of strikes and working days lost has fallen faster than the shrinkage of the unionized share of the workforce. Table 12.3 displays historical strike data.

[57] *TWA* v. *Independent Federation of Flight Attendants*, U. S. Supreme Court, 1989, 130 LRRM 2657.

[58] For arguments supporting this position, see C. R. Greer, S. A. Martin, and T. E. Reusser, "The Effect of Strikes on Shareholder Returns," *Journal of Labor Research*, 1 (1980), pp. 217–229; and M. J. Mauro, "Strikes as a Result of Imperfect Information," *Industrial and Labor Relations Review*, 35 (1982), pp. 522–538.

Incidence of Strikes

Several economic and structural variables are linked to the incidence of economic strikes. Strikes are more frequent when costs of disagreeing or the parties' relative risks have substantially changed since earlier negotiations. For example, declining real wages or failure to win settlements comparable to other contracts increases strike likelihoods.[59] Strike incidence is procyclical; that is, strikes increase as unemployment falls and inflation rises.[60]

Employer and union stability[61] and stability in the employer's supplier market are associated with lower incidence rates.[62] Economic strikes in the auto industry were more prevalent when productivity was low, while intracontract strikes were more frequent when productivity was increasing.[63] Strikes of 14 days or less during the last negotiation increase the odds of strikes in the present round.[64] However, a study of strikes in Ontario found that previous strikes reduced the possibility in the next round, smaller units were less likely to strike, and (not surprisingly in Ontario) strikes were less frequent in winter.[65] Higher proportions of unionized employees in an industry are related to higher strike and wage levels, reflecting successful use of union bargaining power.[66] Unions in high-injury industries strike more frequently, perhaps reflecting willingness to

[59] See O. Ashenfelter and G. Johnson, "Bargaining Theory, Trade Unions, and Industrial Strike Activity," *American Economic Review*, 59 (1969), pp. 35–49; D. J. B. Mitchell, "A Note on Strike Propensities and Wage Developments," *Industrial Relations*, 20 (1981), pp. 123–127; M. I. Naples, "An Analysis of Defensive Strikes," *Industrial Relations*, 26 (1987), pp. 96–105; and C. L. Gramm, "The Determinants of Strike Incidence and Severity: A Micro-Level Study," *Industrial and Labor Relations Review*, 39 (1986), pp. 361–376.

[60] See J. Kennan, "Pareto Optimality and the Economics of Strike Duration," *Journal of Labor Research*, 1 (1980), pp. 77–94; B. E. Kaufman, "The Determinants of Strikes over Time and across Industries," *Journal of Labor Research*, 4 (1983), pp. 159–175; C. L. Gramm, W. E. Hendricks, and L. M. Kahn, "Inflation Uncertainty and Strike Activity," *Industrial Relations*, 27 (1988), pp. 114–129; S. B. Vroman, "A Longitudinal Analysis of Strike Activity in U.S. Manufacturing: 1957–1984," *American Economic Review*, 79 (1989), pp. 816–826; and S. McConnell, "Cyclical Fluctuations in Strike Activity," *Industrial and Labor Relations Review*, 44 (1990), pp. 130–143.

[61] B. E. Kaufman, "The Determinants of Strikes in the United States: 1900–1977," *Industrial and Labor Relations Review*, 35 (1982), pp. 473–490.

[62] J. M. Cousineau and R. Lacroix, "Imperfect Information and Strikes: An Analysis of Canadian Experience, 1967–82," *Industrial and Labor Relations Review*, 39 (1986), pp. 539–549.

[63] S. Flaherty, "Strike Activity, Worker Militancy, and Productivity Change in Manufacturing, 1961–1981," *Industrial and Labor Relations Review*, 40 (1987), pp. 585–600; and S. Flaherty, "Strike Activity and Productivity Change: The U.S. Auto Industry," *Industrial Relations*, 26 (1987), pp. 174–185.

[64] D. Card, "Longitudinal Analysis of Strike Activity," *Journal of Labor Economics*, 6 (1988), pp. 147–176.

[65] M. Campolieti, R. Hebdon, and D. Hyatt, "Strike Incidence and Strike Duration: Some New Evidence from Ontario," *Industrial and Labor Relations Review*, 58 (2005), pp. 610–630.

[66] J. M. Abowd and J. S. Tracy, "Market Structure, Strike Activity, and Union Wage Settlements," *Industrial Relations*, 28 (1989), pp. 227–250.

take risks associated with certain types of jobs.[67] Foreign-owned firms in Canada have lower strike rates, possibly due to more care in sharing information with unions to increase the company's credibility.[68]

A variety of geographic, demographic, and psychological factors are related to strike incidence. Southern, urban, and female-dominated bargaining units strike less often.[69] Younger members appear more militant, while personal hardship decreases militancy.[70] A study of the correlates of the willingness to strike found that economic perceptions played a stronger role than social background or the perceived labor relations climate. Propensities to strike were negatively related to company commitment, the labor relations climate, pay equity, strike hardship, seniority, education, and age; they were positively related to concessions, union loyalty, integrative bargaining views, pay rate, union participation, family employment stability, and blue-collar background.[71]

Public policy has a mixed effect on strikes. Right-to-work laws are related to higher strike rates.[72] Canadian legal mandates for conciliation and strike votes reduce incidence rates.[73] Where public policy reduces risks to strikers, such as where strikers are entitled to unemployment compensation[74] or, as in much of Canada, where employers cannot legally replace them, the incidence rate is higher.[75]

Duration of Strikes

Strike duration is related to a number of variables, increasing during low-performing economic periods.[76] Strikes are longer when companies are not performing well relative to competitors or other industries. But duration is

[67] J. P. Leigh, "Risk Preferences and the Interindustry Propensity to Strike," *Industrial and Labor Relations Review*, 36 (1983), pp. 271–285.

[68] J. M. Cousineau, R. Lacroix, and D. Vachon, "Foreign Ownership and Strike Activity in Canada," *Relations Industrielles*, 46 (1991), pp. 616–629.

[69] Kaufman, "The Determinants of Strikes over Time."

[70] J. E. Martin, "Predictors of Individual Propensity to Strike," *Industrial and Labor Relations Review*, 39 (1986), pp. 214–227; see also A. W. Black, "Some Factors Influencing Attitudes toward Militancy, Solidarity, and Sanctions in a Teachers' Union," *Human Relations*, 36 (1983), pp. 973–985.

[71] J. E. Martin and R. R. Sinclair, "A Multiple Motive Perspective on Strike Propensities," *Journal of Organizational Behavior*, 22 (2001), pp. 387–407.

[72] Gramm, "Determinants of Strike Incidence and Severity."

[73] M. Gunderson and A. Melino, "The Effects of Public Policy on Strike Duration," *Journal of Labor Research*, 8 (1990), pp. 295–316.

[74] Hutchens et al., *Strikes and Subsidies.*

[75] Gunderson and Melino, "Effects of Public Policy."

[76] Kennan, "Pareto Optimality and the Economics of Strike Duration"; Kaufman, "Determinants of Strikes over Time and across Industries"; Vroman, "Longitudinal Analysis of Strike Activity in U.S. Manufacturing; and A. Harrison and M. Stewart, "Cyclical Fluctuations in Strike Duration," *American Economic Review*, 79 (1989), pp. 827–841.

longer in booming industries, suggesting strong earnings by both companies and union members may allow longer holdouts.[77] Employers that are diversified across industries can usually take a longer strike.[78]

Employer costs do not increase at a constant rate as a strike continues since costs may be small for a short strike if shipments can be made from inventory or if customers have stocked up in anticipation. As strikes lengthen, revenue losses from forgone orders increase rapidly, and long-term profits are reduced as market share is lost to more reliable competitors. For strikers, direct marginal costs rise rapidly as savings are exhausted and the disparity between strike benefits and wages becomes apparent. Health care insurance usually ends at the end of the month in which the strike begins. Strikes last longer where union members have relatively low debt-to-income ratios.[79] Striker job security is important; durations are longer in Canada, where strikers cannot be replaced.[80] However, in the United States, either announcing an intent to replace or actually replacing strikers increased strike durations by an average of 30 percent.[81] Strikes are longer if there is a lot of publicity about the negotiations, seemingly hardening the parties' positions.[82]

Issues are related to duration. Renegotiation strikes are almost always over economics (85 percent of cases), while intracontract strikes almost always involve working conditions or job security (90 percent of cases). The median duration of renegotiation strikes in one studied sample was 15 days, while the median for intracontract strikes was just 3 days.[83] Wildcat strikes most frequently involve plant administration issues and generally last three days or less. They are predicted by high unionization rates within the industry, unsafe working conditions, low inventories, a liberal political environment, and a moderate degree of bargaining experience. Wildcat strikes are inhibited by the employer's likelihood of filing a ULP, high unemployment rates, high real wages in the industry, a higher percentage of women in the bargaining unit, location in the South, and a long-term bargaining relationship.[84]

[77] McConnell, "Cyclical Fluctuations in Strike Activity."

[78] D. Rose, "Firm Diversification and Strike Duration: Is There a Connection?" *Industrial Relations*, 33 (1994), pp. 482–491.

[79] Gramm, "Determinants of Strike Incidence and Severity."

[80] Gunderson and Melino, "Effects of Public Policy."

[81] J. F. Schnell and C. L. Gramm, "The Empirical Relations between Employers' Strike Replacement Strategies and Strike Duration," *Industrial and Labor Relations Review*, 47 (1994), pp. 189–206.

[82] F. J. Flynn, "No News Is Good News: The Relationship between Media Attention and Strike Duration," *Industrial Relations*, 39 (2000), pp. 139–160.

[83] S. Flaherty, "Contract Status and the Economic Determinants of Strike Activity," *Industrial Relations*, 22 (1983), pp. 20–33.

[84] D. M. Byrne and R. H. King, "Wildcat Strikes in U.S. Manufacturing, 1960–1977," *Journal of Labor Research*, 7 (1986), pp. 387–401.

Almost 13 percent of strikes are settled in the first day. At the 10th day, the rate drops to 4.8 percent, and at 30 days, to 3.2 percent; at 50 days, only 2.4 percent of the remaining strikes are settled. Once a strike exceeds 50 days, the probability of settling does not change, indicating that the parties' relative costs of continuing the strike do not change.[85]

Health care is an important trigger for recent strikes. With rapidly escalating costs and insurance premiums, employers have increasingly demanded limits on insurance contributions, employee co-pays and deductibles, and elimination of or limits on retiree health care benefits. Unions strongly oppose such concessions, particularly because health care costs are a larger proportion of total expenditures for low- as compared to high-income employees.

In 2003, UFCW-represented grocery workers in Los Angeles struck Vons and Pavilions supermarkets to oppose proposed health care benefit cuts and a two-tier pay structure. In response, Albertson's and Ralph's locked out their workers, and all stores remained open using managers and temporary replacement workers. After 141 days, the 67,300 workers voted to accept a contract that implemented a lower starting pay and lower health care benefits for new hires, gradual implementation of some health insurance co-pays, and retroactive lump-sum pay. The ability to hire replacements, coupled with high short-term barriers to entry in the grocery industry, substantially reduced union bargaining power.

Effects of Strikes

Some argue that strikes are strictly random events not known before they occur. If this were true, outsiders who could be hurt by strikes could not take action to insulate themselves. During the 1960s and early 1970s, steel customers learned to stock up before contract expirations since they expected strikes. Studies of shareholder behavior suggest investors anticipate strikes. Rates of return on shares of struck companies decline in value before a strike occurs. Investors discount stocks as the duration increases over relatively short terms.[86] However, only about one-third of the total decline in share price is discounted before the strike is announced.[87] The costs of strikes spread to supplier industries as well. Auto strikes were associated with declines in stock prices for steel companies roughly equal to those found in autos.[88] On the other hand, there are few intraindustry strike effects on share prices. This may relate to

[85] Kennan, "Pareto Optimality and the Economics of Strike Duration."

[86] G. R. Neumann, "The Predictability of Strikes: Evidence from the Stock Market," *Industrial and Labor Relations Review*, 33 (1980), pp. 525–535.

[87] B. E. Becker and C. A. Olson, "The Impact of Strikes on Shareholder Equity," *Industrial and Labor Relations Review*, 39 (1986), pp. 425–438.

[88] O. S. Persons, "The Effects of Automobile Strikes on the Stock Value of Steel Suppliers," *Industrial and Labor Relations Review*, 49 (1995), pp. 78–87.

defensive strategies such as inventory buildups, expectations of concessions, or pattern-bargaining expectations for other nonstruck firms.[89] Very long strikes appear related to situations in which firms have done better than average before the strike (ability to pay) and investors bid these firms' stocks up after the strike (perhaps anticipating that management gained major concessions).[90] This appears rational because data indicate that wages negotiated after a strike are about 3 percent lower than they are when no strike occurs.[91]

Struck employers suffer short-term profitability and productivity decreases. However, effects are even stronger for suppliers or customers of struck firms. There are two reasons for this. First, it is more difficult for suppliers or customers to predict strikes than for the target employer to do so. Second, suppliers and customers are less likely to lay off workers than are struck firms.[92]

Besides productivity and profitability, quality may also suffer, especially if replacements are hired to continue operating. During the period of 1994 to 1996, Bridgestone/Firestone and the United Rubber Workers (now part of the Steelworkers) engaged in bitter conflict. At its Decatur, Illinois, plant the union worked without a contract from April 1994 until striking in July. The plant continued to operate and hired replacement workers. A sizable minority of union members crossed picket lines and returned to work as replacements were added. On May 22, 1995, the union unconditionally returned to work and the company implemented its last offer. It wasn't until December 1996, when a new agreement was reached, that all the strikers were recalled. Quality levels for tires produced during the strike period were significantly lower than those before or after and as compared to the levels at nonunion Bridgestone/Firestone plants. Many of these tires were used as original equipment on Ford Explorers. Tread separations were blamed for contributing to Explorer rollovers in which drivers and/or passengers were killed or permanently disabled. Ultimately, these problems led to a massive tire recall and replacement campaign and Ford's termination of its almost 100-year supplier relationship with Firestone.[93]

Negotiators may make subjective estimates of the effects of striking when deciding on bargaining tactics. In a study of the perceived results

[89] J. K. Kramer and G. M. Vasconcellos, "The Economic Effect of Strikes on the Shareholders of Nonstruck Competitors," *Industrial and Labor Relations Review*, 49 (1995), pp. 213–222.

[90] Greer et al., "The Effect of Strikes in Shareholder Returns."

[91] S. McConnell, "Strikes, Wages, and Private Information," *American Economic Review*, 79 (1999), pp. 810–815.

[92] R. McHugh, "Productivity Effects of Strikes in Struck and Nonstruck Industries," *Industrial and Labor Relations Review*, 44 (1991), pp. 722–732.

[93] A. B. Krueger and A. Mas, "Strikes, Scabs, and Tread Separations: Labor Strife and the Production of Defective Bridgestone/Firestone Tires," *Journal of Political Economy*, 112 (2004), pp. 253–289.

of striking, chief negotiators believed that management gained more from strikes than did unions. The ability to remain in operation and/or to have a large proportion of a plant's employees involved in the strike increased management's perceived advantage.[94] Strikes may also influence internal union politics. For example, locals voting not to ratify the 1981 United Mine Workers–Bituminous Coal Operators Association agreement were very likely to vote to replace the international's leadership during the next election. Dissidents campaigned actively against the contract.[95]

Strikes are unusual and disruptive activities for both employers and employees. Among employees, there are likely differences in the degree to which they support the strike and the financial stresses they experience. A study of a 16-day strike in Ontario found that employee anger following the conclusion of the strike was related to financial concern and cynicism toward both the employer and the union.[96] Union members who had experienced a five-month-long strike had significantly decreased organizational commitment, job satisfaction, work climate satisfaction, management satisfaction, and union commitment than before the strike.[97]

BOYCOTTS

Boycotts are appeals to the general public not to purchase struck goods. Boycotts are seldom used for a number of reasons: (1) A great deal of publicity is required to alert customers, (2) customers may not respond unless a clear-cut social issue is involved, (3) keeping a boycott from becoming a secondary boycott is sometimes difficult, and (4) boycott effects do not end as quickly as strike effects because the public may continue to identify the producer with poor labor relations after a settlement. Boycotts generally have little economic effect. Stock prices of boycotted companies fall for only about 15 days before returning to preboycott levels.[98]

One boycott technique informs the public of a labor dispute at a location where the struck business's products are sold. However, this activity risks being declared a secondary boycott. Consider the following: A major tire manufacturer is struck by its production employees. To pressure the

[94] A. Shirom, "Strike Characteristics as Determinants of Strike Settlements: A Chief Negotiator's Viewpoint," *Journal of Applied Psychology*, 67 (1982), pp. 45–52.

[95] T. Ghilarducci, "The Impact of Internal Union Politics on the 1981 UMWA Strike," *Industrial Relations*, 27 (1988), pp. 114–129.

[96] C. M. Wickens, "Employee Stress Reactions to a Municipal Government Strike," *Journal of Collective Negotiations*, 31 (2007), pp. 119–139.

[97] K. Chaulk and T. C. Brown, "An Assessment of Work Reaction to Their Union and Employer Post-Strike," *Relations Industrielles*, 63 (2008), pp. 223–245.

[98] S. W. Pruitt, K. C. J. Wei, and R. E. White, "The Impact of Union-Sponsored Boycotts on the Stock Prices of Target Firms," *Journal of Labor Research*, 9 (1988), pp. 285–290.

employer to settle, the union pickets tire stores selling the tires. The signs read, "Don't shop here. This store sells XYZ tires produced under unfair conditions. ABC union on strike for justice against XYZ." Suppose the union uses a different message on its signs: "ABC on strike against XYZ Co. Don't buy XYZ tires while shopping here today. ABC has no dispute with this store." Only the second strategy is legal. In the second instance, the picket calls attention to the labor dispute and the struck product but does not ask persons to boycott the neutral store. If the union follows the second strategy and does not impede customers or deliveries, the action is considered primary and legal.[99]

Print advertisements may be used instead of bannering retail establishments selling the struck product. Figure 12.2 shows an example used by the United Steelworkers in a recent dispute with Goodyear Tire and Rubber. Note the use of the Bridgestone/Firestone labor relations—tire quality relationship results discussed above.

In the 1980s, boycotts were used against Adolph Coors Company (to force recognition) and J. P. Stevens & Co., Inc. (to force recognition and bargaining on initial contracts). The Coors boycott had some effect on the ultimate willingness of the firm to recognize the union, but the J. P. Stevens action was much more difficult because many of its products are produced for sale under retailers' labels and thus were hard to identify with J. P. Stevens.

Unions cannot use boycotts to make political statements. When the International Longshoremen's Association refused to handle Soviet goods after the 1980 Afghanistan invasion, the action was an illegal secondary boycott because there were no primary disputes with the shipping companies.[100]

LOCKOUTS

Lockouts are the flip side of the strike coin. Employers use them most frequently when faced with strikes involving (1) perishable goods or (2) multiemployer bargaining units.

Perishable Goods

An employer dealing with perishable goods is frequently at the mercy of the union. For example, California vegetable canners were struck in 1976 just before harvest. Because their revenues depended on packing the

[99] *NLRB* v. *Fruit & Vegetable Packers, Local 760*, 377 U.S. 58 (1964).

[100] *International Longshoremen's Association, AFL-CIO* v. *Allied International, Inc.*, No. 80-1663, U.S. Supreme Court, 1982; for a critique of this decision, see J. Rubin, "The Primary-Secondary Distinction: The New Secondary Boycott Law of *Allied International, Inc.* v. *International Longshoremen's Association*," *Industrial Relations Law Journal*, 6 (1984), pp. 94–124.

FIGURE 12.2
Advertisement Used by the United Steelworkers in a Recent Dispute with Goodyear Tire and Rubber

Source: United Steelworkers.

CONSUMER SAFETY ALERT

Will Goodyear tires be safe for your family?

The experienced workforce at Goodyear has been forced out on strike due to the company's demands to gut their healthcare, close factories and bring in tires made in China and other low-wage countries.

For now, Goodyear is using replacement workers to make tires to be sold here in America.

Why is this important to you?

An independent Princeton University study has linked labor strife, including the use of replacement workers, with the production of defective tires.

The Princeton study examines the causes of the Firestone and Ford recall of 14.4 million tires in 2000. You may remember the rollover accidents that caused so many deaths and horrific injuries on our nation's highways.

These tires were linked by the National Highway Safety Transportation Administration to complaints involving 271 fatalities and more than 800 injuries.

So ask yourself:

Can you afford to trust Goodyear?

UNITED STEELWORKERS
USW
UNITY AND STRENGTH FOR WORKERS

produce when it was mature, a strike during the pack would have caused the produce to rot. Thus, the employers were under great pressure to settle quickly.

Sometimes the employer has some control over the perishability of goods or services. For a packer, the timing of when a crop matures is not within its control. But a brewer can decide when to start a new batch of beer, and a contractor can elect when to begin the remodeling of a house. For the brewer, once a batch is started, it must be bottled on a certain date or it will spoil. For the contractor, the homeowners may sue because their property is not usable and they have construction loans that have interest payments accruing. Lockouts are legitimate employer tactics to decrease union power in situations when the lockout is done to avoid economic loss[101] or to preserve customer goodwill.[102] In 2004, the National Hockey League locked out its players at the beginning of the season. A settlement was not reached until after the end of the season, with the players making major concessions on salary caps and free agency. A lockout is credible only at the beginning of a season when players are yet to be paid; close to the end of the season, playoffs would be looming, along with the prime opportunities for owners to recognize revenue. Lockouts also put heavy pressure on players because their playing lives are generally quite short. Missing a year of competition and salary has huge consequences on lifetime earnings.[103]

Multiemployer Lockouts

As discussed in Chapter 8, several small employers that are engaged in the same business and whose employees are represented by the same union often form a multiemployer bargaining unit. But if the union strikes only one employer and attempts to break the solidarity of the group by using a **whipsaw** strategy, can the remainder of the employers lock out their employees? When one member of a multiemployer unit is struck and the remaining members lock out their employees, the lockout is defensive in nature, and without its use, the continued integrity of the bargaining unit could not be ensured.[104] Multiemployer groups can also lock out employees when one is struck and temporarily replace them for the duration of the lockout to continue operations.[105]

Single-Employer Lockouts

In a single-employer negotiation, there is no need to defend against a whipsaw. Thus, the question of whether a lockout interferes with employee rights to engage in concerted activities must be scrutinized more closely. Unless an impasse occurs, a lockout cannot be implemented.[106] When an impasse has been reached and the contract has expired, employers are permitted to lock out employees,[107] although refusing to bargain simply to

[101] *Duluth Bottling Association*, 48 NLRB 1335 (1943).

[102] *Betts Cadillac-Olds, Inc.*, 96 NLRB 26 (1951).

[103] For more details, see P. Staudohar, "The Hockey Lockout of 2004–05," *Monthly Labor Review*, 126, no. 12 (2005), pp. 23–29; and E. G. Fisher, "Can Strikes Pay for Management? Pro Sports' Major Turnarounds," *Relations Industrielles*, 62 (2007), pp. 3–30.

[104] *NLRB* v. *Truck Drivers' Local 449*, 353 U.S. 87 (1957).

[105] *NLRB* v. *Brown*, 380 U.S. 278 (1965).

[106] *Quaker State Oil Refining Corp.*, 121 NLRB 334 (1958).

[107] *American Ship Building Co.* v. *NLRB*, 380 U.S. 300 (1965).

gain an impasse to allow the use of a lockout would be unlawful. In addition, single employers may hire temporary replacements to pressure the union after a lockout is imposed.[108]

BANKRUPTCIES

While bankruptcies are not impasses, some firms have used them to gain concessions or to escape existing contracts without negotiating. Bankruptcy law allows companies to abrogate contracts with suppliers and renegotiate on more favorable terms. Under Chapter 11, the firm continues operations and gains protection from its creditors while trying to reorganize. Bankruptcy courts oversee the changes made to contracts to safeguard the interests of both the creditors and the debtor-in-possession.

When companies attempted to abrogate labor agreements, unions filed refusal-to-bargain charges with the NLRB. However, early in 1984, the Supreme Court ruled that bankruptcy courts may allow rejection of collective bargaining agreements if the debtor-in-possession shows their continuance burdens the business.[109] Congress responded by amending the bankruptcy code to require negotiations with unions over changes thought to be necessary. Collective bargaining agreements cannot be abrogated unless the union has refused to renegotiate. Equities of the situation must also be taken into account.[110]

Some argue that relatively liberal provisions of Chapter 11, which don't require insolvency, will lead to "going concerns" electing to file bankruptcy to escape contract terms unavoidable through collective bargaining. Conflicts between labor legislation and bankruptcy law lead to controversy whenever bankruptcy is declared.[111]

During the 2001–2010 decade, four of the largest U.S. airlines entered and emerged from Chapter 11: United, US Air, Delta, and Northwest. All substantially restructured their collective bargaining agreements, gaining major wage and work rule concessions. In addition, both United and Delta terminated their defined benefit pension plans. With Northwest, ultimately all the unions renegotiated and ratified contracts. Before entering bankruptcy, Northwest had locked out its mechanics and replaced them with strikebreakers after the cooling-off period imposed by the NMB

[108] *Harter Equipment, Inc.*, 122 LRRM 1219 (1986).

[109] *NLRB* v. *Bildisco & Bildisco*, 115 LRRM 2805, U.S. Supreme Court, 1984.

[110] M. D. Sousa, "Reconciling the Otherwise Irreconcilable: The Rejection of Collective Bargaining Agreements under Section 1113 of the Bankruptcy Code," *Labor Lawyer*, 18 (2003), pp. 453–483.

[111] For further details, see T. R. Haggard and M. S. Pulliam, *Conflicts between Labor Legislation and Bankruptcy Law*, Labor Relations and Public Policy Series, No. 30 (Philadelphia: Industrial Relations Unit, Wharton School, University of Pennsylvania, 1987).

Exhibit 12.6

NORTHWEST AIRLINES CHAPTER 11 BANKRUPTCY CHRONOLOGY

08/20/05	Mechanics represented by AMFA go on strike and are immediately replaced by workers who have been in training for much of the year in case a strike occurred. Northwest flies its full schedule.
09/15/05	Northwest Airlines files a Chapter 11 bankruptcy petition to restructure debt and contractual obligations while continuing to operate the airline.
10/12/05	Northwest requests permission from bankruptcy judge to void labor agreements unless concessions can be negotiated.
12/21/05	Northwest wins permission from bankruptcy court to temporarily cut pay.
02/03/06	Pilots announce they will hold a strike authorization vote.
03/01/06	Tentative agreement reached between Northwest and flight attendants.
03/07/06	Clerical and customer service workers ratify a new contract, while baggage handlers reject a tentative settlement.
05/03/06	Pilots ratify a 5½-year contract that cuts wages by 24 percent and permits Northwest to start a subsidiary carrier to operate planes with 76 seats or less.
06/07/06	Flight attendants overwhelmingly reject tentative contract agreement.
06/09/06	Baggage handlers ratify a concessionary agreement.
06/19/06	Mark McClain, the Air Line Pilots Association leader at Northwest during the concession negotiations, is ousted by the union's Northwest unit governing board and replaced by Dave Stevens.
07/01/06	A majority of flight attendants vote for the Association of Flight Attendants (CWA) to replace the Professional Flight Attendants Association as bargaining agent.
07/15/06	IAM District 143 president Bobby DePace during the concession negotiations is ousted as leader of the baggage handlers union and replaced by Steve Gordon.
07/31/06	Flight attendants reject second tentative agreement and threaten to strike in 15 days.
08/25/06	Federal judge prohibits flight attendants from implementing their "CHAOS" rolling work stoppage strategy.
11/06/06	AMFA-represented mechanics ratify a new contract that provides recall rights and severance pay. Practically speaking, very few of the mechanics will ever return to Northwest.
01/10/07	Reorganization plan is announced with an emergence from bankruptcy projected for the second quarter of 2007.
03/31/07	Federal appeals court prohibits flight attendants from striking after the company voided its collective bargaining agreement.
04/20/07	New Northwest board of directors members are announced. They will take over on the date the company emerges from bankruptcy.
04/26/07	Flight attendants reach a tentative agreement on a new contract, motivated by the need to have a contract in order to be entitled to an equity claim.
05/29/07	By a 51 to 49 percent margin, flight attendants ratify a concessionary agreement.
05/31/07	Northwest emerges from bankruptcy. Unions decry $26.6 million in stock and stock options that CEO Doug Steenland was awarded by Northwest's board of directors.
07/02/07	Flight attendants receive an average $14,500 equity claim settlement from the bankruptcy proceedings.

expired, and then implemented its final offer. The following month it filed for protection under Chapter 11 and sought to abrogate its contracts with the pilots, ground service workers, and flight attendants. The pilots were the first to settle. During the negotiations with the flight attendants, the bargaining agent was replaced following an NMB election. Two tentative agreements were voted down, and Northwest asked for permission to impose terms. Allen Gropper, the bankruptcy judge in the case, required that both parties resume bargaining, and an agreement was ultimately reached that was ratified. It's clear that concessions were necessary for the airline to return to financial viability, but the judge also saw bargaining as necessary. Given the earlier tentative agreement, it was clear that the flight attendants were continuing to bargain toward a potential solution. Exhibit 12.6 contains a chronology of the bankruptcy and broad details of the concessions that were made.

In 2009, General Motors went through a prepackaged Chapter 11 bankruptcy. Unlike the Northwest Airlines example above, the total time from filing on June 1, 2009, through emerging as a new company was only 40 days. Because the federal government had made substantial loans to the company, it held a whip hand in the structuring of the bankruptcy. As often occurs in bankruptcies, shareholders were wiped out. Secured creditors were first in line and were paid off on a dollar-for-dollar basis. Unsecured creditors received about 10 cents on the dollar. Majority ownership of the new company was held by the U.S. government, with other major stakes going to the governments of Canada and Ontario and the UAW's VEBA. Labor agreements had been renegotiated some time before the bankruptcy filing and were not further altered during the bankruptcy proceedings.

Summary

Impasses occur when the parties fail to reach an agreement during negotiations. Several methods are used to break impasses. The parties may strike or lock out, agree to mediation, or invoke interest arbitration.

Mediation brings the parties together through a third party who helps reopen communications, clarify issues, and introduce a realistic approach to bargaining issues that continue to separate the parties. Interest arbitration turns over the dispute to a neutral party to decide the terms of a final settlement.

In bargaining relationships under the Railway Labor Act, parties cannot engage in self-help until after the NBM declares an impasse and releases the parties to take self-help action.

Typical tactics used by unions in impasses include strikes, slowdowns, picketing, boycotts, and corporate campaigns. Employers respond by hiring replacements, locking out employees, or declaring bankruptcy.

Strikes usually occur as the result of a disagreement on the terms of a new agreement. These strikes are called economic strikes. Other strikes occur over ULPs, in sympathy with other unions, and in violation of no-strike clauses. The strikers' rights to employment in each category have been clearly defined by the courts.

Lockouts involve a refusal to provide work. Although strikes can occur any time after the termination of the contract, lockouts seldom occur because the employer loses revenues when not in operation. Most lockouts involve multiemployer bargaining units whose members seek to preserve the bargaining relationship by countering the strike of a single member.

Strikes occur more often when unions have failed to keep up with relevant comparison settlements. Good economic conditions are also associated with more strikes. Strikes are longer if economic issues are the major concern.

Discussion Questions

1. Why don't more firms use lockouts to break impasses?
2. What conditions are necessary for mediation to assist in settling an impasse?
3. Do you believe the present rights given to strikers by the NLRB are appropriate? Should they be increased or decreased?
4. What are the economic and social consequences of prohibiting the replacement of economic strikers?

Key Terms

Impasse, *399*
Mediation, *400*
Fact-finding, *406*
Interest arbitration, *407*
Rights arbitration, *407*
Economic strike, *409*
Unfair labor practice strike, *409*
Wildcat strike, *409*
Sympathy strike, *409*
Picketing, *411*
Recognitional picketing, *411*
Common situs picketing, *412*
Secondary boycott, *412*
Working to rules, *413*
Corporate campaign, *414*
Ally doctrine, *419*
Whipsaw, *429*

Selected Web Sites

www.fmcs.gov
www.nmb.gov

Case: *GMFC Impasse*

Assume you are director of industrial relations for GMFC. The company and the union have failed to agree on a new contract, and the old contract expired last week. Two issues are unresolved, and no movement has been made on these for more than 10 days. The union is demanding 10 cents an hour more than the company is willing to offer, and management continues to demand some employee co-payments for medical care. This is the first negotiation in 15 years in which a new contract has not been ratified before the old one expired.

Local 384 voted a strike authorization about a month ago, but the leaders have not indicated at this point whether they intend to strike. Production managers are lobbying for a lockout to avoid material losses if the heated steel treating process must be shut down rapidly. Marketing managers want production maintained to meet orders scheduled for shipment. They argue the union doesn't intend to strike because it hasn't already done so.

In the executive council meeting this morning, financial officers briefed the top executives of GMFC and indicated the company could accept a labor cost increase of 5 cents an hour more, but only if this is a firm figure and not subject to increases over the term of the contract. Unfortunately, the union appeared adamant that it will not agree to any health care co-payment.

It is now your turn to recommend strategy to the company in this impasse. Considering the evidence, what action should the company take? Outline the action, including processes used and timetables. Consider the possibility that your strategy may trigger a strike or other union activity.

Union-Management Cooperation

Many labor relations practices are adversarial—organizing, bargaining over wages, disputing contract interpretations, and the like. But many argue that both unions and managements can achieve improved outcomes through cooperation. The catalyst for cooperation is often the financial exigency of the employer and the specter of potentially large job losses.

This chapter explores variations in union-management cooperation and their effects, including interest-based bargaining, employee involvement programs, gainsharing, labor-management partnerships, and work and organization redesign. In reading this chapter, consider the following questions:

1. How are cooperative problem-solving methods different from traditional bargaining?
2. Can a cooperation program violate labor laws?
3. What are some results of cooperative programs? Are they equally likely to lead to successes for both unions and managements?
4. What types of cooperation programs are in current use by employers and unions?
5. Are union-management cooperation programs sustainable in the long run?

LABOR AND MANAGEMENT ROLES AND THE CHANGING ENVIRONMENT

A succession of economic cycles and regulatory changes has influenced outcomes for labor and management. The Railway Labor Act, Norris-LaGuardia Act, Wagner Act, and various state laws enabling public sector collective bargaining strengthened labor's ability to organize. The Taft-Hartley Act and Landrum-Griffin Act increased employer power. At various points, new production technologies substantially reduced the need for lower-skilled union members. Today global competition affects the survival of some employers and the jobs of a diverse set of workers. During the past 40 years, industries that virtually monopolized domestic markets, such as steel, motor vehicles, consumer electric and electronic products, textiles, shoes, and software, now either need to be globally competitive or may hardly exist any longer in the United States. Foreign competitors benefitted from investment, technology transfer, and particularly, lower wages for unskilled workers that boosted their productivity or lowered costs at a faster rate than was the case for domestic producers. Some of this was due to unions' abilities to increase wages and some to employers' failures to invest in technology. Both groups were responsible for not attending to the way work and production were organized as foreign producers implemented new and improved methods.[1] Some companies failed and local unions were decimated, while others survived and prospered. In most cases, companies and unions in basic industries that have survived have changed their approaches to each other considerably.

Organizing and the Evolving Bargaining Relationship

U.S. employers have traditionally fought unionization. Even some employers in heavily unionized industries have implemented active union avoidance programs by fighting new organizing, shifting production from unionized plants to new **greenfield operations**, and reducing investment in unionized plants.[2]

Adversarial relationships carry over from organizing to bargaining and implementing contracts. The union needs bargaining successes for its officers to be reelected and for the union to avoid decertification. The legal specification of mandatory bargaining issues increases the union's emphasis on immediate economic issues and turns emphasis away from employer and union survival issues. As noted earlier, managers have generally been judged on their ability to avoid unionization or to limit its impact. In dealing with the union, managers tend to view a cooperative relationship as one in which the union has an insignificant role in decision making.[3] Thus, neither party's leaders are initially motivated to seek cooperation.

Evidence also suggests that unions win initial certification because employees are interested in exercising their voices in the employment relationship. But to management, coordinating with unions to create opportunities for this to occur may seem like a legitimization of union efforts.

[1] J. Hoerr, *And the Wolf Finally Came* (Pittsburgh: University of Pittsburgh Press, 1989).

[2] T. A. Kochan, H. C. Katz, and R. B. McKersie, *The Transformation of American Industrial Relations* (New York: Free Press, 1986).

[3] M. M. Perline and E. A. Sexton, "Managerial Perceptions of Labor-Management Cooperation," *Industrial Relations*, 33 (1994), pp. 377–385.

Preferences of Management and Labor

Management seeks the highest profit level it can achieve through investing its capital. It makes investment decisions that shift resources from product lines with lower returns to those with higher profits. To do this, it needs to be able to adapt. From an unconstrained standpoint, it would prefer to open, close, and retool plants as needed, hire labor on a flexible basis, and adjust wage rates to meet changing product market conditions and to respond to shifts in the labor market.

Employees are generally assumed to be risk-averse, while employers are assumed to be risk-neutral. This means employers are looking for the highest rate of return, consistent with the risks they expect to encounter, while employees are assumed to accept lower pay if they can simultaneously increase job security and income protection. Employees are risk-averse not because they have an inherent dislike of risk but rather because their skills are often occupationally specific, and perhaps specifically tailored to their present employer's requirements. Thus, their human capital is not diversifiable. They may also own homes and have family ties in the locality in which they work. They depend on continued employment, often with their present employers and in their present occupations, to be able to realize a return on the investments they have made in acquiring their skills.

Levels of Cooperation and Control

Given the way mandatory bargaining issues are defined in the labor acts and employers' antipathy toward organized labor, managers have sought to retain as much control of the workplace as possible. Unions have generally been reluctant to seek shared responsibility for decision making given their adversarial roles and the economic concessions they might have to make to gain a greater say in decision making.

In some situations, in return for economic concessions, unions have won greater claims on the rights to control processes and share in profits. Provisions have been negotiated to increase the proportion of employees' pay that is at risk, usually to help ensure employer survival and increase employment security. The effect of participation in gaining rights can flow along two dimensions: control and return rights. *Control rights* involve the degree to which labor participates in organizational decision making. Unionization, in itself, introduces a degree of control rights because the employer can no longer unilaterally decide wages, hours, and terms and conditions of employment. At the extreme, control rights would include works council arrangements (as in Germany—covered in Chapter 17) and employee representation on corporate boards of directors. *Return rights* begin with wage payments and progress through incentive plans, profit-sharing and gainsharing programs, and ultimately to employee stock ownership of the enterprise.[4]

[4] A. Ben-Ner and D. C. Jones, "Employee Participation, Ownership and Productivity: A Theoretical Framework," *Industrial Relations*, 34 (1995), pp. 532–554.

Conflicts over control rights and unions' general disinterest in broader return rights, the historical antipathy of employers, and adversarial relationships in bargaining have made the creation of joint problem solving difficult.

This chapter explores initiatives in union-management cooperation to jointly accomplish their separate goals. Part of this is done through integrative bargaining during contract negotiations and part through developing ongoing cooperative relationships. Many cooperation experiments are initiated through side letters in the contract or through agreements to suspend contract provisions to experiment with new methods.

INTEGRATIVE BARGAINING

Integrative bargaining is a set of activities leading to the simultaneous accomplishment of nonconflicting objectives that solves a common problem for both parties.[5] Conflict occurs when parties have different goals and either the need to share resources or task interdependencies block one party's goal attainment if the other party pursues a certain course.[6] For example, shared resources may be available hours of work, and different goals may be overtime premium earnings for the union and high profits for management. One party's accomplishment will interfere with the other party's goals. Integrative bargaining seeks solutions that expand resources or remove barriers that interfere with the parties' ability to achieve their individual goals. Parties may not immediately know integrative issues that might emerge from a failure of distributive bargaining to achieve the goals the parties desired.

Two major types of integrative solutions may alleviate this conflict. The first is a situation in which both parties experience an absolute gain over their previous positions. For example, in the 1980s, auto workers at Ford achieved permanent job security in return for new work rules to reduce costs. Second, integrative bargaining may involve both parties' sacrificing simultaneously (in distributive bargaining, one's gain is the other's loss).[7] Steel industry wage concessions in the early 1980s reduced labor costs enough in several situations to induce employers to invest in new technology, thus lengthening the likely employment of many steelworkers.

Change processes in union employment situations require that certain conditions exist. Increasing internal or external pressures felt by both parties should lead to the consideration of new joint ventures. Multiple constituencies within the union and/or management would stimulate

[5] R. E. Walton and R. B. McKersie, *A Behavioral Theory of Labor Negotiations* (New York: McGraw-Hill, 1965), p. 5.

[6] S. M. Schmidt and T. A. Kochan, "Conflict: Toward Conceptual Clarity," *Administrative Science Quarterly*, 17 (1972), pp. 359–370.

[7] Walton and McKersie, *Behavioral Theory*, pp. 128–129.

efforts to arrive at innovative procedures for dealing with joint problems. Where the normal collective bargaining process and its attention to crisis situations is used exclusively, innovation is less likely. Joint commitments are more likely when a program is seen as accomplishing important ends for both and when both are willing to compromise on goals they desire. Programs should enable early measurable progress toward goals for both parties to maintain support from their constituents. Many of each group's members must experience benefits, and these benefits should not detract from accomplishing other important goals. Programs should be insulated from the formal bargaining process, and usual methods for distributive bargaining should continue.[8]

While management may propose integrative bargaining when the effects of economic change need to be addressed, distributive reasons often underlie the overture. If a change can't be negotiated, management may signal its intent to close a facility. Capital is far more mobile than labor. A plant can be sold and resources redeployed, but the financial burdens workers face, especially if the firm is the dominant employer in the area, are often very onerous.[9]

Several conditions are necessary for facilitating problem solving. First, parties must be jointly motivated to reach a solution. Second, communications between parties must reveal as much information about the problem as possible. Third, parties must create a climate of trust to deliberate over the issues without taking advantage of disclosed information.[10]

Integrative bargaining is appropriate for both immediate and long-term problems. For example, an integrative solution may be appropriate when a contract issue causes grievances during the agreement. Rather than waiting until the next negotiation, addressing the problem immediately may lead to positive outcomes for both parties. On the other hand, anticipated consequences of technology changes may be long-term and may require an open-ended relationship extending beyond the contract period.

Mutual-Gains Bargaining

A contract is based on the assumption that current conditions will continue during the length of the agreement. By the time a situation reaches the point that both parties will suffer if the contract is not changed, each may have lost a substantial amount (e.g., employer profits and union members' job security).

[8] T. A. Kochan and L. Dyer, "A Model of Organizational Change in the Context of Union-Management Relations," *Journal of Applied Behavioral Science*, 12 (1976), pp. 59–78.

[9] E. A. Mannix, C. H. Tinsley, and M. Bazerman, "Negotiating over Time: Impediments to Integrative Solutions," *Organizational Behavior and Human Decision Processes*, 62 (1995), pp. 241–251.

[10] Walton and McKersie, *Behavioral Theory*, pp. 139–143.

A climate in which both the employer and the union would be continually concerned with problem solving and mutual improvement in their situations would call for a living agreement.[11] This would require that the parties determine, a priori, what types of events would trigger problem solving. Where contracts typically include the possibility of reopeners based on the passage of time, this would require that certain employer and employee outcomes would trigger joint problem solving to deal with them. In Canada, Saskatoon Chemicals and the Communications, Energy & Paperworkers Union have agreed to continuous bargaining, particularly with relation to interest-based issues and work redesign.[12]

In bargaining, withholding information or threatening opponents breaks down trust. It's difficult to define and address problems straightforwardly unless each party trusts the information the other provides. **Principled negotiations** require that bargaining be on the merits of the issue, providing information that would enable both to arrive at a mutually agreeable solution.[13] Trust does not occur spontaneously, however. It follows from attitudes toward trust itself, and the experience the parties have had with the perceived trustworthiness of their opponents.[14] Where a trust relationship doesn't exist, the parties will need training and an opportunity to build trust in simulated relationships before beginning to bargain in situations where they are at risk. Even trained bargainers may encounter problems because their constituents are primarily interested in tangible outcomes, not necessarily the effort that it takes to build an infrastructure of trust.

FMCS Innovations

The Federal Mediation and Conciliation Service (FMCS) has worked for over 30 years to develop tools that help parties improve their bargaining relationships. These tools include relations by objectives, bucket bargaining, and technology-assisted group solutions. While each of these will be examined separately, aspects of the three innovations may be combined in a particular bargaining situation.

Relations by Objectives

Creating and sustaining a trusting relationship can be difficult because bargaining often involves both distributive and integrative issues simultaneously. **Relations by objectives** programs train negotiators to take a problem-solving approach in negotiations and contract administration.

[11] C. Hecksher and L. Hall, "Improving Negotiations: Two Levels of Mutual-Gains Interventions," *Proceedings of the Industrial Relations Research Association*, 44 (1992), pp. 160–168.

[12] L. Clarke and L. Haiven, "Workplace Change and Continuous Bargaining: Saskatoon Chemicals Then and Now," *Relations Industrielles*, 54 (1999), pp. 168–193.

[13] R. Fisher and W. Ury, *Getting to Yes: Negotiating Agreement without Giving In* (Boston: Houghton Mifflin, 1981).

[14] S. C. Currall, "Labor-Management Trust: Its Dimensions and Correlates," *Proceedings of the Industrial Relations Research Association*, 44 (1992), pp. 465–474.

The technique brings union and management members together outside a negotiating setting to mutually plan actions to reduce future conflict. The program is designed to increase the skills of union and management negotiators in communicating, mutual goal setting, and goal attainment. It assumes that improving problem-solving skills and obtaining increased information will enable each side to better appreciate the other's positions and to specify bargaining issues. Evidence about the effectiveness of these programs is mixed, with some positive effects on the time necessary to negotiate agreements. But adverse economic conditions erase the effects, especially if the negotiator for either side changes.[15]

Bucket Bargaining

The **bucket bargaining** model is based on the idea that there are five types of issues in bargaining: minor issues, past-problem issues, change issues, discussion issues, and economic issues. The bargaining issues that emerge are screened into five "buckets"—update, repair, redesign, discussion, and economic. Figure 13.1 shows the bucket bargaining process. Bargaining begins with the update bucket and moves toward the right. The figure shows tools that are used to assist bargaining within each of the buckets. Studying how other parties have solved similar problems may reveal "best practices" that the negotiators might want to examine or adopt. Another method is to create a team with members from both parties to come up with a "straw design" that they present to the bargaining team. They don't defend the design, but they note comments and criticisms and then modify the proposal by incorporating feedback from both sides in subsequent versions. These are labeled "wood," "tin," and "iron," in turn. The iron version is not debated but is either accepted or rejected.[16]

The economic portion of bucket bargaining uses established guidelines to frame the issues in the economic package, rank or prioritize them, identify and define costs, identify interests of the parties, and agree on the tools for analysis. Then a straw design is developed, and the parties use their problem-solving techniques to develop standards and arrive at a solution that fits the standards. Figure 13.2 details the economic bucket process. The aim is to avoid a strictly sequential approach to bargaining and to deal first with issues that can readily be resolved and then to handle in a final reconciliation those that can't be settled within their bucket.

Technology-Based Group Solutions

Technology-based group solutions (TAGS™) provides bargainers with a network of laptop computers. Participants enter comments and suggestions at their keyboards that are displayed and categorized before

[15] R. Hebdon and M. Mazerolle, "Mending Fences, Building Bridges: The Effect of Relationship by Objectives on Conflict," *Relations Industrielles*, 50 (1995), pp. 164–185.

[16] K. Saunders, "Bucket Bargaining: Best Process in Interest Based Bargaining," *Labor Law Journal*, 50 (1999), pp. 83–96.

FIGURE 13.1 Bucket Bargaining Process

Source: K. Saunders, "Bucket Bargaining: Best Process in Interest-Based Bargaining," *Labor Law Journal*, 50 (1999), p. 87.

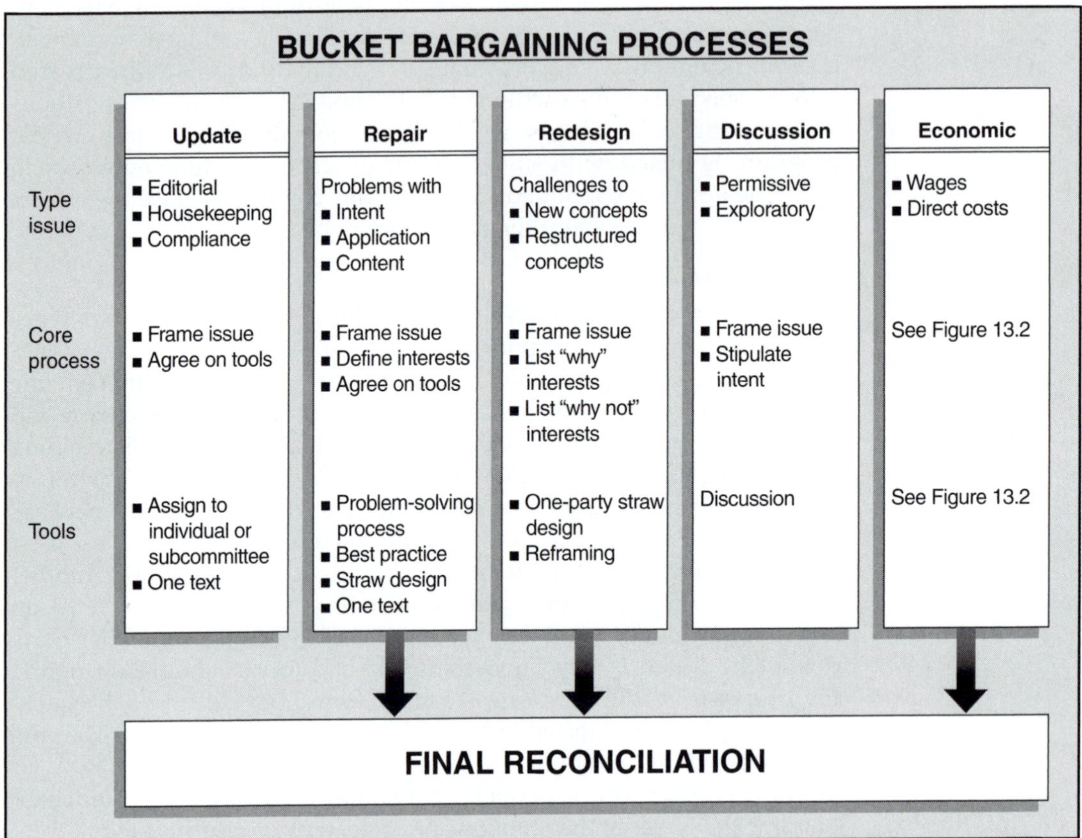

the group. Language for proposals can be changed to reflect suggestions agreed to by the entire group. The time necessary for negotiation, a permanent record of the comments, and the ability to vote secretly all enhance the amount of information that can be transmitted quickly and enhance the ability to reach a consensus.[17]

The Use and Effects of Interest-Based Bargaining

The FMCS compared the results of **interest-based bargaining (IBB)** to negotiations where traditional methods were used.[18] The study found

[17] For more information, see www.fmcs.gov/internet/categoryList.asp?categoryID=23.

[18] J. Cutcher-Gershenfeld, T. Kochan, and J. C. Wells, "In Whose Interest? A First Look at National Survey Data on Interest-Based Bargaining in Labor Relations," *Industrial Relations*, 40 (2001), pp. 1–21.

FIGURE 13.2
Bargaining Economics

Source: K. Saunders, "Bucket Bargaining: Best Process in Interest-Based Bargaining," *Labor Law Journal*, 50 (1999), p. 52.

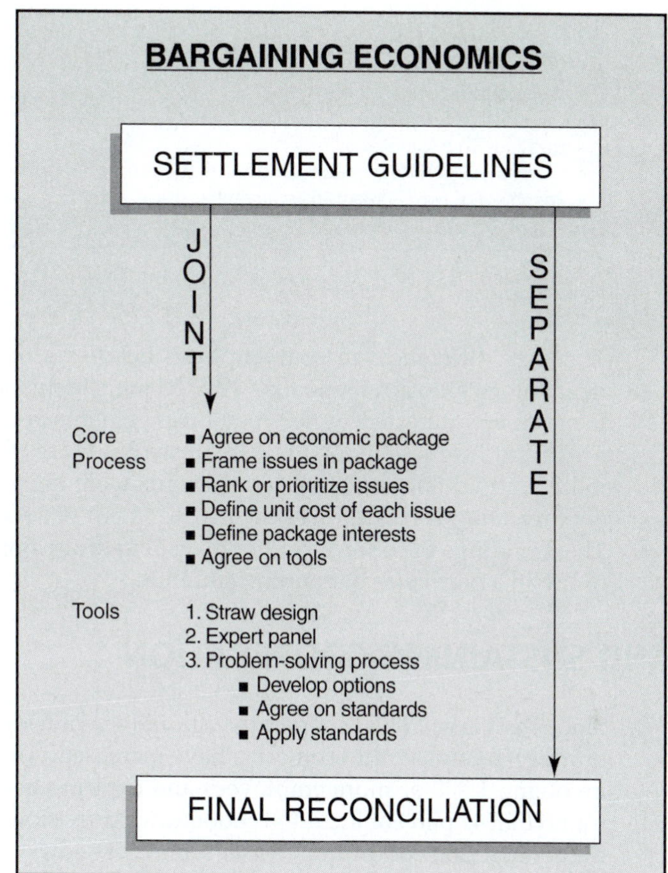

that unions were more likely to use IBB if they had a less experienced negotiator, were in a service industry, and were dealing with a management bargaining team having internal disagreements. Union negotiators' preference for using IBB was associated with having less negotiating experience, being male, dealing with a management team having internal conflict, and not being located in the middle Atlantic states.

For management bargainers, use of IBB was associated with pressure around new technology and with not being in construction, manufacturing, or service industries. Preference for using IBB was associated with less negotiating experience, a perception that the bargaining relationship is cooperative following negotiations, pressure around new technology, and not being in manufacturing, construction, or service industries.

Contracts negotiated using IBB were more likely to have increased work rule flexibility, new pay arrangements, joint committees, and team-based work systems. Most economic issues were not influenced by IBB. The greatest effect seemed to be on the ability to negotiate complex issues.

FIGURE 13.3
The Cooperation Continuum

Source: G. R. Gray, D. W. Myers, and P. S. Myers, "Cooperative Provisions in Labor Agreements: A New Paradigm?" *Monthly Labor Review,* 122, no. 1 (1999), p. 31.

- FULL COOPERATION
- Decisions on strategic issues
- High-performance practices
- Guarantees of employment security
- Decisions on traditional issues
- Committees to review mutual concerns that arise
- Statement of commitment to cooperate
- INTENT TO COOPERATE

There are differences in goal emphasis between union and management negotiators who prefer to use IBB. Management negotiators are more likely to be interested in new pay arrangements and teams, while union negotiators are less likely to be interested in those issues. Work rule flexibility and willingness to reduce benefits were higher for union bargainers preferring IBB but lower for management negotiators preferring IBB. These findings raise some caution flags regarding long-term sustainability of IBB in a particular bargaining situation.

CREATING AND SUSTAINING COOPERATION

Since the early 1980s, cooperative initiatives outside contracts and integrative bargains within contracts have increased. An analysis of contracts involving 1,000 or more employees and expiring between 1997 and 2007 found that 47 percent included cooperative provisions.[19] Figure 13.3 shows the cooperation continuum, while Table 13.1 shows the incidence of cooperative clauses by levels of cooperation.

Given management's long-standing antipathy toward unions, it's reasonable to expect collaboration only where improved performance is expected. Cooperation has been successful where communications between the parties is open, management accepts the representational role of the union, and the union is concerned about the success of the enterprise.[20]

Figure 13.4 models the proposed impact of collaboration on performance. It suggests that the intensity of cooperation is influenced by a cooperative structure and the relative power of the union and the company as modified by organizational constraints. Over time, the labor-management relations climate also influences intensity. Changing labor-management

[19] G. R. Gray, D. W. Myers, and P. S. Myers, "Cooperative Provisions in Labor Agreements: A New Paradigm?" *Monthly Labor Review*, 122, no. 1 (1999), pp. 29–45.

[20] R. W. Miller, R. W. Humphreys, and F. A. Zeller, "Structural Characteristics of Successful Cases of Cooperative Union-Management Relations," *Labor Studies Journal*, 22, no. 2 (1997), pp. 44–65.

TABLE 13.1
Incidence of Cooperative Clauses in Private Sector Collective Bargaining Agreements Expiring between September 1, 1997, and September 30, 2007

Source: G. R. Gray, D. W. Myers, and P. S. Myers, "Cooperative Provisions in Labor Agreements: A New Paradigm?" *Monthly Labor Review*, 122, no. 1 (1999), p. 33.

Provision	Number of Contracts	Percent of All Contracts	Percent of All Employees
Total in sample	1,041	100.0	100.0
All contracts with cooperative provisions	485	46.6	46.2
All contracts with explicit cooperative language	286	27.5	29.2
Stage 1:			
Statement of intent to cooperate only	150	14.4	9.6
Stage 2:			
Joint committees to review issues	163	15.7	16.0
Total at stages 1 and 2 only	160	15.4	13.1
Stage 3:			
Drug programs	72	6.9	4.7
Health care	16	1.5	2.2
Human relations	106	10.2	10.9
Safety	261	25.1	28.8
Stage 4:			
Favored "nation"	46	4.4	3.2
Neutrality toward organizing	49	4.7	4.6
No layoff	22	2.1	2.8
No subcontracting	14	1.3	0.7
Stage 5:			
High-performance work practices	154	14.8	19.1
Stage 6:			
Strategic decision making	27	2.6	4.4

FIGURE 13.4
Model of the Effect of Cooperation on Performance and Labor Relations Outcomes

Source: W. N. Cooke, *Labor–Management Cooperation* (Kalamazoo, MI: W. E. Upjohn Institute for Employment Research, 1990), p. 94. Reprinted with permission.

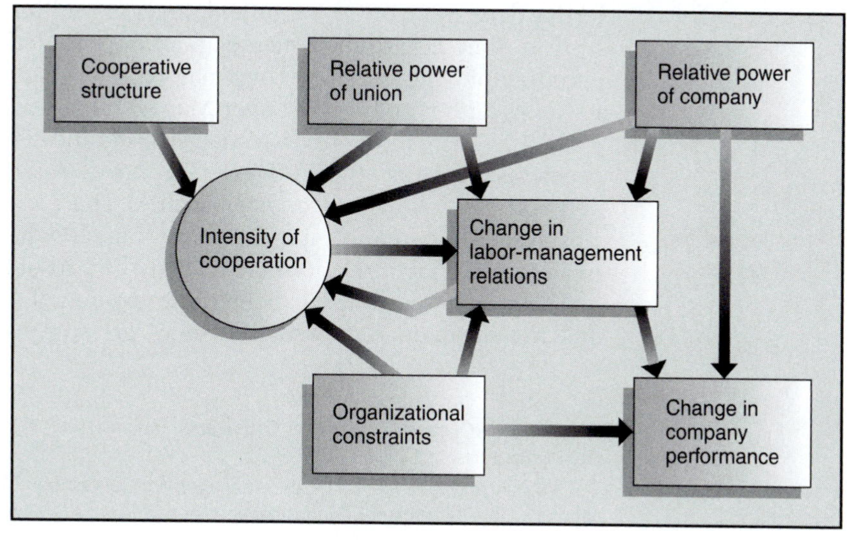

relations, the relative power of the company, and organizational constraints leads to changes in company performance. The availability of union and company power implies they will use it to influence cooperation. Applying relatively equal power should enhance cooperation efforts where both parties prefer it as a mode for achieving important ends for each.[21] A cooperative climate is promoted by the union's willingness to adopt an integrative bargaining approach, management's willingness to share information freely, and perceptions of procedural justice. This study found that cooperation contributed to higher productivity and improved customer service.[22]

METHODS OF COOPERATION

This section examines cooperation methods, covering assumptions about types of cooperation, mechanisms used to achieve it, union and management personnel involved, and results of cooperative efforts. It examines several generic approaches to labor-management cooperation, including areawide labor-management committees, productivity improvement and employee involvement plans, gainsharing, labor-management partnerships, and employee stock ownership plans. Within firms, several of these may be combined to enhance joint outcomes. The section also covers the changing roles of managers and union officials, political changes, and theprocesses involved in the diffusion and institutionalization of innovation in workplace design.

Areawide Labor-Management Committees

Areawide labor-management committees (AWLMCs) are jointly sponsored by unions and employers in a local area. They don't engage in collective bargaining or form multiemployer or multiunion bargaining units. Instead, they advise their members on how to deal with jointly experienced employment issues. They may receive financial support from the FMCS as authorized by the Labor-Management Cooperation Act of 1978.

AWLMCs are most often a response to significant regional employment problems. They have been developed most frequently in the Northeast and Midwest following economic declines. There is often a history of plant closings, with parent companies expanding elsewhere. High wages and/or adversarial labor relations are likely to be part of the problem.

The primary assumption behind the creation of AWLMCs is that labor and management representatives may pressure each other to identify

[21] W. N. Cooke, *Labor-Management Cooperation* (Kalamazoo, MI: W. E. Upjohn Institute for Employment Research, 1990), pp. 93–95.

[22] S. J. Deery and R. D. Iverson, "Labor-Management Cooperation: Antecedents and Impact on Organizational Performance," *Industrial and Labor Relations Review*, 58 (2005), pp. 588–609.

sources of problems and use cooperative methods to reduce or avoid conflict. They provide information to members about cooperation successes and legitimize the use of nonadversarial methods. The identification of joint issues, such as reduced profits and declining job security, may lead to joint efforts to resolve them.

An AWLMC is usually managed by an executive director hired by a coalition of business and union leaders. AWLMCs engage in four major types of activities: (1) sponsoring events to improve labor-management communications, (2) establishing committees in local plants, (3) assisting in negotiations, and (4) fostering economic development.[23] These activities aim to create a problem-solving environment and an appearance of labor-management cooperation.

Generally, evidence suggests that AWLMCs need the backing of major employers in the community and a competent executive director who is willing and able to stay in the post for an extended period to be able to accomplish the goals.[24]

Joint Labor-Management Committees

The retail food industry **joint labor-management committee (JLMC)** involves top union leaders from the UFCW and Teamsters and management leaders of 14 major grocery chains. It helps managers understand the national-local union relationship in a decentralized industry. JLMCs have been successful with research on occupational safety and health issues, introduction of new technology, health care cost containment, and issues relating to competitiveness.[25] JLMCs are most often implemented in industries with many employers and a dominant union with locals in many employers and locations.

Joint labor-management committees have most often been used to deal with specific problems rather than to address the entire scope of the bargaining relationship. Some joint efforts have led to continuing and expanded cooperation efforts. Notable is the employee involvement (EI) program developed by Ford and the United Auto Workers in 1979 to respond to higher levels of quality and value in imported vehicles and decreasing profits and job security in an industry under siege. Since then the program has been institutionalized within the joint UAW-Ford National Program Council encompassing eight programs to promote employee relations, skill development, and productivity. Another example is the introduction of joint building trades–union contractor committees in the construction industry. Here one study found improvements in safety, training, and

[23] R. D. Leone, *The Operation of Area Labor-Management Committees* (Washington, DC: U.S. Department of Labor, Labor-Management Services Administration, 1982).

[24] Ibid.; and R. W. Ahern, "Discussion of Labor-Management Cooperation," *Proceedings of the Industrial Relations Research Association*, 35 (1982), pp. 201–206.

[25] Kochan et al., *Transformation of American Industrial Relations*, pp. 182–189.

absenteeism; a reduction in jurisdictional disputes between unions; and a decline in jobs going to nonunion contractors.[26]

Joint labor-management committees are difficult to sustain when contract negotiations become adversarial. Confronting new economic realities over which the parties have no control strains the relationships. A once successful health care labor-management council in Minneapolis–St. Paul that created extensive cooperation led to improved hospital staffing flexibility, resulting in an increase in hospital income per patient of about $80 per day.[27]

But the demands for cost reductions from health maintenance organizations (HMOs) and the refusal to recognize AFSCME representation by a private hospital organization that was acquiring a large public facility led the Minnesota Nurses Association to question how pervasive a culture of cooperation actually was. Additionally, there was less interest among the hospitals in being part of a multiemployer group since they each began to experience unique problems given their competition to gain and/or retain admissions from large HMOs. The labor-management council is no longer in operation.[28] Thus, joint labor-management cooperation does not, in itself, ensure corporate survival and employee job security.

Workplace Interventions

Workplace interventions are projects usually initiated at a single location within an employer and involve a single union, or they may be part of a larger joint union-management program in a single firm. Typically, changes are sought by employers to improve product quality, productivity, and profitability. Unions seek enhanced employment security, an opportunity for economic gains, and continued operation of local facilities.

Workplace interventions change the design of organizations by increasing the use of lean production, cell manufacturing, self-directed work teams, and the like. Jobs are made broader and classifications are reduced, increasing the employer's flexibility in assigning work as demands change and reducing the likelihood that layoffs might follow a reduction in demand for jobs with narrow skills. Pay programs are often changed so that employees share in productivity or profitability gains while reducing employers' risks during periods of economic difficulty. Base pay levels are more frequently tied to skill level than to current job duties or seniority level.

[26] J. Remington and B. Londrigan, "Construction Industry Labor-Management Cooperation Committees: Defining Essential Elements," *Labor Studies Journal*, 19, no. 2 (1994), pp. 67–80.

[27] G. A. Preuss, "Labor-Management Cooperation and Hospital Adjustment of Practices," *Proceedings of the Industrial Relations Research Association*, 51 (1999), pp. 68–74.

[28] G. A. Preuss and A. C. Frost, "The Rise and Decline of Labor-Management Cooperation: Lessons from Health Care in the Twin Cities," *California Management Review*, 45, no. 2 (2003), pp. 85–106.

TABLE 13.2 Comparative Analysis of Workplace Interventions

Source: Adapted from M. Schuster, *Union Management Cooperation: Structure, Process, and Impact* (Kalamazoo, MI: W. E. Upjohn Institute for Employment Research, 1984), p. 73.

	Gainsharing			Nongainsharing		
Program Dimension	**Scanlon**	**Rucker**	**Impro-Share**	**Labor-Management Committees**	**Employee Involvement (EI) and Quality of Work Life (QWL)**	**Self-Managed Work Teams**
Role of supervisor	Chair, production committee	None	None	None	No direct role	No supervisor
Role of managers	Direct participation in bonus committee assignments	Ideas coordinator evaluates suggestions, committee assignments	None	Committee members	Steering committee membership	Communicates with work team on production targets; problem solving
Bonus formula	Sales/payroll	Bargaining unit payroll/ production value (sales, materials, supplies, services)	Engineered standard × BPF*/total hours worked	All savings/ improvements retained by company	All savings/ improvements retained by company	All savings/ improvements retained by company
Frequency of payout	Monthly	Monthly	Weekly	Not applicable	Not applicable	Not applicable
Role of union	Negotiated provisions, screening committee membership	Negotiated provisions, screening committee membership	Negotiated provisions	Active membership	Negotiated provisions, screening committee membership	Job design negotiated into collective bargaining agreement
Impact on management style	Substantial	Slight	None	Some	Substantial	Substantial

*Base productivity factor.

A variety of workplace interventions has been implemented. Table 13.2 divides them into gainsharing and nongainsharing plans and describes their characteristics. Gainsharing plans (covered in Chapter 9) tie periodic bonuses to labor productivity improvements. Nongainsharing approaches may include a changed reward structure (primarily nonmonetary) in the intervention without a directed relationship between productivity and pay. The table summarizes the guiding philosophy of each method, primary change goal, degree of worker participation, role of supervisors and managers, any bonus formulas, the union's role, and other characteristics.

Gainsharing plans generally benefit both employers and employees. As noted in Chapter 9, their adoption is often followed by increased profits, productivity-related bonuses for employees, and/or a greater ability for a firm to survive and employees to retain jobs during secular decline in an industry. In addition to generally positive economic benefits, a study found that after the introduction of a Scanlon-type plan, grievance and absentee rates permanently decreased over time.[29] A long-term study of a suggestion system found that productivity improved and grievances and disciplinary problems declined but implementation costs more than offset the gains the suggestions generated.[30] The survival of gainsharing plans is related to employees' vote to approve, new employee training, labor intensity, major capital investments, bonus performance, and use of consultants.[31]

Gainsharing plans are often implemented in mature organizations in competitive product markets where there is continuous pressure on all types of costs. Unless barriers to entry exist against new firms, flexible compensation programs inevitably lead to ratchet effects, with the performance base on which bonuses are paid increasing following higher productivity.[32]

Employee Involvement Programs

Employee involvement (EI) programs have three components: (1) improving climate, (2) generating commitment, and (3) implementing change. Union participation in EI programs is related to the progressiveness of the company and increased foreign competition. The implementation of involvement programs in traditional unionized workplaces is related to deregulation, demographic change, and support (but not pressure) from a parent national union. Cooperation in strategic decision making is positively related to foreign competition and negatively related to domestic competition—probably because the national union often bargains with other companies in the industry.[33]

A study of GM-UAW plants found that performance, quality, productivity, grievances, discipline, absenteeism, number of local contract demands, and negotiating time were significantly related. Grievances and

[29] J. B. Arthur and G. S. Jelf, "The Effects of Gainsharing on Grievance Rates and Absenteeism over Time," *Journal of Labor Research*, 20 (1999), pp. 133–146.

[30] D.-O. Kim, "The Benefits and Costs of Employee Suggestion under Gainsharing," *Industrial and Labor Relations Review*, 58 (2005), pp. 631–652.

[31] D.-O. Kim, "The Longevity of Gainsharing Programs: A Survival Analysis," *Proceedings of the Industrial Relations Research Association*, 51 (1999), pp. 200–209.

[32] H. L. Carmichael and W. B. McLeod, "Worker Cooperation and the Ratchet Effect," *Journal of Labor Economics*, 18 (2000), pp. 1–19.

[33] I. Goll, "Environment, Corporate Ideology, and Employee Involvement Programs," *Industrial Relations*, 29 (1990), pp. 501–512.

absenteeism rose when production pressures increased. Product quality and productivity measures decreased as labor problems increased. Managerial attitudes were positively related to both labor relations and productivity-efficiency measures. EI programs were associated with higher product quality and reduced grievances. Absenteeism and quality were related, possibly because less careful workers were gone more.[34] A study of both unionized and nonunion firms in Canada found that in unionized firms grievance rates generally decreased following implementation of EI programs but in nonunion workplaces EI was associated with the development and implementation of grievance procedures but not lower rates.[35]

EI programs are associated with reductions in absences, accidents, grievances, and quits.[36] Desire for union involvement in EI programs is related to dissatisfaction, organizational commitment, and attitudes toward EI.[37] Participation in programs leads to greater loyalty to the union rather than reduced commitment. However, perceived effectiveness of the grievance procedure is a stronger predictor of attitudes toward the union than of participation in EI programs.[38] EI program participation was associated with improved job satisfaction and enhanced communication skills. Union empowerment is a possible outcome.[39] EI programs increased organizational citizenship behavior of participants, both through participation and through changing job characteristics requiring more task sharing. Other employment practices had little effect.[40] Local unions involved in participation programs do not change the nature of their regular functions and activities, but unless they have support from their parent national, they may have a hard time coping with both participation and representation activities simultaneously.[41] Finally, union antagonism toward

[34] H. C. Katz, T. A. Kochan, and K. R. Gobeille, "Industrial Relations Performance, Economic Peformance, and QWL Programs: An Interplant Analysis," *Industrial and Labor Relations Review*, 37 (983), pp. 3–17.

[35] A. J. S. Colvin, "The Relationship between Employee Involvement and Workplace Dispute Resolution," *Relations Industrielles*, 59 (2004), pp. 681–704.

[36] S. J. Havlovic, "Quality of Work Life and Human Resource Outcomes," *Industrial Relations*, 30 (1991), pp. 469–479.

[37] Y. Reshef, M. Kizilos, G. E. Ledford, Jr., and S. G. Cohen, "Employee Involvement Programs: Should Unions Get Involved?" *Journal of Labor Research*, 20 (1999), pp. 557–570.

[38] A. E. Eaton, M. E. Gordon, and J. H. Keefe, "The Impact of Quality of Work Life Programs and Grievance System Effectiveness on Union Commitment," *Industrial and Labor Relations Review*, 45 (1992), pp. 591–604.

[39] T. Juravich, "Empirical Research on Employee Involvement: A Critical Review for Labor," *Labor Studies Journal*, 21, no. 2 (1996), pp. 51–69.

[40] P. Cappelli and N. Rogovsky, "Employee Involvement and Organizational Citizenship: Implications for Labor Law Reform and 'Lean Production'," *Industrial and Labor Relations Review*, 51 (1998), 633–653.

[41] A. E. Eaton and S. Rubinstein, "Tracking Local Unions Involved in Managerial Decision-Making," *Labor Studies Journal*, 31, no. 2, pp. 1–31.

EI doesn't appear to influence employee attitudes, but it does reduce participation.[42]

The evidence suggests that positive outcomes for both employers and employees result from implementing EI programs. However, a study using two large employer and employee data sets found that while employees generally feel that they benefited from EI programs, there is no measurable effect on company sales, even across a 10-year period.[43]

Team-Based Approaches

The organizational restructuring that began in the 1980s has been increasingly team-oriented. A work team is responsible for the output from an area, including work assignment. Each team member is expected to be able to perform all the tasks necessary to produce the output for which the team is responsible. The more skills employees possess, the greater the variety of tasks they can perform. As such, many team-based programs are supported by skill-based pay (SBP) plans. SBP ties employees' pay levels to the number of specific skills they have acquired.[44] Within a team, an employee who has acquired the entire set of applicable skills can perform any of the jobs. Broader skill sets mean the organization can readily accommodate changes in the demand for products because employees can assume new responsibilities quickly. Less equipment downtime occurs because one of the skill sets includes equipment maintenance. Multiskilling also improves an individual's job security.[45]

Team members are expected to learn all skills involved in the jobs performed by the team. The team decides how work will be accomplished. Supervisors facilitate rather than direct work. In organizations where teams have been implemented, relatively small numbers of distinct jobs exist. Employee-supervisor relations improve more when there is substantial union leader participation and teams are very active. They do best where employment has not changed appreciably, where workers are experienced, and where management does not subcontract.[46]

At Chrysler's Jefferson North plant, a **"modern operating agreement"** was implemented as the company's quid pro quo for rebuilding the plant

[42] R. E. Allen and K. L. Van Norman, "Employee Involvement Programs: The Noninvolvement of Unions Revisited," *Journal of Labor Research*, 17 (1996), pp. 479–495.

[43] R. B. Freeman and M. M. Kleiner, "Who Benefits Most from Employee Involvement: Firms or Workers?" *American Economic Review*, 90, no. 2 (2000), pp. 219–223.

[44] For additional details on skill-based pay plans, see G. T. Milkovich and J. Newman, *Compensation*, 8th ed. (Burr Ridge, IL: Irwin/McGraw-Hill, 2005).

[45] C. Ichniowski, "Human Resource Practices and Productive Labor-Management Relations," in D. Lewin, O. S. Mitchell, and P. D. Sherer, eds., *Research Frontiers in Industrial Relations and Human Resources* (Madison, WI: Industrial Relations Research Association, 1992), pp. 239–272.

[46] W. N. Cooke, "Factors Influencing the Effect of Joint Union-Management Programs on Employee-Supervisor Relations," *Industrial and Labor Relations Review*, 43 (1990), pp. 587–603.

in Detroit. Team leaders are elected in this operation as well, but rotation is infrequent. The team structure encourages equal effort and reduced absenteeism. This plant was staffed primarily by senior employees who would have been laid off if a new plant had not been built.[47]

Toyota pioneered the development of lean production methods focused on continuous improvement in both quality and productivity and waste reduction. General Motors (GM) adapted this system together with enhanced employee involvement and attention to union goals to create its Global Manufacturing System program. The company was interested in enhanced productivity and the ability to introduce new products in a more flexible fashion in its assembly plants. The UAW was interested in maintaining job security and employment standards. Since they had agreed on a contract that guaranteed income security and interplant transfer rights, even if employees were furloughed, GM was faced with fixed labor costs. Plants competed with each other to have products allocated to them. Those that received new products were more likely to continue producing in a shrinking auto market. At the Lansing Grand River assembly (LRGA) plant, production workers were trained in problem-solving skills and production teams were formed. Team leaders were elected, taking over the role of supervisors (who became trainers and problem-solving facilitators). Joint Team Concept Area Committees were introduced to ensure that both management and union members were meeting their responsibilities and achieving productivity improvement and waste reduction goals. Teamwork has reduced the need for managers to monitor performance and make production-related decisions. As a result, costs associated with management overhead have decreased. LRGA was awarded the opportunity to be the primary assembler of the expanding Cadillac-badged product line.[48]

Joint labor-management teams are often established to deal with workplace issues such as safety and health. These are standing committees, co-led by labor and management. Stewards who are members of these committees become less likely to file grievances and more likely to settle them at earlier stages in the process. They see their roles as less advocative and more tied to enforcing the contract equally on labor and management. However, they aren't more likely to adopt managerial goals related to plant or firm performance.[49]

[47] H. Shaiken, S. Lopez, and I. Mankita, "Two Routes to Team Production: Saturn and Chrysler Compared," *Industrial Relations*, 36 (1997), pp. 17–45.

[48] R. N. Block and P. Berg, "Joint Responsibility Unionism: A Multi-Plant Model of Collective Bargaining under Employment Security," *Industrial and Labor Relations Review,* 63 (2009), pp. 60–81.

[49] R. Bruno, "Bargaining through Cooperation: The Impact of Labor Management Teams on Steward Identity and Performance," *Proceedings of the Industrial Relations Research Association*, 55 (2003), pp. 264–273.

Labor-Management Partnerships

Labor-management partnerships (LMPs) expand the governance of the organization beyond what is included in union-management cooperation. In a cooperative framework, the union is involved in decisions that would be considered permissive bargaining issues only if management permits. In an LMP, management is agreeing that the union will be involved as an equal partner in forming and implementing the organization's strategy and operations.

In a private for-profit company, true partnership is highly unlikely since the firm's management is ultimately chosen by the representatives of the shareholders. If a firm with an LMP is not accomplishing the performance objectives set by the board of directors, and the board believes that the LMP detracts from performance, it will replace top management with a group that will likely dismantle the LMP. Thus, we might expect to see LMPs more frequently among nonprofits and employee-owned firms in the for-profit sector, or limited to a specific plant or division within a large firm.

Factors that would lead to the formation of an LMP would include changes in the market that increase competition, interdependence of the employer (key employee groups expect their employer will be unionized) and union (which would not exist in the company without employment), recognition of the legitimacy of both actors, and leaders of each who share a vision that outcomes for both would be improved by greater collaboration. The largest HMO in the United States, Kaiser Permanente (KP), has had an LMP for over 15 years. Its existence is particularly noteworthy since KP's organizational structure is very decentralized. It operates in eight states, has 86,000 employees ranging from physicians to unskilled maintenance employees, and bargains with 30 local unions that belong to 10 different internationals, some of whom compete with each other to organize workers in other firms. Since it is highly decentralized, diffusing the LMP throughout the organization required substantial effort on the part of both management and the local and international unions over several years. In order to be sustainable, the LMP had to solve problems and implement solutions that were visibly successful. Workers who had previously had no responsibility for taking on change initiatives were involved in more intensive and potentially stressful work efforts as the LMP went into operation. At the same time, they had increased autonomy and received training to help them acquire and use problem-solving skills. Some managers who were unable or unwilling to cope with the change left the organization. The unions asked some stewards who did not support the change to step down from their positions.[50] The fact that the LMP

[50] The description of the KP LMP is drawn from T. A. Kochan, P. S. Adler, R. B. McKersie, A. E. Eaton, P. Segal, and P. Gerhart, "The Potential and Precariousness of Partnership: The Case of the Kaiser Permanente Labor Management Partnership," *Industrial Relations*, 47 (2008), pp. 36–65.

has been in operation for 15 years and has survived a number of contract negotiations, interunion rivalry, and changes in top leadership of both management and unions gives evidence of its sustainability and contributions to all partners.

Alternative Governance Forms

Union-management cooperation changes both the production process and workplace governance. Employee involvement in decision-making shifts the focus of collective bargaining from structural rules to processes. Traditional collective bargaining offers less participation than other forms of governance.[51] Table 13.3 shows the relationship between employee relations practice and various employee involvement areas influencing governance of the organization.

Union Political Processes and the Diffusion of Change

Collaboration is foreign to an adversarial relationship and requires political change by local and national unions. Firm stability and progressive management ensure the safety net union leaders need to advocate change. Unions adopt one of five reactions to innovative workplace initiatives: (1) "Just say no," (2) let management lead and see what results, (3) become involved for political protection, (4) cooperate or collaborate, or (5) assert union interests.[52] Local union defensiveness is not irrational because sometimes managers view cooperation as a signal of a willingness to make concessions and increase productivity while efforts to undermine the union continue.[53] If unions perceive an unequal power relationship exists with management, cooperation is hard to introduce. Unions can take advantage of economic problems that motivate management to seek cooperation to further worker interests. Cooperative programs offer an opportunity to negotiate permanent participation into contracts.[54]

Developing cooperation programs is enhanced by international union education efforts, and local willingness to risk experimenting with new forms of bargaining and work designs.[55] Participation programs can

[51] A. Verma and J. Cutcher-Gershenfeld, "Joint Governance in the Workplace: Beyond Union Management Cooperation and Worker Participation," in B. E. Kaufman and M. M. Kleiner, eds., *Employee Representation: Alternatives and Future Directions* (Madison, WI: Industrial Relations Research Association, 1993), pp. 197–234.

[52] A. E. Eaton and P. B. Voos, "The Ability of Unions to Adapt to Innovative Workplace Arrangements," *American Economic Review*, 79, no. 2 (1989), pp. 172–176.

[53] P. B. Voos and T. Y. Cheng, "What Do Managers Mean by Cooperative Labor Relations?" *Labor Studies Journal*, 14, no. 1 (1989), pp. 3–19.

[54] J. Cutcher-Gershenfeld, R. B. McKersie, and K. R. Wever, *The Changing Role of Union Leaders* (Washington, DC: Bureau of Labor-Management Relations, U.S. Department of Labor, 1988).

[55] A. E. Eaton, "The Extent and Determinants of Local Union Control of Participative Programs," *Industrial and Labor Relations Review*, 43 (1990), pp. 604–620.

TABLE 13.3 Variations in Governance across Cooperation Methods

Source: A. Verma and J. Cutcher-Gershenfeld, "Joint Governance in the Workplace: Beyond Union-Management Cooperation and Worker Participation," in B. E. Kaufman and M. M. Kleiner, eds., *Employer Alternatives and Future Directions* (Madison, WI: Industrial Relations Research Association, 1993), pp. 204–205.

Dimensions	High-Involvement Nonunion Systems	Traditional Collective Bargaining	Traditional Labor-Management Committees	Labor Representatives on the Board	German-Style Works Councils	Mutually Agreed-to Joint Governance
Conflict vs. cooperation	Heavy emphasis on cooperation; only interpersonal avenues for conflict resolution	Formal conflict resolution procedures with limited emphasis on cooperation	Cooperative forum with no decision-making role and no formal conflict resolution procedure	More of a cooperative forum; some room for expressing conflict	Potential for cooperation; conflicts can be taken to labor courts	Potential for cooperation and room for surfacing and resolving conflicts
Procedural vs. substantive work rules	Few formal work rules; heavy emphasis on informal resolution	Heavy reliance on substantive rules enforced by the grievance procedure	Procedural rule making	Procedural decision making	Heavy emphasis on procedural decision making	Heavy emphasis on procedural decision making
Direct vs. indirect participation	Heavy emphasis on direct participation	Mostly indirect; little emphasis on direct participation	Mostly indirect; little emphasis on direct participation	Indirect	Indirect; informal direct participation	Indirect; creates pressures to introduce direct participation
Administrative vs. political skills	Administrative skills taught to employees at all levels	Management concentrates on administrative skills; union on political skills	Some overlap but lack of decision-making role prevents further diffusion	Labor representatives develop administrative skills but management only develops marginal political skills	Labor develops administrative skills; plant management develops political skills	Labor develops administrative skills; management develops political skills
Joint and equal decision-making power	No	Yes, but in bargainable issues and at bargaining time only	May contain equal number of labor and management reps, but equality is less significant because the role is mostly advisory	No, with the exception of the German law of 1951 covering the iron, steel, and coal industries	Yes	Yes

benefit unions since workers who are active are more satisfied with their union and involved in union activities. Union support is not undermined by member involvement.[56] Union leader involvement in participation lifts member commitment, but members who view the company and union negatively are not changed by a program's success. In situations where several unions represent employees in an organization that is involved in a cooperation program, union leaders need to be supportive of efforts within the company even if they are actual or potential rivals in organizing activities.[57]

Management Strategy

Labor-management cooperation efforts are often focused at the plant level, although some companywide strategies, such as the Ford-UAW EI program, exist. Management may frequently encounter situations in which its employees, across plants, are represented by several different international unions, each with its own approach toward union-management cooperation.

Initial research on management strategies toward collective bargaining, cooperation, union avoidance, and firm performance suggests that firms improve profitability through extensive collaboration between management and labor. Performance is also improved by closing existing unionized facilities and opening or acquiring new nonunion plants. Deunionizing activity in any existing plant has a negative effect on performance.[58]

Evidence from steel minimills indicates they follow either a cost-reduction or product-differentiation strategy. Cost-reduction strategies are associated with conflict and the use of formal grievance procedures, while product differentiation requires flexible manufacturing and is associated with employee commitment, collective bargaining, and the informal solution of problems. Wages in minimills following a product-differentiation strategy are higher and employees add more value to the products.[59]

Research on the Effects of Cooperation across Organizations

A study of several hundred organizations has yielded important information on the effects of contextual and cooperative structures on productivity

[56] A. Verma, "Joint Participation Programs: Self-Help or Suicide for Labor?" *Industrial Relations*, 28 (1989), pp. 401–410.

[57] For information on how the various unions representing Kaiser Permanente employees coordinated union involvement in the LMP, see A. E. Eaton, S. A. Rubinstein, and T. A. Kochan, "Balancing Acts: Dynamics of a Union Coalition in a Labor Management Partnership," *Industrial Relations*, 47 (2008), pp. 10–35.

[58] D. G. Meyer and W. N. Cooke, "Labor Relations in Transition: Strategic Activities and Financial Performance," *British Journal of Industrial Relations*, 31 (1993), pp. 531–552.

[59] J. B. Arthur, "The Link between Business Strategy and Industrial Relations Systems in American Steel Minimills," *Industrial and Labor Relations Review*, 45 (1992), pp. 488–506.

and quality. The more active team-based programs are, the greater their effect. Top union leader participation is important. Larger plants have more difficulty improving productivity through cooperative efforts. Technology changes improve productivity at a rate faster than any negative effects from unilateral management implementation. Higher union security predicts more positive results. Subcontracting and frequent layoffs reduce gains. Interestingly, the larger the proportion of women in the workforce, the greater the productivity gains.[60]

Product quality was higher where joint labor-management programs existed. Adversarial programs produced better results than programs run only by management, which were not better than having no program. Joint programs were as effective as participation programs in nonunion firms. If the firm coupled cooperation with significant capital investments, quality improved substantially. Factors reducing joint-program effectiveness included subcontracting, earlier concessions, downsizing, and larger unit size.[61] Table 13.4 shows the effects of various union-management cooperation plans, demographic characteristics, and program performance on measures of quality, productivity, cost reduction, production processes, and bonus payouts.

A study of company performance across 24 units found that adversarial labor-management relations were associated with higher costs, more scrap, lower productivity, and lower returns to direct labor hours than was found in areas with increased cooperation and improved grievance handling.[62] Employee involvement programs were equally likely in both union and nonunion settings, but unionized firms allowed employees less authority. EI programs were not related to return on assets.[63]

EI programs influence firm performance more in unionized firms, while profit-sharing and gainsharing programs are better in nonunion firms in raising value added per employee. Unionized firms had higher value added, lower labor costs, and more experienced and skilled workforces.[64]

Another study of outcomes across a set of employers found union officer–management relations were positively related to forming general

[60] W. N. Cooke, "Improving Productivity and Quality through Collaboration," *Industrial Relations*, 28 (1989), pp. 299–319.

[61] W. N. Cooke, "Product Quality Improvement through Employee Participation: The Effects of Unionization and Joint Union-Management Administration," *Industrial and Labor Relations Review*, 46 (1992), pp. 119–134.

[62] J. Cutcher-Gershenfeld, "The Impact of Economic Performance of a Transformation in Workplace Relations," *Industrial and Labor Relations Review*, 44 (1991), pp. 241–260.

[63] J. T. Delaney, C. Ichniowski, and D. Lewin, "Employee Involvement Programs and Firm Performance," *Proceedings of the Industrial Relations Research Association*, 41 (1988), pp. 148–158.

[64] W. N. Cooke, "Employee Participation Programs, Group-Based Incentives, and Company Performance: A Union-Nonunion Comparison," *Industrial and Labor Relations Review*, 47 (1994), pp. 594–609.

TABLE 13.4 Perceived Effectiveness of Involvement and Gainsharing Programs on Performance Measures

Source: Adapted from D. -O. Kim, "Factors Influencing Organizational Performance in Gainsharing Programs," *Industrial Relations*, 35 (1996), pp. 232–233.

Program or Characteristic	Improved Quality	Improved Labor Productivity	Cost Reduction	Improved Production Process	Bonus Payout Level
Employee involvement	**			**	
Frequent bonus			*(–)		**
Employee bonus share				***	—
Employee bonus share squared				***(–)	—
Bonus payouts	**	***	***	***	—
Bonus payouts squared		***(–)	**(–)		—
Small bonus group	*				**
Scanlon plan	***			***	
Modified Scanlon plan				**	**(–)
Rucker plan				*	
Customized plan	**			**	
Consultant involvement	*				
Employee vote	***		***	*	**(–)
Labor intensity		*	**		
Market growth				**	**
Financial situation					**
Average education	*(–)				
Average seniority	**	***	***		*
Union	*** (–)	***(–)	**(–)	***(–)	
Program age		*(–)	**(–)	*	***
MU(1)	***	***	***	***	***
Union support (if union present)	**		*	*	***

*Likelihood that effect of program or characteristic is zero is less than 10 percent.
**Likelihood that effect of program or characteristic is zero is less than 5 percent.
***Likelihood that effect of program or characteristic is zero is less than 1 percent.
(–) Direction of effect is negative.
— Effect is not measured in this specification.

committees but not to decisions involving profit sharing or **employee stock ownership plans (ESOPs)**. Grievances were reduced where committees or gainsharing plans were implemented. General labor-management committees kept grievance handling more informal and resolved problems more quickly. Flexibility and reduced absenteeism and turnover were related to all types of participation, as cataloged in "Workplace Interventions." [65] Table 13.5 summarizes the results of this study.

[65] P. G. Voos, "The Influence of Cooperative Programs on Union-Management Relations, Flexibility, and Other Labor Relations Outcomes," *Journal of Labor Research*, 10 (1989), pp. 103–117.

TABLE 13.5 Managers' Mean Evaluations of the Impact of Selected Committees and Programs on Six Labor Relations Outcomes*

Source: Adapted from P. B. Voos, "The Influence of Cooperative Programs on Union-Management Relations, Flexibility, and Other Labor Relations Outcomes," *Journal of Labor Research*, 10 (1989), p. 109.

	Union Officer–Management Relations	Grievance Rate	Ability to Resolve Grievances Informally	Flexibility in Using Labor	Absenteeism	Turnover
General plant committees	1.23	1.03	1.24	0.54	0.41	0.31
Specialized plant committees	0.77	0.71	0.66	0.25	0.32	0.25
Local-area cooperation committees	0.82	NS	0.36	NS	NS	NS
Employee participation programs	0.47	0.53	0.55	0.47	0.30	0.27
Gainsharing plans	0.57	0.78	0.78	0.57	0.57	0.47
Profit-sharing plans	0.36	NS	0.28	0.20	0.25	0.46
Employee stock ownership plans	0.38	NS	NS	NS	NS	0.23

*Only relationships that are statistically significantly different from 0 are shown.
NS = not significantly different from 0.
Evaluations are based on the following response scale: 2 = large positive effect, 1 = small positive effect, 0 = no effect, −1 = small negative effect, and −2 = large negative effect.

Managers perceive greater support from employees who are covered by profit-sharing and participation plans. Employee input on issues and authority to implement suggestions are related to managerial perceptions that employees support change.[66]

Research on the Long-Term Effects of Cooperation

Little research on the long-term effects of union-management cooperation has been reported. One study of cooperation initiatives found large differences in the philosophies underlying projects. Scanlon and quality circle programs have the greatest participation, while Rucker and Impro-Share programs are mostly associated with economic incentives. The plans cannot substitute for good management, but where that does not exist, labor-management committees can be a springboard for progress. In the absence of management commitment to participation, Scanlon and other high-participation programs will fail.[67] Critical factors for the ongoing success of the programs are the training and commitment of supervisors and the construction and understanding of the bonus formulas.

[66] S. Schwochau, J. Delaney, P. Jarley, and J. Fiorito, "Employee Participation and Assessments of Organizational Policy Changes," *Journal of Labor Research*, 18 (1997), pp. 379–401.

[67] Schuster, *Union Management Cooperation*.

Companies and unions generally begin programs to improve labor relations, increase the level of pay available, and so on. Motives of the parties influence the type of plan chosen. Gainsharing affects productivity more than do labor-management committees or EI programs. If a traditional bargaining relationship has enabled both the company and the union to accomplish their objectives, they do not initiate cooperation methods. Those methods are used only when the parties encounter difficulties in accomplishing their goals while using a traditional distributive bargaining approach.

A study of cooperation at 23 sites found productivity improvements in 12 and no change in 10 others. In 16, subsequent experience enabled employees to earn bonuses supplementing what they would have earned solely as a result of collective bargaining. Bonus levels are directly influenced by the rate of suggestions generated by the employees.[68] Employment levels are relatively unaffected by cooperative programs, and labor relations are seen as improved.[69]

It is very difficult to develop and sustain labor-management cooperation. Harley-Davidson and the IAM and PACE unions worked together for over 10 years to increase productivity, quality, and profitability. They implemented substantial changes in work design, worker participation, and gainsharing. Intensive involvement by top management and the national and local unions helped the program succeed. During this period, Harley-Davidson increased its market share and reputation with consumers to an almost "cult" level.[70] But since the economy stalled in 2009, it has forced workers to make significant concessions and demanded incentives from the State of Wisconsin to maintain production at Milwaukee and Tomahawk.

The second example involves the city of Indianapolis and the American Federation of State, County, and Municipal Employees (AFSCME) locals representing employees in the transportation department. Working with the mayor and AFSCME leaders, workers improved productivity sufficiently to undercut private bidders for street maintenance and repair contracts. Several layers of middle management and supervisors were eliminated in a politically volatile environment. Communications between management and the union were substantially enhanced and

[68] M. Schuster, "The Scanlon Plan: A Longitudinal Analysis," *Journal of Applied Behavioral Science*, 20 (1984), pp. 23–38.

[69] M. Schuster, "The Impact of Union-Management Cooperation on Productivity and Employment," *Industrial and Labor Relations Review*, 37 (1983), pp. 415–430.

[70] See J. Young and K. L. Murrell, "Harley-Davidson Motor Company Organizational Design: The Road to High Performance," *Organizational Development Journal*, 16, no. 1 (1998), pp. 65–74; and R. Teerlink and L. Ozley, *More Than a Motorcycle: The Leadership Journey at Harley-Davidson* (Boston: Harvard Business School Press, 2000).

racial segregation in job assignments was successfully addressed.[71] The partnership continues to improve services and lower taxes.[72]

One of the most widely followed innovative cooperative relationships was between the UAW and the Saturn division of GM. Managers and union leaders worked together in a partnership for 13 years from the time the Spring Hill, Tennessee, plant was opened until 1999 when the UAW's local leaders were voted out and replaced by new officers who favored a traditional relationship between the union and the company. Over the next several years, the Saturn operation was fully integrated with General Motors and then with the 2009 bankruptcy, the Saturn brand was retired.

HIGH-PERFORMANCE WORK ORGANIZATIONS

A lot of attention has been paid to the development of so-called high-performance work organizations (HPWOs). These employers have adopted many of the EI and other work practice innovations that have been discussed previously. Recent research finds strong evidence that firms need to implement a coherent set of practices to enhance firm performance.

A study of steel minimills found that plants that implemented a combination of problem-solving teams, flexible job assignments, training for multiple jobs, guaranteed employment security, and flexible pay plans were substantially more productive and profitable than firms that implemented smaller combinations of these or only single practices. Operating uptime and value added were strongly influenced by these types of human resource management practices.[73]

In another study, steelworkers in HPWOs who say they are able to use skills and knowledge, perceive positive employee relations, and balance work and family life are very satisfied. Predictors of satisfaction include perceptions of pay fairness, being a woman, being a high school graduate, job autonomy, use of skills, employee relations, work/family balance, and low job stress.[74]

Workplace Restructuring

A great deal of workplace restructuring has taken place over the past 25 years. Much of this has increased the intensity of work and reduced the

[71] B. Rubin and R. Rubin, "Municipal Service Delivery, Collective Bargaining, and Labor-Management Partnerships," *Journal of Collective Negotiations in the Public Sector*, 30 (2003), pp. 91–112.

[72] www.dol.gov/_sec/media/reports/worktogether/chp2snap.htm.

[73] C. Ichniowski, K. Shaw, and G. Prennushi, "The Effects of Human Resource Management Practices on Productivity: A Study of Steel Finishing Lines," *American Economic Review*, 87 (1997), pp. 29–313.

[74] P. Berg, "The Effects of High Performance Work Practices on Job Satisfaction in the United States Steel Industry," *Relations Industrielles*, 54 (1999), pp. 111–135.

number of employees in production jobs. At the same time, the number of layers of management has been reduced. One study found that workplace restructuring and employer performance outcomes were more successful when the organizational structure and operation of the local union were stronger as reflected by horizontal and vertical communication network ties and internal political vitality.[75]

Companies that implemented HPWOs during the early 1990s had higher layoff rates and no net compensation gain for employees during the decade. Layoffs were negatively related to sales gains, exports, skill levels, employee age, and proportion of female employees, and they were positively related to the proportion of blue-collar workers and the introduction of HPWO practices. Wage gains for core employees were associated with sales gains and were negatively related to employee age and proportion of female employees. Teams, quality circles, and total quality management (TQM) were positively associated with layoffs, while teams were negatively associated with wage gains. Clearly, HPWO practices have not increased job security or pay except in situations where the organization's revenues were growing.[76] This evidence suggests that unions are unlikely to gain from cooperating in implementing HPWO practices. The study found that union status had no effect on layoff or wage gain outcomes among the employers studied.

THE LEGALITY OF COOPERATION PLANS

Among unionized employers, cooperation plans meet the requirements of the labor acts because they are jointly agreed to by unions and managements. Many employers in nonunion companies have established joint management-employee committees to deal with a variety of production and employment issues. However, it's possible these committees violate labor law. Section 8(a)(2) of the Taft-Hartley Act forbids employers to create and operate employer-dominated labor organizations.[77] Discussions of employment issues or proposals by committees for taking action on areas related to wages, hours, and terms and conditions of employment intrude into the mandatory bargaining issues specified in the act.[78]

[75] A. C. Frost, "Explaining Variation in Workplace Restructuring: The Role of Local Union Capabilities," *Industrial and Labor Relations Review*, 53 (2000), pp. 559–578.

[76] P. Osterman, "Work Reorganization in an Era of Restructuring: Trends in Diffusion and Effects on Employee Welfare," *Industrial and Labor Relations Review*, 53 (2000), pp. 179–196.

[77] A. B. Cochran, III, "We Participate, They Decide: The Real Stakes in Revising Section 8(a)(2) of the National Labor Relations Act," *Berkeley Journal of Employment and Labor Law*, 16 (1995), pp. 458–519.

[78] R. Hanson, R. I. Porterfiel, and K. Ames, "Employee Empowerment at Risk: Effects of Recent NLRB Rulings," *Academy of Management Executive*, 9, no. 2 (1995), pp. 45–56.

The NLRB was faced with ruling on the legality of an employer-sponsored committee in the *Electromation* case.[79] In its deliberation the NLRB asked: "When does an employee committee lose its protection as a communication device and become a labor organization?" and "What employer conduct constitutes interference or domination of such committees?"

The company had set up five volunteer committees to look at absenteeism, pay, bonuses, and the like. The company initiated the committees and drafted their goals, and management representatives facilitated discussions. The NLRB ruled this was an employer-dominated labor organization in violation of Section 8(a)(2). But in a later case, it held that employee committees that were delegated management responsibilities for production and personnel decisions that were reviewed by and sometimes reversed by management were not employee dominated. However, these committees neither were elected nor made proposals to management.[80]

At this point, it would be difficult to determine what a legal employee involvement program in a nonunion environment would be since pay will undoubtedly be an issue if productivity is discussed.[81] At the same time, the NLRB has accepted and pursued very few cases alleging 8(a)(2) violations where employers have established teams and committees.

EMPLOYEE STOCK OWNERSHIP PLANS

Employee stock ownership plans (ESOPs) were first permitted by the Employee Retirement Income Security Act (ERISA) of 1974. Employees may receive stock through profit sharing, productivity gains, or subtractions from wages. Since the early 1980s, several companies (e.g., Chrysler, several airlines) have given employees stock in exchange for labor concessions. In most of these cases, particularly in the airline and steel industries, employees in general have experienced an erosion of their shares' value, in some cases even going through bankruptcies.

ESOPs will not, in themselves, improve productivity. Employee-owned firms in Israel don't function much differently than privately-owned firms. Pay, productivity, and job security are somewhat higher.[82] Workers are generally productive regardless of the source of ownership.[83] Ownership

[79] *Electromation, Inc.*, 309 NLRB No. 163 (1992).

[80] *Crown Cork & Seal Co.*, 334 NLRB No. 92 (2001); and J. L. Ditelberg and T. J. Piskorski, "NLRB Breathes New Life into Employee Participation Committees," *Employee Relations Law Journal*, 27, no. 1 (2002), pp. 127–137.

[81] A. E. Perl, "Employee Involvement Groups: The Outcry over the NLRB's *Electromation* Decision," *Labor Law Journal*, 44 (1993), pp. 195–207.

[82] A. Ben-Ner and S. Estrin, "What Happens When Unions Run Firms? Unions as Employee Representatives and as Employees," *Journal of Comparative Economics*, 15 (1991), pp. 65–87.

[83] J. R. Blasi, "The Productivity Ramifications of Union Buyouts," *National Productivity Review*, 9 (1990), pp. 17–34.

affects workers' attitudes by providing greater perceived influence and control and financial value.[84] A study of Ohio ESOPs found that in unionized companies, there were more shop-floor participation methods in companies where employees owned a majority of the stock. Performance was judged to be somewhat higher than that in non-ESOP firms.[85] However, workers may not automatically favor ESOPs either. The firm governance role involved in ESOPs may induce fear and anxiety as well as expanded commitment. Where firm performance is linked to retirement security, workers may wish to avoid ESOPs since their investments lack diversification.[86]

In some cases, employees have bought the companies in which they work in order to protect their jobs and pensions. One of the largest was the purchase of the Weirton Steel works by employees from National Steel Company in 1983 when it had planned to close the mill. Ultimately, the mill went bankrupt in 2003, but by that time, the pensions of employees who worked there at the time of the buyout were protected and many others were able to qualify for more generous pensions over the 20-year period between the buyout and bankruptcy.[87]

THE DIFFUSION AND INSTITUTIONALIZATION OF CHANGE

An important labor-management issue is how successful changes get diffused throughout the organization and become institutionalized. Participation needs a stable environment, especially in the composition of the management team, in order to grow. The parties need to avoid or isolate collective bargaining shocks and strategic shocks. Layoffs create problems for teams because workers use competitive seniority rights to bump in and out. Changes are aided by implementing them in new facilities with new workers. Diffusion of successes can then move toward established settings. Unions can markedly assist change when they have a role in strategic decision making such as plant locations. They may also provide needed concessions and work rule changes to make retrofitting of existing facilities economically feasible. Training to introduce new technology and increase employment security is important to employees and can help

[84] A. A. Buchko, "Effects of Ownership on Employee Attitudes: A Test of Three Theoretical Perspectives," *Work and Occupations*, 19 (1992), pp. 59–78.

[85] J. Yates, "Unions and Employee Ownership: A Road to Economic Democracy?" *Industrial Relations*, 45 (2006), pp. 709–733.

[86] J. L. Pierce, S. A. Rubenfeld, and S. Morgan, "Employee Ownership: A Conceptual Model of Process and Effects," *Academy of Management Review*, 16 (1991), pp. 121–144.

[87] G. Beamer, "Sustaining the Rust Belt: A Retrospective Analysis of the Employee Purchase of Weirton Steel," *Labor History*, 48 (2007), pp. 277–299.

make change permanent. Gainsharing will probably follow as a logical consequence of innovative participation.[88]

The ability to institutionalize change depends on high levels of trust and commitment by union leaders and members, supervisors, plant managers, and corporate executives. Evidence shows that labor and management have substantially different perceptions in many situations regarding the degree of commitment, feelings of manipulation and co-optation, and delivery on promises given that the efforts undertaken have not always followed their planned course. Establishing and continuing trust are critical underlying factors in the success of cooperation programs.[89]

Maintaining Union-Management Cooperation in the Face of External Change

Union-management cooperation is a fragile regime. At the most basic level, the parties have different interests. Creating cooperation requires a political investment by both managers and union officers who see it as a vehicle to achieve their organization's objectives more fully than pursuing a traditional approach. There are always other managers and faction leaders within unions who believe that cooperation is antithetical to labor-management relations. When or if they move into leadership positions, the efforts are likely to flounder.

Besides facing internal political pressures, managers must deal with shareholder demands. Unless a firm with a cooperative labor-management relations climate performs better than comparable firms within its industry during the current operating period, there will be inevitable pressures to try different methods. While most of the evidence cited above suggests that cooperation is generally associated with higher worker satisfaction, lower grievances, and greater organizational commitment, there is no consistent evidence to indicate it universally improves firm performance.

Summary

Employers would like to earn as large a return as possible on their investment, while labor would like continuous economic improvements and employment security. Given the requirements for negotiations on mandatory issues and the inability of unions to demand negotiations on permissive issues, room for cooperation in traditional bargaining environments is sparse.

Integrative bargaining is the set of activities leading to simultaneously accomplishing nonconflicting objectives in solving a common problem. Mutual-gains bargaining is a method to help the parties achieve their objectives. To implement integrative solutions, both parties must have as much information as possible on the problem they are attempting to solve.

[88] T. A. Kochan and J. Cutcher-Gershenfeld, *Institutionalizing and Diffusing Innovations in Industrial Relations* (Washington, DC: U.S. Department of Labor, Bureau of Labor-Management Relations and Cooperative Programs, 1988).

[89] Cooke, *Labor-Management Cooperation*, pp. 121–136.

Employers and unions use a variety of methods to create and sustain cooperation. These include areawide labor-management committees that deal with regional employment problems in unionized environments, joint labor-management committees that operate at the industry or firm level, gainsharing plans (the Scanlon plan, Rucker plan, and Impro-Share), and nongainsharing interventions (labor-management committees, quality circles, employee involvement programs, team-based approaches, and labor-management partnerships).

Increasing numbers of companies are working with unions to implement team-based action groups to improve productivity and quality. Perceived productivity seems to increase most where the union is secure, top union officials are involved in the process, and significant numbers of union members are in team-based activities. The introduction of new technology continues to lead the way in improving productivity. Unions are learning how to participate in and benefit from cooperation while retaining their distributive bargaining roles. Innovation is institutionalized through success and stability in organizations where experiments are tried.

Employee stock ownership plans aim to increase employee commitment to the company through the long-term improvement of the value of ownership gained through higher productivity.

Discussion Questions

1. Why would including such programs as union-management cooperation programs in the collective agreement be difficult?
2. Under what conditions would a Scanlon plan be likely to be effective over relatively long periods?
3. What are the potential long-term problems for unions in agreeing to labor-management cooperation programs?
4. In return for cooperation or participating in partnerships, should unions be guaranteed a seat on an organization's board of directors?
5. Should the *Electromation* decision be overturned?

Key Terms

Greenfield operations, *436*
Principled negotiations, *440*
Relations by objectives, *440*
Bucket bargaining, *441*
Interest-based bargaining (IBB), *442*
Areawide labor-management committees (AWLMCs), *446*
Joint labor-management committee (JLMC), *447*
Employee involvement (EI) program, *450*
Modern operating agreement, *452*
Employee stock ownership plan (ESOP), *459*

Selected Web Sites

www.thejlmc.com/
www.lmpartnership.org/home
www.uawford.com/dandp_frameset.html

Case: *Continuing or Abandoning the Special-Order Fabrication Business*

It is about three months since the effective date of the GMFC–Local 384 contract. In GMFC's executive council meeting this morning, financial officers reported on an in-depth study on the profitability of the special-order fabrication operations. They recommended GMFC take no more orders for this area and close the operation when present commitments were shipped. Their data showed that the operations lost money two out of the last three years, and they argued that the Speedy-Lift assembly lines could be expanded into that area for meeting the increasing demand for GMFC forklift trucks.

Top-level managers in the special-order fabrication operations conceded that profits, when earned, were low, but they pointed out that, from a return-on-investment standpoint, their operations had been among the best in the company during the 2003 to 2007 period. Besides, they argued, many of the special orders were from some of the largest customers in the standard product lines, and GMFC could not afford to lose that business if it was dependent on occasional custom orders as well.

The finance people reiterated their recommendations to terminate the operations, pointing out that labor costs had risen over the past several contracts and, due to the custom nature of the work, productivity gains had been small because new technologies could not be introduced.

After both sides presented their final summations, the chief executive officer announced that the firm should prepare to terminate operations. After the announcement, the industrial relations director pointed out that GMFC would have to negotiate the termination with Local 384. The union might demand severance pay, job transfers, and so forth. The point was also raised that this decision offered the union and the company the opportunity to devise a method for reducing and controlling labor costs.

The CEO designated the vice president of finance, the general manager of special-order fabrications, and the industrial relations director as the bargaining team to present the company's decision and bargain a resolution. The CEO made it clear that the company intended to abandon these operations but could reverse its position with the right kind of labor cost reductions.

Although this meeting was not publicized, Local 384's leadership had been concerned about the special-order fabrications area for some time. Management had frequently grumbled about low productivity, and stewards were frequently harassed about alleged slowdowns. Union members in the shop often grieved about work rule changes. The stack of grievances, coupled with management's lack of action on them, led the leadership to request a meeting with the industrial relations director to solve the problems.

DIRECTIONS

1. Rejoin your original labor or management bargaining team.
2. Reach an agreement for continuation or termination of the special-order fabrication operations.
   a. Company negotiators must reduce labor costs by 10 percent and stabilize them for project bids if operations are to continue (labor costs are 30 percent of the total costs, and ROI would be 7 percent if costs were cut by 10 percent).
   b. Union members are unwilling to have their pay rates cut.
   c. All the employees in this area are level 2 or 3 skilled production workers, and most have more than 20 years' experience.
3. Use the agreement you previously reached or the contract in Chapter 11 to specify current terms for these workers.

Chapter Fourteen

Contract Administration

After a contract is negotiated and ratified, the parties are bound by its terms. But contract clauses may be violated or interpreted differently, so disputes often arise. Almost all contracts contain a grievance procedure to resolve intracontractual disputes. This chapter identifies types and causes of disputes and the contractual means used for resolving them.

As noted in Chapter 13, team-based work designs have reduced the use of first-line supervisors. In these types of work situations, grievances or problems in implementing the contract are increasingly resolved within the work team in consultation with management.

In reading this chapter, keep the following questions in mind:

1. What areas of disagreement emerge while the contract is in effect?
2. What actions by the parties violate the labor acts?
3. Are disagreements resolved by bargaining or by evaluating the merits of a given issue?
4. How can team-based work environments lead to proactive grievance procedures?
5. What does the union owe individual members in grievance processing?

THE DUTY TO BARGAIN

Parties do not end their obligation to bargain by negotiating an agreement. The National Labor Relations Board (NLRB) and courts interpret the duty to bargain as covering the entire relationship from recognition onward. Although the parties have developed a written agreement, there may be situations in which they interpret it differently. There also may be differences about the creation and implementation of rules that are enabled by the contract but not actually within it. To establish an orderly process for handling intracontract disputes, the parties virtually always incorporate a grievance procedure that spells out how they will be resolved. Thus, the duty to bargain is fulfilled by using the agreed-upon steps for any dispute regarding wages, hours, or terms and conditions of employment.

Conventional Contract Administration

Management takes the initiative in **contract administration**. It determines how it will operate facilities and discipline employees. The union reacts if it senses a result is inconsistent with its interpretation of the contract and work rules. The employer does not file a grievance when the union or a worker allegedly violates the contract; it simply acts and waits for a union response. For example, if a worker swears at a supervisor, the company might suspend the worker for five days. The company does not ask the union to discipline its members. If the union believes the discipline is unjust, it protests the action through a grievance. The contract spells out the resolution process, and the management decision stands unless and until it is reversed or modified at some step in the overall process.

When a grievance procedure exists and management changes its operations, employees are expected to conform to the change. If employees believe the change violates the contract considered unjust, they must grieve rather than refuse to follow orders. If the latter occurred, employees could be discharged for insubordination unless their conducted constituted protected concerted activity.

Empowered Work Environments

Many empowered production work environments have developed self-managed work teams. Teams do not have the authority to adjust grievances within the teams. However, they may raise problems with management without making a formal grievance and use their ongoing access to management to identify the likely causes of problems and to more quickly solve them. While this reduces the formal role of the union negotiating committee in resolving grievances, a team member at a Ford stamping plant felt that the team-based approach actually increased the relevance and input of the union.[1]

ISSUES IN CONTRACT ADMINISTRATION

Disputes during the contract may focus on specific contract clauses or the implementation of rules by the employer that are within the purview of the management rights clause. Following are some of the major subjects of grievances.

[1] For a summary of this and other team-based environments, see M. Kaminski, "New Forms of Work Organization and Their Impact on the Grievance Procedure," in A. E. Eaton and J.H. Keefe, eds., *Employment Dispute Resolution and Worker Rights* (Champaign, IL: Industrial Relations Research Association, 1999), pp. 219–246.

Discipline

Discipline imposed for infractions of rules is one of the most frequently disputed issues. Discipline often involves demotion, suspension, or discharge and is meted out for absenteeism, insubordination, dishonesty, rule violations, or poor productivity. Rule violations include issues such as substance abuse and sexual harassment. A discharge almost always leads to a grievance, regardless of its ultimate merit, because political solidarity often requires that the union extend itself in trying to save a member's job.

Discipline is imposed for violations of employer rules. Employees must be aware of the rules to be able to conform to them. Employers use discipline to deter employees from behavior that would damage the employers' performance. Before employers can impose discipline, they must observe employees behaving unsatisfactorily and violating rules. The employer must decide whether violations are important enough for action to be taken. If violations exceed the threshold for requiring punishment, discipline is imposed. Unions want to verify that employers, when imposing discipline, have reliably observed the unsatisfactory behaviors and have consistently applied similar penalties in similar situations and that the magnitude of the penalties is commensurate with the violations.

When an employee has repeatedly breached rules and been disciplined and the employee's behavior does not change, employers and unions may implement a **last chance agreement (LCA)** in an attempt to save the employee's job. In return for not discharging the employee for the most recent offense, the employer, union, and employee draw up a written agreement stipulating that if another violation of the same rule occurs within a specified time period, the employee will be discharged automatically and the union will not grieve.

An LCA might be negotiated, unilaterally imposed by the employer and not grieved by the union, or it may be included in an arbitrator's decision at the final step. LCAs save union resources on having to defend members who chronically violate rules. A study of LCAs found that the largest number involved absentee/tardiness problems (possibly resulting from drug or alcohol abuse). Employees for whom LCAs had been implemented were more likely to be discharged in subsequent years, but a majority was able to avoid discharge. Married and older employees, nonminorities, and higher-wage employees were more likely to remain employed.[2]

Incentives

A contract may have an incentive scheme whereby employees are paid by the piece or receive bonuses for productive efficiency. Frequently, these

[2] P. A. Bamberger and L. H. Donahue, "Employee Discharge and Reinstatement: Moral Hazards and the Mixed Consequences of Last Chance Agreements," *Industrial and Labor Relations Review*, 53 (1999), pp. 3–19.

contracts establish groups of jobs that work on incentive rates and identify others that don't. If an employee is moved from an incentive job to a non-incentive job, wages will probably decrease. If the job seems highly similar to the incentive job, grievances may result. A grievance might also result if the assignment is considered arbitrary or punitive. Problems also may arise if a new production process is introduced and management seeks to establish higher base rates or time standards before incentive earnings begin. New standards must be bargained collectively.

Work Assignments

Disputes may occur over which job classification is entitled to perform certain work. For example, assume that an electrical generating plant using coal-fired boilers to generate steam shuts down a boiler for rebricking. To do this, a wall has to be knocked down with some care to avoid damage to other boiler parts. Who should do the work? General laborers might do the work under a supervisor's direction. But the work requires some care and is preparatory to rebricking, so the job might be assigned to skilled masonry workers. The company may assign the job to helpers because the cost is less and it believes the skill requirements are low. But masons may believe the task is an integral part of their job and thus grieve.

Individual Personnel Assignments

Personnel assignment grievances most often concern promotions, layoffs, transfers, and shift assignments. Most contracts specify that seniority, seniority and merit, or experience on a particular job will govern personnel assignments. Disputes often relate to layoffs and shift preference. People who are laid off may believe they are entitled to jobs of junior workers in other departments who have been retained. While contracts normally specify that employees must be qualified for a job, if a junior employee is bumped by a senior employee, there may be a dispute regarding whether the senior employee actually possesses the claimed qualifications. Bumping has negative consequences not only for those who are laid off but also those who bumped or were in departments where bumping occurred. A survey of unionized employees who bumped or experienced bumping found significantly lower job satisfaction and organizational commitment as compared with those who had not. They also had lower union commitment and perceptions regarding organizational justice.[3]

Hours of Work

Hours grievances involve overtime requirements and work schedules. For example, if the firm has maintained an 8 a.m. to 4 p.m. shift to mail customer orders, and its freight company moves its shipping schedule from

[3] K. G. Stringer and T. C. Brown, "A Special Kind of Downsizing: An Assessment of Union Member Reaction to Bumping," *Relations Industrielles*, 63 (2008), pp. 648–670.

4 p.m. to 3 p.m., then a 7 a.m. to 3 p.m. shift better meets its needs. This change will affect employees, and grievances may result.

Supervisors Doing Production Work

Most contracts forbid supervisors to perform production work except when demonstrating the job to a new employee or handling an emergency. An employee's absence is usually not considered an emergency. This is basically a job security issue.

Production Standards

Employers and unions often agree on output rates in assembly-line technologies or standards for incentives in piece-rate output. If management speeds up the line or reengineers the standards, employees must put forth more effort for the same amount of pay, and grievances often result.

Working Conditions

Working-condition issues involve health, safety, and comfort concerns. This is one of the few areas in which employees might be justified in unilaterally refusing a work assignment they have a valid reason to believe could lead to injury. Arbitrators who hear cases involving grievances against discipline for refusing to perform unsafe work tended to rule narrowly when upholding a worker's right to refuse. They tended to rule for an employee if there was no insubordination, if there was a major danger or reasonable cause to believe that there may have been, if the employee has been loyal, if the employee reported the danger, if the manager was at fault, or if the manager was not at fault but did not respond to the identified problem.[4]

Subcontracting

Unless the contract allows complete discretion to the company in subcontracting, work done by bargaining-unit members may not be subcontracted before bargaining with the union.[5] Subcontracting can affect job security, and if grievances result, management would be involved in a refusal to bargain if it did not discuss the subcontracting issue.

[4] M. Harcourt and S. Harcourt, "When Can an Employee Refuse Unsafe Work and Expect to Be Protected from Discipline? Evidence from Canada," *Industrial and Labor Relations Review*, 53 (2000), pp. 684–703.

[5] The Supreme Court decision in *Fibreboard Paper Products* v. *NLRB*, 379 U.S. 203 (1964) requires bargaining by management if a union requests when subcontracting is being considered, unless the union has expressly waived its right in this area; however, this rule has been relaxed somewhat by *First National Maintenance* v. *NLRB*, 107 LRRM 2705 (U.S. Supreme Court, 1981) and later by the NLRB when it held that removal of union work to another facility of the company would be permissible if bargaining has reached an impasse [*Milwaukee Spring Div. of Illinois Coil Spring Co.*, 115 LRRM 1065 (1984), enforced by the U.S. Court of Appeals, District of Columbia Circuit, 119 LRRM 2801 (1985) or for a legitimate business reason if there were no antiunion animus [*Otis Elevator Co.*, 115 LRRM 1281 (1984)].

Outsourcing

Outsourcing is a form of subcontracting. In this case, part or all of certain processes are subcontracted to another employer that may or may not operate on the current employer's premises and may or may not hire some or all of the current employer's employees who work on that process. An example of this might involve outsourcing call center work currently done by bargaining-unit members to another firm with employees in India.

Past Practice

Many employment practices are not written into contracts, but unions consider them to be obligations. For example, an employer may provide cafeteria food services below cost to workers. If the cafeteria is closed, the union may grieve even though there is no contract language on food services, and management must respond.[6] If stopping work 15 minutes before the end of a shift to wash up is usual practice, then extending working time to the shift's end changes past practice.

Rules

Employers occasionally institute rules to improve efficiency or to govern the workforce. Many contracts establish the employer's right to do so under the management rights clause. Employees may grieve the establishment of rules as altering a term or condition of employment.

Work rules relating to smoking, drug testing, and sexual harassment have the potential to create divisions within the bargaining unit depending on employee attitudes and how the rules are implemented. While a large majority of union members questioned in one survey approved of limited drug testing, those who were subject to testing were more negative about probable cause testing, random testing, and terminating those who tested positive.[7]

Discrimination

Employees may believe they have been adversely affected because employer decisions have been influenced by age, gender, race, religion, color, or national origin. If a contract has a nondiscrimination clause employees can grieve the decisions on this basis. If the contract clearly and unmistakably indicates that arbitration shall be used to determine the merit of discrimination claims, the employee is barred from access to statutory remedies.[8]

[6] *Ford Motor Co.* v. *NLRB*, 441 U.S. 448 (1979).

[7] M. H. LeRoy, "The Presence of Drug Testing in the Workplace and Union Member Attitudes," *Labor Studies Journal*, 16, no. 3 (1991), pp. 33–42.

[8] *14 Penn Plaza* v. *Pyett*, 556 U.S. ___(2009). See G. C. Peterson, "United States Supreme Court Enforces Collective Bargaining Agreement Requiring Arbitration of Employees' ADEA Claims," *Employee Relations Law Journal*, 35, no. 2 (2009), pp. 69–85 for an extended analysis.

FIGURE 14.1
Example of a Written Grievance

Source: Adapted from www.ueunion.org/stwd_grstep2.html.

> Orville Bush is the most senior bidder for the inspection job and should be awarded the job bid. By not giving Orville the job award, the employer is violating Article 3, section 2 of the contract. The employer is also in violation of all other relevant sections of the contract. Make Orville Bush whole, including but not limited to being transferred immediately to the inspection job and paid the $1.00 an hour pay rate difference for the time missed on the inspection job, including overtime.

Prevalence of Issues

Grievances are filed over a number of issues, as noted previously. A study of four organizations in different industries found that the seven largest grievance categories were distributed as follows: pay (17 percent), working conditions (16 percent), performance and permanent job assignments (16 percent), discipline (14 percent), benefits (14 percent), management rights (7 percent), and discrimination (6 percent).[9]

GRIEVANCE PROCEDURES

Most contracts specify procedures for resolving intracontract disputes. While contracts vary, most procedures contain four or five steps. In the absence of a grievance procedure, the employee is still entitled to file grievances individually under guarantees contained in Section 9 of the Taft-Hartley Act. Individual employees may also file grievances if the contract has such a procedure, but they generally do not, depending on which union represents them.

Steps in the Grievance Procedure

The usual steps in the grievance procedure are as follows.

Step 1

This step varies considerably across companies. In some, an employee who believes the company has violated the contract complains to the union steward, who may accept or assist in writing up a grievance. Then the steward presents the grievance to the grievant's supervisor, who has the opportunity to answer or adjust it.

In some companies, few grievances are settled at Step 1. The company won't delegate power to supervisors because their decisions can establish precedents for future grievance settlements. Thus, supervisors often simply deny grievances at Step 1. In other companies, an oral grievance is presented directly to the supervisor, and settlements can be negotiated immediately. (Figure 14.1 is an example of a written grievance.)

[9] D. Lewin and R. B. Peterson, *The Modern Grievance Procedure in the United States* (Westport, CT: Quorum, 1988).

Supervisory style affects grievance rates and their disposition. In a large manufacturing plant, autocratic supervisors had fewer grievances overall and fewer overtime, supervisor-related, and discipline grievances than did democratic supervisors. Higher management was less likely to reverse grievance decisions for autocratic supervisors.[10]

Supervisors and stewards usually do not understand the contract well. Stewards may have more knowledge of the contract if they are experienced and contract administration is their full-time job. About 7 of 10 grievances examined in one study were screened by stewards, and about half of these stewards used their authority to adjust grievances.[11]

Presenting grievances in an informal oral manner may allow supervisors and stewards greater latitude for reaching a quick solution before a written record is established. One study found that supervisors, stewards, union leaders, and top management favored moving toward oral grievances and away from written ones but ultimately failed due to opposition from plant managers who felt their authority was undermined.[12]

Several levels of activity may lead to filing grievances. Stewards may act on complaints from members. A large-scale study of Canadian bargaining units found that stewards reported more complaints from members if the supervisor had little knowledge of the contract and if the work unit was relatively larger. Informal grievance resolution was related to the supervisor's knowledge of the contract and the steward's commitment to the employer, education, and training. The likelihood of a steward initiating a grievance when a union member declined to do so or when the steward observed a contract violation and filed on behalf of the group increased if the supervisor used a considerate supervisory style and had little contract knowledge. It was positively related to union commitment and a contested vote in the unit for the steward's position and negatively related to employer commitment. Grievance rates were related to many of these same factors but were reduced by informal settlements and increased by steward initiation. Steward and supervisor behavior was a more important predictor of initiation and settlement than were workplace characteristics.[13]

Stewards are generally more satisfied in their grievance processing roles if the procedure permits oral grievances and if some grievance committee

[10] R. L. Walker and J. W. Robinson, "The First-Line Supervisor's Role in the Grievance Procedure," *Arbitration Journal*, 32 (1977), pp. 279–292.

[11] S. Briggs, "The Steward, the Supervisor, and the Grievance Process" *Proceedings of the Industrial Relations Research Association*, 34 (1981), pp. 313–319.

[12] V. G. Devinatz, "A Program for Building Cooperative Shop Floor Labor Relations: The UAW, The International Harvester Corporation and the 'New Look' Procedure," *Labor Studies Journal*, 20, no. 3 (1995), pp. 5–18.

[13] B. Bemmels, Y. Reshef, and K. Stratton-Devine, "The Roles of Supervisors, Employees, and Stewards in Grievance Initiation," *Industrial and Labor Relations Review*, 45 (1991), pp. 15–30.

screening takes place. Dissatisfaction is related to high grievance rates and large work groups. Satisfaction is higher if a larger proportion of grievances are resolved, and resolved successfully for the grievant.[14]

Step 2

Many grievances are settled at Step 1. If denied there, the steward presents the grievance to a plant industrial relations (IR) representative. Both are very familiar with the contract, and both are aware of how previous grievances have been settled. In routine cases, the company allows the IR representative to apply and create precedents. If a grievance has major precedent-setting implications or involves potentially major costs but may have merit, the IR representative may deny it. If the case involves an employee discharge, the union is likely to send it to Step 3.

Step 3

Most grievances have been settled by Step 2. The Step 3 participants vary depending on the contract. The grievance may be settled locally, with the union represented by its local negotiating committee and management by its top IR manager or plant manager. In more complex situations or in larger firms, the parties may be an international union representative with or without the local negotiating committee and a corporate-level IR director. Most unresolved grievances are settled at this stage.

Step 4

When a grievance is unresolved at the third step, the parties submit the dispute to an arbitrator who hears evidence from both sides and renders an award. A number of methods are available for choosing an arbitrator. The parties may name a permanent arbitrator **(umpire)** in their contract. They may ask a private agency, such as the American Arbitration Association, for a panel of arbitrators. A panel has an odd number (usually five) from which each party rejects arbitrators in turn until one remains. The remaining person becomes the arbitrator unless one party objects, in which case a new panel is submitted. The same process may be followed by petitioning the Federal Mediation and Conciliation Service, which also supplies panels of arbitrators listed by the agency. There may also be state government agencies that will supply panels of arbitrators. A hearing date is set, and the arbitrator renders an award some time after the evidence is presented. Chapter 15 examines arbitration as a separate topic. Figure 14.2 is an example of a contract clause dealing with grievance handling.

How the grievance procedure operates is very important to local union leaders. Between negotiations this is where the union and employer are most engaged and where "wins" and "losses" may be politically critical

[14] B. Bemmels, "Shop Stewards' Satisfaction with Grievance Procedures," *Industrial Relations*, 34 (1995), pp. 578–592.

FIGURE 14.2
Grievance Procedure Clause

9.02 Grievances

Step 1 The employee and the departmental steward, if the employee desires, shall take the matter up with his or her supervisor. If no settlement is reached in Step 1 within two working days, the grievance shall be reduced to writing on the form provided for that purpose.

Step 2 The written grievance shall be presented to the supervisor or the general supervisor and a copy sent to the production personnel office. Within two working days after receipt of the grievance, the general supervisor shall hold a meeting, unless mutually agreed otherwise, with the supervisor, the employee, the departmental steward, and the chief steward.

Step 3 If no settlement is reached in Step 2, the written grievance shall be presented to the departmental superintendent, who shall hold a meeting within five working days of the original receipt of the grievance in Step 2 unless mutually agreed otherwise. Those in attendance shall normally be the departmental superintendent, the general supervisor, the supervisor, the employee, the chief steward, the departmental steward, a member of the production personnel department, the president of the UNION or his representative, and the divisional committeeman.

Step 4 If no settlement is reached in Step 3, the UNION COMMITTEE and an international representative of the UNION shall meet with the MANAGEMENT committee for the purpose of settling the matter.

Step 5 If no settlement is reached in Step 4, the matter shall be referred to an arbitrator. A representative of the UNION shall meet within five working days with a representative of the COMPANY for the purpose of selecting an arbitrator. If an arbitrator cannot be agreed upon within five working days after Step 4, a request for a list of arbitrators shall be sent to the Federal Mediation and Conciliation Service. Upon obtaining the list, an arbitrator shall be selected within five working days. Prior to arbitration, a representative of the UNION shall meet with a representative of the COMPANY to reduce to writing wherever possible the actual issue to be arbitrated. The decision of the arbitrator shall be final and binding on all parties. The salary, if any, of the arbitrator and any necessary expense incident to the arbitration shall be paid jointly by the COMPANY and the UNION.

for current officers. Satisfaction of union leaders with the process was positively related to autonomy and the proportion of grievances resolved and negatively related to the size of the unit. Satisfaction with the Step 1 process was negatively related to unit size and the rate of grievances and positively related to the importance of issues and early settlement. Satisfaction with the step before arbitration was positively related to issue importance and resolution rate and negatively related to the number and proportion of women in the bargaining unit. Satisfaction with outcomes was positively related to issue importance, resolution rate, and the union success rate and negatively related to size of the unit and cost.[15]

Grievance rates in unionized employers probably run about 10 per 100 employees per year. Of each 100 grievances, between 0.5 and 2.5 require arbitration for resolution.[16] About half of all written grievances are settled

[15] B. Bemmels and D. C. Lau, "Local Union Leaders' Satisfaction with Grievance Procedures," *Journal of Labor Research*, 22 (2001), pp. 653–657.

[16] Lewin and Peterson, *Modern Grievance Procedure*, p. 89.

at Step 1, 60 percent of open grievances at Step 2, and 80 percent of the rest at Step 3.[17] Higher-level settlements are associated with the requirement of written grievances, rigid procedural rules, larger bargaining units, adversarial bargaining relationships, low costs, and low supervisor and steward knowledge of the contract.[18] One study of several employers found that settlement at the first step is higher with written grievances and authorization by management and/or the union to allow supervisors and/or stewards to settle at the first step. Settlement before arbitration is higher where units are larger and where more grievances are filed.[19]

Grievances may be granted, denied, partially granted, or withdrawn at any step in the process. A study of grievances in a Canadian firm found 46 percent were denied, 36 percent partially or fully granted, and 18 percent withdrawn at the first step. Of those proceeding to the second step (which could include some of those partially granted at step 1), 62 percent were denied, 24 percent partially or fully granted, and 14 percent withdrawn. At step 3, 4 percent were partially or fully granted, 80 percent denied, and 16 percent withdrawn. Prior decisions on a particular type of grievance reduce that type's submission for a period of time.[20]

Time Involved

Generally, speedy resolution of grievances is preferred. Typical contracts allow 2 to 5 days for resolution at the first two steps and 3 to 10 days at step 3. If management denies a Step 3 grievance, the union has 10 to 30 days to demand arbitration. If the union does not make a timely demand, the dispute may no longer be arbitrable. If arbitration is demanded, the time frame is less rigid because a panel must be requested and received, an arbitrator selected, hearing dates arranged, the hearing held, and a final award written and rendered. While an unresolved dispute could conceivably be arbitrated in two months or less, the time lapse is usually considerably longer. (See Chapter 15 for information on the length of the entire process when a grievance goes to arbitration.) One study found the average grievance was settled in between 10 and 14 days.[21] Settlements take longer where bargaining units are large, the union requires written grievances, both parties follow procedures closely, an adversarial bargaining relationship exists, and a supervisor's contractual knowledge is low.[22]

[17] Ibid., p. 170.

[18] Ibid., pp. 98–100.

[19] J. A. Davy, G. Stewart, and J. Anderson, "Formalization of Grievance Procedures: A Multi-Firm and Industry Study," *Journal of Labor Research*, 13 (1992), pp. 307–316.

[20] R. P. Chaykowski, G. A. Slotsve, and J. S. Butler, "A Simultaneous Analysis of Grievance Activity and Outcome Decisions," *Industrial and Labor Relations Review*, 45 (1992), pp. 724–737.

[21] Lewin and Peterson, *Modern Grievance Procedure*, p. 89.

[22] Ibid., pp. 98–100.

FIGURE 14.3
Grievance Procedure Steps

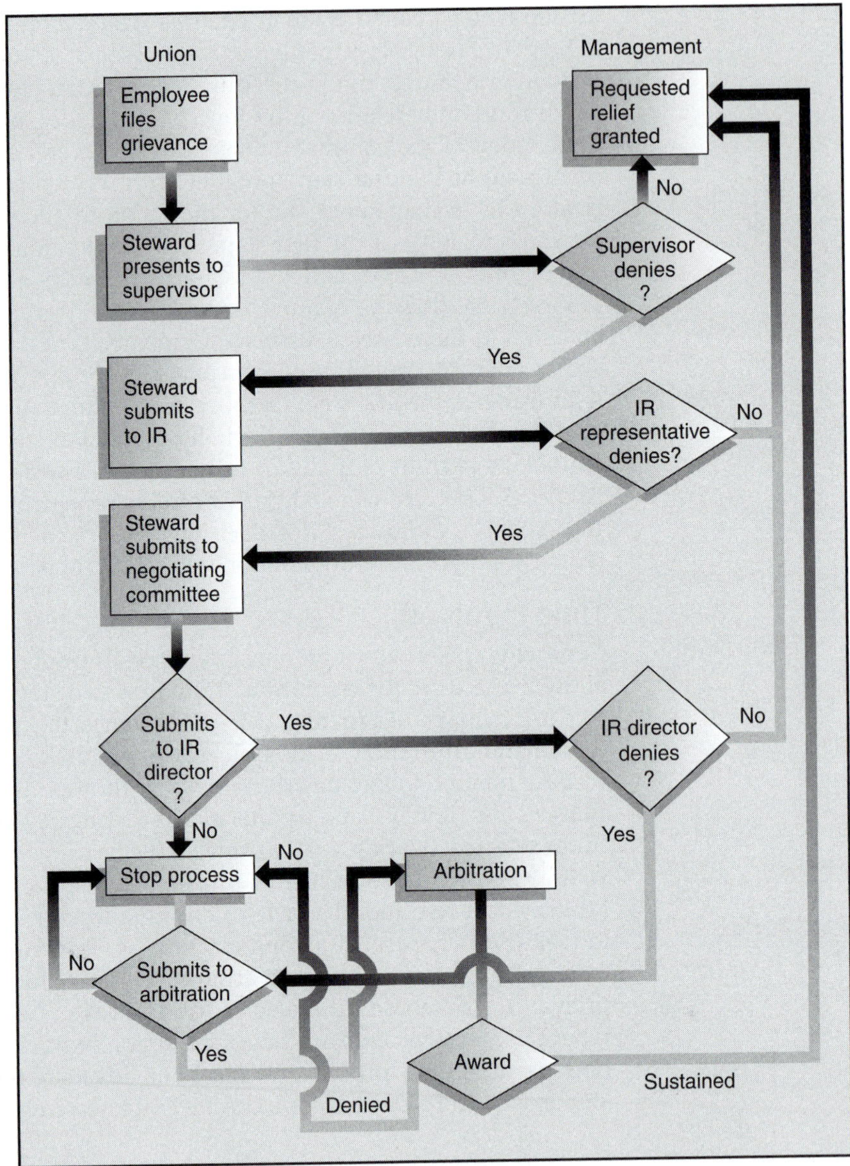

Most contracts rely on a four-step procedure, settlement rates are higher in Steps 2 and 3, contractual procedures and time schedules are closely followed, and few differences exist in filing periods when disciplinary and other contractual grievances are compared.[23] Figure 14.3 presents the flow of decisions in a typical grievance process.

[23] J. A. Davy and G. W. Bohlander, "Recent Findings and Practices in Grievance-Arbitration Procedures," *Labor Law Journal*, 43 (1992), pp. 184–190.

METHODS OF DISPUTE RESOLUTION

Intracontract disputes not resolved through the prescribed steps in the grievance process are generally resolved by arbitration (see Chapter 15). As noted, arbitration is used sparingly by both parties because the process is costly (particularly for the union in a relative sense) and often involves a substantial time lag between the grievance and its resolution. Strikes may be used by the union to pressure management to grant requested relief, but only in situations where a no-strike clause has not been negotiated. Strikes are most likely where time is of the essence. Unions in the building trades seldom avail themselves of arbitration due to the short periods their members work for a given employer. By the time a grievance is arbitrated, the job would be completed, the employer having dictated the working conditions.

The same holds for safety and working-condition grievances in which stable employment relationships exist. When these conditions occur, the union may use a strike to force the employer to interpret the contract as the union demands. With a contract in effect, these strikes may or may not be breaches of the agreement if it contains a no-strike clause.

Project Labor Agreements

Since the 1980s building trades unions and contractors have often negotiated **project labor agreements (PLAs)** prior to bidding on major projects. PLAs cover pay rates, hiring procedures, work rules, and the like that will apply to a specific project during its duration. A PLA also includes dispute resolution procedures, and, per the agreement, unions agree to forgo strikes during its term.[24] In 2001, shortly after taking office, President George W. Bush issued Executive Order 13202 that prohibited union agreements as a condition for being awarded federal construction contracts, effectively banning project labor agreements in federal construction. In 2009, shortly after taking office, President Barack Obama issued Executive Order 13502 that repealed President Bush's order and encouraged project labor agreements for all federal construction projects in excess of $25 million.

Grievance Mediation

An experiment in the mediation of grievances found costs and time to settlement were reduced by using a mediationlike process to deal with contract disputes. Grievance mediation tends to shift the focus from a "rights" (who wins) orientation toward a problem-solving mode. In the experiment, a large share of the grievances headed for arbitration were settled with the help of mediation. The union was highly satisfied with

[24] See *Journal of Labor Research*, 19, no. 1 (1998), for additional details.

mediation, especially if it believed that the mediator understood the grievance. Mediation may allow the parties to uncover and deal with the real reason for the conflict rather than requiring that the conflict be framed as a specific contract violation. Mediation did not increase the likelihood of settlements at lower levels and was not used for discharge grievances or those involving financial claims of more than $5,000.[25] A follow-up study of grievance mediation in coal mining found that about 85 percent of mediated grievances were resolved at an average third-party cost of $500 versus $2,674 for arbitration.[26] A further follow-up study was done on almost 23 years of experience with grievance mediation in coal mining. General findings indicated that 86 percent of cases potentially headed for arbitration were settled through mediation at substantially lower cost and much more quickly. In addition, the parties learned how better to resolve grievances at lower levels because they learned more about the interests of their opposite number in grievances and grew in their beliefs about the trustworthiness of information supplied by their counterpart.[27]

In a utility setting where suspension and discharge grievances were included in grievance mediation, managements were equally satisfied with mediation and arbitration processes but not with the settlements when mediation was used. About two-thirds of all final-step grievances were settled by mediation; thus, the number going to arbitration was cut to one-third. But the overall rate of grievances did not decline as a result of mediation.[28] Evidence from one plant indicates that mediation is unrelated to "win" rates of management or the union.[29]

Wildcat Strikes

If a no-strike clause coupled with the opportunity for binding arbitration has been negotiated, a strike during the agreement period is a wildcat strike because it violates the contract and is unauthorized by the parent national union. Wildcats are particularly prevalent in coal mining.[30]

[25] S. B. Goldberg and J. M. Brett, "An Experiment in the Mediation of Grievances," *Monthly Labor Review*, 106, no. 3 (1983), pp. 23–30.

[26] P. Feuille, "Grievance Mediation," in A. E. Eaton and J.H. Keefe, eds., *Employment Dispute Resolution and Worker Rights* (Champaign, IL: Industrial Relations Research Association, 1999), pp. 187–218.

[27] S. B. Goldberg, "How Interest-Based, Grievance Mediation Performs over the Long Term," *Dispute Resolution Journal*, 59, no. 4 (2004), pp. 8–15.

[28] M. T. Roberts, R. S. Wolters, W. H. Holley Jr., and H. S. Feild, "Management Perceptions of Grievance Mediation," *Arbitration Journal*, 45, no. 3 (1990), pp. 15–23.

[29] R. N. Block and A. R. Olson, "Low Profile/High Potential," *Dispute Resolution Journal*, 51, no. 4 (1996), pp. 54–61.

[30] J. M. Brett and S. B. Goldberg, "Wildcat Strikes in Bituminous Coal Mining," *Industrial and Labor Relations Review*, 32 (1979), pp. 465–483.

Research on the characteristics of wildcat strikes in coal mining found that high-strike mines were larger than low-strike mines, perhaps reflecting the increased formality of grievance handling in large mines. Working conditions were not related to wildcat strikes, but supervisory friction was. Strikes were higher where miners perceived supervisors as being unable to handle grievances and in mines where disputes could not be dealt with locally. Confidence in the grievance procedure did not relate to strike incidence. Miners at both high- and low-strike mines believed strikes resolved disputes in the miners' favor, but high strike incidence rates appeared related to perceptions that this was the best method for getting management to listen.[31]

When companies agree to submit unresolved grievances to arbitration, they are giving up some of their freedom to initiate change. As a quid pro quo, they usually demand and win a no-strike clause. In that case, the union agrees not to strike during the term of the contract, because it has an arbitral forum available. But what if the union strikes? Does the company have a legal recourse? The Norris-LaGuardia Act prohibits injunctions against lawful union activity, which includes strikes. However, the Supreme Court ruled that where a bona fide no-strike clause exists, a grievance procedure terminating in arbitration is available, and the union has not sought to arbitrate its dispute, federal courts could enjoin a wildcat strike.[32]

Discipline for Wildcat Strikes

What tools do employers have to counteract a wildcat strike? First, if the strike was over an unfair labor practice and the union correctly judged that the practice was illegal, the strike would be protected and the employer could not legally retaliate. But if the strike was in violation of a no-strike clause, several factors would come into play.

Both the national and local unions participate in ratifying an agreement. They have a joint responsibility for enforcing it. Unfortunately for management, little can be gained in damages unless a union's leaders clearly fomented a wildcat strike.[33] However, if a union demands that its members return and they fail to obey, they are subject to union discipline as well as to employer retaliation. But employers cannot sue individual union members for breach of contract for violating a no-strike clause.[34] Where a union defies an injunction to return to work, it may be found in contempt of court and fined.[35]

[31] Ibid.

[32] *Boys Markets, Inc.* v. *Retail Clerks Union Local 770*, 398 U.S. 235 (1970).

[33] *Carbon Fuel Co.* v. *United Mine Workers*, 444 U.S. 212 (1979).

[34] *Complete Auto Transit* v. *Reis*, 451 U.S. 401 (1981).

[35] *United Mine Workers* v. *Bagwell*, 512 U.S. 821 (1994).

EMPLOYEE AND UNION RIGHTS IN GRIEVANCE PROCESSING

One important grievance issue concerns an employee's right to union representation in disciplinary proceedings. For example, if a supervisor suspects an employee of leaving work early, which normally merits a suspension, can the supervisor confront and interrogate the employee without allowing union representation? The Supreme Court ruled that members of the bargaining unit who are suspected of offenses that could result in discipline are entitled to union representation if they request it.[36] The employer cannot proceed with the interrogation unless a union steward is present to advise its member. However, neither union nor nonunion employees are entitled to legal counsel during an employment investigation by the employer.[37]

To What Is the Employee Entitled?

Not every grievance constitutes a bona fide contract violation, and not every legitimate grievance is worth pursuing to arbitration. For example, suppose a supervisor performed bargaining-unit work during a short-term peak production period. The union may have a legitimate grievance with workers entitled to be paid for the period the supervisor worked. If it is an isolated incident, bringing it to management's attention should reduce the likelihood of its recurrence, even if management denies the relief requested. The importance of individual cases varies. For example, a discharge is more serious than a claim of entitlement to two hours' pay for overtime given to another employee.

How far can an individual union member pursue a grievance or force a union to process it through arbitration? This subject is not entirely resolved, but opinions of legal experts and court discussions provide some direction. The issue is referred to by terms such as *individual rights* and **fair representation.** In the discussion, the latter term is applied to the vigor and equality of the union's advocacy, not necessarily its competence. (The competence issue is covered in Chapter 15.)

Occasionally a union activist receives harsh discipline for a rule violation. If the individual charges the company with an unfair labor practice (ULP), the NLRB applies the following test: There must be a prima facie case that the discipline was motivated by the employee's union activity.

[36] *NLRB* v. *J. Weingarten, Inc.*, 420 U.S. 251 (1975). The NLRB has ruled that nonunion employees are not entitled to have another employee present during a disciplinary investigation [*IBM Corp.*, 341 NLRB 148 (2004), which reversed *Epilepsy Foundation of Northeast Ohio*, 331 NLRB 676 (2000) enforced, which had extended "Weingarten" rights to nonunion employees].

[37] P. E. Starkman, "The Good, the Bad, and the Uncooperative: Dealing with the Uncooperative Employee during an Internal Investigation," *Employee Relations Law Journal*, 25, no. 1 (1999), pp. 69–92.

Then the employer could rebut a ULP charge if it can show the same punishment would have occurred in the absence of union activity.[38]

Fair Representation

Fair representation is a complex issue in which the rights and duties of those involved are not completely spelled out.[39] All employees, represented or not, are able to seek legal redress for employer actions violating civil rights, wage and hour, or health and safety laws; but in other areas, unrepresented employees have no legal right to review an arbitrary decision.

Individual Rights under the Contract

Several decisions clarify individual rights under collective bargaining agreements. Major decisions before Taft-Hartley helped specify minority rights in grievance processing. In *Elgin, Joliet, and Eastern Railway* v. *Burley*, the Supreme Court held that the concession of a grievance by the union does not necessarily insulate the employer from being sued.[40] The employees must have authorized the union to act for them, and some vigorous defense must be shown. Because the union is the exclusive bargaining agent for all employees, the courts will watch to ensure that all classes and subgroups are entitled to and receive equal protection and advocacy from their representatives.

Taft-Hartley enables represented employees to grieve directly to employers. However, employers cannot process grievances without union observation, if demanded by the union, or adjust the grievance in a manner inconsistent with the contract. For example, if the contract entitles senior employees to promotions, a junior employee cannot personally insist on receiving a promotion to which a senior employee is entitled.

Individual rights under the contract are not clearly established. Three possible positions might be suggested: (1) Individuals have a vested right to use the grievance procedure through arbitration if they choose; (2) individuals should be entitled to process grievances for discharge, seniority, and compensation cases; and (3) the union as a collective body should have freedom to decide what constitutes a meritorious grievance and how far the grievance should be pursued.[41]

The NLRB and courts seldom assert jurisdiction over the merits of grievances. But a few rulings help explain employee entitlements and employer

[38] *Wright Line*, 251 NLRB 1083 (1980).

[39] For a detailed review of fair representation issues, see E. C. Stephens, "The Union's Duty of Fair Representation: Current Examination and Interpretation of Standards," *Labor Law Journal*, 44 (1993), pp. 685–696.

[40] 325 U.S. 711 (1945).

[41] B. Aaron, "The Individual's Legal Rights as an Employee," *Monthly Labor Review*, 86 (1963), pp. 671–672.

and union responsibilities. In *Miranda Fuel Company*, an employee was permitted to start vacation before the date in the contract.[42] After a late return caused by illness, other bargaining-unit members demanded that the union require his discharge. The NLRB ruled this was an unfair labor practice because the union acquiesced to the majority even though the discharged employee had seniority. The second case involved a merger.[43] Here the same union represented employees of both acquired and surviving companies. After the merger, the union credited the seniority of the workers from the acquired company rather than starting at the acquisition date. Several employees from the surviving company claimed they were unfairly represented because their union granted seniority to employees coming from the other firm. The Supreme Court held the employees must use Taft-Hartley remedies for breach of contract rather than using state courts to redress unfair representation.

In *Vaca* v. *Sipes*, an employee returning from sick leave was discharged because the employer believed he was no longer capable of holding a job.[44] He filed a grievance and the union pressed his case, obtained medical evidence, and requested he be given a less physically demanding job. Doctors' reports conflicted on whether the employee could safely continue working. Although the union vigorously pursued the grievance through the final step before arbitration, it did not demand arbitration when the company refused to reinstate the grievant.

The grievant sued his union for unfair representation and his employer for breach of contract. The court held an employee may not go to court on a grievance unless contractual remedies have been exhausted, except where the employer and/or the union have refused to use these remedies. If the grievant contends that the union has unfairly represented the employee, he or she must prove this. The court found that individual bargaining-unit members have no inherent right to invoke arbitration. In representing all bargaining-unit members, the union is both an advocate and an agent that must judge whether claims are frivolous or inconsistent with past practice or contract interpretation. If the union weighs the grievance's merit and treats the grievant similar to others in the same situation, then the representation isn't unfair.

An appeals court decision can place the union "between a rock and a hard place."[45] In this case, the contract provided that promotions would be based on seniority and merit. When the company promoted junior employees, the union processed grievances of senior employees to arbitration.

[42] 140 NLRB 181 (1962).

[43] *Humphrey* v. *Moore*, 375 U.S. 335 (1964).

[44] 386 U.S. 171 (1967).

[45] *Smith* v. *Hussman Refrigerator Co. & Local 13889, United Steelworkers of America* (U.S. Court of Appeals, 8th Circuit, 1979); certiorari denied by U.S. Supreme Court, 105 LRRM 2657 (1980).

The arbitrator awarded the senior employees the jobs. The displaced junior employees sued their union for failing to represent their positions in the arbitration. The court held that the union owed equal obligations to both groups. Although the union certainly favored seniority as the basis for promotion, it must advocate management's position as well because the contract provides benefits to two potential groups with opposite interests.

Another case extends union liability for damages. If an employee can prove the employer violated the contract to the employee's detriment and the union dealt with the grievance in an arbitrary and capricious manner, the employee can collect damages from both. The employee collects damages from the employer up to the point at which the union fails to process a meritorious claim and from the union until relief is granted.[46]

Supreme Court decisions on fair representation yield the following six principles: (1) Employees have the right to have contract terms enforced to their benefit; (2) an employee has no right to insist on a personal interpretation of a contract term; (3) no individual can require that a union process a grievance to arbitration, but each should have equal access to grievance procedures; (4) settlement on the basis of personal motives by union officials constitutes bad faith; (5) the individual should have a grievance decided on its own merits, not traded for other grievance settlements; and (6) while the union is entitled to judge the relative merit of grievances, it must exercise diligence in investigating the situation that led to the grievance.[47]

GRIEVANCES AND BARGAINING

As noted in the chapters on union structure, organizing, and negotiating, the processes involved can be specified, but the actual behavior does not always duplicate the model. The grievance procedure, as described, provides a method for resolving intracontract disputes. The model consigns the union to the role of responding to management's actions. Grievance resolution has been dealt with as a serial process, from both the steps involved (which duplicate reality rather closely) and the presentation order (first in, first out, which is unlikely). This section looks at grievances from a political standpoint and as a bargaining tool.

Union Responses to Management Action

Grievances have a number of ramifications for the union. A novel grievance may establish a precedent for or against the union if it is arbitrated. A situation may have been handled informally on a case-by-case basis,

[46] *Bowen* v. *U.S. Postal Service*, 459 U.S. 212 (1983).

[47] C. W. Summers, "The Individual Employee's Rights under the Collective Agreement: What Constitutes Fair Representation?" in J. T. McKelvey, ed., *Duty of Fair Representation* (Ithaca: New York State School of Industrial and Labor Relations, Cornell University, 1977), pp. 60–83.

usually favorably for the union, so the risks of pursuing it may be too great. Other grievances may lead to internal union disputes, such as entitlements to work or overtime. Politically powerful minorities within the union may need to be accommodated. Upcoming elections may influence grievance activity resolution rates. Candidates may be more militant, and management may grant less relief or take more time, particularly in areas where a candidate it would like to see defeated is leading the advocacy.

Besides the responses of union officials, rank-and-file members may engage in tactics affecting the grievance process. If a large number of grievances builds up, or if settlement is slow (particularly for those alleging a continuing violation), then pressure tactics such as slowdowns, quickie strikes, and working to rules may be used to pressure management to settle or grant the grievances.[48] Grievants might not wait passively for an ultimate response but rather may use tactics to speed a favorable settlement.

Evidence indicates the union gains bargaining power by shaping employee complaints so that they fit a clear grievance category. At the same time, the union is more successful in winning its grievance if the category is different from one particularly important to the employer.[49]

Fractional Bargaining

Because most grievances concern an individual employee or a single work group and relate only to one or a few contract terms, tactics aimed at modifying the way the contract is administered are called **fractional bargaining.**[50] Fractional bargaining affects an establishment in the same way that an employer with multiple bargaining units suffers a reduction in bargaining power. An organization consists of interdependent parts, and if one part is embroiled in disputes that lessen its productivity, it will affect the remainder.

Fractional bargaining occasionally poses problems for the union because one critical group may win grievances that others fail to achieve. If a negotiating committee stops grievances of a powerful small group, internal political pressures increase. A steward of a powerful small group may successfully pressure for settlement at lower levels to avoid local officer involvement. The company may accede to lessen chances of production disruptions.

Management may also take the initiative by treating political opponents of the existing union leadership differently and by handling some disciplinary cases by the book and being lenient with others. These practices may increase internal political pressures and cause more of the union's energies to be devoted to healing such rifts rather than engaging in

[48] J. W. Kuhn, *Bargaining in Grievance Settlement* (New York: Columbia University Press, 1961).

[49] P. Suschnigg, "Measuring Bargaining Power through Grievance Outcomes: Results from an Ontario Steel Mill," *Relations Industrielles*, 48 (1993), pp. 480–500.

[50] Kuhn, *Bargaining in Grievance Settlement*, p. 79.

additional grievance activity. Thus, as in contract negotiations, each side pressures the other, but some mutual accommodation that enables both to survive is usually reached.

Union Initiatives in Grievances

The union may take the initiative with grievances. Stewards may solicit grievances looking for potential contract violations.[51] A violation does not actually need to occur to file a grievance; there need be only the belief that one did occur and a linking of that belief to some contract clause. If the union believes it has problems with one area or supervisor, it may simply flood management with grievances. These create work for management because they must be answered in a certain time frame under the contract. If higher management has to spend more time on grievances, it may simply tell supervisors to "clean up their act," which usually results in a more lenient approach to demonstrate to management that supervision has "cured" the grievance problem.

Union stewards may stockpile grievances as threats or trade-offs for larger issues. If an issue of importance to the steward comes up, the supervisor may be told informally that unless a change is made, a number of grievances will be filed with higher-ups later in the day.

In large plants, the steward has an advantage over the supervisor. Many contracts allow the steward to be a full-time union representative, although the steward is paid by the company. As such, a steward's full-time work involves contract administration, while the supervisor is responsible for personnel, equipment, production, and other matters.

The steward's personality may play a role in grievance resolution. A study found that stewards who informally settled grievances with supervisors were likely to have higher needs for autonomy, affiliation, and dominance than those who used formal processes. It also found that stewards with higher needs for achievement and dominance were involved in greater numbers of grievances.[52] Higher commitment to the union predicted higher grievance activity levels, while higher company commitment and job satisfaction were related to lower grievance activism.[53]

Higher grievance rates are related to inexperienced stewards, union policies that influence grievance filing, and periods close to negotiations or political choice within the union.[54] A longitudinal study of an auto plant with a single UAW local found that grievances with high factual clarity

[51] Ibid., p. 14.

[52] D. R. Dalton and W. D. Todor, "Manifest Needs of Stewards: Propensity to File a Grievance," *Journal of Applied Psychology*, 64 (1979), pp. 654–659.

[53] D. R. Dalton and W. D. Todor, "Antecedents of Grievance-Filing Behavior: Attitude/Behavioral Consistency and the Union Steward," *Academy of Management Journal,* 25 (1982), pp. 158–169.

[54] C. E. Labig Jr. and C. R. Greer, "Grievance Initiation: A Literature Survey and Suggestions for Future Research," *Journal of Labor Economics*, 9 (1988), pp. 1–27.

were decided for the union more often when they occurred during periods of high production importance, such as during model changeovers and heavy schedules; when few grievants were involved; when the steward was politically entrenched; and when they occurred in nonassembly plants. In cases where grievances had low factual clarity, political issues had more effect, such as the shorter the time until the next union election, the lower the settlement rate; the more the grievances, the lower the union win rate; the more likely the grievance claimed a right given to another bargaining-unit member, the lower the union win rate; and the more entrenched the steward, the lower the win rate. Other factors involved with low-clarity outcomes for the union included high-production pressure situations and skilled-trades occupations.[55] All these indicate management's response could be seen as pressuring the union politically and facilitating the production process.

Management practices also have an influence on grievance rates. A study of grievances and productivity in an aircraft manufacturing plant found that highest productivity occurred at a grievance rate significantly above zero. Very low grievance rates might indicate less monitoring and enforcement by management, while high levels consume extra effort in their settlement.[56]

Political competition within a local union may also affect labor relations and contract settlements. A comparison of internal democracy in two UAW locals in aircraft manufacturing found that the one that had well-developed internal political "parties" and frequent changes in local leaders also had better contract settlements but more strikes. The economic gains came at the cost of lost wages during strikes and also through the firm's greater use of subcontracting.[57]

Stewards are often elected. Grievance handling influences the election process. Stewards who file more grievances, who resolve them at lower levels, and who take more time with them are more frequently reelected, with higher margins. As the relationship between supervisors and stewards matures, the process becomes more efficient and effective.[58]

Individual Union Members and Grievances

Employees unionize to exercise a voice in governing the workplace. The negotiation and ratification of a contract by the bargaining unit create an

[55] D. Meyer and W. Cooke, "Economic and Political Factors in Formal Grievance Resolution," *Industrial Relations*, 27 (1988), pp. 318–335.

[56] M. M. Kleiner, G. Nickelsburg, and A. Pilarski, "Monitoring, Grievances, and Plant Performance," *Industrial Relations*, 34 (1995), pp. 169–189.

[57] M. M. Kleiner and A. M. Pilarski, "Does Internal Union Political Competition Enhance Its Effectiveness?" in S. Estreicher, H. Katz, and B. Kaufman, eds., *Internal Governance and Organizational Effectiveness of Unions* (New York: Kluwer Publishing, 2001).

[58] D. Meyer, "The Political Effects of Grievance Handling by Stewards in a Local Union," *Journal of Labor Research*, 15 (1994), pp. 33–51.

employment equilibrium. This equilibrium reflects the bargaining power of both parties and their preferences for the structure of the agreement. In grieving, an individual member exercises a voice to express dissatisfaction or to take advantage of an opportunity for gain that a specific situation, such as increased production rates, might allow. Workers in high-paying jobs or those with few alternative job opportunities are more likely to use the grievance process and less likely to be absent or quit.[59] The strength of the grievance procedure influences the beliefs that employees have about their ability to influence outcomes within their employers since quit rates, in one study, were negatively related to the strength of the grievance procedure.[60] Figure 14.4 portrays a model of the grievant's choices and potential outcomes. Some grievance opportunities occur because of workplace changes or actions taken against the grievant. The model suggests that negative outcomes will occur to the employee and employer unless the process leading to the ultimate outcome is perceived to be procedurally just.[61]

Differences exist among employees in grievance behavior and characteristics. Although the relationships are not strong, evidence shows that younger,[62] male,[63] minority,[64] and better-educated employees[65] have higher grievance rates. Aspects of the work environment appear to interact with race and gender in influencing grievance activity. Women and African-Americans were more likely than men and whites to grieve in situations where they felt supervisory behavior was abusive.[66] An attitudinal study

[59] P. Cappelli and K. Chauvin, "A Test of an Efficiency Model of Grievance Activity," *Industrial and Labor Relations Review*, 45 (1991), pp. 3–14.

[60] D. I. Rees, "Grievance Procedure Strength and Teacher Quits," *Industrial and Labor Relations Review*, 45 (1991), pp. 31–43.

[61] B. S. Klaas, "Determinants of Grievance Activity and the Grievance System's Impact on Employee Behavior: An Integrative Perspective," *Academy of Management Review*, 14 (1989), pp. 445–458.

[62] P. Ash, "The Parties to the Grievance," *Personnel Psychology*, 23 (1970), pp. 13–38; J. Price, J. Dewire, J. Nowack, K. Schenkel, and W. Ronan, "Three Studies of Grievances," *Personnel Journal*, 55, no. 1 (1976), pp. 32–37; Lewin and Peterson, *Modern Grievance Procedures*, p. 174; M. E. Gordon and R. L. Bowlby, "Reactance and Intentionality Attributions as Determinants of the Intent to File a Grievance," *Personnel Psychology*, 42 (1989), pp. 309–329; and D. Lewin and R. B. Peterson, "Behavioral Outcomes of Grievance Activity," *Industrial Relations*, 38 (1999), pp. 554–576.

[63] Lewin and Peterson, *Modern Grievance Procedures*, p. 174; and Lewin and Peterson, "Behavioral Outcomes."

[64] Lewin and Peterson, *Modern Grievance Procedures;* Ash, "Parties to the Grievance"; and Lewin and Peterson, "Behavioral Outcomes."

[65] Ash, "Parties to the Grievance"; Lewin and Peterson, *Modern Grievance Procedures*, p. 174; Price et al., "Three Studies"; but Lewin and Peterson, "Behavioral Outcomes," found the opposite.

[66] P. Bamberger, E. Kohn, I. Nahum-Shani, "Aversive Workplace Conditions and Employee Grievance Filing: The Moderating Effects of Gender and Ethnicity," *Industrial Relations*, 47 (2008), pp. 229–259.

FIGURE 14.4 An Integrative Model of Individual Grieving Behavior

Source: Adapted from B. S. Klaas, "Determinants of Grievance Activity and the Grievance System's Impact on Employee Behavior: An Integrative Perspective," *Academy of Management Review,* 14 (1989), p. 449.

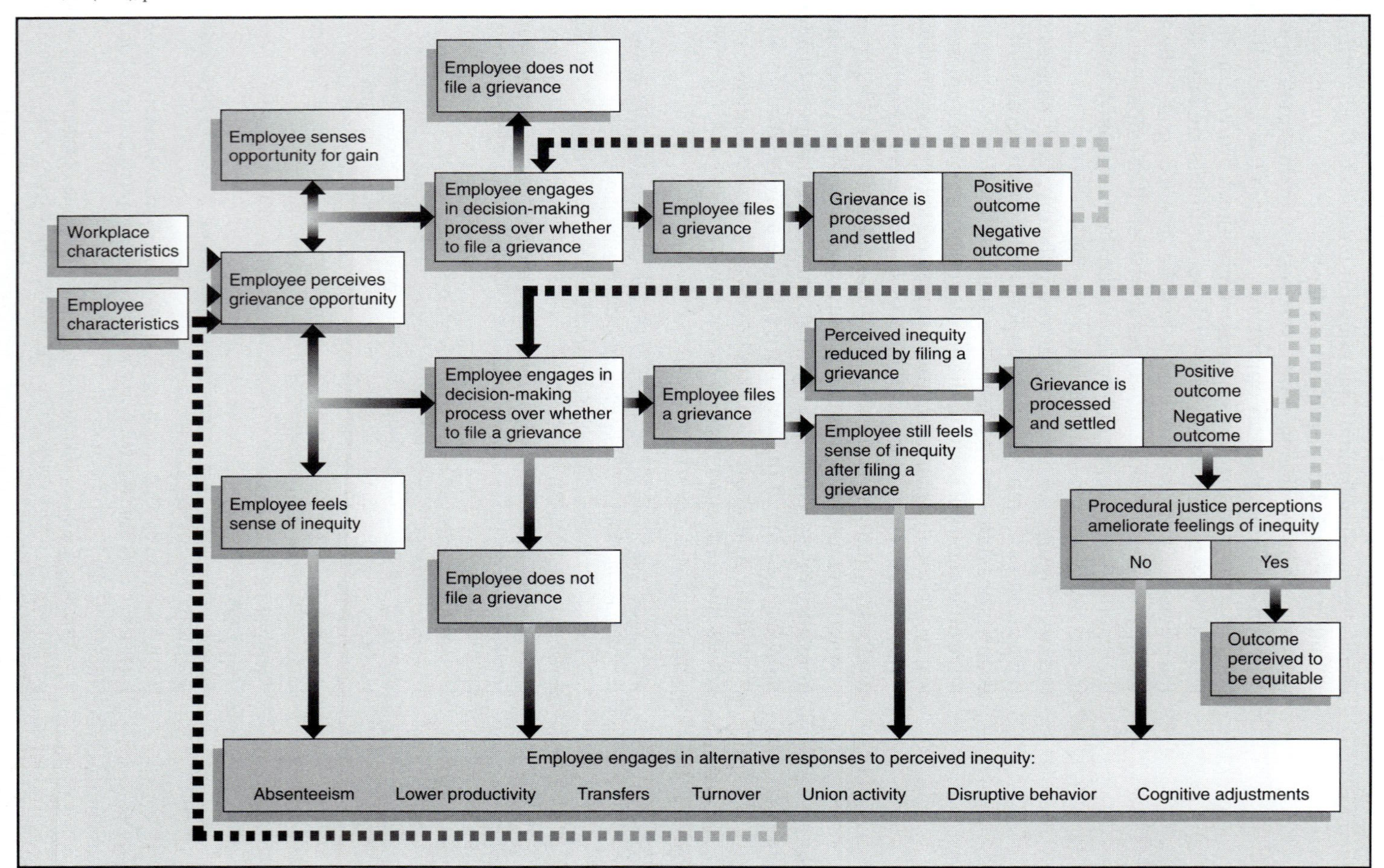

examining employees across many employers found that grievants were more likely to have lower job satisfaction, be more satisfied with the union, and be active participants in union affairs.[67] Another study using the same sample found that employees who filed more grievances had declining job satisfaction during the four years between the waves of the study, were in larger plants, perceived themselves as expending lower effort, and anticipated working for the same employer in five years. Factors relating to perceived union effectiveness, poor or changing working conditions, or the openness of the supervisor did not influence grievance-filing behavior.[68] An experimental study using a hypothetical situation found that union members were more likely to indicate they would file grievances when the situation evoked strong reactions and when management's action was perceived to be intentional.[69]

EFFECTS OF GRIEVANCES ON EMPLOYERS AND EMPLOYEES

Both employers and employees may be influenced by the filing, processing, and outcome of grievances. A study of grievances in a government agency found that employees filing two grievances within one rating period received lower performance ratings. Winning or losing the grievance was not associated with the rating. Employees who grieved were no more likely to transfer; however, employees who filed a second grievance were more likely to receive a disciplinary sanction, and a second negative adjustment to a grievance was associated with an increased probability of quitting. From the employer's standpoint, grievance filing was associated with higher absenteeism and fewer production hours.[70] Absenteeism appears to increase with policy grievances and is reduced by disciplinary grievances. Absenteeism falls following negative outcomes from disciplinary grievances, possibly due to escalating consequences for further discipline problems.[71] In a study of a steel mill, grievants were usually better

[67] R. E. Allen and T. J. Keaveny, "Factors Differentiating Grievants and Nongrievants," *Human Relations*, 38 (1985), pp. 519–534.

[68] B. Klaas and G. G. Dell'Omo, "The Determinants of Grievance Filing Behavior: A Psychological Perspective," paper presented at the Academy of Management meetings, Anaheim, CA, 1988.

[69] Gordon and Bowlby, "Reactance and Intentionality Attributions." For an excellent review of research on the grievance procedure, see D. Lewin, "Theoretical and Empirical Research on the Grievance Procedure and Arbitration: A Critical Review," in A. E. Eaton and J. H. Keefe, eds., *Employment Dispute Resolution and Worker Rights* (Champaign, IL: Industrial Relations Research Association, 1999), pp. 137–186.

[70] B. S. Klaas, H. G. Heneman III, and C. A. Olson, "Grievance Activity and Its Consequences: A Study of the Grievance System and Its Impact on Employee Behavior," unpublished paper, University of South Carolina, Columbia, 1988.

[71] B. S. Klaas, H. G. Heneman III, and C. A. Olson, "Effects of Grievance Activity on Absenteeism," *Journal of Applied Psychology*, 76 (1991), pp. 818–824.

employees during the year in which they grieved; and if their grievance was settled at a low level and/or they lost the grievance, they were more likely to be rated higher, have better attendance, have lower turnover, and be promoted in the subsequent year.[72] Managers and supervisors of units in which grievance rates were higher were somewhat more likely to be rated lower in the next period.[73] In another study, both supervisors and grievance filers were likely to have lower performance ratings, fewer promotions, and higher turnover after they were involved in grievance activity, as compared with employees who were not.[74]

A study of public sector management and union representatives found explicit performance and disciplinary standards were associated with higher grievance rates. Rivalry between unions within the same employer increased grievances. Positive management attitudes and willingness to compromise were related to lower rates, but consultation with the union about items of mutual interest did not reduce grievances.[75]

Managerial perceptions of the effectiveness of discipline systems was related to being in a nonunion organization, having either a very permissive or very restrictive set of rules, high monitoring costs, and pressures for performance. Managers in organizations that invested in training on solving workplace problems were more positive.[76]

Grievance resolution provides information to help resolve subsequent cases at lower levels. Evidence suggests that only management uses prior decisions to guide initial decisions on a grievance. The higher the level of settlement of a grievance, the more likely the parties were to use formal settlements of previous grievances as precedents. Earlier decisions are used most frequently as precedents in discipline and work assignment cases.[77] In a Canadian public sector union, grievances were more likely to be settled favorably in the early steps, for more highly paid employees, and for working-condition rather than work assignment issues.[78] Management may settle grievances to the grievant's and union's benefit "without precedent" for similar future cases.

Employees who frequently grieve do not necessarily have better work outcomes. But what effect do grievances have for employers? Each grievance requires involvement of stewards, the grievant, and supervisors

[72] Lewin and Peterson, *Modern Grievance Procedures*, pp. 185–187.

[73] Ibid., p. 189.

[74] Lewin and Peterson, "Behavioral Outcomes."

[75] C. E. Labig Jr. and I. B. Helburn, "Union and Management Policy Influences on Grievance Initiation," *Journal of Labor Research*, 7 (1986), pp. 269–284.

[76] B. S. Klaas, T. W. Gainey, and G. G. Dell'Omo, "The Determinants of Disciplinary System Effectiveness: A Line Management Perspective," *Industrial Relations*, 38 (1999), pp. 542–553.

[77] T. R. Knight, "Feedback and Grievance Resolution," *Industrial and Labor Relations Review*, 39 (1986), pp. 585–598.

[78] I. Ng and A. Dastmalchian, "Determinants of Grievance Outcomes: A Case Study," *Industrial and Labor Relations Review*, 42 (1989), pp. 393–403.

at the first step; industrial relations representatives, national union representatives, and the union negotiating committee at subsequent steps; and attorneys or representatives, witnesses, and an arbitrator at arbitration. A study of 10 paper mills (9 union and 1 nonunion) found higher grievances associated with lower plant productivity. The presence of a grievance procedure (only in the union mills) was associated with higher productivity, perhaps because employees had an outlet for complaints that would operate while production continued.[79]

When management and union representatives approach grievance resolution in a cooperative relationship, they are better able to achieve integrative resolutions. Those with competitive goals are more likely to take a closed-minded approach. Seniority issues can be dealt with cooperatively more often, while disciplinary issues are often competitive. Cooperative approaches tend to settle at lower steps and lead to more positive reactions among the parties. Competitive approaches are used more often when the parties want to establish a precedent.[80]

Summary

Contract administration is the joint activity in which labor and management spend the most time. Not only do the parties respond voluntarily to differences in interpretation, but they also must, by law, bargain on practices related to mandatory items over the life of the contract.

Both sides deal with a variety of issues, of which job security, seniority, and discipline are among the most important. Methods for handling disputes involve the presentation and resolution of grievances in a stepwise manner, culminating in arbitration, if necessary.

Unions must represent employees in a consistent manner in grievance proceedings, and employees who can show they were not accorded fair treatment may hold the union and the employer in breach of contract.

All grievances are not equally meritorious, and political factions within unions may obtain power to gain more favorable outcomes. Grievances also may accompany periodic union political elections. Management may influence these by the way in which it responds to the source of grievances during campaigning.

Grievants are less satisfied with their jobs, more satisfied with their unions, and more involved in union activities. They are more likely to grieve if they see fewer alternatives (such as quitting) available to them. Grievances, in general, do not lead to stronger positive outcomes for employees. Employers with high grievance rates appear to have slightly lower productivity.

[79] C. Ichniowski, "The Effects of Grievance Activity on Productivity," *Industrial and Labor Relations Review*, 40 (1986), pp. 75–89.

[80] D. Tjosvold and M. Morishima, "Grievance Resolution: Perceived Goal Interdependence and Interaction Patterns," *Relations Industrielles*, 54 (1999), pp. 527–548.

Discussion Questions

1. Should management be required to consult with the union about discipline before it is imposed rather than simply providing for grievance processing after its imposition?
2. Should unions be allowed to drop an employee's grievance if the employee desires arbitration?
3. How does the grievance procedure make subtle changes in the meaning of the contract possible over time?
4. What are the advantages and disadvantages of a program for reducing the number of written grievances?

Key Terms

Contract administration, *470*
Last chance agreement (LCA), *471*
Umpire, *477*
Project labor agreement (PLA), *481*
Fair representation, *484*
Fractional bargaining, *488*

Case: *New Production Equipment: Greater Efficiency with Less Effort or a Speedup?*

Carolyn Foster had just returned to her office from the weekly plant IR representatives' meeting. Her secretary had left a note to call George Lowrey, the superintendent of the forklift assembly operation. She called back and immediately recognized from the seriousness of George's tone that a major problem must be brewing in his area. They both agreed she would come right over.

After George had welcomed her into his office, he leaned forward and, putting his chin in his hands, said, "Carolyn, I feel like I'm sitting on a powder keg here. Last year we put in the new Simplex Process assembly line for our forklifts. It had a rated capacity of 35 units an hour. When we installed it, we started up at 28 units, which is the same as the old line, to shake it down and get the bugs out. The new line automates more of the assembly, so each worker has less of a physical demand than before. Well, last week we figured we had all the bugs ironed out, so we raised the speed to 35. We figure each worker has to put out about the same amount of effort as under the old system.

"This morning, Steve Bonneville, the shop steward, and three of my general supervisors came in, all arguing. Bonneville had a fistful of grievances and was yelling about a 'speedup.' Anyway, the upshot is that he wants the employees to be advanced one skill level to compensate for the additional effort and more difficult working conditions under Section 7.03 of the contract.

"Carolyn, we can't give them a penny more and remain competitive. Besides that, if they get a raise, the whole plant will paper us with classification grievances. Bonneville is running for union president because Matt Duff is retiring, and if he's successful with this grievance, he's a shoo-in. All we need is a long strike over some penny-ante issue and a bunch of hotheads like him running the show. What can you do to help me?"

Carolyn had been busy taking notes about the problem. She asked, "Do you have the grievances?" George nodded and handed them to her. Then she said, "I'll study the grievances, the contract, and the union situation and get back to you in time for us to plan a Step 3 response. I'll be back to you this afternoon."

DIRECTIONS

1. Draft a strategy for the company to follow. Consider the immediate problem and the possibilities of precedents being set by your action. List the advantages and disadvantages of your chosen strategy.
2. Prepare a scenario in which your response is presented to Steve Bonneville. How is he likely to react? What steps do you expect he will take as a result of your response?
3. What conditions do you consider necessary for these grievances to be resolvable at Step 3?

Grievance Arbitration

This chapter covers the procedure used to render a decision about the merits of a grievance when the parties cannot reach agreement. Arbitration is not solely a labor relations process, and within labor relations it does not deal solely with grievances. The chapter covers the definition of arbitration, its legal place in labor relations, the process itself, difficulties associated with its practice, and results associated with arbitration of employee discharge and discipline cases.

In reading this chapter, consider the following questions:

1. How have the Supreme Court's decisions influenced the application and practice of arbitration?
2. How has the NLRB aided or interfered with arbitration?
3. What procedures are used during arbitration?
4. What problems do critics of arbitration point out?

WHAT IS ARBITRATION?

Arbitration is a quasi-judicial process in which parties agree to submit unresolved disputes to a neutral third party for binding settlement. Both parties submit their positions, and the arbitrator decides what each party is entitled to. This chapter is concerned with labor arbitration, but the method is also applied to disputes between buyers and sellers, contractors and real estate developers, stockbrokers and customers, and doctors and patients.

Two major topics of labor arbitration involve *interest* and *rights*. This chapter is primarily concerned with rights arbitration. Chapter 16 covers interest arbitration, which is primarily applied in the public sector. The Supreme Court distinguished between interest and rights arbitration this way:

> [Interest arbitration] relates to disputes over the formation of collective agreements or efforts to secure them. They arise where there is no such agreement or where it is sought to change the terms of one, and therefore the issue is not whether an existing agreement controls the controversy. They look to the acquisition of rights for the future, not to assertion of rights claimed to have vested in the past.

> [Rights arbitration], however, contemplates the existence of a collective agreement already concluded or, at any rate, a situation in which no effort is made to bring about a formal change in terms or to create a new one. The dispute relates either to the meaning or proper application of a particular provision with reference to a specific situation or to an omitted case. In the latter event the claim is founded upon some incident of the employment relation, or asserted one, independent of those covered by the collective agreement. In either case the claim is to rights accrued, not merely to have new ones created for the future.[1]

Thus, rights arbitration applies to interpreting and applying terms of an existing contract, and interest arbitration decides unresolved future issues.

DEVELOPMENT OF ARBITRATION

The Knights of Labor preferred arbitration for resolving interest differences but was never able to use it. In 1925 Congress passed the Arbitration Act establishing the right of parties to a contract to specify the processes to be used to resolve disputes over the interpretation or implementation of the contract. There is no legal requirement to arbitrate private sector labor disputes. However, during World War II the National War Labor Board required that labor contracts provide for arbitration of intracontract disputes.[2] Beginning in 1957, NLRB and Supreme Court decisions have defined and expanded the role of rights arbitration.

Lincoln Mills

Lincoln Mills established arbitration as the final forum for contract disputes.[3] In *Lincoln Mills,* the Supreme Court held that Section 301 of the Taft-Hartley Act required that federal courts enforce collective bargaining agreements, including provisions for arbitrating future grievances. If the contract called for arbitration and if the court agreed with the arbitrator, the award would be enforced by the court if either party failed to comply with it.

Steelworkers' Trilogy

In 1960 the Supreme Court ruled on the legitimacy and finality of rights arbitration for settling intracontract disputes.[4] The Court ruled that arbitrators' decisions were essentially not subject to judicial review, and it laid

[1] *Elgin, Joliet & Eastern Railway Co.* v. *Burley*, 325 U.S. 711 (1945).

[2] F. Elkouri and E. A. Elkouri, *How Arbitration Works*, 3rd ed. (Washington, DC: Bureau of National Affairs, 1973), p. 15.

[3] *Textile Workers Union* v. *Lincoln Mills*, 355 U.S. 448 (1957).

[4] *United Steelworkers of America* v. *Warrior & Gulf Navigation Co.*, 363 U.S. 574; *United Steelworkers of America* v. *Enterprise Wheel and Car Corp.*, 363 U.S. 593; and *United Steelworkers of America* v. *American Manufacturing Co.*, 363 U.S. 564 (1960).

down three basic protections for arbitration. First, contractual arbitration clauses require that parties arbitrate unresolved grievances. Second, the substance of grievances and their **arbitrability** are to be determined by arbitrators, not courts. And third, if an arbitration clause exists, unless a dispute is clearly outside contract provisions, courts will order arbitration. The decisions state that labor arbitrators are presumed to have special competence in labor relations and are thus better able than courts to resolve labor disputes.

In the *Warrior and Gulf* case, the Court held that if a contract includes a broad arbitration clause, a dispute not covered in other sections is still arbitrable. In this case, the employer subcontracted work while its employees were in a partial-layoff status. While lower courts held subcontracting to be a potential management right, the Supreme Court held that the broad arbitration agreement, coupled with the no-strike provision, brought the dispute within the arbitral arena.

The *American Manufacturing* case involved an employee who became disabled and accepted workers' compensation. Later, his doctor certified his ability to return to work, but the company refused to reinstate him. He grieved, but the company refused to process the grievance, claiming it was frivolous. The Supreme Court ordered arbitration.

Enterprise Wheel involved several employees who had been fired for walking out in protest when another employee was fired. After the company refused to arbitrate the discharge grievances, a federal district court ordered arbitration. The arbitrator reinstated the employees with back pay for all but 10 days' lost time. The award was rendered 5 days after the contract expired, but the Supreme Court ordered compliance.

The trilogy decisions enable arbitrators to decide whether disputes are arbitrable and, if they are, to render awards, free from judicial intervention.[5] When companies or unions have gone to court over arbitration procedures or awards, courts most often compel arbitration if a party has tried to avoid it or they enforce awards if awards haven't been implemented. Less than 1 percent of cases end up in court. About a quarter of postarbitration appeals succeed.[6]

The **Steelworkers' trilogy** protects a union's right to insist on arbitration and to have awards enforced without court review. But could management also expect similar treatment if it agreed to arbitrate, received a favorable award, and was struck to prevent enforcement (given that the Norris-LaGuardia Act prevents federal courts from enjoining most union

[5] R. A. Smith and D. L. Jones, "The Supreme Court and Labor Dispute Arbitration," *Michigan Law Review*, 63 (1965), p. 761.

[6] P. Feuille and M. LeRoy, "Grievance Arbitration Appeals in the Federal Courts: Facts and Figures," *Arbitration Journal*, 45, no. 1 (1990), pp. 35–47; M. H. LeRoy and P. Feuille, "The Steelworkers Trilogy and Grievance Arbitration Appeals: How the Federal Courts Respond," *Industrial Relations Law Journal*, 13 (1991), pp. 78–120.

activities, including strikes for any purpose as long as they do not threaten life or property)?

Boys Markets Relaxes Norris-LaGuardia

The Norris-LaGuardia Act forbids courts from enjoining lawful union activity, including strikes. Labor agreements most often contain a no-strike clause forbidding strikes by bargaining-unit members during the life of the agreement. Management is particularly interested in including this clause because it reduces operating risk. On the other hand, labor would like to have the opportunity to protest management conduct that it believes violates the contract. Strikes offer this opportunity, but so do grievance procedures, particularly if they include arbitration as a final step.

In *Boys Markets* the Supreme Court held that where a no-strike clause together with a grievance procedure including arbitration as the final step were included in a collective bargaining agreement, a court could enjoin a strike if the employer were willing to arbitrate the dispute.[7]

14 Penn Plaza and Deferral of Statutory Grievances to Arbitration

In Chapter 3 the various federal statutes outlawing employment discrimination based on race, sex, color, religion, national origin, age, pregnancy, and disability were presented. Individuals who believe that an employer based an employment decision on one of these protected factors can ask the Equal Employment Opportunity Commission (EEOC) to investigate the charge. If it finds merit to the charge, the EEOC can initiate a civil proceeding against the employer or it may give the complainant a "permission to sue" letter.

To avoid the expense and time involved in litigating discrimination claims, many employers have required as a condition of employment in *nonunion* settings that employees agree to have all unresolved employment disputes, including charges of discrimination, submitted to arbitration as a final decision-making forum. The Supreme Court has ruled that this practice is not inconsistent with the statutory due process rights contained in the various civil rights laws.[8]

Terms and conditions of employment are mandatory bargaining issues, so a unionized employer could not impose a requirement to arbitrate discrimination charges of bargaining-unit members without agreement with the union. The Realty Advisory Board (RAB), a collection of building owners, and the SEIU, the bargaining agent for a large group of building maintenance employees, negotiated a multiemployer collective bargaining agreement that contained a nondiscrimination clause requiring that

[7] *Boys Markets, Inc.* v. *Retail Clerks Union Local 770*, 398 U.S. 235 (1970).

[8] *Gilmer* v. *Interstate/Johnson Lane Corp.*, 500 U.S. 20 (1991).

any statutory discrimination claims would have arbitration as their sole and exclusive remedy, and that arbitrators shall apply appropriate law in rendering their decisions. A group of senior employees was reassigned to other lower-wage jobs when their employer subcontracted nighttime security jobs to another unionized affiliate. The employees claimed that, among other reasons, they were reassigned because of their age. Their union grieved arguing that their reassignments violated seniority rules and the nondiscrimination clause in the contract. Because the union had consented to the subcontracting, it did not believe that it could legitimately object to the reassignments and dropped the age claim after the initial arbitration hearing. The arbitrator denied relief for all other aspects of the grievances. The grievants then went to the EEOC, claiming age discrimination. The EEOC investigated and concluded that the evidence failed to support the claim, but gave the grievants a "right to sue" letter. They then sued. The defendant employer argued that the claims must be referred to arbitration under the collective bargaining agreement while the plaintiffs argued that the statute entitled them to litigate the claim. The Supreme Court held that a clear and unmistakable nondiscrimination clause requiring arbitration of statutory claims that directs an arbitrator to apply appropriate law precludes bargaining-unit members from pursuing individual claims in court.[9]

Additional Supreme Court Decisions on Arbitration in Unionized Firms

Four cases involving arbitration procedures and awards modified and reaffirmed the basics of the Steelworkers' trilogy. In the first case, the company and the union couldn't agree on whether the disputed situation involved the contract. The union argued the decision should be made by the arbitrator after appointment, while the company maintained arbitrability should be up to the courts. The Supreme Court agreed with the company and declared the courts ultimately are responsible for deciding the arbitrability of contract disputes. This doesn't mean that an arbitrator can't rule on arbitrability; it means that a decision is subject to court review. If a dispute exists, a party can petition the courts to decide arbitrability before the case is heard.[10]

In the second case an arbitrator had reinstated an employee fired for smoking marijuana. The company appealed the decision, which was overturned in court as inconsistent with public policy on drug use. The Supreme Court reversed, however, holding that in the absence of fraud or dishonesty, courts may not review a decision on its merits, or for errors of fact, or for possible contract misinterpretations. Further, to overturn an

[9] *14 Penn Plaza LLC* v. *Pyett*, 566 U.S. ___ (2009).

[10] *AT&T Technologies, Inc.* v. *Communications Workers of America*, 475 U.S. 643 (1986).

award on the basis of public policy, the court must show that the policy is well defined, dominates the interests of the employee or employer, and has a history of laws and legal precedents to support it.[11] A later Supreme Court decision continued this logic. An arbitrator restored a truck driver to duty who had twice tested positive for marijuana use. The award included a last chance agreement provision. The Court held the ruling did not conflict with the requirements of the Omnibus Employee Testing Act of 1991.[12]

The third case held that where a contract has expired and the employer takes a unilateral action (e.g., a layoff) that had no history under the expired contract, the employer cannot be compelled to arbitrate a grievance where a renewal has not been negotiated.[13]

The fourth case held that arbitration could be compelled only where an agreement had been formed and the dispute had arisen under that agreement. Here, after a bargaining impasse the local union struck the employer. During the strike some of the strikers damaged equipment belonging to the employer. About a month after the strike began, the employer and union agreed on the basis for a new contract. The local asked the company to hold harmless its members for conduct during the strike, which the employer refused to do. The international instructed the local not to ratify the agreement until a hold-harmless clause was added. The company, believing that the agreement had been ratified, sued for ongoing strike damages given that it believed the discipline for strike-related behavior should be arbitrated. The Court held that whether the contract had been ratified was a matter for a federal court to decide and that, unless the parties had actually formed an agreement, there was no definition of an arbitrable dispute.[14]

Substituting arbitration for litigation decreases costs and speeds resolutions relative to litigation. For employers, this is particularly important since it is estimated that employment regulations have increased ninefold since the 1960s.[15] For grievants, there is always the question of whether they would have had a more sympathetic hearing before a judge than an arbitrator. It may be the case in nonunion arbitration, but evidence from a simulation found that labor arbitrators were less likely than either jurors or employment arbitrators to uphold an employer's termination of an employee in either a for-cause or statutory claim situation. Labor arbitrators also gave more weight to issues of procedural compliance, evidence

[11] *United Paperworkers International Union, AFL-CIO* v. *Misco, Inc.*, 484 U.S. 29 (1987).

[12] *Eastern Associated Coal Co.* v. *United Mine Workers of America*, 531 U.S. 57 (2000).

[13] *Litton Financial Printing Division* v. *NLRB*, 501 U.S. 190 (1991).

[14] *Granite Rock Co.* v. *International Brotherhood of Teamsters,* 561 U.S. ___ (2010).

[15] R. L. Seeber and D. B. Lipsky, "The Ascendancy of Employment Arbitrators in U.S. Employment Relations: A New Actor in the American System," *British Journal of Industrial Relations*, 44 (2006), pp. 719–756.

of discrimination, employee work history, and stress-inducing personal circumstances in making their decisions.[16]

NLRB Deferral to Arbitration

Occasionally, a dispute involves both a grievance and an unfair labor practice (ULP) charge. For example, bargaining-unit members might claim certain work has been given to nonunion employees outside the bargaining unit. The grievance would allege a violation of the contract on work assignments, and the union might charge the employer with discrimination based on union membership. To prevent "forum shopping" and to reduce its caseload, the NLRB has adopted rules for deferring to arbitration when a contract violation and a ULP are alleged simultaneously.

In developing its policy, the NLRB first held that where a grievance also alleged a ULP and the arbitration award had been adverse to, say, the union, the union could not then pursue the ULP.[17] The board decreed it would defer to arbitral awards if the parties had agreed in the contract to be bound by the decisions, the proceedings were fair and regular, and the results were consistent with the provisions of the labor acts.

In 1971, the NLRB decided to defer pending ULP-charge hearings until arbitration was completed, as long as the process was consistent with *Spielberg*.[18] In 1977, the NLRB partially retreated from the ***Collyer* doctrine** by limiting deferral to cases where the alleged ULP is not a Section 7 employee rights violation.[19] Ironically, a study of several cases where the board deferred to arbitration in 1977 and 1978 in the Detroit region found that arbitrator decisions on ULPs involving violation of Section 7 rights were seldom incompatible with board decisions, while refusals to bargain ULP decisions were frequently incompatible. Unions frequently received more favorable treatment from arbitrators than they would have before the NLRB.[20] In 1984, the board extended deferral to arbitration awards unless the decision was "palpably wrong."[21] The NLRB declared it would defer to arbitration if the arbitrator had adequately considered the alleged ULP and contractual and ULP issues were essentially parallel. Even before *Olin*, regional directors of the NLRB deferred about 90 percent of cases

[16] B. S. Klaas, D. M. Mahony, and H. N. Wheeler, "Decision-Making about Workplace Disputes: A Policy-Capturing Study of Employment Arbitrators, Labor Arbitrators, and Jurors," *Industrial Relations*, 45 (2006), pp. 68–95.

[17] *Spielberg Manufacturing Co.*, 112 NLRB 1080 (1955).

[18] *Collyer Insulated Wire Co.*, 192 NLRB 150 (1971).

[19] *Roy Robinson Chevrolet*, 228 NLRB 103 (1977); *General American Transportation Corporation*, 228 NLRB 102 (1977).

[20] B. W. Wolkinson, "The Impact of the *Collyer* Policy of Deferral: An Empirical Study," *Industrial and Labor Relations Review*, 38 (1985), pp. 377–391.

[21] *Olin Corporation*, 268 NLRB 574 (1984).

alleging ULPs. Following *Olin*, this rate increased even though appeals courts have not enforced cases similar to *Olin*.[22]

ARBITRATION PROCEDURES

In this section we examine the prearbitration processes, arbitrator selection, conduct of the arbitration hearing, preparing and rendering an award, and the magnitude of arbitration.

Prearbitration Matters

The contract specifies how an unresolved dispute goes to arbitration. Normally, arbitration is used for cases the parties have been unable to settle in one of the preceding steps of the process. If management denies a grievance at the last step or fails to modify its position sufficiently for the union to agree, the union can demand arbitration.

If the parties agree to concessions before arbitration, these may not be communicated to the arbitrator. In most cases, the parties can return to their step 1 positions without establishing precedents. Also, in cases settled before arbitration, the company may explicitly state that the settlement is not precedent-setting for similar future grievances.

The union's request for arbitration must be timely. The contract specifies time limits for the various steps of the grievance process. If management denies the grievance at the last step, the union has a certain time to demand arbitration. If it does not exercise its rights within this period, management's decision becomes final.

Selection of an Arbitrator

Procedures for selecting an arbitrator are specified in the contract. Usually arbitration is performed by one impartial arbitrator, a tripartite board consisting of company and union representatives, and an impartial chairperson who all hear the evidence and render an award. In large organizations or those where a long-term bargaining relationship exists, the contract may name an individual or group of **permanent umpires** to judge disputes. Permanence, however, is relative, because arbitrators continue to serve only as long as both parties are satisfied with their rulings. Permanent umpires may be more vulnerable when a militant union presents less meritorious cases than when a union saves arbitration for very important issues. In dealing with a militant union, an arbitrator would likely more frequently find merit in management's position, and as a result, be rejected by the union quite soon.[23] **Ad hoc arbitrators** are appointed to

[22] P. A. Greenfield, "The NLRB's Deferral to Arbitration before and after *Olin*: An Empirical Analysis," *Industrial and Labor Relations Review*, 42 (1988), pp. 34–49.

[23] M. Marmo, "Acceptability as a Factor in Grievance Arbitration," *Labor Law Journal*, 50 (1999), pp. 97–114.

hear only one case or set of cases. The appointment ends when the award is rendered and implemented.

Both methods of arbitrator selection have advantages and disadvantages. Less may be known about an ad hoc arbitrator, although information about potential arbitrators is usually available through résumés, previously published decisions, fields of expertise, and so on. But the appointment constitutes no continuing obligation by the parties. The permanent umpire has a better grasp of the problems the parties encounter because of his or her continuing experience with both. But because the relationship is continuous, whether the umpire will engage in award splitting may always be open to question.

A study of arbitrator acceptability found that the visibility of the arbitrator rather than personal background or practice characteristics was the factor most highly related to volume of cases heard. Other important factors included being listed by referral agencies, publication of awards, membership in professional organizations, and background as a permanent umpire.[24] Another study suggests managements and unions should not pay too much attention to the personal background characteristics of arbitrators in making choices for a particular case because they account for little variance in arbitrators' rulings.[25] One study of decisions in suspension cases found that male arbitrators were more lenient for female than male grievants, while female arbitrators dealt similarly with both men and women.[26] However, a study focusing on the public sector found that rulings there were more often favorable for men.[27] A study of discharge cases found reinstatement to be less likely when the arbitrator was a professor or was older; reinstatement was more likely when the employee had increased seniority or was assigned to a professional, technical, or skilled/semiskilled job or when the discharge was for work performance rather than a rule violation.[28] How the parties perceive the arbitrator's attention to justice issues influences their evaluation of arbitral performance. Arbitrator selection rates in interest cases are higher for arbitrators who are evaluated highly on attention to procedural

[24] S. S. Briggs and J. C. Anderson, "An Empirical Investigation of Arbitrator Acceptability," *Industrial Relations*, 19 (1980), pp. 163–174.

[25] H. G. Heneman III and M. H. Sandver, "Arbitrators' Backgrounds and Behavior," *Proceedings of the Industrial Relations Research Association*, 35 (1982), pp. 216–223; and N. E. Nelson and S. M. Kim, "A Model of Arbitral Decision Making: Facts, Weights, and Decision Elements," *Industrial Relations*, 47 (2008), pp. 266–283.

[26] B. Bemmels, "Gender Effects in Grievance Arbitration," *Industrial Relations*, 30 (1991), pp. 150–162.

[27] D. J. Mesch, "Arbitration and Gender: An Analysis of Cases Taken to Arbitration in the Public Sector," *Journal of Collective Negotiations in the Public Sector*, 24 (1995), pp. 207–218.

[28] N. E. Nelson and A. N. M. M. Uddin, "The Impact of Delay on Arbitrator's Decisions in Discharge Cases," *Labor Studies Journal*, 23, no. 2 (1998), pp. 3–20.

Exhibit 15.1

GAINING ACCEPTABILITY AS AN ARBITRATOR

"Paul, you've been an active arbitrator for over 25 years. For several of those years arbitration was your principal means of livelihood. At what point did you personally cease to be a fringe arbitrator and consider yourself a mainliner?"

"Not on any one single case, I can assure you. A fringe arbitrator can be broken by a bad opinion in just one arbitration, but becoming a mainliner is a process rather than the result of a single spectacular case."

"Is there any condition or status you can describe which clearly defines a mainline arbitrator?"

"When you put it that way, Pete, I can make the line of demarcation between a fringe arbitrator and a mainliner quite distinct. When I was a fringe arbitrator, the losing party would scrutinize my opinion to find out where I was wrong. I knew I had arrived at the mainline stage when in many cases the loser would study my opinion to find out where he was wrong."

Source: P. Prasow and E. Peters, *Arbitration and Collective Bargaining: Conflict Resolution in Labor Relations* (New York: McGraw-Hill, 1970), pp. 284–285.

justice issues.[29] Exhibit 15.1 reports a conversation between two experienced arbitrators on gaining acceptability.

Sources and Qualifications of Arbitrators

There are no absolute qualifications to be an arbitrator. Anyone can simply declare that he or she is an arbitrator and seek appointments. However, to arbitrate, an individual must be selected by the parties. Where do arbitrators come from? Arbitrators are those who have arbitrated. Arbitrators are generally from two groups: increasingly, attorneys who are full-time arbitrators; and academics who teach labor law, industrial relations, and economics. A typical mainline arbitrator is over 65 and has more than 30 years of experience. One method for becoming an arbitrator is to serve an informal apprenticeship under an experienced arbitrator, gaining practice in writing decisions and learning hearing techniques. Exposure with a highly regarded arbitrator may lead to later appointments. There are few formal training courses for arbitrators; however, programs designed to train minority arbitrators have been quite successful.[30] Evidence suggests arbitrator acceptability of those who complete training is quite high.

[29] R. A. Posthuma, J. B. Dworkin, and M. S. Swift, "Arbitrator Acceptability: Does Justice Matter?" *Industrial Relations*, 39 (2000), pp. 313–335.

[30] W. A. Nowlin, "Arbitrator Development: Career Paths, a Model Program, and Challenges," *Arbitration Journal*, 43, no. 1 (1988), pp. 3–13.

There are three major sources of arbitrators. Each serves a slightly different function, but all have interests in providing arbitrator services in labor disputes.

National Academy of Arbitrators

The National Academy of Arbitrators includes full-time arbitrators, as well as law school, industrial relations, and economics professors who have established excellent arbitral reputations. The academy holds meetings and issues proceedings, commenting on difficult problems in arbitration and offering alternative solutions. The academy's membership directory provides a source of recognized, highly qualified arbitrators the parties can contact directly to request appointments to ad hoc or permanent umpire positions.

American Arbitration Association

Many contracts specify that the parties use American Arbitration Association (AAA) services for their unresolved grievances. The AAA does not employ arbitrators but acts as a clearinghouse to administer matters between the parties and the arbitrators.

If a contract specifies that the AAA assist in choosing an arbitrator, the AAA is notified that a dispute exists. The AAA sends the parties a panel of arbitrators (usually five and almost always an odd number). The arbitrators may have particular expertise in the disputed area (e.g., job evaluation) or may practice in a particular geographic area. The parties reject names alternately until only one remains. This person will be the nominee unless either party objects. If an objection occurs, the AAA sends out another panel. Generally, referral agencies refuse to send more than three panels for any dispute. After a name has been agreed on, the AAA contacts the appointee to offer the dispute, and the appointee accepts or declines. If the appointment is accepted, arrangements are made directly with the parties for a hearing date. The AAA will provide hearing facilities and court reporters if the parties request. Finally, the AAA follows up to see what decisions were rendered.

Federal Mediation and Conciliation Service

The Federal Mediation and Conciliation Service (FMCS) maintains a roster of arbitrators from which it selects panels. The arbitrators are not FMCS employees but private practitioners. If FMCS assistance is specified in a contract, the FMCS would provide panels as the AAA does but would not provide reporting or facilities assistance.

The FMCS screens arbitrators who seek listing. People with obvious conflicts of interest (union organizers, employer labor consultants, etc.) are not included, and listees who fail to be selected are purged from subsequent lists.[31] Figure 15.1 shows some of the listing requirements.

[31] Title 29, Chapter 12, Part 1404, *Code of Federal Regulations*.

FIGURE 15.1 Requirements for Listing as an Arbitrator with the FMCS

Section 1404.5 Listing on the Roster, Criteria for Listing and Retention

Persons seeking to be listed on the Roster must complete and submit an application form which may be obtained from the Office of Arbitration Services. Upon receipt of an executed form, OAS will review the application, assure that it is complete, make such inquiries as are necessary, and submit the application to the Arbitrator Review Board. The Board will review the completed applications under the criteria set forth in paragraphs (a), (b), and (c) of this section, and will forward to the Director its recommendation on each applicant. The Director makes all final decisions as to whether an applicant may be listed. Each applicant shall be notified in writing of the Director's decision and the reasons therefore.

(a) General Criteria. Applicants for the Roster will be listed on the Roster upon a determination that they:
  (1) Are experienced, competent, and acceptable in decision-making roles in the resolution of labor relations disputes; or
  (2) Have extensive experience in relevant positions in collective bargaining; and
  (3) Are capable of conducting an orderly hearing, can analyze testimony and exhibits, and can prepare clear and concise findings and awards within reasonable time limits.

(b) Proof of Qualification. The qualifications listed in paragraph (a) of this section are preferably demonstrated by the submission of actual arbitration awards prepared by the applicant while serving as an impartial arbitrator chosen by the parties to disputes. Equivalent experience acquired in training, internship or other development programs, or experience such as that acquired as a hearing officer or judge in labor relations controversies may also be considered by the Board.

(c) Advocacy
  (1) Definition. An advocate is a person who represents employers, labor organizations, or individuals as an employee, attorney, or consultant, in matters of labor relations, including but not limited to the subjects of union representation and recognition matters, collective bargaining, arbitration, unfair labor practices, equal employment opportunity, and other areas generally recognized as constituting labor relations. The definition includes representatives of employers or employees in individual cases or controversies involving worker's compensation, occupational health or safety, minimum wage, or other labor standards matters. The definition of advocate also includes a person who is directly associated with an advocate in a business or professional relationship as, for example, partners or employees of a law firm.
  (2) Eligibility. Except in the case of persons listed on the Roster before November 17, 1976, no person who is an advocate, as defined above, may be listed. No person who was listed on the Roster at any time who was not an advocate when listed or who did not divulge advocacy at the time of listing may continue to be listed after becoming an advocate or after the fact of advocacy is revealed.

(d) Duration of Listing, Retention. Initial listing may be for a period not to exceed three years, and may be renewed thereafter for periods not to exceed two years, provided upon review that the listing is not canceled by the Director as set forth below. Notice of cancellation may be given to the member whenever the member:
  (1) No longer meets the criteria for admission;
  (2) Has been repeatedly and flagrantly delinquent in submitting awards;
  (3) Has refused to make reasonable and periodic reports to FMCS, as required in Subpart C of this part, concerning activities pertaining to arbitration;
  (4) Has been the subject of complaints by parties who use FMCS facilities and the Director, after appropriate inquiry, concludes that just cause for cancellation has been shown.
  (5) Is determined by the Director to be unacceptable to the parties who use FMCS arbitration facilities; the Director may base a determination of unacceptability on FMCS records showing the number of times the arbitrator's name has been proposed to the parties and the number of times it has been selected.

No listing may be canceled without at least 60 days' notice of the reasons for the proposed removal, unless the Director determines that the FMCS or the parties will be harmed by continued listing. In such cases an arbitrator's listing may be suspended without notice or delay pending final determination in accordance with these procedures. The member shall in either case have an opportunity to submit a written response showing why the listing should not be canceled. The Director may, at his discretion, appoint a hearing officer to conduct an inquiry into the facts of any proposed cancellation and to make recommendations to the Director.

The FMCS follows up on referrals by requiring arbitrators to render awards within 60 days of the hearing's close and the receipt of posthearing briefs.

Once the arbitrator has been selected, processes related to the scheduled hearing begin. The phases of this process include prehearing, hearing, and posthearing activities.

Prehearing

Elkouri and Elkouri detail a number of steps both parties' advocates should go through before an arbitration hearing:

a. Review the history of the case as developed at the prearbitral steps of the grievance procedure.

b. Study the entire collective agreement to ascertain all clauses bearing directly or indirectly on the dispute. Also, compare current provisions with those contained in prior agreements to reveal changes significant to the case.

c. So as to determine the general authority of the arbitrator, and accordingly the scope of the arbitration, examine the instruments used to initiate the arbitration.

d. Talk to all persons (even those the other party might use as witnesses) who might be able to aid development of a full picture of the case, including different viewpoints. You will thus better understand not only your own case but your opponent's as well; if you can anticipate your opponent's case, you can better prepare to rebut it.

e. Interview each of your own witnesses (a) to determine what they know about the case; (b) to make certain they understand the relation of their testimony to the whole case; (c) to cross-examine them to check their testimony and to acquaint them with the process of cross-examination. Make a written summary of the expected testimony of each witness; this can be reviewed when the witness testifies to ensure that no important points are overlooked. Some parties outline in advance the questions to ask each witness.

f. Examine all records and documents that might be relevant to the case. Organize those you expect to use and make copies for use by the arbitrator and the other party at the hearing. If needed documents are in the exclusive possession of the other party, ask that they be made available before or at the hearing.

g. Visit the physical premises involved in the dispute to visualize better what occurred and what the dispute is about. Also, consider the advisability of asking at the hearing that the arbitrator (accompanied by both parties) also visit the site of the dispute.

h. Consider the utility of pictorial or statistical exhibits. One exhibit can be more effective than many words, if the matter is suited to the exhibit form of portrayal. However, exhibits that do not fit the case and those that are inaccurate or misleading are almost certain to be ineffective or to be damaging to their proponent.

i. Consider what the parties' past practices have been in comparable situations.

j. Attempt to determine whether there is some key point on which the case might turn. If there is, it may be to your advantage to concentrate on that point.

k. In interpretation cases, prepare a written argument to support your view as to the proper interpretation of the disputed language.

l. In interests or contract-writing cases, collect and prepare economic and statistical data to aid evaluation of the dispute.

m. Research the parties' prior arbitration awards and the published awards of other parties on the subject of the dispute for an indication of how similar issues have been approached in other cases.

n. [O]utline your case and discuss it with other persons in your group. This ensures better understanding of the case and will strengthen it by uncovering matters that need further attention. Then, too, it will tend to underscore policy and strategy considerations that may be very important in the ultimate handling of the case. Use of the outline at the hearing will facilitate an organized and systematic presentation of the case.[32]

In addition, the parties may continue to seek a settlement or reduce the time necessary to settle a case. Anytime during the prehearing phase, the arbitration request may be withdrawn by joint consent. Contracts will often specify whether withdrawal is final and whether a withdrawal is precedent-setting. The parties also may stipulate certain facts in a case, agree on applicable contract terms, and prepare joint exhibits. Settlement after arbitration is requested, but settlement before the hearing occurs more frequently when the parties' representatives are not attorneys.[33]

Hearing Processes

The actual hearing may take many forms. Most simply, a case may be completely stipulated, with the arbitrator ruling on an interpretation of the contract given the written documents submitted. This option is not

[32] Elkouri and Elkouri, *How Arbitration Works*, pp. 198–199. See also C. A. Borell, "How Unions Can Improve Their Success Rate in Labor Arbitration," *Dispute Resolution Journal*, 61, no. 1 (2006), pp. 28–38; and M. M. Franckiewicz, "How to Win Your Arbitration Case before the Hearing Even Starts," *Labor Law Journal*, 60 (2009), pp. 115–120.

[33] C. R. Deitsch and D. A. Dilts, "Factors Affecting Pre-Arbitral Settlement of Rights Disputes: Predicting the Methods of Rights Dispute Resolution," *Journal of Labor Research*, 7 (1986), pp. 69–78; see also R. Mittenthal, "The Impact of Lawyers on Labor-Management Arbitration," *Dispute Resolution Journal*, 60, no. 3 (2005), pp. 42–44.

entirely up to the parties, however, because the arbitrator may insist on calling witnesses and examining evidence on site.

Representatives of the Parties

The parties' positions may be advocated by anyone they choose, which means the representatives may be attorneys, company or union officials, or the grievant. In most cases involving smaller companies, a national union field representative or local union officer and an industrial relations director or human resource manager are the advocates. Parties represented by an attorney have an advantage when the other side is not represented by one. When only one side retains an attorney, it is more frequently management that does so.[34]

Presentation of the Case

Because the union generally initiates grievances, it presents its case first, except in discipline and discharge cases. The union presents exhibits relevant to its case and calls witnesses. Management may object to exhibits and may cross-examine witnesses. When the union has completed its case, management offers its evidence in a similar manner. Rules of evidence in arbitration are more liberal than those in courts of law. At the end, both sides may present closing arguments. The arbitrator may question witnesses but is not required to do so.

Posthearing

Following the hearing, the parties may submit briefs supporting their positions. The arbitrator studies the evidence, takes briefs into account, and perhaps examines similar cases.

The arbitrator then prepares an award and sends it to the parties. In some cases, the arbitrator maintains jurisdiction until the award has been implemented in case additional proceedings are necessary to iron out differences in its application.

Evidentiary Rules

Where AAA rules apply, Rule 28 states: "The arbitrator shall be the judge of the relevancy and the materiality of the evidence offered, and conformity to legal rules of evidence shall not be necessary."[35] However, arbitrators must weigh the relevance or credibility of evidence when considering a grievance. Evidence is either *direct* or *circumstantial.* Direct evidence is information specifically tying a person to a situation. The search for the "smoking gun" is an attempt to find direct evidence. Circumstantial evidence suggests a connection between events and an individual. For

[34] R. N. Block and J. Stieber, "The Impact of Attorneys and Arbitrators on Arbitration Awards," *Industrial and Labor Relations Review*, 40 (1987), pp. 543–555.

[35] 30 LA 1086, 1089.

example, if shortages in a cash register occur only when one particular employee is scheduled, that circumstance, when connected with others, may establish guilt.

Evidence is relevant if it addresses the issue at hand. For example, if an arbitrator hears a case involving drinking on the job, evidence related to the subject's work assignment is not highly relevant. The evidence must also be material. For example, testimony that the subject bought a six-pack of beer the week before the alleged offense has little impact on establishing a connection with the offense.

In arbitration hearings, the union must prove management violated the contract, except in discipline cases. The level of proof required in discipline cases varies among arbitrators, but it is usually greater if the potential consequences are more severe.

Generally, employees are expected to know that published rules apply and that prior written warnings they received were correctly given unless challenged. Past discipline may be used to corroborate that an employee committed the type of offense at issue; but the longer the time since that discipline, the less weight it usually carries.

If another arbitrator has ruled on the same issue in this company and no contract changes have occurred in the area, the present arbitrator will probably rule that the issue has already been decided. In discipline cases where criminal proceedings have also occurred, the arbitrator is not bound by the same rules for evaluating evidence to prove the offense beyond a reasonable doubt.

Arbitrators weigh the credibility of witnesses. Persons who have little inherent interest in the case might be considered more credible, and an individual's reputation for honesty may also be considered.[36]

Occasionally, one party has information that would aid the other in the preparation of a case. Four rules have been suggested for the production of material held by one party: (1) the information should be produced if the arbitrator requests it; (2) if the party refuses to produce the information, the arbitrator may weigh the refusal as he or she sees fit; (3) the document or information could be used to attack the credibility of a witness; and (4) the arbitrator may admit only the parts of the information that are relevant to the hearing.[37]

For cross-examination and confrontation, (1) depositions and previous testimony should be admitted if a witness is unavailable; (2) hearsay should be accepted when a direct witness declines to testify against a fellow employee; (3) the arbitrator should generally not attempt to investigate; (4) where exposing the witness's identity would damage either

[36] M. Hill Jr. and A. V. Sinicropi, *Evidence in Arbitration* (Washington, DC: Bureau of National Affairs, 1980), pp. 1–108.

[37] R. W. Fleming, *The Labor Arbitration Process* (Urbana: University of Illinois Press, 1965), p. 175.

party's legitimate interests, the witness should be questioned by counsel with only the arbitrator present.[38]

The accused is not required to testify in criminal trials. Arbitrators probably will not grant absolute immunity against self-incrimination and will give evidentiary weight to refusals to testify. However, arbitrators should not sustain a case based on a refusal to testify.[39]

Arbitral Remedies

When a case is submitted to an arbitrator, the issues usually are specified and the grievant has indicated what relief is desired. The relief requested tends to vary depending on the type of case, but generally arbitrators will grant relief, up to but not exceeding the relief desired, when it is found that the aggrieved party has been wronged.

In discipline and discharge cases, requested relief is usually for back pay for periods when an employee was out of work, restoration of employment, rescission of a demotion or transfer, elimination of reprimands from personnel files, and the like. If reinstatement and/or back pay is to be granted, the arbitrator must determine the amount through the likely job history of the grievant, minus pay earned on other jobs, and the like. Arbitrators might also reduce discipline if it exceeds what the offense merits, given similar situations at that employer or other workplaces with similar settings.

More difficult cases to remedy involve such issues as subcontracting, plant closures, entitlements to overtime, assignment of work, and other economic issues. Usual remedies may require the restoration of work to the bargaining unit and payment of wages forgone by employees who would have been entitled to the work.[40]

Preparation of the Award

The award conveys the arbitrator's decision in the case, including (in most cases) a summary of the evidence presented, the reasoning behind the decision, and what action must be taken to satisfy the decision.

To prepare the award, the arbitrator must determine whether the dispute was arbitrable. Did the grievance allege an actual violation of the contract? Were the grievance procedure steps followed in a prescribed manner so that the grievance and the union follow-up were timely? If these criteria are met, the arbitrator examines the merits.

While the arbitrator has no statutory obligation to do so, it is important that the reason for a particular award be included to guide the parties in the future. Even though the grievance may appear trivial, the decision will

[38] Ibid., p. 181.

[39] Ibid., p. 186.

[40] M. Hill Jr. and A. Sinicropi, *Remedies in Arbitration* (Washington, DC: Bureau of National Affairs, 1981).

guide employer and union conduct during the contract, so it is important for them to know why the issue was decided as it was.

The arbitrator must be careful that the award draws from the essence of the contract. Most contracts prohibit arbitrators from adding to, subtracting from, or modifying the agreement. The arbitrator must show how the interpretation is within the parameters of the contract. If there are ambiguities in the contract that apply to the grievance, the arbitrator needs to explain how they are resolved in the award.[41] In general, arbitrators are expected to apply the "plain-meaning rule" to contract language, but the history of how clauses were constructed is also important in understanding the meaning of the words used.[42]

Occasionally, arbitrators find a conflict between contract language and federal labor or civil rights laws or interpretations. No clear-cut guidance for this situation exists. Some argue the arbitrator should give primacy to a contractual interpretation,[43] while others suggest federal employment laws must supersede contract terms and influence the award where they apply.[44] Given the Supreme Court and NLRB's willingness to defer statutory issues to arbitrators, it is likely that courts will expect arbitrators to apply appropriate law in situations where a statutory issue is part of or at the core of a grievance. Arbitrators may also need to explain the rationale for their award if there appears to be a potential conflict with public policy—particularly in substance abuse, dishonesty, or theft discipline cases where the public would potentially or actually be at risk from the disciplined behavior.[45]

PROCEDURAL DIFFICULTIES AND THEIR RESOLUTIONS

Time delays are a major problem in arbitration. Some cases take up to two years to resolve. Table 15.1 provides the time data from almost 600 arbitrated cases in the province of Alberta, Canada, between 1985 and 1988.[46] The total time is quite similar to that in U.S. data.

[41] J. B. LaRocco, "Ambiguities in Labor Contracts: Where Do They Come From?" *Dispute Resolution Journal*, 59, no. 1 (2004), pp. 38–41.

[42] D. A. Dilts, "Of Words and Contracts: Arbitration and Lexicology," *Dispute Resolution Journal*, 60, no. 2 (2005), pp. 40–46.

[43] B. Meltzer, "Ruminations about Ideology, Law, and Labor Arbitration," in *The Arbitrator, the NLRB, and the Courts: Proceedings of the National Academy of Arbitrators* (Washington, DC: Bureau of National Affairs, 1967), p. 1.

[44] R. Howlett, "The Arbitrator, the NLRB, and the Courts," in *The Arbitrator, the NLRB, and the Courts: Proceedings of the National Academy of Arbitrators* (Washington, DC: Bureau of National Affairs, 1967), p. 67.

[45] D. J. Petersen and H. R. Boller, "Applying the Public Policy Exception to Labor Arbitration Awards," *Dispute Resolution Journal*, 58, no. 4 (2003), pp. 14–23.

[46] A. Ponak, W. Zerbe, S. Rose, and C. Olson, "Using Event History Analysis to Model Delay in Grievance Arbitration," *Industrial and Labor Relations Review*, 50 (1996), pp. 105–121.

TABLE 15.1
Time Involved in Arbitrated Grievances

Source: Adapted from A. Ponak, W. Zerbe, S. Rose, and C. Olson, "Using Event History Analysis to Model Delay in Grievance Arbitration," *Industrial and Labor Relations Review*, 50 (1996), p. 112.

	Mean	Median	Minimum	Maximum
Prearbitration grievance steps (days)	54.7	41.5	0	334
Arbitrator selection (days)	77.7	50.0	0	428
Scheduling (days)	128.3	112.0	9	623
Decision preparation (days)	65.2	55.9	0	347
Total procedure (days)	333.6	161.2	14	936
Length of award (pages)	15.1	13	1	105

The arbitral process can take more time, but data indicate an average of 184 days from appointment to award. The 65 days from the end of the hearing to the award date is greater than the 60-day limit established by the FMCS, but it may include time during which briefs are submitted.[47] The median of 50 days is within the FMCS limit. One arbitrator noted that the time between the close of hearings and the rendering of a decision for about 150 cases varied from 0 to 94 days, with a mean of 30 days or less in every industry except railroads. For the 150 cases, the time lapse between the grievance and the hearing was 0 to 1,426 days, with a mean of over 100 days in all industries and a mean of over one year in steel, railroads, and the federal government.[48]

Time delays occur at various points. From the original grievance to referral to arbitration, complexity and nondischarge grievances increase time required. A delay in arbitrator selection is related to using attorneys and the size of the arbitration board. Delays in scheduling relate to use of outside attorneys and hours, wages, benefits, and job entitlement issues. Delays in decisions were related to complexity; discipline, hours, wages, benefits, and other issues; board size; lawyer counsels; and the arbitrator's workload. Public sector arbitrations took longer.[49]

Time delays are difficult for the grievant. The quote "Justice delayed is justice denied" is not an empty platitude. It is important to individuals who have been disciplined to have their cases decided so that they can move on to a new job or return to work made whole. Delays in discharge arbitrations reduce the likelihood of reinstatement. A one-month delay is related to an 8.6 percent decrease in reinstatement odds.[50] For firms, a grievance involving many employees can lead to heavy back pay liabilities if long-delayed findings are adverse.

Arbitration costs also cause problems, particularly for unions. Because unions and managements usually share arbitration costs, a poorly

[47] Ibid.

[48] G. Mangum, "Delay in Arbitration Decisions," *Arbitration Journal*, 42, no. 1 (1987), p. 58.

[49] Ponak et al., "Using Event History Analysis."

[50] Nelson and Uddin, "Impact of Delay."

TABLE 15.2
The Union's Cost of Traditional Arbitration for a 1-Day Hearing

Prehearing	
Lost time: grievant and witnesses @ $20 × 32 hours	$ 640
Lawyer:	
Library research @ $300 × 4 hours	1,200
Interviewing witnesses @ $300 × 4 hours	1,200
Filing fee: AAA (shared equally) $450	225
Total prehearing costs	$ 3,265
Hearing Expense	
Arbitrator:	
Fee (shared equally): 1 hearing day @ $980	$ 490
Expenses for meals, transportation, etc. (shared)	250
Travel time (shared): ½ day	245
Transcript, 200 pages @ $12.50 per page (shared)	1,250
Lawyer: presentation of case @ $300 × 8 hours	2,400
Lost time: grievant and witnesses @ $20 × 32 hours	640
Hearing room (shared)	150
Total hearing	$ 5,425
Posthearing Expense	
Lawyer: preparation of posthearing brief @ $300 × 8 hours	$ 2,400
Arbitrator: study and award preparation time, 2.5 days @ $980 (shared)	1,225
Total posthearing	3,675
Total cost to union	$12,375

financed union may be reluctant to use arbitration as much as it would like. Table 15.2 estimates the costs for a typical, relatively uncomplicated arbitration case, using 2009 per diem figures for arbitrators and increasing most other costs by about 275 percent over the costs when the table was first constructed in 1976.[51] The impact of the total cost of $12,375 can be estimated in relation to union dues. Assume that dues are equal to two hours of pay per month ($20 × 2 = $40). Usually the local retains about 50 percent of the dues ($20). It would take 619 dues payments to pay for an arbitration. If a local union budgeted 50 percent of dues collected for arbitration cases, this would mean that a bargaining unit with about 600 union members could take no more than six cases to arbitration annually. Using the rates at which employees grieve, on average, and the rate at which grievances ultimately are arbitrated as discussed in Chapter 14, a local union with 600 members would be projected to take between 0.3 and 1.5 cases to arbitration annually. Thus, its expected arbitration costs would be between $3,713 and $18,563 annually.

Expedited Arbitration

Since the early 1970s, some larger companies and unions have used **expedited arbitration** to reduce time delays and costs. In expedited arbitration,

[51] www.fmcs.gov/internet/itemDetail.asp?categoryID=185&itemID=16525.

arbitrators hear several cases and submit very short written awards. Most expedited arbitration cases involve individual discipline and discharge or are emergencies. Expedited arbitration facilitates the entry of new arbitrators because relatively simple and straightforward cases are generally handled in this way.

Inadequate Representation

Chapter 14 noted a few cases in which employees were not fairly represented by their unions. Inadequate representation could be either malicious or inept. Because arbitration awards are viewed as final by courts, the quality of advocacy is very important. The Supreme Court reversed an arbitration award discharging an over-the-road trucker accused of padding expenses because an adequate investigation would have found that a motel clerk charged more than the published rate and pocketed the difference. The trucker was actually blameless.[52]

During hearings, arbitrators may recognize quality differences in the preparation of the case. Although arbitrators may question witnesses and probe into other matters, their impartiality could be questioned if it is concentrated on one side's case. Can an arbitrator ethically "make a case" for an advocate who is inadequately prepared? This issue has not been settled. However, if it's clear to the arbitrator that the grievant's rights are not adequately represented, a later appeal could reverse an award based on the inadequately prepared case.[53]

ARBITRATION OF DISCIPLINE CASES

Many arbitration cases are employee appeals to reconsider evidence related to employer discipline or to reassess the severity of a punishment. Any punishment that includes discharge is particularly likely to go to arbitration. What principles do arbitrators apply to evaluate evidence and establish fair punishment in industrial discipline cases?

Role of Discipline

Employees have specified job rights under the contract, and employers are entitled to performance from their workers. An employer expects employees to carry out orders, regardless of the employees' interpretation of the rightness of the orders, unless they are unsafe, unhealthful, or illegal.[54] If employees believe orders violate the contract, they are entitled to file

[52] *Hines* v. *Anchor Motor Freight, Inc.*, 424 U.S. 554 (1976).

[53] See J. T. McKelvey, "The Duty of Fair Representation: Has the Arbitrator a Responsibility?" *Arbitration Journal*, 41, no. 2 (1986), pp. 51–58, for one arbitrator's opinion.

[54] D. L. Jones, *Arbitration and Industrial Discipline* (Ann Arbor: Bureau of Industrial Relations, University of Michigan, 1961), pp. 17–18.

grievances and seek relief. But if employees take matters into their own hands, they are guilty of insubordination and may be punished. Punishment can serve two basic purposes: (1) to motivate employees to avoid similar conduct in the future and (2) by example, to deter others.

Evidence

Because imposed discipline is extremely important to the grievant, arbitrators require that the employer present evidence showing that the grievant actually committed the offense and the punishment was proportional to the violated rule. Arbitrators decide discipline cases based on their assessment of what caused the problem to occur.[55] Arbitrators who overturn discipline decisions generally cite a lack of supporting evidence; mitigating circumstances; arbitrary, capricious, or disparate treatment; inappropriate administration or rules; or procedural errors.[56] Given this evidence, arbitrators may uphold or deny punishment or modify it downward (but not upward) to more closely match the disciplinary breach.

Uses of Punishment

Punishment can be thought of, first, as a legitimate exercise of authority to impose consequences for a breach of rules and, second, as a corrective effort to direct employees' attention to the consequences of their actions and to change their attitudes toward the punished behaviors.[57]

Arbitrators may consider these purposes, but they are more concerned with the procedural regularity of the discipline in the case at hand, in the evenness of its application across persons within the same firm, and in its fundamental fairness given societal norms.[58]

The application of authoritarian or corrective discipline is divided about equally, while a small proportion of cases uses humanitarian discipline, which uses rules only as guidance and takes into account individual intentions. Table 15.3 shows the results. Corrective discipline is used more often for absenteeism and incompetence, while authoritarian approaches are applied more often for dishonesty and illegal strike activity.[59] Corrective discipline is often applied for alcohol use, and punishment is more likely for drug use.[60]

[55] B. Bemmels, "Attribution Theory and Discipline Arbitration," *Industrial and Labor Relations Review*, 44 (1991), pp. 548–562.

[56] G. W. Bohlander and D. Blancero, "A Study of Reversal Determinants in Discipline and Discharge Arbitration Awards: The Impact of Just Cause Standards," *Labor Studies Journal*, 21, no. 3 (1996), pp. 3–18.

[57] Jones, *Arbitration and Industrial Discipline*, pp. 2–4.

[58] Ibid., pp. 16–20.

[59] H. N. Wheeler, "Punishment Theory and Industrial Discipline," *Industrial Relations*, 15 (1976), pp. 235–243.

[60] K. W. Thornicroft, "Arbitrators and Substance Abuse Discharge Grievances: An Empirical Assessment," *Labor Studies Journal*, 14, no. 4 (1989), pp. 40–65.

TABLE 15.3 Analysis of Arbitration Decisions Relating to Discharge and Discipline by Theory of Discipline and Type of Offense, as Reported in *Labor Arbitration Reports,* May 1970–March 1974

Source: Hoyt N. Wheeler, "Punishment Theory and Industrial Discipline," *Industrial Relations,* May 1976, p. 239. Reprinted with permission from Blackwell Publishing.

	Humanitarian	Corrective	Authoritarian	Total
Absenteeism, tardiness, leaving early	2	20	8	30
Dishonesty, theft, falsification of records	2	13	28	43
Incompetence, negligence, poor workmanship, violation of safety rules	1	27	9	37
Illegal strikes, strike violence, deliberate restriction of production	0	12	19	31
Intoxication, bringing intoxicants into plant	1	10	7	18
Fighting, assault, horseplay, troublemaking	3	16	15	34
Insubordination, refusal of job assignment, refusal to work overtime, fight or altercation with supervisor	2	42	54	98
Miscellaneous rule violations	2	20	26	48
Total	13	160	166	339
Percent	4%	47%	49%	

Given that corrective discipline is applied about half the time, is it effective? An intensive study concluded that employees who performed unsatisfactorily and received corrective discipline never performed satisfactorily later. A number of reasons are suggested for this finding. First, the individual is often restored to the original work group, where behavior that resulted in the punishment is reinforced. Second, the grievant may be unclear as to which behavior the punishment was related. And third, in some cases, placing an employee in a probationary status rather than punishing him or her makes the discipline contingent on future rather than past behavior.[61]

An employee's previous work record is predictive of job performance after reinstatement. Poor performance after reinstatement was predicted by the number of warnings and other disciplinary actions before being discharged and by discharges for absenteeism or dishonesty.[62] Among another group of reinstated employees, most discharges had been for attendance problems, and the performance of reinstated employees was about average.[63] These findings are consistent with the results following last-chance agreements, examined in Chapter 14.

[61] Jones, *Arbitration and Industrial Discipline*, pp. 71–74.

[62] C. E. Labig Jr., I. B. Helburn, and R. C. Rodgers, "Discipline History, Seniority, and Reason for Discharge as Predictors of Post-Reinstatement Job Performance," *Arbitration Journal*, 40, no. 3 (1985), pp. 44–52.

[63] W. E. Simkin, "Some Results of Reinstatement by Arbitration," *Arbitration Journal*, 41, no. 3 (1986), pp. 53–58.

Substance Abuse Cases

Increasingly, contracts and/or work rules recognize alcoholism and addiction to narcotics as diseases. Employers and unions have agreed generally to facilitate treatment for employees who make their conditions known and to forgo discipline for the substance abuse.[64] Some abuse problems become known to employers through drug testing. Since abstinence would be a condition of employment, testing is a mandatory bargaining issue. Where probable cause of abuse exists, failure to submit to a drug test will usually lead an arbitrator to uphold a discharge.[65]

In alcohol and drug cases arbitrators uphold company discipline depending on proof of misconduct, the reasonableness of the employer's action, and appropriateness of the penalty. Other factors include proper notice to employees of likely consequences for drug and alcohol offenses, equal treatment, and proper investigation.[66]

Where last chance agreements are violated, courts have held that they supersede the contract and discharges under them are not arbitrable if the facts are uncontroverted.[67]

Sexual Harassment Violations

Sexual harassment is a violation of Title VII of the 1964 Civil Rights Act. Employers are liable for damages if an employee is sexually harassed and the employer has taken no affirmative action to prevent its occurrence. Thus, most employers promulgate policies forbidding supervisors to solicit sexual favors for positive employment treatment and forbidding employees to create and maintain a sexually hostile environment. Courts have generally viewed harassment from the standpoint of the potential target of the harassment (e.g., if the target is a woman, what would a "reasonable woman" consider harassment?). Many companies have "zero-tolerance" policies for harassment (i.e., employees who harass will be terminated).

An analysis of arbitration awards in sexual harassment cases found that 72 percent involved co-workers, 5 percent supervisors, and 4 percent nonemployees, with 92 percent involving complaints of unwanted sexual

[64] T. Schneider-Denenberg and R. V. Denenberg, "Arbitration of Employee Substance Abuse Rehabilitation Issues," *Arbitration Journal*, 46, no. 1 (1991), pp. 17–33.

[65] C. L. Reder and A. Abbey, "The Arbitration of Drug Use and Testing in the Workplace," *Arbitration Journal*, 48, no. 1 (1993), pp. 80–85.

[66] S. M. Crow, E. C. Stephens, and W. H. Sharp, "A New Approach to Decision-Making Research in Labor Arbitration Using Alcohol and Drug Disciplinary Cases," *Labor Studies Journal*, 17, no. 3 (1992), pp. 3–18.

[67] D. S. McPherson and B. R. Metzger, "'Last Chance' Discharges at Arbitration: Emergent Standards of Judicial Review," *Proceedings of the Industrial Relations Research Association*, 46 (1994), pp. 315–323.

advances or hostile work environments.[68] If arbitrators find a violation but don't view it as serious enough to merit discharge, there is a potential problem if a harassing employee is restored to the same work area as the person who was harassed, thereby continuing a threatening or hostile workplace.[69]

Fighting

Employers often discharge employees involved in fights, regardless of their role in the altercation. A study of arbitration awards involving discipline for fighting found that individuals involved in fighting could be assigned to three categories: unprovoked aggressor, provoked aggressor, and victim. Arbitrators reduced discipline in about two-thirds of cases they heard. The role of the grievant was related to the reduction in about half of the cases.[70]

Work-Family Conflicts

There may be situations where an employee is scheduled to work during a period when a child is sick or needs to be picked up from day care or school or when some other conflict occurs. Some of these situations may involve short absences of a few hours or a few days, while others may be for extended periods. If there is a bona fide reason for an extended absence, an employee is normally entitled to take a leave under provisions of the Family Medical Leave Act, but such leaves may not be requested in short, ad hoc situations.

Generally, if an employer disciplines a work-family conflict absence, arbitrators will weigh evidence regarding the grievant's usual attendance record, the severity of the illness of the family member, the effort the grievant took to try to arrange for alternative care, and the length of time or shortness of notice given by the employer regarding the scheduled work.[71]

E-Mail Abuse

Employers may establish reasonable rules under management rights clauses. They may establish codes of conduct regarding the use of an employer's e-mail system and its connection with the Internet. Requirements that computer usage be for business purposes and that content may not be pornographic or abusive are generally seen by arbitrators as

[68] V. E. Hauck and T. G. Pearce, "Sexual Harassment and Arbitration," *Labor Law Journal*, 43 (1992), pp. 31–39.

[69] T. J. Piskorski, "Reinstatement of the Sexual Harasser: The Conflict between Federal Labor Law and Title VII," *Employee Relations Law Journal*, 18 (1993), pp. 617–623.

[70] M. A. Lucero and R. E. Allen, "Fighting on the Job," *Dispute Resolution Journal*, 53, no. 3 (1998), pp. 50–57.

[71] B. Wolkinson and R. Ormiston, "The Reconciliation of Work-Family Conflicts in Arbitration," *Dispute Resolution Journal*, 59, no. 3 (2004), pp. 84–95.

reasonable. An employer must make sure that rules are communicated and that they are enforced in an even manner.

Situations that lead to discipline include e-mails to large numbers of recipients protesting management decisions, intentional or accidental transmission of confidential material, the viewing and/or storing of pornography, distribution of bulk mail or chain letters, or a variety of other personal uses.[72]

ARBITRATION OF PAST-PRACTICE DISPUTES

Certain work practices or benefits may not be written in the contract but may have been applied so consistently that there is an understanding they will continue. Unions may frequently negotiate clauses stating that both parties agree that existing conditions will not be reduced during the agreement.

In a variety of situations, arbitrators have ruled that certain practices not mentioned in the contract are protected to the initiator: union or management. If management confers a benefit but announces special circumstances each time it confers it, the employer does not establish a continuing practice. On the other hand, if management mentions a benefit as a reason for not conceding in some area during negotiations, the benefit assumes binding characteristics. If conditions change and management decides to drop a practice, it must do so within a reasonably short time after the change to defend itself against **past-practice** grievances.[73]

Eight criteria are examined in ruling on past-practice grievances:

1. Does the practice concern a major condition of employment?
2. Was it established unilaterally?
3. Was it administered unilaterally?
4. Did either party seek to incorporate it into the body of the written agreement?
5. What is the frequency of repetition of the practice?
6. Is the practice of long standing?
7. Is it specific and detailed?
8. Do the employees rely on it?[74]

If the answers to these questions are yes, the condition will likely take on the same legitimacy as a negotiated benefit.

[72] A. Lichtash, "Inappropriate Use of E-Mail and the Internet in the Workplace: The Arbitration Picture," *Dispute Resolution Journal*, 59, no. 1 (2004), pp. 26–36.

[73] P. Prasow and E. Peters, *Arbitration and Collective Bargaining: Conflict Resolution in Labor Relations* (New York: McGraw-Hill, 1970), pp. 96–121.

[74] *Jacob Ruppert* v. *Office Employees International Union Local 153*, October 19, 1960, 35 LA 505, Arbitrator, Burton B. Turkus.

TABLE 15.4
Federal Mediation and Conciliation Service Arbitration Statistics for Fiscal Year 2009

Reason for Request	Number of Cases
New or reopened contract terms	13
Contract interpretation	2,109
Arbitrability of grievance involved	64
Procedural	108
Substantive	41
Both	16
Issue or Issues	
Affirmative action	0
Absenteeism	8
Bargaining-unit work	24
Conduct (off-duty/personal)	7
Demotion	10
Discipline (nondischarge)	114
Discipline (discharge)	731
Discrimination (any type)	9
Fringe benefits	36
Grievance mediation	2
Health/hospitalization	17
Hiring practice	1
Job performance	12
Job posting/bidding	34
Jurisdictional dispute	8
Layoffs/bumping/recall	42
Management rights	63
Official time	2
Past practices	24
Pension and welfare plans	4
Pension claim (federal statute)	0
Promotion	24
Retirement	0
Safety/health conditions	19
Seniority	15
Sexual harassment	1
Strikes/lockouts/work stoppages/slowdowns	0
Subcontracting/contracting out	31
Tenure/reappointment	
Wages (overtime, holiday pay, etc.)	114
Work hours/schedule/assignment	40
Working conditions/work orders	15
Violence or threats	4
Public Sector Cases	
Federal sector cases	233
Public sector cases	452

ARBITRAL DECISIONS AND THE ROLE OF ARBITRATION

For arbitration to be accepted by the parties, neither expects to fare worse in the results. In a survey of published decisions, win rates for unions and managements were divided evenly. The party with the burden of proof (management in discipline cases, the union in others) wins in 43 percent of cases.[75]

The parties agree to use arbitration for unresolvable grievances. Most contracts indicate arbitrators cannot add to the agreement or decide a case using criteria outside the agreement. Yet the parties encounter situations in which they cannot agree on the interpretation of the contract. One commentator suggests that the role of the arbitrator is to add to the agreement by setting terms to cover one of a number of infinite work situations the parties could not contemplate when the agreement was negotiated.[76] The method continues to be the choice of parties to resolve intracontractual differences that cannot be negotiated or mediated.

The FMCS gathers data on the number of cases going to arbitration and the issues involved for panels it supplies. Table 15.4 shows the number and distribution of cases by issue for 2009. The number of grievances taken to arbitration for almost all issues has declined substantially since the early 1980s. A good deal of this is probably due to the reduced proportion of workers currently represented by unions as compared to earlier periods.

Summary

Arbitration is a process for resolving disputes through the invitation of a neutral third party. The use of arbitration is encouraged by the courts, and the outcome of arbitral awards is generally considered nonreviewable. Supreme Court decisions in the Steelworkers' trilogy laid the groundwork for the present status of arbitration. Arbitration is the preferred method for settling employment disputes.

Arbitral hearings are quasi-judicial in nature and resolve alleged contract violations. Arbitrators hear evidence from both parties and rule on the issue in dispute.

A large number of arbitration proceedings are associated with individual discipline and discharge cases. Arbitration cases appear to be split about evenly in applying authoritarian or corrective standards in the use of punishment.

Arbitration has been criticized because it can entail substantial time delays and costs and because some decisions seem to go outside the scope of the contract or dispute. But opponents and proponents are relatively satisfied with the system.

[75] D. A. Dilts and C. R. Deitsch, "Arbitration Win-Loss Rates as a Measure of Arbitrator Neutrality," *Arbitration Journal*, 44, no. 3 (1989), pp. 42–47.

[76] D. Feller, "The Remedy Power in Grievance Arbitration," *Industrial Relations Law Journal*, 5 (1982), pp. 128–137.

Discussion Questions

1. Given the Supreme Court and NLRB rulings, what is the scope and finality associated with rights arbitration proceedings in the private sector?
2. What possible drawbacks do you see associated with the expansion of expedited arbitration?
3. What duty, if any, does an arbitrator have to the parties to see that both are competently represented?
4. Give arguments for and against the greater involvement of attorneys in arbitration, as both advocates and umpires.
5. Forecast what you see as the future of labor arbitration in terms of the expansion or contraction of issues within its jurisdiction and the finality of its decisions.

Key Terms

Arbitrability, *500*
Steelworkers' trilogy, *500*
Collyer doctrine, *504*
Permanent umpire, *505*
Ad hoc arbitrator, *505*
Expedited arbitration, *517*
Past practice, *523*

Selected Web Sites

www.adr.org (American Arbitration Association)
www.fmcs.gov (Federal Mediation and Conciliation Service)
www.naarb.org (National Academy of Arbitrators)

Cases

About 6 months after the new GMFC–Local 384 contract was ratified, four grievances were sent to arbitration by the union. The company and the union agreed that all four grievances would be heard on separate dates by the same arbitrator. Your name was on the panel the FMCS sent to the parties, and they selected you to arbitrate the grievances. You agreed and have heard all four grievances over the past three days. Now you have to prepare your awards.

CASE 1

George Jones was a level 1 assembler in the heavy-components assembly department. He worked with six other assemblers of the same grade, constructing cabs for power shovels. The supervisor, Ralph Barnes, was in charge of three of these heavy-assembly crews. George Jones had been with GMFC for about four years. Over the past six months, he had spent all of his time with his present work crew. His work record had been unremarkable. He had two unexcused absences but no problems with supervision.

On May 6, Jones struck a co-worker, Elliot Johnson, with his fist, rendering him unconscious. As soon as Barnes arrived on the scene and gave first aid, he asked the work crew what had happened. They had only seen Jones strike Johnson. After Johnson regained consciousness, Barnes asked him what happened. Johnson stated he and Jones had been talking when Jones suddenly turned and swung at him. Barnes then asked Jones what happened. Jones, who is the only African American employee in his work group, said Johnson had been making racial slurs toward him ever since he joined the crew, and this morning he had been pushed over the brink when Johnson said, "If it weren't for affirmative action, welfare would be the only thing that would keep a shirt on your back."

From his supervisor training course, Barnes knew it was company policy to discharge anyone who struck another employee or started a fight. Thus, he called security to take Jones to the HR department for termination. When Jones arrived there, he demanded to see Ralph Murphy, the union steward in his area. After conferring, Murphy filed a grievance on Jones's behalf, alleging the company had violated Section 4.02 of the contract by discharging him without cause. His grievance stated the attack on Johnson was justified given his past harassment and punching him seemed to be the "only way to get him off my back."

When Murphy gave the grievance to Barnes, it was immediately denied. Barnes said, "The rule is ironclad, as far as I'm concerned. They said we supervisors didn't have any latitude on this issue."

Murphy then presented copies of the grievance to the shift IR representative, Carolyn Foster, and the general supervisor, Neal Young. In her examination of the grievance, Foster called Johnson and Cronholm, Jensen, and Albers (three other employees in the work group) to her office separately. When questioned, Johnson repeated his allegation that Jones's attack was unprovoked and adamantly denied ever making racial slurs toward him. Information from Jensen and Albers supported Johnson's denial of racial slurs, but Cronholm said he had repeatedly heard Johnson make disparaging remarks to Jones and Jones had asked him to stop. After weighing this information and considering company policy on fighting, she upheld Barnes's action.

The union continued to demand Jones's reinstatement with full back pay, and management adamantly refused.

When the case was heard, the union's grievance alleged not only that had Jones been discharged without cause (Section 4.02) but also that the discharge had been racially motivated, violating the EEO section (12.16a). In its opening argument, the company asked you to find the grievance nonarbitrable because Jones could file a charge with the EEOC under Title VII if your award upheld the discharge. The company also said the discrimination issue was not arbitrable because it had not been raised in step 3 as provided in EEO Section 12.16b. You noted the arguments but reserved your ruling on arbitrability for the decision you would prepare.

Both sides presented their evidence. All of it was in substantial agreement with what Barnes and Foster had found in their investigation. Jones and Johnson held to their stories, as did Jensen, Albers, and Cronholm. The company introduced evidence to show that without exception employees had been terminated for fighting. It also provided statistics showing that 12 percent of the eight employees discharged for fighting over the past three years were African American and 14 percent of the production labor force was African American.

In this case, your award should contain:

1. Your ruling on the arbitrability of the grievance.
2. Your rationale in finding on the merits of the case (if arbitrable).
3. If arbitrable, the degree to which you would grant the relief Jones is asking or uphold management.

CASE 2

Until the point at which the present grievance was filed, the company has always used its own janitors for cleaning and maintenance.

Because of operational requirements, most of this work is performed on the third shift. About 16 janitors are required to maintain the Central City facilities. GMFC has always had problems with absences among its janitors, but since the last contract was signed, the absence rate has increased from an average of about 2.5 percent each week to 20 percent. Because of this increase, housekeeping lagged, and GMFC officials were starting to worry about fire code violations resulting from the superficial cleaning. Management considered discharging those who were chronically absent but found on investigation that absences seemed to rotate systematically among members of the crew, as if they were planned.

As a result of management's investigation, Carolyn Foster contacted Matt Duff, Local 384 president, and asked him to enforce the contract and get the janitors' absence rate down. She told Duff that the company considered the action the equivalent of a slowdown, and that strong action would be taken if absence rates were not reduced. Duff protested, saying there was not concerted activity behind the absences.

When the high rate and rotating pattern persisted, the company discharged the janitors and subcontracted their work to Dependa-Kleen, a full-time janitorial service. To the company's pleasure, Dependa-Kleen was able to take over the entire operation at a lower cost than the in-house operation had incurred before the absence problem.

On behalf of the janitors, Duff filed a grievance arguing the discharges violated Section 4.02 of the contract. He also filed a ULP charge with the NLRB, claiming the company violated Section 8(a)(5) of the Taft-Hartley Act through its unilateral action in subcontracting the work without consulting or bargaining with the union.

The company argued it was justified in replacing the janitors because their systematic absences were a violation of the contract's no-strike or slowdown clause (Section 9.05). The company argued it was entitled to replace the participants consistent with the management rights clause in Section 4.02.

Assume the testimony at the hearing does not seriously challenge the evidence management has gathered on the increase in absences among the janitors. In this case, decide the following:

1. Would you find the grievance arbitrable given the ULP charge filed by the union?
2. Assuming you find the grievance arbitrable, frame an award and justify it.

CASE 3

The maintenance electricians in the unit are assigned to repair jobs around the Central City facilities shortly after they report to work at their central shop at the beginning of a shift. Before ratification of the most recent contract, electricians traditionally returned to the shop for their afternoon coffee breaks. All of the electricians left their work so that they would arrive at the shop at the beginning of the break, and they left the shop at the end of the break to return to work.

The electrical shop supervisor, Ken Bates, issued a new policy after the new contract was approved, stating the break would commence once work stopped at the assigned location and end when work was restarted. This policy change meant some electricians would have insufficient time to return to the shop for their breaks.

The union filed a grievance alleging that the company had revoked a prevailing practice that had the effect of a contract term. It also argued it had not been consulted, as Article 12.03 of the contract required. The company denied the grievance, citing the language in Section 12.02.

1. Should the grievance be sustained?
2. If it should be sustained, what is your reasoning and what should the award be? If it

should be denied, what is the basis for the denial?

CASE 4

Two months ago, GMFC decided to change its health care preferred provider organization (PPO) from the Central Indiana Medical Group (CIMG) to UniCare of Indiana, a local affiliate of UniCare of America. This shift has meant that GMFC employees must change from their present family doctors in CIMG to employee doctors of UniCare if they are to receive PPO coverage. If they remain with their present doctors, they will have to pay the difference in treatment costs between the UniCare and CIMG schedules, which are, on average, about 20 percent higher. In addition, UniCare does not cover some of the treatments offered by CIMG, such as chiropractic treatments when referred by a medical doctor.

The union grieved this change, arguing the chosen provider would be expected to remain in place over the term of the agreement. It argues that a significant negotiated benefit issue has been unilaterally changed by the employer, and that employees' compensation would suffer as a result. The union has also filed a refusal-to-bargain ULP charge with the NLRB.

The company argues that Section 12.08 of the negotiated agreement permits it to choose the PPO. It further argues that none of the provisions of Section 12.08 has been changed. The company still stands ready to pay 80 percent of the first $2,500 in treatment provided by the PPO. It simply has made a business decision to change suppliers to maximize performance.

1. Should the grievance be sustained or denied?
2. If it should be sustained, what should the award be?
3. Has a ULP been committed? If so, what action can the NLRB take? Given the evidence in how the NLRB acts in cases where ULPs are charged, how would it likely rule?

Chapter **Sixteen**

Public Sector Labor Relations

This chapter covers collective bargaining practices in the public sector and highlights differences between public and private sectors and within public sector levels. The public sector consists of the myriad of levels and jurisdictions of governmental units (federal, state, municipal, etc.). The "customer" group affected by outcomes in public sector labor relations is generally much larger (e.g., homeowners and apartment dwellers in a garbage collection strike), and settlement costs are much more likely to be directly passed on to users or taxpayers than is the case in the private sector. Little public sector collective bargaining occurred before the early 1960s, compared to the private sector bargaining that occurred in the middle to late 1930s.

This chapter covers the evolution of federal and state labor law, differences in coverage among jurisdictions and across occupations, union structure and organizational issues, bargaining methods and outcomes, and impasse procedures and their effectiveness.

In reading this chapter, consider the following questions:

1. How do public and private sector bargaining relationships differ, particularly with regard to impasse procedures?
2. How do laws regulating labor relations in the public sector differ across states and occupations?
3. How do the conduct of collective bargaining and the determinants of bargaining power differ in the public and private sectors?
4. What variables seem to have the greatest effect on bargaining outcomes?
5. What benefit issues are currently most relevant for public sector employers and unions?

PUBLIC SECTOR LABOR LAW

As noted in Chapter 3, federal labor-management relations are governed by special laws. State and local employees are governed by state or local laws where collective bargaining is permitted.

Federal Labor Relations Law

Federal employees have engaged in union activities since the 1830s. The federal government did not oppose union activities among its employees until the 1880s, when postal employees began to organize. Before the Lloyd-LaFollette Act of 1912, federal employees were forbidden to lobby Congress about their employment. Union activities increased in the 1930s, but President Roosevelt asserted that collective bargaining was not possible in the federal sector.

President Kennedy preempted pending legislation that would have permitted collective bargaining for federal employees with the issuance of Executive Order 10988. The order enabled unions representing a majority of federal employees within a unit to negotiate exclusive written agreements with an agency but only covering noneconomic and nonstaffing issues. Other labor organizations representing less than a majority but more than 10 percent of employees in a unit were entitled to consultation but could not negotiate agreements. Arbitration of grievances was allowed but was advisory to agency heads rather than binding. Most employees were entitled to organize, except managers and nonroutine personnel workers.

Civil Service Reform Act, Title VII

In January 1979, presidential executive orders were supplanted by the Federal Service Labor-Management Relations statute. The act applied to federal agencies except the U.S. Postal Service (covered under the Taft-Hartley Act), the FBI, the General Accountability Office, the National Security Agency, the CIA, and agencies dealing with federal employee labor relations. Under the constitutional separation of powers requirement, employees of the legislative and judicial branches were excluded. The Federal Labor Relations Authority (FLRA) was created to deal with representation and unfair labor practice (ULP) questions. The Federal Mediation and Conciliation Service (FMCS) assists agencies involved in bargaining impasses, and unresolved impasses are referred to the Federal Services Impasses Panel (FSIP). The FSIP deals with approximately 200 to 300 cases per year, all involving noneconomic issues.[1]

Bargaining rights are limited. Federal employees cannot bargain on wages and benefits, participation in political activities, position classification, missions or budgets of agencies, hiring or promotion, or subcontracting. They may consult in these areas and may negotiate on them if the agency allows. Federal labor organizations may not advocate the use of strikes, and unauthorized strikes may lead to decertification and discipline of individual members. Picketing is also unlawful if it disrupts an agency's activities. Grievance procedures must be included in contracts

[1] G. W. Bohlander, "The Federal Services Impasses Panel: A Ten-Year Review and Analysis," *Journal of Collective Negotiations in the Public Sector*, 24 (1995), pp. 193–206.

and must provide for binding arbitration of unresolved issues. The FLRA may review appealed arbitration awards and set them aside if they conflict with laws, rules, or regulations.

The law enumerates a number of ULPs like those in the private sector, except employers and unions must permit third-party impasse interventions. Unions may not call strikes, work stoppages, or slowdowns. If ULPs occur, the FLRA may issue cease-and-desist orders, require renegotiation of agreements, reinstate employees with back pay, or take other actions.[2]

When the Department of Homeland Security (DHS) was created following the 9/11 terrorist attacks, it contained several already unionized units, including some in the Immigration and Naturalization Service from the Justice Department, Customs from the Treasury Department, the Coast Guard from the Transportation Department, and Animal and Plant Health Inspection from the Agriculture Department. President Bush would not accept legislation weakening presidential authority to exempt units from coverage under the FLRA. The law creating the DHS enables a more flexible human resource management system.[3] In 2011, TSA Administrator John Pistole extended limited collective bargaining rights to airport screeners, an action that Republican senators were unable to block. In an election, screeners voted for representation.

Unions are not permitted to negotiate union or agency shop clauses; thus membership is voluntary where a collective bargaining agreement has been negotiated and a union has representation responsibilities for members of the unit. Free-riding in the federal sector is a big problem for unions, reducing their financial viability and decreasing their ability to provide representational services to bargaining-unit members.

State Labor Laws

Public sector labor relations differ widely among the 50 states. Several have no public sector bargaining laws, a few prohibit at least some occupations from bargaining, and most prohibit strikes. Where they exist, state labor laws generally follow the Taft-Hartley Act except for prohibiting strikes.[4] Labor laws are more comprehensive and were passed earlier in states in which private sector unionization is greatest. Unlike the private sector, some states allow supervisors and managers to organize. Many states have established public employment labor relations boards to act in the same role as the National Labor Relations Board (NLRB) with

[2] H. B. Frazier III, "Federal Employment," in M. K. Gibbons, R. B. Hersby, J. Lefkowitz, and B. Z. Tener, eds., *Portrait of a Process—Collective Negotiations in Public Employment* (Fort Washington, PA: Labor Relations Press, 1979), pp. 421–434.

[3] M. F. Masters and R. R. Albright, "Labor Relations in the Department of Homeland Security: Competing Perspectives and Future Possibilities," *Labor Law Journal*, 54 (2003), pp. 66–83.

[4] D. A. Dilts, W. J. Walsh, and C. Hagmann, "State Labor-Management Relations Legislation: Adaptive Modeling," *Journal of Collective Negotiations in the Public Sector*, 22 (1993), pp. 79–86.

regard to recognition and ULP questions. State laws that allow union or agency shops increase the odds that employees will be represented, while right-to-work laws do not reduce coverage to below that of states without union security provisions. The degree of public employee union coverage in a state is related to pay levels.[5] The requirement for compulsory arbitration of negotiation impasses for some employee groups probably reduces dispute costs but results in higher wage costs,[6] although there is probably little effect for police.[7] Reductions of dispute costs may be beneficial to the citizenry, however, even at the cost of higher wages, given disruption of services such as sanitation and education.

Private sector unionization levels within a state predict public sector bargaining statutes. Pro-public sector bargaining legislation is related to low public sector wages relative to the private sector, larger proportions of nonwhite employees, a favorable political climate, and the spread of laws from neighboring states. Prospects for prolabor legislation are reduced by management opposition and single-party dominance of the legislature.[8]

Unlike those in the private sector, public sector employers are simultaneously bargainers and legislators. Thus, they pass the laws under which they bargain. Legislators are elected by voters, who also use state services. Outcomes of prior contract negotiations influence labor law changes. States change public sector bargaining laws and procedures to be more favorable to labor or management depending on difficulties each might have had in recent negotiations.[9] In states that permit direct democracy initiatives, where collective bargaining exists, initiatives aim at cutting wages, but not employment; where collective bargaining is not permitted, initiatives aim at cutting employment, but not wages.[10]

The 2010 election had huge consequences for public sector collective bargaining in several states—particularly in Wisconsin and Ohio—where legislation eliminated the opportunity for unionization for various public sector occupations or severely limited the scope of bargaining issues and/or outcomes. To an extent, at the state level the 2010 elections were a test

[5] G. Hundley, "Collective Bargaining Coverage of Union Members and Nonmembers in the Public Sector," *Industrial Relations*, 32 (1993), pp. 72–93.

[6] J. Currie and S. McConnell, "Collective Bargaining in the Public Sector: The Effect of Legal Structure on Dispute Costs and Wages," *American Economic Review*, 81 (1991), pp. 693–718.

[7] O. Ashenfelter and D. Hyslop, "Measuring the Effect of Arbitration on Wage Levels: The Case of Police Officers," *Industrial and Labor Relations Review*, 54 (2001), pp. 316–328.

[8] M. S. Waters, R. C. Hill, W. J. Moore, and R. J. Newman, "A Simultaneous-Equations Model of the Relationship between Public Sector Bargaining Legislation and Unionization," *Journal of Labor Research*, 15 (1994), pp. 355–372.

[9] S. Schwochau, "Effects of Employment Outcomes on Changes to Policy Covering Police," *Industrial Relations*, 35 (1996), pp. 544–565.

[10] J. G. Matsusaka, "Direct Democracy and Public Employees," *American Economic Review*, 99 (2009), pp. 2227–2246.

of the effectiveness of both pro- and antilabor special interest campaigns. Recall from Chapter 5 that unions representing primarily public sector employees were the most heavily involved in political campaign activity and financial support for candidates and issue advertising. Recall also that almost all of the expenditures by labor unions or their PACs were for the election of Democratic party candidates and issues. Approximately equal amounts were raised and spent by other individuals and interest groups to support Republican party candidates and issues. One of the primary points of contention in many state campaigns was the argument that public sector employee compensation and job security, especially during the difficult economic period beginning in 2008, was substantially higher than in the private sector. It was argued that pensions and health care benefits, in particular, were much more generous and secure for public sector employees and that the playing fields should be leveled. Republican issue-oriented advertising sought to identify the power of public sector unions and the Democratic party legislators they had helped to elect as a major contributor to their states' current fiscal crises and potential long-term solvency problems. The political makeup of states' legislatures is critically important for public sector labor relations because the legislature makes the rules for what may be bargained for and how bargaining occurs. Essentially, the success or failure of public sector unions' political strategies has a direct effect on their bargaining power over and above the ability of state, local governments, and school districts to pay. This chapter will discuss the highly charged public sector labor relations environment and what fiscal issues are actually ones that are amenable to changes in bargaining power.

Jurisdictions and Employees

In the private sector, only agricultural workers, domestic workers, and supervisors and managers are exempt from Taft-Hartley or Railway Labor Act coverage. In the public sector, differences in coverage exist by types of employees and political jurisdictions.

Levels of Government

Large differences exist in the jurisdictions of bargaining units. Within states, a variety of lesser jurisdictions and semiautonomous agencies exist. For example, if a public university's creation predated statehood, its governance may be largely autonomous from the state's legislature. Counties, cities, school boards, sewer districts, transportation authorities, and the like, are all publicly governed, but each is responsible to a different constituency and perhaps dependent on a different source of funding. A state may pass laws that require, forbid, or regulate the conduct of collective bargaining in other governmental units within the state. In situations in which state statutes are silent with regard to public sector bargaining, cities, school districts, and other non-state governmental units may decide to collectively bargain with units of their employees who desire representation.

Types of Employee Groups

Frequently, state labor laws have different provisions based on occupation and jurisdiction, such as teachers, police, firefighters, state employees, and local employees. Large differences exist among states and across employee groups in terms of collective bargaining rights and restrictions.

Teachers Teacher bargaining laws primarily apply to elementary and secondary public school teachers. Most states that permit bargaining for teachers also confer exclusive recognition on a majority union; impose a mutual duty on both the employer and the union to bargain; have defined impasse procedures, normally including some combination of mediation, fact-finding, arbitration; and prohibit strikes. Some states allow strikes when the school district refuses to arbitrate at a bargaining impasse. A study of teacher bargaining laws finds that, all else being equal, the right to strike is associated with an 11.5 percent wage premium and 37 minutes less time in the work day. States that do not grant the right but do not prohibit teacher strikes have a 5.7 percent premium and 49 minutes less time, while a 3.6 percent wage premium and 70 minutes less time are associated with mandatory arbitration. Fact-finding and voluntary arbitration states have no premiums and no less time than states prohibiting strikes and offering no other impasse procedures.[11]

Police Police statutes cover uniformed officers employed by cities or counties. Most states permit collective bargaining for police and grant exclusive recognition to a majority union. Where bargaining is allowed, most impose a mutual duty on both union and employer, but some only allow the union to meet and confer with management, not to bargain. Most laws require mediation or fact-finding at impasse, and many require arbitration if no agreement is reached.

Firefighters The **International Association of Fire Fighters (IAFF)** is one of the oldest public sector unions and has been very successful in obtaining bargaining rights. Most states grant exclusive representation to a majority union and require a mutual duty to bargain. Impasse procedures are generally similar to those for police, and firefighters are forbidden to strike (except in Idaho). In states where public sector bargaining laws were changed in 2011 to limit bargaining, the changes were not applied to police and firefighter bargaining.

State Employees Fewer states permit bargaining for general state employees than for special occupational groups. Where permitted, bargaining

[11] M. A. Zigarelli, "The Linkages between Teacher Unions and Student Achievement," *Journal of Collective Negotiations in the Public Sector*, 23 (1994), pp. 299–320.

is generally a mutual duty. There are fewer formal procedures for breaking impasses than exist for specific occupational groups. Some states allow strikes if an impasse has been reached.

Local Employees Provisions for local employees in nonuniformed occupations are generally similar to those of state employees, with the exception that strikes are more often permitted.

While many states forbid strikes, enforcing the prohibition is often difficult. A long history of public employee strikes shows that legally permissible steps to end strikes are not often taken and that statutorily mandated reprisals, such as discharges, are infrequently invoked. Table 16.1 is a compilation of the basic provisions in state labor laws across the 50 states. In Table 16.1, "codified" means that a law is currently in effect enabling public sector collective bargaining. The mandatory subjects for bargaining specified by the law are in parentheses. W is for wages, H for hours, and TC for terms and conditions of employment. In the second part of the table, basic components of legislated or bargained impasse procedures are included. In the actual statutes, these are usually described across several sections, so if you are researching a particular state, you should go directly to the statutes to determine the sequence of activities that occur in the bargaining and impasse process.

PUBLIC EMPLOYEE UNIONS

Four types of nonfederal public sector labor organizations are (1) all-public sector employee unions, (2) mixed public and private sector unions, (3) state and local employee associations, and (4) unions and associations representing only uniformed protective services.[12] The Service Employees International Union (SEIU) and the Teamsters are major mixed-sector unions. The IAFF and the **Fraternal Order of Police (FOP)** are among the largest all-public sector unions. Several unions exclusively or predominantly represent public sector employees. The American Federation of State, County, and Municipal Employees (AFSCME), AFL-CIO, represents state and local unit employees (see Chapter 4 for a description of its structure). The **American Federation of Government Employees (AFGE),** AFL-CIO, represents federal employees. Postal service employees are represented by several national unions, such as the American Postal Workers Union (APWU). Some postal unions have recently merged with larger, primarily private sector unions (see Chapter 4).

Some public sector bargaining representatives began as professional associations and were primarily involved in establishing standards and occupational licensing requirements and lobbying for improved funding

[12] J. Stieber, *Public Sector Unionism* (Washington, DC: Brookings Institution, 1973).

TABLE 16.1
Provisions of State Labor Laws by Occupational Group

Collective Bargaining Availability				
State	**Police and Fire**	**State Employees**	**Public School Teachers**	**Municipal**
Alabama	Meet and confer	No provision	Permitted	Meet and confer
Alaska	Codified (WHTC)	Codified (WHTC)	Codified (WHTC)	Codified (WHTC)
Arizona	Present proposals	No provision	Permitted	Permitted*
Arkansas	No provision	No provision	Permitted	No provision
California	Meet and confer	Meet and confer	Codified (WHTC)	Meet and confer
Colorado	Permitted	Permitted	Permitted	Permitted
Connecticut	Codified (WHTC)	Codified (WHTC)	Codified (WHTC)	Codified (WHTC)
Delaware	Codified (WHTC)	Codified (HTC)	Codified (WHTC)	Codified (WHTC)
District of Columbia	Codified (WHTC)	(No employees)	Codified (WHTC)	Codified (WHTC)
Florida	Codified (WHTC)	Codified (WHTC)	Codified (WHTC)	Codified (WHTC)
Georgia	Prohibited	Prohibited	Prohibited	Prohibited
Hawaii**	Codified (WHTC)	Codified (WHTC)	Codified (WHTC)	Codified (WHTC)
Idaho	Codified (WHTC)***	No provision	Codified (W)	No provision
Illinois	Codified (WHTC)	Codified (WHTC)	Codified (WHTC)	Codified (WHTC)
Indiana	No provision	Prohibited	Codified (WH)	No provision
Iowa	Codified (WHTC)	Codified (WHTC)	Codified (WHTC)	Codified (WHTC)
Kansas	Meet and confer	Meet and confer	Codified (WHTC)	Meet and confer
Kentucky	Codified (WHTC)	No provision	Permitted	No provision
Louisiana	No provision	No provision	Permitted	No provision
Maine	Codified (WHTC)	Codified (WHTC)	Codified (WHTC)	Codified (WHTC)
Maryland	Local option	Codified (WHTC)	Local option	Local option
Massachusetts	Codified (WHTC)	Codified (WHTC)	Codified (WHTC)	Codified (WHTC)
Michigan	Codified (WHTC)	Codified (WHTC)	Codified (WHTC)	Codified (WHTC)
Minnesota	Codified (WHTC)	Codified (WHTC)	Codified (WHTC)	Codified (WHTC)
Mississippi	No provision	No provision	Permitted	No provision
Missouri****	Codified (WHTC)	Codified (WHTC)	Codified (WHTC)	Codified (WHTC)
Montana	Codified (WHTC)	Codified (WHTC)	Codified (WHTC)	Codified (WHTC)
Nebraska	Codified (WHTC)	Codified (WHTC)	Codified (WHTC)	Codified (WHTC)
Nevada	Codified (WHTC)	No provision	Codified (WHTC)	Codified (WHTC)
New Hampshire	Codified (WHTC)	Codified (WHTC)	Codified (WHTC)	Codified (WHTC)

(*Continued*)

TABLE 16.1
Provisions of State Labor Laws by Occupational Group (continued)

State	Police and Fire	State Employees	Public School Teachers	Municipal
New Jersey	Codified (WHTC)	Codified (WHTC)	Codified (WHTC)	Codified (WHTC)
New Mexico	Codified (WHTC)	Codified (WHTC)	Codified (WHTC)	Codified (WHTC)
New York	Codified (WHTC)	Codified (WHTC)	Codified (WHTC)	Codified (WHTC)
North Carolina	Prohibited	Prohibited	Prohibited	Prohibited
North Dakota	No provision	No provision	Permitted	No provision
Ohio	Codified (WHTC)	Codified (WHTC)	Codified (WHTC)	Codified (WHTC)
Oklahoma	Codified (WHTC)	No provision	Codified (WHTC)	Permitted
Oregon	Codified (WHTC)	Codified (WHTC)	Codified (WHTC)	Codified (WHTC)
Pennsylvania	Codified (WHTC)	Codified (WHTC)	Codified (WHTC)	Codified (WHTC)
Rhode Island	Codified (WHTC)	Codified (WHTC)	Codified (WHTC)	Codified (WHTC)
South Carolina	Prohibited	Prohibited	Prohibited	Prohibited
South Dakota	Codified (WHTC)	Codified (WHTC)	Codified (WHTC)	Codified (WHTC)
Tennessee	No provision	No provision	Codified (WHTC)	No provision
Texas	Permitted*****	Prohibited	Prohibited	Prohibited
Utah	No provision	No provision	Permitted	Permitted******
Vermont	Codified (WHTC)	Codified (WHTC)	Codified (WHTC)	Codified (WHTC)
Virginia	Prohibited	Prohibited	Prohibited	Prohibited
Washington	Codified (WHTC)	Codified (WHTC)	Codified (WHTC)	Codified (WHTC)
West Virginia	No provision	No provision	Permitted	No provision
Wisconsin	Codified (WHTC)	Codified (W)†	Codified (W)†	Codified (W)†
Wyoming	Codified (WHTC)***	No provision	Permitted	No provision

*City of Phoenix bargains with five unions annually.
**Hawaii's constitution establishes public sector collective bargaining rights.
***Firefighters only.
****Missouri Supreme Court ruled in 2007 that CB statute can be construed to include public employees.
*****Local option to allow.
******Salt Lake City permitted.
†W=base wage only not to exceed change in CPI without voter referendum.

Permissibility of Strikes and Impasse Resolution Procedures

State	Police and Fire	State Employees	Public School Teachers	Municipal
Alabama	No provision	No provision	No provision	No provision
Alaska	Mediation, arbitration, strikes prohibited	Mediation, strikes permitted*	Mediation, strikes permitted	Mediation, strikes permitted*
Arizona	No provision	No provision	No provision	No provision

State	Police and Fire	State Employees	Public School Teachers	Municipal
Arkansas	No provision	No provision	No provision	No provision
California		Mediation, fact-finding	Mediation, fact-finding required, arbitration permitted	Mediation, fact-finding
Colorado	No provision	No provision	Strikes permitted	No provision
Connecticut	Final offer arbitration on each issue, strikes prohibited	Mediation, final offer arbitration on each issue, strikes prohibited	Final offer arbitration on package, strikes prohibited	Final offer arbitration on each issue, strikes prohibited
Delaware	Mediation, fact-finding, strikes prohibited	Mediation, fact-finding, strikes prohibited	Mediation, fact finding, strikes prohibited	Mediation, fact-finding, strikes prohibited
District of Columbia	Mediation, fact finding, arbitration as imposed by PERB on case-by-case basis	Mediation, fact finding, arbitration as imposed by PERB on case-by-case basis	Final offer arbitration on economic package, issue by issue on others, strikes prohibited	Mediation, fact finding, arbitration as imposed by PERB on case-by-case basis
Florida	Mediation, fact finding, final resolution by legislative body, strikes prohibited	Mediation, fact finding, final resolution by legislative body, strikes prohibited	Mediation, fact finding, final resolution by legislative body, strikes prohibited	Mediation, fact finding, final resolution by legislative body, strikes prohibited
Georgia	No bargaining	No bargaining	No bargaining	No bargaining
Hawaii	Mediation, arbitration, strikes prohibited	Mediation, strikes permitted	Mediation, fact-finding, arbitration, strikes permitted	Mediation, strikes permitted
Idaho	Fact finding, strikes permitted	No provision	Fact-finding	No provision
Illinois	Final offer arbitration on each issue, strikes prohibited	Fact finding, strikes permitted	Mediation, fact-finding, arbitration, strikes permitted	Fact finding, strikes permitted
Indiana	No bargaining	No bargaining	Mediation, fact-finding, arbitration, strikes prohibited	No bargaining

(*Continued*)

TABLE 16.1
Provisions of State Labor Laws by Occupational Group (continued)

State	Police and Fire	State Employees	Public School Teachers	Municipal
Iowa	Fact-finding, final offer arbitration by issue, strikes prohibited	Fact-finding, final offer arbitration by issue, strikes prohibited	Fact-finding, final offer arbitration by issue, strikes prohibited	Fact-finding, final offer arbitration by issue, strikes prohibited
Kansas	Mediation, fact-finding, final determination by legislative body, strikes prohibited	Mediation, fact-finding, final determination by legislative body, strikes prohibited	Mediation, fact-finding, final determination by legislative body, strikes prohibited	Mediation, fact-finding, final determination by legislative body, strikes prohibited
Kentucky	Fact-finding, strikes prohibited	No bargaining	No bargaining	No bargaining
Louisiana	No provision	No provision	No provision	No provision
Maine	Mediation, fact-finding, binding arbitration on nonwage issues, advisory on wages, strikes prohibited	Mediation, fact-finding, binding arbitration on nonwage issues, advisory on wages, strikes prohibited	Mediation, fact-finding, binding arbitration on nonwage issues, advisory on wages, strikes prohibited	Mediation, fact-finding, binding arbitration on nonwage issues, advisory on wages, strikes prohibited
Maryland	No provision	Fact-finding, final offer arbitration by issue, strikes prohibited	No provision	No provision
Massachusetts	Fact-finding, arbitration, strikes prohibited	Fact-finding, arbitration, strikes prohibited	Fact-finding, arbitration, strikes prohibited	Fact-finding, arbitration, strikes prohibited
Michigan	Final offer arbitration on each issue, strikes prohibited	Mediation, strikes prohibited	Mediation, strikes prohibited	Mediation, strikes prohibited
Minnesota	Arbitration, strikes may be a ULP	Arbitration, strikes permitted	Arbitration, strikes permitted	Arbitration, strikes permitted
Mississippi	No bargaining	No bargaining	Strikes prohibited	No bargaining
Missouri	Mediation, strikes prohibited	Mediation, strikes prohibited	Mediation, strikes prohibited	Mediation, strikes prohibited
Montana	Arbitration, strikes prohibited for police and permitted for firefighters	Fact-finding, arbitration, strikes permitted	Fact-finding, arbitration, strikes permitted	Fact-finding, arbitration, strikes permitted

State	Police and Fire	State Employees	Public School Teachers	Municipal
Nebraska	Mediation, final offer arbitration by issue, strikes prohibited	Mediation, final offer arbitration by issue, strikes prohibited	Mediation, final offer arbitration by issue, strikes prohibited	Mediation, final offer arbitration by issue, strikes prohibited
Nevada	Mediation, fact-finding, arbitration, strikes prohibited and punished	No provision	Mediation, fact-finding, arbitration, strikes prohibited and punished	Mediation, fact-finding, arbitration, strikes prohibited and punished
New Hampshire	Fact-finding, mediation, strikes prohibited	Fact-finding, mediation, strikes prohibited	Fact-finding, mediation, strikes prohibited	Fact-finding, mediation, strikes prohibited
New Jersey	Arbitration, strikes prohibited	Fact-finding, strikes permitted	Fact-finding, strikes permitted	Fact-finding, strikes permitted
New Mexico	Mediation, arbitration, strikes prohibited	Mediation, arbitration, strikes prohibited	Mediation, arbitration, strikes prohibited	Mediation, arbitration, strikes prohibited
New York	Mediation, arbitration, strikes prohibited and punished	Mediation, arbitration, strikes prohibited and punished	Mediation, arbitration, strikes prohibited and punished	Mediation, arbitration, strikes prohibited and punished
North Carolina	Strikes prohibited	Strikes prohibited	Strikes prohibited	Strikes prohibited
North Dakota	No provision	No provision	Strikes prohibited	No provision
Ohio	Final offer arbitration on each issue, strikes prohibited	Fact-finding, other procedures determined by parties, strikes prohibited	Fact-finding, other procedures determined by parties, strikes prohibited	Fact-finding, other procedures determined by parties, strikes prohibited
Oklahoma	Final offer arbitration on total package, strikes prohibited	No bargaining	Fact-finding, strikes prohibited and punished	Mediation, arbitration, strikes prohibited
Oregon	Mediation, arbitration, strikes prohibited	Mediation, fact-finding, arbitration, strikes permitted	Mediation, fact-finding, arbitration, strikes permitted	Mediation, fact-finding, arbitration, strikes permitted
Pennsylvania	Arbitration, strikes not prohibited	Fact-finding, arbitration, strikes permitted	Arbitration, strikes permitted	Fact-finding, arbitration, strikes permitted
Rhode Island	Arbitration, strikes prohibited	Arbitration, strikes prohibited	Arbitration, strikes prohibited	Arbitration, strikes prohibited

(*Continued*)

TABLE 16.1
Provisions of State Labor Laws by Occupational Group (continued)

State	Police and Fire	State Employees	Public School Teachers	Municipal
South Carolina	No bargaining	No bargaining	No bargaining	No bargaining
South Dakota	Mediation, strikes prohibited and punished	Mediation, strikes prohibited and punished	Mediation, final resolution by legislative body, strikes prohibited	Mediation, strikes prohibited and punished
Tennessee	No bargaining	No bargaining	Fact-finding, strikes prohibited	No bargaining
Texas	Arbitration, strikes prohibited and punished	No bargaining	No bargaining	No bargaining
Utah	No bargaining	No bargaining	Mediation, fact-finding, strikes not prohibited	No provision
Vermont	Fact-finding, arbitration, strikes permitted	Final offer arbitration on total package, strikes allowed	Fact-finding with review by legislative body, strikes allowed	Fact-finding, arbitration, strikes allowed
Virginia	No bargaining	No bargaining	No bargaining	No bargaining
Washington	Arbitration, strikes prohibited and punished	Mediation, fact-finding	Fact-finding, arbitration, strikes permitted	Fact-finding with review by legislative body, strikes prohibited
West Virginia	No bargaining	No bargaining	No provision	No bargaining
Wisconsin	Arbitration	No provision	No provision	No provision
Wyoming	Arbitration, strikes not prohibited	No bargaining	No provision	No bargaining

*Strikes may be enjoined and arbitration required if work stoppage leads to a public emergency.

and facilities. Others began as **civil service employee** associations before collective bargaining rights were available. They were primarily involved in meeting and conferring with management and lobbying with legislatures. Some, like the California State Employees Association, were large enough to exercise political influence by having large blocs of voters in districts where state employment was high.

Most national unions bargaining at state and local levels are organized along a federal model, such as the National Education Association (NEA). Because education laws and funding methods vary by state and most bargaining occurs at local school board levels, state-level services primarily involve lobbying and negotiation assistance. Public sector locals seldom need approval from the national for contract ratifications and strikes.

Increased public sector unionization depends on the adoption of state laws permitting expanded bargaining rights and bargaining success. In particular, duty-to-bargain laws substantially increase unionization beyond other public policy measures favorable to public sector unions.[13]

Public sector unions, in general, have a strong interest in promoting social programs, education, municipal services, and uniformed protection because greater focus on these areas leads to greater public sector employment. Public sector unions may have the greatest success in achieving their goals by linking bargaining issues with broader public concerns, such as smaller class sizes and their relationship to educational outcomes (and teacher employment).[14] Actively supporting candidates who favor increasing publicly provided programs is consistent with achieving union goals and also with having elected officials sympathetic to public sector union interests, which proves helpful during negotiations.

BARGAINING RIGHTS AND ORGANIZING

Public employers often bargain with several unions. Bargaining units are generally not as inclusive as those in the private sector. In a given geographic area, public employee unions bargain with a variety of statutory agencies. For example, a large city may have a local government, school board, transit authority, sewer district, public utility, and so forth, all with autonomous powers to bargain, levy taxes, and provide specific services. Separate bargaining units exist within each. For example, a school board may bargain with an American Federation of Teachers (AFT) local representing teachers, an SEIU local representing custodians, an AFSCME local representing clericals, and a Teamsters local representing bus drivers. This situation makes whipsawing an unsophisticated management possible, but the costs ultimately result in higher taxes, which bring either legislative or taxpayer referendums into play.

Bargaining-unit composition depends on what state laws allow and the interests of the organizing union. From the employer's standpoint, bargaining-unit scope is usually limited by the extent of the taxing authority. For example, a statewide clerical bargaining unit would be appropriate for state employees but not for local government clericals, because the city may not have the revenue-producing capabilities necessary to finance wages negotiated at a state level.

[13] J. S. Zax and C. Ichniowski, "Bargaining Laws and Unionization in the Local Public Sector," *Industrial and Labor Relations Review*, 43 (1990), pp. 447–462.

[14] V. G. Devinatz, "The Real Difference between the Old Unionism and the New Unionism: A New Strategy for U.S. Public Sector Unions," *Journal of Collective Negotiations in the Public Sector*, 28 (1999), pp. 29–40.

PUBLIC SECTOR BARGAINING PROCESSES

This section examines differences between public sector and private sector bargaining and evolving bargaining structures found in nonfederal negotiations.

Bargaining Structures

Bargaining is more fragmented in the public sector than in the private sector. This is due partly to legislation imposing different recognition, bargaining, impasse, and strike rules on various jurisdictions and occupations. Another reason relates to the relatively narrow governmental jurisdictions involved. For example, although public school teachers are a relatively homogeneous occupational group, a rather small geographic area may have several municipalities with separate school boards and separate negotiations. Local public employers negotiate contracts within their municipalities but may also belong to associations of cities, school boards, and so on and contract with one consultant or law firm to negotiate all contracts.

In a few states, teacher unions have implemented coordinated bargaining on a regional basis. In Illinois, coordinated bargaining in 45 southern counties led to higher salary levels. Similar efforts have also gone forward in the East San Francisco Bay and Portland, Oregon, areas. In Michigan, teacher union successes in enforcing regional patterns led to legislation outlawing higher-level union approval of negotiated local school contracts.

Management Organization for Bargaining

Unlike the private sector, the public sector has an ambiguous management structure. Top policymakers are elected, while operating managers are usually career civil servants. In some jurisdictions, managers may have their own bargaining units. Although appointed managers may be directly responsible for negotiations, elected officials can pressure them to modify positions toward or against the union. Intraorganizational bargaining may become intense between levels of management in public sector negotiations. Over time, bargaining structures become increasingly centralized to gain budgetary control, apply expertise, and coordinate bargaining within a labor relations office having responsibility for collective bargaining agreements.[15]

Multilateral Bargaining

In the public sector, employees indirectly influence management because they also vote, and their union may be aligned with the current incumbents.

[15] M. Derber, "Management Organization for Collective Bargaining in the Public Sector," in B. Aaron, J. M. Najita, and J. L. Stern, eds., *Public Sector Bargaining*, 2nd ed. (Washington, DC: Bureau of National Affairs, 1988), pp. 90–123.

Also, many voters in a given jurisdiction use services provided by or see their taxes affected by the result of the negotiations. Elected officials who were endorsed by public employee unions may influence negotiations. Thus, public sector bargaining is multilateral, with elected officials developing negotiating positions or pressuring appointed managers to make or avoid concessions. Managers usually continue, regardless of who is elected, but as the political positions of elected officials change given election outcomes, appointed managers must be responsive or risk losing their jobs.

Multilateral bargaining occurs when interests beyond management and the union are injected into bargaining. Multilateral bargaining activities involve (1) public officials attempting to influence negotiations, (2) union representatives discussing contract terms with managers who are not on the bargaining team, (3) community interest groups being involved, (4) city officials not implementing the agreement, and (5) mediation attempts by elected officials. Multilateral bargaining is more frequent where there is internal conflict in the positions of management bargainers, the union is politically active, and the union attempts to use a variety of impasse procedures. Data collected from 228 firefighter negotiations found multilateral bargaining was most strongly related to (in order of importance) four factors: (1) general conflict among city officials, (2) union political pressure tactics, (3) union impasse pressure tactics, and (4) management commitment to collective bargaining. Multilateral bargaining increased with the age of the bargaining relationship, but comprehensiveness of state laws and experience of management negotiators had little impact.[16]

In Texas, cities may hold referenda on whether to permit collective bargaining for police and firefighters. Multilateral activities by unions, employees, and local interests influence the outcomes of these referenda. Cities with high union membership, private sector unions endorsing police and firefighter positions, and cooperation between police and firefighters were associated with votes to permit bargaining. Denials were associated with active business opposition, active opposition by current elected city officials or an ad hoc group, and a concurrent city council election.[17]

Both bargaining outcomes and the ability to bargain may be influenced multilaterally. A study of firefighters' negotiations found that several factors predicted positive union outcomes: (1) fact-finding or compulsory arbitration at impasse, (2) comprehensiveness of state bargaining laws, (3) management negotiator's decision-making power, (4) city

[16] T. A. Kochan, "A Theory of Mulilateral Collective Bargaining in City Government," *Industrial and Labor Relations Review*, 28 (1974), pp. 525–542.

[17] D. T. Barnum and I. B. Helburn, "Influencing the Electorate: Experience with Referenda on Public Employee Bargaining," *Industrial and Labor Relations Review*, 35 (1982), pp. 330–342.

council–negotiator goal incompatibility, and (5) elected official intervention at impasse. The first two factors reflect the legal environment, the next two reflect management characteristics, and the last reflects multilateral bargaining. Union pressure tactics were not related to outcomes.[18]

The scope of public sector bargaining laws reflects the relative wealth of a state.[19] Comprehensive laws and greater ability to pay influence bargaining outcomes toward the union. A comprehensive law legitimizes unions, reduces management's costs of recognition, and may legally decrease management's use of contract rejection, refusals to bargain, and similar tactics.[20] Environmental characteristics affect not only the makeup of bargaining teams and their interrelationships but also the power and tactics available to parties during negotiations.

As noted in Chapter 5 and earlier in this chapter, public sector unions are large contributors to Democratic candidates for office, and unions sponsor a significant amount of anti-Republican candidate advertising. The substantial gains made by Republicans in winning state gubernatorial and/or legislative elections in 2010 has led to initiatives to reduce public sector unions' abilities to use member dues to finance political action and/or to restrict or eliminate collective bargaining for public sector employees: In addition to the initiatives to use a portion of dues for political activity without the express permission of individual union members, legislation has been proposed and/or passed in some states to end the ability of unions to collect dues through checkoff arrangements or requiring "**fair-share**" payments by nonmembers in the bargaining unit, thereby increasing the administrative effort required by the union to maintain its finances and increasing the ability of bargaining unit members to free-ride.

Bargaining Outcomes

Public employees often work in an agency in which the government is the only provider (e.g., police protection). Obtaining better contracts is easier because the government can more easily pass on these costs in the short term. Collective bargaining in the public sector expanded rapidly during the 1970s. Several studies examined the early effects of collective bargaining. One study of cities with either public or private waste management systems found that the effect of unions on wages in privately managed systems was not significant but in public systems the effect was between 10 and 17 percent. In privately managed systems, several

18 T. A. Kochan and H. N. Wheeler, "Municipal Collective Bargaining: A Model and Analysis of Bargaining Outcomes," *Industrial and Labor Relations Review*, 29 (1975), pp. 46–66.

19 T. A. Kochan, "Correlates of State Public Employee Bargaining Laws," *Industrial Relations*, 12 (1973), pp. 322–337.

20 P. F. Gerhart, "Determinants of Bargaining in Local Government Labor Negotiations," *Industrial and Labor Relations Review*, 29 (1976), pp. 331–332.

competing waste haulers were usually involved in the market.[21] These results indicate monopoly power available to public employers can be used to increase wages.

Bargaining outcomes are related to institutions, public opinions, and union political activities. Bargaining outcomes in medium-sized municipalities were better for unions (1) where only certain trades were involved, rather than a large general unit; (2) where no statutory penalty for striking existed; (3) where the union was affiliated with a public sector national; (4) where strike activity in the state was above average; and (5) where public opinion had led to or favored a bargaining law.[22] Political activity can have an indirect effect on union outcomes for particular occupations. For example, police and firefighter union support for better police and fire protection is associated with higher departmental budgets and the employment of larger forces.[23] Police and firefighter unions are also more likely to split political contributions between parties and/or vary their endorsements of candidates across parties, a strategy that has seemed to insulate them fairly well from having their bargaining issues restricted.

Pay for union-represented workers in the public sector is about 10 percent higher than pay for comparable unrepresented employees, somewhat less than the differential in the private sector. Premiums are higher for blue-collar and African American workers. Differentials shrink with increased education and experience. However, public sector unionized employees earn a greater premium for experience than their private sector counterparts.[24] Differences are greatest at the local level, for women and younger workers, in the northeast and central United States, and in occupations most likely to be represented by a craft-type union (e.g., teachers, lawyers, firefighters, and police).[25] Spillovers to unorganized areas also occur.[26]

Firefighter unionization influenced total pay and entry and maximum salary levels, with the greatest effect on benefits, similar to the

[21] L. N. Edwards and F. R. Edwards, "Wellington-Winter Revisited: The Case of Municipal Sanitation Collection," *Industrial and Labor Relations Review*, 36 (1982), pp. 307–318.

[22] Gerhart, "Determinants of Bargaining," p. 349.

[23] R. Gely and T. D. Chandler, "Protective Service Unions' Political Activities and Departmental Expenditures," *Journal of Labor Research*, 16 (1995), pp. 171–185; and K. M. O'Brien, "The Effect of Political Activity by Police Unions on Nonwage Bargaining Outcomes," *Journal of Collective Negotiations in the Public Sector*, 25 (1996), pp. 99–116.

[24] B. Bahrami, J. D. Bitzan, and J. A. Leitch, "Union Worker Wage Effect in the Public Sector," *Journal of Labor Research*, 30 (2009), pp. 35–51.

[25] D. G. Blanchflower and A. Bryson, "What Effect Do Unions Have on Wages Now and Would Freeman and Medoff Be Surprised?" *Journal of Labor Research*, 25 (2004), pp. 385–407.

[26] J. S. Zax, "Wages, Nonwage Compensation, and Municipal Unions," *Industrial Relations*, 27 (1998), pp. 301–317.

private sector.[27] For teachers, unionization leads to lower male/female and elementary/secondary pay differences. Pay increases are more often based on education level, years of experience, and years of experience in the district. A 10 percent increase in union density is associated with 2.6 percent higher teacher wages at the top of the structure and 0.2 percent at the bottom.[28] In many teacher units, the majority of teachers is closer to the top of the structure. In unionized public higher education, faculty pay is about 2 percent higher and is more related to seniority and less related to research than it is in nonunion colleges and universities.[29] While employment usually falls as pay increases, lobbying efforts by unions, unit managers, and election campaigns emphasizing quality or safety issues often lead to net new hiring.[30] Collective bargaining increases expenditures in city departments that are covered, but it does not appear to influence property taxes, total revenues, or total expenditures.[31] Local-unit wages are related to union density, enabling legislation, mandatory arbitration, household income in the local area, and private sector union density. At the state level, wages are positively related to public sector union density and household incomes but negatively related to the right to strike, voluntary arbitration at impasse, and private sector union density.[32] During the 1980s, private sector concessions were much larger, but the union wage advantage was also greater.[33]

Productivity effects vary. In the private sector, only blue-collar unionization was associated with greater productivity. Unionization has little apparent effect on student achievement,[34] or high school dropout rates, but does appear to increase teacher employment by about 5 percent.[35]

[27] C. Ichniowski, "Economic Effects of the Firefighters' Union," *Industrial and Labor Relations Review*, 33 (1980), pp. 198–211.

[28] H. L. Zwerling and T. Thomason, "Collective Bargaining and the Determinants of Teachers' Salaries," *Journal of Labor Research*, 16 (1995), pp. 467–484.

[29] D. A. Barbezat, "The Effect of Collective Bargaining on Salaries in Higher Education," *Industrial and Labor Relations Review*, 42 (1989), pp. 443–455.

[30] L. M. Spizman, "Public Sector Unions: A Study of Economic Power," *Journal of Labor Research*, 1 (1980), pp. 265–274; and J. S. Zax, "Employment and Local Public Sector Unions," *Industrial Relations*, 28 (1989), pp. 21–31.

[31] R. G. Valetta, "The Impact of Unionism on Municipal Expenditures and Revenues," *Industrial and Labor Relations Review*, 42 (1989), pp. 430–442.

[32] D. Belman, J. S. Heywood, and J. Lund, "Public Sector Earnings and the Extent of Unionization," *Industrial and Labor Relations Review*, 50 (1997), pp. 610–628.

[33] D. J. B. Mitchell, "Collective Bargaining and Compensation in the Public Sector," in B. Aaron, J. M. Najita, and J. L. Stern, eds., *Public Sector Bargaining*, 2nd ed. (Washington, DC: Bureau of National Affairs, 1988), pp. 124–159.

[34] R. M. Carini, "Is Collective Bargaining Detrimental to Student Achievement? Evidence from a National Study," *Journal of Collective Negotiations*, 32 (2008), pp. 215–235.

[35] M. F. Lovenheim, "The Effect of Teachers' Unions on Education Production: Evidence from Union Certification Elections in Three Midwestern States," *Journal of Labor Economics*, 27 (2009), pp. 525–588.

Research finds unionized police are slightly less productive with regard to minor crimes.[36]

Public Sector Pensions

The financial crisis and associated recession that began in 2008 substantially decreased state and municipal tax revenues, and simultaneously reduced the market value of assets that produce income to pay public pension obligations. Most state and municipal governments provide defined benefit pension plans as part of their employee benefit programs (see Chapter 9 for how these operate). In their constitutions, many states recognize that pension obligations are the most senior liabilities that they owe. Since states (unlike municipalities) are not permitted to enter bankruptcy, accrued pension liabilities must ultimately be paid.

Future pension liabilities are "off-balance sheet" liabilities. In many cases, states record the liability in terms of the amount that would be necessary to pay off recipients as if they retired at their current salaries with their current years of credited service rather than the likely future salaries and years of service that would be accrued before they retired. In addition, most states assume an 8 percent rate of return on their current pension fund assets, and thus use this figure to discount the present value of future obligations. The defined pension benefit plans of all 50 states are underfunded as of 2009 with the amount of underfunding equal to between 171 and 874 percent of the state's total annual tax revenue.[37]

Developments in the economic and political environment that followed from the effects of the economic crisis place public sector pension benefits in the spotlight. Most private sector workers participate in defined contribution pension plans (detailed in Chapter 9) that experienced significant negative investment returns during the period from late 2007 through early 2009. Even if these losses had not occurred, the magnitude of public sector pensions relative to preretirement pay appeared to many private sector workers to be quite large relative to what they expect to receive. In addition, even outside the uniformed services, the age at which employees with sufficient service are entitled to full retirement benefits is often substantially lower than what most private sector employees experience. And finally, public sector workers did not experience nearly the same risks of layoff that were seen in the private sector. In fact, they were prominent beneficiaries of the 2009 stimulus package, a significant portion of which consisted of grants to states that were used to sustain services and

[36] D. Byrne, H. Dezhbakhsh, and R. King, "Unions and Police Productivity: An Economic Investigation," *Industrial Relations*, 35 (1996), pp. 566–584.

[37] See R. Novy-Marx and J. D. Rauh, "The Liabilities and Risks of State-Sponsored Pension Plans," *Journal of Economic Perspectives*, 23, no. 4 (2009), pp. 191–210 for an extensive discussion of these issues.

employment in the public sector. Thus, the public's opinion of the amount and configuration of public employee compensation has become increasingly negative.

To the extent that Democratic legislatures and governors were replaced by Republicans in the 2010 election, substantial pressure was put on management negotiators to extract concessions from unions on the design of pension plans and the generosity of the benefits they contained. In several states, pension plans have been restructured to increase the percentages that employee participants must contribute and/or to increase the age of retirement for employees who will be hired in the future. Proposals to lower the rate of future accruals of current employees and/or create defined contribution plans to cover all newly hired employees were made in several states.

Union-Management Cooperation

Voters have become more interested in increasing efficiency in public services and offering more choice for users, particularly in public education. In some cities, previously publicly provided services, such as sanitation, have been privatized. In others, union-management cooperation programs have been developed to increase efficiency while maintaining public provision of services. Exhibit 16.1 shows some of the initiatives that have taken place in Indianapolis.

During the 1990s, the Clinton administration required that federal agencies and the unions representing their employees must work toward cooperation and partnership. Keep in mind that bargaining issues for unions in the federal sector are quite limited. Even with that constraint, a study of managers and union representatives noted modest perceived improvement in labor-management relations, fewer disputes, and modestly improved organizational performance. These partnerships were ended early in George W. Bush's first term, and the proportion of grievances requiring arbitration increased.[38] President Obama issued an executive order reinstituting labor-management cooperation programs in December 2009. This new order mandated labor-management forums in all agencies and encouraged forums to include permissive issues in future bargaining.

Perceptions of federal employees were influenced by how quickly programs were implemented or canceled and how broad was the scope of issues considered. Supervisor-employee relations, employee involvement, training, and collaboration were all negatively influenced by cancelation or late adoption of partnership programs. Perceptions of job satisfaction, job security, employment security, and alienation were also negatively

[38] M. F. Masters, R. R. Albright, and D. Eplion, "What Did Partnerships Do? Evidence from the Federal Sector," *Industrial and Labor Relations Review*, 59 (2006), pp. 367–385.

Exhibit 16.1

UNION-MANAGEMENT COOPERATION IN THE PUBLIC SECTOR

When Stephen Goldsmith ran for mayor of Indianapolis, he vowed to engage in widescale privatization; in other words, transferring delivery of services to private contractors. Convinced that Indianapolis was in a struggle with its neighbors for both business and residents, raising taxes to pay for improved city services did not seem a viable option. Goldsmith believed that market forces and competition would ultimately serve citizens better than what he and his staff call the government "monopoly."

Once in office, however, he says he quickly came to realize that the real answer to improving service delivery was not privatization because "monopolies, public or private, are inefficient." Instead, Indianapolis launched a comprehensive effort that features labor-management cooperation and, in some areas, fosters competitions between city departments and private contractors. In these instances, it treats city departments as businesses and gives workers a voice in ways to cut costs. If the department can put in a winning bid against private competitors, the city workers continue to provide that particular service.

In addition, city workers also bid for new work and work that was previously contracted out—returning those services to the public sector when it can be done there in a competitive fashion. For example, both the sign shop and fleet maintenance services are now performing work purchased by community organizations, by other governments and by local utilities.

Although Indianapolis receives much attention for its competitive initiatives, the Task Force found in its site visit that the structured, cooperative relationship pervading city operations is the unsung hero of the service and cost improvements.

In fact, where the union has bid, city and union officials estimate that public employees have won the bulk of the contracts put up for competition by examining methods, systems, and cost structures in conjunction with management.

"I was increasingly impressed with the inherent ability of our own employees to perform better when the system allowed them to; I underestimated what they could do if we unloaded the bureaucracy off the top of their heads," Goldsmith said.*

His goal then became providing the best service at the lowest cost for citizens—a goal embraced by the city's workers, largely represented by the American Federation of State, County and Municipal Employees (AFSCME). AFSCME leadership viewed the competitions as a way to help eliminate the myth that the private sector always is more efficient than the public sector, as well as to take back work that had been contracted out years ago.

"Using the private sector as a yardstick with which to measure ourselves, we're fine with that institutionally," said Steve Fantauzzo, executive director of Indiana's State Council 62, AFSCME. "But to simply say that the private sector is always a better answer, that's simply not true." Fantauzzo points out that under public management, for example, refuse collection routes have been redesigned and worker productivity has doubled, producing annual savings close to $15 million.†

*Rob Gurwitt, "Indianapolis and the Republican Future," *Governing,* February 1994, pp. 24–28.
†"Indianapolis Wins Big on Savings, Safety, Effluent Quality Under Contract O&M," *Public Works Financing*, March 1995, pp. 14–16.

Source: *Working Together for Public Service,* Report of the U.S. Secretary of Labor's Task Force on Excellence in State and Local Government through Labor-Management Cooperation, May 1996, p. 35.

affected by cancelation or late adoption. Councils that had broad agendas for discussion were associated with better worker perceptions.[39]

IMPASSE PROCEDURES

In the public sector the following may occur at impasse: mediation, legal or illegal strikes or "sickouts," fact-finding, interest arbitration, continued work under terms of an expired contract, or legislation mandating an agreement. Experience with bargaining impasses in the public sector primarily dates from the early 1970s since that was when bargaining opportunities were first available and the parties had little experience in how to achieve agreements. As noted in Table 16.1, there are large differences between states in how impasses are handled. Over the last 25 years there have been very few changes among the states in public sector impasse resolution procedures. The occurrence of impasses has decreased over time as the parties have gained experience in negotiating. Following is a discussion of the major impasse resolution variants applied in the public sector in one or more states.

Fact-Finding

Fact-finding began in the private sector through the establishment of fact-finding boards in the Taft-Hartley Act and emergency board procedures in the Railway Labor Act. However, it is presently more prevalent in the public sector.

In a private sector impasse, the fact-finder's role is to establish a reasonable position for settlement by studying the context and issues and preparing a report based on the setting. A primary end result sought by this process is the publication of the disputed issues and a recommended settlement. In this way, public opinion may be galvanized to pressure a settlement on a factual conclusion. Fact-finding may also lead to economizing a legislative body's time when it expects to impose a solution.[40]

The role of fact-finding for a legislature is not very appropriate in the public sector since the legislature is often a party in the dispute (school boards, city councils, etc.). The fact-finder's role, then, is to educate the public about costs of a reasonable settlement. Fact-finding may be sought by parties fearing adverse public opinion if they bargain a settlement. They might expect a fact-finder to recommend something similar to a negotiated settlement, but "facts" from a neutral party may seem more reasonable.[41]

[39] D. M. Mahony, "Making Partnership Work: Inside the Black Box of Labor-Management Participation," *Journal of Collective Negotiations*, 31 (2007), pp. 215–240.

[40] J. T. McKelvey, "Fact-Finding in Public Employment Disputes: Promise or Illusion?" *Industrial and Labor Relations Review*, 23 (1969), pp. 528–530.

[41] Ibid., pp. 530–531.

Statutory Role of the Fact-Finder

Wisconsin had one of the first comprehensive fact-finding statutes. While the law was in effect, fact-finding could be initiated by either party at impasse or at the other's refusal to bargain. The Wisconsin Employee Relations Board (WERB) first attempted to mediate. If that failed, a fact-finder examined the evidence and recommended a settlement. The recommendation was sent to the parties and publicized by the WERB. While parties may have asked for fact-finding, they were not obligated to accept the report's recommendations.[42] If dispute resolution is the criterion, fact-finding is less successful than other methods once an impasse has been reached.

In New York, fact-finding follows mediation for all except police and firefighters. It's mandatory for public school teachers and permissive for others. In the past, the mediation and fact-finding roles were often combined in the same person. Since the roles were split, fact-finding is associated with an increased likelihood of accepting the fact-finder's report. However, the gap between the final offers submitted to the fact-finder by the negotiators has widened.[43]

Criteria for Fact-Finding Recommendations

In early Wisconsin experiences with fact-finding, wage comparisons were most often used for economic recommendations. Ability to pay was also frequently considered. Some fact-finders decided what the wage settlement would have been if the union were permitted to strike. Productivity and cost-of-living issues were seldom mentioned, although management and labor raised them in their presentations.[44]

Arbitration

Some laws require arbitration at impasse. They apply more often to uniformed services and are considered to be a quid pro quo for prohibiting strikes. With arbitration at impasse, the union does not face the prospect of management unilaterally continuing past terms without recourse to some other self-help weapon. Other laws allow unions and managements voluntarily to agree to interest arbitration as a means for settling negotiating impasses.

Arbitrators who handle public sector interest cases are normally selected in the same way as those in private sector ad hoc rights cases. The hearing procedure is also similar. Both sides present evidence supporting their positions, and the arbitrator determines the contract on the basis of the evidence and whatever criteria are to be used for the award. The less

[42] J. L. Stern, "The Wisconsin Public Employee Fact-Finding Procedure," *Industrial and Labor Relations Review*, 20 (1966), pp. 4–5.

[43] R. Hebdon, "Fact-Finding: Evidence from New York State," *Industrial Relations*, 40 (2001), pp. 73–82.

[44] Stern, "Wisconsin Procedure," pp. 15–17.

information the parties have about the arbitrator's decision-making tendencies, the more likely they are to avoid an impasse and settle on their own.[45] Variations in laws among the states lead to several different methods applied in public sector interest arbitration.

Conventional Arbitration

When arbitration is conventionally applied, each party articulates its desired award and presents evidence to support the logic of its position. At impasse, the parties select an ad hoc arbitrator to render a decision. The expiring contract is likely to contain a clause indicating the range of issues and the powers and limits the arbitrator has in fashioning a new agreement. There may also be legislated rules and limits that apply within the state or to the occupational group involved in the hearing. It's possible that the arbitration will involve a tripartite hearing with a management and union representative joining with the arbitrator in rendering a decision. Practically speaking, the award is determined by the neutral arbitrator, but involving partisan representatives may lead the parties to narrow differences or concede positions before a final decision is reached on the shrinking set of unresolved issues.

During early experience with availability of conventional interest arbitration, a concern developed that bargaining might be chilled because negotiators might believe an arbitrator will split their differences. For example, if a union wants 90 cents an hour and management is willing to give 30 cents, they may believe an arbitrator will settle on 60 cents. It was also argued that using arbitration has a **narcotic effect**. Negotiators go directly to impasse, thereby availing themselves of an effortless and less risky remedy. Early evidence suggests a narcotic effect existed because negotiations in states providing for arbitration went to impasse more frequently.[46] Beliefs that a narcotic effect occurs led to implementation of several variants of interest arbitration.

Final-Offer Arbitration

To reduce the use of arbitration, **final-offer arbitration** has been implemented in some states. Final-offer arbitration was proposed as a "medicine" to cure parties from using arbitration. In final-offer arbitration, each party presents its positions, with the arbitrator required to choose one of the positions without modification. This supposedly results in an extreme contract the loser would do anything to avoid in the future.[47]

[45] L. C. Babcock and L. J. Taylor, "The Role of Arbitrator Uncertainty in Negotiation Impasses," *Industrial Relations*, 35 (1996), pp. 604–610.

[46] H. N. Wheeler, "Compulsory Arbitration: A 'Narcotic Effect'?" *Industrial Relations*, 14 (1975), pp. 117–120.

[47] C. M. Stevens, "Is Compulsory Arbitration Compatible with Bargaining?" *Industrial Relations*, 5 (1966), pp. 38–50.

Some states opt for entire-package approaches; others use issue-by-issue methods. Entire-package selections increase the need to make a reasonable final-offer submission because one unreasonable position in an otherwise reasonable package may tip the arbitrator's preferences toward the other party. Where final-offer selection is available on an issue-by-issue basis, more unresolved issues reach the arbitrator.[48] Arbitrators appear to give equal weight to wage and nonwage issues in fashioning awards.[49]

One way interest arbitration and rights arbitration differ is that many contracts and statutes permit parties to alter final offers and to settle after the process begins. Since public sector interest arbitration is often conducted before a tripartite board (one labor, one management, and one neutral member), partisans may sense which direction the neutral appears to be leaning and concede an issue rather than lose entirely.[50]

Results of Final-Offer Laws

Final-offer procedures can be evaluated by examining whether parties accept and comply with awards and whether the process chills or encourages future bargaining.[51]

Michigan Michigan uses issue-by-issue final offers for economic aspects and a conventional approach for others. The process has not had an effect on arbitration frequency in the uniformed services. There has been a slight tendency for deputy sheriff negotiations to use the procedure more often than police or fire, but this may be related to a newer bargaining relationship.[52] Police arbitrations are more frequent in larger cities, where there are more police officers per capita, and where lower property values indicate a decreased ability to pay.[53]

Wisconsin Wisconsin used a package-type final-offer procedure before the 2011 change in its public sector bargaining law. The Wisconsin experience does not support the idea that arbitration use declines in a package-selection environment over time.[54] But evidence does indicate its use

[48] P. Feuille, *Final-Offer Arbitration* (Chicago: International Personnel Management Association, 1976), pp. 35–48.

[49] C. A. Olson, "Arbitrator Decision Making in Multi-Issue Disputes," *Proceedings of the Industrial Relations Research Association*, 44 (1992), pp. 392–401.

[50] Feuille, *Final Offer Arbitration*.

[51] Ibid., pp. 15–16.

[52] J. L. Stern, C. M. Rehmus, J. J. Loewenberg, H. Kasper, and B. D. Dennis, *Final-Offer Arbitration* (Lexington, MA: Lexington Books, 1975), pp. 37–75.

[53] B. R. Johnson, G. Warchol, and K. A. Bailey, "Police-Compulsory Arbitration in Michigan: A Logistic Model Analysis of Environmental Factors," *Journal of Collective Negotiations in the Public Sector*, 26 (1997), pp. 27–42.

[54] Stern et al., *Final-Offer Arbitration*, pp. 77–115.

decreases when management wins.[55] The relative use of arbitration in Wisconsin is less than that in Michigan, an issue-by-issue state.

Negotiators in Wisconsin public teacher negotiations appear to engage in strategic behavior since in about half of all cases referred to arbitrators, the parties either negotiated an agreement after the arbitrator had been appointed or accepted a consent settlement. In 86 percent of cases, the settlement ranges of the parties overlapped.[56] Arbitrators in Wisconsin appear to compare settlements from other schools in the same athletic conference from earlier rounds of teacher negotiations during the same period in fashioning their awards.[57]

Parties that used arbitration in the previous round and lost made better offers to their opponents in the next contract round. Also, variance in settlements was down, and the negotiated wage structure was closer to what the arbitrator imposed in the last settlement.[58]

Massachusetts Massachusetts has a package final-offer procedure. After its passage, arbitrations increased almost 70 percent. Almost 40 percent of negotiations went to impasse, but only 7 percent were ultimately arbitrated. Arbitrators' awards paralleled closely fact-finders' reports issued earlier during the impasse.[59]

New Jersey Bargainers can elect to use conventional arbitration, final-offer arbitration on a single package, final-offer on an issue-by-issue basis, final-offer on the economic package and issue-by-issue on others, or two forms of fact-finding. Parties choose which type of arbitration they want to use. Results indicate relatively fewer negotiations have arbitrated settlements, and arbitrators are acting more frequently in mediating roles.[60]

The evidence suggests that states with issue rather than package approaches have more arbitrations and more issues going before arbitrators.

[55] C. A. Olson, "Final-Offer Arbitration in Wisconsin after Five Years," *Proceedings of the Industrial Relations Research Association*, 31 (1978), pp. 111–119.

[56] L. C. Babcock and C. A. Olson, "The Causes of Impasses in Labor Disputes," *Industrial Relations*, 31 (1992), pp. 348–360; and L. C. Babcock, "Strategic Behavior in Negotiations and the Use of Arbitration," *Proceedings of the Industrial Relations Research Association*, 44 (1992), pp. 375–384.

[57] C. A. Olson and P. Jarley, "Arbitrator Decisions in Wisconsin Teacher Wage Disputes," *Industrial and Labor Relations Review*, 44 (1991), pp. 536–547.

[58] C. A. Olson and B. L. Rau, "Learning from Interest Arbitration: The Next Round," *Industrial and Labor Relations Review*, 50 (1997), pp. 237–251.

[59] D. B. Lipsky and T. A. Barocci, "Final-Offer Arbitration and Public-Safety Employees: The Massachusetts Experience," *Proceedings of the Industrial Relations Research Association*, 30 (1977), pp. 65–76.

[60] R. A. Lester, "Analysis of Experience under New Jersey's Flexible Arbitration System," *Arbitration Journal*, 44, no. 2 (1989), pp. 14–21.

What Is a "Final Offer"?

One problem frequently encountered in final-offer arbitration is, "What is a final offer?" In Wisconsin, parties had to state their positions to the WERB when an impasse was declared. But it has been the practice there and in Michigan (where mediation by the arbitrator is encouraged) to allow negotiations to narrow differences after an arbitration request. Some see this as an advantage because the parties settle the issues. But others see it as a no-win situation because if they adhere to a well-thought-out final position and only their opponent expresses a willingness to move, the arbitrator may award the point to the opponent based on the apparent intransigence of the adamant party. Thus, a party may provoke an impasse to achieve what it believed it could not get from true bargaining. Evidence indicates that unions gained 1 to 5 percent more in economic settlements as a result of arbitration than they would have in bargaining a settlement.[61]

Arbitration and Maturing Labor Relations

Strikes are very selectively permitted in the public sector. Because the private sector model included them and little experience existed with other mechanisms, a great deal of experimentation has occurred. Fact-finding has decreased, both statutorily and at the individual impasse level. Surveys suggest the use of arbitration is low and decreasing.[62] Arbitration's effectiveness may also depend on prehearing processes. Where experienced negotiators are bargaining, mediation may be much more helpful in fashioning an acceptable settlement.[63]

It's difficult for bargainers to determine an appropriate settlement point where third-party interventions exist. Neither knows for certain what an arbitrator would view as appropriate. They also may doubt an imposed solution's workability.

Arbitral Criteria

Arbitrators apply certain criteria in deciding awards. Some state bargaining laws include an extensive set of criteria that arbitrators must consider in determining their awards. There are also precedents that have been established through previous arbitral awards that present day arbitrators recognize and to which they defer.

[61] Stern et al., *Final-Offer Arbitration*, pp. 77–115.

[62] C. A. Olson, "Dispute Resolution in the Public Sector," in B. Aaron, J. M. Najita, and J. L. Stern, eds., *Public Sector Bargaining*, 2nd ed. (Washington, DC: Bureau of National Affairs, 1988), pp. 160–188.

[63] P. F. Gerhart and J. F. Drotning, "The Effectiveness of Public-Sector Impasse Procedures," in D. B. Lipsky and J. Douglas, eds., *Advances in Industrial and Labor Relations*, 2 (Greenwich, CT: JAI Press, 1985), pp. 143–195.

One factor often considered is ability to pay. Nevada requires its assessment in arriving at an award.[64] The ability-to-pay issue may retard gains when revenues do not support wage demands. However, arbitrators are less concerned about the actual ability to pay than are elected officials.[65] A Wisconsin study found that economic awards were most frequently shaped by internal and external comparability of pay packages, less so by cost of living, and least by ability to pay.[66] Comparability in police arbitrations was important, with city offers having greater influence than the union.[67]

Managements and unions have some common and dissimilar preferences in their choice of an arbitrator. A study of New Jersey arbitrations found that management and union preferences were moderately similar and stressed arbitrators' experience levels. Unions preferred lawyer arbitrators, while managements preferred economists. Both sides were influenced by the direction of the arbitrator's previous awards.[68]

The Utility of Arbitration for Unions

Public safety unions strongly advocate binding arbitration to resolve impasses. While arbitration is obviously a method to resolve interest differences where strikes are prohibited, less information is available on its impact on bargaining outcomes. Two studies found relatively minimal wage effects (0 to 5 percent) associated with arbitration.[69] However, arbitration should serve to raise management offers, particularly in final-offer selection states. Management might be expected to concede toward an anticipated award, rather than risk having a union's extreme position chosen. For the union's part, it might likely take a harder line where it has arbitration available and not have to take the risk of an illegal strike. A study of firefighter arbitration laws found that arbitration was associated with higher salaries and shorter working hours the longer the law was in effect. Wage increases averaged about 11 to 22 percent higher in arbitration states.[70]

[64] J. R. Grodin, "Arbitration of Public-Sector Labor Disputes," *Industrial and Labor Relations Review*, 27 (1974), pp. 89–102.

[65] R. D. Horton, "Arbitration, Arbitrators, and the Public Interest," *Industrial and Labor Relations Review*, 27 (1975), pp. 497–507.

[66] G. G. Dell'Omo, "Wage Disputes in Interest Arbitration: Arbitrators Weight the Criteria," *Arbitration Journal*, 44, no. 2 (1989), pp. 4–13.

[67] S. Schwochau and P. Feuille, "Interest Arbitrators and Their Decision Behavior," *Industrial Relations*, 27 (1988), pp. 37–55.

[68] D. E. Bloom and C. L. Cavanagh, "An Analysis of the Selection of Arbitrators," *American Economic Review*, 76 (1986), pp. 408–422.

[69] Stern et al., *Final-Offer Arbitration*, pp. 77–115; and Kochan et al., *Dispute Resolution*, pp. 158–159.

[70] C. A. Olson, "The Impact of Arbitration on the Wages of Firefighters," *Industrial Relations*, 19 (1980), pp. 325–339.

The expected utility of arbitration to settle a dispute depends on the perceived threat presented by arbitration to both sides. The lower the expected utility from arbitration, the less favorable a settlement a party would be willing to accept.[71] Part of utility is related to direct costs. The higher the costs, the more likely parties are to negotiate their own settlement. Where this occurs, the less risk-averse party achieves higher outcomes.[72] In some situations, a union bargainer chooses arbitration where a satisfactory settlement might be negotiated to signal to members that the union isn't shirking negotiations and settling for less than it could have gotten.[73]

Strikes

Most states prohibit public employee strikes and have injunction and penalty provisions if they occur. Although most states forbid strikes, enforcing the prohibition is difficult. A long history of public employee strikes shows that legally permissible steps to end them are not invoked often and that statutorily mandated reprisals, such as discharges, are not frequently used. Job actions are actually about 25 to 30 percent higher in states where either strikes are not permitted or there is no other established final impasse procedure.[74] Strike incidence in the public sector is quite low. About 42 percent of all union members work in the public sector, but only 20 percent of strikes occur there, with only 12 percent of days lost to strikes attributable to the public sector.

More days are lost from strikes by public school teachers, and the duration of strikes is longest for school disputes. One reason for the level and duration of school strikes is that they are often essentially costless to both employers and employees. Legislatures establish school years of certain lengths, so if a strike disrupts the first three weeks of school, the year is simply extended three weeks. The only cost to the school or the teachers is the delay in school aid receipts and wages. The incidence and duration of school strikes are associated with state laws requiring a school year of a particular length and the local district's willingness to tax itself for greater educational costs.[75] Strikes are decreased when

[71] F. C. Champlin and M. F. Bognanno, "A Model for Arbitration and the Incentive to Bargain," in D. Lipsky and J. Douglas, eds., *Advances in Industrial and Labor Relations*, 3 (Greenwich, CT: JAI Press, 1986), pp. 153–390.

[72] H. S. Farber, M. A. Neale, and M. H. Bazerman, "The Role of Arbitration Costs and Risk Aversion in Dispute Outcomes," *Industrial Relations*, 29 (1990), pp. 361–384.

[73] B. P. McCall, "Interest Arbitration and the Incentive to Bargain: A Principal-Agent Approach," *Journal of Conflict Resolution*, 34 (1990), pp. 151–167.

[74] R. Hebdon and R. Stern, "Do Public-Sector Strike Bans Really Prevent Conflict?" *Industrial Relations*, 42 (2003), pp. 493–512.

[75] C. A. Olson, "The Impact of Rescheduled School Days on Teacher Strikes," *Industrial and Labor Relations Review*, 38 (1994), pp. 515–528.

lost school days are not rescheduled. Strike duration was predicted by neighboring districts paying higher salaries, variation in comparison salaries (uncertainty about an appropriate settlement point), and the unemployment rate (reduced bargaining power and willingness to be taxed). Duration was decreased by average income of residents (ability to pay), percent of teachers with master's degrees, and school days not rescheduled (forgone income).[76]

There is mixed evidence regarding the incidence of strikes. For police, the evidence suggests strikes occur less often when there is a provision for collective bargaining and arbitration to settle impasses.[77] On the other hand, strikes appear to be used when they are legal, or not prevented, as vehicles for increasing public employee bargaining power. Well-enforced penalties or threats of firing reduce public sector strikes, while poorly enforced laws have no effect, and permissive laws increase their frequency.[78] Strike incidence declines with both the length of experience of the bargainers and the relative equality of their experience level.[79] Where strikes are banned, grievance rates are higher, particularly on economic issues.[80]

Generally, strikes in the public sector are positively influenced by the rate of wage increases for private sector employees, increases in the cost of living, and fiscal belt-tightening. Private sector unemployment and recessions are related to reduced public sector strike activity.[81]

Studies of teacher strikes suggest they are not used as an offensive weapon to improve relative outcomes but are used as defensive weapons to maintain a relative position or to reverse erosion. Among Illinois and Iowa teachers, strikes are worth only about $285 annually. Overall, the availability of impasse resolution procedures influences wages by about

[76] X. Wang and L. Babcock, "Salary Comparisons and Public School Teachers Strikes," *Proceedings of the Industrial Relations Research Association*, 48 (1996), pp. 224–230.

[77] C. Ichniowski, "Arbitrators and Police Bargaining: Prescriptions for the Blue Flu," *Industrial Relations*, 21 (1982), pp. 149–166; and R. N. Horn, W. J. McGuire, and J. Tomkiewicz, "Work Stoppages by Teachers: An Empirical Analysis," *Journal of Labor Research*, 3 (1982), pp. 487–495.

[78] C. A. Olson, "Strikes, Strike Penalties, and Arbitration in Six States," *Industrial and Labor Relations Review*, 39 (1986), pp. 539–551; and D. M. Partridge, "Teacher Strikes and Public Policy: Does the Law Matter?" *Journal of Collective Negotiations in the Public Sector*, 25 (1996), pp. 3–22.

[79] E. Montgomery and M. E. Benedict, "The Impact of Bargainer Experience on Teacher Strikes," *Industrial and Labor Relations Review*, 42 (1989), pp. 380–392.

[80] R. P. Hebdon and R. N. Stern, "Tradeoffs among Expressions of Industrial Conflict: Public Sector Strike Bans and Grievance Arbitration," *Industrial and Labor Relations Review*, 51 (1998), pp. 204–221.

[81] W. B. Nelson, G. W. Stone Jr., and J. M. Swint, "An Economic Analysis of Public Sector Collective Bargaining and Strike Activity," *Journal of Labor Research*, 2 (1981), pp. 77–98.

10 percent.[82] Evidence from Pennsylvania finds that neither the incidence or duration of strikes is associated with student achievement.[83]

No-strike laws may have the unintended consequence of moving more negotiations to impasse. Without the threat of a strike and the opportunity for binding arbitration, there is a lower ability to elicit information, adjust expectations, and provide catharsis for the negotiating parties. Some illegal strikes in the public sector could have been avoided if a broader set of issues had been discussed and if information on the level and types of grievances under the expiring contract had been made available to mediators.[84]

Summary

The legal environment is a critical factor in public employee unionization because management ultimately determines the scope of bargaining rights. Public opinion predicts changes in the laws in some states, but generally rights are more restrictive in the public sector than in the private sector. Legislation is most conducive to bargaining in the industrialized North and East and is least conducive in rural or southern areas. Right-to-work laws for the private sector predict statutes prohibiting union activity in the public sector.

Where bargaining is permitted, issues are much the same as those in the private sector. Unionization varies, with AFSCME taking an industrial union approach and the uniformed services generally organized on a craft basis.

Unionization benefits public sector employees in the same ways and at roughly the same levels as it benefits employees in the private sector.

Impasse resolution varies widely by jurisdiction and occupation. In the federal government, the Federal Services Impasses Panel resolves disputes. In states providing for impasse resolution by statute, arbitrators usually handle uniformed services disputes. In other areas, fact-finding, mediation, and other methods are prescribed. Strikes are generally forbidden.

Evidence suggests that unions benefit from mandatory interest arbitration and strikes. Final-offer selection may reduce reliance on arbitration, but more recent evidence suggests that experience with arbitration lessens its future usage.

[82] J. T. Delaney, "Strikes, Arbitration, and Teacher Salaries: A Behavioral Analysis," *Industrial and Labor Relations Review*, 37 (1983), pp. 431–446.

[83] H. L. Zwerling, "Pennsylvania Teachers' Strikes and Academic Performance," *Journal of Collective Negotiations*, 32 (2008), pp. 151–172.

[84] R. Hebdon, "Behavioural Dimensions of Public Sector Illegal Strikes: Cases from Canada and the U.S.," *Relations Industrielles*, 53 (1998), pp. 667–690.

Discussion Questions

1. If government employees were to be given a limited right to strike, which occupations should be prohibited from striking, and under what conditions should the prohibition be enforced?
2. Since arbitrators are not responsible to the electorate, should they be allowed to make binding rulings on economic issues?
3. Should public employee unions be barred from making political contributions in jurisdictions in which they represent employees?
4. Civil service rules provide many public employees with a large measure of protection from arbitrary action, so why should public employees be allowed to organize?
5. Because fact-finding publicizes the major areas in dispute and a proposed settlement, why has it not been more successful, given the public's stake in the outcome?

Key Terms

Civil service employee, *542*
International Association of Fire Fighters (IAFF), *535*
Fraternal Order of Police (FOP), *536*
American Federation of Government Employees (AFGE), *536*
Multilateral bargaining, *545*
Fair-share, *546*
Narcotic effect, *554*
Final-offer arbitration, *554*

Case: *Teacher Bargaining at Pleasant Ridge*

The annual contract negotiations between the Pleasant Ridge Board of Education and the Pleasant Ridge Classroom Teachers Association (PRCTA) are due to begin July 1, one week from now. Under state law, the new contract must be signed by September 1 or an impasse will be declared. Following an impasse, state law requires simultaneous mediation and fact-finding. The fact-finder's report must be published no later than September 20. Under the law, the parties could arbitrate unresolved contract issues using a total-package final-offer selection approach if both agree that arbitration would be binding. The state law prohibits teacher strikes, but about 10 short strikes occurred in the state last year at the time school opened.

The contract at Pleasant Ridge was not signed until November 10 last year, even though mediation and fact-finding occurred. The PRCTA repeatedly requested arbitration, but the board refused. Although no strike occurred, two "sickouts" took place in October when teacher absence rates exceeded 90 percent and schools had to be closed. For the upcoming contract, considerable sentiment exists for "hitting the bricks" if negotiations are unsatisfactory.

About 5,000 students are enrolled at Pleasant Ridge in kindergarten through 12th grade. There are 200 teachers, of whom 190 are PRCTA members. Student populations are growing at about 5 percent per year at the secondary level and at 10 percent per year at the elementary level.

The school system's operating budget is funded from two sources: state school aid, based on student enrollments, and local property taxes. The legislature has maintained per-student funding at the current level for the upcoming school year even though the overall budget was cut by 2 percent to avoid a deficit. Local property taxes presently provide the other 60 percent, based on a 22-mill levy against assessed market value. Fifteen mills are permanently required by state law. The other 7 are supplemental and are periodically reconsidered by local voters. Five of the 7 mills expire this November and will be subject to reapproval by the voters in the general election. Residential property values decreased last year by 4 percent, while commercial properties decreased by 2 percent.

School costs are approximately equally divided between salaries and plant, equipment, supplies, lighting and heating, and reduction of bonded indebtedness. Of the 50 percent allocated to salaries, 80 percent is paid to the instructional staff represented by the PRCTA. Costs for equipment and supplies are increasing at an annual rate of 2 percent, while utility costs are increasing by 25 percent. Of the 50 percent not allocated to salaries, about 20 percent was paid for utilities last year.

The teacher contract includes a defined benefit pension plan. Pension benefits are based on the average total pay that teachers earn during their last three years of employment, times 1.5 percent, times number of full school years of service in the district. Since 1990, the contract has contained a "rule of 85" clause. Under that clause, a teacher whose age and years of service in the district equal or exceed 85, and who is under the age of 65, may retire and continue to have the district provide health care benefits at the same level as if he or she were employed full-time until becoming Medicare-eligible at age 65. The district currently has 50 retired teachers, with 15 of those between the ages of 55 and 65 who met "rule of 85" criteria when retiring. During the next five years, about 30 teachers will meet "rule of 85" requirements.

The PRCTA bargaining committee has just completed its contract demands. Major areas in which it demands changes include a 2 percent salary increase, a reduction in maximum class size from 30 to 25 in the elementary grades (K–6), and the granting of tenure after the second year of teaching, instead of the fourth. Because about 2,700 students are in the K–6 program, a reduction in class sizes would boost teacher employment. The tenure change would affect 25 second-year and 25 third-year teachers who are now not covered. In case of staff reductions (which are based on seniority in the district), tenured employees who are terminated are entitled to one year's pay under the contract. As part of its preparations for negotiations, the PRCTA surveyed comparable schools and found its members' pay is about 5 percent below the market rate, tenure is normally granted after three years, and the median elementary class size (by contract) is 27.

As the school's governing body, the Pleasant Ridge Board of Education must ultimately approve the contract if arbitration is not used. The district's superintendent, personnel director, high school principal, and two elementary principals form the management bargaining team. The school board consists of five persons. Two of these are union members, and three (including these two) were endorsed by the Pleasant Ridge Central Labor Union (PRCLU) at the last election. Two other candidates endorsed by the PRCLU lost to the other present board members. At that last election, two mills of the supplementary tax were added, but the margin was only 500 out of 10,000 votes cast.

QUESTIONS

1. What should be the initial bargaining position of the school board? What data justify this position?
2. What should the PRCTA consider a reasonable settlement?
3. If fact-finding occurs, what should the fact-finder use as criteria in recommending a settlement? What should the recommendation be?
4. Should the board go to arbitration if an agreement cannot be negotiated?
5. What strategies should the management and union negotiators use to win their demands?
6. If the negotiations go to arbitration as a final-offer package, what should each party's offer be for the arbitrator?

A Survey of Labor Relations in Market Economies

This chapter provides an overview of labor relations in market economies around the world. Labor organizations vary substantially in their involvement in political activity, collective bargaining, and decision-making within societies, industries, and enterprises. Their organizational structures differ as well. The previous chapters dealt with the development, structure, and process issues that influence and describe labor relations in the United States. This chapter compares the development of labor movements, their structures, and the manner in which processes are implemented in market economies. The chapter focuses on the basics of labor relations among both older and newer European Union (EU) members, Australia, Japan, and the developing economies of East Asia.

Since an entire text could be written on labor relations in any of these countries, this chapter provides only a brief overview that will acquaint you with the topic and direct you to more detailed and analytical treatments.

In reading this chapter, consider the following issues:

1. What are the major differences in the influence and operation of labor unions in North America and Western Europe?
2. How are the plant-level needs of workers addressed in countries where bargaining occurs at the industry and employer association level?
3. How does the role of the government in labor-management relations differ across developed market-based economies?
4. What are the advantages and disadvantages for workers, unions, and employers of the various structures of labor-management relations examined in this chapter?

THE DEVELOPMENT OF LABOR MOVEMENTS

The development of European labor unions roughly paralleled the development of unions in the United States, with some variation across countries depending on political activities. German unions began to form with the 1848 revolution but did not gain momentum until after the antisocialist laws promulgated under Bismarck were repealed.[1] Swedish unions gained adherents in the late 19th and early 20th centuries. British unions began to organize about the same time and in the same manner as did the Knights of Labor in the United States. As discussed in this chapter, only British collective bargaining resembles U.S. labor relations, with recognition initially obtained primarily at the plant level and with generally adversarial bargaining at the establishment or corporate level.

As in the United States, several types of unions emerged in Europe during the formative period. Germany and England were early spawning grounds for revolutionary approaches to government and employment. Karl Marx advocated the takeover of the state by the proletariat (rank and file) together with state ownership of the means of production to end the exploitation of workers. Under this approach, the goals of unions and the state are synonymous. Anarchists and syndicalists advocated abolishing the state and/or capitalistic ownership of the means of production. In Great Britain, the Fabians and other socialists favored state ownership and planned economies to better allocate wealth among a population and to choose desired outputs.

In Sweden in the late 1890s, labor organized into a variety of federations forming the Swedish Confederation of Trade Unions (LO). This was followed around 1900 by employers forming the Swedish Employers' Confederation (SAF). In 1906 the SAF recognized the LO's right to unionize, and the LO recognized managerial prerogatives. Industrywide agreements were negotiated during the 1900 to 1910 decade after major strikes.[2] Substantial conflict continued between labor and management until the 1930s when the government moved into the hands of the Social Democrats, whose agenda meshed closely with labor, separating the political and economic power of employers for the first time. After some adjustments, an era of consultation and cooperation was begun that continues to some extent today.

Japanese unions emerged in the 1890s after the country's industrial revolution. Unions were active before World War II and were encouraged by the United States during the martial law period after the war.

[1] "Germany: Industrial Relations Background," *European Industrial Relations Review*, 216 (1992), pp. 21–27.

[2] W. Korpi, "Industrial Relations and Industrial Conflict: The Case of Sweden," in B. Martin and E. M. Kassalow, eds., *Labor Relations in Advanced Industrial Societies: Issues and Problems* (Washington, DC: Carnegie Endowment for International Peace, 1980), pp. 89–108.

Following the war, unions exhibited Marxist tendencies when real wages were low but became more enterprise-oriented as productivity and wages increased. As in most industrialized countries, unions in Japan affiliate with federations.[3]

While many unions in Europe originally had socialist agendas, they have increasingly accommodated capitalism in free-market economies. In Germany, formerly Marxist unions have increasingly acted as intermediaries, representing worker interests and ameliorating the effects of changes in supporting a dynamic economy within democratic capitalism.[4]

Unions in socialist economies are expected to assist in meeting production goals and maintaining discipline since everyone is expected to conform to statist objectives. The community of interests of the state and its citizens precludes legitimate goal conflict. Pay inequality in most socialist economies was smaller than in capitalist societies except in the old USSR. In economies that switched from socialistic to market oriented, unionization remained high in the state-owned sector but not in the private sector. Private wages are generally higher. When state-owned companies are sold to private investors in Hungary, new owners must establish works councils; while in Poland, one-third of a company's board of directors' seats are given to workers' representatives.[5]

Major changes in unionization in Eastern Europe followed the fall of communism. In Poland, the Solidarity movement was largely responsible for catalyzing the breakdown of the Communist system, and its leader, Lech Wałęsa, led the government following the collapse of martial law. Solidarity accepted the consolidation of owner rights during the transformation period. Governance of organizations shifted from employees to shareholders. Co-governance was seen as a hindrance to a transition to a market economy.[6] In the former East Germany rapid privatization undermined union influence, but extension of the German codetermination law and centralized bargaining offset the decline.[7] After communism, the East Germans, as compared to the Hungarians, had a more centralized union structure with already-existing German unions extended to them. On the other hand, Hungary established primarily enterprise-based unions and

[3] K. Koike, *Understanding Industrial Relations in Modern Japan* (New York: St. Martin's Press, 1988).

[4] O. Jacobi, "World Economic Changes and Industrial Relations in the Federal Republic of Germany," in H. Juris, M. Thompson, and W. Daniels, eds., *Industrial Relations in a Decade of Economic Change* (Madison, WI: Industrial Relations Research Association, 1985), pp. 211–246.

[5] R. J. Flanagan, "Institutional Reformation in Eastern Europe," *Industrial Relations*, 37 (1998), pp. 337–357.

[6] M. Weinstein, "Solidarity's Abandonment of Worker Councils: Redefining Employee Stakeholder Rights in Post-Socialist Poland," *British Journal of Industrial Relations*, 38 (2000), pp. 49–74.

[7] U. Jurgens, L. Klinzing, and L. Turner, "The Transformation of Industrial Relations in Eastern Germany," *Industrial and Labor Relations Review*, 46 (1992), pp. 229–244.

union-controlled mandatory works councils. East Germans were more committed to their unions, while Hungarians had more confidence in their managements. However, Hungarians were more positive about their former Communist unions than were the East Germans.[8]

In Poland changes in union philosophies toward supporting a market economy occurred gradually as state intervention was seen as a decreasingly viable alternative for catalyzing change.[9] Compared to workers in Western countries, ex-Communist country workers were more egalitarian, expressed lower job satisfaction, and more strongly supported trade unions. As wage differentials increased in Eastern Europe following the collapse of communism, support for egalitarianism decreased.[10] In the Polish state-owned sector, employees were more likely to join unions if they intended to make a career with that employer and more likely to quit the union if they planned to change jobs in the future.[11]

Unionization and union membership in affluent economies is strongly influenced by institutional factors and less by economic or solidaristic variables. In general, leftist governments implement policies that promote unionization, while rightist governments reduce the emphasis on worker influence in the workplace and the facilitation of unionization. There is also some evidence that the welfare state acts as a substitute for unionization, in that unionization is lower the higher a country's welfare benefits (all else equal). Economic variables such as the degree of globalization have relatively little effect.[12]

THE STRUCTURE OF LABOR MOVEMENTS

In the United States, the locus of power is vested in the national unions, organized on a craft or industrial basis. This model does not hold for most free-market industrialized nations. Most other nations concentrate union control in labor federations or at the local level.

Swedish unions concentrate power in the LO, which deals with the employers' SAF. In Germany, a small number of national unions do most of the bargaining. British unions organize into nationals, but locals retain

[8] C. M. Frege and A. Tóth, "The Cultural Embeddedness of Labor Relations from Two Post-Communist Economies," *Proceedings of the Industrial Relations Research Association*, 51 (1999), pp. 110–121.

[9] M. Sewerynski, "Changes in Polish Labour Law and Industrial Relations during the Period of Post-Communist Transition," *Bulletin of Comparative Labour Relations*, 31 (1996), pp. 85–108.

[10] D. G. Blanchflower and R. B. Freeman, "The Attitudinal Legacy of Communist Labor Relations," *Industrial and Labor Relations Review*, 50 (1997), pp. 438–459.

[11] P. Zientara and G.Kuczyński, "Employees' Desire to Join or Leave a Union: Evidence from Poland," *Industrial Relations*, 48 (2009), pp. 185–192.

[12] D. Brady, "Institutional, Economic, or Solidaristic? Assessing Explanations for Unionization across Affluent Democracies," *Work and Occupations*, 34 (2007), pp. 67–101.

a good deal of authority. Local unions in many countries have primarily geographic relationships (somewhat similar to the early Knights of Labor in the United States) rather than corporate relationships.[13] Italy, France, and the Netherlands have politically or religiously based national federations. Some employees in the Netherlands also organize along religious lines.[14] National unions are increasingly merging in the EU, similar to the trend in the United States.[15] Union leaders in Europe are more entrenched than those in the United States, particularly at the local level, because in Europe there are fewer elections.[16] In Japan, although most bargaining is conducted at the local or enterprise level, most locals affiliate with a national.[17] Enterprise unions there usually include both blue-collar and white-collar workers.[18]

In the United States, a variety of characteristics are related to interest and participation in union activities. Japanese union member activity is predicted relatively similarly. For example, length of membership in the union, pay levels, dissatisfaction with pay and working conditions, interaction with others in the work group, and perceptions of union effectiveness and democracy predict participation in Japan. Contrary to the case in the United States, age and educational attainment are negatively related, and job status is unrelated.[19]

Because union members and employees in many European countries have little involvement in contract negotiations at the plant or enterprise level, there is little rank-and-file participation in union activities. Since negotiated agreements in major industries are usually adopted by other employers, there is less motivation to join unions in Europe than there is in the United States. Paradoxically, in some countries such as France, where union contract coverage is very high, union membership is even lower than that in the United States.

Works Councils

In Germany, most establishments are required to have **works councils.** These councils advise management on employment matters and may also be consulted in the overall strategy of the organization. In general, works councils have rights to codetermine with management issues such as work

[13] J. P. Windmuller, "Comparative Study of Methods and Practices," in J. P. Windmuller, ed., *Collective Bargaining in Industrialized Market Economies: A Reappraisal* (Geneva: International Labour Office, 1987), pp. 3–158.

[14] T. Kennedy, *European Labor Relations* (Lexington, MA: Lexington Books, 1980).

[15] Windmuller, "Comparative Study."

[16] Poole, *Industrial Relations.*

[17] Koike, *Understanding Industrial Relations in Japan.*

[18] Ibid.

[19] S. Kuruvilla, D. G. Gallagher, J. Fiorito, and M. Wakabayashi, "Union Participation in Japan: Do Western Theories Apply?" *Industrial and Labor Relations Review*, 43 (1990), pp. 374–389.

schedules, pay systems, selection criteria, and training programs. They have veto rights regarding recruitment, restructuring, and dismissal decisions. They are entitled to consultation and information rights regarding health and safety issues, human resource planning, and information about major business plans and anticipated changes in equipment, work processes, or locations of production. Works councils are more likely to be created in larger, older firms with more highly educated workers and where managers support employee participation.[20]

There may be an operational conflict between unions and works councils. Evidence suggests works councils may be more interested in preserving plant interests than those of the union with which many of the plant's employees are associated.[21] In Germany, a corporatist approach is taken, with labor and management operating as "social partners." German unions have extensive technical expertise because they employ an extensive professional administration. German unions are highly consolidated; only 17 major nationals currently exist.[22] Evidence from a study of German companies finds that having a works council is related to the likelihood of a plant closing, especially among newer, smaller, single-establishment employers that have a high proportion of employees whose employment continues for a fixed term.[23] On the other hand, the creation or dissolution of a works council does affect a firm's investment decisions contrary to what happens when unionization or deunionization occurs in the United States.[24]

At the EU level, the European Work Council (EWC) ("Vredeling") directive was passed in 1994 in anticipation of increasing consolidation and creation of transnational industries in Europe as a result of increased economic integration. It was pushed by the European Trade Union Congress and opposed by employers. This corporatist approach was forwarded by social democratic representatives aiming to increase the relative power of labor organizations from what they considered to be a weaker position, although the mechanism for balancing the relationship was through consultation and veto rights rather than collective bargaining.[25]

[20] U. Jirjahn and S. C. Smith, "What Factors Lead Managers to Support or Oppose Employee Participation—With and Without Works Councils? Hypotheses and Evidence from Germany," *Industrial Relations*, 45 (2006), pp. 650–680.

[21] K. R. Wever, "Industrial Relations Developments in France, West Germany, the U.K., and Sweden: An American Assessment," *Proceedings of the Industrial Relations Research Association*, 41 (1988), pp. 361–364.

[22] C. Lane, *Management and Labour in Europe* (Hampshire, England: Edward Elgar, 1989).

[23] J. T. Addison, L. Bellmann, and A Kölling, "Works Councils and Plant Closing in Germany," *British Journal of Industrial Relations*, 42 (2004), pp. 125–148.

[24] J. T. Addison, T. Schank, C. Schnabel, and J. Wagner, "Do Works Councils Inhibit Investment?" *Industrial and Labor Relations Review*, 60 (2007), pp. 187–203.

[25] P. Knutsen, "European Works Councils and the Development of a Euro-Corporatist Model," in I. Fitzgerald and J. Stirling, eds., *European Works Councils: Pessimism of the Intellect, Optimism of the Will?* (London: Routledge, 2004), pp. 17–33.

The directive requires that transnational employers set up works councils with representatives from all the EU countries in which the employer operates.[26] In many situations, the EWCs are more symbolic than influential, and progress in transnational bargaining in EU industries is uneven.[27] In the automobile manufacturing sector, more influential EWCs have emerged to deal with overcapacity problems. Agreements have been concluded that prohibit forced layoffs and provide for spreading the "pain" of employment reductions across facilities rather than concentrating on a specific location. Transnational bargaining, greater information exchange, and EU-wide codes of conduct have been developed, but cross-national wage coordination has not.[28] Volkswagen, Daimler-Benz, and Renault have extended coordinated consultation in voluntarily formed world works councils.[29] EU works council representation within a multinational company seems to represent national interests rather than adopting a European viewpoint.[30]

Globalization

Economic globalization has accelerated since the early 1980s. Various regions have experienced rapid economic development as the result of extensive state or foreign direct investment, primarily in manufacturing. In Asia, development has been most rapid in China, Indonesia, Korea, Malaysia, Singapore, Taiwan, and Thailand. Eastern Europe has shifted from communism toward market economics at varying rates, with faster earlier progress in the Czech Republic, Hungary, and Poland and more recently in Slovakia and Slovenia. Mexico and Latin America have also been strongly influenced by globalization and foreign investment.

During the same period, regional trade treaties have been enacted in various areas. The most prominent include the EU, NAFTA, and Mercosur (Argentina, Brazil, Paraguay, and Uruguay). Regionalization and globalization of the economy have put increasing pressure on unions and reduced their ability to increase wages given the increasingly competitive nature of product markets. Unions have tried to influence the "social

[26] S. Stoop, "'Thriving on Diversity' Revisited," in I. Fitzgerald and J. Stirling, eds., *European Works Councils: Pessimism of the Intellect, Optimism of the Will?* (London: Routledge, 2004), pp. 48–61.

[27] S. LeQueux and G. Fajertag, "Towards Europeanization of Collective Bargaining? Insights from the Chemical Industry," *European Journal of Industrial Relations*, 7 (2001), pp. 117–136.

[28] I. Greer and M. Hauptmeier, "Political Entrepreneurs and Co-Managers: Labour Transnationalism at Four Multinational Companies," *British Journal of Industrial Relations*, 46 (2008), pp. 76–97.

[29] I. Da Costa and U. Rehfeldt, "European Unions and American Automobile Firms: From European Works Councils to World Councils?" *Proceedings of the Labor and Employment Relations Association*, 58 (2006), pp. 105–112.

[30] J. Waddington, "The Performance of European Works Councils in Engineering: Perspectives of the Employee Representatives," *Industrial Relations*, 45 (2006), pp. 681–708.

dimension" of the EU and NAFTA but have had only limited success.[31] One of the major difficulties they face in regionalization and globalization is that they are almost always national organizations that have little ability to coordinate pressure across political boundaries. In Mexico, divisions in the labor movement, labor's political isolation, undemocratic union structures, and a lack of innovative strategies and tactics disabled efforts to influence extension of some protective labor regulations during the development of NAFTA.[32] Militant responses were more likely to come from autonomous and democratic unions that were not part of Mexico's state-corporatist labor confederation.[33]

Transnational organizations and neoconservative political control of developed economies have contributed to market integration and a decline in union bargaining power and interest in the welfare state.[34]

Developing economies may adopt one of two basic approaches (or a mix of them) to industrialize: import-substitution industrialization (ISI) or export-oriented industrialization (EOI). ISI strategies have limited growth implications since there is probably some limit on the potential level of internal consumption, particularly given income levels. EOI strategies require that output be either substantially cheaper or of better quality than the domestic products with which it will compete. Figure 17.1 presents a model of industrialization strategies, national industrial relations policy goals, and their likely consequences.[35]

Figure 17.1 indicates that countries in the first stage of EOI are primarily competing by containing costs. Some of this may result from repressive measures such as relaxing labor standards and banning labor organizations. The second stage, which requires high-quality and higher-value-added output, requires increases in worker skills and productivity. Repression ceases to be an effective strategy as a developing middle class gains the opportunity to exercise political power. Strikes, even if outlawed, are more likely to lead to change.

Competition leads employers and the state to look for ways to attract investment. One way to do this is to enhance labor's effectiveness to the

[31] R. Hyman, "Trade Unions and European Integration," *Work and Occupations*, 24 (1997), pp. 309–331.

[32] W. Vanderbush, "Mexican Labor in the Era of Economic Restructuring and NAFTA: Working to Create a Favorable Investment Climate," *Labor Studies Journal*, 20, no. 4 (1996), pp. 58–86.

[33] J. P. Tuman, "Unions and Restructuring in the Mexican Automobile Industry: A Comparative Assessment," *Industrial Relations Journal*, 27 (1996), pp. 317–330.

[34] T. Boswell and D. Stevis, "Globalization and International Labor Organizing," *Work and Occupations*, 24 (1997), pp. 288–308.

[35] S. C. Kuruvilla, "Economic Development Strategies, Industrial Relations Policies and Workplace IR/HR Practices in Southeast Asia," in K. S. Wever and L. Turner, eds., *The Comparative Political Economy of Industrial Relations* (Madison, WI: Industrial Relations Research Association, 1995), pp. 115–150.

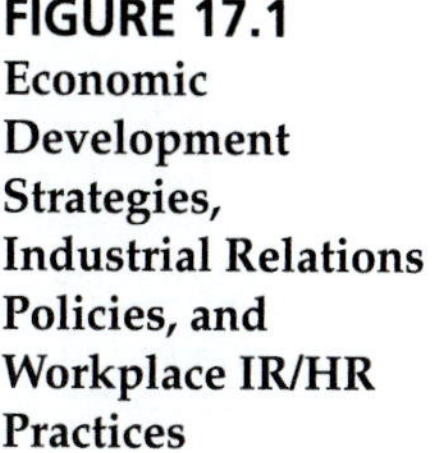

FIGURE 17.1
Economic Development Strategies, Industrial Relations Policies, and Workplace IR/HR Practices

Source: S. C. Kuruvilla, "Economic Development Strategies, Industrial Relations Policies and Workplace IR/HR Practices in Southeast Asia," in K. S. Wever and L. Turner, eds., *The Comparative Political Economy of Industrial Relations* (Madison, WI: Industrial Relations Research Association, 1995), p. 120.

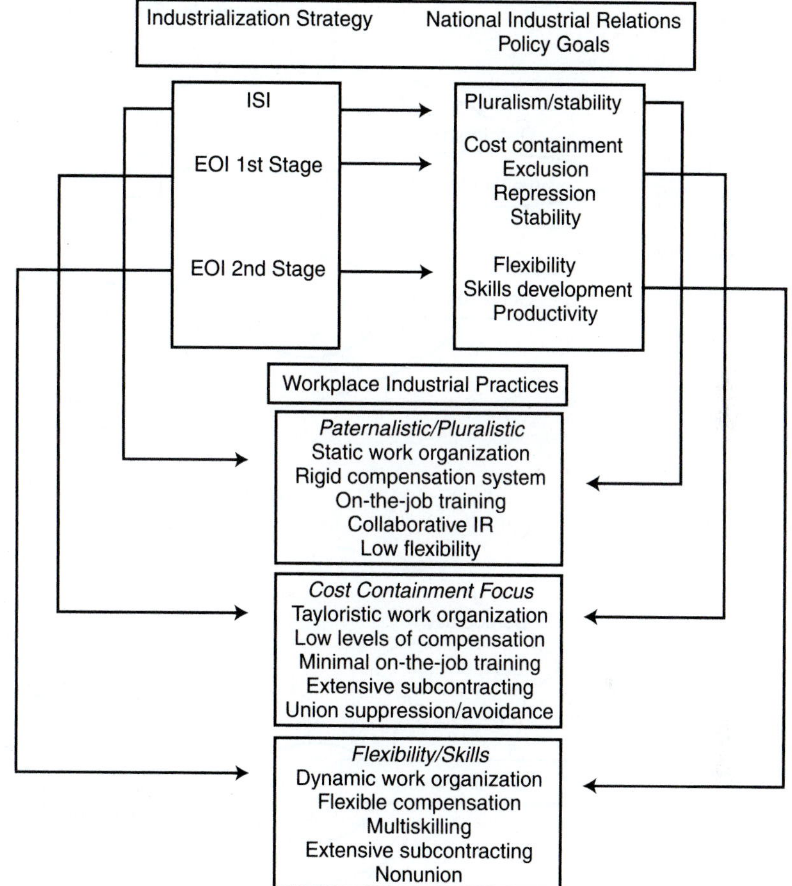

benefit of capital. In the short term, holding down real wages while boosting productivity will accomplish this. The willingness of state-owned employers to participate in this process is related to exposure to foreign investors, but it is also related to the nation's culture and politics.[36]

It is argued that political regimes, especially in countries without a democratic tradition, make a choice about whether to adopt a repressive or benign policy toward labor unions. Where unions are likely to create an opposition political force, repressive approaches are probably more likely. Repressive forces may also be used when the state has a strong need (possibly for corrupt reasons) to tap the results of economic growth. Figure 17.2 depicts systematic relationships between state and labor components

[36] S. J. Frenkel and D. Peetz, "Globalization and Industrial Relations in East Asia: A Three-Century Comparison," *Industrial Relations*, 37 (1998), pp. 282–310.

FIGURE 17.2
State Policy—Unionization Relationships

Source: R. B. Freeman, "Repressive Labor Relations and New Unionism in East Asia," *Proceedings of the Industrial Relations Research Association*, 46 (1994), p. 235.

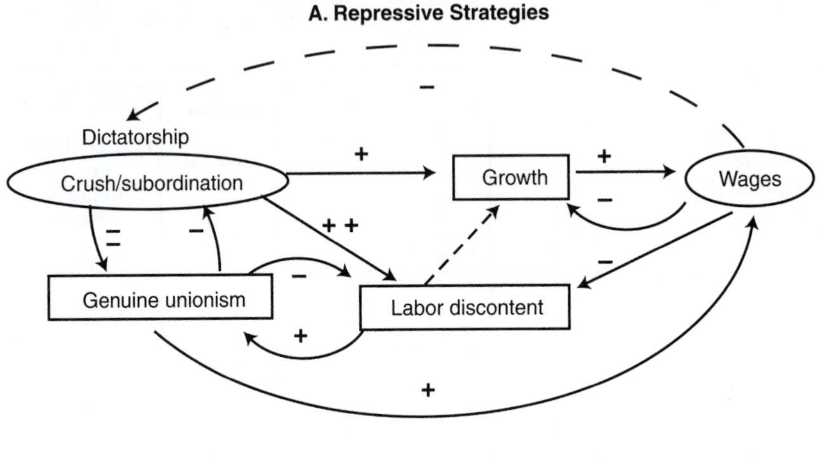

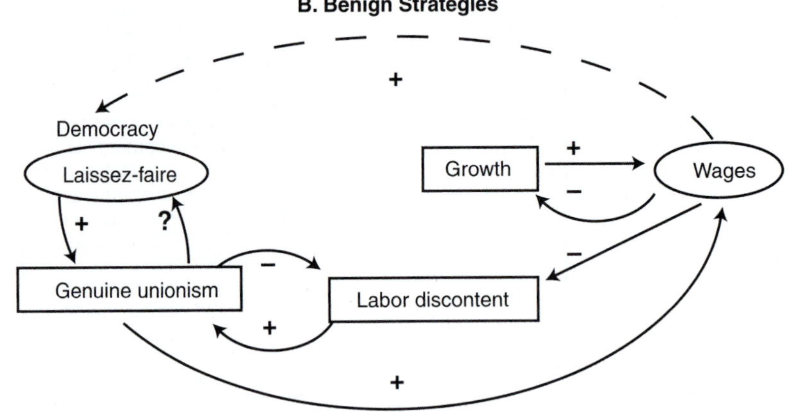

under repressive and benign strategies.[37] In the figure, arrows show the direction of effects, oval shapes relate to state policy variables (labor and wage), and broken lines represent long-term effects. Growth permits wage increases, but rapid wage growth would reduce economic growth. Dictatorships would be likely to repress unionization and directly influence labor discontent that, in the absence of unionization, would have no expression except to reduce growth. In the benign strategy, wage growth could reduce labor discontent, and this would reduce unionization. On the other hand, democracy would also lead to greater opportunities to unionize, which would have a likelihood of raising wages.[38]

[37] R. B. Freeman, "Repressive Labor Relations and New Unionism in East Asia," *Proceedings of the Industrial Relations Research Association*, 46 (1994), pp. 231–238.

[38] Ibid.

For their part, unions in various developing economies face multinational employers in a variety of different manners. A study of union reactions to foreign investment in Argentina, South Korea, and Spain suggests that multinationals may be viewed as "villains," "necessary evils," "arm's-length collaborators," or "partners." In all of these countries, authoritarian governments and unions initially opposed investment by multinationals. Over time the view has shifted in Argentina toward "a necessary evil"; in Korea toward limited collaboration; and in Spain, which has taken a modernist as opposed to a populist approach, toward a partnership.[39]

ORGANIZING AND REPRESENTATION

Organizing and representation outside North America is unlike what occurs in the United States. With the exception of Great Britain, in EU member nations workers do not vote in their workplaces to be represented. Rather, unions are recognized at the national or federation level by their employer counterparts and bargaining over a basic contract occurs at that level.

Exclusive representation is uncommon outside the United States. In some European countries, employers deal with several unions in a workplace, each with slightly different agendas. This situation is prevalent in countries with unions that have religious ties. As discussed below, the multiplicity of representatives and the lack of exclusive jurisdiction do not lead to problems.

Union security differs substantially across Europe. In most countries union security is not an issue since several unions may represent employees in what would be considered a bargaining unit in the United States.[40] In Great Britain, representation is possible only when employers give voluntary recognition. While union membership declined in Great Britain between 1979 and 1991, there was no increase in the rate at which employers declined to recognize worker representatives.[41]

Union density (percentage of the workforce that belongs to unions) varies widely among European nations. Table 17.1 shows differences in membership rates that vary from 86 percent in Iceland to 8 percent in France. The Nordic countries range between 53 and 86 percent, while Belgium is the only other European nation with more than 50 percent membership.

[39] M. F. Guillén, "Organized Labor's Images of Multinational Enterprise: Divergent Foreign Investment Ideologies in Argentina, South Korea, and Spain," *Industrial and Labor Relations Review*, 53 (2000), pp. 419–442.

[40] T. Kennedy, *European Labor Relations*.

[41] M. Wright, "The Collapse of Compulsory Unionism? Collective Organization in Highly Unionized British Companies, 1979–1991," *British Journal of Industrial Relations*, 34 (1996), pp. 497–514; and P. Willman and A. Bryson, "Union Organization in Great Britain," *Journal of Labor Research*, 28 (2007), pp. 93–115.

TABLE 17.1 Union Density (1970–2008) and Union Coverage in Selected Market Economies

Sources: Adapted from J. Visser, "Union Membership Statistics in 24 Countries," *Monthly Labor Review*, 129, no. 1 (2006), pp. 45–46; http://stats.oecd.org/Index.aspx?DataSetCode=UN_DEN (2010); and M. van Klaveren and K. Tijdens, "Trade Union Membership and Collective Bargaining Coverage: Four Options," www.wageindicator.org/documents/publicationslist/publications-2010/Trade-union-membership-and-collective-bargaining-coverage-Four-options.pdf.

	Union Membership Density (%), Year Closest to:					Bargaining Coverage
	1970	1980	1990	2000	2008	
Australia	50.2	49.5	40.5	24.7	18.6	18.9
Austria	62.8	56.7	46.9	36.5	28.9	99.0
Belgium	42.1	54.1	53.9	55.1	51.9	73.0
Canada	31.6	34.7	32.9	28.1	27.1	29.0
Chile	NA	NA	NA	13.5	13.6	28.0
Czech Republic	NA	NA	78.8	27.0	20.2	39.0
Denmark	60.3	78.6	75.3	73.3	67.6	NA
Finland	18.3	69.4	72.5	75.0	67.5	90.0
France	21.7	18.3	10.1	8.2	7.7	95.0
Germany	32.0	34.9	31.2	25.0	19.1	55.0
Greece	NA	NA	NA	26.5	24.0	NA
Hungary	NA	NA	NA	19.9	16.8	55.0
Iceland	NA	NA	NA	81.7	86.4	NA
Ireland	53.2	57.1	51.1	38.4	32.3	34.5
Italy	37.0	49.6	38.8	34.9	33.4	87.0
Japan	35.1	31.1	25.4	21.5	18.2	22.2
Korea	12.6	14.7	17.6	11.1	10.3	NA
Mexico	NA	NA	NA	16.9	17.4	46.0
Netherlands	36.5	34.8	24.3	23.1	18.9	74.0
New Zealand	55.2	69.1	51.0	22.7	20.8	NA
Norway	56.8	58.3	58.5	53.7	53.3	55.5
Poland	NA	NA	53.1	24.2	15.6	49.0
Portugal	NA	NA	NA	21.6	20.4	NA
Slovak Republic	NA	NA	78.7	32.3	16.8	NA
Spain	NA	12.9	12.5	16.1	14.3	67.0
Sweden	67.7	78.0	80.8	79.1	68.3	77.0
Switzerland	28.9	31.1	24.3	19.4	18.3	NA
Turkey	NA	NA	NA	9.9	5.8	NA
United Kingdom	44.8	50.7	39.3	29.7	27.1	34.0
United States	23.5	19.5	15.5	12.8	11.9	12.0

Between 1990 and 2008, union densities declined in every country in Europe except Iceland and Spain.

There are no developed countries outside Europe with a union density rate higher than 27 percent (Canada). Similar to countries in Europe, all other developed economies saw decreases in membership between 1990 and 2008. In general, unions are in decline in Asia and have lower influence there than in Western countries.[42]

[42] S. Kuruvilla, S. Das, H. Kwon, and S. Kwon, "Trade Union Growth and Decline in Asia," *British Journal of Industrial Relations*, 40 (2002), pp. 431–461.

On the other hand, in 1994 union coverage (employment conditions determined by a collective agreement) was 70 percent or more in 7 of the 16 developed economies shown in Table 17.1. Outside Europe, coverage rates are only slightly higher than density rates, while in Europe, coverage rates equal or exceed 90 percent in Austria, Finland, and France.[43]

Union bargaining coverage is quite low in the United States, reflecting, among other things, greater resistance among employers to unionization. Union wage premiums are generally higher in the United States. Additionally, the variation in earnings is decreased more by unionization in the United States than in all other developed countries but Switzerland.[44]

Trade union density has declined in most developed economies in which membership and coverage are substantially equal. Most of the decline is unrelated to adversarial relationships, per se. Demographic, legal, and occupational changes account for about 30 percent of the British decline.[45] Similar declines are beginning to occur in other more heavily unionized industrial countries. In the English-speaking world, evidence indicates that employees exhibit a relatively high degree of job satisfaction and a relatively low demand for union representation except in problem workplaces.[46] Employees in British nonunion workplaces perceive their employers as being more responsive to employee problems and needs than do employees in unionized situations.[47] However, the adoption of human resource management practices in unionized employers is not associated with declining union density in those workplaces.[48] In addition, employment rights that have been previously secured through collective bargaining have increasingly become protected by statute.

Strong local unions and the official institution of work participation mechanisms are associated with higher union density among nations of the EU. The local level is the point at which most workers assess whether union membership is to their benefit. France has unimportant locals with little voice in participation (France also has the lowest density rate), although legislation passed in the early 1980s encouraging participation

[43] J. Visser, "Union Membership Statistics in 24 Countries," *Monthly Labor Review*, 129, no. 1 (2006), pp. 38–49.

[44] D. G. Blanchflower and R. B. Freeman, "Unionism in the United States and Other Advanced OECD Countries," *Industrial Relations*, 31 (1992), pp. 56–79.

[45] F. Green, "Recent Trends in British Trade Union Density," *British Journal of Industrial Relations*, 30 (1992), pp. 445–458.

[46] P. Boxall and P. Haynes, "Employee Voice in the Anglo-American World: An Overview of Five National Surveys," *Proceedings of the Labor and Employment Relations Association*, 57 (2005), pp. 139–150.

[47] A. Bryson, "Managerial Responsiveness to Union and Nonunion Worker Voice in Britain," *Industrial Relations*, 43 (2004), pp. 213–241.

[48] S. Machin and S. Wood, "Human Resource Management as a Substitute for Trade Unions in British Workplaces," *Industrial and Labor Relations Review*, 58 (2005), pp. 201–218.

has led to more bargaining and employee involvement.[49] Great Britain and Italy (with density rates close to 30 percent) have strong locals but no participation mechanisms ensured. Germany, Sweden, and Belgium (with rates between 19 and 68 percent) have strong locals with participation ensured.[50]

Why does union density fall far short of union coverage in most of Europe? Mandatory membership is not important in Europe since there is no exclusive representation requirement in most countries. Probabilities of joining a union are increased among recently hired men who work in the public sector, have a pro-union attitude, perceive the benefits of joining to exceed the costs, expect to use union services, and believe they have limited job mobility opportunities. Leavers are more likely to be female, older when initially joining, longer-term members, becoming unemployed or changing jobs, coming from a nonunion parental family, and having a first child if a woman.[51] In Great Britain desires for unionization are related to job dissatisfaction, left-wing views, and perceived union instrumentality.[52]

High union density and coverage in Europe are found in countries in which unions share responsibility with their national governments in administering the social welfare system, particularly regarding unemployment benefits. Thus, unemployment persons and retired workers who are not labor force participants are likely to continue their memberships to be more closely linked with the welfare programs their unions help administer.[53]

BARGAINING ISSUES

Bargaining issues in countries outside the United States are both broader and narrower. Because most countries do not have a collective bargaining law, bargaining issues or methods are unspecified. Thus, there are no distinctions between mandatory, permissive, or prohibited issues. Bargaining issues and outcomes differ from country to country depending on the economic policies of the government and the degree to which the country has central planning or income policies.[54] Further, except in Sweden and

[49] "France: A Decade of the 'Auroux' Laws," *European Industrial Relations Review*, 233 (1993), pp. 30–32.

[50] B. Hancke, "Trade Union Membership in Europe, 1960–90: Rediscovering Local Unions," *British Journal of Industrial Relations*, 31 (1993), pp. 593–614.

[51] J. Visser, "Why Fewer Workers Join Unions in Europe: A Social Custom Explanation of Membership Trends," *British Journal of Industrial Relations*, 40 (2002), pp. 403–420.

[52] A. Charlwood, "Why Do Non-Union Employees Want to Unionize? Evidence from Britain," *British Journal of Industrial Relations*, 40 (2002), pp. 463–491.

[53] J. Pencavel, "Unionism Viewed Internationally," *Journal of Labor Research*, 26 (2005), pp. 65–96.

[54] Poole, *Industrial Relations*.

France, there is no legal duty to bargain, although it's implied in employer recognition of unions.[55] Work rules and seniority issues are seldom found in contracts and evolve from tradition, particularly in Great Britain. These clauses are less necessary in most EU countries because there is substantial social legislation to deal with **redundancy** due to economic reverses and technological changes.[56] More recent negotiations in Great Britain have introduced changes in traditional work practices, including them in contracts. Where work rules were negotiated, wage settlements were generally higher. Large productivity gains have resulted.[57] Unionized workplaces in Great Britain are more likely to provide parental leave, special paid leaves, and job-sharing options and are less likely to have flexible working hours or work-at-home arrangements.[58] In Germany, the presence of works councils is associated with the institution of family-friendly employment practices, particularly as the proportion of women members of works councils increases.[59]

In France, contracts are usually negotiated annually, but the length of agreements may be indeterminate in some countries.[60] This is very contrary to U.S. approaches, where contracts have tended toward longer periods and the only intracontract issues open to change are wages, and then only annually.

In Japan, unions have little say on promotion procedures but do exert control on transfers between workshops or employee groups. The group's supervisor has great influence on promotion decisions and is usually a union member. Regular and contract workers are from noncompeting groups. Because there is no distinction between classes of bargaining issues in Japan, unions have more influence in managerial decision-making than they do in the United States. Issues requiring consultation or consent at the enterprise level involve improvement in production methods, conditions of labor, shop-floor environment and safety, and fringe benefits. Occasionally, consultation occurs regarding investments, product development, financial situations, recruiting, mergers, and training policies.[61] In Japan

[55] Windmuller, "Comparative Study."

[56] A. Sturmthal, *Comparative Labor Movements* (Belmont, CA: Wadsworth, 1972).

[57] P. N. Ingram, "Changes in Working Practices in British Manufacturing Industry in the 1980s: A Study of Employee Concessions Made during Wage Negotiations," *British Journal of Industrial Relations*, 29 (1991), pp. 1–14.

[58] J. W. Budd and K. Mumford, "Trade Unions and Family-Friendly Policies in Britain," *Industrial and Labor Relations Review*, 57 (2004), pp. 204–222.

[59] J. S. Heywood and U. Jirjahn, "Family Friendly Practices and Worker Representation in Germany," *Industrial Relations*, 48 (2009), pp. 121–145.

[60] S. Dayal, "Collective Bargaining and Contemporary Management-Labor Relations: Analysis and Prospects," in S. B. Prasad, ed., *Advances in International Comparative Management* (Greenwich, CT: JAI Press, 1989), pp. 45–59.

[61] Koike, *Understanding Industrial Relations in Japan*.

unions have successfully resisted deteriorations in working conditions and positively influenced average wage levels. Additionally, wage structures in unionized Japanese employers are substantially flatter than in nonunion firms.[62] In contrast to the situation in the United States, information sharing in Japanese union-management negotiations is associated with lower union wage demands and shorter negotiations.[63]

BARGAINING STRUCTURES

Except for Great Britain, bargaining in most EU countries occurs at the industry level, involving national unions or federations and employer associations. In Italy unions may bargain with the government on social issues, at the employer association and industry levels on economics, and at plant levels on working conditions.[64] Increased economic integration in the EU will require that corporatist deals pay attention to EU-wide economic targets.[65]

Industry-level bargaining, coupled with works councils, enhances the introduction of technological change because contracts address redundancy issues. Unions may take a broader look at employment security, and employers may be able to take the costs of retraining out of competition, since all in the industry would be vulnerable for the same training costs. Great Britain's tendency to negotiate at the enterprise level has been cited as one reason that British firms may be less able to incorporate technological change than other EU members.[66] The fact that several unions frequently represent employees in British firms also leads to employer and employee resistance to workplace concessions involving technological issues.

While most union-management relationships occur within national boundaries, the increasing importance of multinational employers may lead to changes. Changes in local economic climates that increase global competition will make information availability increasingly critical for both labor and management in the future. In turn, this should increase multinational consultation. But due to their interests in maintaining national and geographic pay differentials, employers will resist multinational

[62] H. Hara and D. Kawaguchi, "The Union Wage Effect in Japan," *Industrial Relations*, 47 (2008), pp. 569–590.

[63] M. Morishima, "Information Sharing and Collective Bargaining in Japan: Effects on Wage Negotiations," *Industrial and Labor Relations Review*, 44 (1991), pp. 469–485.

[64] Kennedy, *European Labor Relations*.

[65] P. Teague and J. Donaghey, "European Economic Government and the Corporatist *quid pro quo*," *Industrial Relations Journal*, 33 (2002), pp. 465–483.

[66] W. Brown, "The Effect of Recent Changes in the World Economy on British Industrial Relations," in H. Juris, M. Thompson, and W. Daniels, eds., *Industrial Relations in a Decade of Economic Change* (Madison, WI: Industrial Relations Research Association, 1985), pp. 151–175.

negotiations.[67] In multinational companies, union officials frequently have difficulty accessing executives who make overall industrial relations policies for their companies.[68]

Ironically, as product markets have globalized, the tendency for labor negotiations has been to move from the industry to the local level to cope with increasingly diverse production practices and local job security issues linked with potential plant closings.[69] There are increasing pressures for decentralization in Germany, with joint union-employer involvement in the chemical industry, while the metal workers union still exercises great power over district-level employers.[70] In Ireland, centralized bargaining is practiced in primarily domestic industries where wage gains are closely linked to productivity improvements, while foreign multinationals generally negotiate on an establishment-level basis.[71]

There is a generally corporatist approach to industrial relations in northern and central Europe, although there is beginning to be some decentralization in response to global competition and some proliferation of occupationally based confederations in the Nordic countries.[72] In Sweden and Germany bargaining has taken place at the employer association–national union level. However, increasing competition leading to pressures to reduce labor costs is shifting negotiations toward the enterprise level.[73] Centralized bargaining in Sweden began to break down in the mid-1980s following several rounds of pay increases higher than those in other Organization for Economic Cooperation and Development (OECD) countries. In the 1993 metal working agreement, negotiated at the industry level, a 3.3 percent overall pay increase was provided, but the actual distribution of the increase was left to plant-level decision-making.[74]

[67] H. R. Northrup, D. C. Campbell, and B. J. Slowinski, "Multinational Union-Management Consultation in Europe: Resurgence in the 1980s?" *International Labour Review*, 127 (1988), pp. 525–543.

[68] D. Kujawa, "Labor Relations of U.S.Multinationals Abroad," in B. Martin and E. Kassalow, eds., *Labor Relations in Advanced Industrial Societies: Issues and Problems* (Washington, DC: Carnegie Endowment for International Peace, 1980), pp. 14–42.

[69] R. Locke, T. Kochan, and M. Piore, "Reconceptualizing Comparative Industrial Relations: Lessons from International Research," *International Labour Review*, 134 (1985), pp. 139–164.

[70] M. Behrens and W. Jacoby, "The Rise of Experimentalism in German Collective Bargaining," *British Journal of Industrial Relations*, 42 (2003), pp. 95–123.

[71] L. Baccaro and M. Simoni, "Centralized Wage Bargaining and the 'Celtic Tiger' Phenomenon," *Industrial Relations*, 46 (2007), pp. 426–455.

[72] M. Wallerstein, M. Golden, and P. Lange, "Unions, Employer Associations, and Wage-Setting Institutions in Northern and Central Europe, 1950–1992," *Industrial and Labor Relations Review*, 50 (1997), pp. 379–401.

[73] W. Streeck, "More Uncertainties: German Unions Facing 1992," *Industrial Relations*, 30 (1991), pp. 317–349.

[74] "Sweden: Collective Bargaining in Transition," *European Industrial Relations Review*, 234 (1993), pp. 15–16.

In Germany, IG Metall (one of the largest unions) and Gesantmetall (an employer organization) bargained with Bundesbank (German central bank) involvement. IG Metall has a policy of maintaining or increasing employment of its members. New contracts contain incentives for skill development and keep wages in line with productivity and inflation increases.[75] German and Swedish employers act as cartels to take wages out of competition and sanction whipsaw strikes. Contractual wage terms are often extended to nonrepresented workers, decreasing the incentive to avoid unionization.[76] In Japan unions have occasionally combined to implement a *Shunto* approach in which the state pressures employers to improve wages to union workers in line with productivity and inflation increases.[77]

Developing labor relations in rapidly developing Asian nations has been highly varied. Korean unions developed strongly during the 1980s, but employers are large and involved in several industries simultaneously. In Taiwan, labor is dominated by employers and the ruling political party. Only consultation and constrained collective bargaining are available.[78]

Substantial variance exists between industrialized countries relative to the level at which bargaining takes place, the degree of coordination between unions in bargaining, labor federation involvement, and government involvement. Bargaining is most centralized in Austria, Belgium, France, and Norway and least centralized in Canada, Japan, New Zealand, and the United States. Bargaining coordination is highest in Austria, Germany, and Japan and lowest in Canada, New Zealand, the United Kingdom, and the United States. Coordination in Germany appears to be declining since some unions representing workers with particularly high and/or not easily replaceable skills (such as train drivers) have recently begun demanding nonpattern settlements. Federation involvement is highest in Finland, Norway, and Sweden and lowest in Germany, Italy, Switzerland, the United Kingdom, and the United States. Both Australia and New Zealand have substantially decreased government involvement in determining wage awards and bargaining has been essentially decentralized.[79] Table 17.2 examines these variations.

[75] M. D. Soskice, "The German Wage Bargaining System," *Proceedings of the Industrial Relations Research Association*, 46 (1994), pp. 349–358.

[76] M. Reder and L. Ulman, "Unionism and Unification," in L. Ulman, B. Eichengreen, and W. T. Dickens, eds., *Labor and Integrated Europe* (Washington, DC: Brookings Institution, 1993), pp. 13–44.

[77] L. Ulman and Y. Nakata, "Enterprise Bargaining and Social Contract in Japan," *Proceedings of the Industrial Relations Research Association*, 46 (1994), pp. 339–348.

[78] A. Kleingartner and H. Y. Peng, "Taiwan" An Exploration of Labour Relations in Transition," *British Journal of Industrial Relations*, 29 (1991), pp. 427–446.

[79] R. D. Lansbury, N. Wailes, and C. Yasbeck, "Different Paths to Similar Outcomes: Industrial Relations Reform and Public Policy in Australia and New Zealand," *Journal of Labor Research*, 28 (2007), pp. 629–641.

TABLE 17.2
Characteristics of Industrial Relations Systems in Developed Economies

Source: Adapted from R. J. Flanagan, "Macroeconomic Performance and Collective Bargaining: An International Perspective," *Journal of Economic Literature*, 37 (1999), pp. 1152–1153.

Country	Bargaining Level	Bargaining Coordination	Federation Involvement	Government Involvement
Australia	1.5	1.5	6	10
Austria	2+	3	2	6
Belgium	2+	2	3	4
Canada	1	1	1	2
Denmark	2	2+	1	5
Finland	2+	2+	7	8
France	2	2	3	3
Germany	2	3	1	3
Italy	2	2.5	1	3.7
Japan	1	3	2	4
Netherlands	2	2	2	6
New Zealand	1	1	—	10
Norway	2+	2.5	8	5
Sweden	2	2	7	8
Switzerland	2	2+	1	3
United Kingdom	1.5	1	1	2
United States	1	1	1	2

Coding key: *Bargaining level*, 1 = plant-level bargaining, 2 = industry-level bargaining, 3 = centralized bargaining; *bargaining coordination*, 1 = uncoordinated bargaining, 3 = highly coordinated bargaining; *federation involvement*, 1 = uninvolved in setting wages in any of the subsequent ways, 2 = participates in formulation of wage demands for all affiliates, 3 = negotiates nonwage benefits, 4 = negotiates a part of the wage agreement, 5 = represents affiliates in mediation with centralized ratification, 6 = represents affiliates in arbitration, 7 = negotiates national wage agreement without peace obligations, and 8 = negotiates national wage agreement with peace obligation; *government involvement*, 1 = uninvolved in wage setting, 2 = establishes minimum wage(s), 3 = extends collective agreements, 4 = provides economic forecasts to bargaining partners, 5 = recommends wage guidelines or norms, 6 = negotiates wage guidelines with unions, 7 = imposes cost-of-living adjustments, 8 = formal tripartite agreement for national wage schedule without sanctions, 9 = same with sanctions, 10 = arbitrator imposes wage schedules without sanctions on unions.

IMPASSES

The incidence and duration of strikes vary substantially across industrialized nations. Incidence is relatively higher in Denmark, France, Italy, and Spain. Strikes are longest in the United States, Ireland, and Canada. Italy has frequent intracontract strikes.[80] In Great Britain, strike incidence was higher in plants where employees were represented by several unions. Unlike in the United States, incidence was countercyclical. Preannounced one-day strikes are not unusual. Incidence rates have declined markedly since 1990 in Australia, Canada, Finland, Ireland, Poland, Sweden, and the United Kingdom. Frequency is negatively related to duration and intensity. In general, rates in southern Europe are considerably higher than rates in northern Europe.[81] Table 17.3 details changes in strike data among

[80] Kennedy, *European Labor Relations.*

[81] M. Aligisakis, "Labour Disputes in Western Europe: Typology and Tendencies," *International Labour Review*, 136 (1997), pp. 73–94.

TABLE 17.3
Comparative Strike Data from Selected Nations, 1980–2008

Source: http://laborsta.ilo.org, January 10, 2011.

	1980	1990	2000	2008
Australia	2,429	1,193	698	177
Austria	9	9	4	0
Belgium	132	33	75	NA
Canada	1,028	579	377	187
Denmark	225	232	1,081	335
Finland	2,182	450	96	92
France*	2,118	1,790	2,768	NA
Greece	726	234	99	NA
Ireland	130	49	39	12
Italy	2,238	1,094	966	621
Japan	1,133	284	118	52
Korea†	206	322	250	108
Netherlands	22	29	23	21
New Zealand	360	137	21	NA
Poland‡	NA	250	44	12,765
Spain	NA	1,312	750	811
Sweden	212	126	2	5
United Kingdom	1,330	630	212	144
United States	187	44	39	16

*Number of strikes.
† 1987 = 3,749, 1988 = 1,873, 1989 = 1,616.
‡ 1992 = 6,351, 1993 = 7,443.

19 nations between 1980 and 2008. The evidence overwhelmingly indicates that strike activity has declined substantially in every country except France and Spain. Strikes in France often involve public sector employees who are protesting overall government employment policy initiatives and invite others to participate, making them general strikes.

France requires conciliation when agreements can't be reached. In Sweden, the state has taken a hands-off approach to bargaining disputes since it has a strong need for cooperation and wage restraint because of its export-based economy.[82]

UNION-MANAGEMENT COOPERATION

Different mechanisms have been developed to enhance union-management or worker-manager cooperation. These mechanisms can be involved with three primary levels of decision-making: shop floor (work methods and production processes), core (wages, hours, and terms and conditions of employment), and strategic (production levels, product lines, designs, pricing, etc.). Levels of involvement might roughly be split into three categories: advisory (providing suggestions to management that may be

[82] N. Elvander, "The New Swedish Regime for Collective Bargaining and Conflict Resolution: A Comparative Perspective," *European Journal of Industrial Relations*, 8 (2002), pp. 197–216.

TABLE 17.4
Cooperation Types and Involvement Dimensions

Source: Table adapted from J. Bellace, "Managing Employee Participation in Decision-Making: An Assessment of National Models," *Bulletin of Comparative Labour Relations*, 27 (1993), pp. 5–15.

Country	Involvement Dimension	Advisory	Collective Bargaining	Codetermination
United States	Strategic	No	No	No
	Core	No	Yes	No
	Shop floor	Yes	Yes	No
Japan	Strategic	Yes	No	No
	Core	Yes	Yes	No
	Shop floor	Yes	No	No
Germany	Strategic	Yes	No	Yes
	Core	Yes	Yes	No
	Shop floor	Yes	No	Yes

undertaken), collective bargaining (ability to negotiate and contract on issues), and codetermination (mutual consensus on goals and/or processes).[83] Table 17.4 summarizes the current relationships between cooperation types and involvement dimensions in the United States, Japan, and Germany.

Great variation exists in Europe regarding the degree to which employees are entitled to information, consultation, and participation, even though the development of the European Union has aimed at reducing national differences in a host of business and legal areas. Among the EU countries, only Germany allows unionists on boards of directors. Works councils are legislated in most countries, but union involvement in them varies. With regard to collective bargaining, employers *must* disclose information necessary to unions to assist in preparing their positions.[84]

In Germany, works council members are equally appointed by management and elected by employees. Works council members need not be employees and are often union officials elected by union members in the various plants. Works councils must be involved in all decision-making that has an effect on employment. This means that many strategic decisions are included in their menu of subjects. Evidence as to their effect on organizational performance is mixed. One study finds they have no significant effect on profitability but some positive effect on wages.[85] Turnover and dismissal rates are lower in firms where there is works council representation.[86] One study found that establishments with works councils grew about 16 percent

[83] J. Bellace, "Managing Employee Participation in Decision-Making: An Assessment of National Models," *Bulletin of Comparative Labour Relations*, no. 27 (1993), pp. 5–15.

[84] R. Blainpain, "Management Initiatives and Rights to Information, Consultation, and Workers' Participation in the EC Countries," *Bulletin of Comparative Labour Relations*, no. 27 (1993), pp. 25–42.

[85] J. T. Addison, K. Kraft, and J. Wagner, "German Works Councils and Firm Performance," in B. E. Kaufman and M. M. Kleiner, eds., *Employee Representation: Alternatives and Future Directions* (Madison, WI: Industrial Relations Research Association, 1993), pp. 305–338.

[86] B. Frick, "Co-Determination and Personnel Turnover: The German Experience," *Labour*, 10 (1996), pp. 407–430.

less over an eight-year period and that they did not improve or decrease the likelihood of organizational survival.[87] In larger firms, works councils are associated with positive productivity and negative hiring effects. For firms of fewer than 100 employees, works councils are associated with positive effects on wages and negative effects on productivity.[88]

In Germany, by law, works councils must be allowed in any establishment having five or more employees, but unless the employees demand an election for one, none is required. All establishments with at least 1,000 employees must have a works council. Evidence indicates that any firm with 40 or more employees has a 50-50 chance of having a works council.[89]

In Japan, enterprise-level labor councils exist in steel and auto industries. Managements and unions have negotiated profit sharing to make pay more flexible and to enhance worker job security. Many plants periodically have large-scale job shifts to introduce variety and broaden employee skills.[90] However, participation has not led to greater workplace democracy. Strategic decisions are made at higher levels. Work-floor suggestions are forwarded to supervisors for possible implementation.[91] Employee stock ownership plans (ESOPs) are popular in Japan, with 91 percent of companies listed on Japanese stock exchanges having implemented them. Firms adopting ESOPs were more likely to be more labor-intensive, experience high employment growth, and have below-average business performance. Implementation of an ESOP increased productivity.[92]

In Europe, worker cooperatives are more common than in the United States. In a worker cooperative employees own the firm, hire its managers, and direct its strategy. A study of northern Italian cooperatives found that they have higher productivity, more labor-intensive production functions, low differentials between pay of rank-and-file workers and pay of managers, and more tranquil labor relations than do privately held firms.[93]

Industrial democracy has developed to a much higher degree in most industrialized countries than in the United States. There is also a greater

[87] J. T. Addison and P. Teixeira, "The Effect of Works Councils on Employment Change," *Industrial Relations*, 45 (2006), pp. 1–25.

[88] J. T. Addison, L. Bellman, C. Schnabel, and J. Wagner, "The Reform of the German Works Constitution Act: A Critical Assessment," *Industrial Relations*, 43 (2004), pp. 392–420.

[89] J. T. Addison, "Nonunion Representation in Germany," *Journal of Labor Research*, 20 (1999), pp. 73–91.

[90] K. Kawahito, "Labor Relations in the Japanese Automobile and Steel Industries," *Journal of Labor Research*, 11 (1990), pp. 231–238.

[91] R. M. Marsh, "The Difference between Participation and Power in Japanese Factories," *Industrial and Labor Relations Review*, 45 (1992), pp. 250–257.

[92] D. C. Jones and T. Kato, "The Scope, Nature, and Effects of Employee Stock Ownership Plans in Japan," *Industrial and Labor Relations Review*, 46 (1992), pp. 352–367.

[93] W. Bartlett, J. Cable, S. Estrin, D. C. Jones, and S. C. Smith, "Labor-Managed Cooperatives and Private Firms in North Central Italy: An Empirical Comparison," *Industrial and Labor Relations Review*, 46 (1992), pp. 103–118.

incidence of worker-owned cooperatives, input into managerial selection, and other consultations of unions. Table 17.5 shows types of industrial democracy in industrialized nations.

CONTRACT ADMINISTRATION

Large differences exist in contract administration in different countries because there are such great differences in bargaining structure and because in many countries the contract is simply a basic agreement that individual plants and employees may add to.

In Canada, labor law forbids intracontract strikes and requires binding arbitration of unresolved grievances even if the parties have not negotiated an agreement to arbitrate into an agreement.[94] Where unresolved grievances remain in France, conciliation is required, while in Italy, they are referred to the courts.[95]

In Germany, disputes arise occasionally within works councils with worker and management representatives at odds. Strikes are not permitted to pressure a settlement. By law, disputes over works council discussions must be settled by arbitration.[96]

PUBLIC SECTOR UNIONIZATION

Collective bargaining in the public sector internationally is somewhat akin to the differences found among states in the United States. Its level and practice depends largely on the relative development of private sector unionism and the friendliness of the ruling political party. For example, public sector unions were defensive during most of Margaret Thatcher's term as prime minister in the United Kingdom in the 1980s. As in the United States, a variety of impasse procedures are used and significant differences exist as to what are considered permissible bargaining issues.[97]

COMPARATIVE EFFECTS OF UNIONIZATION

In general, positive wage differentials for unionized workers are negatively associated with union coverage. In countries like Austria and Finland, coverage exceeds 90 percent, thus few nonunion comparisons exist. On the

[94] R. J. Adams, B. Adell, and H. N. Wheeler, "Discipline and Discharge in Canada and the United States," *Labor Law Journal*, 41 (1990), pp. 596–600.

[95] Kennedy, *European Labor Relations*.

[96] International Labour Office, *World Labour Report*, 2 (Geneva: International Labour Office, 1985), pp. 5–52.

[97] International Labor Office, *World Labour Report, 1989* (Geneva: International Labour Office, 1989), pp. 105–125.

TABLE 17.5 A Comparative Analysis of the Main Types of Industrial Democracy

Source: Adapted from M. Poole, *Industrial Relations: Origins and Patterns of National Diversity* (London: Routledge and Kegan Paul, 1986), pp. 154–156.

Type	Defining Characteristics	Structural Properties	Range of Incidence	Key Examples
1. Workers' self-management	Occurs in decentralized socialist economies; a substantial degree of workers' participation on the main decision-making bodies and the overall right of the workforce to use but not to own the assets of the enterprise	Typical organs of administration include workers' assemblies, workers' councils, and representation on management committees	Algeria, Peru, Poland, Yugoslavia, and various Third World and Eastern European societies	Yugoslavia
2. Producer cooperatives	Occur in a variety of political economies; workers' ownership with market mechanisms	Many workers own stock, ownership is widely distributed, workers participate in enterprise management and control and share in the distribution of the surplus (profits)	Very wide ranging, including many Third World countries, France, Italy, Spain, United States, and United Kingdom	Mondragon (Basque provinces of Spain)
3. Codetermination	Rights of workers' representatives to joint decision-making on actual enterprise boards in predominantly private enterprise economies	Single- or two-tier boards (supervisory and management), varying rights to veto and decide proportion of workers' representatives on main board(s)	Widely practiced in Western Europe (e.g., Italy, Norway, Sweden, Germany), Africa (e.g., Egypt), and South America (e.g., Argentina)	Germany
4. Works councils and similar institutions	Varying political economies, bodies that regularly meet with management on enterprise issues	Representatives of workforce elected, varying degree of legalism or voluntarism and extent to which committees are constituted solely by employees and are joint bodies	Broad ranging, including Finland, Indonesia, Netherlands, Spain, Sri Lanka, Germany, and Zambia	Netherlands Germany

5. Trade union action *a.* Disjunctive via collective bargaining	Pluralist societies, acknowledgment of conflicting interests accommodated through trade union-management negotiations	Trade union channel of representation on workers' side, varying degrees of legalism and voluntarism and levels at which bargaining is conducted	The most common form of participation in pluralist societies. Examples include Australia, Canada, United States, and United Kingdom	United States United Kingdom
b. Integrative	State socialism or corporatism; trade union rights to determine various issues within a framework of harmoniously conceived interests of management, trade union, and the state	Trade unions have responsibility for areas such as holiday arrangements and influence decisions over dismissals, safety, welfare, and working conditions but are integrated into both management and the state	The typical role for trade unions in a planned economy whether under state socialism or corporatism	Former USSR
6. Shop-floor programs	Workers' initiatives and new concepts of work organization; participation by employees in the organization of work in various political economies (e.g., autonomous work groups and quality-of-work-life programs)	Influence of workers varies depending on program, though usually task based	Very wide-ranging worker practices and accommodative management techniques in First, Second, and Third Worlds	Scandinavia United States

other hand, among countries with coverage rates below 50 percent, differences appear to be larger in less centralized bargaining environments except where unemployment is very low. Union differentials increased in Australia after firms were given some freedom in negotiating firm- and establishment-level agreements that improved floors established by arbitration tribunals.[98]

There have been a variety of general changes in industrial relations following from increased globalization. Common patterns of transformation include a stronger focus at the enterprise level, increased flexibility in production and job assignments, skill development, and declining unionization. Some of the decline can be attributed to changes in skill mix.[99]

Foreign direct investment (FDI) by U.S. firms is negatively related to union density, centralized collective bargaining, layoff restrictions, and contract extension policies but is positively related to education levels and works councils. This suggests that investors wish to avoid situations in which bargaining power is reduced and prefer situations with skilled workforces and institutionalized methods for continuous conflict resolution and problem solving.[100] Among Organization for Economic Cooperation and Development (OECD) member countries, FDI is negatively influenced by the extensiveness of labor market institutions and positively influenced by neoconservative labor market reforms.[101]

Among European countries, the United Kingdom has the most adversarial system and decentralized bargaining. Many decisions are made at the firm or plant level. Effects of unions in the United Kingdom might be close to those in the United States. Investment rates of firms that recognized manual unions were 23 percent below the rates of nonunion firms. Taking into account the higher wages of their unionized employees, the decrease due primarily to unionization was between 4 and 13 percent.[102] Dual allegiance among British workers is quite low, with less than 10 percent of unionized electronics workers being committed to both union and employer. Most workers had low commitment to both.[103] The introduction

[98] C. J. Waddoups, "Trade Union Decline and Union Wage Effects in Australia," *Industrial Relations*, 44 (2005), pp. 607–624.

[99] R. Locke, "The Transformation of Industrial Relations? A Cross-National Review," in K. S. Wever and L. Turner, eds., *The Comparative Political Economy of Industrial Relations* (Madison, WI: Industrial Relations Research Association, 1995), pp. 9–32.

[100] W. N. Cooke, "The Influence of Industrial Relations Factors on U.S. Foreign Direct Investment," *Industrial and Labor Relations Review*, 51 (1997), pp. 3–17.

[101] H. Ham and M. M. Kleiner, "Do Industrial Relations Institutions Influence Foreign Direct Investment? Evidence from the OECD Nations," *Industrial Relations*, 46 (2007), pp. 306–328.

[102] K. Denny and S. Nickell, "Unions and Investment in British Manufacturing Industry," *British Journal of Industrial Relations*, 29 (1991), pp. 113–122.

[103] D. E. Guest and P. Dewe, "Company or Trade Union: Which Wins Workers' Allegiance? A Study of Commitment in the UK Electronics Industry," *British Journal of Industrial Relations*, 29 (1991), pp. 75–96.

of employee involvement programs has been linked to improved firm performance in nonunion firms but to decreased performance in unionized firms.[104] Unions in Britain have a positive effect on the provision of training by their firms to both manual and nonmanual workers, all else being equal.[105]

In Germany, even though unions see themselves as cooperative rather than conflictual, unionization is related to slightly lower productivity.[106] However, unionization does not reduce the proportional expenditures of firms on research and development (R&D) or employment in R&D activities.[107]

In the Far East, enterprise unionization in Japan has not influenced worker satisfaction but has reduced company commitment. The negative relationship between job satisfaction and unionization in the United States appears to be related to lower job complexity, less worker autonomy in shop-floor decision-making, lower promotional opportunities, and less quality circle membership.[108] Unionized firms in Singapore become more capital-intensive and add technology to improve product quality. More attention is paid to communications and work design, tighter control systems, and dominance of the workplace.[109]

In Korea unionization increases wages and reduces turnover, while works councils are associated with increases in employee satisfaction and productivity (but less so).[110] Interest in works councils was increased by demands for increased democracy in Korea in the late 1980s. Some firms have instituted a bonus policy. Labor productivity is positively influenced by the bonus policy; however, unionization reduces the productivity effect. Under poorer labor relations since 1987, the effect is negative. It increasingly appears that worker participation is necessary for the bonus to have a positive productivity effect.[111]

[104] J. T. Addison, W. S. Siebert, J. Wagner, and X. Wei, "Worker Participation and Firm Performance: Evidence from Germany and Britain," *British Journal of Industrial Relations*, 38 (2000), pp. 7–48.

[105] F. Green, S. Machin, and D. Wilkinson, "Trade Unions and Training Practices in British Workplaces," *Industrial and Labor Relations Review*, 52 (1999), pp. 179–195.

[106] C. Schnabel, "Trade Unions and Productivity: The German Evidence," *British Journal of Industrial Relations*, 29 (1991), pp. 15–24.

[107] C. Schnabel and J. Wagner, "Unions and Innovative Activity in Germany," *Journal of Labor Research*, 13 (1992), pp. 391–406.

[108] J. R. Lincoln and J. N. Boothe, "Unions and Work Attitudes in the United States and Japan," *Industrial Relations*, 32 (1983), pp. 159–187.

[109] C. T. Foo, "Union Presence and Corporate Productivity Practices: Evidence from Singapore," *British Journal of Industrial Relations*, 29 (1991), pp. 123–128.

[110] M. M. Kleiner and Y. M. Lee, "Works Councils and Unionization: Lessons from South Korea," *Industrial Relations*, 36 (1997), pp. 1–16.

[111] M. B. Lee and Y. Rhee, "Bonuses, Unions, and Labor Productivity in South Korea," *Journal of Labor Research*, 17 (1996), pp. 219–238.

Summary

Labor relations in other industrialized countries is conducted in a variety of modes. Generally, union power tends to reside in labor federations on the continent and at the enterprise level in Great Britain and Japan. Works councils are most prominent in Germany and Sweden. Employees may be represented by more than one union in a workplace, and recognition is gained through the bargaining process. Trade unions are continuing to undergo transformations in the former Warsaw Pact nations. In some East Asian nations, unions are either outlawed, highly restricted, or controlled by the government and employers.

Bargaining issues are much more broadly defined in European Union countries than in the United States because there is no legislation in most EU countries differentiating between so-called mandatory and permissive issues. Bargaining structures are more centralized; employer associations represent a large number of employers within an industry, and federations or national unions bargain with them. By contrast, in Japan most decisions are made at the enterprise level.

In most European countries strikes are of shorter duration than in the United States, but strike incidence rates are higher in Australia, New Zealand, Italy, and Finland.

Union-management cooperation is higher in the EU, although there are wide variations. A common mechanism for cooperation is the works council, which is involved in any decisions affecting employment.

Effects of unions on firm performance tend to be similar in Europe and the United States. Wage differences due to unionization are less in Europe than in the United States, and the degree of wage differentiation is associated negatively with the level of investment.

Discussion Questions

1. Given the degree of democracy found in U.S. political jurisdictions, why isn't there more democracy in the workplace?
2. Why are there such large differences in the structure of unions and managements for negotiation in Germany and Japan, yet such similar levels of consultation in the workplace?
3. Could religious or politically affiliated unions have an effective role in labor relations in the United States?
4. Are the concepts of exclusive representation and mandatory bargaining issues anachronisms in a modern industrial society?

Key Terms

Works council, *569*
Redundancy, *579*

Glossary

Ability to pay The economic ability of the employer to grant a wage increase.

Accretion The addition of a group of employees to an existing bargaining unit.

Across-the-board increase An equal cents-per-hour increase for all jobs in a bargaining unit.

Ad hoc arbitrator An arbitrator appointed to hear a particular case or set of cases.

Administrative law judge A judge charged with interpreting the application of federal labor law in unfair labor practice cases that are not settled between the parties.

Agency fee The portion of union dues that nonmembers must pay when employed under a contract with an agency shop clause.

Agency shop A union security clause requiring that employees who are not union members must pay a service fee to the bargaining agent.

Ally doctrine The principle that employees of a secondary employer do not commit an unfair labor practice by refusing to perform struck work.

American Federation of Government Employees (AFGE) An industrial-type union asserting jurisdiction over employees of the federal government.

American Federation of Labor (AFL) The first permanent national labor organization. It brought together a set of craft unions in 1883 and evolved a business unionism approach toward influencing employers and public policy.

American Federation of Labor-Congress of Industrial Organizations (AFL-CIO) The primary labor federation for international union affiliation in the United States. It coordinates national public policy initiatives for the labor movement.

American Federation of State, County, and Municipal Employees (AFSCME) The dominant industrial-type union organizing nonfederal public sector employees.

American Plan A strategy used by employers in the 1920s that aimed at casting organized labor in an outsider role to employees. It fostered company unions and opposed the idea of nonemployees being able to act as bargaining representatives.

Appropriate bargaining unit A group of employees that the National Labor Relations Board determines to be a reasonable unit in which a representation election will be held.

Arbitrability The concept of being arbitrable. A grievance is arbitrable if it alleges a violation under the contract and if the contract terms allow it to be settled through arbitration.

Arbitration A dispute resolution procedure in which a neutral third party hears the positions of the parties and renders a decision binding on both. The arbitrator draws his or her power from the agreement of the parties to abide by the decision and/or the creation of the position in a contract to handle any disputes arising under the contract.

Areawide labor-management committee (AWLMC) An organization of industrial and trade union leaders in a given geographic region whose goal is to deal with employment problems of common concern. Usually these are aimed at promoting labor-management cooperation to enhance job security and competitiveness, especially in an area experiencing economic decline.

Attitudinal structuring The techniques and processes aimed at changing a party's position toward bargaining issues in negotiations.

Authorization card A card signed by an employee to authorize the union to act as his or her bargaining representative. It is necessary for establishing a sufficient interest to request an election from the NLRB.

Bargaining book A collection of contract clauses and their history, the desired position of the party on an issue in negotiation, and acceptable levels for settlement.

Bargaining convention A meeting of union delegates to determine the union's position on mandatory bargaining issues in an upcoming negotiation.

Bargaining order An order from the NLRB requiring that an employer bargain with a union where a representation election failed but the employer's egregious conduct eroded the union's majority.

Bargaining power The ability of one side in a dispute to inflict heavier loss on the other side than it will suffer.

Bargaining structure The organizational nature of the relationship between union(s) and employer(s) in contract negotiations, including a specification of the employees and facilities covered.

Bargaining unit A collection of employees with similar interests who are represented by a single union representative. For organizing purposes, bargaining units would be within the same employer. For bargaining purposes, they might involve several employers.

Benefit-status seniority The seniority in a bargaining unit entitling an employee to a certain level of benefits, usually dating from date of hire (adjusted by layoffs or leaves).

Board-directed (petition) election A representation election in which the NLRB determines the bargaining unit in which the election will be conducted.

Boycott A refusal by individuals not directly involved in a labor dispute to deal with the employer directly involved. For example, if a clerks' union struck a store, a boycott would occur when some segment of the general public (usually union members) refused to patronize the store until the dispute was settled.

Bucket bargaining An FMCS innovation to assist interest-based bargaining by assigning issues to update, repair, redesign, discussion, and economic categories and dealing with them in that sequence.

Bumping The assertion of a competitive status seniority right of an employee who is going to be laid off to claim a different job held by another employee who has lower competitive status seniority.

Business agent A permanent union employee who administers the contract and provides services to union members in a local union representing employees across several employers, particularly in the construction industry.

Business unionism An approach in which collective bargaining is the union's primary objective, leading to the betterment of the workers they represent.

"C" (charge) cases NLRB cases involving allegations of unfair labor practices against an employer or union.

Capital-labor accords A period during the 1950s and 1960s in which employers conceded the legitimacy of unions and negotiated wage increases closely tracked to productivity growth.

Cease-and-desist orders Orders by the NLRB to stop conduct that violates labor law.

Central bodies Collections of local unions at the city or state level for the purposes of political activity. Their support is directly from the AFL-CIO.

Certification The process whereby the NLRB determines the results of a representation election. Certification bars an election in the same unit for one year.

Certification election An election under the auspices of the National Labor Relations Board to determine whether a group of employees desires initially to be represented by a union for collective bargaining purposes.

Change to Win (CTW) A coalition of five major unions that left the AFL-CIO in 2005 to pursue an agenda involving more intensive organizing activities.

Civil service employee A public sector employee who is in a job that is statutorily protected from dismissal as a result of a change in the political party that governs the unit in which the employee is working. Hiring and promotion rules are codified.

Clayton Act An amendment to the Sherman Antitrust Act that, among other things, removed union activities as possible restraints of trade.

Closed shop A collective bargaining clause requiring that a prospective employee be a union member before employment. It is unlawful under federal labor law.

Coalition bargaining A bargaining structure in which a group of unions simultaneously bargains with a single employer.

Collective bargaining The negotiation of labor agreements and their administration during the period in which they are in effect. The collective aspect of collective bargaining is the exclusive representation by the union of the collection of people in a bargaining unit.

***Collyer* doctrine** The NLRB's policy of deferring the disposition of unfair labor practice charges to pending arbitration.

Committee for Industrial Organization (later Congress of Industrial Organizations) (CIO) A group of trade unionists interested, in the early 1930s, in organizing unskilled workers by industry. Later, as they were successful, the unions that were created formed the Congress of Industrial Organizations.

Committee on Political Education (COPE) A department within the AFL-CIO that endorses candidates friendly to labor, provides information on political positions to members, and mobilizes voters.

Common situs picketing The picketing of a facility used by several employers. An action aimed at a single employer may cause unionized employees of other employers to refuse to cross the picket line.

Community action A union tactic seeking to link the interests of a local union with those of the larger community to gain public support for its positions.

Community of interests The degree to which the employees in a proposed unit have common interests in bargaining outcomes. It is one of the most frequent criteria the NLRB uses to determine the scope of a bargaining unit in petition elections.

Company union An employer-established labor organization created for a single firm's employees. It is unlawful under federal labor law.

Competitive-status seniority The seniority levels of employees that entitle them to hold certain jobs, bid on certain jobs, bump, or avoid layoffs. It is usually calculated from the date of promotion into a given job or job group.

Congress of Industrial Organizations (CIO) A federation of industrial unions established in the 1930s.

Consent election A representation election in which there is no dispute between the employer and the union about which employees will be represented if the union wins.

Conspiracy doctrine The legal approach holding that any union activity among a collection of individuals was ultimately aimed at restraining trade by fixing wages.

Contract administration The process a union and management pursue in complying with the contract during its term.

Conventions Periodic national meetings required by the constitutions of labor unions to elect officers, adopt positions, and amend their constitutions (as necessary).

Coordinated bargaining Cooperation between two or more unions in bargaining with a single employer. This method may involve observation of bargaining by other unions or coordinating bargaining demands.

Corporate campaign An activity by unions in difficult organizing or bargaining situations to pressure companies whose officers are members of the board of directors of the targeted company with public relations campaigns. It is frequently used against banks and aimed at informing the public of the connection between the targeted company and potential supporting companies.

Corporatism A labor-management–public policy approach in which employers, unions, and the government work together to create and maintain a stable labor-relations climate involving essentially equal roles for management and labor with government overseeing the relationship.

Cost-of-living adjustments (COLAs) The contract terms that adjust pay in response to changes in the level of the consumer price index. These terms are aimed at keeping the real value of pay constant over the term of the agreement.

Craft severance An action by the NLRB to remove craft employees from a bargaining unit because their community of interests is dissimilar.

Craft union A national union representing predominantly employees in one occupation, such as the Carpenters Union.

Davis-Bacon Act A federal law requiring that employers involved in contract construction work for the federal government pay prevailing area wages for the crafts that they employ.

Decertification election An election to determine whether a majority of bargaining-unit employees still favor union representation.

Defined benefit pension plan A pension plan guaranteeing a certain payment level at retirement. It is usually based on the average of the final two or three years' pay and length of service.

Defined contribution pension plan A pension plan with a specific formula for calculating employer contributions toward retirement. The ultimate level of benefits depends on the amount of contributions and the investment experience of the plan.

Distributive bargaining Bargaining over issues in which one party's gain is the other party's loss.

Doctrinaire organization An employer adopting an employee relations approach aimed at closely duplicating conditions likely under collective bargaining to avoid being a target of unionization.

Drive system A production system in which supervisors have a great deal of power in rewarding and punishing subordinates.

Dual commitment The notion that an individual can be simultaneously committed to his or her employer and union.

Dual governance The notion that individuals have opportunities for the governance of their workplace through electing officers of their bargaining unit local union and voting on contract ratification.

Dues checkoff The provision whereby union members' dues are deducted from their pay by their employer, which forwards the sum directly to their union.

Duty to bargain The duty by both parties under federal labor law, following recognition or certification of a union, to bargain over wages, hours, and terms and conditions of employment.

Economic strike A strike following the expiration of a contract over an impasse on any mandatory bargaining issue. Strikers may be replaced.

Election bar The policy that certification of an election prohibits another election in the same unit for a year.

Employee Any person who is not an employer or supervisor and who is involved in a labor dispute, according to the Taft-Hartley Act.

Employee involvement (EI) programs A name for a variety of plans in which employers provide more employee voice in the operation of the work setting. They are usually included with problem-solving activity.

Employee relations The set of activities engaged in by employers to systematically address employment problems in the workplace.

Employee stock ownership plan (ESOP) A plan in which employees acquire part or all of the shares of stock in a private sector organization.

Employer An organization or manager acting for an organization within the jurisdiction of the labor acts.

Establishment An employment facility, e.g., plant or regional office, that contains all the employees on a contiguous site.

Excelsior list A list of employees and their addresses that employers must turn over to the union when the NLRB authorizes a representation election.

Exclusive representation The union's representation of all individuals within a bargaining unit for purposes of collective bargaining regardless of whether they voted for representation or whether they are union members.

Executive committee The elected executive officers of a local union.

Executive Order 10988 An order issued by President Kennedy allowing federal employee bargaining units where a majority of employees vote for representation. Bargaining was limited to terms and conditions of employment.

Exempt An employee who is in an occupation that is not subject to the overtime pay provisions of the Fair Labor Standards Act.

Expedited arbitration An arbitration method that speeds the process and reduces the formality of the proceedings.

Fact-finding A third-party method used to develop information about the issues in dispute and recommend a potential settlement.

Fair Labor Standards Act (FLSA) A federal law requiring that employers pay overtime premiums when covered employees exceed 40 hours of work in a week and that at least a minimum wage be paid.

Fair representation The requirement that the union treat all bargaining-unit members equally in processing grievances.

Fair-share In public-sector unions, the amount that nonmembers within the bargaining unit are required to pay to the union in lieu of dues for the cost of representation services by the union.

Federal Labor Relations Authority The federal employment equivalent of the National Labor Relations Board. It oversees representation elections and rules on unfair labor practice allegations.

Federal Mediation and Conciliation Service (FMCS) A federal agency created by the Taft-Hartley Act to assist employers and unions in bargaining through mediation, particularly in situations where they have reached impasses.

Field representatives The full-time international union employees who provide organizing services and services to local unions in negotiations and grievance processing.

Final-offer arbitration A variant of interest arbitration in which the arbitrator must choose one of the offers of the parties. Variants of final-offer arbitration may require that an arbitrator select the entire package or select one or the other party's offers on each issue.

Fractional bargaining A tactic a union might use in contract administration to pressure the employer to make concessions on issues that could not be won in bargaining.

Fraternal Order of Police (FOP) A major collective bargaining representative for police. It began as a benevolent organization and turned to collective bargaining when legislation enabled it and unions to begin to organize police.

Free riding A condition in which a bargaining-unit member does not pay dues; occurs under an open shop or in a right-to-work law state.

Functional democracy The availability of union members' checks on their environment by voting for local union members and ratifying contracts in their establishments.

Gainsharing A flexible compensation system in which employees receive bonuses based on labor and/or material savings as compared to a base period.

Good-faith bargaining The willingness of the parties to meet at reasonable times and places to discuss mandatory bargaining issues.

Greenfield operation A newly opened plant in a location in which the employer has never had operations previously. It is usually part of an employer strategy to avoid unions or reduce the proportion of employees represented.

Grievance Any complaint any employee has against an employer; in collective bargaining, an allegation that the employer has violated the collective bargaining agreement.

Grievance procedures The negotiated provisions in the contract that specify how alleged contract violations will be resolved.

Hiring hall The union office, in the building trades, at which tradespeople congregate to take available jobs for which employers have asked the unions to provide workers.

Hot cargo The goods made by nonunion labor that unionized employees refuse to transport or install.

Human resource manager A person responsible for developing and implementing employment policies and practices and advising line managers on employment issues.

Impasse An inability to agree on a contract that follows an unwillingness by both parties to concede further.

Impro-Share A gainsharing plan in which groups of employees receive bonuses as a result of producing products in fewer hours than standards require.

Industrial relations manager In a unionized employer, a person responsible for developing and implementing policies and practices consistent with the collective bargaining agreement and for negotiating and administering contracts.

Industrial union A national union representing predominantly employees employed in a single industry, such as the United Auto Workers.

Industrial Workers of the World (IWW) A revolutionary union founded in the late 1800s that urged the end of the capitalistic system and worker control of the means of production. It was strongly opposed by employers, and its leaders were jailed during World War I for opposing the war.

Industrywide bargaining A bargaining structure in which all (or many) employers in an industry bargain simultaneously with a single union.

Injunctions The court orders requiring that certain actions be stopped.

Integrative bargaining Bargaining over issues in which both parties may achieve a better position than the one held previously.

Interest arbitration Arbitration over the contents of the contract.

Interest-based bargaining (IBB) An approach to bargaining in which both sides indicate at the outset what issues are most important to them in a new agreement.

International Association of Fire Fighters (IAFF) The dominant craft-type union organizing firefighters. The IAFF has been highly successful in influencing public sector legislation enabling bargaining for municipal employees.

International union *See* National unions.

Intraorganizational bargaining The activities that occur within a bargaining team that lead to agreements on positions and concessions in negotiations.

Job evaluation A procedure used to measure the relative value of jobs to an organization. It usually examines factors such as skill, effort, responsibility, and working conditions.

Job security The retaining of employment with a given employer until the employee voluntarily retires or quits once a probationary period is completed.

Joint labor-management committee (JLMC) An organization of employers and a labor union designed to deal with common industrywide problems in an integrative manner.

Journeyman The job level in a skilled trade that an individual attains following successful completion of an apprentice program.

Jurisdictional dispute A dispute between two unions over the representation of a specific group of employees.

Knights of Labor A post–Civil War national union movement in which employees joined city central unions. Leaders advocated arbitration to settle disputes. The Knights declined rapidly after the formation of the American Federation of Labor in 1883.

Labor relations The activities of unions and management in negotiating and implementing collective bargaining agreements.

Laboratory conditions The environment the NLRB has desired to surround union representation elections to allow the employee to make a free and uncoerced choice regarding representation.

Landrum-Griffin Act A law passed in 1959 aimed at increasing democracy in unions and ensuring individual rights. It also modified the Taft-Hartley Act.

Last chance agreement (LCA) In lieu of possible termination for a disciplinary infraction, an arrangement in which an employee, the union, and management agree that another instance of a similar violation will result in immediate termination without access to the grievance procedure.

Line manager A manager who has responsibility for some part of the actual process of producing or delivering an organization's products or services.

Local union The union body closest to the members. It is usually established in a particular geographic location to represent employees in either one employer or one industry. Officers are elected and frequently remain employed full time.

Logrolling A practice in bargaining in which sets of dissimilar issues are traded.

Maintenance of membership A union security clause in which employees who become union members during the agreement are required to remain members.

Management rights clause A contract clause specifying certain areas in which management reserves the right to make and implement decisions.

Mandatory bargaining issue An issue that is statutorily required to be discussed if one of the parties in bargaining raises it.

Marginal revenue product The value of the additional production resulting from a 1-unit addition of a productive input (usually the value of production produced by adding an additional worker, all else being equal).

Marginal supply curve The functional representation of the additional costs associated with hiring each additional unit of labor.

Median voter The middle person, from an opinion perspective, in a bargaining unit. For any two alternate decisions, assuming that voter opinions lie along a continuum, the winning alternative must include the median voter.

Mediation A process involving a neutral party who maintains communications between bargainers in an attempt to gain agreement.

Mediators Neutral individuals who attempt to help parties settle disputes. Mediators have no power to impose solutions but rather focus on keeping lines of communication open and exploring alternative settlements with disputing parties.

Modern operating agreement The agreement between Chrysler Corporation and the United Auto Workers in which the amount of supervision was reduced and team concepts and broader jobs were introduced in return for rebuilding a plant in Detroit.

Modified union shop A union security clause in which employees who are hired after a specified date are required to become union members.

Mohawk Valley formula An employer approach toward organizing campaigns in the 1930s in which organizers were branded as outsiders and Communists and local public interests were stirred against organizing.

Monopoly power The ability of a union to increase wages as a result of controlling the labor supply to the firm.

Multiemployer bargaining A consensual relationship between employers and a union in which bargaining on a contract involves all employers in the unit and in which the terms and conditions of the ultimate agreement apply equally to all employers.

Multiemployer bargaining unit A bargaining unit for contract negotiations that contains a collection of employers and the union with which they negotiate. A multiemployer bargaining unit is voluntarily formed by the employers and the union. Once formed, members are not free to leave while a contract is in effect or being negotiated, unless an impasse has been reached.

Multilateral bargaining The tendency of elected officials to become involved in public sector labor negotiations, thus creating a tripartite bargaining situation in which the employer, the union, and elected officials are the parties.

Mutual-gains bargaining An approach to bargaining in which labor and management enter negotiations with the objective of simultaneously improving the outcomes of both.

Narcotic effect The assumption that parties who have experienced interest arbitration will be more likely to use it in the future than those who have not.

National departments The offices within unions created to bargain and administer contracts with major national employers.

National Education Association (NEA) A professional association of elementary, secondary, and college and university public school teachers with chapters in all states that is now involved in organizing and collective bargaining where permitted.

National Labor Relations Board (NLRB) The federal agency created by the Wagner Act that has responsibility for investigating and ruling on unfair labor practice charges and holding and certifying the results of representation elections.

National Labor Union (NLU) A post–Civil War uplift union.

National Mediation Board (NMB) The agency that mediates contract disputes between employees and unions covered by the Railway Labor Act. It also holds representation elections.

National Railroad Adjustment Board (NRAB) The group originally designed to handle unresolved grievances under the Railway Labor Act. Since there were equal numbers of management and union representatives, an independent arbitrator renders the decision.

National unions Organizations chartering general unions or local unions representing certain crafts or industries. National unions are the level at which control ultimately resides in the labor movement.

Negotiation committee The local union committee responsible for contract negotiations and decisions on grievance handling above the entry-level steps.

Nonexempt An employee who is in an occupation in which the Fair Labor Standards Act requires the employer to pay at least a 50 percent premium for all work beyond 40 hours in a given regularly defined work week.

Norris-LaGuardia Act An act passed in 1932 prohibiting federal courts from enjoining lawful union activities and forbidding enforcement of yellow-dog contracts.

Open door policy A policy in which employees have access to higher-level management to complain about problems in their work unit. Such programs are usually accompanied by investigative units and formal feedback to the employee about the disposition of the problem raised.

Open shop An employment arrangement in which an employee would never be required to join a union as a condition of continued employment.

Organizing campaign The set of activities involved in attempting to gain recognition for a union and representation for employees to collectively bargain with their employer.

Past practice A traditional work practice or rule on which the employees rely even though it is not a part of the collective agreement.

Pattern bargaining A bargaining tactic in which employers or unions seek agreements that imitate those previously concluded in other bargaining rounds in the industry.

Pay form The manner in which pay is provided, such as cash, deferred compensation, insurance, and paid time off.

Pay level A comparison between the average pay rates of a given employer and the market averages for comparison jobs.

Pay structure The rates and ranges of pay assigned to different jobs in the organization.

Pay system The set of rules used by an organization or included in a contract to determine how an individual employee's pay will change.

Permanent umpire An arbitrator named in a contract who hears all cases within his or her area that may come up under the agreement.

Permissive bargaining issue An issue that does not statutorily require bargaining and one that cannot be used to go to impasse.

Philosophy-laden Employee relations programs that consistently follow a particular value system that simultaneously renders unionization superfluous to employees.

Picketing The act of parading at an employer's site to inform the public about the existence of a labor dispute and ask other union members and the public not to cross the picket line.

Political action committee (PAC) An employer or union organization that raises and disburses funds to support political candidates.

Predatory unionism A situation in which the primary goal of the union is to gain the dues of the employees and extract side payments from employers in return for beneficial contracts.

Principled negotiation A negotiating process in which parties reveal all information necessary to reach an agreement early in the process and whenever asked by an opponent.

Production committee A work-unit-level committee consisting of rank-and-file employees and the unit's supervisor that acts on employee suggestions in the Scanlon plan.

Professional employee An employee, under the Wagner Act, with substantial education and working without close supervision in a professional job. The employee cannot be included in a nonprofessional bargaining unit without majority vote of the professionals.

Profit-sharing plan A flexible compensation system in which employees receive bonuses based on the profitability of a unit or firm.

Prohibited bargaining issue An issue the parties are statutorily forbidden to include in their contract.

Project labor agreement (PLA) In construction, an agreement that covers the period during which a project will be undertaken. Usually unions agree not to strike and employers agree to hire only union labor.

"R" (representation) cases Petitions for certification elections.

Raid election An election to determine whether a new union should succeed the present bargaining agent.

Railway Labor Act (RLA) The labor act passed in 1926 that applies to the rail and airline industries. It established craft-oriented bargaining units and requires bargaining with majority representatives who have exclusive rights to bargain for employees in the unit. The act established the National Mediation Board and the National Railroad Board of Adjustment.

Recognitional picketing The act of picketing to inform the public that the employer is not represented and to request recognition. It is prohibited after 30 days if the employer requests and wins an election.

Redundancy In Europe, a situation in which technological or economic conditions lead to surplus workers who will be permanently terminated.

Regional director The top NLRB official in each of the board's regions who has broad power to deal with representation election certifications and unfair labor practice charges and investigations.

Relations by objectives A program initiated by the FMCS to train parties who have strained bargaining relationships to improve communications and focus more closely on desired bargaining outcomes.

Representation The union's role as the employees' agent in employment matters.

Representation election An election to determine whether unrepresented employees desire to be represented by a union for the purposes of collective bargaining.

Revolutionary unionism An approach in which the union movement mobilizes to change the ownership of the means of production, commonly toward a socialist approach.

Right-to-work law A state law, permitted under Section 14(b) of the Taft-Hartley Act, prohibiting the negotiation of union or agency shop clauses, thereby forbidding the requirement of union membership as a condition of continued employment.

Rights arbitration Arbitration over interpretation of the meaning of contract terms or entitlements to outcomes.

Roll-up The amount by which overtime payments and fringe benefits increase as the base wage rate is increased.

Rucker plan A gainsharing program in which employees, as a group, receive bonuses for improvements in labor productivity and reductions in material costs.

Salary reduction plan An employee retirement plan in which the employee's retirement assets accumulate through pre-tax salary reductions. The employer may or may not provide a supplementary matching payment. These are permitted under Internal Revenue Code sections 401(k) for private-sector, and 403(b) for public-sector employees.

Scanlon plan A gainsharing program in which employees, as a group, receive bonuses for improvements in labor productivity.

Screening committee A committee of employee and management representatives under the Scanlon plan that handles suggestions referred to it from lower-level production committees.

Secondary boycott An action asking the public not to patronize an uninvolved party doing business with an employer that is involved in a labor dispute. It is unlawful under federal labor law.

Self-help A legally permitted action taken by a union or employer against the other to pressure a settlement in its terms. For the union, this usually means a strike; for the employer, either using a lockout or hiring strike replacements.

Seniority The period between the time an individual is hired or moved into a current job and the present.

Sherman Antitrust Act A federal law prohibiting organizations from fixing prices or a single organization from becoming and acting as a monopolist.

Sit-down strike An illegal strike in which employees cease work in place and refuse to leave. This type of strike denies the employer the use of the facility.

Skill-based pay (SBP) A pay plan basing pay rates on the acquired skills of employees specific to the work environment. Pay is based on skills or knowledge rather than on the job the person happens to be assigned to.

Spillover The adoption of an outcome from collective bargaining to nonrepresented employees.

Spillover effect The tendency for economic gains won in collective bargaining to influence pay practices for nonunion employees and employers.

Standard of living The absolute level of goods and services an individual can purchase with his or her pay.

Steelworkers' trilogy A set of three Supreme Court decisions essentially establishing arbitration as the *final* decision-making step in the grievance procedure when the parties have agreed to include it in a contract.

Stewards The elected or appointed shop-floor union representatives responsible for interpreting the contract for union members and processing grievances.

Subcontracting Contracting with another employer to perform work that bargaining-unit employees could perform.

Superseniority The state of having greater seniority than any other individual in the bargaining unit. It is usually conferred on stewards to protect union governance in case of layoffs.

Supervisor An employee who is an agent of management and who has the power to effectively hire, fire, and make compensation decisions for subordinates.

Supplementary unemployment benefits (SUB) An employer-provided benefit added to unemployment benefits to bring an employee's payments during unemployment closer to pay for work.

Sympathy strike A strike by a union not involved in negotiations in support of a union that is.

Taft-Hartley Act The act amending and extending the Wagner Act to include union unfair labor practices. It also established the FMCS, provided for dealing with national emergency strikes, and regulated suits by union members against their unions.

Team concept A work design in which groups of employees are assigned to produce a given product, assembly, or service. All employees in the group are expected to be able to perform all tasks. Worker autonomy is increased because the group is responsible for supervising its own activities.

Totality of conduct The sum total of conduct of employers or unions, rather than each individual act, in organizing campaigns or bargaining that may be determinative of unfair labor practices.

Trusteeship A situation in which a national union takes over operation of a local union as a result of its violation of the union constitution.

Twenty-four-hour rule The NLRB rule forbidding union and management campaigning in certification elections in the last full day before the election.

Two-tier pay plan A pay structure variant in which groups of employees are paid different rates for performing the same job. It is usually included as a concessionary clause, with newly hired employees being paid at lower rates. Some plans merge employees after a period of time, while others create permanent differences.

Umpire An arbitrator designated by name in a collective bargaining agreement to hear and rule on disputes between the parties during the life of the agreement.

Unfair labor practice strike A strike by employees to pressure an employer to stop an unfair labor practice. Employees are entitled to reinstatement if they are fired or replaced.

Unfair labor practices (ULPs) Activities by a management or union that violate Section 8 of the Taft-Hartley Act.

Union An organization established to represent the interests of employees. Under U.S. statutes, to be considered a union, an organization must seek to represent groups of nonsupervisory employees, and after being designated as a representative must collectively bargain for the employees it represents.

Union-free An employer strategy to either remain or become free of union representation for any of its employees.

Union security The level of permanency in representation negotiated into a labor agreement, such as a union shop.

Union shop A contract clause requiring that all employees who are members of the bargaining unit must become union members following completion of a probationary period as new employees.

Uplift unionism An approach in which the labor movement's primary goal is to better society as a whole.

Voice power The ability that unionization provides to empower employees to have their complaints heard and acted on by management.

Voluntary employee benefits association (VEBA) A trust set up to receive payments and administer benefits to its members. In the context of labor relations, a company makes a lump sum or series of payments to eliminate future benefit liabilities to the VEBA and the union's trustee becomes responsible for investing the sum and making medical and retirement benefit payments as they are incurred.

Wagner Act The law that provided for collective bargaining for handling labor disputes, recognized the right to representations, established the National Labor Relations Board, initiated exclusive representation within bargaining units, defined employer unfair labor practices, and specified rights and duties of employers and unions in bargaining.

Walsh-Healy Act A federal law requiring that employers that are producing goods for the federal government must pay industry prevailing wage rates and comply with overtime pay requirements.

Whipsaw A bargaining tactic in which a union settles contracts sequentially, demanding a higher settlement in each subsequent negotiation.

Wildcat strike An intracontract strike in violation of a no-strike clause.

Working to rules The act of meticulously following the contract and work rules to degrade productivity and pressure an employer to settle on the union's terms.

Works council A bipartite board in Germany involving employee and management representatives in consultation over issues involving staffing, strategy, health and safety, technological change, and other issues of concern to workers in the organization.

Yellow-dog contract An agreement between an employee and an employer in which the employee indicates that he or she is not a member of a labor union and that joining a labor union in the future will be sufficient grounds for dismissal.

Author Index

Aaron, B., 485*n*, 544*n*, 548*n*, 557*n*
Abbey, A., 521*n*
Abowd, J. S., 321*n*, 421*n*
Abraham, K. G., 319*n*
Abraham, S. E., 9*n*, 70*n*
Adams, R. J., 62*n*, 91*n*, 587*n*
Addison, J. T., 322*n*, 570*n*, 585*n*, 586*n*, 591*n*
Adell, B., 587*n*
Adler, P. S., 454*n*
Ahern, R. W., 447*n*
Ahlburg, D. A., 215*n*
Aiman-Smith, L., 282*n*
Albright, R. R., 532*n*, 550*n*
Alexander, S., 226*n*
Aligisakis, M., 583*n*
Allen, R. E., 452*n*, 493*n*, 522*n*
Allen, S. G., 251*n*, 294*n*, 295*n*, 296*n*, 309*n*
Allen, W. D., 418*n*
Amann, R. J., 189*n*
Ames, K., 463*n*
Anderson, J. C., 98*n*, 215*n*, 479*n*, 506*n*
Andiappan, P., 134*n*
Angle, H. L., 138*n*
Arnold, E., 187*n*
Arthur, J. B., 282*n*, 450*n*, 457*n*
Artz, B., 325*n*
Ash, M., 296*n*
Ash, P., 491*n*
Ashenfelter, O., 290*n*, 421*n*, 533*n*
Asher, M. A., 258*n*
Atkin, R. S., 75*n*, 122*n*, 142*n*, 150*n*
Avgar, A., 325*n*
Azfar, O., 259*n*

Babcock, L. C., 292*n*, 351*n*, 554*n*, 556*n*, 560*n*
Baccaro, L., 581*n*
Bae, J., 200*n*
Bahrami, B., 547*n*
Bai, M., 58*n*
Bailey, K. A., 555*n*
Bamberger, P. A., 136*n*, 137*n*, 471*n*, 491*n*
Banning, K., 200*n*
Barbash, J., 95*n*
Barber, A. E., 311*n*
Barbezat, D. A., 548*n*
Barboza, D., 415*n*
Barfield, R., 324*n*
Barling, J., 132*n*, 133*n*, 135*n*, 138*n*, 189*n*
Barnum, D. T., 545*n*
Barocci, T. A., 556*n*
Bartlett, W., 586*n*
Batt, R., 181*n*, 249*n*, 308*n*
Baugher, J. E., 318*n*
Bazerman, M. H., 351*n*, 354*n*, 401*n*, 439*n*, 559*n*
Beadles, N. A., 174*n*
Beale, D., 309*n*
Beales, N. A., II, 70*n*
Beamer, G., 465*n*
Becker, B. E., 47*n*, 199*n*, 200*n*, 296*n*, 297*n*, 424*n*
Behrens, M., 581*n*
Behringer, K., 207*n*
Belfield, C. R., 137*n*, 322*n*
Bell, L. A., 289*n*
Bellace, J., 585*n*
Bellman, L., 586*n*
Belman, D., 290*n*, 548*n*
Belzer, M. H., 225*n*, 244*n*
Bemmels, B., 137*n*, 138*n*, 307*n*, 476*n*, 477*n*, 478*n*, 506*n*, 519*n*
Benedict, M. E., 560*n*
Ben-Ner, A., 437*n*, 464*n*
Bennett, J. T., 317*n*
Bennett, R. J., 351*n*
Berg, P., 453*n*, 462*n*
Berger, C. J., 324*n*, 325*n*
Bernbeim, R., 205*n*
Berthiaume, R. D., 139*n*, 357*n*
Bitzan, J. D., 547*n*
Black, A. W., 422*n*
Blackburn, M. L., 289*n*
Blainpain, R., 585*n*
Blancero, D., 207*n*, 519*n*
Blanchflower, D. G., 127*n*, 288*n*, 291*n*, 547*n*, 568*n*, 577*n*
Blasi, J. R., 464*n*
Block, R. N., 91*n*, 174*n*, 200*n*, 322*n*, 453*n*, 482*n*, 512*n*
Bloom, D. E., 558*n*
Blount, S., 341*n*
Bodah, M. M., 178*n*, 179*n*
Bognanno, M. F., 143*n*, 247*n*, 559*n*
Bohlander, G. W., 118*n*, 207*n*, 480*n*, 519*n*, 531*n*
Boles, T. L., 348*n*
Boller, H. R., 515*n*
Booth, J. E., 127*n*
Boothe, J. N., 591*n*
Borell, C. A., 511*n*
Boroff, K. E., 250*n*, 251*n*, 324*n*
Boswell, T., 572*n*
Boudreau, J. W., 325*n*
Bowker, A. L., 123*n*
Bowlby, R. C., 352*n*, 491*n*, 493*n*
Boxall, P., 577*n*
Boyle, K., 48*n*
Bozeman, D. P., 188*n*
Brady, D., 568*n*
Bratsberg, B., 287*n*, 289*n*
Bremermann, E. H., 189*n*
Brett, J. M., 9*n*, 350*n*, 351*n*, 352*n*, 482*n*, 483*n*
Briggs, S., 476*n*, 506*n*
Briskin, L., 134*n*
Brister, J., 178*n*
Broadbent, B., 96*n*
Brockner, J., 220*n*, 221*n*
Brody, D., 143*n*
Bronars, S. G., 199*n*, 297*n*
Bronfenbrenner, K., 158*n*, 170*n*, 171*n*, 176*n*, 177*n*, 180*n*, 183*n*, 202*n*, 415*n*, 416*n*, 418*n*
Brooks, F. P., 181*n*
Brotherton, C. J., 353*n*, 404*n*
Brown, B. R., 341*n*, 349*n*, 350*n*, 351*n*, 352*n*
Brown, R. B., 104*n*
Brown, T. C., 426*n*, 472*n*
Brown, W., 580*n*
Bruning, N. S., 178*n*
Bruno, R., 100*n*, 453*n*
Bryson, A., 178*n*, 288*n*, 291*n*, 547*n*, 575*n*, 577*n*
Buchko, A. A., 465*n*
Budd, J. W., 127*n*, 159*n*, 246*n*, 289*n*, 290n, 291*n*, 293*n*, 294*n*, 323*n*, 338*n*, 340*n*, 418*n*, 579*n*
Burke, D. R., 357*n*
Busman, G., 215*n*
Bussell, R., 176*n*, 190*n*
Butler, J. S., 479*n*
Buttigieg, D. M., 130*n*, 410*n*
Byrne, D. M., 423*n*, 549*n*
Byrne, J., 415*n*

Cable, J., 586*n*
Caldwell, P. J., 174*n*
Camerer, C., 351*n*
Cameron, C. D. R., 178*n*
Campbell, D. C., 581*n*
Campolieti, M., 421*n*
Cantell, R. S., 322*n*
Cappelli, P., 244*n*, 245*n*, 451*n*, 491*n*
Card, D., 225*n*, 292*n*, 421*n*
Carini, R. M., 548*n*
Carmichael, H. L., 450*n*
Carnevale, P. J. D., 403*n*
Carsten, J. M., 10*n*
Carter, N. W., 237*n*
Carter, W. H., 288*n*
Cavanagh, C. L., 558*n*
Cavanaugh, J. K., 287*n*, 360*n*
Cebula, R. J., 290*n*
Chachere, D. R., 153*n*
Chacko, T. I., 135*n*
Chaison, G. N., 18*n*, 20*n*, 121*n*, 129*n*, 134*n*
Chalykoff, J., 214*n*
Chamberlain, N. W., 32*n*, 33*n*, 41*n*, 99*n*, 237*n*
Champlin, F. C., 559*n*
Chandler, T. D., 547*n*
Chang, T. F. H., 96*n*
Charlwood, A., 578*n*
Chaulk, K., 426*n*
Chauvin, K., 491*n*
Chaykowski, R. P., 292*n*, 479*n*
Chelius, J., 77*n*
Chen, S. J., 200*n*
Cheng, T. Y., 455*n*
Chiles, T., 200*n*
Christenson, S., 317*n*
Christofides, L. N., 289*n*
Chun, J. J., 178*n*
Clark, D. A., 177*n*, 188*n*, 311*n*

Clark, P. F., 114*n*, 115*n*, 128*n*, 149*n*, 177*n*, 181*n*, 184*n*, 188*n*, 244*n*, 249*n*, 250*n*, 311*n*
Clark, R. L., 294*n*
Clarke, L., 440*n*
Clawson, D., 142*n*
Cleveland, G., 292*n*
Cobble, D. S., 240*n*
Cochran, A. B., III, 463*n*
Coggins, J. S., 290*n*
Cohen, S., 338*n*
Cohen, S. G., 451*n*
Collomo, C., 31*n*
Colvin, A. J. S., 208*n*, 451*n*
Commons, J. R., 29*n*
Conlin, M., 339*n*
Conlon, D. E., 348*n*
Constantine, J. R., 36*n*
Cook, A. H., 99*n*, 142*n*
Cooke, W. N., 89*n*, 184*n*, 189*n*, 347*n*, 445*n*, 446*n*, 452*n*, 457*n*, 458*n*, 466*n*, 490*n*, 590*n*
Copping, J., 209*n*
Cousineau, J. M., 313*n*, 421*n*, 422*n*
Cowie, J., 92*n*
Craft, J. A., 16*n*
Crain, M., 178*n*
Cramton, P. C., 410*n*, 418*n*
Craypo, C., 16*n*, 247*n*
Cross, J. G., 341*n*, 352*n*
Crow, S. M., 521*n*
Cullen, D. E., 32*n*, 33*n*, 41*n*, 99*n*, 237*n*
Culpepper, R., 180*n*
Cunningham, J. D., 322*n*
Currall, S. C., 440*n*
Currie, J., 533*n*
Currivan, D. B., 133*n*
Curtis, T. D., 153*n*
Cutcher-Gershenfeld, J., 190*n*, 350*n*, 359*n*, 360*n*, 442*n*, 455*n*, 456*n*, 458*n*, 466*n*

Da Costa, I., 571*n*
Dalton, D. R., 489*n*
Daniels, W., 567*n*, 580*n*
Dark, T. E., III, 151*n*
Das, S., 576*n*
Dastmalchian, A., 494*n*
Datz, H., 414*n*
Davis, J. C., 317*n*
Davis, K. M., 413*n*
Davy, J. A., 479*n*, 480*n*
Day, D. V., 177*n*, 188*n*
Dayal, S., 579*n*
DeBreu, C. K. W., 348*n*
Deere, D. R., 199*n*, 297*n*
Deery, S. J., 129*n*, 130*n*, 410*n*, 446*n*
DeFina, R. H., 258*n*
DeFreitas, G., 188*n*
Deitsch, C. R., 511*n*, 525*n*
Delaney, J. T., 88*n*, 104*n*, 115*n*, 116*n*, 149*n*, 150*n*, 152*n*, 153*n*, 180*n*, 181*n*, 184*n*, 208*n*, 220*n*, 221*n*, 244*n*, 249*n*, 250*n*, 253*n*, 458*n*, 460*n*, 561*n*
Dell'Omo, G. G., 493*n*, 494*n*, 558*n*
Delp, L., 181*n*
Demsetz, R. S., 188*n*
Denenberg, R. V., 521*n*
DeNisi, A. S., 325*n*
Dennis, B. D., 555*n*
Denny, K., 590*n*
Denton, M., 85*n*
Derber, M., 544*n*
DeRue, D. S., 348*n*
Deshpande, S. P., 14*n*
DeSouza, G., 178*n*
Devinatz, V. G., 104*n*, 135*n*, 178*n*, 180*n*, 187*n*, 476*n*, 543*n*
Dewe, P., 590*n*
Dewire, J., 491*n*
Dhavale, D. G., 129*n*
Diamond, W. J., 115*n*
Dickens, W. T., 214*n*, 582*n*
Dilts, D. A., 511*n*, 515*n*, 525*n*, 532*n*
DiNardo, J., 20*n*, 258*n*
Ditelberg, J. L., 464*n*
Dolin, K. R., 89*n*
Donaghey, J., 580*n*
Donahue, L. H., 471*n*
Donn, C. B., 245*n*
Donohue, S. M., 288*n*
Donovan, E., 322*n*
Dotson, D. L., 88*n*
Doucouliagos, H., 299*n*
Douglas, J. M., 324*n*, 557*n*, 559*n*
Drotning, J. E., 404*n*, 557*n*
Dulles, F. R., 31*n*, 32*n*, 33*n*, 35*n*, 36*n*, 37*n*, 38*n*, 39*n*, 40*n*, 43*n*, 46*n*, 47*n*, 53*n*, 54*n*
Dunham, R. B., 311*n*
Dunlop, J. T., 115*n*
Dunn, S., 78*n*
Dworkin, J. B., 215*n*, 250*n*, 507*n*
Dyer, L. D., 79*n*, 318*n*, 439*n*

Eade, V. H., 250*n*
Earle, J. S., 311*n*
Eaton, A. E., 182*n*, 348*n*, 451*n*, 454*n*, 455*n*, 457*n*, 470*n*, 482*n*, 493*n*
Eaton, J., 116*n*
Eberts, R. W., 296*n*
Edwards, F. R., 547*n*
Edwards, L. N., 547*n*
Eflal, B., 410*n*
Eichengreen, B., 582*n*
Eichstedt, J. L., 142*n*
Eischen, D. E., 204*n*, 318*n*
Elkouri, E. A., 499*n*, 511*n*
Elkouri, F., 499*n*, 511*n*
Ellwood, D. T., 188*n*
Elvander, N., 584*n*
Endersby, J. W., 150*n*
Engberg, J., 292*n*
Eplion, D., 550*n*
Eren, O., 286*n*
Erickson, C. L., 21*n*, 92*n*, 246*n*
Eriksen, S., 142*n*
Ernst, D., 41*n*
Erwin, P. J., 129*n*
Estreicher, S., 23*n*, 97*n*, 119*n*, 414*n*, 490*n*
Estrin, S., 464*n*, 586*n*
Euwema, M. C., 402*n*
Evansohn, J., 19*n*
Ewing, D. W., 207*n*

Fajertag, G., 571*n*
Fallick, B. C., 200*n*
Farber, H. S., 4*n*, 15*n*, 16*n*, 18*n*, 20*n*, 172*n*, 319*n*, 321*n*, 352*n*, 559*n*
Feild, H. S., 482*n*
Feller, D., 525*n*
Ferguson, J.-P., 190*n*
Ferris, G., 9*n*
Feuille, P., 200*n*, 208*n*, 482*n*, 500*n*, 555*n*, 558*n*
Fields, M. W., 140*n*
Fine, G., 188*n*
Fine, S., 44*n*
Finnegan, B., 176*n*, 177*n*
Fiorito, J., 7*n*, 9*n*, 10*n*, 11*n*, 14*n*, 15*n*, 95*n*, 104*n*, 105*n*, 106*n*, 115*n*, 116*n*, 135*n*, 141*n*, 142*n*, 143*n*, 149*n*, 180*n*, 187*n*, 188*n*, 249*n*, 460*n*, 569*n*
Fisher, E. G., 330*n*, 429*n*
Fisher, R., 440*n*
Fisk, C. L., 246*n*
Fitzgerald, I., 570*n*, 571*n*
Fitzpatrick, T., 103*n*
Flaherty, S., 421*n*, 423*n*
Flanagan, R. J., 4*n*, 20*n*, 22*n*, 82*n*, 567*n*, 583*n*
Fleming, R. W., 513*n*, 514*n*
Flood, P., 131*n*, 132*n*
Florkowski, G. W., 75*n*
Flynn, F. J., 423*n*
Foner, P. S., 417*n*
Fong, M., 5*n*
Foo, C. T., 591*n*
Forbath, W. E., 39*n*, 62*n*
Fortin, N. M., 258*n*
Fossum, J. A., 79*n*, 184*n*, 204*n*, 205*n*, 271*n*, 318*n*
Foulkes, F. K., 201*n*, 203*n*, 205*n*, 206*n*
Fox, A. L., II, 117*n*
Fox, E. S., 87*n*
Franckiewicz, M. M., 511*n*
Franke, W. H., 245*n*
Frazier, H. B., III, 56*n*, 532*n*
Freedman, A., 182*n*, 198*n*, 210*n*, 223*n*, 245*n*, 262*n*, 336*n*, 358*n*, 359*n*
Freeman, R. B., 5*n*, 14*n*, 15*n*, 16*n*, 18*n*, 21*n*, 115*n*, 183*n*, 199*n*, 214*n*, 228*n*, 236*n*, 288*n*, 289*n*, 290*n*, 292*n*, 293*n*, 295*n*, 299*n*, 322*n*, 323*n*, 325*n*, 452*n*, 568*n*, 574*n*, 577*n*
Frege, C. M., 568*n*
Frenkel, S. J., 573*n*
Frick, B., 585*n*
Fried, Y., 139*n*
Friedman, B. A., 9*n*
Friedman, R. A., 340*n*, 350*n*, 351*n*, 353*n*, 354*n*
Friedman, S., 92*n*, 158*n*
Frost, A. C., 114*n*, 181*n*, 184*n*, 244*n*, 249*n*, 250*n*, 448*n*, 463*n*
Frost, C. F., 280*n*, 282*n*
Fukami, C. V., 137*n*
Fullager, C., 128*n*, 138*n*
Fuller, J. B., 129*n*, 133*n*, 136*n*
Fuller, S. H., 345*n*, 347*n*
Funkhouser, R., 189*n*
Furusawa, T., 339*n*

Gabriel, J., 181*n*
Gainey, T. W., 494*n*
Gallagher, D. G., 7*n*, 9*n*, 10*n*, 11*n*, 95*n*, 105*n*, 106*n*, 115*n*, 128*n*, 135*n*, 136*n*, 141*n*, 142*n*, 143*n*, 188*n*, 569*n*
Galloway, L., 91*n*
Gamm, S., 117*n*
Gannon, M. J., 42*n*
Garen, J., 295*n*

Garren, B., 87*n*
Gattiker, U. E., 307*n*
Geffner, L., 414*n*
Gely, R., 547*n*
Gerhart, B., 263*n*
Gerhart, P. F., 404*n*, 454*n*, 546*n*, 547*n*, 557*n*
Getman, J. G., 183*n*, 325*n*
Ghilarducci, T., 426*n*
Gibbons, J. M., 14*n*
Gibbons, M. K., 532*n*
Gibney, R., 119*n*, 149*n*
Gifford, C. D., 102*n*
Gobeille, K. R., 451*n*
Godard, J., 91*n*, 307*n*, 347*n*, 410*n*
Goldberg, M. J., 95*n*
Goldberg, S. B., 183*n*, 325*n*, 482*n*, 483*n*
Golden, M., 581*n*
Goll, J., 450*n*
Gomez, R., 178*n*
Gompers, S., 40*n*
Goodman, L. M., 279*n*
Gordon, D., 153*n*
Gordon, D. M., 53*n*, 197*n*
Gordon, M. E., 16*n*, 128*n*, 325*n*, 451*n*, 491*n*, 493*n*
Gould, W. B., IV, 89*n*, 198*n*
Gramm, C. L., 105*n*, 106*n*, 249*n*, 309*n*, 417*n*, 421*n*, 422*n*, 423*n*
Granof, M. H., 332*n*, 335*n*
Gray, G. R., 444*n*, 445*n*
Gray, L. S., 114*n*, 115*n*
Gray, W. B., 78*n*
Green, F., 326*n*, 577*n*, 591*n*
Greenfield, P. A., 505*n*
Greenhouse, S., 165*n*
Greer, C. R., 9*n*, 420*n*, 425*n*, 489*n*
Greer, I., 571*n*
Grenier, G., 82*n*
Grier, K. B., 150*n*
Griffin, C. J., Jr., 314*n*
Griffin, M. A., 340*n*
Grodin, J. R., 558*n*
Gu, W., 339*n*
Guest, D. E., 590*n*
Guillen, M. F., 575*n*
Gunderson, M., 178*n*, 292*n*, 418*n*, 422*n*, 423*n*
Gurwitt, R., 551*n*
Guy, F., 309*n*

Haggard, T. R., 430*n*
Haggerty, M. E., 289*n*
Hagmann, C., 532*n*
Haiven, L., 440*n*
Hall, A., 324*n*
Hall, L., 440*n*
Ham, H., 590*n*
Hammer, T. H., 139*n*, 325*n*
Hamner, W. C., 10*n*
Hancke, B., 578*n*
Hanslowe, N. B., 186*n*
Hanson, R., 463*n*
Hara, H., 580*n*
Harcourt, M., 473*n*
Harcourt, S., 473*n*
Harrison, A., 422*n*
Hartmann, P. T., 245*n*
Hassett, K. A., 200*n*
Hauck, V. E., 522*n*
Hauptmeier, M., 571*n*
Havlovic, S. J., 451*n*
Hayes, K., 292*n*
Haynes, P., 577*n*
Hebdon, R., 340*n*, 421*n*, 441*n*, 553*n*, 559*n*, 560*n*, 561*n*
Hecksher, C., 440*n*
Heinz, P. K., 159*n*
Helburn, I. B., 494*n*, 520*n*, 545*n*
Hendricks, W. E., 105*n*, 106*n*, 249*n*, 421*n*
Hendrix, W. H., 322*n*
Heneman, H. G., III, 79*n*, 260*n*, 318*n*, 493*n*, 506*n*
Herman, J. B., 183*n*, 325*n*
Hersby, R. B., 532*n*
Hester, K., 129*n*, 133*n*, 136*n*
Heywood, J. S., 137*n*, 321*n*, 548*n*, 579*n*
Heywood, J. W., 288*n*
Hill, M., Jr., 513*n*, 514*n*
Hill, R. C., 533*n*
Hills, S. M., 178*n*
Hirsch, B. T., 6*n*, 297*n*
Hirschman, A. O., 7*n*, 205*n*
Hochner, A., 116*n*
Hodson, R., 134*n*
Hoell, R. C., 137*n*
Hoerr, J. P., 57*n*, 246*n*, 258*n*, 436*n*
Hogler, R. L., 82*n*
Holl, P., 318*n*
Holley, W. H., Jr., 482*n*
Horn, R. N., 560*n*
Horton, R. D., 558*n*
Howlett, R., 515*n*
Hoxie, R. F., 28*n*
Hoyman, M. M., 134*n*
Humphreys, R. W., 444*n*
Hundley, G., 6*n*, 321*n*, 533*n*
Hunter, J. M., 173*n*
Hunter, L. W., 326*n*
Hurd, R. W., 100*n*, 158*n*, 181*n*, 190*n*
Huston, J. H., 317*n*
Hutchens, R, 422*n*
Hyatt, D., 292*n*, 340*n*, 421*n*
Hyman, R., 572*n*
Hyslop, D., 533*n*

Ichniowski, C., 77*n*, 315*n*, 452*n*, 458*n*, 462*n*, 495*n*, 543*n*, 548*n*, 560*n*
Idson, T. L., 323*n*
Ingram, P. N., 579*n*
Issacharoff, S., 351*n*
Iverson, R. D., 129*n*, 130*n*, 133*n*, 410*n*, 446*n*

Jacobi, O., 567*n*
Jacobs, D., 153*n*
Jacobs, J. B., 112*n*
Jacobs, R. R., 340*n*
Jacoby, S. M., 46*n*, 101*n*, 197*n*, 267*n*, 313*n*
Jacoby, W., 581*n*
Jain, H. C., 418*n*
Janus, C. J., 121*n*
Jarley, P., 104*n*, 115*n*, 116*n*, 180*n*, 460*n*, 556*n*
Jarrell, S. P., 289*n*
Jelf, G. S., 450*n*
Jick, T., 402*n*
Jirjahn, U., 570*n*, 579*n*
Johansson, R. C., 290*n*
Johns, D. V., 69*n*
Johnson, B. R., 555*n*
Johnson, G., 421*n*
Johnson, G. E., 290*n*
Johnson, M. H., 317*n*
Johnson, N. B., 297*n*
Johnson, S., 182*n*
Johnson, T. R., 324*n*
Jones, D. C., 437*n*, 586*n*
Jones, D. L., 40*n*, 500*n*, 518*n*, 519*n*, 520*n*
Jones, M. A., 314*n*
Juravich, T., 415*n*, 416*n*, 418*n*, 451*n*
Jurgens, U., 567*n*
Juris, H., 567*n*, 580*n*

Kahn, L. M., 421*n*
Kaminski, M., 470*n*
Karim, A., 402*n*
Kasper, H., 555*n*
Kassalow, E. M., 566*n*, 581*n*
Katchanovski, I., 9*n*
Kato, T., 586*n*
Katz, H. C., 21*n*, 211*n*, 245*n*, 249*n*, 265*n*, 267*n*, 307*n*, 436*n*, 451*n*, 490*n*
Katz, L. F., 291*n*
Kaufman, B. E., 8*n*, 16*n*, 18*n*, 82*n*, 152*n*, 182*n*, 208*n*, 209*n*, 421*n*, 422*n*, 455*n*, 456*n*, 490*n*, 585*n*
Kaufman, R. S., 296*n*
Kaufman, R. T., 285*n*, 296*n*
Kawaguchi, D., 580*n*
Kawahito, K., 586*n*
Keane, M. P., 247*n*
Keaveny, T. J., 184*n*, 493*n*
Keefe, J. H., 181*n*, 249*n*, 250*n*, 251*n*, 307*n*, 309*n*, 451*n*, 470*n*, 482*n*, 493*n*
Kelley, M. R., 308*n*
Kellock, S., 414*n*
Kelloway, E. K., 132*n*, 133*n*, 135*n*, 189*n*
Kennan, J., 421*n*, 422*n*, 424*n*
Kennedy, T., 408*n*, 569*n*, 575*n*, 580*n*, 583*n*, 587*n*
Keppler, M. J., 204*n*, 207*n*
Kessler, D. P., 291*n*
Ketkar, K. W., 324*n*
Kilborn, P. T., 147*n*
Kilpatrick, J. G., 120*n*
Kim, D.-O., 285*n*, 450*n*, 459*n*
Kim, S. M., 506*n*
Kim, Y. M., 401*n*
King, R. H., 423*n*, 549*n*
Kizilos, M., 326*n*, 451*n*
Klaas, B. S., 411*n*, 412*n*, 491*n*, 492*n*, 493*n*, 494*n*, 504*n*
Kleiner, M. M., 16*n*, 18*n*, 152*n*, 183*n*, 184*n*, 199*n*, 200*n*, 208*n*, 268*n*, 290*n*, 299*n*, 316*n*, 452*n*, 455*n*, 456*n*, 490*n*, 585*n*, 590*n*, 591*n*
Kleingartner, A., 582*n*
Klinzing, L., 567*n*
Kluger, A. N., 136*n*, 137*n*
Knauss, K., 308*n*
Knight, T. R., 494*n*
Knoke, D., 13*n*
Knutsen, P., 570*n*
Koch, M. J., 321*n*
Kochan, T. A., 21*n*, 23*n*, 190*n*, 211*n*, 214*n*, 265*n*, 267*n*, 307*n*, 309*n*, 348*n*, 359*n*, 400*n*, 402*n*, 436*n*, 438*n*, 439*n*, 442*n*, 447*n*, 451*n*, 454*n*, 457*n*, 466*n*, 545*n*, 546*n*, 581*n*
Kohn, E., 491*n*

Koike, K., 567*n*, 569*n*, 579*n*
Kolb, D. M., 402*n*, 404*n*
Kolodinsky, R. W., 115*n*
Korpi, W., 566*n*
Koziara, K., 116*n*
Kraft, K., 585*n*
Kramer, J. K., 425*n*
Kressel, K., 402*n*
Kriesky, J., 182*n*
Krol, R., 297*n*
Krueger, A. B., 16*n*, 18*n*, 425*n*
Kruse, D. L., 286*n*
Kuczynski, G., 568*n*
Kuhn, J. W., 174*n*, 488*n*, 489*n*
Kuhn, P., 322*n*, 339*n*
Kujawa, D., 581*n*
Kuruvilla, S., 21*n*, 136*n*, 569*n*, 572*n*, 576*n*
Kutler, S. I., 40*n*
Kwon, H., 576*n*
Kwon, S., 576*n*

Labig, C. E., Jr., 489*n*, 494*n*, 520*n*
Lacroix, R., 313*n*, 421*n*, 422*n*
Lane, C., 570*n*
Lange, P., 581*n*
Langsner, A., 264*n*
Lansbury, R. D., 582*n*
LaRocco, J. B., 515*n*
Laroche, P., 299*n*
Larrick, R. P., 341*n*
Larson, E. W., 137*n*
Latham, G. P., 140*n*
Lau, D. C., 478*n*
Lawler, J. J., 158*n*, 175*n*, 181*n*, 183*n*, 184*n*, 200*n*, 211*n*, 212*n*, 213*n*, 214*n*
Leap, T. L., 322*n*
Ledford, G. E., Jr., 451*n*
Lee, B. A., 77*n*
Lee, M. B., 591*n*
Lee, R. T., 268*n*
Lee, T. W., 176*n*, 177*n*
Lee, Y. M., 591*n*
Leff, P. J., 185*n*
Lefkowitz, J., 532*n*
Leigh, D. E., 289*n*
Leigh, J. P., 422*n*
Leitch, J. A., 547*n*
Lemare, J. R., 151*n*
Lemieux, T., 20*n*, 258*n*, 292*n*
Leonard, J. S., 297*n*, 321*n*
Leone, R. D., 447*n*
Le Queux, S., 129*n*, 571*n*
LeRoy, M. H., 412*n*, 418*n*, 474*n*, 500*n*
Lester, R. A., 556*n*
Lévesque, C., 129*n*
Levinson, M., 233*n*
Lewchuk, W., 201*n*
Lewin, D., 62*n*, 208*n*, 452*n*, 458*n*, 475*n*, 478*n*, 479*n*, 491*n*, 493*n*, 494*n*
Lichtash, A., 523*n*
Lichtenstein, N., 28*n*, 47*n*, 306*n*
Lillie, N., 244*n*
Lim, R. G., 403*n*
Lim, S. G. S., 357*n*
Lincoln, J. R., 591*n*
Linneman, P. D., 288*n*
Lipset, S. M., 9*n*
Lipsky, D. B., 208*n*, 245*n*, 324*n*, 503*n*, 556*n*, 557*n*, 559*n*
Locke, R., 581*n*, 590*n*
Loewenberg, J. J., 555*n*
Loewenstein, G., 351*n*
Logan, J., 214*n*
Londrigan, B., 448*n*
Long, L. N., 16*n*
Long, R. J., 297*n*
Lopez, S., 453*n*
Lovenheim, M. F., 548*n*
Lowe, G. S., 139*n*
Lowery, C. M., 174*n*
Lucas, M. D., 158*n*
Lucero, M. A., 522*n*
Lukas, J. A., 38*n*
Lund, J., 548*n*
Lynn, M. L., 178*n*
Lytle, A. E., 350*n*

Mace, R. F., 169*n*
Machin, S., 577*n*, 591*n*
Macpherson, D. A., 6*n*
Magenau, J. M., 141*n*, 353*n*
Magnani, E., 297*n*, 309*n*
Maher, K., 5*n*
Mahoney, T. A., 208*n*
Mahony, D. M., 504*n*, 552*n*
Maki, D., 317*n*
Mangum, G., 516*n*
Mankita, I., 453*n*
Mannix, E. A., 439*n*
Maranto, C. L., 180*n*, 187*n*
Mareschal, P. M., 153*n*, 181*n*, 404*n*
Marmo, M., 505*n*
Marsh, R. M., 586*n*
Marshall, A., 230*n*
Martin, A. W., 119*n*
Martin, B., 566*n*, 581*n*
Martin, J. E., 139*n*, 141*n*, 268*n*, 357*n*, 422*n*
Martin, S. A., 420*n*
Martindale, S., 415*n*
Martinez-Pecino, R., 402*n*
Mas, A., 425*n*
Masters, M. F., 75*n*, 112*n*, 119*n*, 122*n*, 129*n*, 142*n*, 149*n*, 150*n*, 153*n*, 532*n*, 550*n*
Matsusaka, J. G., 533*n*
Mattson, J., 204*n*, 205*n*
Matuszak, M., 308*n*
Mauro, M. J., 420*n*
Mautz, R. D., Jr., 359*n*
Mayfield, J., 186*n*
Mayfield, M., 186*n*
Mazerolle, M., 340*n*, 441*n*
McCabe, D. M., 206*n*
McCall, B. P., 323*n*, 356*n*, 559*n*
McCammon, H. J., 39*n*
McCarthy, M. A., 100*n*
McClendon, J. A., 10*n*, 11*n*, 188*n*, 411*n*, 412*n*
McClurg, L. N., 136*n*
McConnell, S., 421*n*, 423*n*, 425*n*, 533*n*
McDermott, T. J., 406*n*
McElroy, J. C., 136*n*
McGuire, W. J., 560*n*
McHugh, P. P., 178*n*, 179*n*, 360*n*
McHugh, R., 425*n*
McIntosh, S., 326*n*
McKelvey, J. T., 487*n*, 518*n*, 552*n*
McKersie, R. B., 21*n*, 214*n*, 265*n*, 267*n*, 295*n*, 307*n*, 342*n*, 343*n*, 344*n*, 345*n*, 347*n*, 348*n*, 355*n*, 356*n*, 436*n*, 438*n*, 439*n*, 454*n*, 455*n*
McLaughlin, J. M., 414*n*
McLaughlin, M. E., 403*n*
McLeod, W. B., 450*n*
McPherson, D. S., 521*n*
McShane, S. L., 134*n*
Meany, G., 54*n*, 55*n*, 56*n*
Medina, F. J., 402*n*
Medoff, J. L., 5*n*, 199*n*, 288*n*, 289*n*, 295*n*, 323*n*
Melcher, D., 142*n*
Melino, A., 422*n*, 423*n*
Mello, J. A., 175*n*
Mellor, S., 134*n*, 136*n*
Meltz, N., 178*n*
Meltzer, B., 515*n*
Mendeloff, J. M., 78*n*
Mesch, D. J., 506*n*
Metzger, B. R., 521*n*
Meyer, D. G., 347*n*, 457*n*, 490*n*
Meyer, L. L., 349*n*
Milkman, R., 181*n*, 202*n*
Milkovich, G. T., 263*n*, 265*n*, 452*n*
Miller, C. S., 282*n*
Miller, R. W., 444*n*
Mills, D. Q., 295*n*
Mishel, L., 240*n*
Mishra, A. K., 89*n*
Mitchell, D. J. B., 91*n*, 92*n*, 246*n*, 262*n*, 267*n*, 313*n*, 421*n*, 548*n*
Mitchell, M., 202*n*
Mitchell, O. S., 62*n*, 208*n*, 452*n*
Mittenthal, R., 511*n*
Montgomery, B. R., 179*n*
Montgomery, D., 19*n*
Montgomery, E., 560*n*
Moon, H., 348*n*
Moore, W. J., 153*n*, 533*n*
Morgan, J., 324*n*
Morgan, S., 465*n*
Morgenstern, M., 348*n*
Morishima, M., 138*n*, 495*n*, 580*n*
Morrow, P. C., 136*n*
Mumford, K., 579*n*
Munday, K. M., 127*n*
Munduate, L., 402*n*
Munger, M. C., 150*n*
Murnighan, J. K., 351*n*, 356*n*, 357*n*
Murphy, K. J., 313*n*
Murray, G., 129*n*
Murrell, K. L., 461*n*
Murrman, K. F., 182*n*, 183*n*
Myers, D. W., 444*n*, 445*n*
Myers, P. S., 444*n*, 445*n*

Nahum-Shani, I., 491*n*
Nair-Reichert, U., 290*n*
Najita, J. M., 544*n*, 548*n*, 557*n*
Nakata, Y., 582*n*
Naples, M. I., 421*n*
Navasky, V., 49*n*
Neale, M. A., 349*n*, 351*n*, 354*n*, 401*n*, 559*n*
Nelson, D., 46*n*, 197*n*
Nelson, N. E., 506*n*, 516*n*
Nelson, W. B., 560*n*
Neufeld, M. F., 28*n*

Neumann, G. R., 424*n*
Newman, J. M., 263*n*, 265*n*, 452*n*
Newman, R. J., 533*n*
Newstrom, J. W., 311*n*
Newton, L. A., 13*n*
Ng, I., 494*n*
Nho, Y., 290*n*
Nickell, S., 590*n*
Nickelsburg, G., 316*n*, 490*n*
Nieswiadomy, M., 292*n*
Nilsson, E. A., 215*n*
Nissen, B., 16*n*, 22*n*, 23*n*
Norris, J. A., 87*n*
Northcott, H. C., 139*n*
Northcraft, G. B., 352*n*
Northrup, H. R., 180*n*, 312*n*, 581*n*
Norwood, S. H., 47*n*
Novy-Marx, R., 549*n*
Nowack, J., 491*n*
Nowlin, W. A., 507*n*

O'Brien, C. N., 174*n*
O'Brien, K. M., 149*n*, 547*n*
O'Brien, R., 52*n*
Ochs, J., 344*n*
O'Connell, J. F., 89*n*
Officer, D., 297*n*
Okunade, A. A., 290*n*
Olson, C. A., 47*n*, 199*n*, 296*n*, 324*n*, 325*n*, 424*n*, 482*n*, 493*n*, 515*n*, 516*n*, 555*n*, 556*n*, 557*n*, 558*n*, 559*n*, 560*n*
O'Reilly, C. A., III, 215*n*
Ormiston, R., 522*n*
Osterman, P., 308*n*, 463*n*
Oswald, R. A., 158*n*
Ozley, L., 461*n*

Paci, P., 318*n*
Park, H., 178*n*
Partridge, D. M., 411*n*, 560*n*
Paulson, D., 307*n*
Pearce, T. G., 522*n*
Pearlstein, G., 282*n*
Peetz, D., 573*n*
Pegnetter, R., 402*n*, 403*n*
Peled, N. O., 288*n*
Pencavel, J., 289*n*, 311*n*, 578*n*
Peng, H. Y., 582*n*
Peoples, J., 225*n*
Perl, A. E., 464*n*
Perline, M. M., 436*n*
Perry, J. L., 138*n*
Persons, O. S., 424*n*
Peters, E., 507*n*, 523*n*
Petersen, D. J., 515*n*
Petersen, J. S., 294*n*
Peterson, G. C., 474*n*
Peterson, M. F., 141*n*
Peterson, R. B., 176*n*, 177*n*, 208*n*, 475*n*, 478*n*, 479*n*, 491*n*, 494*n*
Pierce, B., 69*n*
Pierce, J. L., 311*n*, 465*n*
Piilutla, M. M., 351*n*
Pilarski, A., 316*n*, 490*n*
Pinkley, R. L., 349*n*, 352*n*
Piore, M. J., 7*n*, 19*n*, 581*n*
Piskorski, T. J., 162*n*, 187*n*, 464*n*, 522*n*
Pollack, S. D., 69*n*
Polodny, J., 351*n*
Ponak, A., 515*n*, 516*n*
Poole, M., 569*n*, 578*n*, 588*n*
Porter, A. A., 182*n*, 183*n*
Porterfield, R. I., 463*n*
Portnoi, D. D., 112*n*
Posthuma, R. A., 250*n*, 507*n*
Power, D., 360*n*
Prasow, P., 507*n*, 523*n*
Prennushi, G., 462*n*
Prentice, D., 297*n*, 309*n*
Preston, A., 77*n*
Preuss, G. A., 448*n*
Price, J., 491*n*
Pritchett, W. E., 338*n*
Pruitt, D. G., 353*n*, 402*n*
Pruitt, S. W., 426*n*
Pulliam, M. S., 430*n*

Quaglieri, P. L., 117*n*
Quan, K., 181*n*
Quigley, J. M., 78*n*

Ragan, J. F., Jr., 287*n*, 289*n*
Ramirez, M., 309*n*
Raphael, S., 289*n*
Raskin, A. H., 404*n*, 405*n*
Rasp, J., 187*n*
Rau, B. L., 556*n*
Rauh, J. D., 549*n*
Rayback, J. G., 38*n*, 39*n*, 43*n*, 44*n*, 48*n*, 49*n*
Ready, K. J., 143*n*, 180*n*, 246*n*
Reder, C. L., 521*n*
Reder, M. W., 18*n*, 582*n*
Reed, T. F., 189*n*
Rees, D. I., 491*n*
Rehfeldt, U., 571*n*
Rehmus, C. M., 338*n*, 406*n*, 555*n*
Reilly, B., 318*n*
Remington, J., 448*n*
Reshef, Y., 104*n*, 121*n*, 307*n*, 326*n*, 451*n*, 476*n*
Reusser, T. E., 420*n*
Rhee, Y., 591*n*
Rich, D. P., 180*n*, 187*n*
Richardson, F. M., 359*n*
Riddell, C., 182*n*, 183*n*
Riddell, W. C., 292*n*
Roberts, J. T., 318*n*
Roberts, M. T., 482*n*
Robfogel, S. S., 174*n*
Robinson, J. W., 476*n*
Roby, P. A., 96*n*, 140*n*
Rodgers, R. C., 520*n*
Rogers, J., 14*n*, 15*n*, 16*n*, 236*n*
Rogovsky, N., 451*n*
Ronan, W., 491*n*
Roomkin, M., 90*n*, 200*n*
Roose, P. D., 401*n*
Rose, D., 423*n*
Rose, D. C., 247*n*
Rose, J. B., 18*n*, 20*n*
Rose, K. M., 312*n*
Rose, S., 515*n*, 516*n*
Rosenblum, J. D., 58*n*
Rosenthal, L. A., 78*n*
Rosse, J., 184*n*
Roth, A. E., 344*n*, 356*n*
Rowland, K., 9*n*
Ruback, R. S., 199*n*
Rubenfeld, S. A., 311*n*, 465*n*
Rubin, B., 462*n*
Rubin, J., 427*n*
Rubin, J. Z., 341*n*, 349*n*, 350*n*, 351*n*, 352*n*
Rubin, L., 357*n*
Rubin, R., 462*n*
Rubinstein, S., 451*n*, 457*n*
Ruh, R. A., 280*n*, 282*n*
Ryan, T. F., 413*n*
Ryder, M. S., 338*n*

Saad, L., 14*n*
Safford, S., 19*n*
Salem, G. R., 185*n*
Salsburg, S. W., 200*n*
Saltzman, G. M., 150*n*, 212*n*, 411*n*
Sandver, M. H., 180*n*, 506*n*
Saunders, K., 441*n*, 443*n*
Savino, D. M., 178*n*
Sayles, L. R., 96*n*, 98*n*, 100*n*
Schank, T., 570*n*
Schenkel, K., 491*n*
Schmidt, S. M., 116*n*, 438*n*
Schnabel, C., 570*n*, 586*n*, 591*n*
Schneider-Denenberg, T., 521*n*
Schnell, J. F., 309*n*, 319*n*, 423*n*
Schoenfeld, G., 142*n*
Schoumaker, F., 356*n*
Schriver, W. R., 352*n*
Schuster, M., 282*n*, 283*n*, 449*n*, 460*n*, 461*n*
Schwab, C. M., 41*n*
Schwab, D. P., 79*n*, 260*n*, 318*n*
Schwartz, R. M., 96*n*
Schwochau, S., 150*n*, 152*n*, 325*n*, 460*n*, 533*n*, 558*n*
Scott, C., 70*n*, 180*n*, 187*n*
Seago, J. A., 296*n*
Seeber, R. L., 158*n*, 208*n*, 503*n*
Seers, A., 180*n*
Segal, P., 454*n*
Selekman, B. M., 345*n*, 347*n*
Selekman, S. K., 345*n*, 347*n*
Selvin, D. F., 43*n*
Sewerynski, M., 568*n*
Sexton, E. A., 436*n*
Shaiken, H., 453*n*
Shapiro, D. L., 350*n*
Sharp, W. H., 521*n*
Sharpe, T., 348*n*
Shaw, K., 462*n*
Shea, D. G., 177*n*, 188*n*
Sherer, P. D., 62*n*, 138*n*, 208*n*, 452*n*
Sherman, M. P., 141*n*
Shirom, A., 426*n*
Shore, L. M., 13*n*, 136*m*
Siebert, W. S., 591*n*
Siegel, R., 414*n*
Sikorski, J. C., 117*n*
Silverblatt, R., 189*n*
Simkin, W. E., 401*n*, 404*n*, 520*n*
Simoni, M., 581*n*
Simpson, P. A., 139*n*
Sinclair, R. R., 422*n*
Singh, P., 418*n*
Sinicropi, A. V., 513*n*, 514*n*
Skarlicki, D. P., 140*n*
Slaughter, M. J., 226*n*

Slotsve, G. A., 292*n*, 479*n*
Slottje, D. J., 292*n*
Slowinski, B. J., 581*n*
Smith, F. J., 10*n*
Smith, R. A., 500*n*
Smith, S. C., 570*n*, 586*n*
Sobel, R. S., 129*n*, 317*n*
Sockell, D., 220*n*, 221*n*, 253*n*
Soskice, M. D., 582*n*
Sousa, M. D., 430*n*
Spector, P. E., 10*n*
Sperka, S., 186*n*
Spizman, L. M., 548*n*
Spognardi, M. A., 158*n*, 214*n*
Spreitzer, G. M., 89*n*
Stagner, R., 410*n*
Stallworth, L., 88*n*, 134*n*
Stamatakos, T. C., 162*n*, 187*n*
Stanley, M. C., 120*n*
Stanley, T. D., 289*n*
Starkman, P. E., 484*n*
Staudohar, P., 429*n*
Stengos, T., 289*n*
Stephan, P. E., 182*n*
Stephens, E. C., 485*n*, 521*n*
Stephenson, G. M., 353*n*, 404*n*
Stepina, L. P., 188*n*
Stern, J. L., 544*n*, 548*n*, 553*n*, 555*n*, 557*n*, 558*n*
Stern, R. N., 559*n*, 560*n*
Stevens, C. M., 5*n*, 341*n*, 342*n*, 554*n*
Stevis, D., 572*n*
Stewart, G., 479*n*
Stewart, J., 324*n*
Stewart, M., 422*n*
Stieber, J., 295*n*, 512*n*, 536*n*
Stirling, J., 570*n*, 571*n*
Stone, G. W., Jr., 560*n*
Stoop, S., 571*n*
Story, A., 174*n*
Stratton, K., 104*n*
Stratton-Devine, K., 104*n*, 121*n*, 476*n*
Strauss, G., 7*n*, 10*n*, 11*n*, 95*n*, 96*n*, 98*n*, 100*n*, 105*n*, 106*n*, 115*n*, 135*n*, 141*n*, 142*n*, 143*n*, 188*n*, 348*n*
Streeck, W., 581*n*
Stringer, K. G., 472*n*
Stuhlmacher, A. F., 349*n*
Sturmthal, A., 579*n*
Suchard, R., 136*n*, 137*n*
Suffern, A., 50*n*
Summers, C. W., 487*n*
Suschnigg, P., 488*n*
Svorny, S., 297*n*
Sweetman, A., 322*n*
Swift, M. S., 507*n*
Swint, J. M., 560*n*

Taft, P., 32*n*, 41*n*, 50*n*, 51*n*, 54*n*
Taras, D. G., 201*n*, 209*n*
Taylor, B. J., 47*n*
Taylor, G. S., 322*n*
Taylor, J. A., 419*n*
Taylor, L. J., 554*n*
Teague, P., 580*n*
Teerlink, R., 461*n*
Teixeira, P., 586*n*
Tener, B. Z., 532*n*
Tesluk, P. E., 340*n*
Tetrick, L. E., 136*n*
Thacker, J. W., 140*n*
Theilmann, J., 150*n*
Thieblot, A. J., 123*n*
Thomas, R. K., 9*n*
Thomas, S. L., 268*n*, 297*n*
Thomason, T., 548*n*
Thompson, L., 349*n*
Thompson, M., 567*n*, 580*n*
Thornicroft, K. W., 519*n*
Threlkeld, T. S., 173*n*
Tiegs, R. B., 139*n*
Tijdens, K., 576*n*
Tinsley, C. H., 439*n*
Tjosvold, D., 495*n*
Todor, W. D., 489*n*
Tomkiewicz, J., 560*n*
Torigian, M., 51*n*
Toth, A., 568*n*
Tracy, J. S., 297*n*, 410*n*, 418*n*, 421*n*
Traxler, F., 241*n*
Truesdale, J. C., 87*n*
Tschirhart, M., 89*n*
Tuman, J. P., 572*n*
Turkus, Burton B., 523*n*
Turnbull, P. J., 233*n*
Turner, L., 567*n*, 572*n*, 573*n*, 590*n*
Turner, T., 131*n*, 132*n*

Uddin, A. N. M. M., 506*n*, 516*n*
Ulman, L., 582*n*
Ury, W., 440*n*

Vachon, D., 422*n*
Valletta, R. G., 323*n*, 548*n*
Valley, K. L., 354*n*, 401*n*
Vandenberg, R. V., 136*n*
Vanderbush, W., 572*n*
van Jaarsveld, D. D., 169*n*
van Klaveren, M., 576*n*
Van Norman, K. L., 452*n*
Varma, A., 88*n*
Vasconcellos, G. M., 425*n*
Vedder, R., 91*n*
Verma, A., 23*n*, 101*n*, 295*n*, 455*n*, 456*n*, 457*n*
Visnic, B., 231*n*
Visser, J., 576*n*, 577*n*, 578*n*
von Nordenflycht, A., 400*n*
Voos, P. B., 70*n*, 173*n*, 251*n*, 290*n*, 455*n*, 459*n*, 460*n*
Vroman, S. B., 291*n*, 421*n*

Wachter, M. L., 4*n*, 91*n*, 288*n*
Waddington, J., 130*n*, 571*n*
Waddoups, C. J., 250*n*, 291*n*, 590*n*
Wagner, J., 570*n*, 585*n*, 586*n*, 591*n*
Wailes, N., 582*n*
Wakabayashi, M., 569*n*
Wakeley, J. H., 280*n*, 282*n*
Waldstein, W., 103*n*
Walker, J. M., 175*n*
Walker, R. L., 476*n*
Wall, J. A., Jr., 404*n*
Wallerstein, M., 581*n*
Walsh, D. J., 267*n*
Walsh, W. J., 532*n*
Walsworth, S., 297*n*
Walters, A. E., 349*n*
Walters, V., 85*n*
Walton, R. E., 342*n*, 343*n*, 344*n*, 345*n*, 347*n*, 355*n*, 356*n*, 438*n*, 439*n*
Wang, X., 560*n*
Wang, Y., 418*n*
Warchol, G., 555*n*
Wass, V. J., 233*n*
Waters, M. S., 533*n*
Watson, M. R., 208*n*
Wazeter, D. L., 139*n*
Webb, J., 404*n*
Wei, K. C. J., 426*n*
Wei, X., 591*n*
Weil, D., 318*n*
Weiler, P. C., 18*n*
Weingart, L. R., 351*n*
Weinstein, M., 567*n*
Wells, D., 104*n*, 201*n*, 241*n*
Wells, J. C., 86*n*, 442*n*
Wermuth, A., 69*n*
Wesman, E. C., 204*n*, 318*n*
Wessels, W. J., 291*n*
West, R., 214*n*
Western, B., 4*n*, 20*n*
Wetzel, K., 136*n*
Wever, K. R., 455*n*, 570*n*, 572*n*, 573*n*, 590*n*
Wheeler, H. N., 10*n*, 11*n*, 23*n*, 188*n*, 504*n*, 519*n*, 546*n*, 554*n*, 587*n*
White, J. K., 283*n*
White, M. D., 17*n*, 237*n*
White, R. E., 426*n*
White, S. B., 349*n*, 354*n*
Wickens, C. M., 426*n*
Wilhite, A., 150*n*
Wilkinson, D., 591*n*
Willaby, H. W., 348*n*
Williams, J. S., 29*n*, 30*n*
Willman, P., 131*n*, 132*n*, 575*n*
Wilson, J. T., 312*n*
Windmuller, J. P., 569*n*, 579*n*
Witney, F., 47*n*
Wolkinson, B. W., 174*n*, 196*n*, 504*n*, 522*n*
Wolters, R. S., 482*n*
Wong, K., 246*n*
Wood, S., 23*n*, 92*n*, 577*n*
Wright, M., 575*n*
Wunnava, P. V., 288*n*, 290*n*

Yager, D. V., 173*n*
Yang, D., 247*n*
Yasbeck, C., 582*n*
Yates, J., 465*n*
Yellen, J., 203*n*
Yellowitz, I., 42*n*
Young, J., 461*n*

Zagenczyk, T. J., 149*n*
Zajac, E. J., 401*n*
Zax, J. S., 543*n*, 547*n*, 548*n*
Zeller, F. A., 444*n*
Zerbe, W., 515*n*, 516*n*
Zeuthen, F., 342*n*
Zieger, R. H., 53*n*
Zientara, P., 568*n*
Zigarelli, M. A., 535*n*
Zimmerman, M. B., 199*n*
Zollitsch, H., 264*n*
Zullo, R., 151*n*
Zumbolo, A., 401*n*
Zwerling, H. L., 548*n*, 561*n*

Subject Index

Ability to pay
  arbitration and, 558
  pay-level changes and, 261
  wage demands and, 258–259, 260*f*
Absenteeism, 448, 450, 451, 453, 459, 460*t*, 464, 493
Absorption, merger by, 120–121
Accelerated depreciation practices, 359
Accretion, 168
Ad hoc arbitrators, 505–506
Administrative law judge, 88
Adolph Coors Company, 427
AFL (American Federation of Labor). *See* American Federation of Labor (AFL)
AFL-CIO. *See* American Federation of Labor-Congress of Industrial Organizations (AFL-CIO)
African Americans, 188
AFSCME. *See* American Federation of State, County, and Municipal Employees (AFSCME)
Age Discrimination in Employment Act (ADEA), 79*t*
Agency fees, 127, 128
Agency shop
  explanation of, 317
  prohibitions against, 129
  right-to-work states and, 73
Aircraft industry, 315–316
Aircraft Mechanics Fraternal Association, 65, 406
Airline industry
  bankruptcies in, 430–432
  bargaining units in, 249
  consolidation in, 169–170
  deregulation in, 225
  passenger check-ins in, 233
  pattern bargaining in, 245
  unions representing, 21–22
Air Line Pilots Association, 413
Air traffic controllers, 129
Allied Industrial Workers, 54
Ally doctrine, 419
Alternative Dispute Resolution Act, 86
Amalgamated Clothing and Textile Workers (ACTWU), 190
Amalgamated Meat Cutters, 121
Amalgamation, merger by, 121
Ambulatory site picketing, 413
American Arbitration Association (AAA), 477, 508, 512
American Conservative Union, 153
American Federation of Government Employees (AFGE), 122, 536
American Federation of Labor (AFL)
  craft unions in, 104
  creation of, 27, 33
  Danbury Hatters and, 39
  leadership in, 53, 56
  membership statistics for, 40
  during 1920s, 42
  organization of, 33–34
  World War II and, 50
American Federation of Labor-Congress of Industrial Organizations (AFL-CIO)
  Change to Win coalition and, 118–119
  Committee on Political Education, 153
  corruption investigations by, 54–55
  creation of, 27, 53–54
  hierarchy in, 120
  International Brotherhood of Teamsters and, 56, 110
  leadership in, 58
  membership in, 54, 101–102, 118
  organizing strategies of, 176
  per capita tax of, 122
  political positions of, 152
  profile of, 117–118
  relationship with state and local central bodies and, 119–120, 120*f*
  UNITE HERE and, 105
American Federation of State, County, and Municipal Employees (AFSCME), 112, 113, 113*f*, 448, 461, 551
American Federation of Teachers (AFT), 543
American Manufacturing case, 500
American Nurses Association, 180
American Plan, 41, 47, 197
American Railway Union (ARU), 36
Americans for Democratic Action (ADA), 153
Americans with Disabilities Act of 1990 (ADA), 79*t*
America West Airlines, 413–414
Appeal Boards, 86
Appropriate bargaining unit, 161
Arbitrability, 500
Arbitration
  cases on, 526–529
  costs of, 516–517, 517*t*
  deferral of statutory grievances to, 501–502
  of discipline cases, 518–523
  early use of, 32
  evidentiary rules in, 512–514
  expedited, 517–518
  explanation of, 498–499
  Federal Mediation and Conciliation Service statistics for, 524*t*
  final-offer, 554–557
  function of, 481
  hearing procedures for, 511–513, 518
  historical background of, 499–502
  interest, 407, 498
  NLRB deferral to, 504–505
  of past practices disputes, 523
  posthearing in, 512
  prehearing steps for, 510–511
  preparation of award in, 514–515
  presentation of case in, 512
  procedural difficulties and resolutions in, 515–517
  processes prior to, 505
  in public sector, 553–559
  remedies in, 514
  representation in, 518
  representatives of parties in, 512
  rights, 407, 498–499
  role of, 525
  substituted for litigation, 503–504
  Supreme Court decisions on, 499–504, 515
  time delays in, 515–516
Arbitrators
  ad hoc, 505–506
  methods to choose, 477
  qualifications for, 507
  selection of, 477, 505–507
  sources of, 508, 509*f*, 510
Areawide labor-management committees (AWLMCs), 446–447
Argentina, 575
AT&T, 181
Attitudinal structuring, 344, 347, 347*f*
Authorization card campaign, 158–159
Authorization cards, 160*f*
Automobile industry
  global competition in, 226–228
  market share losses in, 20–21
  organization in, 43–44, 49
  pattern bargaining in, 245
  work design in, 305–306

Bakers Union, 54–55
Bakery and Confectionery Workers Union, 54
Bankruptcies, 430–432
Bankruptcy courts, 430
Bankruptcy law, 430
Bargaining/bargaining process
  attitudinal structuring as, 344, 347, 347*f*
  basic rules for, 342–343
  from behavioral perspective, 342
  Congress and, 45
  distributive, 343–344, 345*t*–346*t*, 355–356, 406
  from economic perspective, 341–342
  election of 2010 and, 533–534, 550
  explanation of, 4, 219–220
  fractional, 488–489
  in global market economies, 578–580
  good-faith, 220

Bargaining/bargaining process—*Cont.*
grievances and, 487–491, 492*f*, 493
integrative, 344, 407, 438–444, 442*f*, 443*f*
interest-based, 350
interorganizational, 347–348
multilateral, 545–546
mutual-gains, 344, 350, 439–440
nonwage issues in, 302–326 (*See also* Nonwage bargaining issues)
pay administration and, 259–260 (*See also* Pay programs)
public sector, 535–536, 537*t*–542*t*, 543–552 (*See also* Public sector bargaining)
sequence of activities in, 328, 329*f*, 330
specific issues and, 355
types of issues in, 220, 221*f*
during World War II, 50–51
Bargaining books, 335, 338
Bargaining convention, 339–340
Bargaining environment
actor roles and, 353–354, 353*f*
attributes of parties and, 348–350
bargaining power and, 237–240
competition and concentration in markets and, 224–225
consumer demand and, 229–230
employee interests and, 236–237
employer interests and, 230–232, 232*f*
global competition and, 226–228
labor-capital substitution and, 234*f*, 233–235
labor force demographics and employer growth and, 228–229
labor markets and, 235–236
legal and political structure and, 219–223
negotiation process and, 350–352
perceptions of bargainers and, 352–353
public policy and, 223–224, 251–252
regulation and deregulation and, 225–226
union interests and, 237
Bargaining orders, 185, 186
Bargaining power
elasticity of demand for products and, 238
elements of, 237–238
influence of, 252–253, 253*f*
union, 240
wage negotiations and, 235
Bargaining structures
centralization and decentralization in, 249
change in industrial, 250–251
coalition, 248–249, 251
conglomerate and multinational, 246–247
coordinated, 247–249, 251
craft units within employer, 249
explanation of, 240–241
in global market economies, 580–582, 583*t*
industrywide, 243–244
influence of, 252–253, 253*f*
multiemployer, 241–243, 242*f*
national/local, 244
pattern, 245–246
wide-area and multicraft, 244–245
Bargaining units
accretion and, 168
appropriate, 161
court decisions and, 251–252
desired employer, 165–166
desired union, 164
explanation of, 163, 251
female-dominated, 177–178
joint employers and, 169
legal constraints and, 163–164
in local unions, 99–100
NLRB policy and, 166–168, 251
public sector, 543
reorganization and reclassification and, 168–169
successor organizations and, 169
Beck, Dave, 54, 110
Belgium, 575, 578
Bell Atlantic, 312
Benefits. *See* Employee benefits; Pay form
Benefit status seniority, 278–279
Benefit-status seniority, 319
Beverly Enterprises, 183–184
Binding arbitration, 208
Bipartisan Campaign Reform Act of 2002, 147–148
Blue Cross-Blue Shield, 180
Bluffing, 352
Board-directed elections, 162
Borden Co. case, 166
Boston Journeymen Bootmakers' Society, 29–30
Boycotts
function of, 39–40, 426–427
secondary, 52, 412
Supreme Court and, 40
Boyle, Emmett, 416
Boys Markets case, 501
Bridgestone/Firestone, 425, 427
Bucket bargaining, 441, 442*f*
Bucks Stove case, 39
Bumping, 319
Bundesbank, 582
Bureau of Apprenticeship and Training (Employment and Training Administration), 85
Bureau of International Labor Affairs, 85
Bureau of Labor Statistics (BLS), 85
Burger, Anna, 59
Bush, George H. W., 146
Bush, George W.
Department of Homeland Security and, 532
Executive Order 13202 and, 481
steel tariffs and, 226
threatened aircraft mechanics strike and, 65, 406
unions relations and, 550
West Coast Dock Workers and, 74
Business agents, for local unions, 95–96
Business unionism, 28
Butcher Workers, 121
Byrnes Act of 1936, 76
California State Employees Association (NEA), 542
Canada
company unions in, 209
grievance issues in, 476, 479, 494
income distribution in, 20
integrative bargaining in, 440
NAFTA and, 146
private sector unions in, 20
strikes in, 418, 422, 423
Capistrano (California) United School District, 415
Capital, 233–235, 234*f*
Capitalists, 196
Card check agreements, 181–182
Carey, Ron, 112, 122
Carnegie Steel Company, 35
Carpenters (UBC)
Change to Win coalition and, 58, 119
explanation of, 54
Carter, Jimmy, 74
Cases
Continuing or Abandoning the Special-Order Fabrication Business, 468
GMFC Attitude Survey, 327
GMFC Custom Conveyer Division, 193–194
GMFC Impasse, 434
grievance arbitration, 526–529
Health Care Bargaining and the PPACA, 301
Locating the New Recreational Vehicle Plant, 217
Material Handling Equipment Association Bargaining Group, 255
New Production Equipment: Greater Efficiency with Less Effort or a Speedup?, 496–497
Teacher Bargaining at Pleasant Ridge, 562–564
Center for Faith-Based and Neighborhood Partnerships, 86
Central bodies, state and local, 119–120, 120*f*
CenturyLink, 181, 226
Certification elections
employer size and, 172–173
explanation of, 160
Chamber of Commerce, 153
Change to Win (CTW)
early actions of, 22–23, 27, 58–59
profile of, 118–119
unions affiliated with, 101
CHAOS tactic, 413–414
Chapter 11 bankruptcies, 430–432
Chicago Transit Authority (CTA), 415
Ching, Cyrus, 404, 405
Chrysler
economic crisis of 2008 and, 228
organization of, 44, 49
team approach at, 452–453
CIO (Congress of Industrial Organizations). *See* Congress of Industrial Organizations (CIO)
Civil Rights Act of 1964, Title VII, 79*t*, 521
Civil service employee associations, 542

Civil Service Reform Act of 1978, Title VII, 56, 63*f*, 531–532
Class consciousness, 7–8
Clayton Act of 1914, 40
Clinton, Bill
  NAFTA and, 146
  public sector unions and, 550
  Team Act and, 90
Closed shop, 316
Coalition bargaining, 248–249, 251
Cohesiveness
  relationship between threat and, 8–9, 8*f*
  role of group, 7, 23
Collective bargaining. *See* Bargaining/bargaining process
Collective Bargaining and Negotiations Survey, 320
Collective behavior
  class consciousness and, 7–8
  explanation of, 7
  external threat and, 8–9
  group cohesiveness and, 7
Collyer doctrine, 504
Colorado Fuel and Iron Company, 39
Commensalistic mergers, 121
Commerce clause, 47
Commitment
  dual, 137–138, 138*f*, 140–141
  elements of union, 135–137
  model of union, 137*f*
Committee for Industrial Organization (CIO), 43
Committee on Political Education (COPE) (AFL-CIO), 153
Common situs picketing, 412
Commonwealth v. Hunt (1842), 30
Communications, Energy & Paperworkers Union, 440
Communications Workers of America (CWA), 181, 226, 248–249, 251
Communities, 16
Community action, 176
Community-based movements, 22
Community of interests, 166
Company unions
  in Canada, 209
  explanation of, 46, 197
  Wagner Act and, 209
Competition
  global, 226–228
  in markets, 224–225
Competitive markets, 224
Competitive-status seniority, 319
Conglomerates, 246–247
Congress, U.S.
  collective bargaining and, 45
  investigation of attempts to thwart or rebuff union activities, 46
  labor law reform in, 90–92
  NAFTA and, 147
  regulation of employer activities by, 47
  right-to-work laws and, 52
Congress of Industrial Organizations (CIO)
  creation of, 27
  industrial unions in, 104
  leadership in, 53
  membership statistics for, 44
  during 1930s, 48, 49
  World War II and, 50
Consent elections, 162
Conspiracy doctrine
  explanation of, 29, 39
  Norris-LaGuardia Act and, 67
Construction industry, 251
Construction unions, 72
Continental Airlines, 169, 170
Continued operations, 416–417
Continuing or Abandoning the Special-Order Fabrication Business Case, 468
Contract administration
  dispute resolution methods and, 481–483
  employee and union rights in grievance processing and, 484–487
  explanation of, 469, 470
  in global market economies, 587
  grievance effects on employers and employees and, 493–495
  grievance procedures and, 475–480, 478*f*, 480*f*
  grievances and bargaining and, 487–491, 492*f*, 493
  issues in, 470–475
Contracting out, during strikes, 419
Contract negotiation exercise, 362–375
Contract negotiation preparation
  bargaining books for, 335, 338
  costing the contract as, 332, 333*t*–334*t*, 335
  data collection as, 331
  identifying probable union demands as, 331–332
  management planning for, 336*t*–337*t*
  review of expiring contract as, 330
  setting objectives as, 330
  strategies and logistics for, 338
  strike preparation and, 338
  by unions, 339–340
Contract negotiations
  bargaining environment and, 348–354, 354*f*, 358–360, 359*t*
  bargaining function and, 341–343
  behavior theories of, 343–344, 345*t*–346*t*, 347–348, 347*f*
  committing to position in, 356
  deadlines in, 356–357
  distributive bargaining and, 355–356
  duty to bargain and, 469–470
  hot cargo issues and, 72
  initial presentation in, 354–355
  management preparation for, 330–338, 333*t*–334*f*, 336*t*–337*t*
  mock exercise in, 362–375
  National Mediation Board and, 64–65, 328
  with newly organized employers, 190
  nonagreement in, 358
  outcomes and, 358–360, 359*t*
  overview of, 328
  process of, 328, 329*f*, 330
  under Railway Labor Act, 64–65
  requests for, 341
  settlements and ratifications in, 357–358
  in specific issues, 355
  union and management representations rights for, 313–314
Contracts
  costing methods for, 332, 333*t*–334*t*, 335
  discipline and discharge clauses in, 314–315
  dues checkoff in, 317
  function of, 1
  between General Manufacturing & Fabrication Company and Local 384, United Steelworkers of America, 376–398
  grievance procedures clause in, 477, 478*f*
  individual rights in, 485–487
  length of, 313
  no-strike clauses in, 481, 483
  review of expiring, 330
  setting objectives for, 330
  wage clauses in, 298*t*, 299
  yellow-dog, 41, 45, 66–67
Control rights, 437–438
Conventions, national union, 103
Cooling-off period, 400
Cooperation. *See also* Union-management cooperation
  creating and sustaining, 444, 446
  methods of, 446–455, 456*t*, 457
  model of effective, 445*f*
  research on effects across organizations, 457–460, 459t, *460*t
  research on long-term effects of, 460–462
Cooperative clauses, 444, 445*f*
Cooperative continuum, 444, 444*f*
Coordinated bargaining, 247–249, 251
Coordinated campaigns, 415, 416
Copeland Anti-Kickback Act of 1934, 76
Cordwainers, 29–30, 196
Corporate campaigns, 104, 414–415
Corporations. *See also* Employers
  ownership of, 1–2
  political contributions by, 52, 74, 147–148
  shareholders in, 2, 3
  tax rate for, 57
Corporatism/corporatist environment
  explanation of, 28, 219
  historical period of, 197–198, 306
  labor relations and, 222–223
  work design and, 306
Corruption
  extent of union, 54–55, 100
  related to finances, 122–123
Cost-of-living adjustment (COLA), 259
Craft severance, 167–168
Craft unions. *See also* Unions
  in American Federation of Labor, 104
  development of, 27
  pension and welfare benefits and, 121, 123
Craft units, 249

Danbury Hatters case, 39, 67
Darrow, Clarence, 38
Davis-Bacon Act of 1931, 79*t*, 310

Deadlines, negotiation, 356–357
Debs, Eugene, 36, 37
Decertification elections, 160
Decertifications, 214–215
Defined benefit pension plans
  explanation of, 90, 272, 274*t*, 275
  public sector, 549
Defined contribution pension plans, 272, 274*t*
Delphi Corporation, 230, 231
Delta Airlines, 169–170
Democracy
  functional, 99
  industrial, 586–587, 588*t*–589*t*
  in local unions, 98–101, 129
Democratic Party
  campaign contributions to, 148
  election of 2010 and, 534
  endorsements and, 151
  unions and, 23, 146–147
  voting behaviors and positions of, 151
Demographics
  for contract negotiations, 331
  employee benefits and, 277–278
  employer growth and labor force, 228–229
Denver Building Trades Council cases, 412
Department of Homeland Security (DHS), 532
Deregulation, 225
Detroit Free Press-Detroit News, 417
Detroit Newspaper Association, 418–419
Discharge
  contract clauses related to, 314–315
  as grievance issue, 471
Discipline
  arbitration for cases involving, 518–523, 520*t*
  contract clauses related to, 314–315, 471
  corrective, 519–520
  for email abuse, 522–523
  for fighting, 522
  role of, 518–519
  for sexual harassment, 521–522
  for substance abuse, 521
  of union activists, 484–485
  for work-family conflicts, 522
Discipline proceedings
  right to union representation in, 484
  for wildcat strikes, 483
Discrimination
  as contract issue, 474
  against prounion job applicants, 321–322
Dispute resolution
  explanation of, 481
  grievance mediation as, 481–482
  project labor agreements and, 481
  for wildcat strikes, 482–483
Dissatisfaction, job, 10, 14. *See also* Job satisfaction
Distillers Union, 54
Distributive bargaining
  explanation of, 343–344, 345*t*–346*t*
  fact-finding and, 406
  tactics in, 355–356
Doctrinaire organizations, 201
Drive system, 53, 306
Dual commitment
  explanation of, 137–138, 138*f*
  of stewards, 140–141
Dual governance, in local unions, 99–101, 99*f*
Due process, 207
Dues
  collection and administration of, 122
  cost of, 172
  requirements for, 129
  used for political activity, 154
Dues checkoff, 317
Dumping, 145
Duty to bargain, 72, 469–470

Economic issues
  effect of unemployment rate on wages, 290
  employee relations and, 21
  inflation in late 1960s as, 222
  in 1970s, 56–57, 197–198
  in 2008, 228
  in unionized vs. nonunionized organizations, 198–201
  union outcome and, 143–144
Economic strikes. *See also* Strikes
  explanation of, 409
  incidence of, 421
  replacements for, 418
  rights of strikers in, 419–420
Efficiency, 305
Election ballot, NLRB, 162, 163*f*
Elections
  board-directed, 162
  certification, 160, 172–173
  consent, 162
  consequences of 2010, 533–534, 550
  decertification, 160
  environmental characteristics and, 188
  NLRB role in, 73, 160–162, 162*f*, 172, 184–187, 189, 190, 215
  petitions for, 161–162
  raid, 160
  representation, 10, 73, 110, 160–162 (*See also* Representation elections)
  rerun, 185–186
  union characteristics and, 187
  worker characteristics and, 188–189
Electrical Workers, 248–249
Electromation case, 209, 464
Electronic Workers, 248
Email abuse, 522–523
Employee benefits. *See also* Pay form; specific benefits
  demographics and, 229, 277–278
  health insurance, 269–272, 271*t*, 273*t*, 274*t*
  miscellaneous, 277, 298*t*
  pension plans and, 272, 274*t*, 275–276
  wage- and person-tied, 269
Employee Benefits Security Administration (EBSA), 83
Employee Free Choice Act (EFCA), 91
Employee involvement programs (EIPs), 136, 450–452
Employee relations
  economy and shift in, 21
  practices in nonunion, 209–211, 210*t*
  success of, 4
Employee Retirement Income Security Act of 1974 (ERISA)
  compliance with, 83
  employee stock ownership plans and, 464
  explanation of, 78, 80*t*
  pension administration and, 123, 272, 275, 276
Employee review boards, 206
Employees. *See also* Unskilled workers
  effect of grievances on, 493–495
  election results and, 188–289
  employer interests vs. interests of, 236–237
  employer interrogation of, 175
  exempt, 310
  local, 536
  nonexempt, 310
  professional, 70
  state, 535–536
  Wagner Act definition of, 69
Employee stock ownership plans (ESOPs), 459, 464–465, 586
Employer-employee committees, 209
Employer interests
  labor as derived demand and, 230–232, 232*f*
  labor-capital substitution and, 233–235, 234*f*
  labor markets and, 235, 236
Employers. *See also* Union-management cooperation
  bargaining unit goals of, 165–166, 166*f*
  contract representation rights for, 313–314
  effect of grievances on, 493–495
  goals and objectives of, 4, 437
  interrogation of employees by, 175
  joint, 169
  neutral, 412
  opposition to Wagner Act by, 46, 47
  organizing campaign strategies and tactics used by, 182–184
  primary, 412
  responses to strikes, 415–419
  rights and responsibilities of, 1
  unfair labor practices of, 71, 183, 184, 214
  unionization and investments by, 200
  union resistance by, 46–47, 212, 213*t*, 214, 436 (*See also* Union avoidance)
  Wagner Act definition of, 68–69
Employment
  changes in union membership and, 6, 6*t*
  functional democracy of, 99
  government regulation of, 17–18
  regulation of, 220–222
  risks associated with, 2
  unionized, 99
Employment and Training Administration (ETA), 85
Employment practices, 474
Energy issues of 1970s, 20, 197, 222

Enterprise Wheel case, 500
Environmental factors
  election results and, 188
  union avoidance and, 201–202
  union member participation and, 135
Equal Employment Opportunity Commission (EEOC), 501, 502
Equal Pay Act of 1963 (EPA), 79*t*
Equity
  pay-level changes and, 261–262
  wage demands and, 257–258, 260*f*
Erdman Act of 1898, 40
Establishments, 1
Europe, 566–571, 575–587, 576*t*, 588*t*–589*t*, 590–591. *See also* Labor movements in global market economies
European Trade Union Congress, 570
European Union (EU), 92, 570–572, 575, 577, 579, 580, 585. *See also* Labor movements in global market economies
European Work Council (EWC), 570, 571
Evidentiary rules, 512–514
Excelsior list, 162
Exclusive representation, 46, 156
Executive committees, in local unions, 96
Executive Order 10988, 55, 531
Executive Order 11246, 83
Executive Order 11491, 55
Executive Order 11616, 55–56
Executive Order 13202, 481
Executive Order 13496, 92
Executive Order 13502, 481
Exempt employees, 310
Expedited arbitration, 517–518
Export-oriented industrialization (EOI), 572, 573*f*

Fact-finding
  effects of, 407–408
  explanation of, 406
  in public sector, 552–553
  uses for, 406–407
Fair Labor Standards Act of 1937 (FLSA), 79*t*, 310
Fair representation
  explanation of, 484, 485
  individual rights and, 485–487
  Supreme Court and, 487
Fair-share payments, 546
Family and Medical Leave Act of 1993, 78, 81*t*
Farm Workers (UFW), 58, 119
Federal Aviation Administration, 57
Federal Aviation Authorization Act of 1996, 64
Federal employee unions, 122, 129–130, 130*t*
Federal government, 222–223
Federal Impass Panel, 55
Federal Labor Relations Authority (FLRA), 56, 531, 532
Federal Mediation and Conciliation Service (FMCS)
  arbitration statistics for 2009, 524*t*
  arbitrators supplied by, 477, 508, 509*f*, 510
  areawide labor-management committees and, 446
  bargaining tools developed by, 440–442, 442*f*
  contract modification and, 72
  establishment of, 52, 86
  function of, 74, 75, 86, 219, 222, 404, 531
  mediation data from, 404, 405*t*, 406
  notifications and caseloads for, 404, 405*t*
  strikes or picketing at health care facilities and, 73
Federal Mine Safety Act of 1977, 81*t*
Federal Reserve Bank, 56, 57
Federal Services Impasses Panel (FSIP), 531
Federal Society of Journeyman Cordwainers, 29
Federal Trade Commission, 223
Federal Unemployment Tax Act, 80*t*
FedEx, 64
Fees
  agency, 127, 128
  collection and administration of, 122
Field representatives, 103
Fighting, 522
Final-offer arbitration
  elements of, 557
  explanation of, 554–555
  results of, 555–556
Finance
  categories of union, 121–122
  corruption in union, 122–123
  revenue sources and, 122
Firefighters
  bargaining laws covering, 535, 537*t*–542*t*
  pay and benefits for, 547–548, 558
527 organizations, 148, 150
Flextime, 312
FMCS. *See* Federal Mediation and Conciliation Service (FMCS)
Food and Commercial Workers (UFCW), 119
Ford, Henry, 43, 305–306
Fordism, 305–306
Ford Motor Company, 47, 49, 230, 447, 457
Foreign direct investment (FDI), 590
Foremen, 197
403(b) plans, 274*t*, 275
401(k) plans, 274*t*, 275
Fractional bargaining, 141, 488–489
France, 569, 577–579, 584
Franken, Al, 91
Fraser, Douglas, 258
Fraternal Order of Police (FOP), 536
Free riding
  factors contributing to, 129
  in federal employee unions, 122, 129–130, 130*t*
  right-to-work rules and, 317
  statistics related to, 131*t*
Frick, Henry, 35
Functional democracy, 98–101

Gainsharing plans
  comparative analysis of, 449*t*
  effectiveness of, 459*t*, 460
  function of, 279, 285*t*, 449, 450
  Impro-Share, 283–285, 284*t*, 285*t*, 449*t*
  negotiations over, 358
  Rucker, 283, 283*t*, 285*t*, 449*t*
  Scanlon, 279–280, 281*f*, 282–283, 285*t*, 449*t*, 450
Gender. *See also* Women
  negotiating behavior and, 349–350
  promotions and, 323–324
  representation preferences of, 188–189
  union member participation among, 133
General Electric (GE), 247–248
General Motors
  bankruptcy filings for, 432
  cooperative programs and, 450–451, 453, 462
  Delphi Corporation and, 230, 231
  economic crisis of 2008 and, 228
  reorganization of, 277
  sit-down strike at, 44, 48
Germany, 566–568, 570, 578, 579, 581, 582, 585–586, 591
Gesantmetall, 582
Get-out-the-vote campaigns, 150–152
Gibbons, James Cardinal, 32
Gissel case, 185
Globalization. *See also* Labor movements in global market economies
  competition and, 226–228
  effects on labor of, 436
  employment regulation and, 91
  labor movements and, 571–575
  oil embargo of 1972-1973 and, 222–223
  organized labor and, 144–146
  of production, 21
  union bargaining power and, 4, 21
GMFC Attitude Survey Case, 327
GMFC Custom Conveyer Division Case, 193–194
GMFC Impasse Case, 434
Goldsmith, Stephen, 551
Gompers, Samuel, 34, 39, 40, 54, 56
Good-faith bargaining, 220
Goodyear Tire and Rubber, 427, 428*f*
Gould, Jay, 32
Great Britain, 566, 568–569, 575, 577–579, 583, 590–591
Green, William, 53, 56
Greenback Party, 31
Grievance arbitration. *See* Arbitration
Grievance issues
  categories of, 475
  discipline, 471, 484
  discrimination, 474
  incentives, 471–472
  outsourcing, 474
  past employment practices, 474
  personnel assignments, 472
  production standards, 473
  rules, 474
  stewards and, 476–477, 489, 490
  subcontracting, 473
  supervisors doing production work, 473
  teams and, 470
  work assignments, 472
  work hours, 472–473
  working conditions, 473

Grievance procedures
as bargaining issue, 315–316, 322
employee rights in, 485–487
in individual union members, 490–491, 492*f*, 493
in public sector, 531–532
steps in, 475–479, 478*f*, 480*f*
time involved in, 479–480
in unionized vs. nonunionized organizations, 205–208, 322
Grievances
bargaining and, 487–491, 492*f*, 493
disputes involving both ULPs and, 504–505
effects on employers and employees of, 493–495
example of written, 475*f*
mediation of, 481–482
past-practice, 523
ramifications for unions related to, 487–488
rates of, 315–316, 478–479, 489–490
time for resolution of, 479
union initiatives in, 489–490
Grocery works, 424
Gropper, Allen, 432
Group cohesiveness, 7, 23

Harley-Davidson, 461
Haywood, "Big Bill," 37–39
Health care
costs of, 269–271, 278*f*
self-insure, 270
strikes over, 424
Health Care Bargaining and the PPACA Case, 301
Health care benefits
cost containment and, 271
cost of, 270
overview of, 269–270
wages and, 270–271, 270*f*
Health care facilities, 73
Health care industry, 73, 250
Health care labor-management council (Minneapolis-St. Paul), 448
Health care reform
bargaining and, 229
Patient Protection and Affordable Care Act and, 78, 81, 272, 273*t*–274*t*
Henry, Mary Kay, 59
High-performance work organizations (HPWO), 307, 462–463
Hilton hotels, 181
Hiring, 321–322, 321*f*
Hiring halls, 22
Hoffa, James P., 112
Hoffa, James R., 54, 110
Holidays, 312, 320
Homestead strike (1892), 35
Hot cargo, 72
Human resource expenditures, 204
Human resource managers, 4
Hungary, 567–568
Hutcheson, "Big Bill," 42

IBM, 206
IBT. *See* International Brotherhood of Teamsters (IBT)
IG Metal, 582
Immigrants/immigration
labor movement and, 27, 41
organizing campaigns and, 181
quotas on, 42
Impasses. *See also* Strikes
bankruptcies and, 430–432
boycotts and, 39–40, 52, 426–427
coordinated campaigns and, 415, 416
corporate campaigns and, 414–415
employer responses to, 415–419
explanation of, 220, 399–400
in global market economies, 583–584, 584*t*
interest arbitration for, 407
lockouts and, 427–430
mediation for, 400–406, 403*t*, 405*t*
picketing and, 411–413
in public sector, 552–561
slowdowns and, 413–414
third-party involvement in, 400, 407–408
Imperial Oil, 209
Import-substitution industrialization (ISI), 572
Impro-Share Plan, 283–285, 284*t*, 285*t*, 449*t*, 460
Incentives, as contract issue, 471–472
Income distribution
perceptions of, 19–20
trends in, 257–258
unions and, 257
Incorporation, 1
Independent local unions (ILUs), 101. *See also* Local unions
Individual rights, 485–487
Industrial democracy, 586–587, 588*t*–589*t*
Industrial relations managers, 4
Industrial relations systems, 20–22
Industrial structure, 200–201
Industrial unions, 104. *See also* Unions
explanation of, 42
leadership in, 42–43, 48
organization of, 43–44
Industrial Workers of the World (IWW), 37–41
Industries
global competition in, 226–228
organizing in concentrated, 224–225
public policy and concentration within, 223–224
regulation of, 225
unionization rates within, 202
Industrywide bargaining, 243–244
Information technology (IT), 115, 180
Injunctions
effects of, 39
national emergencies and, 74
Norris-LaGuardia Act and, 66–67, 483
restrictions on, 45, 66, 67
Integrative bargaining
explanation of, 344, 438–439
fact-finding and, 407
Federal Mediation and Conciliation Service tools for, 440–442
interest-based bargaining and, 442–444
mutual-gains bargaining and, 439–440
Interest arbitration, 407, 498
Interest-based bargaining (IBB)
explanation of, 350
use and effects of, 442–444
Internal Revenue Code, Section 527, 148
International Association of Fire Fighters (IAFF), 535
International Brotherhood of Electrical Workers (IBEW), 108, 110
International Brotherhood of Teamsters (IBT)
AFL-CIO affiliation and, 56, 110
Change to Win coalition and, 58, 119
collective bargaining and, 243
corruption in, 54–55, 122
deregulation and, 225
membership in, 104
National Master Freight Agreement with, 123
organizational structure of, 111*f*
profile of, 110, 112
International representatives, 114
International unions, 101
Interorganizational bargaining, 347–348
Interstate Commerce Act of 1887, 225
Investment
unionization and, 296–297
in unionized vs. nonunionized organizations, 200
Italy, 569

Jackson, Andrew, 31
Japan, 20–21, 198, 566–567, 569, 579–580, 586
JCPenney, 190
Job classifications, 307
Job Corps, 85
Job evaluation, 263, 264*t*
Job grade structure, 263–264, 266*f*
Job postings, 203
Job satisfaction
member participation and, 132–134
trends in, 10, 14
union commitment and, 136
union effects on, 324–326
Job security
bargaining and, 9, 308
union avoidance and, 204–205
in unionized vs. nonunionized organizations, 204–205
Job structuring, 215
Joint labor-management committee (JLMC), 447–448
Joint Unity Committee, 53
Jones & Laughlin Steel, 47
Journeyman printers, 29
J.P. Stevens & Co., 427
Jurisdictional disputes, 48
Justice for Janitors 2001 Campaign, 179, *179*, 246

Kaiser Permanente (KP), 165, 454
Kennedy, John F., 55, 531
Kirk, Ron, 227
Kirkland, Lane, 56, 58
Kmart, 190
Knights of Labor, 32–33, 499
Korea, 582, 591

Labor
  as creator of wealth, 28, 257
  as derived demand, 230–232, 232*f*
  preferences of, 437
Labor-capital substitution, 233–235, 234*f*
Labor Department
  establishment of, 82–83
  organization of, 83, 84*f*, 85–86
  overtime pay and, 310
Laborers (LIUNA), 58, 119
Labor force demographics, 228–229
Labor law. *See also specific laws*
  Byrnes Act, 76
  Civil Service Reform Act, Title VII, 56, 63*f*, 531–532
  Copeland Anti-Kickback Act, 76
  discussion of miscellaneous, 77–81
  effects of implementation of, 82
  Landrum-Griffin Act, 55, 63*t*, 68, 75–76, 98, 115, 411, 435
  listing of, 79*t*–81*t*
  Norris-LaGuardia Act, 45, 63*t*, 66–68, 409, 435, 483, 501
  overview of, 62–63, 143
  public sector, 530–536, 537*t*–542*t*
  Racketeer Influenced and Corrupt Organizations Act, 76–77
  Railway Labor Act, 44, 63*t*, 64–66, 86, 164, 219, 328, 400, 406–407, 435, 552
  reform of, 90–92
  state, 532–536, 537*t*–542*t*
  Taft-Hartley Act, 51, 52, 63*f*, 68–75, 86, 90–91, 164, 175–176, 209, 219, 220, 222, 321–322, 328, 341, 400, 404, 406, 419, 435, 463, 485, 499, 552
  union support for, 221–222
  Wagner Act, 23, 46–48, 55, 63*t*, 68–74, 82, 87, 156, 164, 197, 435
Labor-management committees
  areawide, 446–447
  comparative analysis of, 449*t*
  joint, 447–448
Labor-Management Cooperation Act of 1978, 446
Labor-management partnerships (LMPs), 454–455
Labor-management relations
  adversarial nature of, 5
  in federal service, 56
  institutionalization of change and, 465–466
  during World War II period, 48–51
Labor Management Relations Act of 1947. *See* Taft-Hartley Act of 1947
Labor-Management Reporting and Disclosure Act of 1959 (LMRDA). *See* Landrum-Griffin Act of 1959
Labor movement
  American Plan and, 41
  corruption in, 54–55
  crisis and transition in, 56–59
  decline in, 18–20
  employee intransigence and, 46–48
  historical background of, 29–31
  industrial relations system transformation and, 20–22
  industrial unions and, 42–44
  in late nineteenth century to World War I, 34–40
  legislation and, 40, 44–48, 51–52
  milestones in, 27
  in 1920s, 42
  in 1930s-1940s, 48–51
  officer commitment to, 142
  origins of national unions and, 31–34, 143
  in public sector, 55–56
  retrenchment and merger in, 53–54
  union philosophies and, 28
  union strategies and, 22–23
  values influencing, 28
  World War I and, 40
  World War II and, 50–51
Labor movements in global market economies
  bargaining issues in, 578–580
  bargaining structures in, 580–582, 583*t*
  comparative effects of unionization in, 587, 588*t*–589*t*, 590–591
  contract administration and, 587
  development of, 566–568
  impasses and, 583–584
  organization and representation in, 575–578, 576*t*
  public sector unionization and, 587
  structure of, 568–575, 573*f*, 574*f*
  union-management cooperation and, 584–587, 585*t*
Labor relations
  explanation of, 1
  function of, 3
  present state of, 4–5
  public sector, 3, 535–536, 537*t*–542*t*, 543 (*See also* Public sector unions)
Labor Relations Act 1947. *See* Taft-Hartley Act of 1947
Labor supply, 235, 238
Labor unions. *See* Unions
Landrum-Griffin Act of 1959
  coverage and provisions of, 63*f*, 68, 75–76
  elections and, 98, 115
  explanation of, 55, 68
  function of, 435
  picketing and, 411
Lane-and-step plans, 265–266, 267*f*
Last chance agreement (LCA), 471
Last-in, first-out (LIFO) inventory valuation, 359
Laundry Workers, 54–55
Layoffs
  effect on teams, 465
  procedures for, 319–320
  unionized employees and, 323
  work design change and, 307–308
Legislation. *See* Labor law; *specific laws*, Public sector labor law
Lewis, John L., 42, 43, 48, 49
Lincoln Mills case, 499
Line managers, 4
Litigation, 503–504
Little Steel, 49
Lloyd-LaFollette Act of 1912, 531
Lobbying, 152–153
Local employees, 536
Local officers, 141–142
Local unions. *See also* Unions
  affiliation of, 95
  business agents in, 95–96
  commitment to, 135–138, 137*f*, 138*f*
  contract negotiation preparation and, 340
  effectiveness of, 139
  explanation of, 94–95, 101
  functional democracy and, 98–101
  governance in, 96–98, 99*f*
  independent, 101
  influence of, 17
  joining, socializing, and leaving, 127–130, 130*t*
  jurisdiction of, 95
  member participation in, 130–135, 131*t*, 132*t*, 133*f*
  officers in, 141–142
  organization of, 96
  political competition within, 490
  relations between national and, 113–114
  stewards in, 96, 139–141
Locating the New Recreational Vehicle Plant Case, 217
Lockouts
  as bargaining issue, 316
  function of, 408, 427
  multiemployer, 429
  single-employer, 429–430
  in strikes involving perishable goods, 427–429
Logrolling, 351

Mackay case, 418
Management. *See* Employers
Management-employer committees, 209
Management rights clauses, 314
Mandatory bargaining issues
  cooperation and control in dealing with, 437–438
  explanation of, 220, 221*f*
Marginal revenue product, 231–232
Marginal supply curve, 235, 236*f*
Marx, Karl, 566
Material Handling Equipment Association Bargaining Group Case, 255
McCain-Feingold Act of 2002. *See* Bipartisan Campaign Reform Act of 2002
McCormick Harvester, 35
McKinley, William, 38
McParlan, James, 35, 38
Meany, George, 53, 54, 56
Median voter concept, 17
Mediation/mediators
  approaches of, 401–402, 403*t*
  background and training for, 404
  explanation of, 86, 400–401
  function of, 402, 408
  grievance, 481–482
  management view of, 402–403
  role of, 400–401
  Taft-Hartley Act requirements for, 404
Mercosur, 571

Mergers
in airline industry, 169–170
forms of union, 120–121
in labor movement, 53–54
Merit pay, 203, 279
Mexico, 146, 572
Middle class, 19–20
Mine Safety Act of 1977, 78
Mine Safety and Health Administration (MSHA), 85
Mineworkers Union, 117
Minimum wages, 77, 83
Mining industry, 35, 38, 39, 50, 482–483
Minneapolis Federation of Teachers (AFT), 266, 266*f*
Minnesota Nurses Association, 448
Minorities
interest in unionization, 178
as local officers, 142
representation preferences of, 188
union interest and, 9
Miranda Fuel Company case, 486
Modern operating agreement, 452–453
Modified union shop, 317
Mohawk Valley formula, 46, 47, 197
Molly Maguires, 35
Multicost Scanlon Plan, 285*t*
Multicraft bargaining, 244–245
Multiemployer bargaining units, 163, 241–243, 242*f*
Multiemployer lockouts, 429
Multilateral bargaining, 545–546
Multinational organizations, 247
Murphy, Frank, 44
Murray, Philip, 42, 43, 49, 53
Mutual-gains bargaining, 344, 350, 439–440

NAFTA. *See* North American Free Trade Agreement (NAFTA)
Narcotic effect, 554
National Academy of Arbitrators, 508
National Education Association (NEA), 104, 542
National emergencies, 74
National Industrial Recovery Act of 1933 (NIRA), 45–47
National Labor Relations Act of 1935. *See* Wagner Act of 1935
National Labor Relations Board (NLRB)
bargaining units and, 163–168, 251
company unions and, 46
craft severance and, 167
decisions of, 88–90
deferral to arbitration, 504–505, 515
duty to bargain and, 369
elections and, 73, 160–162, 162*f*, 172, 184–187, 189, 190, 215
employer-sponsored committees and, 464
establishment of, 45–46, 87
functions of, 70, 87–88
grievances and, 485–486
Jones & Laughlin Steel and, 47
jurisdiction of, 87
local unions and, 101
organization of, 88
politics and, 46, 88–89, 223
refusal-to-bargain charges filed with, 430
strikes and, 418, 419
unfair labor practices and, 73, 82, 173, 486
union organizing campaigns and, 156, 162, 184–187
National Labor Union (NLU)
explanation of, 31, 32
work hours and, 310
National/local bargaining, 244
National Master Freight Agreement, 123, 225
National Mediation Board (NMB)
contract negotiations and, 64–65, 328
establishment of, 86, 219
function of, 86–87
impasse and, 400
union organizing campaigns and, 156
National Molders' Union, 31
National Railroad Adjustment Board (NRAB), 65–66, 219
National Right-to-Work Committee, 153
National Steel Company, 465
National Union of Healthcare Workers (NUHW), 105, 165
National unions. *See also* Unions
contract negotiation preparation and, 339–340
economy and, 143–144
finance in, 121–123
formation of, 27
function of, 101–103, 142
globalization and, 144–146
goals of, 103–104
governance and politics in, 116–117
headquarters operations of, 114–116
hierarchy in, 120
jurisdictions of, 104–105
labor law and administration and, 143
leadership in, 103
lobbying and, 152–153
mergers of, 120–121
organizing campaigns by, 157–158 (*See also* Union organizing campaigns)
pension administration in, 123
planning in, 104
political action and, 146–152
public policy and, 117
relations between local and, 113–114
statistics related to, 101–102, 102*t*
strategies of, 104
structure of, 105–106, 106*f*, 109*f*, 111*f*, 113*f*
use of dues by, 154
National War Labor Board (NWLB), 40, 50, 51, 407, 499
Negotiated Rulemaking Act, 86
Negotiating committee, 96, 176, 357–358
The Netherlands, 569
Neutral employers, 412
Neutrality pledges, 181–182
New Production Equipment: Greater Efficiency with Less Effort or a Speedup Case, 496–497
New York Daily News, 417
Nixon, Richard, 222
NLRB. *See* National Labor Relations Board (NLRB)
NMB. *See* National Mediation Board (NMB)
No-distribution rules, 173–174
Nonexempt employees, 310
Nonunion organizations. *See also* Union avoidance
doctrinaire, 201
economic rationale for, 198–201
employee input systems and, 205–208
employee relations practices in, 209–211, 210*t*
employment security in, 204–205
environmental factors associated with, 201–202
explanation of, 201
innovative techniques in, 208–209
nonwage policies in, 203–204
philosophy-laden, 201
preventative practices in, 211–212
strategies of, 198
wage policies in, 202–203
Nonwage bargaining issues
contract length as, 313
discipline and discharge as, 314–315
grievance procedures as, 315–316
list of, 303*t*–304*t*
seniority and job security as, 319–320
strikes and lockouts as, 316
union and management goals for, 304
union and management rights in, 313–314
union effects on, 320–326
union security as, 316–317
work design as, 304–309
work hours as, 310–312
working conditions and safety as, 318
Norris-LaGuardia Act of 1932
conspiracy doctrine and, 67
coverage and provisions of, 45, 63*t*, 66–68
function of, 435
injunctions and, 66–67, 483
union rights in strikes and, 409, 501
North American Free Trade Agreement (NAFTA), 92, 145–147, 571, 572
Northwest Airlines, 65, 169–170, 406, 414, 430–432
No-solicitation rules, 173–174
No-strike clauses, 481, 483

Obama, Barack
Executive Order 13496 and, 92
Executive Order 13502 and, 481
labor-management forums and, 550
tariffs on tire imports and, 227
Occupational Safety and Health Act of 1970 (OSH Act), 78, 81*t*, 318
Occupational Safety and Health Administration (OSHA)
functions of, 83, 85
inspections by, 78
Office cleaning industry, 246
Office of Disability Employment Policy (ODEP), 85

Office of Federal Contract Compliance Programs (Labor Department), 83
Office of Labor-Management Standards (Labor Department), 83
Older workers, 9
Olin case, 505
Omnibus Employee Testing Act of 1991, 503
Open-door policies, 206. *See also* Grievance procedures
Open shop, 41
Open-shop committees, 41
Open-shop industry, 99–100
Operating Engineers Union, 54
Organization for Economic Cooperation and Development (OECD) countries, 581, 590
Organizing campaigns. *See* Union organizing campaigns
Outsourcing, 474
Overtime
  entitlements to and restrictions on, 311
  as grievance issue, 472–473
  legislation addressing, 310

Paid time off, 312, 320
Past-practice grievances, 523
Patient Protection and Affordable Care Act of 2010 (PPACA)
  collective bargaining and, 272
  implementation of, 83, 273
  provisions of, 78, 81*t*, 272, 273*t*–274*t*
Pattern bargaining, 245–246
Pay form. *See also* Employee benefits
  demographics and, 277–278
  explanation of, 260, 268
  health insurance and, 269–272, 271*t*, 273*t*, 274*t*
  miscellaneous benefits and, 277, 298*t*
  pension plans and, 272, 274*t*, 275–276
  union effects on, 293–294, 294*t*
  voluntary employee benefits associations and, 276–277
  wage- and person-tied benefits and, 269
Pay level
  components of, 260*f*, 261–262
  explanation of, 260, 261
  in public sector, 547–548
  union effects on, 286–291, 287*t*, 288*t*
Payne v. Western Atlantic Railroad (1884), 77
Pay programs
  explanation of, 259–261
  pay form and, 268–272, 271*t*, 273*t*–274*t*, 278, 278*f*, 293–294
  pay level and, 261–262, 286–291, 287*t*, 288*t*
  pay structure and, 262–268, 264*t*, 265*f*–267*f*, 292
  pay system and, 278–280, 280*t*, 281*f*, 282–285, 282*t*–286*t*, 294–295
  union effects and, 286–295
Pay structure
  explanation of, 260, 262–263
  grade structures and, 263–264, 266*f*
  job evaluation and, 263, 264*t*
  lane-and-step plans and, 265–266, 267*t*
  skill-based, 264–265, 266*f*
  two-tier, 267–268
  union effects on, 292, 293*f*
Pay system
  explanation of, 260–261, 278
  gainsharing plans and, 279–280, 279*t*, 280*f*, 281*t*, 282–284, 282*t*–285*t*
  membership in organization and, 278
  merit and, 279
  productive efficiency and, 279
  profit sharing and, 285–286, 286*t*
  seniority and, 278–279
  time not worked and, 286
  time worked and, 279
  union effects on, 294–295
Peer review panels, 207
Pension Benefit Guaranty Corporation (PBGC), 90
Pension plans. *See also* Retirement benefits
  administration of, 121, 123
  public sector, 276, 549–550
  regulation of, 272, 275
  types of, 272, 274*t*, 275–276
Perishable goods, 427–429
Permanent umpires, 505
Permissive bargaining issues, 220, 221*f*
Personnel assignments, 472
Phelps-Dodge Corporation, 58, 417
Philadelphia Cordwainers, 29–30, 196
Philosophy-laden organizations, 201, 203
Picketing
  ambulatory site, 413
  common situs, 412
  explanation of, 411
  function of, 411–412
  multiple-use site, 413
  recognitional, 411
Piece rates, 279
Pistole, John, 532
Plain-meaning rule, 515
Plant size, 202
Poland, 567
Police
  bargaining laws covering, 535, 537*t*–542*t*
  strikes by, 560
Political action. *See also* Lobbying
  campaign contributions as, 147–150
  effectiveness of, 153
  endorsements and get-out-the-vote drives as, 150–152, 152*t*
  forms of union, 148–149
  overview of, 146–147
Political action committees (PACs)
  campaign contributions from union, 147–148, 150
  effects of, 153
  explanation of, 104
Political campaign contributions
  election of 2000 and, 147–148
  election of 2010 and, 148
  union characteristics and, 149–150
  unions and corporations and, 52, 74, 147–148
Political campaigns
  candidate characteristics and, 150
  endorsements and get-out-the-vote drives for, 150–152
Political endorsements, 150–151
Politics
  labor law reform and, 90–92
  labor movement decline and, 18
  in national unions, 116–117
  public sector collective bargaining and, 18, 533–534, 550
Polls. *See* Public opinion
Powderly, Terence, 32, 33
PPACA. *See* Patient Protection and Affordable Care Act of 2010 (PPACA)
Predatory unionism, 28
Pressman, Lee, 49
Primary employers, 412
Principled negotiations, 440
Private sector unions, 20, 21. *See also* Unions
Probationary periods, 203
Production committee, 280, 281*f*
Production standards, 473
Productivity
  grievance rates and, 315–316
  labor force composition and, 228–229
  post-World War II, 53, 197, 198
  in public sector, 548–549
  strikes and, 425
  unionization and, 295–296
  in unionized vs. nonunionized organizations, 200
Professional Air Traffic Controllers Organization, 57
Professional employees, 70
Profitability
  strikes and, 425
  unionization and, 297, 299
  in unionized vs. nonunionized organizations, 199
Profit-sharing plans, 285–286, 286*t*
Prohibited bargaining issues, 220
Promotions
  seniority and, 320, 323–324
  union effects on, 322–324
Public employee unions, 536, 542–543
Public Law Boards, 66
Public opinion, 14
Public policy
  business interests and, 19
  court decisions and, 251–252
  industrial organization and, 223–224
  national unions and, 117
  in 1930s, 44–46
  strikes and, 418–419, 422
Public sector
  arbitration in, 553–559
  cooperation between unions and management in, 550–552
  fact-finding in, 552–553
  labor laws covering, 536, 537*t*–542*t*, 542–543
  management structure in, 544
  strikes in, 557, 559–561
  wages and benefits in, 546–548

Public sector bargaining
bargaining units and, 543
labor organizations and, 536, 542–543
management organization for, 544
multilateral, 544–546
outcomes of, 546–549
pensions and, 549–550
public sector labor laws and, 537*t*–542*t*
structures for, 544
union-management cooperation and, 550–552
Public sector defined benefit plans, 276
Public sector labor law
federal, 531–532, 537*t*–542*t*
state, 532–536, 546
Public sector unions. *See also* Unions
cooperation between management and, 550–552
federal executive orders effecting, 55–56
in global market economies, 587
grievances and, 494
growth in, 55–56
politics and, 18, 149
Pullman Company, 35, 36
Punishment, 519–520. *See also* Discipline

Quality, 458
Qwest, 226

Racketeer Influenced and Corrupt Organizations Act of 1970 (RICO), 76–77
Raid elections, 160
Railroad industry
bargaining units in, 249
Erdman Act and, 40
job security and, 407
strikes in, 32, 35, 36
Railway Labor Act of 1926 (RLA)
amendment to, 86
bargaining units and, 164
contract negotiations under, 64–65, 328
coverage and provisions of, 63*t*, 64, 86, 249
disputes under, 66
emergency board procedures and, 552
function of, 435
impasse under, 400, 406–407
National Railroad Adjustment Board and, 65–66, 219
Ratification, contract, 357–358
Reagan, Ronald
air traffic controllers and, 57
economic policies of, 56–57
labor relations and, 223
Realty Advisory Board (RAB), 501
Recognitional picketing, 411
Redundancy, 579
Refusal-to-bargain charges, 430
Regional director, NLRB, 162
Regulation, industrial, 225
Relations by objectives, 440–441
Religious issues, 73
Representation, exclusive, 46, 156
Representation elections
explanation of, 10, 110, 160
management campaign tactics in, 212, 213*t*, 214
petitions for, 161–162
requirements for, 73
results of, 187–189
secret-ballot, 162
types of, 162
Republican Party
campaign contributions to, 148, 534
unions and, 23
voting behaviors and positions of, 151
Republic Steel, 47
Retail Clerks, 121
Retirement benefits, 324. *See also* Pension plans
Return rights, 437
Reuther, Walter, 53, 258
Revolutionary unionism, 28
Rich, Marc, 416
Rights arbitration, 407, 498–499
Right-to-work laws
election results and, 188
free riding and, 317
function of, 52, 73, 533
wages and, 290–291
RLA. *See* Railway Labor Act of 1926 (RLA)
Rockefeller, John D., 39
Roll-up, 332
Roman Catholic Church, 32
Roosevelt, Franklin D., 47–50, 531
Rosselli, Sal, 165
Rucker Plan, 283, 283*t*, 285*t*, 449*t*, 460
Rules. *See* Work rules

S. Lichtenberg case, 190
Safety requirements, 78, 318
Salary reduction plans, 272, 274*t*, 275
Saskatoon Chemicals, 440
Satisfaction, 134–135. *See also* Job satisfaction
Scabs, 417
Scale mergers, 121
Scanlon, Joseph, 280
Scanlon Plan, 279–280, 281*f*, 282–283, 285*t*, 449*t*, 450, 460
Schwab, Charles M., 41
Scientific management, 305
Screening committee, 280
Secondary boycotts, 52, 412
SEIU. *See* Service Employees International Union (SEIU)
Selective Service Act, 50
Self-help, 86
Self-managed work teams, 449*t*
Seniority
as bargaining issue, 323
benefit-status, 319
competitive-status, 319
promotion and transfer and, 320
union interests in, 304
Service Contracts Act, 79*t*
Service Employees International Union (SEIU)
Change to Win coalition and, 58, 119
friction within, 105, 165
Justice for Janitors campaign and, 179, *179*, 246
leadership in, 58
lobbying activities of, 153
National Union of Healthcare Workers and, 165
organizing campaigns of, 178, 180–181
profile of, 106–107
Realty Advisory Board and, 501–502
Workers United and, 59
Service industries, 200
Sexual harassment, 521–522
Shareholders
function of, 2, 3
risk-adjusted return interests of, 230
unionization and returns to, 297, 299
Shareholder value, 199–200
Sherman Antitrust Act of 1890, 39, 40, 223
Shifts, 311
Shutdowns, 416
Singapore, 591
Single-employer lockouts, 429–430
Sit-down strikes, 44, 48, 49
Skill-based pay (SBP)
explanation of, 264–265, 266*f*
teams-based programs and, 452
Slowdowns, 413–414
Social networking, 115–116
Social Security Act, 79*t*
Social security taxes, 78
Solidarity days, 176
Spain, 584
Special Boards of Adjustment, 66
Spielberg case, 504
Spillover, 5
Standard of living
pay-level changes and, 262
wage demands and, 259, 260*f*
Starwood hotels, 181
State employees, bargaining laws covering, 535–536, 537*t*–542*t*
State labor laws
election of 2010 and, 533–534
employee groups and, 535–536
function of, 532–533, 546
jurisdictions and employees and, 532
levels of government and, 534–535
by occupational group, 537*t*–542*t*
Steel industry
dumping in, 145
global competition and, 226
1949 negotiations with United Steelworkers of America, 405
wage concessions in, 438
Steelworkers, 35–36, 43
Steel Workers Organizing Committee (SWOC), 43
Steelworkers' trilogy, 500–502
Stephens, Uriah, 32
Stern, Andy, 9, 58, 119, 165
Steunenberg, Frank, 37–38
Stewards
dual commitment of, 140–141
enrollment duties of, 128
function of, 96, 97, 128, 139–140
grievance issues and, 476–477, 489, 490
Stidham, Dan, 416

Strasser, Adolph, 28, 34
Strike replacements
  explanation of, 418
  public policy and, 57, 418–419
  sources of, 239
Strikers, 419–420
Strikes. *See also* Impasses
  air traffic controllers, 57
  authorization votes for, 409–410
  as bargaining issue, 316
  bargaining power and, 238–240
  boycotts to support, 39–40
  Carnegie Steel, 35–36
  companies vulnerable to, 359
  contracting out during, 419
  contract negotiations and preparation for, 338
  duration of, 422–424
  early use of, 31
  economic, 57, 409, 419–420
  effects of, 424–426
  employer responses to, 415–419
  function of, 408, 411, 420
  in global market economies, 583–584, 584*t*
  incidence of, 420–422, 420*t*
  Knights of Labor and, 32–33
  McCormick Harvester, 35
  mine, 35, 38, 39, 50
  to obtain union recognition, 46
  picketing and, 411–413
  in public sector, 557, 559–561
  railroad, 32, 35, 36
  reasons for, 410–411, 481
  right after World War II, 51
  rights of, 419–420
  sit-down, 44
  state labor laws and, 532
  sympathy, 409
  Taft-Hartley Act and, 52, 55
  textile workers, 38
  time lost to, 399
  unfair labor practice, 409
  wildcat, 316, 409, 423, 482–483
  during World War I, 40
  during World War II, 49–50
Subcontracting, 358, 473
Substance abuse, 521
Superseniority, 96
Supervisors
  doing production work, 473
  grievances related to, 476
  power of, 197, 489
  Wagner Act definition of, 69–70
Supplementary unemployment benefits (SUBs), 286
Supreme Court, U.S.
  arbitration and, 498–504, 515
  bargaining issues and, 252, 499
  Bipartisan Campaign Reform Act and, 148
  boycott cases and, 40
  fair representation and, 487
  grievance issues and, 485
  National Industrial Recovery Act and, 46, 47
  organizing campaigns and, 183, 185
  union dues and, 154
  Wagner Act and, 47–48, 82
  yellow-dog contracts and, 66
Sweden, 566, 568, 578, 581, 582
Swedish Confederation of Trade Unions (LO), 566
Swedish Employers' Confederation (SAF), 566
Sweeney, John, 58, 59, 119
Sylvis, William, 31
Symbiotic mergers, 121
Sympathy strikes, 409. *See also* Strikes

Taft-Hartley Act of 1947
  amendments to, 68–74, 90–91, 164, 222
  bargaining unit determination and, 164
  contract negotiations and, 328, 341
  fact-finding boards and, 552
  Federal Mediation and Conciliation Service and, 86, 219
  function of, 435
  grievances and, 485, 499
  impasse under, 400, 404, 406
  passage of, 51, 75
  provisions of, 52, 55, 63*f*, 68, 175–176, 209, 219–220, 321–322, 463
  strikes and, 419
Taylor, Fredrick, 305
Taylor, Myron, 43
Taylorism, 305, 306
Teacher Bargaining at Pleasant Ridge Case, 562–564
Teachers
  bargaining laws covering, 535, 537*t*–542*t*
  pay and benefits for, 548
  strikes by, 559–561
Team Act of 1996, 90
Team-based programs, 452–453
Teams
  grievance issues and, 470
  responsibilities of, 210–211
Teamsters Local 705 (Chicago), 100
Teamsters Union. *See* International Brotherhood of Teamsters (IBT)
Teamwork, 308
Technological change, 115, 180, 308–309
Technology-based group solutions (TAGS), 441–442
Telecommunications industry, 308–309
Textile industry, 144–145
Textile Workers, 38, 54
Third-party involvement, in impasses, 400, 407–408
Threat, relationship between cohesiveness and, 8–9, 8*f*
Totality of conduct, 185
Toyota, 453
Trade, 233
Trade treaties
  globalization and, 144–146, 571–572
  minimum labor standards and, 92
Transfers
  seniority and, 320
  union effects on, 322–324
Transportation Communications International Union (TCIU), 66
Trucking industry, 225, 243–244
Trucking Management Inc., 225
Truman, Harry, 52
Trumka, Ron, 59
Trusteeships, 76
Turnover rates
  dissatisfaction and, 10
  union effects on, 322–324
  in unionized vs. nonunionized organizations, 203, 205, 296
24-hour rule, 175
Two-tier pay plans, 269

UAW. *See* United Auto Workers (UAW)
ULPs. *See* Unfair labor practices (ULPs)
Umpires, 477
Unemployment
  in 1970s, 56, 57
  in 2010, 17
  wages and, 290
Unemployment insurance, 78
Unfair labor practice strikes, 409. *See also* Strikes
Unfair labor practices (ULPs)
  disputes involving both grievance and, 504–505
  employer, 71, 183, 184, 214
  explanation of, 70–71
  NLRB and, 73, 82, 173, 486
  in public sector, 532
  strike replacements and, 418, 419
  surveillance and, 175
  union, 71–72, 409
  union activists and charges of, 484–485
Union avoidance. *See also* Nonunion organizations
  decertification and, 214–215
  economic rationale for, 198–201
  employee input systems and, 205–208
  employee relations practices and, 209–211, 210*t*
  environmental factors associated with, 201–202
  historical background of, 196–198
  innovative techniques for, 46–47, 208–209
  job security and, 204–205
  job structuring and, 215
  management tactics for, 212, 213*t*, 214, 436
  nonunion organizations and, 201–211
  nonwage policies and, 203–204
  preventative programs and, 211–212, 211*t*
  wage policies and, 202–203
Union density, global, 575–577, 576*t*
Union-free organizations, 157. *See also* Nonunion organizations
Unionization
  beliefs about, 12–13, 12*f*
  benefits of, 5
  catalysts for, 7–8, 170
  community attitudes about, 16
  decline in, 18–20
  economic issues related to, 198–201
  effects on hiring practices, 321–322, 321*f*
  effects on job satisfaction, 324–326
  effects on pay form, 293–294, 294*t*

Unionization—*Cont.*
effects on pay level, 286–291, 287*t*, 288*t*
effects on pay structure, 292, 293*f*
effects on pay system, 293–294, 294*f*
effects on promotions, transfers, and turnover, 322–324
effects on retirement programs, 324
function of, 2, 5, 257
in global market economies, 573–578, 587, 590–591
individuals and, 10–13, 11*f*
labor supply and, 235, 238
monopoly power over labor supply and, 235
organizational investment and growth decisions and, 296–297
productivity and, 295–296
profitability and shareholder returns and, 297, 299
reasons employees support, 9–13, 11*f*, 12*f*
variations in degree of, 5–6
willingness to vote for, 14–16
Union-management cooperation
across organizations, 457–460
alternative governance forms and, 445, 456*t*
areawide labor-management committees and, 446–447
creating and sustaining, 444, 445*t*, 446
diffusion and institutionalization of change and, 465–466
economic and regulatory environment and, 435–438
employee stock ownership plans and, 464–465
in global market economies, 584–587, 585*t*
high-performance work organizations and, 462–463
integrative bargaining and, 438–444
joint labor-management committees and, 447–448
legal issues related to, 463–464
long-term effects of, 460–462
management strategies and, 457
union political processes and diffusion of chance and, 455, 457
workplace interventions and, 448–455, 449*t*
Union member participation
in administration, 134
by category and activity, 131–132, 132*t*
environmental factors related to, 135
explanation of, 130–134, 131*t*
predictors of, 132–133, 133*f*
satisfaction and, 134–135
Union members
beliefs and preferences of, 16
bill of rights for, 75
cohesiveness of, 8–9
individual grievance behavior of, 490–491, 492*f*, 493
in local unions, 127–135, 130*t*–132*t*, 133*f*
philosophy of, 196
Union membership
challenges related to, 22–23
as condition of continued employment, 71
discrimination based on, 71
in 1830s, 31
geographic regions and, 201
maintenance of, 317
reasons for decline in, 15–16
statistics for, 5, 6, 6*t*
Union organizing campaigns
actions in, 157–158, 159*f*
aims of, 170–172
airline mergers and, 169–170
bargaining-unit determination and, 163–166, 168–169
catalysts for, 170
conditions for, 10
election results and, 187–189
employer resistance to, 195–198 (*See also* Union avoidance)
employer size and, 172–173
first contracts and, 189–190
framework for, 158–160
general rules for, 173–175
global, 575
goals of, 13, 218
management strategies and tactics for, 182–184, 212, 213*t*, 214
in national unions, 104
neutrality pledges and card check agreements in, 181–182
NLRB policy and, 162, 166–168, 184–187
overview of, 156
representation elections and, 160–163
success factors for, 180–181
union effectiveness and, 157
union strategies and tactics for, 175–179, 177*t*
wages and, 289–290
Union representation elections. *See* Representation elections
Unions. *See also* Private sector unions; Public sector unions
bargaining power of, 240
bargaining unit goals of, 164, 166*f*
beliefs about, 13–16, 15*t*
challenges facing, 22–23
company, 46, 197
contract negotiation preparation by, 339–340
contract representation rights for, 313–314
corruption in, 54–55, 100, 122–123
craft, 27, 104, 121, 123
development of industrial, 42–44
in Europe, 566–568 (*See also* Labor movements in global market economies)
explanation of, 101–103
finance in, 121–123
formation of, 27
function of, 2–5, 16–17, 28
goals of, 103–104, 237
governance and politics in, 116–117
headquarters operations of, 114–116
hierarchy in, 120
historical perspective on, 19, 29–30
industrial, 42–44, 48
innovative workplace initiatives and, 455–456
international, 101
jurisdictions of, 104–105, 164
leadership in, 103
local, 17, 94–101, 127–142 (*See also* Local unions)
mergers of, 120–121
national, 101–117, 142–154 (*See also* National unions)
"new normal" for, 17–18
origins of national, 31–34
pension administration in, 123
political contributions by, 52, 74, 147–148
pre-Civil War, 30–31
public employee, 536, 542–543
public policy and, 117
relationship between local and, 113–114
reports required by, 75–76
rights and responsibilities of, 1
strategies of, 28
structure of, 102–103, 106*f*, 109*f*, 111*f*, 113*f*
unfair labor practices of, 71–72, 409
work design changes and, 307
Union security
as bargaining issue, 317
explanation of, 316
types of, 316–317
Union shop
explanation of, 71, 128, 316
modified, 317
prohibitions against, 129
Union stewards. *See* Stewards
United Airlines, 169, 170, 413
United Auto Workers (UAW)
AFL-CIO affiliation and, 56
cooperative programs and, 447, 450–451, 453, 457, 462
creation of, 43–44
General Motors strike and, 48
internal democracy in locals, 490
membership in, 104
organizational structure of, 109*f*
pattern bargaining and, 246
profile of, 107–108
voluntary employee benefits association and, 123, 277
United Electrical Workers, 248
United Food and Commercial Workers (UFCW)
Change to Win coalition and, 58
formation of, 121
organizing campaigns by, 180
United Hatters, 39
United Healthcare Workers (UAW), 105, 165
United Mine Workers (UMW), 42, 49, 50, 53, 74, 426
United Parcel Service (UPS), 64
United Rubber Workers, 425
United States International Trade Commission, 227
United Steelworkers of America
advertisement use by, 427, 428*f*
1949 negotiations of, 405
Phelps Dodge Corporation and, 58
regionally elected executive board and, 117

United Textile Workers, 54
United Transportation Union (UTU), 66
UNITE HERE
  AFL-CIO and, 119
  Change to Win coalition and, 58–59, 119
  establishment of, 105
  neutrality pledge agreements and, 181
Unpaid leave, 320
Unskilled workers
  consumer demand and, 229
  employer resistance and, 197
  global competition and, 228
Uplift unionism, 28
U.S. Steel, 43

Vacations, 312, 320
Vaca v. Sipes, 486
Van Buren, Martin, 31
Verizon, 181, 312
Vertical staff meetings, 208
Veterans Employment and Training Service (VETS), 85
Vietnam Era Veterans' Readjustment Act, 83
Vietnam War, 197–198
Visteon, 230
Volcker, Paul, 56
Voluntary employee benefits association (VEBA), 123, 276–277
Voting behavior, 151–152, 152*t*

Wabash Railroad, 32
Wage and Hour Division (Labor Department), 83
Wage demands
  ability to pay and, 258–259, 260*f*
  equity and, 257–258, 260*f*
  standard of living and, 259, 260*f*
Wages. *See also* Pay programs
  in competitive market, 242, 242*f*
  deregulation and, 225
  federal and state laws related to, 77–78
  in international local union members, 101
  monopsony, 235, 236*f*
  in multiemployer bargaining units, 242–243, 243*f*
  in public sector, 546–548, 558
  right-to-work laws and, 290–291
  trade treaties and, 146
  in unionized vs. nonunionized organizations, 198–199, 202–203
Wagner Act of 1935. *See also* Taft-Hartley Act of 1947
  amendment to, 51, 68–74
  bargaining units and, 164
  constitutionality of, 47–48, 82
  employer opposition to, 46, 47
  function of, 435
  National Labor Relations Board and, 87
  provisions of, 23, 45–46, 156, 197
Walsh-Healy Act, 79*t*, 310
War Labor Disputes Act of 1943, 50–51
Warrior and Gulf case, 500
Wealth, 28, 257
Weirton Steel, 465
West Coast Dock Workers, 74
Western Federation of Miners (WFM), 37
Whipsaw strategy, 429
Wide-area bargaining, 244–245
Wildcat strikes
  in coal mining industry, 482–483
  discipline for, 483
  explanation of, 316, 409, 423
Wilhelm. John, 105
Wilkie, Wendell, 48
Williams, Roy Lee, 112
Wilson, Woodrow, 39
"Winner-take-all" rules, 23
Wisconsin Employee Relations Board (WERB), 553
Women. *See also* Gender
  in bargaining units, 177–178
  in leadership positions, 134
  negotiating behavior and, 349–350
  promotions and, 323–324
  representation preferences of, 188–189
  union interest by, 9
  union participation by, 133
Women's Bureau, 85
Work assignments, 472
Work design
  explanation of, 304–305
  historical background of, 305–306
  transformation in, 307–309
Worker Adjustment and Retraining Notification Act of 1988, 78, 81*t*
Worker cooperatives, 586, 587
Workers' compensation, 78, 80*t*
Workers' compensation programs, 83
Workers United (WU), 59, 105
Work-family conflicts, 522
Work hours
  as bargaining issue, 310–312
  as contract issue, 472–473
  legislation concerning, 310
  overtime and, 311
  shift assignments and differentials and, 311
Working conditions, 318, 473
Working to rules, 413
Workplace interventions, 448–450, 448*t*
Workplace restructuring, 462–463
Work rules
  as bargaining issue, 309
  as contract issue, 474
  in unionized vs. nonunionized organizations, 199
  violations of, 471
Work schedules, 311–312
Works councils, 569–571
World Trade Organization (WTO), 226, 227
World War I
  International Workers of the World and, 38–39
  labor activity during, 40
World War II
  collective bargaining during, 222
  industrial union leaders and, 48
  labor-management relations during, 48–51

Yellow-dog contracts
  explanation of, 41, 45
  Norris-LaGuardia Act and, 66–67
Young employees, 178
Youngstown Sheet and Tube, 46–47

Zero-tolerance policies, 521